Earlier

HOUSING POLICY MATTERS

HOUSING POLICY MATTERS
A Global Analysis

Shlomo Angel

OXFORD
UNIVERSITY PRESS

2000

OXFORD

UNIVERSITY PRESS

Oxford   New York
Athens   Auckland   Bangkok   Bogotá   Buenos Aires   Calcutta
Cape Town   Chennai   Dar es Salaam   Delhi   Florence   Hong Kong   Istanbul
Karachi   Kuala Lumpur   Madrid   Melbourne   Mexico City   Mumbai
Nairobi   Paris   São Paulo   Shanghai   Singapore
Taipei   Tokyo   Toronto   Warsaw

and associated companies in
Berlin   Ibadan

Library of Congress Cataloging-in-Publication Data
Angel, Shlomo.
Housing policy matters : a global analysis / Shlomo Angel.
p. cm.
Includes bibliographical references and index.
ISBN 0-19-513715-9
1. Housing policy.   2. Housing surveys.   I. Title.

HD7287.3 .A53 2000
363.5—dc21   99-053984

1 3 5 7 9 8 6 4 2

Printed in the United States of America
on acid-free paper

To Lucy, for the many joys of building together.

Preface

One evening in 1962, on a long walk past Israeli army barracks, my friend David Schutz asked me what I wanted to do with my life. "Architecture," I said, "I want to build houses." "Why waste your time building houses for the rich?" he asked. "I want to build houses for the poor," I replied.

In 1969, I spent a month in Pampa de Comas — the largest *barriada* in Lima, Peru at the time — and designed a beautiful and unaffordable house for the poor as part of a prestigious international competition.

In 1973, I met Stanley Benjamin in Bangkok and he told me that if I was really interested in housing the poor I should forget architecture. House costs have a way of escalating, he said, whenever architects are involved. I forgot architecture right there and then, and stayed in Bangkok (at the Asian Institute of Technology) for a decade to confront the housing question head on. One of my first questions was "how many people lived in slums and squatter settlements in Bangkok?" Nobody really knew. Some said 300,000, others said 600,000. Receiving no satisfactory answer, my students and I counted them using air photographs. We found them to number 1 million, and we discovered that only fifteen percent of them were squatters. The rest paid land rent — they were slum dwellers all right, but not squatters. A big difference. My first lesson.

That same year, the governor of the newly formed National Housing Authority of Thailand announced — like all new housing ministers before and after him — that he was going to build many thousands of apartments for the poor, surely clearing slums here and there in the process, and somehow handing out the new units to the not-so-poor. Stan and I published a polemical article in the *Bangkok Post* entitled "Seventeen Reasons Why the Housing Problem Can't Be Solved." The governor ignored it, but some people listened and started to get together regularly to talk about housing. In the following years, I conducted housing research in many cities in Asia, discovering that the poor had dozens of ingenious ways to obtain shelter, that there was a housing delivery system in operation that ensured that everyone was housed somehow, and that virtually no one remained homeless. Unfortunately, this system was largely invisible to those engaged in policy because much of it was substandard, repulsive, and illegal.

In 1976, Paul Chamniern and I organized a Muslim slum community in Bangkok to upgrade itself. The community decided that its highest priority was to protect itself against fire by building a fire station, improving its wooden walkways, and training a local fire brigade. We helped make it happen by arranging for some matching funds from the Canadian Embassy, and by helping with the engineering.

In 1978, following a visit to El Salvador that was arranged by Jesuit housing activists, we decided to organize slum dwellers to build a new community for themselves. We distributed leaflets in slums, interviewed prospective dwellers, and started the *Building Together Project* in Bangkok. It took us almost five years to build 200 units by self-help and mutual aid. Groups of 20 families were organized into clusters – producing concrete blocks, beams, piles, and stairs on site and building basic houses during their evenings and weekends. When the basic houses were complete – they took seven to twelve months to build – cluster members conducted a lottery to decided which family would get which house, and then the families completed the houses on their own. The houses were impressive. They were all different. And the community was beautiful, graced by colorful murals on its walls painted by local artists. The last few clusters were eventually built, for the same cost and much more quickly, by a small contractor. Quite a few families defaulted on their mortgages, but the Government Housing Bank was quite patient and no one was forcefully evicted. The few that sold out made good profits. It was a wonderful experience, except for the interminable cash-flow headaches.

By 1982 I concluded that the housing problem in the mega-cities of the developing countries was largely a land problem, and that if land were available, the poor could house themselves. I organized a workshop and edited a book entitled *Land for Housing the Poor*, drafted a United Nations position paper on the same subject, and immersed myself in land policy, informal land subdivisions, and property rights issues.

In 1986, I was asked to head a study of the land and housing markets of Bangkok, in collaboration with David Dowall. David introduced me to the study of the formal housing sector. We found out that there were several dozen private-sector projects that produced houses that were less expensive than the subsidized houses built by the National Housing Authority at the time. Using local surveys and air photographs for 1974 and 1984, we were able to detect significant improvements in the housing stock. Looking at the housing sector as a whole, we found that housing development exceeded population growth, that the slum population declined, and that affordability increased. Announcing these uplifting conclusions distanced many of my local housing comrades, who kept insisting that matters were getting worse, and fell short of calling me a traitor to the cause. But Bangkok now had a reality check, and I learned to look at the housing sector as a whole.

In 1988, Stephen Mayo and I were summoned to Habitat – the United Nations Center for Human Settlements in Nairobi – to edit the United Nations's *Global Strategy for Shelter for the Year 2000*. Steve introduced me to the view of the housing sector as a major economic sector with backward and forward linkages — real, fiscal and financial — to the rest of the economy, where policy errors could be extremely costly. This "top-down" economic perspective fused rather elegantly with my earlier sense of the rightness of the "bottom-up" efforts of people to house themselves. We drafted the *Global Strategy for Shelter* for the United Nations, and the strategy was later endorsed by the General Assembly. The report emphasized the *enabling* functions of governments, urging them to facilitate the production of housing by any and all, in contrast to governments' attempts to produce and manage an insignificant amount of housing by themselves.

In 1990, we were asked to come to Nairobi again, to propose a mechanism for monitoring the United Nations shelter strategy. We proposed a set of housing indicators. The chief of research disagreed, citing the low quality of government data which the United Nations was usually forced to use. His deputy asserted that countries did not like to be compared. Fortunately, Mark Hildebrand, the technical assistance chief, walked in. He liked the indicators and obtained some funds for us to pursue them. That same year, Steve and I initiated the *Housing Indicators Program* as a joint program of the World Bank and the United Nations, and embarked on a Global Survey of Housing Indicators. In parallel, we wrote the World Bank housing policy paper, calling it *Housing: Enabling Markets to Work*. In this paper, published in 1992, we were able to champion the enabling approach and to focus more clearly on its essential components. But we did not have the results of the Global Survey of 1990 to support our contention that the enabling approach did indeed work. For three years hence, amidst other commitments, we tried to put together the results of the survey and the policy paper into a single book. We worked together on cleaning up the data, on the basic conceptual framework, on developing the analytical methodology, and on refining our understanding of the various housing policy instruments. Steve shares the credit, of course, for these earlier phases of the work. But we never managed to write a manuscript together. This book is my own interpretation of our earlier joint endeavors. It has taken me several years to articulate its main ideas, to develop and test the numerous econometric models, and to complete the manuscript to my satisfaction.

This, then, is my housing story. In 30 years, I have moved from a naive attempt at architectural design of unaffordable housing to conducting housing research in many countries, to community organizing in slums, to administering a self-help and mutual-aid housing project, to advising governments on housing policy, and to drafting the policy statements of international organizations. All this experience now enables me to write about housing in the world at large, as well as about the day-to-day tasks of building houses; about the theory of housing and about the practice of housing; and, hopefully, about grounding good housing practice in good housing theory, a challenge well worth the effort demanded by this book.

Shlomo Angel
New York, September 1999

Acknowledgments

The quality and comprehensiveness of the Global Survey of Housing Indicators on which this book is based would not have been possible without the disciplined and meticulous work of the housing experts in each country. They participated both in articulating and refining the survey instrument, in obtaining the data for the indicators in their countries and cities, and in patiently reviewing and refining it over a long time period.

I thank them all: Dalila Tadjerouni (Algeria), Joe Flood (Australia), Walter Matznetter (Austria), Nazrul Islam (Bangladesh), Rosa Maria Ramalho Massena (Brazil), George Bryans Fallis (Canada), Mario Aristides Torche Lazo (Chile), Li Zhiqun (China), Enrique Villabona (Colombia), Attahi Koffi (Côte d'Ivoire), Peter Michalovic (the former Czechoslovakia), Gonzalo B.Rodriguez (Ecuador), E. El-Gabaly (Egypt), Martti Lujanen (Finland), Vincent Renard (France), Eduard Stupening (Germany), Frank Tackie (Ghana), Anna Hardman and Dimitris Oikonomou (Greece), Yue-Man Yeung (Hong Kong), Joszef Hegedus and Ivan Tosics (Hungary), Vinai Lall (India), Robert Rerimassie (Indonesia), Barry Cherniavsky (Israel), the late Derek Gordon (Jamaica), Keiko Ono and Yasuyoshi Hayashi (Japan), Ramzi N. Kawar (Jordan), Bosire Ogero (Kenya), Kim Kyung-Hwan (Republic of Korea), Michel Rabariharivelo (Madagascar), Wycliffe R.Chilowa (Malawi), Gurgit Singh and Ravindra Das (Malaysia), Ernesto Rodriguez Quintanilla (Mexico), Abdelilah Mkinsi (Morocco), Hugo Priemus (the Netherlands), Adepoju G. Onibokun (Nigeria), Dagfinn As and Per Ahren (Norway), Hafiz Pasha (Pakistan), Wtadystaw Jan Brzeski and Jasek Laszek (Poland), Oleg Pchelnitsev, Tatiana Belkina, Grigory Ronkin, and Ekaterina Tcherbakova (The Russian Federation), Mamadou Dione (Senegal), Lim Lan Yuan (Singapore), Baralides Alberdi-Alonso (Spain), Leif Colleen (Sweden), Jossy Siril Materu (Tanzania), the late Sidhijai Tanphiphat (Thailand), Ridha Ferchiou (Tunisia), Aysin Arguden (Turkey), Duncan Maclennan and Kenneth Gibb (United Kingdom), George Grier (United States), Jose Miguel Menendez (Venezuela), and Luke Mabvudza and Walter Garaba (Zimbabwe). I would also like to thank Marja Hoek, who toured Southern Africa and assisted the local consultants during the Global Survey.

I thank Mark Hildebrand of the United Nations Centre for Human Settlements (Habitat) in Nairobi for his enthusiasm and financial support and Arcot Ramachandran, the former Executive Director of Habitat, for his trust and support in initiating the Housing Indicators Program; Steve Mayo, for his cooperation, his insights, and his untiring effort in codirecting the Housing Indicators Program at the World Bank, and his family for their gracious hospitality during the years of my commute to Washington, D.C.; William Stephens and Michael Heller for helping to articulate and coordinate the Program; Demetra Relos and Laura Lewis for helping to administer it; Gregory Ingram of the World Bank's Research Committee for trusting us with the considerable research funds needed for the Global Survey of Housing Indicators; and Michael Cohen of the World Bank for offering me the opportunity to coauthor the Bank's Housing Policy Paper together with Steve Mayo. The present work is a direct offshoot of the Housing Indicators Program and that policy paper.

I thank Christopher Clague, the Director of the Project on Institutional Reform and the Informal Sector (IRIS) at the University of Maryland who provided the financial support for the initial work on the Enabling Index; Dixie Blackley and Gershon Ben-Shakhar who gave me invaluable help in formulating and interpreting the statistical and econometric models; Robert Buckley who read the manuscript in various stages from cover to cover through the years, made many useful suggestions, and provided me with the encouragement and prodding necessary to finish it; Carol Roberts, who prepared the index meticulously; and finally, my little family — Lucy, Adam, and Daniella — who gave me the patience, the resilience, the protection, the tenacity, and the love necessary to embark upon and finish this work.

Contents

HOUSING POLICY MATTERS

Introduction

Housing has lost its voice. Not because housing needs have been satisfied. They have not: the 1995 urban housing stock will need to double by 2030 [United Nations, 1998, 97]. Not because housing has become more affordable or easier to acquire, either. It has not: in both richer and poorer countries, housing now requires a larger, not a smaller, share of family incomes, and the very poor are expected to pay a greater share of their incomes for housing, a major cause for homelessness. Housing has simply squandered its voice on defective visions. The slum tenements of the poor were a potent symbol for revolutionaries — the most visible sign of the unjust society they wanted to destroy. The high-rise apartment block was the ultimate vision of modernity, the choice weapon of postwar utopian dreamers who believed they could impose order and design on the chaos and decadence of cities bursting at their seams. Public housing was the battle cry of paternalistic governments vowing to overpower monstrous housing deficits and dedicating themselves to providing decent housing for all those in need. For a while, sites-and-services mimicking the housing process of the poor were the rage at the World Bank, that, while committed to the development of housing markets unencumbered by government intervention, lent money to governments — and only to governments — for "public" projects. And now, at the start of the new millennium, with the cooling of revolutionary fervor, the disillusion with urban utopias, the shrinking of government ambitions, and the miserable performance of a great number of projects, housing visions have been blurred and tired housing voices have fallen silent. Exasperated housing advocates have deserted the field in droves in search of more fashionable development alternatives, and reborn urban planners have found a new mission in the commitment to protect nature from the assaults of housing. And good riddance.

For in the meantime, while the trumpets blared, entire urban populations silently housed themselves and, all in all, an overwhelming majority of people in the world are now housed in one way or another. Yes, there are homeless people everywhere, but very few — of the order of one person in a thousand (see table 23.2) — in comparison with vacancies, or with the number of those who

3

would be left without any shelter at all were the responsibility for housing left to visionaries – be they revolutionaries, utopian dreamers, paternalistic govern-ments, charitable organizations, or international agencies.

It has now become abundantly clear that any attempt to "provide" housing on any meaningful scale is misguided. Society houses itself, day in and day out, because families need houses and are willing to invest considerable time, effort, and savings in acquiring them or building them, and because people make a living by building houses for others. In short, society can house itself because there is a housing market. Market relations can be observed in the poorest of slums in Jakarta, where minimal customary rights to shelter are bought and sold on faith and without the protection of the law. They can also be observed in complicated informal chains of exchanges of rent-controlled apartments in Polish cities. And rarely, if ever, does a nonmarket allocation remain free of market transactions except in a fanatic police state. Public land belonging to the Pakistani air force, for example, was sold illegally to squatters who built permanent homes on it. Nontransferable public flats allocated to displaced slum dwellers in Bangkok were sold for a pittance to middle-class families. Wherever possible – from Singapore to England to Hungary – public housing was sold, often at bargain prices, to sitting tenants. Housing is now perceived everywhere – China being the last bastion of paternalist housing, which has also started to crumble – as a commodity with an exchange value, rather than as a basic need with a use value allocated, as of right, outside the marketplace.

The facts concerning the existence of housing markets and their critical role in the provision of housing are indisputable. Individual market transactions are also – by their very nature – relatively silent, and there is no a priori reason to believe that the housing market is always alive and well. It rarely is. The housing market is a sensitive, complex, and largely unknowable entity, subject to fits and starts, unpredictable, merciless, unstable, and almost totally dependent on forces outside itself. Still, it is a valuable and irreplaceable social construct, one that needs to be handled with care, especially since it is the now the repository of vast personal wealth – the monetary value of the world's urban housing stock in 1990, for example, was already of the order of $50 trillion, roughly 2.25 times the gross national products of the world at that time (see calculation, 288), and this great wealth was largely in the hands of home-owning families. Fortunately, many of the housing policies which have ignored the market have been abandoned. Others survive, through bureaucratic inertia and political cowardice on the one hand, or by maniacal despotism and illusions of grandeur on the other. There is no doubt, however, that each new housing policy must face the housing mar-ket – take it by the horns, so to speak, and make it behave. There is too much at stake.

The challenge then is to understand, limit, and support the housing market in a manner that serves the fundamental interests of society – in other words to *enable* the housing market to work. Anyone interested in housing policy now has no choice but to confront the issue of housing market performance. Instead of looking for deep cultural differences to explain why the Japanese live in small houses, we should ask instead why a house in Tokyo cost three times as much as a house in Washington, D.C., in 1990 (see table A24), and try to devise policies to bring house prices down. And bringing house prices down requires two kinds of knowledge. First, we must know or suspect that prices are unreasonably high. We must have some understanding of what are the expected price norms in a well-functioning housing market. Second, we must know or suspect what conditions are responsible for bringing about and maintaining high prices.

Unfortunately, these conditions are, more often than not, outside the housing market. The housing market operates in a policy environment, and this policy environment significantly affects its performance. What must be done, therefore, is to bring the concerns about the performance of the housing market into the policy environment that affects it. To conserve human resources, this requires the abandonment of earlier attempts of housing enthusiasts to focus on single projects. Many of us were involved in individual housing projects and programs that have often fallen short of expectations even though they were properly executed. Why? Kaufmann [1991] provided one convincing answer. He compared the productivity of some 1,200 World Bank investment projects in several economic sectors in 58 developing countries, and showed that projects in countries that had less trade restrictions, black markets, price distortions, negative interest rates, and fiscal deficits had significantly higher levels of productivity. In short, the overall economic policy environment affected, and often determined, the degree of success or failure of individual programs and projects. And it is precisely this policy environment that needs to be addressed if project performance is to improve. Projects by themselves have no voice nor vision. Properly designed, they may be useful teaching laboratories, but they cannot serve as examples for doing things correctly as long as the policy environment remains contorted.

A new vision and an effective voice for housing requires dismantling the public institutions myopically engaged in the construction and management of public housing. They are at best marginal, and at worst they drain the limited public energies and resources needed to press for housing policy reform. New knowledge-rich government institutions must come into being, agencies that accumulate information about the workings of the housing sector as a key economic sector, monitor the pulse of the sector, understand the effects of the housing policy environment on the sector's performance, and implement minimal corrective mechanisms to support it in the attainment of realistic social objectives. There is no alternative to articulating market-sensitive housing policies that can better gauge, limit, or support housing activity, and campaigning for their acceptance. Individual actors and institutions in the housing arena — be they political parties, government agencies, research institutions, international organizations, nongovernment agencies, professional associations, nonprofit organizations, community groups, builders, financial institutions, landowners, land and housing developers, squatter movements, and (last but not least) dwellers themselves — have now attained different degrees of understanding of how to formulate such market-sensitive policies and how to marshal their campaigns. This book is, in some sense, a manual for the articulation of the housing policies that can inform and empower such campaigns. Articulating such policies is by no means a simple matter. They cannot be easily reduced to simple visions and translated into simple programs for industrial production or public provision. In every city, the housing system is created through millions of large and small decisions, all aimed at tailoring dwellings to the minute needs, resources, and constraints of their inhabitants. Those of us concerned with housing policy can only seek the broad view, looking for general patterns and general prescriptions and relying on gross measures of overall sector performance, but well aware that between our broad policy concerns and the minute concerns of individual households there is inevitably a distance. And lest we get lost in policy abstractions that bear no relation to the reality of people's housing, we have no choice but to listen. Our challenge is to articulate these many voices into a few simple objectives, to devise simple policies that can help attain these objectives, and to design simple measuring systems that can detect progress toward meeting these objectives, all the while remaining connected to the private agendas of those who actually build and dwell.

The book can be best understood as an extended essay on the myriad relationships between housing policy and housing market performance. My single objective is to demonstrate to the reader — both analytically and statistically — that *housing policy matters*, namely that significant differences in important housing outcomes are attributable, at least in part, to differences in the housing policy regimes of cities and countries. When I once told a vice president of the World Bank, during an elevator ride, that I was writing a book that showed that policy mattered in housing, he dismissed it with "What else is new?" Surely, it must matter, that much is trivial. But how it matters, why it matters, when it matters, how can we be sure it matters, and how much it matters are important questions that cannot be simply brushed away with "What else is new?" This book seeks to provide answers to these questions.

The book is divided into three interrelated parts. Part I presents its underlying conceptual framework, and distinguishes in broad brush strokes between enabling and nonenabling housing policy regimes. Each of the chapters in Part I is devoted to one key aspect of this conceptual framework, and together these chapters aim to bring housing policy into a new perspective. Such a perspective provides us with an empirical definition of housing policy. It also transforms our perception of the housing policy agenda from the administration of housing subsidies in one form or another, to the management of a major economic sector — a sector where vast personal wealth is now concentrated. It refocuses our attention on the critical role of cities in the formulation and implementation of housing policy. This new perspective stresses the urgent need for measurement — both for monitoring and for investigating cause and effect — in the conduct of policy, and positions policy analysis and evaluation in a global context.

Part I also introduces the Global Survey of Housing Indicators — conducted in 1990 as a joint venture of the World Bank and the United Nations — on which the statistical analysis in this book is largely based. And, finally, it formalizes these disparate elements of the conceptual framework into a simple policy-sensitive model of the housing market, a model that allows us to explore and explain the variations in housing market conditions and outcomes in different cities and countries.

Part II of the book distinguishes in greater detail between enabling and nonenabling policies in each of the five essential components of an enabling housing policy regime — the property rights regime, the housing finance regime, housing subsidies, residential infrastructure, and the regulatory regime. This part of the book is, in large measure, a presentation of the case for an enabling housing policy regime. It is designed as a rounded presentation of housing policy as one whole, a presentation that makes it possible for anyone versed in one area of housing policy to understand and embrace the other critical policy perspectives. In the process of presenting the case for enabling policies, each chapter in Part II also quantifies the degree of enabling of any given housing policy regime along one of its five key components. The end result is a composite measure of the degree of enabling of the housing policy regime as a whole — the Enabling Index. Variations in this index among different countries are found to be positively associated with higher levels of economic development and political freedoms.

Part III of this book presents the available statistical evidence to support the case for an enabling housing policy regime — a global comparison of the housing sectors of 53 major cities in 53 countries in 1990. Since the focus of the present study is on investigating similarities and differences — as well as what accounts for them — in a broad cross-section of countries, it matters less that a number of years have passed since the data were collected. The 100 housing indicators and composite indices available from the Global Survey of Housing Indicators of 1990 are the best comparative global data set on the housing sector available for the time being, clearly sufficient to discern a large number of patterns and connections that were largely hidden before.

This part of the book is essentially a quantitative analysis of the effects of the economic, social, and political context and the housing policy environment on housing market conditions — the availability of land, conditions in the residential construction sector, and the availability of mortgage credit, plus the effect of all three on housing market outcomes. Housing market outcomes are measured from a number of perspectives: prices, rents, and affordability; dwelling units and living space; housing quality; the value of housing; housing production and investment, vacancy, and mobility; and home ownership, tenure status, and homelessness. A large number of the econometric models posit housing market conditions or outcomes as dependent variables, and they use the Enabling Index as one of a number of explanatory variables. The majority of these models demonstrate — often with a high level of confidence — that an enabling housing policy regime indeed results in better housing conditions and outcomes, even after controlling for differences in levels of economic development and demographic circumstances. Housing in enabling policy environments is, on the whole, significantly better and less expensive, despite minor differences in levels of new production and significantly lower levels of subsidies. Other than the significantly lower rents — largely due to rent control — found in nonenabling regimes, such regimes almost never resulted in better housing sector performance, in terms of most of the measures analyzed in this book. In other words, the statistical analysis confirms that housing policy matters. Enabling housing policies, logical and sensible as they may be in and of themselves, also result in more favorable housing outcomes.

Part I

Housing Policy: A Conceptual Framework

1

The Enabling Approach
to Governing Housing

In the absence of a clear and accepted definition of what constitutes housing policy and who attends to it, we can only speak of the housing policy environment — the set of policies or government interventions that motivate, enable, and constrain housing action. We define the housing policy environment as follows:

The *housing policy environment* is the set of government interventions that have a critical and measurable effect on the performance of the housing sector.

This is an empirical definition. It implies, for example, that policies which do not have any effect on the housing sector are not and should not be considered part of the housing policy environment. In light of the difficulty of associating housing policy with a single well defined institution of government, this definition is also open and inclusive, rather than closed and exclusive.

Housing is not a discrete entity. Housing production is a part of the construction sector, housing investment is a part of overall capital formation, residential property is a part of the real estate sector, housing finance is a part of the financial sector, housing subsidies are a part of social welfare expenditures, and residential development is a part of urban development. They are, no doubt, large parts, but they still are parts of many larger wholes, each with its own bundle of policies. We cannot, therefore, hope to carve out an autonomous housing policy from these disjunct parts of so many different policy wholes, so as to distinguish housing policy from other kinds of policy. We must satisfy ourselves with examining the policy environment of the housing sector in pursuit of policies that matter to dwellers, builders, lenders, and government agencies concerned with housing.

To make matters more complicated, housing policies are often championed in pursuit of nonhousing agendas, further blurring the definition of what constitutes housing policy. For the actors in the housing arena, a well functioning housing sector is, first and foremost, one that meets *housing* needs in an efficient, equitable, and sustainable manner, while freeing resources and energies to meet a host of other important needs. Beyond that, the housing sector can indeed provide an efficient and effective mechanism for meeting other needs that transcend the basic need for shelter — redistributing income, jump-starting a stagnant economy, expanding the financial system or spearheading urban renewal, to cite a few examples. We must bear in mind, however, that it is never absolutely necessarily that housing policies be used to further other agendas, but also that housing does attract many political constituencies that can help further its own agenda. Indeed, the housing sector may have to compete, from time to time, with other economic and social sectors vying for the same resources.

The housing policy environment consists then of a set of interventions in the housing sector by different government agencies. As expected, not all such interventions sustain a well functioning housing sector. In the discussion that follows, we seek to make meaningful distinctions among them. In general terms, some of these interventions are said to be enabling, while others are nonenabling. We define enabling in the simplest terms as "setting boundaries and giving support while relinquishing control."

The easiest way to perceive the deeper meaning of the term "enabling" is by borrowing an insight from psychotherapy: looking at governance by analogy to child-rearing, where government is taken to be the adult parent and the rest of the actors in the housing sector are taken to be newborn children. Alice Miller distinguishes between two kinds of pedagogy: a nurturing one, which we may call enabling, one the one hand, and a poisonous one, which we may call non-enabling, on the other. The poisonous or nonenabling rules, which unfortunately still govern much of what goes by the term child-rearing, take for granted that adults are masters of the dependent child; they determine in godlike fashion what is right and what is wrong; the child's life-affirming feelings pose a threat to the autocratic adult; the child must be "broken" as soon as possible; and all this must happen at a very early age so that the child "won't notice" and will therefore not be able to expose the adult. In contrast, the nurturing or enabling rules assume that the child's aggressive impulses can be neutralized because they do not threaten the parent; the child's striving for autonomy is not a threat to the parent; the child does not have to please the parent and can develop his or her own needs at his or her own developmental pace; the child can depend on and use his or her parents because they are separate from the child; and the parents' independence and good boundaries allow the child to "separate self and object representation" [Bradshaw, 1988,43–44, paraphrasing Miller, 1981].

Enabling and nonenabling housing policy environments may be distinguished along five different lines as:

1. special cases of government intervention in the economy as a whole;
2. systems where housing needs are met by markets and governments oversee markets and correct market failure, versus systems where governments are directly responsible for meeting housing needs;
3. systems governed by the rule of law versus systems governed by decree;
4. pluralist versus centralist systems, allowing multiple visions to coexist rather than advancing a single shared vision; or
5. consisting of two different sets of government interventions, each single intervention being enabling or nonenabling in itself.

Enabling and Government Intervention

The enabling and nonenabling debate could be cast as a simple reformulation of the old dichotomy between laissez faire and planning, between letting the market work versus abandoning the market in favor of a centrally planned economy. It should not be. Neither laissez faire nor the centrally planned economy have survived the test of time. A real economy cannot function without government intervention or without markets. And given that there has to be some government intervention in the economy, the debate must be refocused on precisely what form intervention should take.

The more modern version of the enabling–interventionist debate has been the focus of discussion on strategies for African development during the 1980s, a debate not restricted to housing but to economic development as a whole. The World Bank and the International Monetary Fund (IMF) have focused their efforts on structural adjustment—the liberalization of African economies through shrinking public spending, privatizing public enterprises, removing price controls, reducing rampant subsidies, and increasing the capacities of governments for managing market-based economies. The key argument advanced by the liberalization school is that the role of the state is to create an enabling environment for the market to work by relinquishing control over the economy.

The key argument advanced by those supporting the interventionist approach in Africa pointed to the failure of the market to meet basic needs, the inability of the private sector to raise sufficient capital or to compete in international markets, and the domination of national markets by foreign concerns. But these arguments do not directly apply to the urban housing sector. Even at the very low levels of income in African countries, this sector does perform as a market, using prices and rents to allocate the resources of both producers and consumers. It does meet basic needs, in so far as it produces cheap housing that does not consume in an inordinate share of household incomes. That the quality of much of such housing reflects poverty goes without saying. But its elementary building technology does not require access to capital markets, is not subject to international competition, and is not dominated by foreign concerns. There is no fundamental reason, then, for government intervention in the housing sector in lieu of the private sector.

Why, we may ask, has the enabling approach to markets now come of age? One answer to that question focuses on the current disenchantment with the interventionist manifestos of radical and revolutionary vanguards on both the left and the right of the political spectrum. The enabling paradigm goes hand in hand with a centrist agenda of a liberal democracy, trying to restrain the predatory instincts of both capitalist and state monopolies in an age where information is no longer the prerogative of the few. In that regard, it is a product of recent historical developments — most notably the collapse of the Communist regimes in Eastern Europe and in the former Soviet Union, and the anxieties engendered by the approaching spending limits of the welfare state in Western Europe and North America. These developments have engendered a renewed faith in the efficiency of markets and in the role of regulations and policies as boundaries protecting society from market failure.

The change in focus is also a result of the frustration with much of the development assistance to Africa, Asia, and Latin America has failed to produce meaningful economic growth, because development assistance has often been predicated on doing business with government bureaucrats that had a major stake in the nonenabling status quo. Needed reforms have turned out to require much more — a shift from "better- management" concerns that leave corrupt systems intact to a call for reinventing government through the political process. Distortions in the operation of economies have turned out to be structural, calling for revisions of laws and established (and often corrupt) practices and requiring considerable political will, much beyond the leverage of international organizations, powerful as they are perceived to be.

Enabling and Market Failure

The housing sector is undoubtedly a market, but it is not a single, unfettered market — houses vary by location, quality, design, quantity, form of tenure, degree of legality, and neighborhood amenities. It is composed of a number of fragmented submarkets, which may be quite insulated from each other with little or no crossover between them. Most second-generation families in the established neighborhoods of Rio de Janeiro, for example, would rather squeeze into a small space in an old apartment than move back to the *favela*, the crowded squatter settlement on the hill. Once they have turned their back on the *favela*, it is no longer part of their housing market. The apartment is, however, part of the market of the *favela* dwellers who may be saving for a down payment. Moreover, *favelas* are built with the same building materials as apartment blocks. And when there is an apartment building boom, building on the hills becomes more expensive as well. The markets for apartments and squatter houses are, in short, connected. So are the markets for suburban or inner-city housing, rental or owner-occupied housing, public or private housing, legal or illegal housing. To go even further, there is already some evidence that as financial markets become more integrated, building booms and busts in different countries are now becoming connected as well.

Fortunately, many of the housing policies which have turned their back on the market, or proceeded as if it did not exist, have been abandoned or laid to rest. Many others still survive, by bureaucratic inertia and political cowardice on the one hand, or by maniacal despotism and corrupted visions of grandeur on the other. Be that as it may, we can safely say that new housing policies will have no choice but to face the housing market, to take it by the horns, so to speak, and make it behave.

Enabling housing policy regimes do precisely that. Instead of ignoring markets and proceeding to produce or allocate housing subsidies without regard to and outside housing markets, they allow markets to produce and allocate housing, while ensuring that they do so in an efficient and equitable manner. Enabling, in this sense, is enabling markets to work and protecting them from failure. And in housing, as we shall see, markets do fail. They fail to meet the primary social objective of ensuring "a decent home for every family at a price within their means" [Department of the Environment, 1977a, 214 quoted in Whitehead, 1991, 872]. They fail because society regards shelter as a basic need, a basic necessity which everyone should have regardless of income, a necessity that economists refer to as a merit good. And markets left to themselves will not necessarily insure that everyone is indeed housed at a level acceptable to society as a whole. Housing markets also fail because one's bad housing affects another's well–being, either by being a threat to health and safety, by being a fire hazard, or by being an eyesore — effects that economists call externalities. Left to themselves, housing consumers in an unregulated housing market can therefore impose unacceptable risk on others, risks against which everyone must be protected. Finally, housing markets also fail "from lack of appropriate markets to insure against risk, from inadequate or asymmetric information, or from differences between private and social discount rates" [Whitehead, 1991, 873]. Still, in spite of such failures, enabling housing policy regimes seek to correct them, rather than to assume that they are incorrigible and to take over the responsibility for meeting housing needs directly, through administrative allocations outside the market.

Rule of Law versus Rule by Decree

The actors in an enabling policy environment pursue their own goals and objectives, subject to a set of rules that determine the relationships between them and constrain their behavior. When such rules, or laws, are fair, impersonal, predictable, transparent, and well understood, they enable or empower the actors to exercise their maximum energy and creativity to attain their goals without diminishing the energy and creativity of other actors. When such rules are arbitrary and unpredictable — subject to the whims of autocrats or bureaucrats who themselves are not subject to the rule of law — they weaken first some of the actors and eventually all of the actors. Hayek describes the rules that underlie a mature market system in similar terms:

> Neither his reason nor his innate "natural goodness" leads man this way, only the bitter necessity of submitting to rules he does not like in order to maintain himself against competing groups that had already begun to expand because they stumbled upon such rules earlier. . . . To the naive mind that can conceive of order only as a product of deliberate arrangement, it may seem absurd that in complex conditions order, and adaptation to the unknown, can be achieved more effectively by decentralizing decisions, and that a division of authority will actually extend the possibility of overall order. Yet that decentralization actually leads to more information being taken into account. [Hayek, 1988, 76–77]

It is intuitively clear that such a complex and vibrant an enterprise as the urban housing sector can never be properly coordinated by a central authority, no matter how informed and intelligent it is. In fact, it works because it is not coordinated by a hierarchical organization governed by omniscient helmsmen who impose decrees, centralize control, and silence feedback as subversive. If every little decision about what to build, where to build, how to build, or when to build had to be coordinated with every other decision, nothing would ever get built. The fact that so much does get built and that it does meet needs has to do with breaking down the linkages that coordination demands, realizing that beyond the need for minimal coordination, every action can move along in total disregard of all other actions.

Just as a child-rearing environment is not nurturing if it is permissive, enabling policies do not call for the deregulation of the housing sector in the spirit of laissez-faire. Good laws are indeed deemed essential for its smooth operation, for establishing and protecting property rights, for resolving disputes among different stakeholders, for protecting the interests of urban dwellers from the unwanted consequences of spontaneous residential development (such as traffic congestion, pollution, and environmental degradation), and for the provision of essential public services. But enabling laws do call for relinquishing control over the residential development process, for recognizing that unwarranted and heavy-handed "plans" are stifling and destructive, and for assessing the costs and risks of regulation as part of a broader calculus of the costs and benefits of urban development. De Soto [1989] articulates this view in *The Other Path:*

> Peruvian laws are predominantly bad. . . . The most tangible proof of the unsuitability of these laws is that the vast majority of the economically active population has chosen to operate informally. . . . In other words, they have chosen to operate outside these bad laws, which entail such high costs and such complex regulations. . . . [I]f the state provides good laws, it makes specialization possible and exchange far easier, enabling human and material resources to be used in the best possible way. An appropriate system of property rights, contracts, and extra-contractual liability can spontaneously generate the efficient use of resources without a bureaucracy to decide or authorize how the resources must be used. Citizens dependent on this system will have sufficient incentives to produce, through a multi-plicity of efforts and private transactions, an economic system which is exceptionally sensitive to the opportunities for development. [182-184]

Sandbrook [1993] summarizes the dismal fate of interventionist governments, committed to rule by decree, in sub-Saharan Africa in the 1980s:

> Bloated public administrations operate inefficiently, erratically and some-times dishonestly, partly as a result of the many officials who are appointed and promoted on the basis of nepotistic, factional, and personal ties. Corruption creates administrative bottlenecks. The economic infrastructure deteriorates or operates irregularly. Breakdowns in the administration of

justice and political instability foster uncertainty as to the sanctity of private property and contracts. Heavy handed regulation of civil society by suspicious autocrats discourages autonomous, grassroots initiatives and provokes people to flee into the unregulated informal sector, into illegal activities like smuggling, or even into exile. Ambitious individuals seek to make their fortunes through parasitical manipulation of the government's regulatory and spending powers. Risk-taking entrepreneurial activities are seldom the quickest and easiest road to wealth. Manipulating state offices, contracts, regulations, licensed monopolies, access to foreign exchange and other underpriced goods and services is far more lucrative. [17]

Having said that, we must bear in mind that the enabling–interventionist spectrum should be clearly distinguished from the order–chaos spectrum. Both the enabling order and the interventionist order are forms of order, even when we argue than the enabling order is a higher form of order. And both must distinguished from chaos. Unfortunately, chaos devastates economic performance in general, and housing sector performance in particular. Both enabling and interventionist regimes "cannot succeed without the will to back productive rather than parasitical behavior, and without the necessary extractive, political and administrative capacities to support their responsibilities" [Sandbrook, 1993, 23].

Enabling and Nonenabling as Pluralist versus Centralist Systems

A third distinction between an enabling and a nonenabling housing policy environment pertains to the origins of the rule system — were they derived as a response to a real-world need or with reference to first principles? In an enabling environment, all that is necessary for the housing sector to function properly is a basic and minimal set of well-understood rules, rules that are invented in response to need, established in the law, and gradually refined over time. The housing sector in an enabling environment is, almost without exception, a self-organizing system, an "adaptive system [which] continues to achieve its objectives in the face of a changing environment or deterioration in the performance of some of its elements" through self-correcting feedback mechanisms [Hughes, 1969, 8]. Enabling policies in the housing sector call for a style of governance based on intelligence, on the gathering of information about the housing system, and on the evolution of a sensitive rule system that can effectively guide the sector in a manner that promotes, in as broad a way as possible, the interests of the stake holders in the system. The enabling order seeks to structure the real incentives of the different actors, so that the goals they pursue may not undermine the overall performance of the system. As such it is also a learning system, a dynamic system that is continually modified and corrected as new understanding accumulates.

Complete rule systems may not, however, be transferred as a block from one place to another because every place contains so many unwritten rules. Building codes, freehold titles, zoning restrictions, growth controls, cooperative societies, or infrastructure standards cannot be transplanted from one country to another without sufficient regard for the particular cultural context and the specific modes of interaction and exchange in the two countries. Unfortunately, the evolution of housing policy, especially in the former colonies of the European imperialist powers, abounds with the imposition of inappropriate policies on unsuspecting victims.

Lai [1988], in his discussion of law as the invisible web underlying urban development, sees a distinct difference between the empiricist approaches to the law in Great Britain and the United States, on the one hand, and the rationalist approaches to the law in continental Europe on the other. In the former, the law evolved as a practical response to real-world situations, while in the latter "reason, independent of the senses, constitutes a superior form of knowledge," and laws were derived from intellectual principles and received doctrine rather than from practical experience [39]. In Lai's view, "The authoritarian nature of this latter form of civil law suited continental autocracies in carrying out rationally conceived goals in Renaissance urban design" [22]. In England, on the other hand, after the Great London Fire of 1666, Charles II had to forego his plans for reconstructing the city according to Renaissance design principles because "he lacked the power, under English law, to exercise the necessary authority, despite the devastation" [30]. Power in London was already too decentralized among the different stake holders to admit an authoritarian master plan into their midst, a plan that disregarded the hard-won property boundaries that protected them from the state. The city of London was quickly rebuilt, but essentially along the existing property lines.

Enabling strategies necessarily assume a multiplicity of actors in the housing sector, for if there were only one actor there would be no one to enable. In fact, the enabling policy environment acts to empower governments to act as well. Local governments and central governments also need a set of functional rules, an adequate inflow of resources, professional capabilities, and correct incentives to be able to carry out their responsibilities. They also need to be isolated from intimidation and influence-peddling by interest groups that may distort their actions and render them incapable of attending to their essential goals: under-funded municipalities cannot be expected to maintain residential infrastructure, and low-paid building inspectors cannot be expected to enforce building codes. Similarly, new roads cannot be planned if landowners have the power to refuse to give up their lands and taxpayers have the power to choke municipal infra-structure budgets. The central government, on its part, cannot reform inequitable off-budget housing subsidies under crude political pressure from home owners. Neither can it act on the relaxation of the rent controls in the face of political pressure from sitting tenants. Macrae, in his 1960 paper entitled *To Let?* sums up this predicament: "Rent control has held the British people back from enjoyment of the full standard of life and happiness that they might have achieved. . . . It is not ignorance of economic realities, but sheer and confirmed electoral cowardice that has stayed the statesmen's hands" [Macrae, in Minford et al., 1987, xii].

In short, the enabling paradigm pertains to all the actors in the housing sector, not just to some. A balance of power may be implied in this concept, a sense that no one actor has a monopoly on the truth or a divine mandate to act outside established rules. In a well functioning housing *sector all* actors – dwellers, builders, lenders, local governments and national governments – must be able to carry out their objectives and not some at the expense of others. National governments must be enabled to govern as well, as has been amply demonstrated by the breakdown of governance in Africa: "Willing compliance is the only sure basis for a stable and effective government. As consent declines, so too does the governability of a society in which the coercive force at the center is meagre or unreliable. This has been the unhappy story of many sub-Saharan countries" [Sandbrook, 1993, 50].

The present appeal of the more–pluralist enabling regimes can be attributed to the greater influence of broad–based market forces, to the amplified voices of smaller political constituencies in modern societies, and to the general retreat of governments from undertaking bold unpopular measures in the face of organized and decentralized resistance. In this sense, the enabling paradigm takes as given the motives and the power of diverse interest groups and tries to devise appropriate rules and incentives that will prevent these interest groups from becoming predatory.

The Enabling Housing Policy Environment
as a Set of Enabling Interventions

The housing policy environment can be said to be enabling if it attends to the five key policy instruments that have an inordinate effect on housing sector performance:

1. adjudication of property rights in land and housing;
2. development and regulation of housing finance institutions;
3. administration of housing subsidies;
4. provision and maintenance of residential infrastructure; and
5. regulation of land and housing development.

The first three can be taken to affect the demand side of the housing market, while the last two can be said to affect the supply side. Each of these five components of a comprehensive housing policy can be enabling or nonenabling in and of itself. A housing policy environment can indeed be said to be enabling only in so far as these five components are enabling in and of themselves. In fact, for the sector as a whole to function well, all these components need to be enabling. If only the demand side is enabling and the supply side is not, the housing sector may not gain as much in performance as when both sides are in balance. Enabling mortgage finance and subsidy policies, for example, can increase the demand for housing, while heavy-handed regulations and infrastructure shortages can constrain supply. The overall result can be a shortage of housing, accompanied by high prices and low affordability for all. If, on the other hand, supply-side policies are also enabling, then housing supply may be able to expand quickly to meet demand, with the result that higher demand will result in more housing at affordable prices.

We can illustrate the differences between the enabling and nonenabling components of the housing policy environment with an example. In 1990, informal land subdivisions in Bangkok occurred within a highly enabling housing policy environment [Angel and Pornchokchai, 1990], while high-rise apartment construction in Moscow occurred within a highly nonenabling one. Let us compare the components of these two housing policy environments one by one:

1. *the property right regimes*: Buyers of a plot in a land subdivision in Bangkok obtained a legal land title, properly registered in the Land Department, which could be sold or mortgaged even though the house they built did not meet building and land subdivision regulations. The tenants obtaining an apartment in Moscow did not yet have a clear legal right to the apartment, could only sell or trade it illegally, and could not move out without losing it.

2. *the housing finance regimes*: Typically, Bangkok land subdivision residents paid for their plots in installments to a land broker for 18 months, and then mortgaged the plot to any local bank and, using the plot as collateral, paid for it in installments in three and a half years. Houses were constructed gradually, largely without access to mortgage finance. In Moscow, tenants could not pay more of their savings for better housing even if they wished to do so, nor could they obtain a mortgage loan for securing such housing.

3. *housing subsidies*: Informal land subdivisions in Bangkok were not subsidized. Electricity, water, and building materials were supplied by the land broker at market prices. In Moscow, the entire investment in construction was subsidized. So were rents, as well as the costs of maintenance, energy, and repair without regard to income or need. As a result, the majority of dwellers balked at government efforts to transfer apartments to sitting tenants, even free of charge.

4. *residential infrastructure*: Informal land subdivisions on the outskirts of Bangkok were served by unpaved secondary roads that connected them to the few arterial highways leading into the city. Right-of-way for these roads was quickly negotiated by village headmen along the edges of land holdings — owners donated the edge of their land in exchange for road access, and those who refused were bypassed. The local authorities obtained the title to the roads and paved them in due time. Land brokers provided water wells, roads on landfill, and electricity lines to the plots, where owners could quickly build start-up houses they could inhabit. All infrastructure was constructed in response to demand. In Moscow, all infrastructure construction, and all other construction for that matter, was

coordinated by the Moscow Construction Committee, which, in 1994 for example, employed more than half a million people and had unlimited access to urban land. The committee was charged with the design, finance, execution, and management of all construction in Moscow, implementing its programs without regard to demand.

5. *the regulatory regime*: In Bangkok, there were very few official restrictions on the shape or form of the house, rarely a difficulty in obtaining the necessary permits, and rarely a fine for not obtaining the necessary per-mits. People designed and built what they wanted within the constraints of what they could afford, and they never had to wait for anyone. In Moscow, dwellers had to wait for years before obtaining an apartment. They could not participate in any decision on the shape and size of the unit, let alone help in its construction, nor take responsibility for its maintenance regardless of what they could afford: "[I]n 1992 income, whether from the socialist or informal sector, had no influence on housing allocation.... [I]t was the rationing system rather than households beating the system that determined how much housing households had." [Buckley and Gurenko, 1995, 17]

Bangkok thus had a more enabling housing policy environment than Moscow in each one of the five components of the housing policy environment. The housing policy environment in Moscow in 1990, at the end of the era of central planning, was very similar to the situation in other eastern European countries at that time, succinctly characterized by Hegedus, Mayo, and Tosics [1996]:

Incentives to key stakeholders in the sector have been contradictory, unclear and perverse; institutions have been unsustainable in the context of mar-ket–driven demand and supply. Housing outcomes have deviated signifi-cantly from those in the West, with more limited and highly regulated tenure choice and property rights, more limited choices concerning the type and location of housing, low residential mobility and housing turnover, a monopolistic and inefficient building industry, underdeveloped financial institutions and instruments, distortionary and poorly targeted subsidies, a planning and regulatory framework largely unresponsive to either consumer needs or environmental sustainability, and policies and programs largely divorced from the inputs of major stakeholders concerning their needs and preferences. [9]

The distinction between an enabling and an interventionist policy environment is not black and white. It is really a matter of degree. Kuala Lumpur, for example, while similar to Bangkok in many ways, showed a number of differences in its housing policy environment: permits took much longer, regulations were stricter, and construction monopolies abounded. Similarly, Budapest was a more enabling environment than Moscow, even though both were committed to central planning. It is indeed the degree of enabling that we shall focus on (see chapter 12).

* * *

In conclusion, we must acknowledge that while the enabling paradigm presents an attractive alternative to a control-based regime, its continued ascent is not at all assured and should not be taken for granted. The hope that this more sensitive and guarded intervention will work in the long run can only be conditional upon its ability to deliver results in practice, that is to guarantee good housing sector performance. The enabling paradigm is only a *theory* then, a theory arising out of particular historical conditions and clarifying these conditions in the process. Political action based on this paradigm will change these conditions and will lead to a revision, enrichment, or rejection of the paradigm. There are many who still believe that human society is "out of control," and, lacking a grand vision of the future, has lost its bearings. The radical no-growth agendas, for example, that prescribe uncompromising controls on "urban sprawl" in the name of nature conservation are clearly in the interventionist tradition. They already herald the rejection of the enabling paradigm as being too prone to the predatory practices of unrepentant and conspiratorial "urban growth machines" building cities gone astray. For its true believers, the more benign chant of *Nimby!* — "not in my backyard" — has already been replaced by the more comprehensive chant of *Banana!* — "build absolutely nothing anywhere near anything."

Even the term "enabling" has now acquired a derogatory connotation: in current use in psychotherapy, it is a term describing the behavior of weak-willed family members of violent spouse abusers, drug addicts, and alcoholics who enable them to continue their abusive behavior. Giving unconditional support while failing to set proper boundaries is, needless to say, exactly the opposite of what is meant by enabling in the housing context.

2

Housing as a Key Economic Sector

Comprehensiveness, insofar as it stands for the development of a policy and an institutional framework for managing the housing sector as a whole, is an essential feature of an enabling housing policy environment. It stands in sharp contrast to housing policies that focus , for example, only on the *public* provision of housing while neglecting the private sector and the informal sector; or to policies that focus on one or another component of housing policy — say housing finance or housing subsidies — while neglecting others.

The enabling paradigm calls for a housing policy environment that oversees and regulates the sector, keeping the government out of the direct supply of housing and thus leaving the actual production and delivery of housing to the housing market — be it formal, informal, voluntary, or involving the consumers themselves as producers. This paradigm rejects the interventionist provision of public housing by the nation-state, which is based on the premise that the other actors in the housing sector — dwellers, builders and lenders to name a few — cannot be trusted to supply the kind of housing that society demands as a constitutional "right" for its members.

The now-bankrupt public-housing agenda, by requiring a massive commitment on the part of government to engage in the production, distribution, and management of housing, has stood in the way of pointing government housing efforts in the direction of assuming responsibility for the performance of the housing sector as a whole. As long as housing policy essentially meant public housing, the policy essentially squandered the limited human resources available to society for managing the housing problem, while the great bulk of housing activity continued to take place outside the myopic focus of government efforts.

An enabling housing policy environment gives rise to institutions that take as their goal the performance of the housing sector as a whole, monitor that performance, understand what policies and institutional practices affect it and how they affect it, and intervene in all these policy areas in the name of better housing for all. Nonenabling housing institutions are typically those that have a limited view of housing, that focus on a small segment of the housing sector, and that direct an undue amount of resources toward meeting the housing needs of the few while ignoring the bulk of public interventions affecting the performance of the housing sector as a whole.

Modern housing policy agendas are now motivated by three key concerns: the realization of the importance of the housing sector as a major economic sector; the need to redefine public assistance in the housing sector as part of the overall reform of the welfare state agenda; and the commitment to good governance (the maintenance of public order, the resolution of social conflicts, upholding the country's international reputation, and securing its dominance over its internal affairs) — all of which have a direct bearing on housing policy.

Indeed, the key to understanding the perspective of central governments with regard to what constitutes a well-functioning housing sector is to focus on the shift in its perception of itself — from regarding its role mainly as a direct provider of housing assistance, essentially as a component of social welfare policy, to that of managing the housing sector as a key component of the economy. This shift has not occurred everywhere, by any means. In many countries there is an active and committed "housing policy community" — a coalition of elected and career officials, voluntary-sector activists, and academics — with personal and altruistic interests to channel the nation-state's resources to the housing sector to remedy social ills. Typically, housing activists campaign for establishing minimum standards of housing, defining what constitutes housing unfit for human habitation, and harnessing government with a legal mandate to ensure that everyone is adequately housed. Commendable as such pursuits are, their myopic view of housing policy as a component of social welfare policy demeans it, belittles it, and marginalizes it. The housing sector is thus demoted to an inferior position in the grand scheme of things — as one of many instruments for distributing welfare — a considerably less central position that its role in the economy merits.

Public assistance in housing is, of course, a necessary component of housing policy as we shall see later (Chapter 9), but it is not to be confused with housing policy in its broadest sense. The nation-state has an overriding interest in accumulating wealth and in promoting and managing economic growth and stability; as such, it is committed to encouraging investment, fostering savings, generating employment, containing inflation, exercising fiscal responsibility, promoting fair competition, smoothing out the effects of business cycles, and deepening financial markets. A well-functioning housing sector supports the attainment of each of these objectives, and it needs to be perceived as such.

First, nation-states have an interest in increasing and maintaining national wealth. And because housing assets form the bulk of personal wealth worldwide, all nation-states have an interest in managing, protecting, and maintaining these housing assets, a major form of national wealth.[1]

Second, housing investment normally accounts for 20% to 30% of gross fixed capital formation, and between 3 and 8 percent of the gross domestic product (GDP).[2] Housing services typically account for an additional 5% to 10% of GNP [World Bank, 1993, 2]. Nation-states, in their pursuit of economic growth, seek to encourage the production, sales, rental, maintenance, and rehabilitation of housing in all forms. To do so, they must enable home builders to function effectively in a competitive and open economy. They must also remove barriers to increasing the efficiency of construction activities, to the adoption of technological innovation, and to the regular supply of materials and machinery.

Third, nation-states have an interest in generating household savings and in mobilizing household productive resources, and therefore they have a preference for housing alternatives that encourage, rather than discourage, household investment in homes, as well as the maintenance and care of buildings and neighborhoods to maintain the value of this investment. Housing savings in the form of housing assets are also a form of social security, enabling elderly homeowners to sustain themselves by gradually withdrawing equity from their homes, thus contracting their housing assets while increasing their consumer expenditures. At the same time, nation-states are wary of rapid increases in the value of housing assets which may lead households to withdraw equity and to increase their consumer spending, thereby reducing savings and causing higher inflation (or adversely affecting the balance of payments if people buy foreign goods). Muellbauer [1990] has argued that in Britain, "[t]he ending of mortgage rationing has led to a large rise in the personal sector's debt to income ratio and the phenomenon of mortgage cash withdrawal or 'equity withdrawal' from the housing market. . . . Much of the explanation for the decline of the personal sector savings rate in the 1980s and the boom in consumer imports is to be found here" [49].

Fourth, nation-states have an interest in both full employment and low inflation. Full employment is easier to achieve when people can move freely in search of job opportunities, and hence in a housing sector that facilitates high residential mobility and promotes the exchange of units. This usually means that they have an interest in maintaining a healthy market in rentals. Furthermore, the housing sector itself generates employment and creates a least twice the employment it generates directly through multiplier effects. To prevent the loss of jobs, as well as to control inflation, nation-states also have an interest in keeping land and house prices low through the promotion of a healthy and competitive building industry. High land and house prices compromise the international competitive position of the nation's cities because of their pressure on wages.

Fifth, to exercise fiscal responsibility and to reduce or eliminate budgetary deficits that increase inflation and slow down economic growth, nation-states must ensure that overall public housing expenditures, at both the central and local levels, are sufficient to maintain their basic commitments without unduly straining their budgets. In addition, as mentioned earlier, they may have an interest in restricting the flow of financial resources into the housing sector to "cool" an overheated economy so as to restrain inflation. Conversely, they have an interest in directing financial resources into the housing sector, especially in periods of economic slumps when housing investments can be used to stimulate a stagnant economy.

And sixth, nation-states have an interest in ensuring the growth and deepening of financial markets, and thus in encouraging the growth of mortgage lending and the trading in mortgage-backed securities, both considered to be highly efficient and low-risk financial instruments. Financial development is not simply an outcome of economic growth, but an important contributor to economic growth. Levine [1997] confirms, based on a study of 80 countries over the period 1960–1989, that financial depth in 1960 was "a good predictor of subsequent rates of economic growth, physical capital accumulation, and economic efficiency improvements over the next 30 years even after controlling for income, education, political stability, and measures of monetary, trade, and fiscal policy" [707, citing King and Levine, 1993]. Reviewing the evidence, Levine concludes that "[a] growing body of empirical analyses . . . demonstrate a strong positive link between the functioning of the financial system and long-run economic growth" [720]. Mortgage lending for housing forms a considerable share (of the order of 15%, see table 16.1) of all lending by financial institutions and plays a crucial role in financial sector development. Nation-states have an interest in promoting lending for housing, and in ensuring that mortgage borrowing is on a level playing field with borrowing for other productive capital investments, without resorting to the rationing of financial resources [Carrizosa and Suescun, 1982]. And hand in hand with promoting financial development, nation-states also have an interest in regulating and supporting the financial sector — including the variety of housing-finance institutions — to protect the sector from undue risk and from collapse due to over-exposure.

Because the health of the housing sector is of such importance to the management of the economy, nation-states have an interest in integrating sector policy with overall macroeconomic policy; in having sufficient tools to study, monitor, and guide the sector; in investing in social experiments that can reduce risk and pave the way for other stakeholders to enter and become active in the sector (for example, by introducing fully-amortized mortgages and secondary mortgage markets); and in ensuring that municipalities conform with national sector policy objectives and have sufficient means to attain their goals. The primary role of the nation-state in housing, then, is to oversee the housing sector as a whole and enable it to work efficiently and equitably.

The need to provide and administer public assistance in housing is only a secondary concern of nation-states. All nation-states, without exception, have been forced to attend to severe housing shortages — especially following wars and natural disasters — and to respond to calls that "something must be done" to ameliorate the miserable housing conditions of the poor, the destitute, and the homeless. From the perspective of nation-states, a well-functioning housing sector is one in which every household is housed in a manner that equals or exceeds an adequate minimum standard acceptable to society at large. Defining this minimum standard is a serious commitment on the part of nation-states, for simply by defining it, the government accepts the responsibility for ensuring that everyone is adequately housed, at standards determined by society which may exceed those affordable (or for that matter desirable) by individual households. Even without defining it, by taking the moral position that such a standard exists the government recognizes the right of citizens to some minimum standard housing. It must then assume the role of "houser of last resort," and take responsibility for creating a social safety net that guarantees that households that cannot afford minimum standard housing be provided with such housing or with some form of assistance to enable them to procure it or create it themselves.

In most countries, this commitment has entailed the creation of a host of housing programs and institutions, some more successful than others, whose chief aim is to provide access to housing for people who cannot obtain minimum standard housing with their own resources. These are usually subsidized from the general tax fund, competing for public funds with other socially desirable programs. In general, the better housing welfare programs target housing subsidies to the people who need them most, and administer them efficiently — achieving broad coverage even within severe fiscal constraints. We must bear in mind, however, that in the present political climate — with the weakening of the demand for urban manual labor, the rise of the middle classes, the increased mobility of capital investments, the fiscal pressures on many debt-ridden governments in many developing countries, and the collapse of the Communist regimes in eastern Europe — the political support for government housing programs with a major focus on redistribution has considerably weakened. In the words of one social activist: "A movement for social justice, if it is to mobilize large numbers of people, must focus less on the protection of the most deprived and more on broad benefits, less on the rights of the oppressed and more on security. Most people would prefer economic growth, if any of it trickles down to them, to redistribution, if redistribution does not produce an improvement in their standards of living" [Fainstein, 1997, 38].

Finally, a third major concern of nation-states is their commitment to good governance. The commitment to public order and political stability requires nation-states to reduce racial, religious, or gender discrimination in general, and in access to housing in particular; to avoid riots and civil disturbances that may result from the forced eviction of squatters or slum dwellers; to rehabilitate and secure crime-infested neighborhoods and housing estates; to promote home ownership as a form of giving citizens a stake in maintaining the political status quo; and to prevent tenant exploitation — especially during wartime or in times of severe housing shortages — through the regulation of the relationship between landlords and tenants. Nation-states are also responsible for protecting property rights, and for ensuring that laws are obeyed — by preventing the erosion of respect for the legal system through widespread non-conformance.

* * *

In conclusion, we note again that housing policy in its broadest sense can no longer be restricted to issues of government housing assistance, be it to the masses, the poor, or the homeless. It must be broadened to managing the housing sector as a whole, including the formal and informal sector; the rich and the poor; the private, the voluntary, and the public sectors; the inner city and the suburb. It must encompass all housing activity and all the stakeholders in the housing sector. And it must bring the concerns of the housing sector — as a key economic sector — into the dialogues and debates that guide national macroeconomic policy.

3

Housing Policy and the City

There is no question that municipalities and local governments play a key role in the formulation and execution of housing policy, but this role is often glossed over or rendered invisible in the now-common perception — both in the housing literature and among policy-makers — that housing policy is a national concern and a national prerogative. This perception has been dominant in international forums, such as the United Nations and the World Bank, which, since their creation in the mid-twentieth century, have been held hostage by nation-states insisting on being the sole source of legitimate authority over their internal affairs, housing being one of them. In turn, the World Bank's insistence on central-government guarantees of all its loans further reinforced this perception.

In reality, municipalities and nation-states have overlapping and intertwined responsibilities for the housing sector, and there is no a priori division of these responsibilities between them — one that assigns an exclusive set of housing-sector functions to local governments and another to national governments. At present, there is no question that nation-states have the upper hand in both policy decisions and taxing powers, and that local government powers are fundamentally limited to those powers granted to them by nation-states. But the precise balance of power between municipalities and nation-states is dynamic and sometimes subject to rather radical change: "[G]overnment bureaucracies are the present traces of past struggles over public policies, and cannot really be understood outside of that historical context" [Jones, 1995, 82].

In the cities studied, local autonomy in decisions affecting the housing sector is a matter of degree. At one end of the spectrum, we find appointed city governments that are agents of the nation-state — they have little power to initiate local action and are not immune from oversight by higher levels of government. At the other end, we find elected local governments with a relatively high degree of local participation in decision-making and local powers of land acquisition and taxation. German cities, for instance, are closer to this end of the spectrum, guaranteed the right to regulate all the affairs of the local community within the

limits set by law [Hesse, 1991, 364, in Goldsmith, 1995, 245]. So are the autonomous suburban communities within the metropolitan areas of the United States:

> The proliferation of politically autonomous suburbs during the first half of
> this century may have played as important a part in social and political life
> in the U.S. as the growth of the joint stock company has played in the
> development of its economic life. In particular, the incorporation of thou-
> sands of new suburbs has contributed to what is probably the dominant
> characteristic of metropolitan government in the United States: its fragmen-
> tation in combination with a large measure of municipal autonomy. [New-
> ton and Wulff, 1985, 83–84]

In general, regardless of national legislation and nation–state attempts at
domination, local governments exert a substantial influence in local decisions.
Even when they act as agents, local governments have a considerable degree of
autonomy in local matters because they have the privileged information needed
to tailor policy implementation to unique local conditions, and because they focus
more acutely on the day–to–day activities that give rise to the built urban environment. Even when they do rely on grants from higher levels of government—
usually accompanied by mandates or directives—in practice local governments
appear to exert significant control over budget allocations and to have a distinct
voice in housing policy matters. A distinction can indeed be drawn between the
actual responsibilities of municipalities and those of nation–states in the housing
sector: while both are now directly involved in promoting economic development,
local governments are more directly involved in regulating construction and land
development, in the provision of urban infrastructure services, and in the implementation of a variety of welfare programs as agents of the nation–state. The
nation–state, on its part, is more directly involved in regulating the economy as
a whole, in the administration of property rights, and in the creation and administration of redistributive policies (including housing subsidies) that cannot be
effectively instituted at the local level. With this distinction in mind, we can now
properly focus on the perceptions of local officials as to what constitutes a
well–functioning housing sector. Local governments typically have five principle
concerns which have a bearing on the housing sector: promoting local economic
growth; regulating urban development; providing public infrastructure services;
administering welfare programs; and maintaining an effective bureaucracy.

    Many municipalities within metropolitan areas and many cities the world over
now compete among themselves by creating conditions aimed at attracting both
businesses and higher–income dwellers, encouraging both to choose their
preferred locations by "voting with their feet." They aim to foster local economic
growth by luring the kinds of capital investment which will create good jobs,
maintain and enhance property values, and increase their local tax base. To this
effect, beyond offering a rich array of sometimes–embarrassing incentives, they
feel obliged or expected to transform their cities in the global mold:

[T]he world economy has progressively been producing elements of a global culture to which ruling elites and national bourgeoisies increasingly adhere. In this sense, relatively clean, well-ordered cities, boasting tower blocks and shopping malls in the latest "international" (modern or post-modern) architectural styles and building materials, and filled with luxury restaurants and specialist shops selling imported designer label fashions and other quality goods, symbolize the pinnacle of modernization and development to which they aspire." [Simon, 1992, 155]

This push often means either reversing the decline of dilapidated, older districts — usually through their redevelopment or historic preservation — or opening up new lands for development. At one extreme, the pursuit of "City Beautiful" — often necessary to attract new commercial and residential investment or to promote tourism — may often involve displacing the urban poor or making them invisible. Aggressive cleanup campaigns usually result in the demolition of considerable quantities of affordable housing units, without proper consultation with the local community, without adequate compensation and without the provision of alternative housing arrangements. "City Beautiful" objectives may also reach absurd compromises, such as the construction of walls along important thoroughfares to hide slums from passing cars. In Dakar, Senegal, for example, this " 'philosophy of embellishment' reached its zenith when the motorway was constructed" [Arecchi, 1985, 209, quoted in Simon, 1992, 151].

At the other extreme, where effective resistance is offered by sitting residents, local authorities can and often do negotiate effective compromises that allow communities to have a voice in project design, share in the benefits of development, and obtain adequate housing in exchange for their cooperation in accelerating project implementation. In a well-functioning housing sector, local authorities can negotiate and administer large urban development and redevelopment projects, negotiating quickly and effectively with private-sector interests, national power brokers, and residential community groups. Such projects lead to improvements as well as additions to the housing stock, maintaining the variety of housing options in the city. They also increase the local tax base needed to provide and maintain an acceptable level of local infrastructure services commensurate with the increased demand generated by the new developments.

A second concern of local authorities is ensuring the provision of urban infrastructure services — roads, water, sewage and drainage networks, electricity supply, garbage collection and processing, public transport, communication facilities, schools, and parks and playgrounds — all of which are essential components of a well-functioning residential environment (see chapter 10). In a well-functioning housing sector, local authorities have adequate powers and budgets to plan, acquire land, construct, operate, maintain, and regulate the full range of infrastructure services desired by the citizenry. Local governments should be able to respond to demand for new services without undue delays. They should be able to tailor infrastructure standards to those in demand by users and to adjust standards in different communities to levels of affordability. Local authorities should be able to cover the costs of the provision of services through a variety of user charges, through a variety of local taxes designed to capture part of the increased value of properties resulting from service provision – property taxes, building permit fees, and development fees, to cite a few examples, through a variety of government transfers and through effective privatization. They should also have adequate access to loans so that they can streamline their capital investment and overcome their inability to operate in the face of severe cash–flow problems.

A third concern of local governments, and the one with the most far–reaching implications for housing sector performance, is the regulation of urban development – regulating land use, urban expansion, and building standards (see chapter 11). Local government coordinates and regulates land use through zoning ordinances and land use plans, with the aim of protecting health and safety by reducing land use conflicts (keeping noxious industries away from residential areas, ensuring sufficient daylight and air circulation in buildings, and controlling densities to limit congestion and ensure the adequate provision of urban services); maintaining a healthy local tax base; and, increasingly, shutting out undesirable land uses – from incinerators and major highways to drug rehabilitation centers and, of course, low–income housing.

Using land use controls, in conjunction with controls on the location and timing of urban infrastructure, local government coordinates and regulates the expansion of the city to meet population and economic growth requirements, while seeking to protect the property values of sitting residents by restricting unregulated urban growth. It is a mistake, however, to expect local government (or higher levels of government for that matter) to put effective limits on urban growth. Even when it can restrict development, say within a specified administrative boundary or within a "green belt," no government has the power to block migration into the metropolitan area as a whole. When cities are under strong population pressures – as most cities in the developing countries currently are – restricting urban growth only acts to increase overcrowding, or to the formation of illegal settlements on the urban fringe. Draconian measures to restrain population movements and expel migrants from cities – such as those attempted in China, Indonesia, South Africa, and Cuba – are all doomed to fail. Putting limits on the amount of land available for housing construction in the name of restricting migration only results in the creation of artificial housing shortages and higher prices.

Urban local governments in developed countries now increasingly focus on the need for "sustainable" urban development, a need that inevitably positions them against further urban expansion. Many urban officials increasingly see themselves as protectors of nature against an all–powerful "growth machine," one that seeks unlimited urban expansion at the expense of radical nature preservation. In 1991, the city parliament of Frankfurt, for example, unanimously passed a Greenbelt Constitution, creating a 250-km^2 ring around the city core. In the words of one of the its advocates: "As part of the city, a greenbelt symbolizes the attempt to limit and/or control urban economic growth; building activities are restricted according to a political decision" [Husung and Lieser, 1996]. Needless to say, such restrictions on urban expansion normally harm housing affordability by making residential land scarcer than it needs to be. Many suburban planning officials have now aligned themselves with a form of radical environmentalism that is often hostile to sinister "developers" as though developers build housing for their own benefit, rather than for those who need them, demand them, and pay for them. Surely, maintaining a growth-machine conspiracy theory in today's pluralist policy environment is questionable. In the words of one analyst: "The rentiers of the growth machine thesis are a dying breed" [Harding, 1995, 45]. It must be borne in mind, however, that unnecessarily harsh antimarket restrictions aimed at controlling "suburban sprawl," and wishful thinking about compact cities with more restricted car travel [Hillman,1996] are likely to increase house prices and commuting times for low-income families, while not necessarily increasing their access to parks and greens.

The nonmarket allocation of fringe urban land in Soviet cities – in the name of suppressing speculation, rather than in the name of the preserving open space and the suburban quality of life – provides an important lesson in this regard. Because of the absence of land markets and the tendency of bureaucratic house builders to minimize costs, residential densities in Moscow and St. Petersburg increase, rather than decrease, with distance from their city centers, resulting in a highly inefficient use of land:

> Perhaps the most important lesson of the failed Socialist experiment is that the well-meaning attempt to socialize the collection of the land rent through public ownership and administrative allocation of land has not achieved the intended results. . . . Soviet cities remind us that what is most valuable in urban land market institutions is their ability to signal through prices how the current and future use of land is valued by individuals and society. [Bertaud and Renaud, 1997, 150]

Over and above land use controls, which can and often do restrict residential development, local governments also administer building codes and standards with the aim of protecting public health and safety. Their mandates often include the powers to demolish unsanitary tenements, rickety structures, fire-prone shacks, earthquake-prone buildings, and flood-prone neighborhoods, or to insist on their upgrading. Demolition always diminishes the affordable housing stock, while effective insistence on standards clearly affects affordability – poor tenants in U.S. cities in the 1970s, to cite one example, could not afford the costly upgrading of their apartments to meet local codes. Between 1970 and 1981, 341,000 housing units were abandoned in New York City [Paccione,1990, 118] when landlords, refusing to maintain them at their own expense, gave up possession and turned them over to the municipality. More generally, many building codes in the cities of the developing countries are still out of touch with the ability of their residents to pay for them, and the codes are largely ignored. Non- compliance with unaffordable codes is generally of little consequence, except when a

major natural disaster, such as the earthquakes in Turkey or the floods in Hondu-
ras, Nicaragua, and Venezuela in the late 1990s, obliterate a significant portion
of the housing stock. In a well-functioning housing sector, local authorities have
the power and the means to regulate urban development, to manage urban
growth in an orderly fashion, and to protect and maintain the standards desired
by the community without infringing on the ability of all segments of the population to obtain adequate and affordable shelter. In conditions of severe resource
limitations, attaining this delicate balance is by no means an easy task.

A fourth concern of local authorities involves the effective administration of
a host of redistributive programs aimed at people who need government assistance, many of them concentrated in blighted housing areas in the older sections
of central cities. As mentioned earlier, local governments are appropriately
limited in initiating and financing major redistributive programs on their own,
and they are therefore dependent on central governments for funding them.
Unfortunately, in the present atmosphere of fiscal restraint, often verging on
austerity, many national governments require local governments to administer
such programs without adequate funding, passing on to local authorities "un-
funded mandates." The government of Hungary, for example, in the wake of the
transition to a market economy, transferred substantial responsibilities for housing
to local governments without much regard to the fiscal ability of these local
authorities to handle such responsibilities [Alm and Buckley, 1994].

A fifth concern of local authorities centers on attaining their own institutional
objectives: accumulating and maintaining their power and reputation, their
popularity, and their effectiveness. To this effect, they have to withstand considerable pressure from business, from the community, and from the nation-state.
They must exercise fiscal responsibility and work within a balanced budget, while
avoiding unpopular cuts in service provision. They must increasingly operate in
the market — sometimes participating as entrepreneurs, sometimes regulating the
market, sometimes purchasing services, sometimes privatizing services, sometimes selling uneconomic assets, and sometimes providing a safety net to mitigate
market failure by channeling subsidized services to targeted groups. There are
increasing pressures on local officials to become more professional and more
technically sophisticated so as to be able to handle more complex problems.
Unfortunately, this renders them more isolated from the day-to-day political
pressures for greater public participation in local decision-making, and in turn
makes it more difficult for local elected representatives to exercise control over
the bureaucracy in the name of the electorate. On top of that, there are pressures
on local agencies to coordinate their activities, to eliminate duplication, and to
stamp out the corruption that is often flagrant in local housing construction: "In
the city of Birmingham, for example, a regional building firm maintained a
'Christmas list' of two thousand local authority employees, including a corrupt
city architect, and in the period 1966–1973 received 110 million pounds worth of
public housing work" [Paccione, 1990, 32]. The attainment of these multiple
internal objectives — in addition to fulfilling their other roles in the urban develop-

ment process discussed earlier — places serious limits on the human and financial resources that they can commit to managing and regulating the housing sector, and on their ability to coordinate a large number of separate service agencies in new land development projects or in inner-city redevelopment projects, both of which are essential to increasing housing supply.

Local governments are not a homogeneous group. They include the regional governments of large metropolitan areas, which may span across several sub national jurisdictions. They also include the governments of municipalities, cities, and villages within these metropolitan areas, as well as local boroughs and communities within these municipalities, and the many offices, agencies, authorities, special districts, and semi-government organizations that make up local governments. These different groups do not necessarily share a common vision of a well-functioning housing sector, and several conflicts are usually found among them.

The first conflict is between the regulation of land use, urban expansion, and building standards on the one hand and the cost of housing on the other. Fischel [1995], for example, has shown that California house prices increased five times faster that those in the rest of the country, largely as the result of the anti-development posture of the California Supreme Court in the 1970s [see chapter 11]. A second conflict, between the rich suburbs and the fiscally- constrained central cities merits further elaboration. As an example, the fragmentation of metropolitan areas in the United States into autonomous communities has allowed the wealthier suburban municipalities to exclude the poor by insisting on higher standards of environmental amenities which forbid higher-density housing and rental housing, and by insisting on a fiscal conservatism that highly constrains redistribution. It has been charged that metropolitan fragmentation reduced political conflict at the local level, which thereby reduced political conflict as a whole because moving it to higher levels of government entailed higher costs that poorer citizens could not afford. In fact, it tended to depoliticize the system altogether: "small issues rule the day for want of a political structure that could handle anything larger. . . In short, since conflict cannot be easily or effectively handled by the formal institutions of urban government, it expresses itself in a different form, and this helps explain why interpersonal violence is relatively high in the United States, while political conflict is subdued" [Newton and Wulff, 1985, 90]. Rich suburbs can therefore continue to exclude the poor, retaining them in poor urban neighborhoods in the city, while making full use of the city in their business pursuits. It is interesting to note too that in the United Kingdom, which has powerful area-wide metropolitan authorities that are not politically fragmented at all, the same phenomenon has occurred. It has not been possible to open up the suburbs to lower-income families. In this case, legislation was largely frustrated during the implementation stage through various tactics of procrastination by suburban officials, usually disguised as protocol [Young and Kramer, 1978].

* * *

To conclude, local authorities have considerable power to influence both housing policy and its implementation. They often have broad legal mandates, taxing powers, and considerable land at their disposal. They also have a crowded agenda which colors, constrains, and motivates their actions in the housing sector. On the one hand, they are often inherently averse to unsanitary housing, illegal housing, unplanned and substandard housing, structurally-unsound housing, housing for new migrants, housing that stands in the way of infrastructure provision or lucrative new development, and housing occupied by the "less-desirable" elements of society. Why? Because such housing makes it more difficult for them to meet their key goals: local economic development, "City Beautiful," the regulation of construction and land development, the administration of redistributive programs, and the provision of infrastructure services. On the other hand, housing is viewed by local officials as a major instrument in the attainment of these key goals: it is a leading component in new development or redevelopment schemes, a major source of tax revenue, a principal venue for funneling central-government funds to localities, and a central element in targeted programs to assist poor neighborhoods. It is therefore unimaginable that housing policy could be effectively developed and implemented without the active participation and involvement of local authorities. Housing policy, in light of the importance of the urban housing sector to the economy as a whole, is indeed a major concern for national governments. But it is necessarily a concern which must be shared with the local governments of metropolitan regions, municipalities, and neighborhoods in which the bulk of housing is located.

4

Housing Indicators
as Instruments of Policy

An enabling housing policy regime requires a system of measurement and feedback that will make it possible to set limits and provide support to all the actors in the housing sector, while relinquishing control over the actors. Once policy makers recognize that housing activity is largely "out of their hands," they have no choice but to listen, to discover how the housing sector behaves over time and across space, to set policies in motion to correct its failures, and then to measure whether these policies have their intended effect. What are the essential characteristics of such a measurement system for the housing sector?

Measurement as an Instrument of Policy

One sweltering afternoon I found myself crossing a rickety bridge into a Bangkok slum, accompanied by one of my students. The slum was built on private land in a swamp along a noisy railway line, but the landlord also lived there, and he collected land rent and supplied the houses with water and electricity. We walked from one house to the other, inquiring, among other things, how much people paid in land rent. We got the same answer everywhere: One baht (5 U.S. cents in 1975) per square meter per month. The landlord told us so himself: everyone pays the same land rent—one baht per square meter per month. But when we paced a few of the plots we noticed that the total rent paid by each family did not correspond to how much land it had: Some had 40 m² and were paying 60 baht, and some had 60 m² and were paying 40 baht. It turned out that the price per square meter was indeed the same for everyone, but that the *amount* of land they occupied was not an actual measure but a number fixed arbitrarily by the landlord. Nobody argued.

Numbers liberate and empower. They challenge accepted doctrine, be it divine authority, the vision of the supreme leader, the dictums of the plan, the assertions of the experts, and even the outcomes of the invisible hand itself. Numbers expose; they make the invisible visible. The information age has rendered us more *numerate* than before, over and above being more literate. We like and expect to hear numbers now, because they feel real, because they can be checked and refuted, and because they render politicians and bureaucrats more accountable to their constituencies.

Modern politicians who now have a telegenic commitment to "keeping it simple" have also come to prefer using numbers — numbers make excellent sound bites. Politicians' facility with numbers now demonstrates that they have a solid grasp of the dimensions of the problem they are talking about. Numbers are usually also quite easy to interpret as well, given a simple assumption of "which way is up?": More space per person is good, more homelessness is not good. And so if the floor area per person goes up, things are looking up. Similarly, if the level of homelessness goes up, things are looking down. Unfortunately, if both space per person and homelessness go up or down together, the numbers become more difficult to interpret and it is no longer a simple matter whether "things" are looking up or down. Questions of the relative value of one as against the other become of paramount importance, and the answer given becomes political. If, moreover, there are 100 such numbers all pertaining to the performance of, say, the housing sector, some going up and others going down, then both politicians and their constituencies lose interest and move on to simpler matters.

In our age of information overload, society demands a reductionist approach to numbers — a drive toward a smaller set of numbers that tell the whole story. Those of us committed to telling the whole story need many more numbers, at least initially, before we can agree that a few numbers can tell the story. Good indicators evolve gradually. There is an evolutionary process whereby the experts, through a dialogue with society at large, gradually develop and refine the basic set of numbers that characterize society — the cost of living index as an overall measure of inflation is one such example. And while society gradually becomes more comfortable with numbers, more in tune with what numbers say and what they hide, society in turn becomes more dependent on them in arriving at critical decisions.

Reliance on numbers has been on the increase since the onset of the scientific revolution, and, in an important sense, all modern states are now built on numbers. In 1992, for example, the Central Bureau of Statistics of the Netherlands, a country with a population of 15 million, employed some 2,500 people and had a budget of $140 million for generating and interpreting numbers [Heerma, 1993, 126]. Not surprisingly, the increasing reliance of the state on statistics and quantitative measures for its critical policy decisions exposes it to new pitfalls:

> [T]he statistics–oriented, problem–solving, meliorative state, while vastly preferable to many variants of rule previously experienced, nevertheless poses new and unfamiliar hazards to mankind. . . . What will befall people . . . when the meliorative actions of their own far–reaching states turn out to be animated by inaccurate data, to be informed by a misreading of available information, or simply to intrude into the wide reaches wherein

numbers — though generated — cannot be expected to provide informed and reliable guidance? [Eberstadt, 1995, 2, 15]

States as well as markets in the information age rely on larger and larger sets of numbers, and it becomes imperative for us to understand what these numbers do: how they can be used to illuminate, enlighten, and instruct; and how they can be abused to mystify, misinform, distort, and misrepresent. In this chapter we focus on the critical roles that numbers play in the housing sector, to press home the point that one must become at least moderately numerate to be a player, so to speak, in the housing game.

With or without numbers, policies affecting the housing sector do get formulated, implemented, and evaluated. In the absence of "cool and clean" indicators — solid, carefully updated accounting systems depending on formal reporting requirements, analytical tools, and systematic surveys — the housing sector and its policy environment will be profitably evaluated only by "good journalism" with "hot and dirty" information — qualitative descriptions of chosen aspects of the sector, depending on insightful observations, interviews with street-level informants, and careful story telling [Schon, 1987, 372]. The indicators approach and the case study approach are, of course, complementary, but no number of case studies can yield the information — and the influence — that a carefully crafted measure of a specific aspect of the housing sector discloses.

To give an example: Numbers are often used to inform society about the relative sizes of specific social concerns, in our case concerns with housing. Houses in slums and squatter settlements in many countries are still not counted as part of the housing stock, even when they house millions of people. For example, Maharashstra, the Indian state in which Bombay (now Mumbai) is located, had a law called "The Maharashstra Vacant Lands (Summary Eviction) Act" that considered all land occupied by squatter settlements to be legally vacant, making their inhabitants invisible [Das,1981, 162–163]. For these slum dwellers, simply getting their houses counted mattered, for counting means visibility.

In contrast, endemically weak housing ministries around the world have been touting ridiculous numbers to draw attention (and larger budgets) to their questionable pursuit of a final solution to the housing problem. For example, since the end of World War II, the most prevalent (and sometimes the singular) indicator of housing sector performance in the developing countries has been the housing deficit, which simply measured the difference between the number of households and the number of adequate housing units. It was usually awesome. The United Nations, following suit, often repeated the contention that "more than one billion people have shelter unfit for human habitation, and this number will expand dramatically unless determined measures are taken immediately" [U.N. Commission on Human Settlements, 1988, 5]. But this number is clearly based on a definition which still considers all housing which does not meet some arbitrary standard as unfit for human habitation, and therefore invisible and not part of the housing stock.

Needless to say, this dim view is clearly not shared by the great majority of the inhabitants of slums, squatter settlements, unauthorized housing, and informal subdivisions who live in houses which meet *their* needs given their means, while failing to meet official standards that have little to do with the economic realities they face. Furthermore, the housing deficit portrays the housing problem as so daunting that it relieves us from taking it seriously at all. It renders us immune to it. If, instead, we focused on the fact that homelessness, for example, afflicts one person in 1,000 of the world's urban population (see table 23.2) while 35 dwelling units in a 1,000 are usually vacant (see table 22.1), then housing the homeless will at least sound more manageable, and will hence become more manageable.

The absurd preoccupation of public housing agencies with housing deficits on the one hand, and their equally absurd efforts to eliminate it themselves on the other, have ensured that the true dimensions of the housing sector remain largely invisible. Surely, miscellaneous indicators of overall housing sector performance, some more useful than others, have been collected systematically in the industrialized countries in the past 50 years. But this has not been done in the developing countries, where systematic data collection has been generally unsatisfactory and sometimes dismal. Annual international compilations of country data, such as the World Bank's *World Development Report* [e.g., World Bank, 1994] and the United Nations Development Programme's *Human Development Report* [e.g., UNDP, 1990] contain no housing indicators at all.

But, beyond the examples given here, numbers have now taken on a role much more important than drawing attention to the dimensions of the housing problem. They have come to be relied on for monitoring and guiding the development of the largely self-organizing cities that we inhabit today. Contemporary cities can no longer be conceived as visual wholes, as having a recognizable form that is the result of a rational plan. The attempt to plan cities has utterly failed. The drive towards some balanced equilibrium of a formalistic urban utopia — be it Frank Lloyd Wright's Broadacre city or Corbusier's Ville Radieuse — has been frustrated by the dynamics of modern technological developments. Rapid innovation harnessed by market forces has forced cities beyond their planned boundaries and their projected sizes, beyond the wildest projections of their designers, and beyond any imposed order. The city of today is nothing but a collage of disparate projects large and small, each claiming to be a more or less integrated whole in and of itself, and each inserted, sometimes rather forcefully, into the existing urban fabric. Surely, each such project changes the whole and informs it in an incremental way, but none of these projects should be mistaken for the whole. The city as a whole is greater than the sum of its parts, and is not defined by its parts. The master plan as a common vision toward which the city advances no longer matters in the least.

In fact, as Tafuri [1976] notes, "in the struggle between architecture and the city, between the demand for order and the will to formlessness" [16] architecture has lost. It lost because it sought to give cities a stable structure, a form that celebrates permanent values, an urban morphology in equilibrium:

> [B]ut this was not possible. The city of development does not accept "equilibriums" within it. Thus the ideology of equilibration also proved a failure. . . Indeed the present effort to make equilibriums work, to connect crisis and development, technological revolutions and radical changes in the organic composition of capital, are simply impossible. To aim at the pacific equilibration of the city and its territory is not an alternative solution, but merely an anachronism [Tafuri, 1976, 120, 173].

The demotion of planning and urban design to the level of projects has left the largely formless cities of today without a unified vision of their future, and without the nostalgic and picturesque "unity in variety" of the towns of old. Instead, our urban vision of the future has necessarily turned into a set of practical expectations regarding the performance of cities along a large number of dimensions, in fact a set of norms that measure their productivity and the quality of life within them. Indicators, then, have taken over the visionary function of the plan, as the realistic, though nonvisual, goals that the city strives to attain.

Housing indicators, as an important subset of urban indicators, therefore function as norms. They can be and often are set as goals to be attained and are then monitored over time to measure progress towards their attainment. There is no need, however, for such norms to be utopian, absolute, or permanent. They can be set realistically with reference to existing historical conditions, or with reference to other cities and countries in similar circumstances. The housing situation of Nicaragua, which was not included in the our sample survey of housing indicators, provides a good example of the importance of such norms. The 1995 Nicaraguan Housing Census reported that 58% of the population lived in overcrowded conditions, with more than two persons per room; that 47% of families inhabited houses without proper legal title; that 39% of dwellings were constructed of impermanent materials; that 38% of dwellings were not connected to the electricity network, 44% were not connected to the water supply network, and 83% were not connected to the sewage network.[1] These adverse housing conditions in Nicaragua were, first and foremost, the result of abject poverty and stunted economic growth. Housing conditions are only a reflection of poverty, and we cannot expect housing in Nicaragua to be better than what its level of economic development merits.

We should be concerned, however, if housing conditions in Nicaragua are indeed below expected conditions, given its level of economic development. This can best be understood by comparing the value of housing in Nicaragua with housing values in our sample. A 1998 survey of 520 households in 13 informal settlements in Nicaraguan cities [Internationale Projekt Consult, 1998] found that the median house value–to–income ratio was of the order of 0.7–1.4. Some urban households invested less than one annual income in their housing. In comparison, the global median house value–to–income ratio in low–income countries in our sample was 3.3 in 1990, and the global average for Latin America and the Caribbean was 3.8 in 1995.[2]

We should therefore expect, given these global norms, that Nicaraguans will have houses that are worth 3–4 annual household incomes. If the median annual household income in Nicaragua was of the order of $1,400 in 1998,[3] a median-income family should be living in a house that was worth $4,200–5,600. According to the recent household survey mentioned earlier, a family in Managua (the capital) with this annual income lived in an informal settlement, in a house with a total estimated value of $1,840 [Internationale Projekt Consult, 1998, 17], or 1.3 times its annual income. Nicaraguans, one strongly suspects, were not investing adequate resources in their housing, possibly because of the traumatic effects of the 1972 earthquake that leveled Managua; the prolonged civil war; the lack of confidence in the economy, in land tenure, and in secure transactions; and the nearly complete absence of housing finance.

Such global norms can and do change over time and from place to place, because they depend, in the final analysis, on what is attainable. And just as new norms replace ones that have been attained, so do new norms replace ones that have turned out to be unattainable. Such changes can be both quantitative and qualitative. Just as the demand for new housing units varies with cycles of urbanization and international migration or in the aftermath of wars and environmental disasters, so do the perceptions of housing quality and domestic comfort evolve and change over time:

> [T]he idea of comfort has developed historically. It is an idea that has meant different things at different times. In the seventeenth century, comfort has meant privacy, which lead to intimacy, and, in turn, to domesticity. The eighteenth century shifted the emphasis to leisure and ease, the nineteenth to mechanically aided comforts — light, heat and ventilation. The twentieth century domestic engineers stressed efficiency and convenience [Rybczynski, 1986, 230–231].

The twenty-first century is now gearing for the electronic house. In Japan, for example, the Matsushita house of the future is expected to "become affordable soon, perhaps in a couple of years. At the front door, the moving picture of a visitor is sent to screens in each room. . . . In the living room, a 50–inch plasma display television — like a theater screen in miniature — offers video on demand. . . . In the children's bedroom, on–line education allows them to participate in classroom discussions. . . . In the bathroom, a health–monitoring toilet seat" and so on [WuDunn, 1999, A8].

As new concerns with housing arise, so does the need to find good indicators to measure them. Housing policy analysts often lament the fact that "the national census — which in most European countries contains no information on income, condition or neighborhood quality — is still directed at issues that were pertinent 40 years ago" [Maclennan and Gibb, 1993, 49]. This observation is pertinent in the case of homelessness, for example, which has recently afflicted European and

North American cities again after a long near-absence. Measuring homelessness, like measuring any other controversial phenomenon, is not a trivial matter at all, and, as we shall see later, there has been a vivid debate on how to construct such a measure (see chapter 23). Comfort itself, while rather noncontroversial, is an important aspect of housing quality which still cannot be adequately measured: "The fallacy of the scientific definition of comfort is that it considers only those aspects of comfort that are measurable, and with not atypical arrogance denies the existence of the rest. . . . It is impossible, for example, to describe scientifically what distinguishes a great wine from a mediocre one, although a group of wine experts would have no difficulty establishing which was which" [Rybczynski, 1986, 228].

The difficulties in constructing appropriate and telling measures aside, housing indicators, regardless of their quality, have two important functions — that of monitoring sector performance and that of modeling it. The first function, that of monitoring, serves all the participants in the housing sector — be they dwellers, builders, financial institutions, or local and central governments — by providing each with the information necessary for action. Successful and profitable action in this sector requires good information, some gained through long experience and some obtained through monitoring a variety of indicators of sector performance. For example, in developed market economies, housing starts are carefully watched. The number of housing starts is an important signal of the level of confidence that consumers and producers have in the economy, because it measures their commitment to make long-term investments [Frumkin, 1994, 182–184]. But exactly what information is used and how it is interpreted is never entirely clear and for good reason:

> The information that individuals or organizations can use to adapt to the unknown is necessarily partial, and is conveyed by signals (e.g. prices) through long chains of individuals, each person passing on in modified form a combination of streams of abstract market signals. Nonetheless, the whole structure of activities tends to adapt, through these partial and fragmentary signals, to conditions foreseen by and known to no individual, even if this adaptation is never perfect. This is why this structure survives, and why those who use it also survive and prosper. There can be no deliberately planned substitutes for such a self-ordering process of adaptation to the unknown. [Hayek, 1988, 76–77]

Beyond measuring the degree to which accepted norms are being attained, society needs to monitor housing sector performance for three other reasons: (1) to ensure that the housing market works smoothly on both the demand and the supply side, (2) to take action when the market gets out of control, and (3) to allocate public resources (such as infrastructure services) in response to market demand when there are no markets for these resources.[4] And all this must be done with sensitive and minimal regulation of the housing market — an entity that is not well understood and that should never be trusted blindly. Markets are similar, in this sense, to unruly and energetic teenagers who love to be on their own but never fail to call their parents (read governments) to bail them out when they get into trouble. To keep them out of trouble we must keep looking over their shoulder, insisting that they call home from time to time. This calling home— especially early enough, before things get out of hand—is the least indicators can, occasionally, do for the amorphous markets they measure.

In this sense, indicators need not be perfect, and they need not tell the whole story. They may indicate, they may point, but they are always partial insights into phenomena we do not completely understand. A housing indicator is like a thermometer that measures body temperature. If it varies from the expected norm of 37° Celsius then we suspect we are sick, and when it varies greatly we know we are very sick. We don't know what the sickness is, and we might be very sick even if our temperature does not vary from the norm. But if our fever is high, our attention to our bodies is elevated, and we can conduct a battery of more elaborate tests and detect more. Indicators are indeed only indirect, summary measures of housing sector performance and can therefore only be expected to give indications, possibly as gross measures of performance, sometimes in the form of early warnings or as initial diagnoses of the presence of problems that require more testing and measurement. They are not infallible, especially in the early stage of their development. Good indicators can only evolve over time, as experience is gained in their design, collection, and interpretation. Even so, a small set of well-defined and adequately measured housing indicators can usually be relied upon to give us some new and fresh insights about aspects of the housing sector which were previously hidden from the street-level observer.

Earlier indicators for monitoring housing sector performance over time and space usually came from three sources: population censuses, economic statistics, and social indicators. Demographic indicators pertaining to urban households and the basic characteristics and tenure of the housing stock have the longest history. Economic housing indicators—such as housing investment, production, and prices—have been used in national accounts in some countries for many decades. Social indicators of housing sector performance, beyond those associated with the population census, have come into being in the 1960s. The social indicators movement developed the idea of creating "statistics that enable us to assess where we stand and are going with respect to our values and goals" [e.g., Bauer, 1966]. Social indicators in general, and social housing indicators in particular, focus on final *outcomes*—such as the percentage of families who own their own homes—and rarely ever on intermediate outcomes such as land prices or mortgage interest rates [e.g., OECD, 1982, 10]. This often makes them less useful for policy analysis. The three indicators of housing conditions in the Organization for Economic Cooperation and Development (OECD) list of 33 social indicators, for example, measure only persons per room, access to outdoor space, and the existence of basic amenities [OECD, 1982, 39-40]. The indicators do not measure prices, intermediate outcomes such as levels of production, or policy variables such as the extent of rent control that would make it possible to study causal relationships. This is, indeed, the limitation of pure outcome monitoring.

Indicators of housing sector performance measure the degree to which the sector is functioning in the view of some or all of the actors in the sector. Measured over time, these indicators can tell us whether conditions are improving or becoming worse. Measured in a comparative context, they can tell us whether conditions in one city are better or worse than in another city or than some norm. But they do not necessarily tell us why the conditions are different. To understand why, we need to know how changes in the values of some indicators affect others. More specifically, we would like to know, for example, how changes in the level of economic development or in the housing policy environment affect housing outcomes. Monitoring alone cannot tell us. To accomplish this, we need to use the indicators in *modeling* cause and effect in the housing sector. Such modeling need not be formal. All actors in the sector engage in modeling, structuring the limited data at their disposal in a manner that informs their actions. Housing analysts, however, engage in more formal modeling, studying the statistical relationships among different indicators, often with the aim of arriving at policy prescriptions or recommendations. Indeed, it is our modeling framework, whether articulated formally or suspected intuitively, that suggests to us what needs to be monitored. As our understanding of the "wiring diagrams" of the housing sector grows, our perception of what is relevant becomes more refined, and our ability to invent simple, powerful indicators that contain adequate information to guide policy is increased.

In the absence of a final plan, the dynamism of self–organizing cities requires the implementation of self–correcting policies that are regularly updated and refined to respond, guide, regulate, and motivate evolving housing markets. To be self–correcting, such policies need accepted norms on the one hand, regular feedback to monitor deviations from these norms on the other, and better explanations on how and why these variations occur. There is no choice, therefore, but to accept the need for reliable and robust housing indicators as essential instruments in the conduct of housing policy. That this requires a shift of focus and a shift of resources on the part of governments goes without saying.

The paucity of good housing indicator data, both in the private and in the public sector, can be partially explained by the intrinsic failure to market such data profitably. Information collection is costly, and selling it profitably is almost impossible, because it can be easily copied and because, once produced, it is in boundless supply. Because of the failure of the market to supply such information, most of the burden falls on governments, who may or may not have the incentive, the ability or the resources to collect it [Goodman, 1992]. In the housing sector — as in other sectors with interactive and public–good aspects — governments cannot rely on measurement by self–interested parties and must engage in the collection and dissemination of public information for the sector to function efficiently and equitably. Yet many governments do not, in fact, mandate the public disclosure of information they do have, often leading to further distortions of decisions — both by public and private actors — affecting housing outcomes. To make matters worse, there has been little interest or incentive for governments to collect indicators that can be internationally compared — using identical definitions and collection methods — with the minimal objective of obtaining a broader sense of practical and attainable norms.[5] And to top it all, the question "What is measured?" is often one that is decided by central-government statisticians, usually capable technocrats with a limited understanding of the housing sector and limited contact with its key actors.

In the final analysis, we note again that the question "What is measured?" can never be free of political bias. In a pluralistic society, all the key actors in the housing sector have a clear interest in having their particular concerns translated into numbers and measured regularly. The selection of indicators for the Global Survey of Housing Indicators, described in chapter 5, aimed at incorporating the major concerns of the key actors in the sector. It was constrained by the understanding that almost all housing sectors are now market driven, and that any attempt that ignores the role of the market is likely to end in utter failure. Thus indicators which were used primarily in the nonmarket allocation of resources — the amount of square meters of public residential construction in any given year is one such example, a typical indicator in Soviet-era statistics — have been downgraded in favor of market-based indicators.

This constraint on the selection of indicators raises an important question: Does a system of market-based housing indicators pay adequate attention to the role of housing in the redistribution of income? In the words of Turner [1993]:

> For example, consider two countries with very different housing–policy objectives. One is using housing as a supplement to tax policy; subsidies, a regulated housing provision, and rent control are used to redistribute disposable income between households. . . The other country lies at the other extreme. Its objective is to achieve an efficient housing market, while giving little consideration to fairness or redistributive effects. It avoids using housing policy as a redistributive measure. . . . How could a set of single indicators compare these systems in a fair way?" [62–63]

Whether housing policy can and should be used for redistributing societal resources is a separate matter that will be taken up later. There is, however, no question that a good system of housing indicators must measure the distributive features of the housing sector as well as its overall efficiency. Similarly, it must focus on the performance of public-sector as well as private-sector housing, and on informal as well as formal sector housing. All these demands act in the opposite direction to that of reductionism, that is, the push to reduce the number of housing indicators to a small and manageable set. At this point in time, we do not yet have such a set. Some progress has been made towards distilling the more useful indicators into a system that begins to tell a coherent story. In the next section we focus on the technical and methodological aspects of "What is measured?" as we examine the selection, construction, and measurement of both indicators and composite indices in housing.

Housing Indicators and Composite Indices

What are the basic criteria for generating the indicators and composite indices that make up a system that can both monitor and model the housing sector, as well as compare its policy and performance across the globe? In this section we outline the requirements of such a system, the same requirements that guided the construction of the system of indicators used in this study.

We already know from our earlier discussion that measurement can never be value–free or independent of political agendas. At the same time, we must acknowledge that measurement does free us from petty political concerns, making our predicament more transparent, and allowing persons of different convictions to examine and interpret real data about the sector as a whole rather than exchange opinions based on their own limited observations. Setting up a system for organizing this data has a number of technical requirements. In a technical sense, then, a measurement system of indicators for the housing sector has to fulfil the following five requirements:

1. it should be comprehensive and address the main concerns of the key actors in the sector;
2. it should contain useful measures of both cause and effect, indicators and composite indices that characterize the economic, social and political context; the housing policy environment; housing market conditions; and housing market performance;
3. the measures should be both temporal and global, monitoring the sector over time and comparing the sector across cities and countries;
4. the measurement system should be balanced between efficiency and distributive measures, so that judgments can be made; and
5. to be effective, the set of chosen indicators and composite indices should be as small as possible and with as little overlap as possible.

As the components of the measurement system, each individual indicator or composite index should fulfil the following four criteria:

1. it should be unambiguous, clearly indicating "Which way is up?" and making it possible to use it as a means of monitoring whether objectives are being met;
2. it should be simple and precise, sensitive to change, transparent, consistent, and cost–effective;
3. indicators and indices should be insightful inventions, discovered and developed over time to shed light on aspects of the housing sector which would otherwise remain hidden from view; and

4. where a simple ratio is insufficient, composite indices should be con-
    structed in a consistent and transparent manner, assigning self-evident
    weights to each element of the index.

The rest of this section elaborates on these requirements and illustrates them with
specific examples.

Comprehensiveness: It is not difficult to see that many of the concerns of the key
actors in the housing sector can be translated into measures of the performance
of the sector. The concerns of dwellers with adequate shelter (see chapter 18) can
be translated into a system of measurements by collecting data on living space;
the quality of structures and neighborhoods; the availability of amenities; the
existence of sufficient variety of dwellings; and the absence of homelessness,
overcrowding, or the doubling up of households. These data can be supplemented with information on the social safety net for housing, the security of
tenure, the availability of mortgage finance and nondiscrimination in lending, and
the potential for public participation in decision-making.

The concerns of builders (see chapter 15) can also be accommodated in a
measurement system by collecting statistical information on the cost and availability of the necessary inputs for residential construction – labor, professional
assistance, materials, land, and capital; on conditions in the economy as a whole
which affect the demand for housing; on the legal environment for residential
construction; and on the competitive conditions in the sector. The concerns of
lenders (see chapters 8 and 16) can be addressed by collecting regular data on
conditions in the economy and in the financial sector as a whole; on the demand
for mortgage and construction finance; on the regulatory environment of the
financial sector; and on laws affecting the foreclosure of properties. Such data can
be supplemented by information on the size of the mortgage sector, on the types
and sizes of different mortgages, on the various levels of risks in mortgage
lending, or on secondary mortgage markets.

The concerns of municipalities (see chapter 3) can be translated into measures
of urban population growth, density, and the growth of the built-up area; land
needs for development; the demand for infrastructure and environmental
amenities; the demand for welfare services; the conditions of the housing stock;
and projected needs for replacement, rehabilitation, or redevelopment. The
concerns of nation-states (see chapter 2) can be measured as well. States are
interested, as we noted earlier, in the contribution of the housing sector to overall
economic growth, investment, employment, savings, lending, or labor mobility,
to name a few. They are interested in measures of housing affordability, housing
assistance, housing standards, homelessness, home ownership, and the safety of
residential areas. They are also concerned with the effects of urban development
on the natural environment and on the energy economy.

Many of the measures suggested here are in fact shared concerns of most of
the key actors in the sector. And all of these concerns are, and indeed have

already been, subject to measurement, as we shall see in later chapters. All in all, more than 200 different indicators related to the housing sector have been proposed, tested, and measured—some better than others, some more cost effective than others. No system can be expected to measure everything. The comprehensiveness issue, however, rests on developing a measurement system that combines and balances the concerns of the key actors, eliminating duplication and inefficiency in the process. Such a system usually focuses first on indicators of common concern, and there are many, and then proceeds to include indicators of special concern which can usually be generalized to meet the needs of others.

Balancing efficiency and distribution: There is no question that any individual indicator—for example, floor area per person—can be used to construct a single measure of the efficiency of the housing sector as a whole, or as a number of separate measures pertaining to different income groups, racial groups, gender groups, or age groups. The latter approach may be essential to understanding the distributional aspects of the sector in any given city, but it considerably increases the number of indicators to be measured.

A second approach, and the one adopted in this study, involves the inclusion of single indicators that, in and of themselves, have distributional qualities. Indicators that measure coverage have this quality: for example, the percent of homes with piped water connection or permanent structures. So do indicators such as targeted subsidies, which measure the percentage of subsidies reaching families with below-median incomes.

A third approach involves the construction of special measures of distribution, such as the percentage of housing wealth owned by lowest 40% of the household income distribution. Unfortunately, those kinds of indicators are often difficult to measure. A variant of this approach, one adopted in this study, is to use medians, rather than averages, as the more distribution-oriented global measures of the sector as a whole. For example, half the population lives in less expensive houses, and half in more expensive ones, than the median-priced house. The average price of a house, on the other hand, may be misleading as a measure of the distribution of house prices—it may be considerably higher, for example, because of a relatively small number of very expensive houses in the city.

Finally, there are indicators that focus directly on the housing conditions of the poor—measurements of the percentage of unauthorized housing, squatter housing, or homelessness, to name a few. Because the housing problem often afflicts the weaker segments of society, efficiency measures that overlook distributional aspects may hide significant aspects of the housing sector which require social action.

Measuring both cause and effect: There is no question that monitoring housing sector outcomes, in and of itself, is an invaluable facet of any enabling housing policy regime. Monitoring is equivalent to listening. It provides the feedback and the reality check necessary for the conduct of policy. Yet a system of indicators which measures only housing outcomes, whatever they may be, will be found lacking when we come to act on these outcomes. Knowing that houses are expensive does not tell us why they are expensive, and, without knowing why, we are likely to fumble when we seek corrective measures. As we noted earlier, indicators not only describe the end-states of the housing system, they are also explanations of why the system has come to be what it is. They must be used in modeling the sector, as well as in monitoring it. And to model cause and effect in the sector, we need to have a set of indicators that contains the essential indicators in each of the four components of the model of the sector described in chapter 6: the economic, social and political context; the housing policy environment; housing market conditions; and housing market outcomes. Without discovering and measuring the key indicators that are postulated to affect housing sector outcomes, no diagnosis of its condition is possible, let alone an effective cure.

Monitoring and global comparisons: Any carefully constructed statistical measure—say the total urban population, the number of homeowners, the median house size, or the median house price—can be used to monitor housing sector performance in a given city over time. Measures in different time periods can be easily compared to indicate whether change has occurred—has the city grown or shrunk in size? Are houses bigger or smaller? Or are they less expensive or more expensive? But absolute measures such as those cannot be of value in place-to-place comparisons without undergoing a process of normalization so as to render them comparable. We cannot thoughtfully compare the number of homeowners between two cities, but we can compare the percentage of households who own their homes, that is, the ratio of owner-occupied households to all households. Indeed, most well-tested indicators are ratios of one kind or another. The denominator in the ratio can be the total population of the city, as in dwelling units per 1,000 people; it can be the total number of households, as in the rate of household formation; it can be the total housing stock, as in housing stock growth; it can be median household income, as in the house price-to-income ratio; and it can also be an area measure, as in residential density which is measured in persons per square kilometer.

It is interesting to note that in global comparisons, one round of normalization may not be enough. Let us look at one example. Stren [1989] suggested infrastructure expenditures per capita as a measure of the degree to which the public sector was spending on the construction, operation, and maintenance of infrastructure networks in a number of African cities; he noted that significant reductions in levels of per capita expenditures on infrastructure in the 1970s and 1980s were detrimental to the functioning of these cities. This proposed measure normalized infrastructure expenditures by the city population. And as long as cities with similar household incomes were compared, this measure gave us a sense of which city was spending more on infrastructure. But when we compare countries with vastly different incomes, the comparison is no longer valid. Helsinki, for example, spent 1,000 times more on infrastructure per capita than Dar es Salaam in 1990 — $2,610 as against $2 per annum — but had a per capita income 250 times larger — $26,040 as against $110. To compare the two cities, we normalized infrastructure expenditure per capita by per capita income. According to this measure, Helsinki spent only four to five times as much on infrastructure as Dar es Salaam, still a significant multiple, but now a more realistic comparison.

Over and above issues of proper normalization, there are indicators that are of concern in some countries and of no concern in others. Unauthorized housing and squatter housing are hardly serious problems in industrialized countries or in ex-Communist ones. Neither are measures of piped water supply or permanent structures which hover near 100%. Similarly, measures of maintenance and upkeep of public-sector housing or waiting lists for public housing are of no concern in countries with an insignificant amount of public housing, while measures of citizen participation in the urban decision-making process are of no concern in countries where such participation hovers near zero. A measurement system designed for global application may need to balance the concerns of both industrialized and developing countries when focusing on a basic set of comparable indicators of common concern, which can then be supplemented by other indicators of special concern that need not be shared globally.

A small finite set: The amount of money spent on the collection of housing indicators is itself a housing indicator, and one for which data are not yet available for comparative analysis. It is still a very small fraction of the value of the housing stock in the industrialized countries, and an even a smaller fraction in developing countries. Poorer countries are likely to spend much less on information gathering than richer ones, and therefore they can only rely on a more-modest measurement system. For global comparisons that include both rich and poor countries, we must make do with a more modest system containing as few indicators as possible. But the fewer the indicators, the lower their power of explanation, and the less useful they may be in going beyond a cursory pulse-taking of sector performance. Analysts of the sector will usually opt for more rather than less, while politicians and laymen will prefer less rather than more. For the latter, just one global measure of housing sector performance is ideal, or maybe one composite index for each element of the simple model — a context index, a policy index, a market conditions index, and a market outcomes index — and that is all. For the time being, this goal remains elusive although the present study does offer a beginning: a single Development Index as a composite measure of the context and a single housing policy index — the Enabling Index — as a composite measure of the housing policy environment.

We now turn to the discussion of the criteria for the construction of individual indicators and composite indices.

Unambiguous measures: It is best to use indicators where it is clear "Which way is up?" More floor space is better than less floor space, less homelessness is better than more. There are other indicators, however, where an "optimal" amount may be desired, rather than simply more or less. One such indicator is home owner-ship. At low levels of home ownership, more may be desirable and encouraged. But home ownership, almost certainly, is not desirable by all. There is a need for a certain amount of rental housing for those who are not interested in home ownership or unable to afford it — students, single persons, temporary workers, or young married couples. Rental housing fulfils an important function in ensuring residential mobility and therefore cannot and should not be allowed to disappear. A second such indicator, one with a similar (though a bit different) ambiguity, is housing investment. A high level of housing investment can mean one of two things — either that many new units are being built at affordable prices, or that house prices are high and only a small number of expensive units are being built. The measure itself does not reveal this information. Moreover, too high a level of housing investment may be undesirable — there may be good reasons for discouraging it to ensure an adequate supply of capital for other productive uses, or it may be that too much investment is taking place without sufficient regard to demand. All three reasons make it difficult to judge "Which way is up?" in this case. Indeed, other indicators may need to be looked at simultaneously with housing investment to determine "Which way is up?"

Simplicity and precision: Some indicators are more sensitive to change than others. Some are sensitive in the short term (house prices or housing starts, for example), some in the medium term (floor area per person or home ownership, for example), and some in the long term (residential density or household size, for example). Policies aimed at short-term changes should not be expected to change indicators that are insensitive in the short term. More important, indicators that do not change rapidly need not be measured frequently.

The best indicators are often transparent indicators, especially when their name makes it completely clear exactly what they measure. Floor area per person is quite simple and transparent, as its name suggests, but there are still a number of ambiguities as to what constitutes floor area exactly: Should passageways be included? What about the areas occupied by walls, nonliving spaces, or semi-covered outdoor spaces such as balconies? And so on. Nothing is simple yet, but definitions are becoming clearer over time. To be of use in any comparative framework, floor area must be precisely defined. That is relatively simple. Access to residential amenities, on the other hand, is considerably less transparent. What precisely is access? What constitutes amenity? How do we measure amenity levels? How do we combine levels of access to different amenities? Similarly, while the concept of residential segregation is intuitively clear, there are no simple measurements than can render it transparent. But there should be.

Some indicators can be measured more precisely than others. Where sampling can be used, for example, it is quite possible to obtain exact measures of household size, dwelling unit size, or floor area per person. It is more difficult to obtain measures of the stock as a whole, such as the total number of existing or new dwelling units, both of which may be easier to measure in cities with a very small informal sector and good building departments, but more difficult to measure in cities with crowded slums. The average price of serviced land on the urban fringe is much more difficult to measure, because of the difficulty in defining the fringe and sampling similar plots of land on the fringe. And while typical values may be obtained (and such typical values are used in this study), a precise measure for such an indicator is inherently difficult to construct.

Finally, data collection for the construction of indicators is not free. It usually requires precise surveys, sample surveys, and census taking — which, when it comes to collecting housing data, is never very useful. It was a pleasant surprise to find, contrary to the prediction of Africa experts that bemoaned the scarcity of housing data, that a significant amount of data for housing indicators did exist in all the African cities we considered. In cities everywhere,[6] surveys *are* being conducted by a host of different organizations, but rarely are they coordinated or pooled together in a useful way. As data systems gradually become more organized, data collection can be expected to become more cost-effective. Still, whenever possible, housing indicators should make use of, and make do with, available information or data that can be realistically collected without resorting to complicated and exotic procedures.

Indicators as insightful inventions: Measurement in housing is still in its infancy. Early surveys of housing conditions in the slums of Europe are now almost 200 years old. But, as we noted earlier, there are still no agreed-upon measures that are in wide use globally. And there is even a consensus among analysts and policy makers that measures that are collected regularly are not of much use in either understanding the workings of the sector or in evaluating the effectiveness of actions in the sector. Instead of bemoaning the situation, however, one should look at it as a field wide open for invention and discovery. As we gain under-standing, we can improve our measurement system and vice versa; as our measurement system improves so does our understanding. There is an important and interesting role for housing scholars here. Given our increased understanding of the workings of the sector, we must aim to discover and invent new and effective measures, arrive at a consensus as to their usefulness, and accelerate their adoption by government bureaucracies and international organizations.

In this study, although the emphasis was on accepted and tested measures, several new indicators were developed that shed new light on housing sector performance. A few examples are in order. The first example concerns the down-market penetration of the formal housing sector. To what extent is the formal sector involved in building low-cost housing? Does it concentrate only on the upper-end of the market, leaving the rest to the informal or to the public sector, or does it produce cheap housing as well? An indicator, entitled "down-market penetration," was constructed in a similar way to the house price-to-income ratio. It was defined as the ratio between the price of the lowest-priced house produced and marketed by the formal private sector in significant quantities (not less than 2% of annual housing production) and the median household income.

A second example concerns the premium attached to land on the urban fringe when the authorities allow its owner to convert it from agricultural to urban use. When residential land is in artificially short supply because the regulatory environment restricts such conversion, this premium is expected to be high. Conversely, when the regulatory environment does not impede conversion, it is expected to be low. An indicator, entitled the "land conversion multiplier," was constructed to measure this premium. It was defined as a typical ratio between the median land price of an unserviced plot on the urban fringe given planning permission for residential development, and the median price of a nearby plot in rural/agricultural use without such permission.

A third example concern the measurement of the stringency of the rent control regime. Rent control has several important dimensions: there is the extent and prevalence of rent control – does it affect the entire rental sector or only a small segment of it? And there is the severity of rent control, the degree to which controlled rents are different from market rents. We can construct one indicator which measures the extent of rent control (the percentage of rental units that are under rent control), and a second indicator which measures the distortion produced by rent control (the average ratio of controlled rents to market rents). Given that, in an enabling housing policy regime, less rent control is more desirable, a simple index of rent control can then be constructed (see chapter 9) from the product of the two indicators:

$$\text{Rent Control Index} = 1 - \text{Extent} \times (1 - \text{Distortion})$$

Composite indices: The Rent Control Index is already a simple form of a composite index, as it brings together two separate measurements into one single index. In this study, several composite indices were constructed, all using similar procedures. Except for the Rent Control Index, which used a product, every index was constructed in a similar fashion – from *equally weighted* sums of the component values of the index:

1. The component values of the index were all transformed into z-scores [see, e.g., Freund and Simon, 1997, 89] by subtracting the average value and dividing the result by the standard deviation of the sample, so that they all would be dimensionless and contribute equally to the sum;
2. Depending on "Which way is up?" the resulting z-scores for each country in the sample were then added together (or subtracted from each other) each one given the same weight; and

3. The index values for all the countries were then calculated by transforming their individual sums so that the minimum value of the sample as a whole was 0 and the maximum value 100.

For example, the Residential Infrastructure Index was constructed from three values for each country: (1) the percentage of houses with piped water supply; (2) the length of the journey to work (in minutes); and (3) the per capita infrastructure expenditures-to-income ratio. In this case, the z-scores for the Journey to Work were subtracted from the sum of the other two z-scores to obtain the Index, as a longer journey implied a lower quality of residential infrastructure. More details on the construction of specific composite indices will be provided in the chapters that follow.

* * *

This chapter established the methodological foundations for measurement in the housing sector — the criteria used to design housing indicators, composite indices, and a measurement system that can monitor as well as model the sector both locally and globally. The need for a global measurement system becomes clearer in the next chapter, which examines the housing sector in a global perspective, and further elaborates on the actual data collection procedures used in the Global Survey of Housing Indicators of 1990.

5

Housing in Global Perspective

The Globalization of Housing Policy

In any given country, let alone in a single city, it is extremely difficult to compare housing policies or judge their effects, because there is usually only one policy in operation at any given time. This limits individual cities and countries to "before-and-after" comparisons of their own performance over time, a practice that usually hides the inherent structural weaknesses of their housing sectors. To move beyond these limitations, we must embark on a global analysis of the sector, comparing among different cities and countries with different policy regimes. Previously, in the absence of reliable international comparative statistics, this was impossible to do.

The housing sector — unlike more fortunate sectors such as population, education, or the macro-economy — has always suffered from a dearth of comparative statistics. Worse than that, there are virtually no books with an analytical — rather than a descriptive — global perspective of the housing sector.[1] Housing policy books that adopt a global perspective are usually collections of case studies which may share a common terminology, but which contain few overriding theses to hold them together. They contain almost no data to explain similarities and differences among countries, let alone to evaluate statistically the sources of place-to-place differences.[2] Needless to say, this lack of data makes comparisons between countries less than useful, and inhibits cross-country learning. There is, no doubt, a serious need for comparative housing research that overcomes these limitations: "There is scope for extending the examination of similarities and differences in housing systems. This should be done by reasoned hypothesis testing rather than the application of plausible ideas which seem to fit the facts. This again points to the distinction between a social scientific approach and the use of terminology to tie things together" [Oxley, 1991, 71].

To compare housing sector performance among countries, we must first "recognize that comparison is about commonalities and differences" [Oxley, 1991, 68]. The sources of commonality in the housing predicament of different countries are obvious: housing problems are, by and large, a residue of urbanization — the rapid transformation of modern societies from a predominantly rural to a predominantly urban mode of existence. The early phases of urbanization were accompanied by symptoms that were almost universal: the burgeoning of the urban population was clearly not matched either by the supply of accommodations or by the capacity of urban infrastructure, resulting in overcrowding and congestion, filth and disease, high unaffordable rents, and concerns about the breakdown of the social order. The severe housing problems that accompanied the urbanization process always generated both a private and a public response. Massive financial resources were transferred to the housing sector; a variety of producers, including individual households engaged in housing construction; households also adjusted their housing budgets to pay more for housing; and governments responded by introducing legislation to regulate the sector as well as to provide public funds to support it.

And as governments sought corrective measures to the housing problem, they faced similar dilemmas:

- Should slums be cleared and eradicated or rehabilitated and improved?
- Should rents be controlled, arbitrated, or determined by the forces of supply and demand in a free market?
- Should minimum health and safety standards be mandatory even though they raise housing costs?
- Should illegal and unauthorized buildings be destroyed or improved and legalized?
- How can government accept the responsibility for ensuring that everyone is adequately housed, given government's limited fiscal resources?
- How should the government's limited fiscal resources best be used in the housing sector?
- Should government participate directly in housing production or in land development, or should it limit itself to regulating and enabling private- and voluntary-sector housing production?
- Should home ownership be favored over tenancy?
- How should new housing be financed?
- How should expenditures on housing and infrastructure by government be recovered?
- How can discrimination in housing be eradicated?
- What responsibilities in the housing sector should be with the central government, and what responsibilities should be with local authorities?
- How should housing policy, economic policy, social policy, and urban policy be coordinated?
- How can the bureaucratic stranglehold on housing activity be relaxed?

These questions, in one form or another, have been hotly debated for the past two centuries, and, broadly speaking, all of them are still contested today. In every country, without exception, there is a modern history of housing policy debates and housing legislation that attempt to provide lasting answers to these questions. In every society there are key actors that try to influence the outcomes of these debates to protect and enhance their group interests or their benevolent concerns for the weak and vulnerable. And in every country, innovations in housing policy and practice are continually imported, reinvented, and implemented, with or without adequate care as to their efficacy, their appropriateness, or their impact.

The spread of innovations results in the preponderance of similarities between cities across the globe: high-rise central business districts; suburbs and bedroom communities; transportation grids and limited-access highways; urban renewal and redevelopment; international architectural styles; historic preservation; green belts and suburban growth controls; and the privatization of local infrastructure services, to cite but a few, are spreading everywhere. Property rights in urban housing are now defined within very strict limits, and, almost without exception, these rights are limited to owner-occupation, cooperative ownership, rental from private, nonprofit, or public landlords, free or subsidized accommodation in employer or institutional housing, or customary tribal ownership. Residential buildings — although varying in size, shape, and construction materials — now take on one of four basic forms: the single-family house, the row-house (or compound), the walk-up apartment building, and the high-rise. Construction materials, such as cement, steel, and lumber, are becoming universal commodities. New mortgage instruments are quickly adopted everywhere and sources of mortgage capital are fast becoming internationalized. Overcrowded slum conditions in migrant or immigrant neighborhoods are similar everywhere, or remind one how conditions used to be. Squatter settlements as well as homelessness are almost universal, and even the eviction rhetoric is practically the same everywhere. Infrastructure standards and technologies are becoming globalized as well, and new multinational consortiums seek to establish municipal infrastructure monopolies — in water and sewerage, electricity, toll roads, and telecommunications — in cities around the globe. There are signs that real estate cycles are becoming global as well, spurred by the globalization of financial markets and the increasing influence of international capital flows on these cycles at the national level.[3]

We are now in a period of globalization of policies as well, where increasing competition among cities and countries in the global marketplace [Porter, 1990; Kresl and Singh, 1994] is forcing policy-makers to compare policies and outcomes in the housing sector, and to submit to the necessity of adopting successful policies from other places, so as not to be left behind. In other words, a well functioning housing sector is increasingly understood as an essential ingredient of a competitive economy and a vibrant society that can overcome adversity and forge ahead into a leadership position in the global village.

> [I]n the politics of planning and development, cities are subjected to a wide range of pressures for homogenization, of urban built form, of urban physical structure, and of administrative and political arrangements, as a

result of technological and economic developments that are global in scope. At the same time, local governance asserts local particularity — local ideas about how cities should be governed, how they should look, and what the social milieu should be — in the face of these homogenizing pressures. [Leo, 1997, 78]

Furthermore, with the collapse and abandonment of central planning regimes in a large number of countries by 1991, the range of policies to be emulated has been considerably narrowed. Essentially, this has meant that policies which have turned their backs on markets and individual property rights have been essentially discredited. The common focus is now shifting to the selective intervention in complex housing markets that are in a state of constant flux, moving away from the intense involvement of the paternalistic governments of the past.

Beyond the narrowing choices for housing policies within individual countries, social and human concerns are becoming globalized as well. International organizations, among them the United Nations and the World Bank, are pressuring governments to pursue housing policies such as protecting the human rights of citizens against forced eviction,[4] preserving and enhancing the environmental quality of cities, or designing housing programs that do not worsen fiscal deficits, intervening in matters that were once considered the sole purview of national governments. In a number of important dimensions, globalization is bringing into serious question the sovereignty of states and their ability to govern their territories: "With respect to economic organization, public health, social services and even 'security', sovereignty seems increasingly like a 'show' that offers a comforting illusion of national control over national destinies" [Magnussen, 1996, 291].

Pressure for the globalization of policies and the narrowing of policy choices necessarily means that the housing policies of different countries are indeed "converging." It has been conjectured that housing policies and market structures in industrial countries are becoming increasingly similar regardless of their political and institutional regimes [Donnison, 1967; Donnison and Ungerson, 1982]. There is no question that this is indeed the case in housing, as the present study will clearly demonstrate. Surely, most housing policy regimes are still entrenched in historical institutional commitments that cannot be easily reversed and still bound in structural constraints that cannot be easily removed.[5] But there is no doubt that as economies mature their housing policy regimes become more similar, and that policy differences among industrialized countries are narrower than the policy differences among the less-developed countries.

In broad terms, convergence to efficient, equitable, and sustainable housing policies appears to be gradually taking place with increased learning and cross-fertilization between countries. But, in practice, this convergence is replete with mistakes, reversals, and failures. To cite one example, building codes were often transferred from richer countries to poorer ones, where they were often swollen whole without being properly digested, and then largely ignored.[6] There has been much less of a tendency, unfortunately, to adopt well tried practices and policies from countries in *similar* circumstances, for reasons of nationalistic pride or sheer ignorance. To make matters worse, there is no accepted way of measuring the success or failure of such practices and policies, making it difficult to decide which ones are worth adopting and which ones are not. None of these bode well for an early global convergence on the better policies in the near future.

This book seeks to assist actors in the housing arena in attaining a global perspective of housing policy and housing sector performance, by providing them with broad international comparisons of the policy differences that account for differences in performance. Furthermore, by demonstrating that housing policy matters, it should indeed lead to a more sensible evaluation of policy experiences in different countries. It should focus attention on the limitations of their entrenched policies, accelerate the adoption of sensible new policies, and occasionally prevent the blind embrace of new policies without a true understanding either of their context or of their effects.

The Global Survey of Housing Indicators

The Global Survey of Housing Indicators of 1990 [Housing Indicators Program, 1994] was conducted under the direction of Stephen Mayo and myself, as a joint program of the United Nations Centre for Human Settlements (Habitat) and the World Bank. The overall objectives of the survey were to create a comprehensive basic set of indicators for the housing sector, to obtain current estimates for these indicators in a large number of countries across the entire income distribution, and to use these estimates to build econometric models that examined the statistical relationships among these indicators. This book is the final outcome of this investigation, incorporating the statistical analysis of the Global Survey data.

The more practical aims of the survey were to provide an analytical tool for governments for measuring the performance of the housing sector in a comparative, consistent, and policy–oriented perspective; to create a framework for comparing housing sector performance between cities and countries, as well as between different time periods; to contribute toward establishing a new institutional framework within countries for formulating and implementing sector–wide housing policies; and to work toward the creation of an international network of experts and institutions capable of measuring and overseeing the development of the housing sector. It is pleasant to report that many of these practical objectives were met, and that housing indicator work is now proceeding productively in many cities — both in industrialized and in developing countries — supported by a host of government institutions, international organizations and aid agencies. The United Nations Centre for Human Settlements (Habitat) has spearheaded national efforts among all its members to collect housing and urban indicators and to present them in the Habitat II conference in Istanbul in 1996. It has continued to sponsor indicator work and to function as a clearinghouse for global indicator information on human settlements.[7] The World Bank, in turn, has now embraced the housing indicators framework, and has incorporated the development of performance indicators as an integral part of project preparation in all its lending sectors.

The Global Survey of Housing Indicators focused on the global housing situation in the year 1990. To maximize coverage, the composition of cities and countries selected for inclusion in the survey (see table 5.1) was determined by the need to include as many large countries and large cities as possible. Of the 30 countries with a population exceeding 30 million people in 1990, only seven countries were not included in the survey. The population in the countries that were included accounted for more than 80% of the total world population [World Bank, 1992, table 1, 218–199].

Generally speaking, global comparative studies either focus exclusively on the industrialized countries, where data is plentiful and more easily comparable, or exclusively on developing countries where donor support usually prohibits research in developed countries. The Global Survey, in contrast, aimed at a balanced selection of countries from all income groups. Of the 53 countries selected for the Survey, 10 (19%) were in the first gross national product (GNP) per capita quartile, 13 (25%) in the second, 12 (23%) in the third, and 18 (34%) in the fourth [World Bank, 1992, table 1, 218–219]. The unintended preponderance of countries in the highest–income quartile corresponded to the number of researchers in the European Housing Research Network who volunteered to conduct the survey in their countries without seeking remuneration.[8]

The Global Survey also aimed at a balanced geographical distribution of countries, ensuring adequate representations of all continents as well as their major subregions; 10 were selected from Sub–Saharan Africa; 6 from the Middle East and North Africa; 11 from Western Europe; 4 from Eastern Europe; 3 from South Asia; 10 from East Asia and the Pacific; 2 from North America; and 7 from Latin America and the Caribbean. Table 5.1 presents the population and GNP per capita, the city size, and the geographic region for the countries in the survey.

At the outset of the survey a comprehensive list of housing indicators was assembled from the literature, and additional indicators were designed to fill apparent gaps in coverage. All the indicators focused on the housing sector as a whole and attempted to capture the key quantitative objectives of all the main actors in the sector. The list was then narrowed down to a basic set, ensuring that all the indicators had a clear relevance to policy, were unambiguous when applied in different countries, and could be measured or estimated inexpensively and reliably within the available budgets, without resorting to new household surveys. Each indicator was then precisely defined, and alternative procedures for collecting and calculating its value were outlined in a survey instrument. The survey instrument was then tested in a pilot survey of five cities, definitions were refined and procedures for data collection were corrected and improved. The resulting data collection instrument [Housing Indicators Program, 1991] was supplemented by a videotaped introduction to the Survey, and both were sent to participating consultants during the months of May–August, 1991.[9]

Table 5.1. The Countries and Cities in the Global Survey, 1990.

Country (City)	Label	Country Population (millions)	GNP per capita ($)	City Population	Geographic Region [a]
Tanzania (Dar es Salaam)	TZ	24.5	110	1,566,290	1
Malawi (Lilongwe)	ML	8.5	200	378,867	1
Bangladesh (Dhaka)	BN	106.7	210	5,225,000	2
Madagascar (Antananarivo)	MD	11.7	230	852,500	1
Nigeria (Ibadan)	NI	115.5	290	5,668,978	1
India (New Delhi)	IN	849.5	350	8,427,083	2
Kenya (Nairobi)	KN	24.2	370	1,413,300	1
China (Beijing)	CH	1,133.7	370	6,984,000	2
Pakistan (Karachi)	PK	112.4	380	8,160,000	2
Ghana (Kumasi)	GH	14.9	390	1,387,873	1
Indonesia (Jakarta)	ID	178.2	570	8,222,515	2
Egypt (Cairo)	EG	52.1	600	6,068,695	3
Zimbabwe (Harare)	ZI	9.8	640	1,474,500	1
Senegal (Dakar)	SE	7.4	710	1,630,000	1
Philippines (Manila)	PH	61.5	730	7,928,867	2
Côte d'Ivoire (Abidjan)	CI	11.9	750	1,934,398	1
Morocco (Rabat)	MR	25.1	950	1,050,700	3
Ecuador (Quito)	EC	10.3	980	1,100,847	4
Jordan (Amman)	JR	3.2	1,240	1,300,000	3
Colombia (Bogota)	CO	32.3	1,260	4,907,600	4
Thailand (Bangkok)	TH	55.8	1,420	6,019,055	2
Tunisia (Tunis)	TU	8.1	1,440	1,631,000	3
Jamaica (Kingston)	JA	2.4	1,500	587,798	4
Turkey (Istanbul)	TR	56.1	1,630	7,309,190	3
Poland (Warsaw)	PO	38.2	1,690	1,655,700	5
Slovakia (Bratislava)	CZ	15.7	1,710	441,000	5
Chile (Santiago)	CL	13.2	1,940	4,767,638	4
Algeria (Algiers)	AL	25.1	2,060	1,826,617	3
Malaysia (Kuala Lumpur)	MY	17.9	2,320	1,232,900	2
Russia (Moscow)	RU	148.1	2,330	8,789,200	5
Mexico (Monterrey)	MX	86.2	2,490	2,532,349	4
South Africa (Johannesburg)	SA	35.9	2,530	8,740,700	1
Venezuela (Caracas)	VE	19.7	2,560	3,775,897	4
Brazil (Rio de Janeiro)	BR	150.4	2,680	6,009,397	4
Hungary (Budapest)	HU	10.6	2,780	2,016,774	5
Korea (Seoul)	KO	42.8	5,400	10,618,500	2
Greece (Athens)	GR	10.1	5,990	3,075,000	6
Israel (Tel Aviv)	IS	4.7	10,920	1,318,000	6
Spain (Madrid)	SP	39.0	11,020	4,845,851	6
Singapore (Singapore)	SI	3.0	11,160	2,690,100	6
Hong Kong (Hong Kong)	HK	5.8	11,490	5,800,600	6
United Kingdom (London)	UK	57.4	16,100	6,760,000	6
Australia (Melbourne)	AS	17.1	17,000	3,035,758	6
Netherlands (Amsterdam)	NT	14.9	17,320	695,221	6
Austria (Vienna)	AU	7.7	19,060	1,503,194	6
France (Paris)	FR	56.4	19,490	10,650,600	6
Canada (Toronto)	CA	26.5	20,470	3,838,744	6
United States (Washington, D.C.)	US	250.0	21,790	3,923,574	6
Germany (Munich)	GM	79.5	22,320	1,277,576	6
Norway (Oslo)	NR	4.2	23,120	462,000	6
Sweden (Stockholm)	SW	8.6	23,660	1,500,000	6
Japan (Tokyo)	JP	123.5	25,430	8,163,573	6
Finland (Helsinki)	FL	5.0	26,040	830,600	6

Sources: Housing Indicators Program [1994]; World Bank [1992, table 1, 218–219].

[a] 1 — Southern Africa, 2 — Asia and the Pacific, 3 — Middle East and North Africa, 4 — Latin America and the Caribbean, 5 — Eastern Europe, 6 — Industrialized Countries.

Initial results were received and reviewed by the program staff during the period October 1991–January 1992. Each return was examined for internal consistency as well as for results that appeared anomalous and required further justification. Reviews were then sent to the participating consultants, in preparation for regional meetings where these results were discussed in greater detail.

Three regional meetings on the Global Survey were conducted. The first was hosted by the Government Housing Bank in Bangkok, Thailand in November of 1991 and was attended by Asian consultants. The second was hosted by the United Nations Centre for Human Settlements (Habitat) in Nairobi, Kenya in January of 1992 and was attended by consultants from Africa, Europe, the Middle East, and North America. The third was hosted by the Ecuadorean Housing Bank (BEV) in Quito in February 1992 and was attended by Latin American and Carribean consultants.

The purpose of these regional meetings was to revise and streamline the survey instrument, to discuss how best to institutionalize the process of collecting housing indicators in the future, and to review the preliminary results. The meetings consisted of plenary discussions focused on conceptual and methodological issues, workshops focused on data gathering problems and on definitions, and one–to–one meetings with individual consultants to discuss their particular submissions. Based on discussions in the regional meetings, the survey instrument was further revised and some indicators and methods of collection or calculation were replaced or refined. The consultants were asked to submit their revised results, and all the completed submissions were received by mid–1993. A complete data matrix was compiled in 1993–1994 [Housing Indicators Program, 1994].

The survey instrument asked for final indicator values, as well as for the intermediary values used in their calculation. For example, in calculating the median house price–to–income ratio, intermediate values were obtained for the median house price as well as for the median household income. Intermediate data were later used to construct new indicators and composite indices. For example, intermediate values for the urban population, dwelling unit stock, and housing production were used to construct a new indicator – Housing Stock Growth. Several data items were yes/no answers that were later used to construct composite indices, and for these reasons, it is impossible to say exactly how many indicators were collected in the Global Survey. In addition, these indicators were later supplemented with published data on the overall economic, social, and political context. In the final analysis, a number of indicators for which data were collected were discarded as well, when too many values were missing or unreliable.

Given the resource limitations of the Global Survey, as well as the difficulty and in obtaining reliable values for some indicators (especially in the less–developed countries), it was necessary to limit the number of indicators while ensuring that data were collected for all four elements of the model presented earlier. This set of indicators was seen as minimal for purposes of comparative empirical research. However, given the total absence of good comparative housing data, the leap to a complete system of indicators was indeed a major challenge. The complete system was deemed too large to maintain over the long run, and considerable pressure was applied in subsequent collection efforts to radically reduce this list to a more manageable number. A provisional list of ten indicators was adopted by the U.N. Human Settlements Commission and in 1993,[10] with the proviso that this list will be revisited following the analysis of the original survey data along the lines of this book.

All in all, about 100 housing–sector indicators and composite indices are presented and discussed in this book. They are distributed, approximately evenly among the four components of our model of the housing sector presented here (see chapter 6). Summary values for all these indicators are presented and discussed in the text, while individual values for countries (cities) appear in tables in the Appendix.

All the Global Survey data was obtained for the year 1990. Following the survey, a minimal list of 10 housing indicators was collected by UNCHS (Habitat) in 1995, when indicator information was obtained from 236 cities in 109 countries in preparation for the United Nations City Summit (Habitat II) held in Istanbul in 1996. A summary of the 1995 data was published in 1997 [Flood,1997] and is reproduced here in table A27. Unfortunately, the 1995 data collection effort, like many earlier efforts, focused mainly on housing outcomes and did not include information on the context, the housing policy environment, or housing market conditions. This is lamentable, if only because it restricts our present analysis to the more comprehensive 1990 data set, given that our key interest in this book is not simply to present descriptive data on housing sector outcomes, but to understand and explain how the variations in these outcomes come about.

The Global Survey of Housing Indicators was conducted within a set of specific constraints that define the limits of the foregoing statistical analysis. Four of its limitations merit special attention:

1. *city rather than country data:* The Global Survey focused on a profile of the housing sector in one major city, in most cases the capital, in 53 countries; 16 out of the world's 30 largest urban agglomeration were included in the survey [United Nations, 1993, table A–10, 127]. In addition, 38 out of 53 of the cities surveyed were the largest in the country; and 9 were the second largest [United Nations,1993, table A–11, 128-133]. Forty two of the cities were capital cities. Each country was thus represented by one major city. Given the paucity of data, especially in the developing countries, national data collection was deemed impractical. Furthermore, the key problems in the housing sector are and have always been urban in nature, hence the decision to focus on urban housing. Finally, the emphasis on the policy environment also dictated the selection of the city as the proper framework, given the considerable power of cities to dictate and influence housing policy. For purposes of international comparisons,

however, the major cities were not necessarily typical for countries as a whole. Indeed, Maclennan and Gibb [1993], in reviewing the methodology of the Global Survey, suggested that:

> Single capital cities, as discussed below [*sic*], do not represent "national" profiles. Nor do they represent an unbiased sample of cities. In the West European economies, at least, capital cities tend to have:
>
> - denser development patterns;
> - higher growth rates (in the metropolitan area as a whole);
> - growth–related housing problems pertaining to affordability and homelessness;
> - higher mobility rates;
> - larger private rental sectors;
> - larger social rental sectors;
> - proportionally fewer rehabilitation problems;
> - higher and more volatile land prices.
>
> In consequence, a sample of such cities may over–emphasize problems related to homelessness and affordability. [51]

This criticism must be kept in mind in the foregoing analysis. The capital city and the primate city (the largest city in the country) usually do experience the most difficult housing challenges and are often the central focus of national housing policy. To the extent that these cities in different countries share common characteristics, however, the results of the survey may be consistently biased, and thus they provide a reliable picture of housing conditions in capital cities, from which it should be possible to infer about conditions in other cities.

2. *the absence of distributional measures*: The system of indicators chosen for the Global Survey could not distinguish between two countries that had, say, the same median value but different distributions of this value. The median house sizes in Sweden and in the United Kingdom were roughly identical—75.0 m^2 and 75.9 m^2, respectively. This tells us that in both countries half the households had house sizes below 75 m^2. It could be, however, that in one country most of those houses were in the 25-50 m^2 range, while in the other most were in the 50-75 m^2 range. The single median value does not tell us anything about the distribution of those values. Additional measures, such as the standard deviation of house size, will tell us more about distributional characteristics. But data on such measures were more difficult to find. Since the distributional aspect of housing sector performance is of paramount importance, the absence of such measures does bias the results in favor of cities and countries with higher medians or means — of, say, house size — and against countries that may have lower medians or means but tighter and more equitable distributions.

3. *reliance on available data*: The Global Survey did not rely only on official
    publications; it included a variety of sources of data from academic
    institutions and nongovernmental organizations as well. Budget limita-
    tions did, however, limit data collection to indicators that could be calcu-
    lated from existing sources without necessitating new surveys. This meant
    that in a number of cases no data were available. This was particularly
    critical in the cases of the subsidies and targeted subsidies indicators, both
    of which required complicated calculations as well as data that could not
    be obtained.

4. *a limited set of indicators:* A number of important aspects of housing sector
    performance — such as environmental quality, access to amenities, residen-
    tial segregation, eviction, discrimination in mortgage lending, regulatory
    barriers to affordable housing, or personal safety in residential neighbor-
    hoods — could not be measured either because of lack of data or because
    of lack of solid and unambiguous indicators to measure them.

* * *

Given these constraints, the comparisons between cities and countries in the
ensuing analysis should be approached with due caution. Although cities and
countries are being used interchangeably, the reader should keep in mind that the
data pertains to the city and not to the country as a whole; that it is a single
measure that may hide a more or a less equitable distribution; and that the data
system is incomplete, relying as it does on available data. Still, for the first time,
we have a comprehensive set of housing indicators, all collected by experienced
housing experts, using identical definitions, and covering a very large number
of countries. And since the focus of the present study is on investigating similarities and differences — as well as what accounts for them — in a broad cross section
of countries, it matters less that a number of years have passed since the data were
collected. The Global Survey of Housing Indicators of 1990 yielded the best
comparative global data set on the housing sector available for the time being,
clearly sufficient, as we shall see below, to discern a large number of patterns and
connections that were largely hidden before.

6

Measuring the Effect of Policy on Performance

A Policy-Sensitive Model of the Housing Sector

The actual performance of the housing sector has as much to do with *not building* as it does with building, and in the future the balance will surely tilt in favor of the former. Surely, houses are all too real. They are the actual places in which we all live and they can be seen, touched and experienced directly. The construction process is real as well. It too can be seen, touched, and experienced directly. But neither can be understood, let alone changed for the better, without shifting our focus to not building, and to the connections between building and not building. This shift is essential for anyone concerned with improving housing conditions. It is quite clear – as any squatter family involved in a political struggle to resist eviction knows – that there is often more housing value in activities related to nonbuilding than there is in building.

This chapter aims at widening our understanding of the relationships between housing policy on the one hand, and building and dwelling on the other. We accomplish this first by putting them both in a broader economic, social, and political context, and second, by relating them both to the housing market. Not surprisingly, while all three elements – the broad context, the housing policy environment, and the housing market – are all situated in the virtual realm of neither building nor dwelling, they have an overriding effect on both. This chapter introduces a simple model of the housing sector which focuses on the causal relationships between contexts, policies, housing market conditions, and housing market outcomes – the quantities, qualities, prices and rents of the actual stock of housing. Six such causal relationships are studied in detail in this book.[1] They are illustrated by the arrows in figure 6.1.

The overall economic, social, and political context of the housing sector is expected to affect housing market outcomes both directly and indirectly (through its effect on the housing policy environment and on housing market conditions). The housing policy environment is also expected to affect housing market outcomes both directly and indirectly (through its effect on housing market

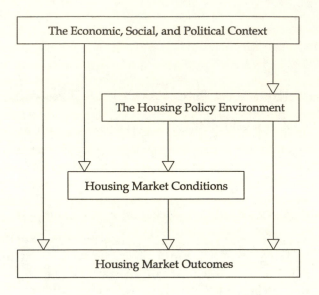

Figure 6.1. A Policy–Sensitive Model of the Housing Sector.

conditions). Finally, housing market conditions are expected to affect housing market outcomes directly.

The Economic, Social, and Political Context

There are five dimensions of the overall economic, social, and political context of the housing sector which are especially critical for the sector:

1. *income and the level of economic development*: Household income, the distribution of income, and the growth of incomes are all expected to have a strong direct impact on housing sector outcomes, especially through their influence on housing demand. Higher–income households can be expected to have bigger and better houses. More developed countries, as measured by higher household incomes or per capita gross national product (GNP), can be expected to have slower–growing cities, smaller households, less unauthorized housing, fewer squatters, more mortgage lending, and better–articulated housing policies.

2. *the political and social context*: First, political freedoms are expected to increase housing choice and residential mobility; they are also expected to be associated with more developed housing markets and with a more enabling housing policy environment. Conversely, restricted freedoms are often associated with restricted housing choice and distorted markets. Housing policy is, in large measure, a direct outcome of a nation's overall political outlook. For example, the encumbrance of public enterprises in

China with serious responsibilities for housing their workers, has continued to burden both their efficient management and their housing output, long after similar practices have been abandoned elsewhere. Also, states like China, which are preoccupied with maintaining strict control over the citizenry, are expected to (and in fact do) have fewer squatter settlements.

At the opposite end of the spectrum, anarchy and the breakdown of the social order in periods of political upheaval often lead to lax and corrupt enforcement of building regulation and property-right protection, resulting in the formation of squatter settlements and in illegal construction. More commonly, the housing sector is badly affected by any political instability as it reduces the level of confidence needed for people to invest in housing. The housing sector is ultimately devastated by wars and civil wars. Wars either decimate the housing stock or paralyze housing production, while creating floods of refugees with no roofs over their heads. In 1944 for example, at the height of World War II, housing production in the United States was reduced to 16% of the long-term trend-line estimate for that year [Doan, 1997, table A, 182-183]. To cite a more recent example, a Bosnian government survey in 1995, found 18% of all housing units destroyed and 63% damaged by the war there. Rebuilding them was estimated to cost many times the total annual revenues of the government at that time [Wren, 1995, 14].

In social terms, the ready availability of human capital — entrepreneurial and managerial talent, skilled craftsmen, and trained professionals in the public, private and voluntary sectors — is expected to improve both the quality of production and the supply response to changing conditions in the housing market. Social structure, family and clan cohesiveness, community organization, and the existence of social networks and voluntary associations all have an effect on the political organization of dwellers that is often crucial to the attainment of housing goals, be they the accumulation of savings for construction, the exchange of labor or information, the common struggle to obtain tenure or services, or the cohesiveness and safety of residential neighborhoods.

3. *demography and geography*: City size, the rate of urban growth, the level of urbanization, household size, and the rate of household formation can all be expected to affect housing market outcomes through their effect on housing demand. Population densities can, on the other hand, can be expected to have a direct effect on land prices, and therefore an indirect one on housing supply. Natural endowments of building materials and energy resources can be expected to lower construction costs, for example, while a mountainous or marshy terrains that limit residential expansion can be expected to increase cost. Similarly, the frequency and force of natural disasters — earthquakes, volcanic eruptions, violent storms, mud slides and floods — all tend to increase construction costs, to place additional burdens on residential infrastructure, and to increase risk.

4. *the overall fiscal regime*: The overall fiscal regime, characterized by the structure of central–government and local–government budgets and tax policies, affect both housing markets and the housing policy environment and are therefore expected to have an indirect effect on housing market outcomes. Cutting housing subsidies, as well as increasing taxes on residential property or construction, are often the instruments of choice of governments faced with budget shortfalls and seeking fiscal austerity measures. Conversely, flooding the housing sector with subsidies is often seen as an effective instrument for jump–starting a stagnant economy.

5. *the financial and monetary regime:* The availability of credit for housing depends, to a large measure, on the overall development of the banking industry. For example, a general credit squeeze has an immediate effect on the availability of mortgage finance. When credit is in short supply, governments and banks often ration credit to priority investments and away from housing—a policy pursued by South Korea for many years which eventually led to severe housing shortages. Mortgage lending is also at the mercy of the overall rate of inflation. As we shall see later, when inflation climbs beyond a certain threshold, mortgage lending ceases altogether.

It is not difficult to see that these five elements of the economic, social, and political context of the housing sector exert an enormous impact on housing market outcomes, both directly and indirectly. But, while the influence of the overall context cannot and should not be ignored, the housing policy environment in and of itself does matter as well.

The Housing Policy Environment

The housing policy environment, as we noted earlier, is the set of policies and government interventions that motivate, enable, and constrain housing action. Many of the policies which are discussed in the pages that follow are, in fact, part of the overall policy context of the housing sector, and are not particular or unique to the housing sector. They are presented here as elements of the housing policy environment because they have an overriding effect on housing market outcomes and are therefore of concern to those engaged in identifying and modifying policies that matter to housing. There are five major components of the housing policy environment which are especially critical for the sector:

1. *the property rights regime*: The freedom to own and exchange land and housing, the transparency of the land registration system and the assignment of different rights in housing, the rules governing the extension of ownership rights to squatters, and rules governing eviction, demolition, and resettlement can all be expected to affect both housing market conditions and outcomes.

2. *the housing finance regime:* The development of housing finance institutions, mortgage insurance, mortgage banking regulations, prudential regulations, restrictions on capital flows, and the market or nonmarket allocation of capital can all be expected to have a direct effect on the availability and extent of mortgage credit and construction finance, and hence an effect on housing market conditions.

3. *the housing subsidies regime*: Public involvement in actual housing construction, management and maintenance; public ownership of land and housing; public management of housing finance institutions; demand-side subsidies such as housing vouchers and rent supplements; and various forms of price and rent controls can all be expected to have an impact on housing market outcomes, such as prices and rents, overcrowding, the doubling-up of households, home ownership, or residential mobility.

4. *residential Infrastructure:* Government expenditures on urban infra- structure can be expected to have a direct effect on the availability of serviced urban land for residential expansion, and hence on land prices and on the supply of housing. Similarly, the availability and quality of urban infrastructure services — uncongested roads, public transport, water, sewerage, drainage, electricity, parks and playgrounds, schools, garbage collection, and police and fire protection — can all be expected to increase the quality, and hence the value, of residential communities.

5. *the regulatory regime*: Restrictive building codes, zoning and subdivision regulations, delays in obtaining permits, and strict urban growth controls, can all be expected to affect housing supply — making construction more expensive, limiting production and investment, and rendering the supply side less able to respond to changes in demand.

Housing Market Conditions

The overall context and the housing policy environment both affect housing outcomes directly, and also indirectly — through their effects on housing market conditions. In the ensuing discussion we distinguish between housing market conditions and housing market outcomes. Housing market conditions constitute the third element in our model. They are the economic conditions affecting housing demand and supply. On the demand side, they are likely to include the availability of mortgage finance and housing subsidies. On the supply side, they are likely to include the availability and cost of housing inputs — land, building materials, labor, and capital. We can postulate a causal relationship between the conditions governing the housing market and the resulting housing market outcomes. The availability of credit and housing subsidies can be expected to increase housing demand by households, making them able to purchase more and better housing. Similarly, low costs of land and construction can be expected to increase the supply of affordable housing by producers.

Housing Market Outcomes

Generally speaking, housing market outcomes are house prices and rents on one hand, and the quantity and quality of housing on the other, which are, in effect, mutually determined through the interaction of housing demand and housing supply. Housing market outcomes, in fact, form the fourth element of our model. These outcomes are affected by all three other elements – the context, the policy environment, and housing market conditions. What ultimately matters in any well functioning housing sector are, of course, the attributes and qualities of the housing stock and its ability to meet quantitative needs, that is to ensure adequate shelter for everyone. Not only are the physical features of buildings important. Their utility and usefulness to the people who dwell in them are important as well: Are they habitable? Are they comfortable? Are they safe? Will they last? Are they pleasant to behold? Are they well located?

Houses perform functions that make dwelling in them possible and valuable. Housing outcomes are therefore of two kinds, so to speak: the state of the houses themselves and the state of dwelling in these houses. As a literary preference, we are using the noun "house" here to refer to the mundane statistical entity known as a dwelling unit. I have yet to meet someone who refers to a home as a dwelling unit, as in "I'll meet you at my dwelling unit at twelve." By house I also mean flat, shack, dorm, barracks, tent, mobile home, and any other encampment – solid or transitory as it may be – that serves for human habitation.

In more mundane terms, when we speak of housing market outcomes it is of interest to know if home ownership and rental housing are well balanced, if there are substantial quantities of unauthorized housing or squatter housing, and if there are homeless people who are not housed at all. It is important to know whether there is sufficient dwelling space or whether families are overcrowded, whether families need to double-up because of a shortage of dwelling units, and whether newly- weds can find a place to dwell or need to stay with their parents. It is also important to know if a sufficient number of new dwelling units are being produced to meet new demand, whether the housing stock is growing at an adequate rate, and whether a sufficient amount of savings is invested in housing. Finally, it may also be of interest to know whether there is sufficient flexibility, variety, choice, and mobility within the housing sector, and whether it can respond to the changing conditions in the city. Housing market outcomes, in short, focus on the actual performance characteristics of the housing stock and on its ability to satisfy the diverse needs and expectations of dwellers.

This summary provides a brief description of the model illustrated in figure 6.1. The four elements in the model will be described in much greater detail in later chapters. The six arrows in the figure should be regarded as cause-and-effect relationships. As we shall see later, the statistical data are highly suggestive of the presence of cause-and-effect among the different elements of the model, but the data cannot constitute proof beyond reasonable doubt. For every arrow in the model, there may be another arrow pointing in the opposite direction. This may be particularly important, for example, in the relationship between market conditions and outcomes, which in the longer term may be bidirectional.[2]

To take another example, there are good reasons to believe that housing market outcomes may, in turn, affect the overall economic, social, and political context. We noted earlier that housing activity has important effects on, among other things, the GNP, household savings, the accumulation of wealth, and wages. Some writers note an effect on political stability as well. For example, the growth of home ownership, a housing market outcome, is assumed by some writers to have dissipated the revolutionary fervor of the masses. Kemeny [1977], for example, argued that home ownership "is undoubtedly the most powerful ideology in Australian social and political life," and "the main bulwark against social, economic and political unrest" [47–48]. Harvey [1977] contended that "[t]he evident social discontent of the 1930s has, to a great degree, been successfully diffused by a governmental policy which created a large wedge of debt-encumbered home owners who are unlikely to rock the boat" [125]. Although there may not have been a conscious effort on the part of governments to promote home ownership in order to diffuse revolutionary zeal, home ownership may well have engendered a bourgeois political outlook. Little wonder that Friedrich Engels [1872], the author of *The Housing Question,* was so adamantly against it.

It is important to note, in conclusion, that in this model the relationship between housing policy and housing outcomes is determined by the housing market, through the interaction of supply and demand. Both policy and outcomes are, in turn, influenced by the overall economic, social, and political context. There is, therefore, no simple, directly observable, and measurable relationship between policy and outcomes. When governments build public housing, they can simply count the annual number of units built, and take that as a measure of their effect on housing market outcomes. When governments do not build, but instead conduct housing policies that eventually result in improved housing market outcomes, they need to measure and model what other actors in the sector do in order to determine whether policies are succeeding or failing. A critical need for more sophisticated measurement and modeling arises when policies are no longer directly related to outcomes but affect outcomes through the operations of the market.

The Housing Market: Conditions versus Outcomes

One spring afternoon in 1993, I found myself sitting at the coffee lounge on top floor of an elegant hotel overlooking the onion–shaped domes of the church of Saint Basil in Moscow's Red Square. This was the final meeting of a World Bank mission charged with preparing a substantial loan to the Russian Federation, aimed at reforming its housing sector. We were drafting the aide–mémoire, our official communiqué to the Russian government, outlining the proposed loan instruments and their respective objectives. At some point, in a truly innocent effort to bring some order into the discussion, I suggested that we distinguish between instruments that aimed at the supply side of the housing market from those that aimed at the demand side. The mission chief confidently dismissed my comment as being "too academic." I knew then and there that I was an incorrigible troublemaker.

By now it should be clear that the most important effects of the housing policy environment on housing outcomes occur through its effects on the housing market. This is indeed an unpleasant realization for those few good but impatient souls who would like to act on the housing sector directly — to go out there and built "affordable" housing for the poor, for example. Why? Because the price of housing is determined by market forces. And if affordable houses are rare, then their price will increase to reflect their market value and they will no longer be affordable. Even in the most repressive of states they will usually end up in the hands of the not–so–poor. As Ramirez [1978] has pointed out, there is a universal "housing queue" that makes it virtually impossible for the poor to have decent houses while the not–so–poor remain overcrowded and ill–housed. It follows also that there is little merit in a housing policy that solely focuses on the poor, hoping against hope that "the market" will take care of the rest, without paying any attention to whether the market is functioning properly. When the market is not functioning properly, the poor are squeezed as well.

For those with a serious interest in improving housing sector outcomes in any city, even with a special focus on the poor, there is no choice but to study the machinations of the housing market as a whole, the forces affecting it, and the constraints governing its behavior with the view of influencing its course rather than ignoring it. In this discussion, we can only paint the urban housing sector with broad brush strokes as a market, where the equilibrium between demand and supply determines the prices, rents, quantities, types of tenure, and qualities of housing. And it is by no means a perfect market either, because of the unique nature of housing as a commodity: it is both an asset and a flow of services; no two houses are the same; location matters; there are many externalities; new production forms only a small part of overall supply; and there are delays in attaining market equilibrium because of the time lag between the rise in demand and the completion of new units. Still, it is a market.[3]

Housing sector performance is thus described and explained as a set of market outcomes. More specifically, we assume that housing market outcomes come about through the interaction of demand and supply in the market place. This essentially implies that housing quantity outcomes, such as the median house size or the volume of new production, cannot be explained without reference to prices; conversely, it implies that house prices and rents cannot be explained without reference to how much housing, and of what quality, is in fact being delivered. The great value of adopting such a conceptual framework is that it unifies our model and gives every disparate indicator a specific place in the model. In fact, housing market outcomes can be conveniently divided into two types: house prices, rents, and measures of affordability on the one hand; and housing quantity and quality (measured in quantitative terms) on the other.[4]

In conceptual terms, our model of the housing sector presented in the previous section can be understood as having three levels of statistical or econometric models:

1. *policy models* that explain the housing policy environment (P) as a function of the economic, social and political context (X);
2. *market conditions models* that explain housing market conditions (H) as a function of the economic, social and political context X, and the policy environment P; and
3. *housing market models* that explain housing market outcomes (M) in terms of the context X, the policy environment P, and the housing market conditions H.

In algebraic terms, we can express these models in three equations:

(1) $P = f(X)$;

(2) $H = f(X,P)$; and

(3) $M = f(X, P, H)$.

The first set of models, the policy models, will be discussed in chapter 12; market conditions models will be discussed in chapters 14–16; and housing market models will be presented and discussed in detail in chapters 17–23.

Housing market outcomes are best understood with reference to models of the housing market in common use in basic econometric textbooks [see for example Ramanathan, 1992, 527]. These models postulate that housing market outcomes — reduced to basic quantities and prices — are determined by a long–term equilibrium of demand and supply. This equilibrium can be expressed as a set of three equations — a demand equation, a supply equation, and an equilibrium equation.

In the models discussed here, the demand equation expresses the demand for housing (Q_d) as a function of Household Income (Y), demographic variables such as population growth or household size (D), the price of housing (p_h), and other variables which may affect demand such as housing finance (F) or subsidies (S), and the housing policy environment P. The supply equation expresses the supply of housing (Q_s) as a function of the price of housing p_h, other variables that may affect supply such as the cost of land (L), the construction cost (C), the cost of capital (I), and the housing policy environment P. And the equilibrium equation requires that in the long run, housing demand, Q_d, will equal housing supply, Q_s. Again, in algebraic terms, these equations take the form:

(4) $Q_d = f(Y, D, p_h, F, S, P)$;

(5) $Q_s = f(C, L, I, p_h, P)$; and

(6) $Q_d = Q_s$.

The data limitations of the Global Survey of Housing Indicators prevented us from including information on subsidies and on the cost of construction capital in the models. Both will, therefore, be excluded in the foregoing discussion. The three structural equation are simplified in this case:

(4) $Q_d = f(Y, D, p_h, F, P)$;

(5) $Q_s = f(C, L, p_h, P)$; and

(6) $Q_d = Q_s$.

The only unknowns in these equations are assumed to be the two housing market outcomes — the equilibrium quantity $Q = Q_d = Q_s$, and the equilibrium price p_h. All the other variables are assumed to be given and exogenous to these models. Upon closer examination, we see that the exogenous variables in equations (4) – (6) break into three groups: the household income variable Y and the demographic variables D belong to the context X; P expresses the housing policy environment; and the rest of the variables — the availability of housing finance F, or subsidies S, and the costs of land L, construction C, and capital I, belong neither to the context nor to the housing policy environment. These, then, are the housing market conditions H, discussed earlier. The three equations (4) – (6) which describe demand, supply, and the equilibrium between them are, in fact, an elaboration of the conceptual equation (3) for the housing market models. Housing market conditions, H, are postulated to be affected both by the context X and by the policy environment P, but they are different and separate from both. The postulated causal relation between these three groups of variables was expressed algebraically in Equation (2).

Housing market conditions — which are expected to have an effect on housing supply and demand, over and above the effects of the economic, social, and political context and the housing policy environment — are of five major types. Three kinds of conditions affect the supply side of the market: the availability of land, conditions in the construction sector, and the availability of construction finance. Two kinds of conditions affect the demand side of the market: the availability of mortgage credit and the availability of subsidies. The first three conditions reflect the costs of necessary inputs to the production of houses, and, in terms of housing supply, can be viewed as exogenous conditions. We should expect, for example, that lower construction, land, and interest costs will have a positive effect on housing supply, or that lower construction time will increase the responsiveness of the construction sector to changes in demand. In parallel, a greater availability of mortgage finance on one hand and housing subsidies on the other can both be expected to have a positive effect on housing demand.

In Part III of this book, we elaborate on three of these housing market conditions — the availability of land, conditions in the construction sector, and the availability of mortgage credit — and construct statistical models that seek to account for variations in their values in terms of a variety of context and policy variables.[5]

Modeling Prices, Quantities, and Supply and Demand

In parallel, in Part III, a large number of measures — prices, rents, and measures of affordability; numbers of dwelling units, crowding, and living space; housing quality; new production and investment; home ownership rates, unauthorized and squatter housing, homelessness, and residential mobility — are presented as housing market outcomes for a large number of cities and countries. As we shall see, such a comprehensive housing data set is interesting and significant it itself. At last we have, for the first time, comparative data on housing sector outcomes that gives us a truly global perspective on the housing sector. Our key interest in this book, however, is not simply to present descriptive data on housing sector outcomes, but to understand how the variations in these outcomes occur.

In our discussion, therefore, we are interested in two questions. First, given our data, can we determine statistically which of the exogenous variables has a significant effect on housing prices and quantities, and how strong is this effect? More specifically, can we determine whether the housing policy environment has a significant effect on housing outcomes? Second, given our data, can we determine the structural characteristics of housing demand and supply? More specifically, can we determine whether the housing policy environment has a significant effect on housing demand and supply?

To answer these two questions, we assume that the functional form of equations (4) – (6) is linear. We can then rewrite the equations:

(4) $Q_d = a_0 + a_1Y + a_2D + a_3p_h + a_4F + a_5P;$

(5) $Q_s = b_0 + b_1C + b_2L + b_3p_h + b_4P;$ and

(6) $Q_d = Q_s.$

We can now obtain an expression for the price of housing p_h as a linear combination of all the exogenous variables:

(7) $p_h = (b_0 - a_0)/(a_3 - b_3) - a_1Y/(a_3 - b_3) - a_2D/(a_3 - b_3) + a_4F/(a_3 - b_3)$
$+ a_5P/(a_3 - b_3) + b_1C/(a_3 - b_3) + b_2L/(a_3 - b_3).$

We can replace $(b_0 - a_0)/(a_3 - b_3)$ by a new coefficient c_0, where $c_0 = (b_0 - a_0)/(a_3 - b_3)$. We can similarly replace all the other coefficients to obtain a new equation for the price of housing p_h :

(8) $p_h = c_0 + c_1Y + c_2D + c_3F + c_4P + c_5C + c_6L.$

This equation is referred to in the literature as the reduced–form equation for the price of housing. It expresses the price of housing as a function of all the exogenous variables, both on the demand side and on the supply side. This equation forms the basic model for all the price, rent, and affordability models presented in chapter 17. We use this equation in a series of multiple–regression models that estimate all the coefficients, c_i, of the equation and determine statistically how confident we can be that each coefficient is different from zero. In other words, these models tell us whether a particular exogenous variable — for example, household income — exerts a significant positive or negative influence on the price of housing.

Following a similar procedure, a reduced-form equation can be obtained for the equilibrium quantity Q:

(9) $Q = d_0 + d_1Y + d_2D + d_3F + d_4P + d_5C + d_6L.$

In chapters 19-23, we follow the same procedure to estimate all the coefficients d_i and to determine whether any of the exogenous variables exerts a statistically significant influence on different measures of housing quantity outcomes, such as the amount of housing or the quality of housing that a household occupies.

If, in addition, we linearly transform each of the independent variables so that its average value for the sample as a whole is 0 and its standard deviation is 1, then the corresponding coefficients d_i will be standardized β-coefficients.[6] "Their value is that we no longer have the problem of units of measure. . ., and the beta coefficient reflects the impact on the criterion variable of a change of one standard deviation in either variable. Now we have a common unit of measure, and the coefficients tell us which variable is most influential" [Hair et al., 1979, 58]. If the β-coefficient for the income variable is 0.5, for example, it suggests that a change of one standard deviation in median household income corresponds to a change of one standard deviation in the price or quantity in question.

To estimate the structural characteristics of housing supply and demand, however, we cannot use two independent reduced-form equations — one for the price and one for the equilibrium quantity — to obtain consistent estimates of the various coefficients, because the equation system may be over-identified. Instead, we can use the two-stage least-squares (TSLS) method, which can be applied to obtain a unique set of estimates which are consistent [Ramanathan, 1992, 539-540]. To apply this method, we must first estimate the reduced-form equation (8) for the price of housing. Given the estimated coefficients c_i, we can then calculate a *predicted* value for the price of housing p^*_h for each country in our sample. We then estimate the demand and supply equations (4) and (5) using the predicted value for the price of housing, p^*_h:

(4) $Q_d = a_0 + a_1Y + a_2D + a_3p^*_h + a_4F + a_5P;$

and

(5) $Q_s = b_0 + b_1C + b_2L + b_3p^*_h + b_4P.$

While the earlier reduced-form equation (9) for the equilibrium quantity of housing can enlighten us about the effects of all the exogenous variables on housing quantity, these equations (4) and (5) tell us more about the parameters of demand and supply that equation (9) does not reveal. Five of these parameters merit special attention:

1. the income elasticity of demand, defined as the incremental change in the quantity demanded associated with an incremental change in income;
2. the price elasticity of demand, defined as the incremental change in the quantity demanded associated with an incremental change in price;

3. the price elasticity of supply, defined as the incremental change in the quantity supplied associated with an incremental change in price;
4. the policy elasticity of demand, defined as the incremental change in the quantity demanded associated with an incremental change increase in the degree of enabling of the housing policy environment; and
5. the policy elasticity of supply, defined as the incremental change in the quantity demanded associated with an incremental change increase in the degree of enabling of the housing policy environment.

As income increases, household are expected to demand more housing, and so the income elasticity of demand is expected to be positive. The question is whether a 1% change in income will lead to a change in the quantity demanded which is less than, equal or greater than 1%. A 1% increase in the latter clearly implies an income elasticity of 1.

Similarly, as house prices increase, the quantity demanded is expected to fall, and so the price elasticity of demand is expected to be negative. Again, the question is how negative. As house prices increase, the quantity supplied is also expected to increase, and so the price elasticity of supply is expected to be positive. Similarly, as the housing policy environment becomes more enabling, both housing demand and housing supply are expected to increase, and so both the policy elasticity of demand and the policy elasticity of supply are expected to be positive. How positive?

The concept of elasticity is closely related to logarithms [Ramanathan, 1992, 155–156]. The elasticity of Y with respect to X, for example, is the same as the derivative of ln Y with respect to ln X. This suggests that if we posit our demand and supply equations with all the variables in logarithmic form, then the estimated coefficients will, in fact, be their respective elasticities. We can therefore rewrite the demand and supply equations as:

$$(10) \quad \ln Q_d = e_0 + e_1 \ln Y + e_2 \ln D + e_3 \ln p^*_h + e_4 \ln F + e_5 \ln P;$$

and

$$(11) \quad \ln Q_s = f_0 + f_1 \ln C + f_2 \ln L + f_3 \ln p^*_h + f_4 \ln P.$$

In these equations, e_1 is the income elasticity of demand, e_3 is the price elasticity of demand, e_5 is the policy elasticity of demand, f_3 is the price elasticity of supply, and f_4 is the policy elasticity of supply.[7] In chapters 19–23, we construct demand and supply models for a large number of housing quantities and qualities and show how they are affected by incomes, prices, and policies. These elasticity measures are, in fact, similar to the β–coefficients already discussed, except that instead of measuring changes in standard deviations, they measure the effects of an incremental change in the independent variable on the dependent one.

* * *

This chapter concludes the discussion of the conceptual framework required for a global analysis of housing policy. Part II will refine the distinction between an enabling and a nonenabling housing policy regime by focusing on its five key components: the property rights regime, the housing finance regime, housing subsidies, residential infrastructure, and the regulatory regime.

Part II

The Components of an Enabling
Policy Regime

7

The Property Rights Regime

The establishment of a regime of individual property rights in land and housing is the cornerstone of an enabling housing policy regime. The formal and informal rules governing property acquisition, sale, development, and use are of critical importance in creating predictable, vibrant, and efficient housing markets; adherence to these rules is what makes these markets work. In the absence of such rules, housing development is subject to the whims of unpredictable political intervention. And intervention by decree, as we shall see, usually impedes and constrains housing sector performance.

The rules that pertain to the development of real property are included in the laws, regulations, and policies governing private property in general, but they assume a special importance in land and housing policy because housing is by far the most important and the most widely distributed form of private wealth. Housing policy concerns have therefore often had a crucial influence on the evolution of the property rights regime as a whole. In recent years, for example, such concerns have focused on the regularization of squatter settlements in the developing countries, on the massive privatization of the public housing stock in Eastern Europe, and on securing property transactions and strengthening foreclosure laws as preconditions for the development of housing finance regimes.

This chapter establishes the critical role of the property rights regime in an enabling housing policy environment, by exploring a number of related questions: What are property rights in land and housing? Why is a property rights regime a necessary component of an enabling housing policy environment? How are property rights in land and housing established and maintained, and what is the role of the public sector in a property rights regime? What are the necessary limits to a property rights regime? How can we measure the degree to which a property rights regime is enabling?

Property Rights in Land and Housing

Property rights in land and housing are legal or customary arrangements or "rules" that make human behavior in this realm predictable. These rules, which can be both formal and informal in nature, define the "relations among individuals that arise from the existence of scarce goods and pertain to their use" [Pejovich, 1995, 65]. The rules do not pertain to relations between people and their land or houses, but to the relations between people and other people. The property rights regime is, in this sense, a social institution. As Rose [1994] notes:

> Indeed, an entire private property regime—whether governmental or customary—may be understood as a managed commons: a private property *regime* is itself a meta- property, held in common by those who understand and follow its precepts. In a sense, when we divide up the commons into private property, we are only moving from a commons as a physical resource to a commons in the social structure that safeguards individualized resource management. [127]

As a social institution governing relations among people, the property rights regime defines the major forms of ownership: private ownership, state ownership, and common ownership [Pejovich, 1995, 66]. Private ownership, which is of particular interest in our discussion of housing, has three basic characteristics: exclusivity, transferability, and constitutional guarantees of ownership. Pejovich further elaborates on these characteristics: "Exclusivity provides incentives for owners to put their assets into the highest-valued uses; transferability provides incentives for resources to move from less productive to more productive owners; and the constitutional guarantee of ownership separates the accumulation of economic wealth from the accumulation of political power" [Pejovich, 1995, 66-68].

The first of these characteristics grants the owner of house and land the right to exclude others, and guarantees the private use of the land for the owner's enjoyment. The second grants the owner the right to enjoy to the fullest the fruits of the investment in the property. And the third characteristic is a form of insurance that limits the power of the regime, the elite, or the majority in exercising control over an individual's private property. This third factor is, in a true sense, the historical outcome of a long struggle against the absolute powers of rulers. It transfers these powers from the state to individuals, groups, and firms, thereby greatly constraining the power of the state in matters of property in general and housing in particular. This does not mean that private property rights are absolute and that the state cannot define and limit these rights through, for example, zoning restrictions, taxation, or compulsory acquisition for public use. But such rights are protected and defended against arbitrary "takings" by the state without due compensation.

Pejovich [1990] further defines the first two characteristics of a private property rights regime:

The right of ownership contains the following four elements: (i) the right to use an asset (*usus*), (ii) the right to capture benefits from that asset (*usus fructus*), (iii) the right to change its form and substance (*abusus*), and (iv) the right to transfer all or some of the rights specified under (i), (ii) and (iii) to others at a mutually agreed upon price. [28]

In a well-functioning property rights regime, such rights are respected and acknowledged by all both formally and informally. As Pejovich [1995] notes, "[e]vidence shows that informal rules matter, that similar formal rules imposed on different societies produce different outcomes, and that informal rules have frequently outlived formal rules" [32]. In the absence of such a regime, land and housing are usually either in some form of common ownership (such as cooperative or tribal ownership), in state ownership, or in informal occupation by squatters of common, unused, underutilized, or disputed lands. For better or worse, in the active and growing urban agglomerations where there is a strong competition for land and housing, none of the alternatives to a private property regime provides the right combination of incentives to the main actors in the housing sector.

The Rationale for a Property Rights Regime

A private property rights regime is a key component of an enabling housing policy environment precisely because of its powers to exclude others, arguably its most important feature. Rose[1994] explains the incentives created by the institution of private property in terms of the well-being of the community at large:

Because they can exclude outsiders, owners alone may capture the value of their individual investments in the things they own, and as a consequence property rights encourage them to put time, labor and care into the development of resources. Moreover, exclusive control makes it possible for owners to identify other owners and for all to exchange the things upon which they have labored until these things arrive in the hands of those who value them most highly — to the great cumulative advantage of all. For these reasons, it is said, exclusive private property fosters the well-being of the community and gives its members a medium in which resources are used, conserved and exchanged to their greatest advantage. [105]

A similar rationale pertains to the incentives for caring and maintaining housing property. Because home owners have to bear the costs of maintenance and repair of their homes, and because they have a long-term interest in preserving the value of their homes, they take better care of their houses, their gardens, and their neighborhoods than those who occupy dwellings without a stake in them or those who rent dwellings with the intention of moving on.

But beyond that, individual home owners have a greater incentive to care for and maintain their property than do state and municipal authorities. Publicly owned housing is generally given or rented to beneficiaries below cost, with the remainder paid from the general tax fund. As Pejovich [1995]notes,

> No matter what the state agency charges for its product, neither its officers nor their superiors can appropriate the residual. . . . [S]tate ownership provides public decision makers with weak incentives to pursue efficient outcomes. Therein lies the problem with state ownership. Inefficiencies in government have less to do with professionalism, work habits or integrity of public decision makers than with the penalty-reward system arising from state ownership. [Pejovich, 1995, 69–70]

While there is a certain rationale for public ownership of some public goods — such as urban roads — state ownership of land and housing has been problematic. Housing investment incentives by public authorities have usually been unrelated to demand, consumer preferences, or willingness to pay. Low rents have usually prevented such authorities from generating sufficient funds to cover maintenance and repair expenditures, let alone construction costs, and there has been no incentive on the part of the state to maintain the value of its housing stock over time. Lack of maintenance and discipline has often invited vandalism and carelessness by residents, further enhanced by their lack of a sense of ownership of their living environment. The deterioration of public housing estates in the United States, Great Britain, and France has often reached an irreversible stage where nothing but demolition was deemed to be an adequate response.

Public housing authorities in Singapore and Hong Kong, the only agencies that were successful in creating and maintaining a massive public housing stock, have embarked on successful privatization programs — transferring properties to households and replacing rental arrangements with condominium ownership.

Similar attempts at privatization have been pursued in Russia and Eastern Europe since the early 1990s. But it has not been an unmitigated good. The valuable apartments of the better-off have been privatized almost immediately, and there are now thriving real estate markets in prime residential properties in most cities. For retirees who have lost the value of their pensions through inflation, home ownership has provided an asset that may be invaluable to them in old age. But as privatization was pursued hand in hand with the decontrol of rents, housing expenditures for the poorer residents have gone up in many instances despite the safety nets set to prevent their impoverishment. A majority of Soviet citizens surveyed in 1988, for example, "stated categorically that they did not want to buy the apartment they occupied" [Vosokovsky, quoted in Struyk and Kosareva, 1994, 64]. Privatization was viewed by many as making many people worse off than before, fueling the yearning for the return of the old Communist regime, when rents were negligible and maintenance expenses were borne by the state. Similar difficulties surfaced in the now largely privatized council houses in Great Britain, where increasing mortgage–interest rates in the late 1980s led to a large number of defaults and foreclosures [Dorling, 1994].

Privatization is by no means a complete answer to state policy failure. Dilapidated public housing still makes up a substantial component of the housing stock in many countries, and wholesale demolition is not a realistic answer. Neither can these buildings be allowed to deteriorate further, to attract crime, or to become the ultimate destination of the destitute. A safety net is an essential complement of successful privatization, and it must be designed with a view to maintaining affordability while engendering a true sense of ownership of house and land. This is considerably more difficult in the apartment complexes of Chicago or Cheliabinsk than in the terraced houses in Glasgow, again because much of the housing environment needs to be held in common. Common ownership may create incentives for some members to overutilize or under-maintain common spaces with impunity, and enforcement or group regulations to control these members may prove ineffective.

Common (or group) ownership rights in land and housing are also problem-atic. The rules usually preclude individuals from selling their shares of these rights freely to others. Individuals lose some or all of these rights upon leaving the group, and they are thus constrained in their mobility – a condition that may not be detrimental in tightly knit rural communities but can definitely be a liability in loosely structured urban communities. Urban housing cooperatives in develop-ing countries, for example, have often failed to institute effective policing mea-sures to force recalcitrant members to pay their dues. In his study of informal settlements in Lima, Peru, for example, De Soto [1989] found that "the absence of coercive mechanisms substantially reduces the potential scope of an informal partnership. In other words, although there are people who are highly altruistic, there are also conflicts of interest which cannot be resolved by informal coordina-tion" [161]. Group ownership may be successful when communities are stable and homogeneous, and share common values and beliefs. But these conditions, desirable as they are, cannot simply be willed into existence. They may be easier to attain in some cultures, while in others they may require the dedicated long–term efforts of community organization.

The absence of a secure property rights regime has been particularly detri-mental and costly in the squatter settlements on the fringes of Asian, African and Latin American cities. De Soto [1989], in his study of Lima, arrived at three conclusions regarding the absence of these rights:

> Our first conclusion is that informals do not use or preserve the resources available to them as efficiently as they might if they were sure of their rights. . . . [T]he ratio of the value of settlements with title and those without is 9 to 1. Everything indicates, then, that the existence or absence of property rights has a direct bearing on the level of investment. The second conclusion is that informals cannot transfer their property easily. They cannot use it for more valuable purposes or as collateral. . . . The third conclusion is that informals incur substantial costs in defending

their possessions and satisfying the need for public property by establishing and operating thousands of different organizations. [159–160]

These conclusions exactly parallel the three characteristics of a private
property rights regime. Of crucial importance in the case of squatter settlements
is the fact that the absence of secure property rights renders them vulnerable to
eviction by state authorities. In general, where tenure remained insecure and
governments engaged in mass eviction and demolition, housing investment in
squatter settlements remained predictably low. Under such a threat it was
irrational for squatters to invest in housing. On the other hand, when the threat
of eviction was removed investment in housing flourished. This has been well
documented in the 1970s in Chile [Merrill, 1971], Mexico [Ward, 1978], and
Pakistan [Van der Linden, 1977], for example. In Lima in 1982, to take another
example, the average squatter dwelling had a replacement value of $22,000, and
the total squatter housing stock had a replacement value of $8.3 billion [De Soto,
1989,18]. We should note, however, that this association between tenure security
and housing investment is not universal. In conditions of dire poverty, such as
in the tenement gardens of Colombo [Indrakumar, 1977], or in places where
people are not committed to staying in the urban area and prefer to invest in
housing in their home villages, such as in Papua New Guinea [Norwood, 1979],
improved tenure did not necessarily led to increased housing investment.

The Development of Property Rights

Private property rights to land are usually established by alienating land from
the commons, using it intensively, and declaring to the world one's intent to
appropriate it. Intensive use and notice to the world establish possession, and
common law grants the land to those who established first possession. Conversely, the abandonment of land and the maintenance of a long silence with
respect to one's claim returns the land to the commons, whereby others can
establish *adverse* possession. Laws of adverse possession in many countries
establish a statute of limitations on claims to land. "In the Maghreb, when
information about a piece of land is lacking ... it belongs to the person in whose
hand it is held, even if the manner in which it became that person's property is
unknown" [Al-Wansharisi, 1909, quoted in Leveau, 1985, 64].

Squatters who occupy unused common land on the fringes of cities are
similarly engaged in establishing private property rights to land by using it
intensively for housing, by linking it to their labor, and by declaring their occupation to the world. It is important to note, for example, that there are virtually no
squatters on land in agricultural cultivation, on private land in current intensive
use for commerce or industry, or on public land in current intensive use. Squatters mostly occupy the commons, idle lands, lands belonging to absentee owners,
and lands in disputed ownership. Such disputed lands usually become available
for squatting in the wake of major political upheavals.

In general, as long as land is plentiful and used sporadically (for hunting and gathering, for example) property rights do not come into being. Rose [1994] explains the rationale for the emergence of property rights regimes:

> [E]conomic thinkers for several centuries have been telling us that the more important a given kind of thing becomes for us, the more likely we are to work towards hard-edged rules to manage it. We draw ever more sharper rules around our entitlements so that we can identify the relevant players and so that we can trade instead of getting into confusions and disputes — confusions and disputes that would otherwise only escalate as the goods in question become scarcer and more highly valued. At the root of these economic analyses lies the perception that it costs something to establish clear rules about things, and we won't bother to undertake the task unless it is worth it to us to do so. What makes it worth it? Increasing scarcity of resources and the conflicts attendant on scarcity. . . . In effect, as competition for a resource raises the costs of conflict over it, the conflict itself comes to seem costlier than setting up a property regime. We then try to establish a system of clear entitlements in the resource so that we can barter and trade for what we want instead of fighting. [199–200]

Urbanization in Asia, Africa, and Latin America during this century has proceeded hand in hand with the gradual alienation of common or underutilized lands surrounding the cities for private and public use. The lack of earlier competition for these lands postponed the development of a strong property rights regime, and its development has been concomitant with urbanization and economic growth. This historical conjunction enabled millions of poor rural migrants to alienate common land through squatting, and to establish valid claims to that land through occupation, investment, and political pressure. Governments, for their part, had no overriding interest in protecting common or idle lands from invasion and encroachment of peripheral lands, and they were caught in a weak moral position when attempting to evict squatters while unable to assist them in obtaining proper housing.

The rapid growth of Asian, African, and Latin American cities during the twentieth century did, however, generate intense competition for urban land. The land rights of well-located squatter settlements were disputed, and conflicts between squatters and the state have been the sharpest when private developers or powerful public authorities eyed these lands. The failure of the state to prevent the occupation of urban land by squatters weakened its position to evict them at will and allowed squatters to establish their land rights through their labor, their investments, and their continued, uninterrupted presence. Squatters have thus established exclusive rights to land, and they have traded it on the informal market. But the lack of official recognition of their squatters' rights has underlined their vulnerability to state interference in their property rights.

There is, therefore, a long history of eviction struggles, street battles won and lost, demonstrations and demolitions, populist governments pursuing votes in the settlements, and law-an-order governments bent on getting rid of illegality everywhere. These struggles usually resulted in one of three outcomes: outright eviction, resettlement, or regularization. In singular situations in Bangkok and Karachi, for example, these battles resulted in "land sharing" agreements whereby the community relocated to a part of the site, freeing the remainder for commercial development [Angel and Boonyabancha, 1988]. All in all, however, the majority of squatter settlements have remained in place and a comparative study of squatter settlements in Asia and Latin America concluded that in recent years regularization has become more acceptable to governments: "Two basic phenomena have affected the major cities in the last decade: firstly, the enduring and sometimes worsening nature of irregular situations, and secondly, the ever increasing willingness of the authorities to overcome this problem, by the implementation of regularization policies" [Durand-Lasserve and Pajoni, 1995, 13].

For example, since 1992, the Municipality of Guayaquil, Ecuador, has been engaged in the systematic legalization of lands and the issuing of proper land titles. The Office of Land Legalization employed 70 people in 2000, and issued approximately 15,000 land titles per year at little net cost to the Municipality. The process of legalization in Guayaquil involved the use of a special law which allowed Congress to approve the purchase of invaded private lands by the municipality for their assessed value (approximately 10% of market value) or on another politically-determined value. Once land was transferred to the Municipality, the Office of Land Legalization could issue title documents.

The objective of regularization is precisely to grant squatters security of tenure — that third characteristic of property rights mentioned earlier, the one that will protect them from outright eviction without full compensation. But the granting and policing of this right are not without cost. In fact, the administration of tenure change is fraught with complications, the settling of claims and counter-claims, and the refusal of home owners to pay the charges for obtaining title adjudication, cadastre mapping, and title registration.

Neither is land tenure an unmitigated blessing. On the one hand, the more insecure a place is, the less valuable it is as a place to build a house on, and the less likely one is to invest in construction of a permanent dwelling. The illegal occupation of land tends to absolve government from its responsibility to provide infrastructure services. It may also render settlers vulnerable to manipulation and intimidation by government officials. On the other hand, the more insecure a place is, the more affordable it is to a poor family that can only afford to live in a shack, and that can only care about adequate living space and a good location rather than amenities and secure tenure. Secure land tenure often results in the displacement of earlier settlers who can no longer afford to live in the community, especially tenants. Some squatters may also be reluctant to accept legal tenure for fear of future taxation or of identifying themselves to the authorities, as has been observed in Mexico City [Ward, 1978]. Tenure security is thus a characteristic of housing that may not be preferred by all.

Moreover, the security and confidence associated with rights to land and housing should not be confused with full-fledged title registration. Many squatter communities in Karachi, for example, were satisfied with the de facto tenure security they felt when the state agreed to provide infrastructure services, and refused to pay for land title documents [Schuringa et al, 1979, 66]. When de facto tenure is secure — or very secure, as it is in Guayaquil, for example — title documents may add little economic value to land in squatter occupation. A study in Guayaquil estimated it to be of the order of 25% [Lanjouw and Levy, 1998, i]. In African squatter settlements, for example, informal property rights regimes adjudicated by local elders have been functioning adequately. In Lusaka, Zambia, a simple register of occupancy rights based on air photographs was deemed adequate for regulating property ownership and transactions. [Martin, 1979, 21–24]. Such rights can be upgraded to full freehold titles over time.

What is important to note is that the development of property rights regimes proceeded hand in hand with urbanization in the developing countries, allowing millions of low-income families to stake claims to commons land and to have their claims gradually recognized. Such a process must eventually come to an end when urban property rights regimes attain full maturity and squatting is no longer tolerated. Indeed, as noted earlier, in most countries squatting has been almost totally replaced during the last decades of the 20th century by the purchase of land in informal subdivisions [Baross, 1990,69]. These subdivisions do not conform to zoning laws, do not meet infrastructure standards, and may involve illegal transactions, but secure property rights are assured.

The Limits to a Property Rights Regime

The rules that make up the property rights regime are essential for securing investments in housing, for the operation of land and housing markets, and for enhancing the performance of the housing sector. These rules constitute a "meta-property" of society as a whole, as noted earlier, and (in principle) their function is to promote the common good. Unfortunately, hard-edged, crystal-clear private property rights cannot be established without compromising the common good. The absolute right to private property — as advocated by Blackstone, for example, in his *Commentaries on the Laws of England* (1765–1769) — cannot be upheld without damaging basic social norms. Blackstone, for his part, wanted to defend private property rights to the point of denial of the existence of the common good altogether:

> So great, moreover, is the regard for private property, that it will not authorize the least violation of it, no not even for the general good of the whole community. In vain, it may be urged that the good of the individual ought to yield to that of the community; for it would be dangerous

to allow any private, or even any public tribunal to be the judge of this common good, and to decide whether it be expedient or no. Besides the public good is in nothing more essentially interested, than in the protection of every individual's private rights, as modeled by the municipal law. [Blackstone, quoted in Shrader–Frechette, 1993, 232]

Property rights in land and housing must necessarily be limited by society in defense of the common good, even though what constitutes the common good is a moving target that is difficult to agree upon or define in clear–cut terms. Generally, there are three types of acceptable limitations on these rights: regulations governing use, compulsory acquisition, and property taxation.

The rationale for regulating the use of one's property is, first and foremost, to limit its potential for endangering the health, safety, and well–being of the community at large. Informal rules are often insufficient to ensure conformity to the common welfare. Zoning regulations, fire and public health codes, limitations on groundwater pumping that causes land subsidence, and pollution and noise controls may be necessary to protect the interests of other members of society from the abuse of one's property rights. These regulations and restrictions, taken together, constitute the regulatory regime, and will be discussed in greater detail in chapter 11. It is important to note here, however, that there are limits to this regulatory regime as well. Such a regime becomes dysfunctional when it limits the supply of residential land; when it imposes high costs on land and housing development so as to render it inefficient, unaffordable, or discriminatory; or when it reduces the value of a property radically, as has been the case with severe rent control, for example.

Second, the public must retain the right to acquire any property deemed necessary for public use, through its power of eminent domain. When such a public need arises, property owners must sometimes part with their land involuntarily, and to receive a fair market price in return: "This power to force a sale of private property to the public at fair market price is typically authorized where a government-sponsored project — such as a road — requires assembly of a number of pieces of land. If these projects had to rely on voluntary sales, any individual landowner might hold out for a prohibitively high price and block the entire project" [Rose, 1994, 128]. In the absence of an effective practice of eminent domain, public agencies cannot provide the infrastructure necessary for expanding cities or for revitalizing and upgrading established neighborhoods. Often, the success of slum and squatter upgrading projects, for example, has hinged on the ability of the community to negotiate agreements to clear sufficient right–of–way for roads and public facilities.

Third, the public has the right to tax private properties, thereby limiting the enjoyment of the increased value of such properties by their owners. The rationale for the right to tax is twofold. First, providing adequate infrastructure services to the land and maintaining the property rights regime in good order are not costless. Second, the increased value of properties is in large measure attributable to public actions in service provision, to actions by other citizens to enhance the property values of the neighborhood, and to the growth and development of the community- at-large, all of which lead to increased demand for properties. Property owners cannot, therefore, claim the right to appropriate all the surplus value of their property, and part of this surplus can and should be taxed to cover the cost of public improvements. Issues of property taxation will be further elaborated upon in chapter 9.

The Property Rights Index

How can we measure the degree to which a property rights regime is enabling? A survey of the literature did not yield useful measures of a property rights regime, beyond measures of the shares of the housing stock in different tenures, which will be discussed later. There is no question that more research is needed to define, test, and collect data on good indicators of the property rights regime of the housing sector.

The Global Survey of Housing Indicators limited its investigation to three aspects of this regime: the freedom to exchange land and housing property without restriction, the development of land registration systems, and the orientation of the government vis-à-vis regularization of squatter settlements as opposed to the eviction of settlers.

Unfortunately, the third aspect — focusing on issues of eviction and regularization — did not yield the expected results. Data for squatter eviction, defined as the average annual number of squatter households evicted and their dwelling demolished during the past five years, were sparse. An indicator for regularization, such as the rate of regularization (defined as the proportion of the housing stock in squatter occupation given partial or full tenure rights during the year) was not included in the survey. These omissions should not minimize the importance of national, as well as global, monitoring of eviction and regularization — both of which are important indicators of the degree of enabling in housing policy regimes. A fourth aspect of the property rights regime — the privatization of the public housing stock, measured, for example, by the rate of privatization (defined as the proportion of the public housing stock privatized during the year) — was altogether missing from the survey.

In this study we define the *Property Rights Index* as a normalized sum of two secondary indices: the *Freedom of Exchange Index* and the *Land Registration Index*. The Freedom of Exchange Index was calculated from answers to yes/no questions about the existence of restrictions on the exchange of land and housing:

- Are there restrictions limiting ownership of land and housing?
- Are there restrictions on who can own land and housing?
- On the amount that can be owned?
- On sales?
- On the price to be charged?
- On inheritance of land and housing?
- On the sale and resale of public housing units?

A property rights regime that does not restrict the ownership and exchange of land and housing was deemed to be enabling, while a regime that institutes such restrictions was deemed to be nonenabling.

The Land Registration Index was defined as the average of two tertiary indices: *Land Registration Coverage* and the *Land Registration System*. The former was defined as the percentage of the metropolitan area covered by a land registration system which allows for buying, selling, long-term leasing, or mortgaging of urban land; the latter is a the sum of positive answers to four yes/no questions about the accuracy and efficiency of the land registration system. The cost of registration (measured, for example, by the median ratio of the cost of registering the least expensive plot and the market value of the plot) was not included in the survey.

The summary values of the Property Rights Index and its components, calculated from the Global Survey, are given in table 7.1. There is not much difference between developing countries and industrialized countries on the Freedom of Exchange Index. Latin American countries, in fact, have higher value than industrialized countries, largely the result of the onset of stricter regulations in the latter in recent years. All in all, 10 countries attained the maximum value of 100 for this measure. China received the minimum value of 0, followed by Madagascar (9), and Russia (14).

Results for the Land Registration Index were quite different. This index did vary significantly by income, rising from a median value of 56 in the low–

Table 7.1. The Property Rights Index, 1990.

Country Groupings	Freedom of Exchange Index	Land Registration Index	Property Rights Index
Low–Income Countries	55	56	32
Low–Middle Income Countries	91	64	69
Upper Middle Income Countries	73	100	70
High–Income Countries	82	100	88
Southern Africa	71	57	38
Asia and the Pacific	73	93	74
Middle East and North Africa	86	68	62
Latin America and the Caribbean	91	64	66
Eastern Europe	73	53	36
All Developing Countries	81	69	62
Industrialized Countries	86	100	90
Global Average	73	77	65
Global Minimum	0	0	0
Global Median	82	89	73
Global Maximum	100	100	100
Global Standard Deviation	27	30	29
Correlation w. Development Index	0.14	0.55	0.45

Source: Housing Indicators Program [1994].

income countries to a median value of 100 in high-income countries, in line with our earlier observation that registration accelerates as land and housing gain in value. Among the developing countries, land registration was especially advanced in Asian nations. Eight developing countries, four of them in Asia, had a median value of 100: Zimbabwe, South Africa, Thailand, the Philippines, Malaysia, Korea, Jordan, and Brazil.

The resulting Property Rights Index does appear to vary with the level of economic development, from a median value of 32 in low-income countries to a value of 88 in high-income countries, and a median value of 62 for the developing countries as a whole as against a median value of 90 for the industrialized countries. A correlation value of 0.45 with the Development Index appears to corroborate this relationship as well. Among the regional groupings, Eastern Europe has the lowest median value for this index (36), followed by Southern Africa (38). Among the developing countries, both Jordan and Thailand had a value of 100 on this index, while among the industrialized countries three countries — Greece, the United Kingdom, and Norway attain this value. Madagascar had the lowest value on this index, followed by Ghana, India and Tanzania.

* * *

To conclude, a functional and effective property rights regime must evolve a set of transparent, predictable, nondiscriminatory and stable rules that preserve the rights of individuals to use, invest, maintain, rent, mortgage, and sell their land and housing properties without hindrance and with the full protection against arbitrary action by the authorities. Private property rights regimes need to be extended to squatter settlements as well as to public housing estates. Land registration systems must be organized, maintained, and adjudicated to reduce conflicts and disputes arising from conflicting claims to land and housing. Such systems can, and often do, develop from low-cost temporary permits to full-scale title registration as lands gain in value. Squatters on common or idle lands that are not required for essential public uses should be recognized and their land tenure regularized, as in now common in numerous countries. Eviction and demolition without compensation or voluntary resettlement should be resisted and discouraged. Regulations and restrictions on the exercise of private property rights should be subject to a review of their effects on the performance of the housing and real property market, so as to balance and spread the costs and benefits of regulation and to avoid increasing the overall prices of land and housing.

8

The Housing Finance Regime

The mortgage, which uses the house as collateral for fully securing a long-term loan, is an invention that has transformed housing beyond recognition, much as the internal combustion engine has transformed transportation. It originated with the self-help "terminating" building clubs in eighteenth century England,[1] where participants pooled their savings to finance the house building of individual members. As the clubs grew and matured, they were gradually displaced by the more impersonal building societies, which could no longer rely on peer pressure to enforce compliance and needed the mortgage contract as a way of reducing lender's risk. The growth of building societies provided increased financial resources for building complete houses and enabled borrowers to pay for houses over a long period of time. Housing producers could now operate with improved cash flow. As transactions grew in volume, the courts were called upon to enforce and secure these transactions through the legal sanction of foreclosure in the case of default. Governments acted to support the development of mortgage markets by promoting the establishment of financial institutions, by regulating them, by guaranteeing and insuring mortgages, and by providing numerous subsidies to home owners. Mortgage instruments were further modified to withstand inflation and financial liberalization, and secondary mortgage markets were created to increase the flow of long-term funds to the housing sector. As a further refinement, a new generation of policies to remove discrimination and other inequities created by the home mortgage system were adopted, directing mortgage credit to lower-income families. In a broad perspective, the evolution of housing finance can be viewed as an interplay of complementary and mutually supportive actions of the private sector and the public sector.

This chapter focuses on the role of the policy regime in the housing finance sector and sharpens our understanding of the difference between an enabling housing finance regime — one that, according to our earlier definition, sets boundaries and provides support while relinquishing control — and a nonenabling one. In general, governments have four interrelated objectives in the development of housing finance:

1. Developing a vibrant and healthy housing finance sector as an integral component of the financial sector;
2. Improving overall housing conditions by promoting the development of the housing sector as a key economic sector in terms of savings, investment, production, employment, and the creation of wealth;
3. Making home ownership more affordable by increasing popular access to mortgage finance; and
4. Ensuring that credit is allocated in accordance with social objectives.

To achieve these objectives, governments may employ three different sets of often-conflicting policy instruments in the housing finance sector:

1. Regulating the housing finance sector to ensure its viability, without impeding its ability to meet a broad spectrum of housing needs;
2. Supporting the creation and development of housing finance institutions; and
3. Channeling housing subsidies through, or in conjunction with, housing finance.

As we elaborate on these policy instruments, it shall become clearer which are enabling and which are not.

Creating and Maintaining a Regulatory Regime for the Housing Finance Sector

There are three sets of quite different regulatory instruments that are employed in the housing finance sector: (a) enforceable contracts and foreclosure laws that can guarantee secure transactions; (b) prudential regulations that ensure the health of financial institutions; and (c) restrictions that aim at controlling mortgage lending by rationing credit.

The most basic policy instrument for the development of a vibrant housing finance regime is the creation of a property rights regime that makes it possible to own, buy, sell, and mortgage houses and apartments, as discussed in the previous chapter.[2] In the absence of clear and undisputed ownership rights — properly documented and legally transferable — the dwelling unit cannot function effectively as collateral for a mortgage loan. Furthermore, in the specific case of the development of the home-mortgage contract, the key regulatory instrument is an effective and enforceable foreclosure law, the law that makes it possible to evict a home owner who fails to meet the contractual obligations toward the mortgage lender. In most developing countries, as noted by Buckley [1996], "relatively little mortgage credit is voluntarily supplied. The main reason for this is the lack of credible contracts. . . . The cost of post-contract governance rather than the cost of producing contracts explains this restrained supply of mortgage credit" [11].

In the 1970s and 1980s, a large number of sites–and–services projects in developing countries suffered from defaults on mortgages, defaults that spread quickly once it became clear that the enforcement of foreclosure laws was lax or involved long delays. In contrast, for example, prompt and immediate enforcement in the Community Development program in Hyderabad, India (relying more on pressure by community organizers than on the due process of law) reduced default rates to a minimum, enabling the program to expand and to assist very low-income households [Kumar,1980]. In El Salvador, to take another example, the Foundation for Minimum Housing and Development set up a special fund and a team of social workers to deal with families that had difficulties in meeting mortgage payments, again keeping defaults and evictions to a minimum.

There is no question that foreclosure, with or without due process, can generate a violent response, especially if it follows in the wake of the loss of employment, sickness, or the death of a breadwinner. In South Africa in the early 1990s, for example, court orders for the repossession of vacated homes could not usually be made effective without a violent reaction. When dwellings were vacated, they were frequently vandalized or burnt down. It was alleged that new occupiers following an eviction could themselves become victims of a violent attack [Milne, 1992, 15].

Once defaults become widespread, eviction becomes impractical, resulting in lending institutions having to write off loans and threatening the viability of the housing finance system. In an enabling housing policy environment, borrowers seeking mortgage loans must understand and honor their contractual obligations, and those obligations must be strictly enforced, preferably through the swift and efficient application of foreclosure laws by the judiciary. In parallel, there must be procedures for rescheduling payments and for short–term financial assistance to families that cannot maintain prompt payment schedules as a result of an emergency.

A second regulatory instrument necessary for the development of a vibrant housing finance regime is the system of prudential regulations required to ensure the viability and health of housing finance institutions. The objectives of such a system are:

> [T]o protect the public interest from the consequences of fraudulent bankruptcies, to foster growth and diversification, to insure the financial integrity of housing finance institutions, to establish net worth requirements for the safety of depositors, to restrict conflict of interest and to insure the proper management of risks. Managing the regulatory environment requires norms for portfolio structure, the supervision of financial management, accounting, auditing and reporting requirements and the capacity to enforce the regulatory framework. [Buckley and Renaud, 1987, 68]

A large number of housing finance systems collapsed as a result of lax (or nonexistent) enforcement of prudential regulations, regulations that were considerably weakened during a period of financial liberalization and rapid rates of innovation in the expanding financial markets of the 1980s and 1990s. The absence of proper monitoring of adherence to prudential regulations that restrain lending — minimum capital requirements, balance sheet constraints, adequate valuation and borrower selection services, and maximum loan-to-value ratios and loan-to-income ratios — allowed savings and loan associations (S&Ls) in the United States to take inordinately high risks with their insured deposits. For example, "[r]esidential home mortgage borrowers paid a much lower rate at failing or failed S&Ls during the 1980s than they did at solvent S&Ls" [Do and Schilling, 11, 1993]. Overoptimistic real estate loans (largely to commercial real-estate ventures) inflated real estate markets to dizzying heights, leading to a crash that brought down a large number of S&Ls in the early 1990s; the S&L failures also resulted in a massive liability to American taxpayers that had to be met by legislated appropriations totaling hundreds of billions of dollars.

In another example, a similar failure to enforce adequate protection against foreign exchange risks allowed a large number of privately run housing finance institutions in Thailand to borrow abroad and lend locally at interest rates lower than those required to cover that risk: "Inflows through resident banks borrowing abroad. . . have accounted for about 37% of total inflows in 1988-96" [Renaud, Zhang and Koeberle, 1998, 15]. While this practice was sustainable as long as exchange rates were stable, more than 50 of these institutions collapsed once exchange rates could not be sustained and the Thai currency lost 30%–50% of its value in 1997–1998. The same fate met Chilean housing finance institutions when the country was forced to switch from fixed to floating exchange rates [Buckley and Renaud, 1987, 79]. An enabling housing policy environment protects the viability of housing finance institutions (often against their own recklessness) by insisting on adherence to conservative banking practices that restrain short-term greed in the name of long-term sustainability. Such practices assess and account for *all* the risks associated with mortgage lending — including inflation risk, maturity and early-repayment risk, default risk, or risks that houses are damaged or destroyed — and cover such risks by setting appropriate interest rates or by the design of specific mortgage instruments that take such risks into account.

A third group of regulatory instruments often found in housing finance regimes are restrictions that aim at controlling mortgage lending by rationing credit: (a) limiting mortgage lending to specific types of housing; (b) limiting lending to specific segments of the population; or (c) placing ceilings on deposit and mortgage interest rates that, in effect, ration credit to the housing sector as a whole. While some of these restrictions may be well-meaning and others purely discriminatory, together they tend to distort lending patterns, depress the development of a healthy housing finance sector, and ultimately bring about the collapse of housing finance institutions.

In some countries, housing finance is restricted to new owner-occupied housing, a small segment (of the order of a few percent) of the housing market as a whole. In the United kingdom, for example, where there were no such restrictions, building society loans in 1985 were distributed quite differently: 20% for the construction of new houses, 58% for the purchase of existing houses, and 22% for other forms of housing (largely repairs and improvements of the existing stock) [Boleat and Coles, 1987, 21]. In an enabling housing finance regime, mortgage lending responds to demand and serves the entire housing market. It is available for all forms of housing, for the construction and purchase of rental units as well as owner–occupied units, for the purchase of land and the construction of land subdivisions, and for infrastructure and land development. Similarly, lending restrictions are not discriminatory — there are no restrictions that exclude potential borrowers on the basis of income, race, or gender. In countries prone to inflation, mortgages are protected by appropriate indexation and variable-rate mortgages are permitted. In general, in an enabling housing policy environment lending institutions can offer a wide array of financial products that are in demand by borrowers without any restrictions except those that threaten the long-term sustainability of the housing finance system.

Finally, there is a short and painful history of regulatory instruments that rationed credit to the housing sector. The oft-repeated underlying logic of credit rationing was that credit was in short supply, and that this limited supply of credit should be channeled to priority economic sectors — infrastructure and other public-sector projects on the one hand, and productive or export-oriented sectors on the other. The housing sector was perceived as an "unproductive" form of consumption: it was seen as a low priority for directed credit and one that would take limited financial resources away from more productive sectors. This position is no longer tenable. Analysis of historical data for Europe and the United States suggests that housing investment was indeed a complement, not a substitute for, other forms of productive investment:

> [T]here is no long-term relationship between increases in the availability of mortgage credit and decreases in non-residential capital investment. . . In fact, if there is any relationship it appears to be positive. That is, increased mortgage debt is positively correlated with investment in plant and equipment and with the per capita growth rate of total national assets. In market economies, housing credit does not appear to "crowd out" other investments to finance consumption. [Buckley and Renaud, 1987, 10]

On the contrary, evidence from the comparison of rates of economic growth with rates of housing investment suggests that the causal relationship between them is actually reversed — economic expansion leads to higher rates of investment in housing [Boleat and Coles, 1987, 134-135]. Once we recognize the housing sector as a key *economic* sector — with a major role in the attraction of savings and in the creation of personal wealth — directed credit must be discredited as a policy instrument. Directed credit policies make credit available at below-market rates to preferred sectors, resulting in less-than-efficient investments while preventing more productive investments from competing fairly for such funds. In an enabling policy environment, both deposit and mortgage interest rates are determined by market supply and demand: they are not artificially restricted. An enabling policy regime abandons ceilings on deposit rates (such ceilings make it difficult to attract savings for housing), and eliminates ceilings on mortgage rates (such ceilings drain mortgage credit when competition for credit forces the rates up). Housing finance institutions are able to compete for funds on a level playing field, offering market rates of interest for deposits and lending at market rates.

Supporting the Creation and Development
of Housing Finance Institutions

The history of the housing finance sector is replete with examples of governments playing key roles in the development of housing finance institutions by: (a) leading by example, through the creation of novel financial institutions that are later emulated by the private sector; (b) creating support institutions that reduce the financial risk associated with long-term mortgage lending and that facilitate the entry of private lenders into housing finance; and (c) removing barriers to entry of a wide variety of financial institutions into housing finance, thereby increasing competition and improving the efficiency of financial intermediation.

A number of governments led by example by establishing government housing banks that floated government bonds to attract savings and offered long-term mortgage loans at near-market rates, a practice that was later followed by private-sector institutions. Support institutions, such as those that guarantee deposits intended for mortgage loans, induce the private sector to enter the housing finance market at a lower "perceived" financial risk. The government of the United States, for example, became engaged in the development of the housing finance sector housing through the National Housing Act of 1934 which set up the Federal Housing Administration to insure long-term, low-interest mortgages. Similar guarantees were provided by the governments of Belgium, the Netherlands, Sweden, and Switzerland [Roman et al, 1994, 113].

In addition to guaranteeing mortgage financing to home owners, other countries initiated a variety of programs to attract households savings into the housing sector. Norway and Finland created government banks that provided loans for social housing. Canada, Finland, Germany, and France created low-interest savings programs that entitled savers to low-interest mortgage loans. [Roman et al., 1994, 113] Other countries – particularly in Latin America – created housing savings funds which relied on mandatory savings by employers and employees.

An enabling housing policy environment does not restrict entry by a wide spectrum of private- and voluntary-sector institutions, large or small, from engaging in the collection of deposits and in the issuing of mortgage loans. Such institutions are not forced to take undue financial risks in the making of loans, and can compete for deposits, both locally and abroad, on an equal footing with all other institutions. Competition among lenders encourages greater efficiency in lending and results in reduced spreads between deposit and mortgage interest rates. Government itself does not monopolize mortgage lending, and, even if the government is involved initially in setting up housing finance institutions, it ensures that its contingent liabilities in mortgage lending are explicit and minimal, and withdraws from the business of issuing and administering or guaranteeing mortgage loans as nongovernment institutions come into being.

Channeling Housing Subsidies through, or in Conjunction with, Housing Finance

Governments have often sought to make housing more affordable by mandating forced savings for housing and the issuing of mortgage loans at below-market interest rates. Such programs, although they have a number of built-in inefficiencies, have been common practice because (a) their administrative costs are lower than those associated with direct housing subsidies, (b) they do not appear in government budgets as direct costs to the government, (c) their basic inefficiency is often not well understood [Buckley and Renaud, 1987, 24], and (d) below-market mortgage rates often rely on forced savings that do not maintain their value over time.

Direct and transparent credit-related subsidies, which will be elaborated upon in the next chapter, should be distinguished from indirect ones. Direct subsidies, for example, may take the form of a one-time grant payment to the borrower or to the lender at the time of contract. Such subsidies are transparent, measurable, finite, and predictable, and they are a clear expenditure item in the government budget. Indirect subsidies that are channeled through or appended to the housing finance system take a number of forms: (a) providing mortgages at below-market interest rates through public finance institutions – such as government housing banks – or allowing arrears on such loans to accumulate; (b) forcing lending quotas for housing, at below-market rates, on private-sector financial institutions or placing ceilings on lending rates; (c) providing government guarantees of deposits in private-sector institutions with high mortgage interest-rate risk exposure; (d) promising below-market mortgage interest rates for those who save for housing over a period of time at below-market deposit rates; or (e) providing tax relief on mortgage interest payments or on construction loans.

All such subsidies are not transparent. They are difficult to estimate correctly, and they are in principle unmeasurable since they are subject to fluctuations in credit markets. When measurement has been attempted, it was shown that the costs of such programs often far exceeded those of direct housing subsidies. More dangerous still, since they are often unmeasurable, these subsidies create hidden contingent liabilities for governments, liabilities that may be surprisingly large if the U.S. savings and loan crisis is a harbinger of things to come.

There is no evidence, moreover, that subsidizing mortgage credit indirectly leads to more housing being produced. "It is now widely agreed that such schemes are less efficient as a long-term stimulus to investment than are programs that directly subsidize the good in question, be it housing services or otherwise" [Buckley and Renaud, 1987, 22]. It is clear, though, that these programs impose significant obstacles to the creation of healthy, viable, and sustainable housing finance institutions.

Interest–rate subsidies create obstacles in a number of different ways. First, public housing–finance organizations that lend at below–market interest rates make it impossible for the private sector to compete with them for borrowers. And since public funds for lending are limited, the growth of mortgage finance is stunted. It can only grow if the private sector is free to attract depositors by offering them attractive deposit rates and by lending at higher rates that cover both the risks and the administrative costs of lending. Second, forcing (unprofitable) mortgage lending quotas on private-sector institutions amounts to requiring these institutions to use their profitable operations to subsidize their loss making operations, exposing them to risks of insolvency. Third, compelling housing finance institutions — both public, semipublic, or private — to lend at negative interest rates (lower than the ongoing inflation rate) eventually leads to their collapse, the fate that befell the mortgage banking system in a number of Latin American countries in the 1970s and the 1980s. Fourth, government guarantees of deposits without adequate and vigilant enforcement of prudential regulations — another form of an indirect interest-rate subsidy — places serious liabilities on the general public, as the S&L cautionary tale suggests. Finally, tying below–market mortgage lending to below–market deposit taking, while making funds available for subsidized housing, forces savers to subsidize beneficiaries.

For example, since 1994, INFONAVIT, the obligatory saving–for–housing fund in Mexico, accounted for 55% of new mortgage originations. The fund was governed by the trade unions, the private sector, and the government and was aimed at private-sector employees. FOVISSSTE, the obligatory fund aimed at public sector employees, accounted for an additional 7.5% of new mortgage originations. Both funds used the mandated savings of their participants to subsidize those who win the housing lottery. But because savers were not allowed access to competitive deposit instruments that offer market rates, they lost the value of their pensions in the process. Yet, these funds were the major source of long-term savings which were needed to raise long-term capital for mortgage loans in the financial markets.

It should be emphasized that for many people who need better housing the primary issue is access to credit, with the cost of this credit being a secondary issue. Interventions that restrict and choke interest rates at below–market rates create artificial shortages of credit for housing, leaving large numbers of people without housing finance at all. In an enabling housing policy environment, the growth and development of the housing finance sector is disengaged from policies aimed at subsidizing housing for the greater social good. Saving and lending for housing should be at positive real interest rates with a sufficient margin to maintain the health of lending institutions — be they public, private or voluntary.

The Housing Finance Regime Index

How can we measure whether the housing finance regime is enabling or non-enabling in the light of the previous discussion? It is difficult to establish a clear separation between the performance of the housing finance regime, on the one hand, and the performance of the housing finance system on the other. In this study, indicators that measure the housing finance regime are those that focus on the regulatory environment, on the development of institutions, and on credit–related subsidies. Indicators that measure the performance of the system are those that measure the resulting availability and extent of mortgage credit, its cost, and its reliability. These are an integral part of housing market conditions, and they will be elaborated upon later.

Following the previous discussion, we can divide the measures of the housing finance regime into three types:

1. Measures of the regulatory environment of the regime;
2. Measures of the development of housing finance institutions; and
3. Measures of the existence of indirect subsidies that are channeled through or appended to the housing finance system.

The key measures of the regulatory environment of the housing finance regime are the existence or nonexistence of prudential regulations, and the effectiveness of foreclosure laws, measured, for example, by foreclosure delay.[3] The key measures of the development of housing finance institutions focus on the existence or nonexistence of novel financial institutions that are later emulated by the private sector; the existence or nonexistence of support institutions that reduce the financial risk associated with long–term mortgage lending and facilitate the entry of private lenders into housing finance; and the existence or nonexistence of barriers to entry of a wide variety of financial institutions into housing finance. Conversely, the existence or nonexistence of monopolies in this sector can also be measured. Measures of the existence of support institutions may include the number of mortgage insurance applications received and endorsed [U.S. Dept. of Housing & Urban Development, 1994, 18], and residential mortgage sales on the secondary mortgage market as a percent of mortgage originations [McGuire, 1981, 151]. The key measures of the existence or nonexistence of indirect subsidies that are channeled through the housing finance system include the prevalence of mortgages at below–market interest rates, the presence of lending quotas for housing, the presence of government guarantees of deposits, the presence of forced saving programs, or the availability and extent of tax relief on mortgage interest payments or on construction loans.

The Global Survey of Housing Indicators of 1990 provided some, but certainly not all, of the data necessary to measure the degree of enabling of the housing finance regime. The *Housing Finance Regime Index* constructed to measure this regime was defined as an equally weighted sum of three component indices: the *Financial Viability Index*, the *Credit Rationing Index*, and the *Financial Institutions Index*.

The Financial Viability Index was defined as an equally weighted sum of two components — the existence or nonexistence of a number of *prudential regulations*, plus *foreclosure delay*. Questions concerning prudential regulations included inquiries about the existence of maximum loan–to–income and loan–to–value ratios, appraisal requirements, and true–value assessments. Foreclosure delay was defined as the typical time in months from the initiation to the conclusion of foreclosure proceedings (including eviction) on a seriously delinquent mortgage.

Summary values for the components of the Financial Viability Index are given in table 8.1. Given the rather simplistic measure of prudential regulation, there is no observed difference between the level of prudential regulation between industrialized countries and developing countries. Quite a number of industrialized countries – notably Australia, Austria, France, Germany, Norway, and the United Kingdom – did not regulate loan–to–income and loan–to–value ratios. China reported no prudential regulation at all, while Turkey and Germany reported only minimal prudential regulation. Twelve countries attained the maximum value on this index.

Foreclosure delay varied considerably among countries. In some countries it was reported to be virtually impossible to foreclose on a mortgage. For example, delay of seven years or more was reported for India.[4] Foreclosure took almost twice as long in developing countries than in industrialized countries, and was found to be negatively correlated with the Development Index (-0.33). It was especially lax in low–income countries, especially in Asia, the Middle East and North Africa, and in Latin America. It was not particularly lax in Southern Africa.

A number of developing countries, notably Malaysia, Jordan and Korea, reported delays of two to three months only, a delay common in a large number

Table 8.1: The Components of the Financial Viability Index, 1990

Country Groupings	Prudential Regulations Index	Foreclosure Delay (months)	Financial Viability Index
Low–Income Countries	51	36	44
Low–Middle Income Countries	76	9	75
Upper Middle Income Countries	76	6	76
High–Income Countries	76	4	78
Southern Africa	63	6	72
Asia and the Pacific	76	15	44
Middle East and North Africa	69	15	67
Latin America and the Caribbean	100	12	91
Eastern Europe	63	0	37
All Developing Countries	76	7	67
Industrialized Countries	76	4	84
Global Average	65	14	67
Global Minimum	0	2	0
Global Median	76	6	71
Global Maximum	100	84	100
Global Standard Deviation	29	19	24
Correlation with Development Index	-0.06	-0.33	0.11

Source: Housing Indicators Program, [1994].

of industrialized countries. Of the industrialized countries, only Spain reported a surprisingly long delay (24 months).

The second housing finance index, the Credit Rationing Index, was created to measure the distortions on lending brought about by restrictions that limit the ability of financial institutions to respond to demand for housing finance, and that force them to lend at negative real interest rates. It is an equally weighted sum of two measures, the *Lending Restrictions Index* and — if the prevailing mortgage interest rate at that time was indeed negative — the actual *negative real interest rate* in 1990.[5] The first index is a normalized equally weighted sum of answers to three kinds of questions: (a) those inquiring about restrictions on lending for land purchases, for rental housing, for residential subdivisions, or for houses on land leased for the long-term; (b) those inquiring about restrictions on lending based on gender; and (c) those requiring banks to lend for housing or fixing ceilings on deposit and mortgage rates, or on term-to-maturity — the number of years allowed for the repayment of loans. Following our usual convention, a higher value on this index implies that there are less restrictions on lending. As can be seen from table 8.2, this index again varied with income. In general, there were fewer restrictions in the industrialized countries than in the developing countries, but among developing-country regions no significant differences could be observed.

The nominal mortgage interest rate was defined as the weighted average of fixed-rate and variable rate mortgages, and the Negative Real Interest Rate was

Table 8.2. The Components of the Credit Rationing Index, 1990.

Country Groupings	Lending Restrictions Index	Negative Real Interest Rate (%)	Credit Rationing Index
Low-Income Countries	64	-6.9	78
Low-Middle Income Countries	73	-11.3	78
Upper Middle Income Countries	77	-18.0	75
High-Income Countries	91	0.0	94
Southern Africa	73	-4.8	81
Asia and the Pacific	64	-6.1	78
Middle East and North Africa	64	-12.2	67
Latin America and the Caribbean	64	-19.4	78
Eastern Europe	77	-21.3	70
All Developing Countries	73	-15.0	78
Industrialized Countries	91	-0.4	94
Global Average	77	-14.4	80
Global Minimum	0	-40.0	0
Global Median	82	-12.5	83
Global Maximum	100	0.0	100
Global Standard Deviation	21	11.9	21
Correlation with Development Index	0.37	-0.25	0.29

Source: Housing Indicators Program, [1994].

calculated by subtracting the rate of inflation for 1990 from the nominal value. Negative real mortgage interest rates were found in 15 of the 53 countries in the sample. In general, there were many more negative values found among the developing countries than in the industrialized countries, and there was a negative correlation (–0.25) between negative real interest rates and the Development Index. Among the industrialized countries, only Greece had a slightly negative real interest rate (–0.4%), and among the high–income countries there were no negative rates to be found. Among the developing countries, Asia and Africa had lower negative rates than the Middle East and North Africa, Latin America and Eastern Europe. Brazil and Poland, countries that both had hyperinflation in 1990, had negative rates of several hundred percent.

The resulting Credit Rationing Index was also found to vary with income, with a positive, though small, correlation (+0.29) with the Development Index. There were no significant differences between developing–country regions. Six industrialized countries and five developing countries had maximum values on this index, the latter being Madagascar, the Philippines, Kenya, Turkey, and Chile. Brazil had the lowest value, followed by Poland and China.

The third housing finance index, the Financial Development Index, focused on the existence or nonexistence of a variety of private–sector institutions that are found in developed housing finance regimes. There are three types of such institutions: (a) those that provide mortgage finance; (b) those that supply credit to mortgage finance institutions; and (c) those that facilitate the development of mortgage finance. The index is a normalized equally weighted sum of yes/no answers to three sets of questions: (a) those inquiring about the presence of commercial banks and finance companies, building societies and savings and loan associations, credit unions, and credit cooperatives and group credit associations that lend for housing; (b) those inquiring about the existence of wage, tax, and provident funds; insurance companies; pension funds; development finance institutions; mutual funds and unit trusts; or stock exchange investment trusts that supply funds for mortgage lending; and (c) those inquiring about the existence of private mortgage insurance companies, rediscounting facilities, issuers of mortgage–backed securities, issuers of mortgage bonds, and traders of mortgage–backed securities or mortgage bonds on the stock exchange.[6] The values for this index, as well as the resulting values for the Housing Finance Regime Index appear in table 8.3.

In general, industrialized countries have slightly higher than median values for this index than developing countries do, with the United States attaining the highest value for this index, followed by Germany, France, Mexico and Jamaica; China attained the lowest value, with Russia and Hungary just slightly better. Among developing country regions, Latin America was found to have a more developed housing finance sector, and Eastern Europe a less developed one. Southern Africa in 1990 was found to have more housing finance institutions than Asia or the Middle East and North Africa.

Table 8.3. The Housing Finance Regime Index, 1990.

Country Groupings	Financial Viability Index	Credit Rationing Index	Financial Development Index	Housing Finance Regime index
Low–Income Countries	44	78	35	51
Low–Middle Income Countries	75	78	38	57
Upper Middle Income Countries	76	75	35	58
High–Income Countries	78	94	50	73
Southern Africa	72	81	44	59
Asia and the Pacific	44	78	29	54
Middle East and North Africa	67	67	24	54
Latin America and the Caribbean	91	78	59	59
Eastern Europe	37	70	18	36
All Developing Countries	67	78	38	55
Industrialized Countries	84	94	47	73
Global Average	67	80	44	61
Global Minimum	0	0	0	0
Global Median	71	83	41	62
Global Maximum	100	100	100	100
Global Standard Deviation	24	21	24	19
Correlation with Development Index	0.11	0.29	0.18	0.30

Source: Housing Indicators Program [1994].

The Housing Finance Regime Index provides a broad measure of the degree of enabling in a housing finance regime. Higher income countries were found to have higher median values for this index, and industrialized countries have higher median values than the developing countries as a whole. There was a positive correlation of +0.30 with the Development Index; and among developing countries, Eastern Europe had lower median values.

* * *

To recapitulate and summarize our discussion, an enabling housing finance regime is one that enables a large variety of deposit–taking and mortgage–lending institutions to come into being, that regulates them with a view to ensuring their long–term viability, that does not ration credit, and that does not attach subsidies to mortgage finance. The Housing Finance Regime Index — which is a composite index of measures of financial viability, credit rationing and financial development — is a proxy measure of the degree of enabling in the regime. It remains to be seen, of course, whether an enabling housing finance regime leads to the availability of more housing finance, to lower interest rates and lower rates of default, and ultimately to better housing–sector performance, topics which will be taken up in later parts of this study.

9

Housing Subsidies

For many of the key actors in the housing sector, the issue of housing subsidies — and by extension of housing-related taxes[1] — is considered *the* central issue of housing policy. It has been unfortunate that discussions of subsidies have dominated so many housing policy debates, with the result that the effects of other aspects of the policy environment — from property rights to the regulatory regime — on the performance of the housing sector as a whole, and especially on housing the poor, have been neglected. This is not to suggest, however, that housing subsidies and taxes are not essential parts of housing policy. They are essential and they should continue to be, in the face of the present onslaught on most housing subsidies as fiscally irresponsible, risky, distorting, regressive, humiliating, or failing to achieve their designated goals. In our definition of enabling housing policies — that is, setting boundaries and providing support, while relinquishing control — subsidies are, in essence, one of the fundamental supports needed to make the housing sector work efficiently and equitably and to overcome market and policy failures.

All housing subsidies are inherently political. They come into being when broad political coalitions press for them, and they are kept alive when new coalitions can sustain them. When support is no longer forthcoming, they are sometimes withdrawn, rarely without a struggle, and sometimes they are kept on the books with a force of inertia that is impossible to resist. The quintessential example is rent control. Introduced (among many long-abandoned price controls) in the war economies of World War I, it is still with us nearly a century later.

The presence or absence of housing subsidies cannot be understood outside the broader framework of overall fiscal policy. These subsidies are just a part of a wide range of subsidies and taxes that together form the budgets of federal, regional, and municipal governments. Earlier in the twentieth century they were often driven by utopian dreams of planned societies; by the need to rebuild cities ravaged by war; by the surpluses generated by continuous economic prosperity; by government spending to reverse economic decline; or by the conviction that the allocation of resources by government is inherently more desirable than market allocation. Housing subsidies are now affected, like other subsidies and taxes, by demands to contain budget deficits; by calls for fiscal austerity or "smaller government"; by moves toward privatization of government services; by political alliances that support a market–based allocation of resources in the name of efficiency; by the "structural adjustment" interventions of the World Bank and the International Monetary Fund; by pressures on governments for better risk management; by the devolution of responsibilities from the federal governments to states, regions, and municipalities; by the insistence on transparency and accountability in fiscal management; by the recent Communist debacle; or by the public disenchantment with the ability of welfare programs to redistribute income and wealth effectively.

In this chapter, we survey the limited experience with housing subsidies during the twentieth century, with two difficult aims: articulating the key distinctions between enabling and nonenabling housing subsidy regimes; and inquiring whether or not such distinctions have an effect on the availability and targeting of housing subsidies.

The rigorous study of housing subsidies is still in its infancy. Little is known — and what little is known is controversial — about the efficiency and effectiveness of different kinds of housing subsidies. Every subsidy regime is, in principal, a social experiment that must be measured and evaluated as to its efficacy, so that it can be corrected if it fails to meet its objectives. Few subsidies have been subjected to such systematic study.[2] In an enabling policy environment, housing subsidies and their effects are subject to regular study and measurement, aimed at ensuring that they are efficient and equitable, and providing the feedback necessary to modify them if they fail to meet their designated goals.

In general, there are three different groups of housing subsidies:

1. supply-side subsidies targeted at the producers, lenders, and owners of housing units;
2. demand-side subsidies targeted at dwellers as consumers of housing services; and
3. price controls — in the form of limits on rent, house price, or interest rates — targeted at both consumers and producers of houses and related services.

Before looking at these types of subsidies in greater detail, we must first establish the general criteria for evaluating housing subsidies. Only then can we begin to understand whether a given subsidy or tax is enabling or nonenabling.

The Underlying Logic of Housing Subsidies

The most important aspect of housing subsidies is that they can and do modify, and sometimes inadvertently distort, the behavior of consumers and producers by affecting the prices of housing inputs, units, and services. In fact, such subsidies are designed to affect housing market behavior and to change it in accordance with political objectives. Neoclassical economic theory sees the involvement of the state in housing as the result of market failure, namely the failure of the autonomous interactions among the actors in the sector to produce results that meet their basic interests and the interests of society as a whole. A typical description of market failure is provided by Engels [1872], in his famous treatise on *The Housing Question*: "What is meant today by the housing shortage is the peculiar intensification of the bad housing conditions of the workers as the result of the sudden rush of population to the big towns; a colossal increase in rents, and a still further aggravation of overcrowding in the individual houses, and, for some, the impossibility of finding a place to live in at all" [21].

Severe and chronic housing shortages, unaffordable housing, and substandard housing are three typical market failures that have often required state intervention in one form or another. They are market failures in the sense that the market fails to meet a basic social norm — the expectation that everyone should be housed in accordance with some basic standard of decency and that decent housing be affordable. But these three market failures may lead to three distinct and separate policy goals: increased housing production, increased affordability, or improved housing conditions, each of which requires a different subsidy and tax regime. Increased production may entail directing more resources to residential construction; increased affordability may be achieved by building low-cost housing or by supplementing housing expenditures; and improved housing conditions can be attained by supporting rehabilitation or new construction, by supplementing the housing budgets of households, or by promoting home ownership.

A central question arises at the outset: Is it really necessary to provide housing subsidies to meet housing goals such as these, or can these goals be met by other means? The answer to this question is clouded by the fact that there are ample nonhousing goals that may mandate directing public resources to the housing sector. Typical nonhousing-related goals that are often found to drive housing subsidy campaigns (either explicitly or implicitly) are redistributing income; creating employment; generating savings; slum clearance and redevelopment; jump-starting the economy; reviving the construction industry; maintaining peace and political stability; or reducing deficits and balancing budgets. There is no question that housing subsidies often come into being in response to a confusing array of both housing and nonhousing goals, making it exceedingly difficult to understand or gauge their effects. But using housing subsidies to attain nonhousing goals leaves open the question of whether or not they are necessary to meet *housing* needs.

The answer to this question goes beyond subsidies to examine the entire policy environment of the housing sector. There are, we note again, a number of policy instruments that can effect housing supply without resort to subsidies — for example, a more enabling regulatory environment and an adequate infrastructure that increases access to adequate residential land and improves residential amenities. And there are a number of policy instruments that can greatly affect housing demand without resort to subsidies — an organized property rights regime and an effective housing finance regime, for example. Removing supply restrictions and bottlenecks and increasing demand by organizing property rights and housing finance can make housing more plentiful and more affordable. There is no doubt that, wherever possible, the application of such instruments will be more effective and more economical than resorting to subsidies. Not only that, but in a well-functioning housing sector, a plentiful supply of housing keeps costs down and increases the effect of a given level of subsidies by reducing their per-unit cost.

Still, even if artificial constraints can be removed and supply can be made to respond to demand (with or without subsidies), not everyone will be able to afford decent housing, and not everyone will be housed in decent housing. There are two separate issues here that remain unresolved: the issue of affordability on the one hand, and the issue of ensuring that everyone is decently housed on the other. The lack of affordability can be characterized as the lack of ability to pay, while the lack of decent housing may also entail the lack of willingness to pay.

The affordability problem can be attacked both within and without the housing sector. It can be met by reducing housing cost (a supply-side intervention); by housing allowances, rent supplements or tax relief on mortgage interest that bridge the gap between prices or rents and ability to pay (a demand-side intervention); or by direct transfers aimed at redistributing income so as to make housing more affordable.

There is no question that inadequate housing is strongly associated with poverty or the lack of ability to pay – cities with higher household incomes have significantly better housing, as we shall see later. The affordability problem is, therefore, first and foremost a poverty issue and not a housing issue. The solution to this problem must therefore rely primarily on policies for the alleviation of poverty, and not on policies that aim at the provision of adequate housing. Donnison, a committed British housing advocate, conceded this point:

> The first concern of anyone engaged in housing must be with jobs and opportunities for earning money, and next with child benefits, pensions and other provisions of social security and fiscal systems for redistributing this money. Rising numbers out of work, coupled with cuts in the real value of child benefits and insurance benefits must now be producing growing poverty. This will make it harder for many people to meet their rent or mortgage payments. Most housing problems are really problems of unemployment, poverty and inequality. [Donnison, 1980, 283]

Keeping this in mind, we should restrain our expectations that the housing problem of the poor can be adequately addressed amidst persistent poverty. It simply cannot be done.

Moreover, it is doubtful that housing subsidies in any form are an especially useful form of redistributing income or reducing social inequality. Hughes [1980], for example, reviews the rather dismal distributional consequences of British housing policies and argues that, because the income elasticity of demand for housing is rather low,[3] then "a tax or subsidy on housing consumption would probably prove a relatively inefficient method of income redistribution and have a significant distortionary effect on the overall pattern of housing expenditure." [70] There is indeed no a priori reason to suspect that housing subsidies would be an effective instrument for redistributing income: "Indeed housing would only be the most suitable vehicle for intervention if it turned out to have the most desirable income and substitution attributes as compared to other goods and services" [Whitehead, 1991, 874].

There are two arguments, however, for state support in the form of direct housing subsidies, in addition to general income support or other redistributive social welfare programs that improve people's ability to pay for housing. The first argument rests on our earlier observation that housing is a "merit good" — wherein the state intervenes to ensure that people consume adequate amounts of housing because it is in their best long-term interest and in the public interest. The merit good argument is strengthened by focusing on the externalities associated with the underconsumption of housing — its adverse (or beneficial) effect on the immediate neighborhood, on the quality of life in the city as a whole, or on social and economic stability. If such externalities were severe, the public would have an interest in making adequate housing available to everyone, regardless of their ability or willingness to pay. Homelessness is a case in point. Most citizens find homelessness intolerable and require governments to act — in benign and less- benign ways — to get homeless people off the streets. But beyond the obvious case of homelessness, most governments — especially in the developing countries — have not been able to define a "decent housing" standard that they can attain on a broad scale with their limited subsidy resources. This has led, as we noted before, to an incessant trickle of showcase housing projects the world over, projects that meet arbitrarily high standards at great cost but can never be replicated on any meaningful scale.

The second argument in favor of housing subsidies rests on the fact that housing-related poverty exacerbates and multiplies other inequalities. An inquiry into British housing, for example, noted that "[t]he negative aspects of our lives — ill health, vandalism and crime, racial prejudice, loneliness, mental illness, family break-up — are multiplied and exaggerated by housing shortages and bad housing conditions" [Hills, 1991b, 13]. In addition, segregated communities, which house a disproportionate numbers of the poor and disadvantaged, restrict their residents' access to health, education, and recreation facilities, as well as to employment and market opportunities. Inadequate housing is thus a source of poverty, as well as a consequence of poverty. It stands to reason, therefore, that a direct attack on housing ills — as part of a more comprehensive antipoverty program — would be an efficient way to assist the poor in combating other social ills.

In the last analysis, there is, therefore, indeed an inherent logic in incorporating housing subsidies in an overall subsidy regime. And given that such subsidies may seek to meet different housing and nonhousing policy goals, the question still arises as to what criteria would enable us to distinguish between enabling and nonenabling housing subsidy regimes.

The overall level of housing subsidies is not necessarily an important distinguishing criterion. More is not necessarily better than less. Subsidies, after all, can only be created through taxing wages, salaries, and profits. The higher the subsidies, the higher the taxes needed to finance them. Conversely, the overall level of revenues from housing-related taxes may not be important, although the taxation of housing wealth, for example, may be a source of tax revenue that, in an efficient fiscal policy regime, has no better substitutes.

There are three general criteria that aim at avoiding or correcting the market distortions associated with housing subsidies and taxes — in other words, leveling the playing field. In a well-functioning housing market, investment in housing should not be less (nor more) lucrative than any other investment, housing consumers should be indifferent between owning and renting their homes, and housing producers should be indifferent between building for rental or for owner-occupation for all income groups. In other words, enabling housing subsidies and taxes should not tilt the balance against investment in housing or against the construction and rehabilitation of rental housing or low-income housing, and they should allow housing consumers to choose freely between owning and renting.

There are six additional criteria for evaluating housing subsidies that have to do with fiscal responsibility:

1. Are they transparent and measurable? It is already well known that subsidies that are "off the books" (and therefore not nearly as transparent and measurable) are often larger than those that are on the books. Typical off the books examples are various tax breaks for home owners or housing producers or the cession of public land for squatter housing.

2. Are their costs finite and predictable? Subsidies, such as those that take the form of entitlements to minimum housing, rent supplements, or government guarantees, are subject to contingencies that cannot be assessed or predicted. Commitments for assistance may thus expose public budgets to undue and incalculable risks.

3. Are they resistant to inflation? Subsidies or taxes that are not calculated in real — as against nominal — terms may be grossly regressive or lose their efficacy over time.

4. Are they sustainable if replicated on an adequate scale? There is no merit in subsidy programs that start with a bang and finish with a whimper. Subsidies need to be administered justly and to large numbers of those in need, rather than to the select few. If resources are limited, then those in greatest need should be targeted first. This unfortunately requires that limited subsidies, to be efficient, must be means-tested, a requirement than makes them less attractive than subsidies available to one and all. Broad-

based programs can command broader political support and should be preferred when adequate resources are available.

5. Are they progressive, or at least not flagrantly regressive? It is one thing to concede that housing subsidies are not an efficient way to redistribute income, and quite another to administer housing subsidies that further skew the income distribution.

6. Can they be efficiently administered? The cost of administration of a subsidy program should be a small fraction of program costs, and together with the transfers involved should be a small fraction of the benefits generated.

Finally, there are a number of specific criteria for determining whether housing subsidies are effective and efficient in meeting housing policy goals. Do they lead to significant housing improvement? Do they increase housing affordability? Do they increase the stock of housing units? Do they increase access to housing finance? Do they increase access to home ownership? Do they improve living conditions in low-income communities? Do they ensure adequate variety in the housing stock? Enabling housing subsidies seek to give affirmative answers to these questions, but there is no a priori reason to believe that they are internally consistent. For example, significant physical improvements in any segment of the low-income housing stock may lead to increased rents and thus to reduced affordability. Over and above the consistency issue, it is not easy to determine whether a given housing subsidy program meets any and all of the criteria just discussed. As we noted earlier, the evidence is scarce. In the sections that follow, we take a closer look at particular types of subsidies and attempt to determine, from the available evidence, which ones are more enabling than others.

Supply-side Subsidies

There are four types of suppliers that are targets of supply-side subsidies: government agencies that construct public housing, private sector developers and builders that construct subsidized private housing, intermediary nonprofit organizations that built or rehabilitate houses in poor neighborhoods, and individual households or groups of households (e.g., cooperatives) engaged in building or improving their dwellings.

Massive subsidies for social housing to be built and managed by state and local governments were premised on the total failure of the market to provide adequate housing for all. Social housing was then considered to be an integral element of social policy, together with universal health coverage, compulsory education, unemployment benefits, retirement pensions, and welfare payments. Harlow [1995], in his comprehensive study of social housing in Europe and the United States distinguished between two types of social housing — mass social housing and residual social housing [Harlow, 1995, 522–527]. Mass social housing usually pertained to rental-housing programs aimed broadly at the middle class and the better-off segments of the working class. Such ambitious programs gained wide political support for short periods in Western Europe and the United States after each world war — particularly after World War II — "to house the war heroes and their families quickly" [Saunders,1990, 26]. After the acute shortages were met, however, these programs gradually declined in importance. Quantitatively, they were most important in Great Britain and in the Netherlands, and least important in the United States [Harlow, 1995, 523]. In Russia, immediately following the October Revolution of 1917, the state nationalized land and housing [Andrusz, 1984, 13] and became the major provider of mass housing. Similar mass housing programs were instituted in eastern Europe after the World War II and later in urban China, Hong Kong, and Singapore.

Broadly speaking, these programs relied on substantial housing subsidies in government budgets, on non-market allocation, on state production monopolies, and on low, controlled rents. In Russia and eastern Europe, where subsidies and production capacity were insufficient, long waiting lists were the order of the day. In the mid-1980s, for example, 1.8 million families were on the waiting list for cooperative housing in Poland, and the waiting period for an apartment was 15–30 years [Woodfield, 1989, 39]. Nonmarket, administrative allocation was often found to be corrupt and unjust. Lack of cost-consciousness in state production monopolies frequently resulted in the shortages of building materials, in the preponderance of energy-wasteful and obsolete technologies, in inordinate construction delays, and in low rents that were insufficient to cover the costs of maintenance and repair. Evidence from a number of non-Communist countries [e.g., Weicher, 1990, 285; Angel et al.,1987, 38–49] suggests that public housing was considerably more expensive to build than private housing of similar quality.

Residual social housing programs involved more restricted building of public housing targeted on the poor. In many countries these programs were historically linked to slum clearance. Unlike mass housing programs, which often excluded the poor, these programs were usually means-tested and often became stigmatized as a result.[4] Residual social housing was often created to replace housing destroyed by public works, or as a means to bolster a sagging building industry. In the United States, during the Depression of the 1930s, for example, the "National Recovery Act of 1933 established the Public Works Administration (PWA) that immediately began to clear slums and redevelop the sites with public housing" [Pugh, 1980,175]. Virtually every country experimented with residual social housing at one time or another, abandoning it at a later date for lack or funds or political support, only to pick it up again later when funds and support became temporarily available. Quantitatively, however, residual social housing was insignificant in most countries.

The alternative to subsidizing public housing relies on subsidies to the private sector aimed at creating incentives for increasing housing supply or specifically for building low-cost housing. Malpass and Murie [1982] summarize the issue facing the state when it opts for this approach: "From the point of view of the state, the real problem in its private sector housing policy is to manage the market by a strategy that on the one hand guarantees standards but on the other hand retains profitability and therefore an adequate supply of dwellings that people can afford"[10]. Supply-side subsidies to the private sector may support both construction and the excess of operating expenses over rents.[5] Subsidy support for residential construction may entail subsidized interest rates or mortgage guarantees, tax credits, tax exemptions, outright grants, tax-free bonds, acquisition and sale of land at below-market prices to developers (as in Korea, for example), sale of subsidized building materials (as in Sri Lanka, for example), depreciation allowances on rental properties, taxation or nontaxation of the imputed rent of owner-occupiers,[6] and the collection or noncollection of property taxes[7] and betterment levies. While it is difficult to focus on each individual subsidy, a few remarks are in order. Evidence from the United States [Murray, 1993, 2] suggests that subsidized low-cost housing did not increase the housing stock as a whole, because it displaced an equivalent amount of non-subsidized housing. Other evidence suggests that benefits to developers, that are inherently difficult to measure, are often excessive [Case, 1991] and sometimes actually exceed the benefits generated for low-income households [Peterson, 1973, 116]. Such subsidies often favor large developers as the expense of small ones [Yoon, 1994, 64], are not subject to competitive bidding, and create many opportunities for "rent-seeking behavior" on the part of developers while subjecting governments to undue risks.

When such supply-side subsidies are channeled through non-profit intermediary organizations engaged in the rehabilitation (or new construction) of low-income housing, however, there are more assurances that rents will remain low, and that subsidies will be better targeted, better suited to the needs of low-income families and special groups not served by the market, and more cost-effective (particularly when focusing on rehabilitation that is cheaper than new construction). Earlier critiques of such suppliers charged that they were inefficient, and that they could not operate at an adequate scale. As experience accumulated, however, both critiques have lost much of their sting. Housing associations in Great Britain built or rehabilitated 50,000 units per year in 1993 and 1994 [Best, 1996, 552], and "in New York City, the bulk of the 124,000 low-and moderate-income housing units built or rehabilitated under the city's multi-billion dollar capital budget housing program have been developed by non-profit organizations" [Bratt et al., 1994, quoted in Keyes et al., 1996, 206]. Similarly, infrastructure improvements in slums and squatter settlements have proven to be effective devices for targeting subsidies, even when they were directed at suppliers such as municipal agencies. In the majority of cases, these subsidies proved to be progressive because they largely benefitted the poor.

Supply-side subsidies to individual households or to groups of homeowners may include any of these instruments. Of particular importance are improvement grants for the renovation of run-down property, that lead to significant improvements, both in living conditions and in the housing stock. An additional and important supply-side subsidy that has made a critical difference for low-income housing in the developing countries has been governments' lack of action in the face of invasion of public land by squatters, an omission that amounted to the transfer of public land to individuals, at practically no charge, for house construction. This action by itself — off the books, not transparent, and impossible to estimate — has enabled millions of low-income people to gain access to minimum housing that in time has improved and now constitutes the bulk of the low- and middle-income housing stock in many countries.

Demand-side Subsidies

The key advantage of demand-side subsidies is that they do not distort housing supply. The rationale for demand-side subsidies rests on the belief that housing supply will be more plentiful and less expensive if governments retreated from attempts to participate in it directly; under this rationale, governments should instead limit their supply-side involvement to regulating construction and land use and providing support in the form of infrastructure for land development. This requires that house prices and rents attain market levels. Demand-side subsidies then open the entire market for consumers and increase housing choice, while breaking down the previous concentrations of low-income people in "projects," an acknowledged policy failure of public housing.

The central objective of demand-side housing subsidies is to increase access to decent housing by those who cannot afford it otherwise. Such subsidies take on a number of different forms: Housing allowances or rent supplements that close the gap between a fixed proportion of income (say 25%) and prevalent market rents; lump-sum one-time subsidies for first-home buyers; mortgage-interest deductions from income taxes and exemption of the sale of principal residences from capital gains tax; forgiveness of mortgage loans in default to public housing finance institutions; and the giveaway or discounted sale of public housing to sitting tenants in the process of privatization. More demand-side subsidies that involve price, rent, or interest-rate *controls* will be discussed in the following section.

Housing allowances and rent supplements are, in effect, income supplements that enable low-income families to find housing in the open market. There is evidence that they do so without leading to rent inflation [Weicher, 1990, 289], but there is no clear evidence that they lead to an appropriate supply response — increasing the supply of needed housing in specific submarkets [Yates, 1994, 180]. There is scant evidence that such supplements fail to reach those in worst housing [Weicher, 1990, 270]; and, since they target low-*income* families — regardless of their housing conditions — they lead to rather minor improvements of the housing stock. Because they are means-tested, they raise questions of stigma and have limited take-up rates. Providing them to millions of households tends to be bureaucratic, their administrative costs are high, and the programs are often plagued with delays and mistakes. Also, because they are means-tested, they are withdrawn when families no longer qualify — "the equivalent of taxing income at a prohibitive level" [Best, 1996, 550]; and finally, because they are subject to the supply-side risk that rents will climb uncontrollably, they cannot be estimated accurately.

Lump-sum one-time subsidies have been provided in Chile, Colombia, Venezuela, Ecuador, Russia, Saudi Arabia, and a number of other countries to first-time home buyers. They are unquestionably the least problematic of all subsidies: "The only subsidy that would be equitable, neutral between methods of finance, and non-distortionary as regards the allocation of resources at the margin would be a lump sum subsidy fixed in real terms. It could be paid directly to the household or incorporated into a general tax-credit or negative-income-tax scheme" [Hughes, 1980, 89].

The most important demand-side subsidy in the industrialized countries is the mortgage interest income-tax deduction, an off the books subsidy that has accompanied government promotion of home ownership since its earliest days. Its effect has been to lower the cost of borrowing for housing, favoring those who do not have sufficient equity and need to resort to housing loans. For those who borrow, it does indeed significantly lower the cost of housing, and it does so even more significantly in periods of high inflation when its acts as a cushion for the heavy "tilt" towards higher monthly payments in the early years. Furthermore, while the deduction is regressive—since the more one borrows the higher the deduction—it is available to all, and the great bulk of mortgages appears to be targeted to low- and middle-income homeowners. In the United States in 1987, for example, where median household income was of the order of $40,000, 57% of mortgages had a balance of less than $40,000, and 97% had a balance of less than $100,000; the average annual deduction was of the order of $1,000 [Woodward and Weicher, 1989, 311]. The deduction has come under strong criticism in recent years, focusing on the massive loss in tax revenue it entails, on its regressive nature and on the need to cap it, on the diversion of excessive resources into housing, and on its favored treatment of homeowners. Similar criticisms have been leveled against the exemption of the sale of principal residences from capital gains tax. While these criticisms may have considerable merit, we must note that withdrawing these benefits will have the short-term effects of lowering housing demand, making home ownership less affordable, and adjusting the market toward consuming smaller houses in the longer run.

Finally, the privatization of public housing in many industrialized countries, particularly in Eastern Europe and the Russian Federation after 1990, resulted in massive housing subsidies in the form of giveaways and discounted sales of public housing apartments to sitting tenants. Sales to sitting tenants could never command a market price. Yet in the United Kingdom, for example, the sale of council houses, at roughly half their market value, resulted in a windfall gain to the government exceeding £30 billion [Best, 1996, 542]. In Eastern Europe and Russia, such high values were not forthcoming. Buckley [1996], for example, argued that over the years households "financed capital subsidies for past investments with 'forced savings' through the wage repression mechanism," and advocated giving away the housing stock [40–41]. Privatization has also been a mixed blessing. In some cases the better units were sold and the low–quality units had no takers; in other cases low–income families, lured by the prospect of home ownership, took on loan burdens that they could not sustain, or they were unable to keep their homes in good repair [Karn and Wolman, 1992, 217, 222].

Price Controls

Price controls in the housing sector take four main forms: ceilings on the sale price of houses and apartments, ceilings on collected rents (commonly known as rent control), ceilings on deposit rates in mandated "saving–for–housing" schemes, and ceilings on mortgage interest rates. The objectives of such ceilings is to choke off speculation (or price inflation) in times of economic crisis, when strong demand faces a limited supply. The problem with such ceilings is that, if they persist, they choke off supply altogether — as potential suppliers, realizing that they cannot make the same profits in housing that they can obtain in other forms of production and investment, move away from housing.

House price controls are often mandated in conjunction with supply–side subsidies. In Seoul, South Korea, during the 1980s, for example, the Korea Land Development Corporation could force landowners to sell their land at assessed, less–than–market prices; the corporation could then develop the land itself and sell it to builders, again at assessed, less–than–market prices. In exchange, all new construction was subject to price controls. Two fixed prices were set, one for small apartments and one for larger ones, without regard to location or quality of construction. The controlled prices were not adjusted to reflect construction cost increases, with several results: Overall supply of new apartments was reduced, new apartments were built in outlying locations with inferior materials, and prices of existing housing rose appreciably [Yoon, 1994, 73–75].

Rent ceilings were introduced in many European countries during and after the World War I, as part of a package of general price controls deemed necessary to manage their war economies. Once introduced, however, rent controls tended to outlive their usefulness. Where they persisted, as in Great Britain for example, they choked off profitability and effectively destroyed the rental housing sector. Largely but not wholly as the result of rent control, the private rental sector in Britain — that housed 90% of the households in 1914 — housed less than 7% of households in 1990, compared with 66% in Switzerland, 43% in former West Germany, and 30% in Canada, Belgium, and Portugal [Forest and Murie, 1985, 101; Hagred, 1994, 22]. Households in rent-controlled dwellings spent less of their income on housing, but they occupied housing that may have been less desirable than what they would have otherwise chosen. In addition, since rent-controlled units were usually not transferable, households were often obliged to forego better housing and may have spent less on housing than they desired. They may also have been prevented from seeking better employment in distant locations because they could not afford to move.

Rent control amounts to a tax on landlords given as a subsidy to sitting tenants, and as such it is kept off the books. Since it is not a subsidy from government, its volume remains unknown. It often comes to the attention of governments only when controlled rents are lower than operating expenses — utilities, maintenance, repair, and property taxes. If no subsidy support or property-tax relief to landlords is forthcoming, there is no longer any incentive for them to keep their properties. They can, and do, abandon them. Peterson [1973], writing in the United States in the early 1970s, reported that:

> In many cities, housing abandonment has reached crisis proportions. In Newark, no less than 7.5 percent of the total housing stock has been abandoned in the last four years alone. In Chicago, between 15 and 20 percent of the structures in Woodlawn and Lawndale which are older than ten years "have been demolished or boarded up , or stand vacant and vandalized." In St. Louis, one-sixth of the structures in the Montgomery-Hyde Park, Murphy-Blair, and Yeatman areas are reported to have been abandoned. In Philadelphia, some 20,000 units were abandoned as of 1970; in Detroit it is estimated that 20,000 structures under the FHA insurance program alone have been or will be abandoned. [117]

As noted in chapter 8, ceilings on mortgage interest rates have similar effects. Such ceilings, when applied to government-backed projects, entail an interest-rate subsidy that is, in fact, equivalent to the difference between the market rate and the subsidized rate. Between 1984 and 1988, the Low-cost Home Ownership Program in Indonesia (KPR) issued mortgage loans to 12,416 households, roughly 0.03% of all households. The estimated cost of this subsidy was equal to approximately "17% of the 1988/89 government development expenditure" [Flagler Management Group, 1989, 1, 14]. There is no question that such subsidies could not be, and indeed were not, sustained for long.

A similar fate met a World Bank housing program, the Sites-and-Services Program which was very popular during the 1970s, and to a lesser extent, in the 1980s. The program involved more than 100 demonstration projects in more than 50 countries; it sought to harness self-help and mutual-aid in house construction through the provision of serviced sites and mortgage loans. It was hoped that, by reducing subdivision and infrastructure standards and by not providing completed houses, such projects could provide houses to low-income groups without subsidies. It was further hoped that these projects would be replicated by the private sector on a larger scale. Neither hope materialized. A detailed 1987 World Bank study on subsidies in sites-and-services projects reported substantial interest-rate subsidies (not counting loans in default, of which there were many) in 78 projects carried out between 1972 and 1984 [Mayo and Gross, 1987]. Because of the prevalence of interest-rate subsidies as well as supply-side subsidies — less expensive land and off the books technical assistance, for example — sites-and-services projects were not replicated, neither by the private sector nor by governments.

Price controls in the form of ceilings on mortgage interest rates discourage or prohibit private lenders from entering the mortgage market. If lenders are forced to lend a certain percentage of their loans at controlled interest rates, they have to absorb the implicit subsidy as a form of a tax, not necessarily an efficient one, or impose it on depositors that are forced to save at bellow-market interest rates. In either case, low- interest loans are, in fact, rationed, and continue to be in short supply, choking off housing demand by many deserving households.

An Enabling Housing Subsidy Regime

The structure of housing subsidies has been changing over the last three decades of the twentieth century, largely toward more enabling subsidy regimes. The two most important trends were (a) the general retreat from public housing construction, usually followed by the privatization of the public housing stock; and (b) the retreat from price controls toward market prices, usually followed by increased housing allowances, construction grants, and rent supplements. Both these trends are welcome developments. They are clearly in the spirit of the enabling paradigm, because they provide support while relinquishing control.

Public housing was largely a policy failure, and is now in retreat, except possibly in Singapore where speaking of "relinquishing control" may still land a person in jail. Abandoned tenements were another visible sign of policy failure; squatter settlements still another. And while a minority of cities with little or no public housing, abandoned tenements, or squatter settlements may not be saddled with the legacy of such failures, many other cities will continue to be tormented with the concentrated mix of difficult social problems that plague such places. It is unimaginable that all of these sites will simply be evacuated and dynamited out of existence, although many have been (and will be) destroyed. Many others, however, are (and should continue to be) sustainable communities. It is difficult to envision, therefore, a total retreat from supply-side subsidies that focus on the gradual repair and rehabilitation of structures and dwelling units in such communities, in conjunction with other assistance programs. Such revival may be partially assisted by housing allowances and rent supplements, but because it must focus on the improvement of the community as a whole it must continue to need supply-side subsidies that focus on home and neighborhood improvements. Such supply-side subsidies are indeed enabling and are best administered by nonprofit organizations, community-based organizations, individual households, and groups of households that share a commitment to the creation of sustainable communities. The rehabilitation and renovation of existing units is indeed a worthwhile target for enabling supply-side subsidies. They are still likely to be less expensive, on a per unit basis, than new housing, if standards can be relaxed to meet the needs of low-income residents, a subject we shall take up at greater length later.

Supply-side subsidies to developers of *new* low-income housing are more problematic. They are still attractive to activist government functionaries who get energized by making things happen—seeing lovely houses and apartments springing up in their districts—regardless of the cost of land, labor or materials and regardless of the subsidies involved, on the books and off the books. There is no question, however, that supply-side subsidies must be subject to greater scrutiny. On initial examination, it is not at all clear that their merits justify their costs. To give just one example, the U.S. Tax Reform Act of 1986 gave a tax credit to developers of low-income housing: "For conventionally financed, mixed income projects that receive no rent subsidies, the credit amounts to 9 percent of total construction costs per year *for ten years*. A set number of units in each project must be set aside for low- or moderate-income tenants. . . . The present value of marketable credits is $5,194 per $10,000 of development costs. . . Developers are willing to spend large sums of money to compete for these credits. That fact by itself indicates that the *full* rate of return is significantly in excess of the return required to secure private financing" [Case, 1991, 350–352].

The argument that subsidized new low-income housing is needed to meet special needs is without merit, because any housing, new and old, can be easily remodeled to meet special needs (if regulations permit it). As we noted earlier, subsidized new housing does not necessarily increase the housing stock as a whole, because it tends to displace new nonsubsidized housing. The lack of a supply response on behalf of private-sector developers to low-income housing needs does not require subsidies but a more benign policy regime. Down-market penetration by the private sector—its ability to provide low-income housing without subsidies at all—already occurs in many countries [see table A20]. This activity does not need to depend on lucrative subsidies to the private sector.

A more benign policy regime should also remove the distortions that presently discriminate against the production and ownership of rental housing. The key advantage to owners of private residences in most countries (and, as it turns out, to rent-control tenants as well) is the nontaxation of imputed rental income, and not the deduction of mortgage interest from income taxes. Mortgage deduction can easily also apply to owners of rental accommodations, to remove such an advantage to owner-occupiers. And correcting this distortion does not necessitate a direct transfer of subsidies to builders or owners of rental properties.

Targeted demand-side subsidies are generally more enabling than supply-side subsidies for new housing: they do not create supply distortions; they allow greater choice to dwellers; they can be better targeted; they increase housing affordability; and, if supply is responsive, they increase housing supply. With the advent of data-processing technology, the cost of administering these subsidies accurately should markedly decrease. Whenever possible, one-time construction grants or contributions toward a down payment for a house are to be preferred to rent supplements, to the mortgage interest tax deduction, and definitely to any form of price control. It is not clear, however, whether the mortgage interest tax deduction should be removed. At present, it enables many people of modest incomes to gain access to better housing, and it is highly likely that its removal, still politically unacceptable in many countries, will burden the sector as a whole.

Capping it, on the other hand, so as to exclude higher–income families, may be a more acceptable alternative.

It is virtually impossible to recommend an appropriate optimal mix of supply–side and demand–side subsidies, given that both can be enabling. Best [1996], for example, compared the structure of subsidies in Great Britain in 1980–1981 and 1995–1996 in 1995 prices: subsidies for public housing fell from £4.8 billion pounds to –£0.3 billion. Subsidies for housing allowances, referred to as housing benefits, rose from £1.9 billion to £5.5 billion. And mortgage–interest tax relief fell from £9.2 billion to £2.7 billion, largely as a result of falling interest rates. The total volume of subsidy fell from £15.9 billion to £7.9 billion [548–549]. Papa [1992] made similar comparisons for the Netherlands and France between 1981 and 1988. In the Netherlands, for example, where housing policies were generally less enabling, housing subsidies as a percentage of gross domestic product (GDP) increased from 2.66% in 1981 to 3.54% in 1988. The share of supply–side subsidies increased from 42% to 54%, the share of housing allowances remained around 12%, and the share of mortgage interest tax relief declined from 46% to 34%. In France, which by contrast had more enabling policies, housing subsidies as a percentage of GDP declined from 1.46% to 1.32% during this period, the share of supply–side subsidies declined from 42% to 34%, the share of housing allowances increased from 12% to 24%, and the share of mortgage–interest tax relief decreased from 45% to 42% [table 10.8, 172]. Marginal increases or decreases in the overall level of housing subsidies should not be alarming — particularly if important components of the subsidy are regressive or nonenabling — as long as the fundamental need for an effective and ongoing housing subsidy program is not questioned.

The Housing Subsidies Index

How do we measure the degree to which a subsidy regime is enabling or nonenabling? The meager number of measures of the total volume and structure of housing subsidies make such a distinction difficult. The volume of subsidies is measured by housing subsidies as a percent of GNP, GDP, or total public expenditure [Hårsman and Quigley, 191, 15; Papa, 1992, 176], or by housing subsidies as a percentage of housing investment [Papa, 1992, 176]. The structure of subsidies is measured by the percentage of new dwellings given state aid [U.N. data, in McGuire, 1981, 190]; the annual percentage of subsidized new dwellings in the total number of completions [Papa, 1992, 175]; the annual number of housing allowance recipients [139]; the average amount of housing allowance in fixed prices [140]; the volume of mortgage interest tax relief [Hills, 1991b, 198]; and property subsidies, housing allowances and foregone fiscal income as percent of GDP or GNP [Papa, 1992, 172; Roman et al, 1994, 125–134; Lujanen, 1993, 82].

The measure of the total volume of subsidies, and its variation over time, may be an important indicator to gauge the importance of housing in overall policy making, but it is of limited value in determining the degree to which the subsidy regime is enabling. Good measures of the structure of subsidies are invaluable, but not in their present form. A good structural measure must distinguish between different forms of supply–side and demand–side subsidies. On the supply side, it must distinguish between public housing, subsidized new private housing, and support for renovation and rehabilitation. There may also be measures of the distribution of recipients of supply–side subsidies, to distinguish between public authorities, private developers, nonprofit organizations, and individual households. Other measures may be needed to assess the levels of per–unit subsidies in each supply–side subsidy type. Off the books supply–side giveaways of public land, public housing, subsidized building materials, and tax deductions will also need to be measured, at least occasionally, to get a sense of their volume and importance.

On the demand side, existing measures already make the key distinction between housing allowances or rent supplements on one hand, and mortgage interest tax relief on the other. Measures of subsidies involving price controls are needed to assess the distortions created by these controls. The Rent Control Index discussed earlier is one such measure. The positive real interest rate discussed earlier is another. The estimated volume of off the books subsidies involving price controls in general, and rent control in particular, may be an important addition to the structural indicators suggested above as well.

Unfortunately, the Global Survey of Housing Indicators failed miserably in collecting information on the volume and structure of subsidies, largely because good published data simply did not exist in most participating countries. Data collected on the overall volume of subsidies were incomplete, as were data on targeted subsidies reaching the lower half of the income distribution. In the absence of good measures of the structure of subsidies, two indicators give us an indirect measure of whether housing subsidies are enabling or nonenabling — the relative size of the public housing stock, and the degree of rent control:

1. *the public housing stock* is defined as the percentage of the total number of dwelling units in the urban area that is owned, managed and controlled by the public sector.[8]

There have been earlier attempts to construct rent control indices; one example is a rent control index that was based on a rating of enforcement, coverage, fairness, indexation, cost pass–through, treatment of new construction, rents reset on new tenancy, and tenure security [Malpezzi and Ball, 1991, 24–32]. The *Rent Control Index* uses only two measures:

2. *the rental price distortion,* defined as the average ratio of controlled rents to market rents; and
3. *the extent of rent control,* defined as the percentage of rental units that are under rent control.
4. *the Rent Control Index* is a measure of the product of the two indicators: Rent Control Index = 1 – Extent × (1 – Distortion).

When rent control is pervasive, the extent is high and the index would be low. When controlled rents are only a small fraction of market rents, the rent ratio is low and the index is low. It is high where there is little or no rent control, and low where rent control is pervasive.

The *Housing Subsidies Index* is a composite index of two measures: the public housing stock and the Rent Control Index. Summary values for the public housing stock, the components of the Rent Control Index, the index itself, and the Housing Subsidies Index appear in table 9.1.

The public housing stock as a percentage of total stock had a global median of 12%. Overall, it was slightly higher in the cities of the industrialized countries (15%) than in those in the developing countries as a whole (13%). It appeared to vary with income and had a weak, yet positive, correlation with the Development Index (+0.23). Among regions, it was exceptionally high in Eastern Europe (88%) and especially low in Africa (9%) and Latin America (10%). It attained a global maximum value in China (97%). Among the industrialized countries, it was especially high in Singapore (79%), the Netherlands (69%), and Hong Kong (64%).Rental price distortion, measured as the ratio of controlled rent to market rent, was more pronounced in developing countries (55%) than in industrialized countries (73%), and it appeared to decrease with income. Higher–income countries had less distorted rents, and the correlation of this indicator with the Development Index was weak, but positive (+0.23). Among geographical regions, Eastern Europe stood out as having the most distorted rents (7% of market rents

Table 9.1. The Components of the Housing Subsidies Index, 1990

Country Groupings	Public Housing Stock (%)	Rental Price Distortion (%)	Extent of Rent Control (%)	Rent Control Index	Housing Subsidies Index
Low–Income Countries	10	44	8	98	96
Low–Middle Income Countries	12	67	17	96	93
Upper Middle Income Countries	22	56	30	87	87
High–Income Countries	18	71	17	94	85
Southern Africa	9	55	12	94	94
Asia and the Pacific	15	65	5	98	92
Middle East and North Africa	15	47	29	76	82
Latin America and the Caribbean	10	88	0	100	94
Eastern Europe	88	7	100	7	9
All Developing Countries	12	55	14	95	91
Industrialized Countries	15	73	18	93	85
Global Average	22	59	33	82	79
Global Minimum	0	2	0	0	0
Global Median	12	66	15	94	88
Global Maximum	97	100	100	100	100
Global Standard Deviation	24	36	38	29	26
Correlation with Development Index	0.23	0.12	0.07	–0.07	–0.18

Source: Housing Indicators Program [1994].

in 1990), and Latin America as having the least distorted ones (88%). China and Russia stood out as having the lowest controlled rents (2% of market rents), and, by contrast, 14 countries reported no price distortions at all.

The extent of rent control varied considerably among regions. Its median value was very low in Latin America (0%), Asia (5%), and Africa (12%), higher in the industrialized countries (18%), and considerably higher in the Middle East and North Africa (29%) and Eastern Europe (100%). The only countries outside Eastern Europe and China reporting that their total rental stock was under rent control were Jordan and Canada. The resulting Rent Control Index was low in Eastern Europe and China, and much higher in the Middle East and North Africa. It attained high values in all the other regions, did not vary with income, and did not have a significant correlation, either positive or negative, with the Development Index.

The Housing Subsidies Index is an equally weighted composite measure of the Public Housing Stock and the Rent Control Index. It was slightly lower in the industrialized countries than in the developing countries, and had a small negative correlation with the Development Index (-0.18). It had a consistently negative relationship to income, becoming smaller as income increased from 96 in the low–income countries to 85 in the high–income countries. Among regions, it was again lowest in Eastern Europe, with a median value of 9. Its median value was lower in the Middle East and North Africa (82), than in the rest of the regions, which were all in the 90s. Two developing countries, Kenya and Indonesia, that had very little public housing and no rent control, attained the maximum value for this index. Among the industrialized countries, Hong Kong (56), Singapore (57), and the Netherlands (64), attained low values, while the United States (99), Germany (97), and Australia (95) attained high values.

The Availability and Targeting of Subsidies

Given the Housing Subsidies Index, we can now seek to answer the question: What affect, if any, does a more enabling housing subsidy regime have on the availability and targeting of housing subsidies? The availability and targeting of subsidies are essential components of Housing Market Conditions, the third building block of our model of the housing sector. This discussion indeed belongs in Part III of the book that describes housing market conditions. It is introduced in this chapter as a taste of things to follow, a first demonstration of the causal relationship between the housing policy environment and housing market conditions, a relationship that will become evident in Part III. The Global Survey of Housing Indicators attempted, with very little success, to collect data on two indicators of housing subsidies:

1. *housing subsidies*, defined as housing subsidies as a percentage of the government budget during the last year; and

2.   *targeted subsidies*, defined as the percentage of housing subsidies reaching
     below–median–income households.

The participating consultants had great difficulty in obtaining reliable information on either of the two indicators. The first involved a complicated calculation
of a large variety of different subsidies. The second involved an empirical
assessment of each one of these subsidies with regards to their distribution among
income groups. Needless to say, both calculations were clearly beyond the
capabilities and resources available to consultants in most of the countries. Data
were more forthcoming from the industrialized countries, and virtually nonexistent in many poor ones. The results presented here should therefore be taken with
great caution. They are presented simply to reflect a first effort at articulating a
comparative framework, paving the way for more comprehensive comparative
studies of housing subsidies in the future. The summary of the results of the
Global Survey regarding housing subsidies are given in table 9.2.

The volume of housing subsidies did not appear to vary with income or with
the level of development. The median values for the developing countries as a
whole and for the industrialized countries were the same (6%), and the correlation
with the Development Index was positive, but rather low (+0.14). The global
median value, 6%, did suggest, however, that housing subsidies formed a
substantial part of government budgets. The availability of subsidies varied
considerably by geographic regions, however. The median value was minimal
in Southern Africa and Asia (1%). It was similar to the overall median of 6% in
the Middle East, North Africa, and Latin America, and 11% in Eastern Europe.
Russia reported the maximum value for this indicator (35%), a surprisingly high
number, and one that is definitely on the decrease with the advent of housing
privatization since the early 1990s. Five developing countries reported values of
less than 1% for this indicator: Bangladesh, Senegal, Colombia, Thailand, and
South Africa. Among industrialized countries, two (Israel and Canada) reported
values of less than 2%, and six (Hong Kong, Australia, Austria, France, Sweden
and Finland) reported values in excess of 8%. Six developing countries, not
including Russia, also reported values in excess of 8%: Nigeria, Jordan, the former
Czechoslovakia, Hungary, Brazil, and South Korea.

Targeted subsidies, in contrast with the volume of subsidies, did appear to
increase with the level of economic development. The developing countries as
a whole reported a median value of 26%, while the industrialized countries
reported a value of 50%. The share of housing subsidies targeted at below–
median–income households increased from 9% in low–income countries to 50%
in high–income ones, and the indicator did have a positive correlation (+0.36) with
the Development Index. All in all, these numbers suggest that housing subsidies
were not well targeted and, on the whole, not especially redistributive. Eastern
Europe, among developing–country regions, reported the lowest percentage (22%)
reaching below–median–income groups, followed by Asia and Southern Africa.
The Middle East and North Africa region reported a higher than expected median

Table 9.2. Housing Subsidies, 1990.

Country Grouping	Housing Subsidies (%)	Targeted Subsidies (%)
Low–Income Countries	5	7
Low–Middle Income Countries	8	39
Upper Middle Income Countries	4	70
High–Income Countries	9	0
Southern Africa	1	27
Asia and the Pacific	1	25
Middle East and North Africa	6	43
Latin America and the Caribbean	6	32
Eastern Europe	11	22
All developing Countries	6	26
Industrialized Countries	6	50
Global Average	7	40
Global Minimum	0	0
Global Median	6	39
Global Maximum	35	100
Global Standard Deviation	7	26
Correlation with the Development Index	0.14	0.36

Source: Housing Indicators Program [1994].

value (43%). Seven countries, all developing countries (Malawi, Bangladesh, Madagascar, Nigeria, the Philippines, Ecuador, and Poland), reported that 10% or less of their housing subsidies reached below–median–income groups. Among the industrialized countries, only two countries reported a value of less than 30% for this indicator: the United States (15%) and Norway (23%). In contrast, eight countries (Senegal, Jordan, Israel, Spain, Singapore, the Netherlands, France and Canada) reported values of 60% or more. The availability and targeting of housing subsidies are best viewed as outcomes of variations in the economic, social, and political context of the housing sector and the housing policy environment — in this case especially that part of the policy environment concerned with the housing subsidy regime, the Housing Subsidies Index.

Two statistical models were constructed to study the effects of variations in the context and the Index on Housing Subsidies and Targeted Subsidies. It was expected that three explanatory variables may have an effect on the actual availability and targeting of housing subsidies — the level of economic development, measured by GNP per capita, the Welfare expenditures of government as a percentage of all government expenditure, and the Housing Subsidies Index. Unfortunately, data on subsidies were only available for less than half the countries in the survey, and the data themselves could not be sufficiently corroborated. Given these qualifications, the first statistical model of the availability of housing subsidies is summarized in table 9.3.

Table 9.3. The Determinants of Housing Subsidies, 1990.

Variable	β–coefficient [a]	t–statistic
Log of GNP per capita	0.26	0.76
Government welfare expenditures as % of all expen.	0.17	0.52
Housing Subsidies Index	–0.50	–2.26** [b]
Number of Observations	25	
R–squared and Adjusted R–squared	0.32	0.22
$F_{3,21}$	3.22**	

Source: Housing Indicators Program [1994].
[a]   For a definition of the β–coefficient, see chapter 6.
[b]   ***,**, and * denote 1%, 5%, and 10% levels of confidence, respectively.

This model had an R–squared of 0.32, suggesting that these three variables explained only one–third of the variation in the subsidies indicator. As we saw earlier, the level of economic development had no significant effect on the availability of subsidies. The model also failed to find any significant effect of the overall welfare orientation of government on housing subsidies. It did uncover, however, a significant *negative* relationship between the Housing Subsidies Index and the volume of subsidies. Countries with less public housing and less rent control were found to devote a considerably lower share of government funds to housing. An enabling housing policy regime, as defined here, was found to be associated with less, rather than more, public resources going into housing. A high level of housing subsidies is not a necessary attribute of the enabling regime. Indeed, if it were shown that an enabling policy regime had a positive effect on housing outcomes, it will have accomplished this effect despite the allocation of less, rather than more, public resources to housing.

A second statistical model, focusing on Targeted Subsidies, is presented in table 9.4. This model had an R–squared of 0.35, suggesting that the three independent variables again explained only one–third of the variation in this indicator. As we noted earlier, the level of economic development did have a significant positive effect on the targeting of housing subsidies. More developed countries had significantly better targeted housing subsidies. Again, it was found that the Housing Subsidies Index had a weak negative effect, this time on the targeting of subsidies. Housing subsidies appeared to be somewhat less efficiently targeted,

Table 9.4. The Determinants of Targeted Housing Subsidies, 1990.

Variable	β–coefficient [a]	t–statistic
Log of GNP per capita	0.45	1.58* [b]
Government welfare expenditures as % of all expen.	–0.01	–0.04
Housing Subsidies Index	–0.34	–1.45*
Number of Observations	27	
R–squared and Adjusted R–squared	0.35	0.27
$F_{3,23}$	4.13**	

Source: Housing Indicators Program [1994].
[a]   For a definition of the β–coefficient, see chapter 6.
[b]   ***,**, and * denote 1%, 5%, and 10% levels of confidence, respectively.

and definitely not better targeted, in more enabling housing policy regimes as defined here. On the whole, however, given the paucity of data both for constructing the Subsidies Index and for measuring levels of subsidies, this initial result only points to the need for more studies of this relationship.

* * *

To conclude, we stress again that an enabling housing policy environment requires the inclusion of a housing subsidy component as one of its essential parts. A well- functioning housing subsidy regime creates a level playing field for housing investors, producers, and consumers — it does not discriminate against investment in housing, nor among owner- occupiers, renters, and landlords of rental properties. En abling housing subsidies are required both on the supply side and on the demand side, but they call for the phasing out of pric e, rent, and interest rate ceilings. On the supply side, the support of low-inco me house holds, groups of house holds, and residential communities with land tenure or home ownership and one-time grants for rehabilitation and improvement, either directly or through nonprofit organizations, is enabling. Subsidies for the construction of new public housing are nonenabling, but may be required for sustaining and upgrading existing public housing. Subsidies for private-sector developers to induce them to build new low-income housing require very close scrutiny and are generally suspect of generating "rent-seeking behavior" and of distorting housing supply. Such subsidies should, in general, be avoided. Housing allowances, one-time grants to first-time home buyers, and rent supplements are enabling subsidies that increase choice, promote social integration, and do not distort housing supply. The mortgage interest tax relief is, on the whole, enabling — it increases access to home ownership and reduces its cost — but can be made more progressive by a ceiling on deductions. Discounted sales and the free transfer of public housing to sitting tenants are both enabling strategies that restore housing market demand and increase mobility and housing choice. Ceilings on deposit interest rates in mandatory "saving-for-housing" schemes, coupled with ceilings on mortgage interest rates to beneficiaries of such schemes, force depositors to subsidize borrowers and should, therefore, be avoided.

10

Residential Infrastructure

Discussions of urban infrastructure do not generally look at it from the perspective of the housing sector, even though the housing sector is *the* primary consumer of infrastructure services. In industrialized countries, residential buildings typically constitute more than half of all non–infrastructure investment in construction,[1] and occupies more than half of all developed urban land not in use for roads and highways.[2] The efficient and equitable provision of residential infrastructure is, without doubt, an essential component of an enabling housing policy environment. In other words, the housing sector cannot function at an adequate, let alone optimal, level unless it is supported by an adequate supply of infrastructure services. Conversely, as we shall see, infrastructure services cannot be optimally produced and paid for if their symbiotic relations with the housing sector are ignored.

This chapter is not a state–of–the–art report on infrastructure in general, or on urban infrastructure in particular.[3] Instead, it focuses on the interaction between infrastructure services and housing, with the principal aim of gaining a better understanding of what constitutes an enabling infrastructure regime for the housing sector. More specifically, five aspects of this relationship are examined here in greater detail:

1. infrastructure services and housing quality;
2. housing, infrastructure, and public health;
3. infrastructure, urban land development, and housing supply;
4. the housing sector and the privatization of infrastructure services; and
5. housing, infrastructure, and the poor.

One serious criticism of the present production and delivery of infrastructure services concerns its multiplicity of goals. The public authority, it is claimed, is ill–suited for the production and delivery of these services "since it pursues diverse objectives that override one another and reduce its productive efficiency" [Lorrain, 1997, 11]. Such an agency is often required, for example, to serve as an employer of last resort, to provide patronage, or to deliver services below cost [World Bank, 1994, 7]. To ensure efficient provision, the task of any agency engaged in the production and delivery of public services can, and should be, simplified. Introducing the housing sector perspective, therefore, should not result in adding more objectives to an already loaded agenda. Indeed, it does not. Rather, it helps us sharpen our understanding of what simple and minimal goals of infrastructure service delivery should be, by introducing the critical perspective of its primary user.

Infrastructure Services and Housing Quality

From the perspective of the housing sector urban infrastructure is defined here as minimally comprising the basic physical networks: roads and walkways; water, sewerage, and drainage; power; and telecommunication. A wider definition also includes (a) mobile services: public transport, solid–waste disposal, police and fire protection; and (b) public facilities: schools, parks and playgrounds, sports and cultural facilities, and health services. These infrastructure services are essential to increasing *housing* quality.

Housing quality increases when it is properly serviced by infrastructure networks, mobile services, and public facilities, and when it is accessible to jobs and markets throughout the city through an efficient transport system. Conversely, housing quality declines when roads are in disrepair, when drinking water is contaminated, when neighborhoods are flooded, when sewage and garbage remain uncollected, when there are power brownouts, when traffic congestion results in long commutes, when the waiting time for telephones in the neighborhood is impossibly long, or when neighborhoods are crime–infested or fire prone. Moreover, the cost of transport and utilities is an inherent part of the cost of housing services.

There is no question that the quality and cost of these services affects the market value of houses. This effect is best understood as an effect on the value of residential land. Where infrastructure quality is high, land is more valuable and therefore houses are more valuable. Where quality is low, land is less valuable and therefore houses are less valuable. The market value of housing, in short, is intimately bound with its supporting infrastructure, while the latter does not command a market value – its value is transferred to the houses surrounding it and feeding on it. The deterioration and failure of infrastructure systems are, by extension, major setbacks for the housing sector. For example Becker et al. [1994] describe the conditions in Africa in the 1980s, where:

> virtually *all* countries have experienced a deterioration in urban infrastructure in the past decade, and at least most do not foresee major improvements as imminent. . . Kinshasa, with a population of three million, has increased in size from six thousand hectares in 1960 to twenty–five thousand hectares today. . . Yet the paved road network has remained virtually unchanged during that period. Paralleling these deficiencies is the absence of storm drains or the obstruction of existing drains with uncollected solid

wastes. As a result the potential coverage of public transport facilities is severely limited. [40]

In the developing countries, infrastructure investment typically represents "about 20 percent of total investment and 40 to 60 percent of public investment" [World Bank, 1994, 14]. Structural adjustment policies that reduced needed new investments the name of reduced public deficits have often led to disproportionally sharp cuts in infrastructure investments. In the long run, such cuts are unsustainable and nonenabling. Such investments are preconditions for both housing and nonhousing investments, and they are therefore critical to the renewal of economic growth. Furthermore, more radical budget cuts, cuts that not only reduce investments to a trickle but also curtail maintenance budgets, are disastrous: "For instance, in Costa Rica during the 1980s current non–wage expenditures (principally operations and maintenance) fell from 1.6 percent of GDP to a mere 0.3 percent, and the share of the national road network in poor or very poor condition rose to 70 percent" [World Bank, 1994, 19].

An efficient and affordable urban infrastructure is an essential component of an enabling housing policy environment — it is a support system without which a well–functioning housing sector cannot be sustained. In the simplest terms, policies that support and sustain urban infrastructure systems are, in general, enabling. Conversely, those that perpetuate inefficient, undermaintained, and undercapitalized urban infrastructure systems are nonenabling.

Housing, Infrastructure, and Public Health

Historically, the initial concern of governments with the "housing problem" — the intolerable housing conditions in the cities resulting from the influx of new migrants — was motivated by the fear and concern of civic groups that the ill health (and moral degradation) of the slums would spread to the rest of the city. For example, Mearns [1883], in his pamphlet *The Bitter Cry of Outcast London*, decried the conditions in the London slums in much similar terms to the descriptions we still hear today:

> To get into them you have to penetrate courts reeking with poisonous and malodorous gases arising from accumulations of sewage and refuse scattered in all directions and often flowing beneath your feet; courts, many of them which the sun never penetrates, which are never visited by a breath of fresh air, and which rarely know the virtue of a drop of cleansing water ... [W]ho can wonder that every evil flourishes in such hotbeds of vice and disease ... Entire courts are filled with thieves, prostitutes and liberated convicts. [173]

Governments have traditionally responded to these threats with two major policy instruments: first, by providing public infrastructure services — particularly water supply, sewerage, drainage, and garbage collection — to contain the spread of disease, especially waterborne disease; and second, by issuing minimum building standards to remove or upgrade structures unfit for human habitation, a policy instrument we shall elaborate upon in chapter 11. Engels [1872] captured this reaction to public health concerns in his description of nineteenth century Manchester:

> I have already mentioned the unusual activity of the health authorities at the time of the cholera [in 1831–2]. When the epidemic threatened, the middle–classes in Manchester were panic stricken. They suddenly remembered the existence of the unhealthy dwellings of the poor; and they were greatly alarmed lest every one of these slums should become a centre from which this pestilence should spread death in all directions, and so reach the dwellings of the wealthier classes. [76]

The reaction in New York during the same period was not atypical:

> The sanitary movement . . . accelerated after the devastating cholera epidemic of 1832 when lot owners and aldermen, fearful of the miasmic vapors arising from the neighborhood wetlands, embarked upon a century–long program of sewer construction. . . . [S]ewer locations did not necessarily correspond to the wealthiest enclaves. . . . The importance of a pure [water] supply grew even more urgent in 1832. [Moehring, 1981, 20, 27]

Public health is a civic concern that transcends the economic decisions of individual households, in the sense that society as a whole may want individuals to consume residential water, sewerage, drainage, and garbage services in higher quantities that they would choose themselves in order to protect the public at large. As a result, these utilities will often tend to be undersupplied unless the public participates in supplying them at its own expense. This was indeed the motivation for the public provision of water, sewerage, drainage, and garbage services in the growing cities of the nineteenth century.

Unfortunately, while cities in the now–industrialized countries built such systems over time and at great expense, for a large number of rapidly growing cities in the developing countries today the construction of citywide waterborne sewer systems and storm drainage systems are now low–priority luxuries, and the massive funds needed to build them are simply not forthcoming. There is a serious lack of both ability and willingness to pay for the installation of such systems for the city as a whole and considerable pessimism about whether the systems can be built in the foreseeable future. Moreover, individual neighborhoods the world over, that now believe — with the advent of modern medicine — that they can better shield themselves against the spread of disease than before, prefer to take care of their own needs in isolation. In some countries, usually in drier climes, small–scale sewerage collection and treatment is feasible at the small town, neighborhood, or household level, leaving nearby places to fend for themselves. The public health outcry of yesteryear does not echo there as loudly as before.

No so in the many cities situated at sea level in the flood plains of river deltas — such as Dhaka, Ho Chi Minh City, Bangkok, and Shanghai — where storm water cannot be properly drained; where contaminated water mixes with the rainwater flooding the city; and where water wells, as well as piped water, are contaminated by sewage and salt–water intrusion. To make matters worse, these cities also continue to subside, sometimes below sea level, as a result of excessive water–pumping from unregulated wells, largely caused by the absence of a piped water supply. Subsidence then further exacerbates the drainage problem, and it will only stop when adequate, citywide piped–water systems replace water pumping from wells. In these cities, only a systematic commitment to citywide water, sewerage, and drainage systems can overcome this vicious circle.

To conclude, the spillover effects from inadequate residential infrastructure — especially in the areas of sewerage and drainage and sometimes in solid-waste disposal — call for public intervention to ensure adequate supply in the name of public health. Such intervention will necessarily involve the public purse.[4] It follows that public intervention in water, sewerage, and drainage is enabling, and that nonintervention is nonenabling because it leaves the housing sector undersupplied with essential services.

Infrastructure, Urban Land Development, and Housing Supply

What distinguishes the network elements of infrastructure from the mobile services and the public facilities is that they require a public right–of–way, a system connecting stretches of land reaching each and every plot. Indeed, what distinguishes urbanized land from rural or agricultural land is precisely that — land is subdivided into relatively small building plots, so that each plot is immediately adjacent to a public right–of–way. Network infrastructure services are then provided, either gradually or simultaneously, along that public right–of–way, connecting houses, apartment buildings, and other land uses to the existing networks. The most basic, and usually the first, infrastructure element is the road system that provides access to and from building plots, with the rest of the services provided along the roads. Once a road is built, primitive as it may be, sites are accessible for the mobile services previously listed, as well as to public facilities, jobs, and markets. Such sites, if not beyond commuting range, then become parts of the metropolitan area. So from the perspective of the housing sector, the extension of the road network, followed (or accompanied) by the provision of the other basic network services, is *the* essential mode of increasing the supply of residential land, and hence the supply of housing. By extension, the road network is also a key factor is keeping housing affordable — when residential land is in short supply housing is not affordable.

Unfortunately, the urban road network cannot and will not be adequately supplied by the market. This is a typical instance of market failure. Except for a few major highways — usually connecting cities to each other — where tolls can be levied to recover some of the costs,[5] the use of most urban roads cannot be properly priced — they are "public goods" teeming with free riders. The enthusiastic movement for the privatization of infrastructure services, which we shall discuss greater length later, is practically silent about roads. There is no economic incentive to build them, and — like sewerage and drainage networks — they are left to governments, who also have no clear incentive to provide them where needed in adequate supply.

A national road (and rail) grid that can gradually integrate the country into one society and one market is inevitably an important national development goal, to be implemented by the central government and financed by road-based and vehicle-based taxes, as well as by general revenues. But it should come as no surprise to anyone that, regardless of that lofty goal, the national grid becomes an urban commuter network by default. Intercity roads become the main directions of fingerlike urban expansion. Soon as they are built, they become clogged with urban commuters, while closer lands in other directions often remain in rural use.

Why is this? First, because the timely introduction of new roads to meet rising needs for serviced urban land is not, and has rarely been, an important national development goal. Growing cities of all sizes are usually considered by their residents to be "exploding," and there has been a general reluctance to let them grow further. They inevitably do grow, but governments are often shy of preparing for such growth, lest they be (wrongly) accused of accelerating it. They prefer, paradoxically, to focus on the national grid, and then to supply urban infrastructure after the fact at considerably greater expense — when obtaining rights-of-way involves many more landowners demanding higher land prices as well as compensation for the demolition of structures. Opening up land for urbanization is the most effective policy instrument for responding to housing demand and for keeping land and house prices low, and the one most often resisted so as to deflect misplaced blame for urban growth. Second, since the use of urban roads can still not be properly priced, the budgets for building them usually come out of the general tax fund, where funds are limited and must be rationed. The incentive rarely exists to provide roads in sufficient quantity where people are willing and able to pay for them.

There are two established ways to create such an incentive. One pertains to the road network and the accompanying services within planned land subdivisions and within small, integrated communities. In such cases, infrastructure provision is seen as part of the price of developed land, to be paid for by those who buy or own land there. Since all the services are immediately adjacent to residential plots, and can be clearly associated with such plots, adding the cost of providing them to the price of plots is rarely disputed.

The second method focuses on land-based taxes and levies. Roads and other services outside land subdivisions and small communities can, and should be, financed from taxing increased land values. A typical land-based levy is the valorization assessment in Colombia, that captured some of the unearned increment in land value resulting from the provision of road access and infrastructure services. In 1972-1973, for example, more than two-thirds of the revenue used to finance local street paving in Bogota was from valorization contributions

[Doebele et al., 1979, table 3, 85]. Unfortunately, recovering the cost of infrastructure provision and maintenance by taxing increased land values on a regular basis has been slow in coming. While land taxes have been levied throughout history, modern taxation systems have moved away from taxing land. The closest alternative to taxing land directly is the more-common property tax, that bundles together investments in building improvements as well as increased land values, and as such is not the best mechanism to capture the unearned increment.[6] Moreover, in industrialized countries, because the property tax is so visible, there is often strong political pressure to reduce it. In developing countries, there are additional obstacles to the efficient collection of property taxes—such as the absence of cadastre information, unwillingness to assess properties regularly, corrupt collectors, and arrears. Harare, Zimbabwe, for example, has recently combined property tax bills with water bills in an attempt to reduce arrears [Kim, 1997, 1611]. But on the whole, the lack of political will (in rich and poor countries alike) to tax residential land—so as to recover fully the cost of servicing it with the gamut of public utilities—still prevails.

One example of a more interventionist method to increase urban land supply while recovering costs has been attempted in South Korea, where a government agency (the Korea Land Development Corporation) was empowered to force the sale of rural land at appraised below-market prices, develop the land, and then sell it (also at appraised below-market prices) to private corporations for residential development. A variant on this method was "land readjustment," whereby the rural land owners came together themselves, pooled their land, built infrastructure, and then sold it as urbanized land. But land readjustment, formerly common in South Korea, Japan, Germany, and Norway, has never been practiced on a grand scale [Doebele, 1982]. It requires considerable voluntary cooperation, technical expertise, financial resources, and long time horizons that are not commonly available. Both methods require a degree of control over the urban development process that is both unnecessary and rarely forthcoming.

In an enabling residential infrastructure regime, urban land development is *the* overall infrastructure objective—the efficient delivery of an expanding network of high-quality services to new and existing urban lands, while ensuring cost recovery. Right-of-way networks are planned long in advance. Legal methods of acquiring land for public right-of-way[7] are efficient and not time consuming, compensation is at near-market prices, and disputes with landowners are quickly resolved by the courts. On-site infrastructure costs are absorbed by local residents as part of their land costs, while off-site urban infrastructure—in ample supply—is financed from land-based taxes that visibly capture the unearned increment in land values in specific jurisdictions, and visibly use the proceeds to pay for the construction and maintenance of such services in those self-same jurisdictions.[8]

The expropriation of private lands for the construction of roads and the concomitant payment of compensation was already in practice by Pope Sixtus IV in Rome as early as 1480 [Lai, 1988, 33]. During the Middle Ages in Germany lands were owned by the ruling princes and leased to users, and the princes had no difficulty in reserving land for public thoroughfares, as well as for open spaces and public buildings, outside the established towns. This power of eminent domain to reserve and acquire the right–of–way for public thoroughfares (*Flucht-linien*) was later transferred to the German states and municipalities. It became the basic instrument for planning town extensions, and for increasing the supply of land for urban development [Sutcliffe, 1981, 9–19]. Moreover, it laid the foundations for sensible town planning. " 'Germany,' wrote Patrick Abercrombie in 1913, '... has concretely achieved more modern Town Planning than any other country' " [Sutcliffe, 1981, 9].

Responsiveness to non–market demand for urban infrastructure – by the road, sewerage, and drainage networks in particular – can hardly be expected at the national level. It calls for the decentralization of authority – both in the provision of infrastructure and in revenue generation from increased land values – to smaller jurisdictions, where the relation between the demand and supply of services is indeed more visible. In summary, then, we can postulate at least three levels of hierarchy in the delivery of such public services: the national level at one end and the subdivision level at the other, with one or more levels in between – the region or state, the metropolitan area, and service districts within the metropolitan area. The process of decentralization of infrastructure expenditures appears to accelerate with increased levels of economic development: "A study using comparable data from twenty industrial and developing countries found that decentralized expenditures accounted for one–half of infrastructure spending in industrialized countries and one–quarter in developing countries" [World Bank, 1994, 74].

In the case of nonmarket demand, the primary goal or incentive of infrastructure agencies should be the maximization of land values in their jurisdiction through the provision and maintenance of a high–quality infrastructure network. To accomplish that, these agencies need to be involved both in revenue generation (through the taxation of increased land values) and in service provision, as indeed many municipal governments already are. In an enabling residential- infrastructure environment the connection between infrastructure and land development should not be a marginal one (as it often is now) but rather the key thrust of infrastructure policy and the basic method for ensuring cost recovery in the nonmarket provision of urban infrastructure services: "Greater effectiveness in raising revenues locally – getting users who benefit most from the local public goods to provide the required resources – is the key to equating revenues with expenditures" [World Bank, 1994, 76]. Building road, sewerage, and drainage networks that maximize the value of – and therefore the tax returns from – developed land will both provide the necessary incentive and impose the necessary discipline on public infrastructure agencies engaged in service delivery. Such discipline is necessary both to prevent unnecessary oversupply and to ensure an adequate response to consumer demand.

Housing and the Privatization of Infrastructure Services

According to the World Bank [1994], in developing countries "[g]overnments at present provide or broker the bulk of infrastructure financing: about 90 percent of financial flows for infrastructure are channeled through a government sponsor, which bears almost all project risks" [89]. The record of public provision both in the developing and the industrialized countries has been problematic, largely because of the lack of proper incentives for efficient, responsive, and responsible operation. This has been partly due to the monopolistic position of public agencies and the resulting absence of competition. In recent years, however, government agencies in many countries have been undergoing fundamental changes: "The Citizen's Charter in the UK requires competition on all service delivery fields, measurement and public disclosure of service performance, and inclusion of users on service management committees" [Urban Institute, 1996, in Kim, 1997, 1615].

The provision of urban infrastructure services is currently undergoing major reforms, and the thrust of these reforms is the privatization of those services where costs can be recovered and profits be made by charging user fees. This pertains especially to the provision of piped water, to the production and distribution of electricity, and to telecommunications; to a lesser extent it can also apply to sewerage and solid-waste collection and disposal. There are numerous examples of successful privatization. In the Côte d'Ivoire, for example, a French-Ivorian joint venture has been providing water and sewerage services under a management contract: "The company manages all the installations at its own risk and takes up all operations and maintenance without government subsidies. . . . [R]evenue from water sales has fully recovered capital as well as operating and maintenance costs. This has been possible by keeping unaccounted for water at less than 15 percent and the level of collection from private consumers at 97–98 percent" [Bi, 1996 in Kim, 1997, 1609]. The competitive privatization of solid waste services in Phoenix, Arizona, for example, "is estimated to have made cost savings of almost 50 percent, despite a nearly 50 percent increase in population since late 1970s" [Donovan, 1994 and Jensen,1995, in Kim, 1997, 1615].

From the perspective of the housing sector, it is immaterial whether infrastructure services financed by user charges are provided by a public or a private agency, as long as services are provided efficiently and reliably, respond to user needs, and attain maximum coverage. There are two issues, however, that specifically concern the housing sector: (a) coordination, and (b) the imbalance of power between monopoly suppliers on the one hand, and weak municipalities and a fragmented housing sector on the other.

Coordination is an aspect of urban land development that is not typically the concern of individual service agencies. While individual agencies—such as the highway agency, the water agency, the sewerage and drainage agency, the power agency, and the telecommunication agency—may all share the goal of network expansion, they may not necessary share plans for expansion into specific locations. Surely, to function efficiently and rapidly, each agency should be free to pursue its own objectives without being constrained or delayed by other agencies. Stubborn insistence on coordination necessarily slows everyone down, and gives veto power to the weakest element in the system. Yet residential development is hampered if less than a full contingent of services is provided before people move in; the lack of water, or the lack of telephone services, can and does delay the occupation of a new neighborhood. In an enabling policy environment, minimal coordination occurs, expansion plans are voluntarily shared, and capital improvement programs are agreed upon in advance, allowing all agencies to move independently at their own speed without centralized control.[9]

The imbalance of power between monopoly suppliers on the one hand, and weak municipalities and a fragmented housing sector on the other, may prove to be a more complicated problem. In the new globalized economy, large public works contracts are now being pursued aggressively by multinational conglomerates. Municipalities and local authorities are retreating from direct productive activity, introducing competition and contracting at all levels; and these local authorities are also taking on new regulatory or overseer roles over private companies, companies that far outweigh them in many respects:

> The important point remains that major multi-sector groups are being formed in all industrialized countries; they are set on being present everywhere, bringing their solutions, methods, standards, and principles. They are backed up in this role by a number of securities firms, engineering companies, and international organizations preparing major reforms in these sectors, and this represents a significant change. Hitherto the initiative was with the public sector, and firms would intervene according to a prearranged scenario. This has all changed. The public and the private arena now balance each other out. Large-scale enterprises are directly involved in the agenda because they have very considerable resources at their disposal. [Lorraine, 1997, 23]

A weakly organized housing sector may find its voice compromised if monopoly producers of infrastructure services import inappropriate standards, reduce variety in service provision, and are less responsive to user needs. Small residential communities, groups that used to have a voice in local elections, may be left unheard. And while monopolies are highly unlikely to emerge in housing production, two critical inputs to housing—housing finance and urban infrastructure—are undergoing global transformations that may result in global oligopolies that are going to be difficult to regulate, especially at the local level.

Housing, Infrastructure, and the Poor

Infrastructure provision has a critical effect on the housing of the urban poor. First, agencies that provide infrastructure services often discriminate against low-income neighborhoods. For example, in 1990, in the urban areas of Paraguay,

54% of the poorest quintile and 89% of the richest quintile had access to public water supply, 10% as against 62% had access to sewers, and 95% as against 99% had access to electricity [World Bank, 1994, table 1.4, 32]. Second, there is also abundant evidence of what has come to be called "environmental injustice" — the location of power lines, garbage transfer points, hazardous waste sites, and sanitary landfills in disproportionate numbers near poor neighborhoods. A U.S. study by the United Church of Christ in 1987 found that "the proportion of residents who are minorities in communities that have a commercial hazardous waste facility is about double the proportion of minorities in communities without such facilities. Where two or more such facilities are located, the proportion of residents who are minorities is more than triple." The report concluded that "it is 'virtually impossible' that the nation's commercial hazardous waste facilities are distributed disproportionately in minority communities merely by chance" [Mohai and Bryant, 1992, 163]. Third, there is abundant evidence concerning the displacement of disproportionate numbers of poor people, usually without adequate compensation, to make way for public works.

Fourth, the poor often pay more for basic services than the rich, having to rely on water vendors or indirect power lines from neighbors that inevitably cost more than regular services: "During the mid-1970s to the early 1980s, people in seventeen cities surveyed were paying private water vendors an average of twenty-five times the prices charged by the utility. In Nouakchott, Mauritania and Port au Prince, Haiti, vendors were charging up to a hundred times the public utility price" [World Bank, 1994, 49]. As a result, "poor urban neighborhoods show much worse conditions than those in the city as a whole or in rural areas. In Manila, for example, infant mortality rates are three times higher in the slums than in the rest of the city. Rates of tuberculosis are nine times higher, and diarrhea is twice as common. . . . In Singapore, the incidence of hookworm, ascariasis, and trichuris was found to be more than double among squatters than among flat dwellers" [World Bank, 1993a, 131].

Urbanization in the developing countries during most of the twentieth century has proceeded without the coordinated supply of infrastructure services prior to the construction and occupation of houses. House building has usually preceded the provision of most infrastructure services [Baross, 1990]. Relying on a minimal rural road network to provide access to the city, residential neighborhoods have been laid out on the urban fringe by subdividing land into small plots, while leaving minimal right-of-way for future roads and pedestrian paths. Houses were then gradually built, supplied with water by vendors or by digging wells. These subdivisions were initially established by squatter groups invading land, and later by private landowners subdividing land informally. None abided by land subdivision regulations that universally required a full contingent of services before the area could be inhabited. Regular services to such communities — paved roads, piped water, electricity, sewerage, and drainage — were often long in coming. Delays were either caused by supply bottlenecks or by the refusal of the authorities to legitimize these settlements, even though willingness to pay for services exceeded the cost of providing them. There is considerable evidence [e.g., van der Linden, 1977] that the provision of infrastructure in slums and squatter settlements accelerated housing investment. A survey of Lima, Peru showed that the rate of housing improvement roughly doubled with access to infrastructure — especially water and sewerage — and that investment in improvements far outweighed access cost [Strassmann, 1984, 743]. Investment ensued because service provision was viewed as a form of recognition by the authorities, reducing the fear of eviction and instilling confidence in the community that houses would not be demolished. Put another way, the provision of infrastructure, as mentioned earlier, increased the value of the land and made investments in improvements more attractive.

There are a number of instances where the self-building of infrastructure acted to empower poor communities. In Orangi, a large squatter settlement in Karachi with 700,000 inhabitants, residents built and maintained a sewerage network at a much lower cost than public provision. By 1985, over half the streets in Orangi had community-built sewage systems [Hassan, 1989]. There are many other examples of private provision of infrastructure in informal land subdivisions, especially water and electricity. There are also many instances of the public sector trying its hand at low-cost land subdivision, spearheaded by the World Bank-sponsored sites-and- services projects in the 1970s. But the latter have not been nearly as successful as informal land subdivisions in creating profitable businesses, largely because these public sector efforts were held to higher standards and involved very complex (and expensive) management. They usually did not recover costs, nor were they replicated on any meaningful scale. Informal land subdivisions, however, are ubiquitous [see Baross and van der Linden, 1990]. The success of these subdivisions has led numerous governments, notably in Colombia [Hamer, 1985] and later in the Philippines and in Ecuador, to issue lower initial subdivision standards that could later be upgraded.

The provision of improved infrastructure services in slums, squatter settlements, and poor neighborhoods has proven to be one of the more successful forms of housing subsidy, whether administered on the supply side or the demand side. It has the advantage of being a well-targeted, one-time investment that is relatively small and can reach a large number of the urban poor. During a 10-year period in Indonesia, for example, the Kampung Improvement Program (KIP) reached more than 3.3 million people with basic infrastructure — streets and pedestrian paths, water, sewerage, and drainage — at the cost of $160 per household [Taylor, 1987]. In Tijuana, Mexico, to take another example, the municipality subsidized 40%–60% of internal community improvements: "Community groups select priorities, pay for the residual cost, and perform the work themselves either by hiring local contractors or on a self-help basis. Through this programme, streets have been built at much less expense than if the municipality had handled the work" [Urban Institute 1996, in Kim, 1997, 1615]. Such subsidies also have the added advantage of often generating considerable investments on the part of dwellers in their houses, and of improved road maintenance. Connecting slum houses to the water and electricity supply network usually reduces the residents' utility costs.[10] The poor are willing to pay for such services, and they may be helped either by one-time subsidies to cover the cost of the initial connections,[11] or, if these are not forthcoming, by access to loans. In short, it is much more important to create efficient citywide services that can recover costs, and then target subsidies to low-income communities, than to provide services below cost to the city as a whole, resulting in enormous subsidies that are not targeted at all: "In Mexico City at the end of the 1980s, neglect of maintenance and the lag between tariff increases and cost increases in the water sector required a federal subsidy amounting to 0.6 percent of GDP a year" [World Bank, 1994, 48].

Infrastructure provision is a fundamental form of support for housing the poor. The poor benefit most if they have access to citywide services, even without any subsidies, because they usually pay more if they are not part of the system. Extending infrastructure networks to poor communities is thus a highly enabling housing policy. It reduces utility costs for the poor; it also reduces discrimination against the poor in the provision of services. In addition it improves overall public health, and it generates new housing investment.[12] One-time subsidies for extending infrastructure networks to low-income communities are usually the most well-targeted of subsidies. There is no need, however, for public authorities to be involved in supplying infrastructure services at the household level. Such services are better supplied by communities themselves or by private sector developers. Direct government involvement in the provision of individual serviced sites is a form of micro-management that detracts from the key tasks of managing the infrastructure systems at the district and urban level.

The Residential Infrastructure Index

There is, at present, no single indicator that measures either the availability or the adequacy of the urban infrastructure system as a whole. There are, however, a large number of indicators that measure the performance of specific infrastructure elements — the transport system, the water supply system, the waste disposal system, and so forth. The Urban Indicators Programme of the United Nations and the World Bank has defined and collected information for a large number of such indicators in preparation for Habitat II, the U.N. Conference on Cities held in Istanbul in 1996 [Flood, 1997, 1662–1663].

Generally, we can divide residential infrastructure indicators into three distinct types: coverage, performance, and fiscal management. Coverage is usually measured either by household connection levels or by measuring overall system capacity. Coverage indicators measure household connection levels to piped water, waterborne sewerage, electricity, telephone service [UNCHS, 1994, 30], regular solid-waste collection, central heating [United Nations, 1992, table 18, 92–99], paved roads, and access to public transport and outdoor space within walking distance [OECD, 1982, 39]. They also measure infrastructure system capacity such as kilometers of roads per capita, automobile ownership per capita, road length per vehicle, size of the public transport fleet (buses or seats), volume of water supplied, volume of solid–waste disposed and treated, energy usage per person, or the amount of public open space per capita.

Infrastructure system performance indicators measure travel time to work, water leakage, line losses, proportion of roads in disrepair, vehicle emissions per capita, traffic accidents per capita, telephone call completion rates, housing destroyed to make way for public works, or disaster mortality. Fiscal manage-ment indicators measure infrastructure capital and operating expen-ditures per capita, revenue–to–operating cost ratios, cost recovery rates, public/private provision ratios, centralized/decentralized provision ratios, sources of income ratios (local tax versus grants, user fees versus grants), infrastructure sub-sidy–to–cost ratios, and targeted infrastructure subsidies.

The relationships between these different types of indicators are often not clear. There is no question, for example, that connection levels are closely linked to capacity and coverage. The two are generally higher where larger capacities are provided. A more tenuous relationship exists between capacity and coverage on the one hand, and performance on the other. A World Bank study [1994] noted that while capacity and coverage tended to be correlated with economic develop-ment (as measured by, say, GNP per capita), efficiency and effectiveness were not. There were very weak correlations between the amount of paved roads and the percentage of roads in good condition, the amount of telephone main lines and faults per main line, the percentage of population with access to safe water and the percentage of accounted–for water, or the percentage of households with access to electricity and the percentage of power delivered. Furthermore, "there is no close correlation between a country's efficiency of provision in one sector and its performance in another" [26]. Finally, there are a few indications that better management of infrastructure services does indeed result in better coverage and in better performance. As we noted earlier, under-investment and under-funding of infrastructure reduces performance. There are also a number of studies that attempt to compare private and public provision with a view to measuring performance differences, but their results are not easy to interpret [OECD, 1982, 39].

The Global Survey of Housing Indicators of 1990 could not collect comprehen-sive data on coverage and connection levels, let alone data on the performance or fiscal management of infrastructure systems. In each type, however, it was possible to collect one sample indicator: a sample connection level indicator, a sample performance indicator, and a sample fiscal management indicator:

1. *piped water supply*, defined as the percentage of dwelling units with a water connection in the plot they occupy;
2. *journey to work*, defined as the average length (in minutes) of a one–way commute during rush hour in the urban area, by all modes of transport (including home–based workers); and

3. *infrastructure expenditures per capita*, defined as the ratio of total expenditures (operations, maintenance, and capital) by all levels of government (including private utilities and para-statal agencies) on infrastructure services (roads, sewerage, drainage, water supply, electricity, and garbage collection) during the current year and the urban population.

Needless to say, data for the latter indicator were difficult to collect, and its accuracy must therefore be suspected. As expected, it was found to be highly correlated with per capita household income. This correlation made it less than useful for global comparisons. It was therefore further normalized to yield:

4. *the infrastructure expenditures-to-income ratio*, defined as the ratio of the infrastructure expenditures per capita and the per capita annual median household income.

The Residential Infrastructure index is an equally weighted measure of three indicators: piped water supply, the journey to work, and the infrastructure expenditures-to-income ratio. Summary values for these three indicators and for the index appear in table 10.1.

As the table shows, piped water supply had a global median of 95%. There is no question that it increased with income. In fact, this indicator could not distinguish among the higher-income countries at all. Among the developing country regions, it was especially low in Southern Africa, higher in Asia, and 90%

Table 10.1. The Components of the Residential Infrastructure Index, 1990.

Country Groupings	Piped Water Supply (%)	Journey to Work (minutes)	Infrastructure Expenditures-to-Income Ratio(%)	Residential Infrastructure index
Low-Income Countries	60	45	4.4	36
Low-Middle Income Countries	87	40	7.9	53
Upper Middle Income Countries	98	40	4.9	55
High-Income Countries	100	30	7.2	74
Southern Africa	49	44	3.2	31
Asia and the Pacific	66	40	7.7	48
Middle East and North Africa	90	34	8.1	64
Latin America and the Caribbean	91	56	4.1	45
Eastern Europe	99	43	5.7	62
All Developing Countries	86	40	5.7	46
Industrialized Countries	100	30	7.2	74
Global Average	83	41	6.3	57
Global Minimum	31	18	0.8	0
Global Median	95	37	5.9	56
Global Maximum	100	107	13.8	100
Global Standard Deviation	21	18	3.7	22
Correlation with Development Index	0.73	−0.32	0.26	0.71

Source: Housing Indicators Program [1994].

or more in all other regions. It was especially high (99%) in Eastern Europe. Piped water connection reached a global minimum of 31% in Malawi, and was lower than 40% in Madagascar, India, and the Côte d'Ivoire. Among the up-per–middle and high–income countries it was lower than 90% only in Venezuela and South Africa. As expected, this indicator was highly correlated with the Development Index (+0.73).

The length of the journey to work, measured in minutes, was not very different among countries with different levels of income or among regions. Its median value was somewhat lower (30 minutes) in high–income countries as against a value of 40 minutes for the developing countries; it was negatively correlated with the Development Index (-0.32). The only region with a slightly higher value than others was Latin America, with a median value of 56 minutes. Amsterdam attained the global minimum for this indicator (18 minutes), and eight cities had values of 25 minutes or less—Nairobi, Beijing, Monterrey, Melbourne, Vienna, Munich, Oslo, and Helsinki. Rio de Janeiro, Bangkok, and Bogota reported exceptionally high values for this indicator (107, 91, and 90 minutes respectively). Three additional cities (Lilongwe, Antananarivo and Kingston) reported median commuting times of an hour or more.

The infrastructure expenditures–to–income ratio did not display a regular increase with income, although the median value for the industrialized countries (7.2%) was higher than the median value for the developing countries as a whole (5.7%). It therefore exhibited only a weak positive correlation with the Develop-ment Index (+0.26). Median expenditure ratios in Asia and the Middle East and North Africa were higher than in the industrialized countries—7.7% and 8.1% as against 7.2%. It was lowest, however, in the low–income countries (4.4%), and, among regions, in Southern Africa (3.2%). The indicator attained a minimum value in Antananarivo (0.8%), and five cities (Dar–es–Salaam, Jakarta, Rabat, Algiers, and Munich) reported values of 2% or less. Eight cities reported values of 10% or more—Beijing, Kumasi, Bangkok, Tunis, Rio, Vienna, Tokyo, and Helsinki.

The resulting Residential Infrastructure Index did display a regular increase with increased income, and a high positive correlation (+0.71) with the Develop-ment Index. Median values for this indicator were 74 for the industrialized countries, and 46 for the developing countries as a whole. Among developing regions, the index attained the lowest value (31) in Southern Africa, and higher–than– median values in the Middle East and North Africa (64) and in Eastern Europe (62). Madagascar and Malawi attained the lowest values for this indicator (0 and 5 respectively), while four countries attained values of 90 or higher— Finland (100); Austria (94); China (92); and the Netherlands (90).

* * *

To summarize our discussion, the efficient provision of urban infrastructure services is, on the whole, a key enabling strategy for housing. Infrastructure services are directly responsible for increasing housing quality, and their provision is an essential supporting framework for the housing sector. The extension of infrastructure services into new areas is the most important policy for ensuring the adequate supply of residential land, and therefore for ensuring a responsive housing supply and for keeping house prices low and affordable. Service provision is directly responsible for increasing the economic value of houses, particularly through increasing land value. Taxing that increased value is the most appropriate way to pay for infrastructure elements that cannot be easily financed from user charges—particularly the road, sewerage, and drainage networks—and should be the primary incentive for extending these services. Other services, where costs can be recovered from user charges—particularly the water, solid-waste disposal, power, and telecommunication networks—should be provided more efficiently through the market or through public provision that simulates the market. Poor housing is especially sensitive to infrastructure provision and can benefit most from extending service networks to poor communities, from collecting regular charges, and from one-time subsidies for service installation.

11

The Regulatory Regime

Laws and regulations affect housing performance both on the demand side and on the supply side. In the preceding chapters we discussed in passing the laws and regulations that affect the demand-side of housing — the adjudication of property rights, the regulation of housing finance institutions, and the regulation of prices and rents. In this chapter we focus on regulations that affect the supply-side of housing, those that constrain and guide the process of building, developing, owning, and managing the urban housing stock. As we shall see, the proper regulation of the supply of housing is indeed a key component of any enabling housing policy environment.

We should note at the outset that, in the industrialized countries in particular, the regulatory regimes have gained in importance since the early 1970s, overshadowing earlier forms of state involvement in domestic affairs. As governments gradually withdrew from their intensive involvement in the direct production and provision of public services, the regulation of market agents became the prime focus of political agendas. In fact, the mode of governance itself can be said to have fundamentally changed, most likely in response to greater international competition, the globalization of markets, and the weakening of the welfare state: "Strategic adaptation to the new realities has resulted in a reduced role for the positive, interventionist state and a corresponding increase in the role of the regulatory state: rule making is replacing taxing and spending... [I]t is important to realize that international competition takes place not only among producers of goods and services but also, increasingly, among regulatory regimes" [Majone, 1997, 139].

Enabling housing policies are an integral part of this overall shift, because they stress the setting of limits while relinquishing control. In this new global climate, however, many regulations affecting housing are espoused with different motives in mind, motives that have little to do with meeting housing needs. Unfortunately, the housing sector has often been caught unawares in a regulatory maze not of its own making, saddled with rules and regulations that are less than enabling — restricting the supply of residential land, increasing the cost of production, making housing less affordable than it can be under more enlightened regulatory regimes, keeping poor people in bad neighborhoods, and forcing millions of families to live in houses that continue to violate laws and municipal regulations.

Laws and regulations affecting the sector are by no means "a single set of legislative decisions. Rather, regulation of most housing systems has arisen through a series of unrelated acts" [Barlow and King, 1992, 381]. Such laws and regulations are not necessarily initiated within the sector or created with housing goals in mind, and therefore they cannot be understood or analyzed without understanding the political motives behind them. These laws and regulations are usually advanced in the name of the public interest and are nominally aimed at achieving the greatest overall good of society as a whole, but they often turn out to be the initiatives of interest groups seeking to gain a specific advantage over other groups. Typical public–interest rationales for regulation are: correcting market failures, checking "speculation," reducing risks to health and safety, increasing the quality of life, protecting nature, setting reasonable limits to laissez faire, or stabilizing volatile markets. Typical interest–group motives are: maintaining the social values or cultural norms of dominant groups, maintaining property values, excluding newcomers to the city or the neighborhood, protecting businesses from competition, and other forms of "rent-seeking" — pursuing monetary gains from the manipulation of the rules [Francis, 1993, 1–17].

Unlike the more transparent budgetary transfers that take place in tax–and–spend regimes, the impact of regulations is often more difficult to understand, measure, and evaluate. This makes regulators dependent on information and knowledge that may only be available to specialist interest groups, making it possible for such groups to "capture" regulatory regimes and to move these regimes further away from their original public–interest objectives. Many of the interest–group motives underlying regulations that affect housing sector performance are incompatible with the basic housing goals of both dwellers and builders. And, unfortunately, while "decent housing for all" is clearly in the public interest, it is not a prime motive for those already decently housed.

The rationale for regulating the housing sector and the underlying motives guiding it are best understood by focusing on three interrelated components of a typical regulatory regime:

1. urban growth controls that reduce and ration the amount of land available for housing, restricting housing supply, and making housing less affordable;
2. residential zoning and land development regulations that limit the options available to builders; such regulations also impose infrastructure and planning standards that raise the cost of land subdivision and development; and

3. building codes and standards that increase the cost of building or maintaining houses and, while increasing housing quality, reduce its affordability.

Urban Growth Controls

Cities, their older inhabitants typically claim, are not what they used to be before the newcomers arrived. Soon enough, the newcomers say the same about the newer arrivals. Nostalgia, in other words, is not what it used to be. Influential "sitting" urban dwellers the world over share a rather hypocritical "antigrowth" attitude. Having arrived earlier, they proclaim that any later intruders adversely impinge on their quality of life. The specific motives for resisting urban growth do change, as we shall see, but the resistance is as strong as ever. Growth controls are, in fact, as ubiquitous as urbanization itself. They were instituted in London and Paris as early as the sixteenth century, as the move to the cities started to assert itself:

> In 1580, under pressure from the influential guilds, which were fearful of competition from recently arrived craftsmen, Queen Elisabeth issued a proclamation restricting development near and within the city. Enacted by Parliament in 1592, her decree had three major provisions: to prohibit "any new building of any house or tenement within three miles of any of the gates of the said city of London"; to restrict the construction of habitations "where no former house has been known to have been"; and to forbid in any house "any more families than one only to be placed". . . [B]etween 1602 and 1630, no fewer than fourteen proclamations were enacted in attempts to limit London's growth. . . The rulers of Paris passed eleven laws between 1548 and 1789 that limited settlement to within the city's successive walls. [Lai, 1988, 27–33]

In this early instance, growth controls prohibiting further housing construction were instituted in the name of protecting a specific interest group from competition. Such regulations must have reduced housing supply without restricting migration, undoubtedly further aggravating the already miserable housing conditions. To judge by the subsequent growth of London and Paris, they were of little effect.

Friedrich Engels [1872], observing the deplorable housing conditions in the European cities of the nineteenth century, arrived at typically anti–urban conclusions as well: "To want to solve the housing question while at the same time desiring to maintain the modern big cities is an absurdity. The modern big cities, however, will be abolished only by the abolition of the capitalist mode of production, and when this is once on the way then there will be quite other things to do than supplying each worker with a little house for his own possession" [54].

The twentieth century Chinese and Khmer disciples of Marx and Engels took such fanciful observations seriously, attempting not only to control urban growth but to reverse it aggressively: "China's rustication program sent many millions of people from cities to rural areas between 1961 and 1976. The program demanded strong administrative control and was resented both by the rusticated and by those who had to receive them. Once the controls were removed or weakened, the process reversed itself naturally. The most drastic rustication effort was made by the Khmer Rouge armies upon their entry to Phnom Penh in April 1975. Perhaps as many as three out of four million people were forcibly sent to the country side, but most eventually returned" [UNDP, 1990, 89].

Almost all countries toyed with population redistribution policies at one time or another aimed at controlling the growth of big cities, and almost all still champion growth controls. Several countries experimented with residence permits and restrictions on rural–urban movements, only to abandon them later — African countries during World War II [Stren, 1989, 36], and Communist countries until the late 1980s [Sillince, 1990, 27, 34]. Vietnam, for example, did not remove migration controls until 1986 [Mathey, 1990, 9]. Other countries initiated programs of rural development or attempted to shift growth to smaller cities or to new towns in the name of curtailing urban growth.[1] Those valiant efforts notwithstanding, there is no question that, on the whole, attempts to control urban growth in the face of the massive drift of populations from the countryside into the cities have been utter failures.

Fears of societal breakdown, political instability, and economic decline resulting from overurbanization have largely proved groundless. Contrary to many earlier claims, urban growth and expansion have no natural limits, and urban areas have outgrown any magical round number put forth as the absolute number of people a city can sustain. As cities grow, so does the knowledge, expertise, and sophistication of the institutions needed to manage them. In fact, judging by the economic dominance of large cities, there are advantages to size, because larger cities can better compete in the global marketplace than smaller ones. Surely, while the larger cities are indeed engines of economic growth, they also require that the benefits of growth be channeled into the needed public infrastructure to sustain the urban environment — to maintain safe water supplies, to dispose of wastes properly, to reduce traffic congestion, to curtail air and noise pollution, to increase access to parks and open spaces, to preserve their historical heritage, to reduce the risk of natural disasters, and to ensure public safety.

The urban environmental agenda is, no doubt, essential both to ensuring the quality of life of urban residents and to the continued competitiveness of cities in the global marketplace. There is no reason, however, for this agenda to place limits on urban growth. It is therefore quite surprising that environmental groups are the most recent converts to the growth–control cult, the more radical among them championing "no–growth" at all. The reason it is surprising is that urban areas (in general) are intensive, rather than extensive, forms of land use. In the United States in 1990, for example, urban areas (cities and towns housing more than 2,500 people) housed 75.2% of the population and occupied only 2.5% of the total land area of the country. Urbanized areas (cities housing more than 50,000 people) housed 63.6% of the population and occupied only 1.7% of the total land area of the country [U.S. Bureau of Census, 1993, table 6, 7].

There is no question that the great bulk of the world primary growth forests and natural habitats have always been — and are presently being — destroyed by agriculture, not by cities. For example, by 1983 Thailand was only 18% urbanized, a much lower rate than other countries with similar levels of economic development. Between 1961 and 1982, its rural population grew by 19 million, but only 4 million settled in urban areas and in government-sponsored land development schemes. "The rest were pioneer settlers who cleared land in government-owned forests and settled there illegally. . . 40 per cent of the Thai farmers are officially considered illegal squatters on public land, mostly forest reserve. . . Thailand did experience a severe rate of deforestation, averaging 2.5 percent, during the period in question. Forest cover was reduced by 11,035,000 hectares, from 27,365,000 in 1961, to 16,330,000 in 1982" [Angel, 1986, 42]. Instead of moving to the cities, which are more friendly to forests, the Thai rural population cleared vast areas of forests.

Rapid urbanization is, no doubt, the surest way to save the remaining forests and to use land more intensively. But this has not, however, been the position of most environmental groups; since the early 1970s, many of these groups have championed legislation and engaged in court battles aimed at reducing the amount of land surrounding the cities that is available for residential development.

Modern urban growth controls are implemented by the following methods:

- zoning legislation to protect wetlands and endangered species near urban areas;
- green belt legislation aimed at prohibiting the transformation of rural to urban land at the perimeters of cities;
- establishing quotas for building permit and residential subdivisions;
- delaying the release of public lands for urban development;
- delaying the development of water resources;
- declaring moratoria on the development of sewerage networks;
- increasing the cost of acquiring right-of-way for new roads;
- prohibiting development that will further congest existing roads;
- restricting the ability of municipalities to raise the necessary capital to extend infrastructure networks;
- requiring lengthy and costly studies and permit procedures; and
- increasing the risks to residential developers of litigation by environmental groups.

The application of these instruments, alone and in combination, was especially successful in California, which has been a leader of the growth-control movement since the late 1960s. Until that time, residential development and conservation could be said to have been in balance, but this balance was overturned with a number of key decisions of the California Supreme Court, which during the early

1970s became "the most antidevelopment in the nation" [Fischel, 1995, 226]. Fischel's detailed study of the effect of court decisions on housing prices concludes:

> California houses appreciated five times faster than those of the rest of the country between 1971 and 1989. . . California housing prices rose faster than those of the rest of the country, and faster than at any other time in the state's recent history. To explain this, one needs to find something that happened in the early 1970s that was (a) different from the rest of the country, and (b) different from California's post-war history. I submit that only the California Supreme Court's unprecedented and largely unmitigated war against developers covers both conditions. [235-237]

The increase in land prices in California no doubt had a number of positive effects, from protecting wetlands to making house owners richer by choking housing supply. But, apart from making housing less affordable both for renters and new owners, it also had a severe negative effect on the state's economy: increasing housing costs made it more difficult to attract professional and skilled labor, leading to a significant migration of jobs and enterprises to neighboring states.

There are by now numerous studies linking increased house prices to growth controls. Malpezzi and Green [1996], for example, have shown that, in U.S. metropolitan areas, growth controls that restrict the supply of *any* new housing by limiting land supply, also affect the availability, prices, and rents of existing low-cost housing. They conclude: "To the extent that a city makes it easy for *any* type of housing to be built, it will also enhance the available stock of low-cost housing. Conversely, restrictions on any kind of housing will also restrict the available stock of low-cost housing" [1811-1812].

The continued appeal of urban growth controls hides the fact that those espousing them ignore the substantial housing costs they impose on others. In an enabling housing policy environment, the regressive economic effects of growth-control regulations are not overlooked. Surely, there is ample room for keeping parts of the natural environment surrounding cities for the use and enjoyment of their inhabitants, and there is ample potential for densification of existing built-up areas. But there is no need to restrict urban growth or to insist on eliminating urban "sprawl." Sprawl is but a part of a dynamic process of extension and later in-fill of urban built-up areas. Instead of blocking or stifling urban extension, it should be managed intelligently, with the understanding that an urban order only emerges over time. The ample supply of serviced urban land — a key to an ample and affordable housing supply — is a fundamental element of such intelligent management. This was well understood in nineteenth century New York, for example, that in 1811 adopted a plan to expand its street network to prepare for a more than *tenfold* population increase. The Commissioners who presented the plan remarked: "To some it may be a matter of surprise that the whole island has not been laid out as a city. To others it may be a subject of merriment that the commissioners have provided space for a greater population than is collected at any spot on this side of China" [Morris, De Witt and Rutherford, quoted in Mackay, 1987, 20]. In contrast, attempts at stunting urban growth have been neither viable nor equitable.

Residential Zoning and Land Use Regulations

Over and above the growth controls that prohibit residential development altogether, there are many zoning and land use regulations that restrict or specify what type of residential development is permissible (if and when it is permissible at all). Typically, upper limits are imposed on residential density, restricting the intensive use of land in the name of health and safety — specifically ensuring that adequate amounts of air and sunlight penetrate into rooms and that residents have adequate access to open space. These restrictions take the form of allowable floor-area ratios, plot coverages, height restrictions, and off-street parking and open space requirements. They essentially dictate the form of high-density residential communities, generally forcing them into high-rise towers surrounded by open spaces. High-density low-rise development, which has typically housed equivalent numbers of people in abutting dwellings with small courtyards for centuries, is usually disallowed. In large part, such restrictions have little to do with health and safety, and more with the desire of governments to champion the transition from tradition to modernity that high-rise towers have come to symbolize. Andrusz captures this spirit in post-revolutionary Russia:

> Since the city housed socialism and represented a radical break with the past — the "idiocy" associated with the countryside, the conservative peasantry and the tsarist cities, which anyway were nothing more than 'overgrown villages' — its housing and architecture had to be distinguished from that past. . . And when the Party turned its back on the *muzhik* and his wooden *izba*, low-rise development did not enter into consideration as part of a housing strategy for urban areas. The workers of tomorrow would be accommodated in high-rise, standardized blocks of flats. [Andrusz, 1984, 275]

Insistence that high-rise towers replace high-density low-rise housing essentially limits the ability of individual families to build houses on small, or very small, plots of land, forcing them either to consume larger quantities of land at a higher cost or to live in flats. It also excludes small, undercapitalized builders from entry into the market, as only large builders can build high-rise towers. In fact, restrictions on high-density low-rise housing often affect the structure of the building industry, shifting the emphasis from a large number of small builders to a small number of large ones, thus increasing industrial concentration. Industrial concentration, as any other oligopoly, tends to increase the opportunities for collusion in price setting as well as in competitive bidding, often leading to higher costs of construction.[2]

Citywide zoning typically distinguishes between neighborhoods by restricting the kinds of housing that could be built there. The most typical restrictions distinguish between central-city high density and suburban low-density housing, with medium-density housing in between. Suburban zoning regulations, in pursuit of the dream of Garden Cities, mitigate against the intensive use of urban land, favoring low-density housing that consumes much more land. The zoning laws pertaining to low-density housing further reduce allowable densities. Among the more common zoning restraints in low-density suburbs are "exclusive single-family use; one structure per lot; minimum lot size; maximum lot- coverage; minimum floor area of the house; off-street parking; front, side, and rear-yard setbacks; maximum height restrictions... and requirements for the provision of infrastructure at the developer's expense" [Fischel, 1995, 221]. On-site infrastructure requirements may also require wide streets and open spaces, expensive sewage treatment facilities, and other "gold-plated" local improvements. Regardless of the zeal with which zoning regulations are pursued, however, it is important to bear in mind that all low-density zoning and land use regulations, without exception, have no functional justification in the sense of being necessary for healthy and safe living. Downs [1973], who has written extensively on zoning laws in American cities, summarizes the common motivations behind them, none of which has to do with health and safety:

> [A]ll minimum size requirements and many construction method requirements incorporated in most suburban (and other) codes are based almost entirely upon cultural and even political considerations, not upon health and safety requirements. This is true even though the basic legal justification for such ordinances — the police power — is founded on the community's right to protect its health and safety. I believe that prevailing minimum housing standards are really based upon four objectives of the people who already live in each community: (1) meeting their culturally conditioned (often social-class-related) perceptions of what is "desirable" or "socially acceptable"; (2) protecting their own property values; (3) avoiding certain consequences of higher density living, such as greater traffic congestion; and (4) excluding low- and moderate-income households by making local housing too expensive. [Downs, 1973, 52]

In the United States, the structure of local government is such that small suburban communities can and do enforce zoning laws and are thus able to effectively exclude low-income housing. Practically all suburban towns have now adopted strict zoning laws and cumbersome regulations that make the construction of higher-density low-income housing practically impossible. They also forbid the voluntary remodeling of single-family houses to allow for adding low-income rental units, a simple regulation that, if reversed, could vastly expand the supply of affordable housing [Downs, 1991, 1113]. And so, while suburban job vacancies are on the increase and central city unemployment remains high, inner-city residents, who are excluded from housing in proximity to suburban jobs, schools, and natural amenities, are forced into long reverse commutes into the suburbs in search of work. Federal legislation in the United States has been emphatic, declaring exclusionary zoning regulations unconstitutional and requiring municipalities to shoulder "a fair share of the present and prospective regional need." But, as it became clear in the 1980s that the electoral power of the suburbs was of decisive importance in federal elections, the affirmative penetration of lower- income families into the suburbs remained a drip rather than a flood, further aggravating the housing problems of the inner cities.[3]

Residential zoning, which segregates cities into areas of different densities, is by no means a necessary component of modern urban planning. The precursors of zoning laws — the law of nuisance on the one hand and regulations allowing for restrictive covenants on the other — fulfilled a similar function adequately without resorting to land use controls. The doctrine of nuisance, originating in the Middle Ages, was "*sic utere tuo ut alienum non laedas* – use your property so as not to harm that of others" [Platt, 1991, 53]. It legally protects one's residence from nearby houses blocking its light and air, or generating air pollution or excessive noise.

A restrictive covenant is "a promise made by the purchaser or lessee of real estate that the use of the premises will conform to conditions specified by the seller or lessor" [Platt, 1991, 59]. It may include similar, and even more stringent, restrictions on the use of land and on the character and appearance of buildings than typical zoning regulations. But it is a contractual agreement, governed by civil law, rather than a regulation backed by police power. Restrictive covenants responded to the need for upper-income housing estates, and provided the legal framework for the Baroque squares of seventeenth and eighteenth century Europe. Houston, Texas, for example, still relies on the law of nuisance and on restrictive covenants, and the city does not have any zoning law at all. And while there are no observable differences in its overall urban structure, lot sizes in Houston tend to be smaller than those in other U.S. cities [Holcombe, 1995, 64].

Developing-country cities typically do not have large swaths of exclusive suburban housing communities, nor do they have concentrations of poor families in the inner cities. Their urban structure is of much smaller grain, with intermingled commercial, productive, and residential land uses in close proximity to each other everywhere. Poor communities border on rich housing estates, separated only by walls, in older central districts as well as in newly developed areas. Small shops and productive enterprises are often found on the ground floor of houses and on all floors of apartment buildings, allowing residents to intensify the use of their residences and to gain additional income without creating a nuisance to their neighbors.

Unfortunately, many developing countries have been saddled with the legacy of colonial zoning laws that have been left unchanged even though they were never appropriate for any but a small minority of high-income neighborhoods. Other countries, advised by foreign consultants unfamiliar with local conditions, have copied complete zoning codes from industrialized countries. None, however, considered affordability as a key constraint on residential land development. Recently, in a few instances (the Philippines and Ecuador, for example), governments have acted to initiate regulatory reforms that improve the access of the poor to residential subdivisions. In an important innovation, the government of Colombia created regulations, aimed at providing legal alternatives to informal land subdivisions, which do not mandate high infrastructure standards as a condition for occupancy but allow infrastructure standards to be improved over time [Hamer, 1985].

In an enabling housing policy environment, pervasive exclusionary zoning practices that prevent low-income people from access to employment and increase their housing costs are replaced with minimal nuisance prevention, and with ample opportunities to build small exclusive communities based on restrictive covenants that are enforced through contractual obligations among buyers and sellers. Mixed occupation of land is encouraged, both among competing commercial, productive, and residential uses and among different income groups. No unnecessary restrictions are imposed on builders and developers of residential land, allowing them to choose the most efficient combination of land, labor, and capital for constructing housing; similarly, there are no regulations prohibiting or restricting any kind of housing development from locating in any jurisdiction. The minimal regulations necessary to promote health and safety are transparent and well-understood, there are no inordinate delays in obtaining permits, and developers do not bear any undue risk of litigation by groups politically opposed to the construction of affordable housing in their vicinity.

A special case can and should be made, however, for regulations that aim at the preservation of the aesthetic values of historical districts, for controlling the timing and form of development in archaeologically sensitive districts, and for the selective regulation of the form and shape of buildings in new special districts in the name of urban design. The preservation of urban cultural treasures in the public interest has often been protected by law: "As early as 1262, the Italian city of Siena passed an ordinance governing the character and height of private structures facing the city's Piazza del Campo" [Lai, 1988, 22]. We should keep in mind, though, that nuisance and aesthetic motivations are different in their perception of the need for regulation. The first motivation aims at limiting the free use of property because of the distress it forces on others, which the market fails to take into account. The second seeks to restrict the free enjoyment of individual property rights in the name of a greater good — the promotion and preservation of common cultural artifacts for the enjoyment of all — which cannot emerge from simple market transactions. And because the aesthetic motivation imposes restrictions and costs on individual tenants and home owners — many of which cannot afford them — it should necessarily be selective, minimalist in its application, and protected from "capture" by those intent on appropriating it to block any and all development.

Building Codes and Standards

In contrast to zoning ordinances and residential land use regulations, building codes, and standards have often been imposed precisely to promote the health and safety of cities. In first century Rome, for example, in the time of the emperor Augustus, there is evidence that residential quarters reached a high degree of congestion that threatened public health and posed a serious fire hazard. The height of buildings exceeded the decreed height limit of 70 feet, often reaching 100 feet, and allowed little light and air to penetrate from the narrow streets. In the reconstruction that followed the burning of the city during the reign of the emperor Nero, new regulations were put in place whereby hasty and irregular constructions were forbidden, and the height of private houses was apparently limited to twice the width of the street. Similarly, "wooden floors in lower storeys were forbidden, and porticoes were ordered to be built in front of the dwellings to give the passer–by protection from rain and heat. The later building act of Trajan fixed the height of tenement houses at 60 feet" [Hiorns, 1956, 66–67].

Early instances of the application of building codes during the Middle Ages in Europe consisted of similar laws, motivated by the doctrine of nuisance, to prevent the spread of fire and to safeguard against unsanitary conditions; for example, some cities regulated the use of roof construction materials or outlawed pigsties facing the street, as London did in 1297. The essence of the nuisance argument for codes and standards has since remained fundamentally the same — the state can and should use its police powers to enforce building codes and standards in the name of public health and safety.

A second argument for codes and standards, the "decent minimum housing" argument discussed in earlier chapters, poses housing as a *merit good*, whereby society–at–large insists that everyone be decently housed, sometimes at a higher standard of housing than that which consumers may be willing or able to purchase by themselves. This is a second instance of market failure in the housing sector, and possibly as serious as the first failure which sees substandard housing as a public health and safety nuisance. There is no doubt that uniform standards that prescribe the basic necessities of good housing often lead to improvements in housing conditions. For example, according to Burnett, the imposition of minimum standards in Great Britain in the nineteenth century did precisely that: "The development of a sanitary house, with adequate standards of construction, water supply, and sewerage, was the product of the Public Health acts and, more especially of the building by–laws from 1875 onwards, which brought about a major, and largely unrecognized, advance in working–class housing standards" [Burnett, 1986, 335].

There is, however, a fundamental problem with housing codes and standards. The problem revolves around the question of who defines what is minimally acceptable. Throughout the world, official standards have been set by the dominant groups in society, essentially reflecting their own standards of health and comfort. All such standards make it illegal to construct or inhabit substan-

dard housing without regard to either the views or the resources of large segments of society unable to afford them. Jacobs [1961] articulated this problem by
bringing the perspective of low-income dwellers into focus: "To overcome slums,
we must regard slum dwellers as people capable of understanding and acting
upon their own self-interests, which they certainly are" [271]. Turner [1972]
expressed the same belief: "[W]e must know how much money the inhabitant of
a slum has, what his expectations are, and what his alternatives are, before we can
be sure that the slum, alleged or actual, is doing him more harm than good" [175].

Surely, buildings codes and standards can be enforced selectively in small
communities within the metropolitan area that can afford them. But there will
always be people in the city who cannot afford them, sometimes a very large
number of people. What about them? There are four possible avenues available
to policy-makers who confront the problem of establishing and enforcing
areawide standards: (1) use police powers to demolish housing unfit for human
habitation; (2) provide adequate public subsidies to raise all housing to a socially
acceptable minimum standard of decency; (3) allow different housing standards
for different income groups; and (4) tolerate the continued existence of illegal
sub-standard housing. All four approaches, alone and in combination, have been
with us for centuries.

Demolition and slum clearance as methods of ridding society of the evil of
bad housing were the favored options of urban visionaries, from Haussmann and
Le Corbusier to Robert Moses and Jagmohan. Haussmann, for example, aggressively implemented clearance measures to construct the *Grandes Boulevards* in
Paris during the reign of Napoleon III. The narrow residential streets — where
barricades were easily constructed during the revolutions of 1789-1848 — gave
way to wide tree-lined avenues, "a move intended to facilitate both sanitary
measures and troop movements" [Benevolo, 1993, 169-173]. Le Corbusier [1943],
in his modernist *Athens Charter*, echoed a similar sentiment: "An elementary
knowledge of the principal notions of health and sanitation is sufficient to detect
a slum building and to discriminate a clearly unsanitary city block. These blocks
must be demolished, and this should be an opportunity to replace them with
parks" [70]. Moses [1970], the forceful New York City Parks Commissioner,
concurred: "The first prescription for slum dwellers in the ghettos of the big cities
is total, immediate, uncompromising surgical removal. Anything else is palpable
fraud and a sure failure. It's a tough prescription and no panacea. But the
physicians are going to have to choose between good housing and riots" [473].

As late as 1976, the Indian government used military force to evict and
relocate more than 600,000 slum dwellers in New Delhi, citing unsanitary environmental conditions as its rationale. Hundreds died in the resulting clashes [Dayal
and Bose, 1977, 36; Jagmohan, 1978, 15] Massive slum clearance campaigns, on
a city scale, occurred in many other countries in the 1980s and 1990s — Bangladesh,
Korea, the Philippines, Myanmar, the Sudan, Nigeria, Brazil, and the Dominican
Republic, to name a few [Audefroy, 1994, 11] — often to make way for the redevelopment of cleared land for commercial uses or for higher-income residences.

Surely, smaller-scale demolition and redevelopment in central locations is still a recurring news story in many cities, but, all in all, demolition and clearance have never been a serious response to the substandard housing problem. Demolition cannot make poor housing disappear. It usually only displaces it to another location, imposing additional costs on the original inhabitants and worsening their housing situation. This was already clear to earlier practitioners of this method in nineteenth century Britain. The Artizans' and Laborers' Dwellings Act of 1868, for example, decreed that landlords were obliged to maintain their buildings in fit conditions, otherwise local governments were authorized to destroy them without compensation. According to Pugh, however, this act was never pursued with great zeal: "Local government was disinclined to act because of the injustice in the consequences, and also because closures and demolitions added to housing vexation when there were already shortages of low-income housing" [Pugh, 1980, 155].

Only Singapore—with no rural hinterland and hence with no rural-urban migration—remains today as an example of a successful combination of the first two approaches—demolition coupled with adequate subsidies. It has succeeded, without doubt, in gradually demolishing its slums and squatter settlements and in replacing them with high-rise publicly built housing estates that ensure an adequate standard of living, a standard that has risen over time as its economy developed. By the mid-1990s, its Housing Development Board had constructed more than half a million units, housing more than 85% of the island's population [Beng-Huat, 1997, i]. Governments in centrally-planned economies have also attempted, with lesser success, to channel massive subsidies into the public housing sector while using police powers to prevent the emergence of slums. Without exception, the fiscal burden of providing decent housing as a right has proved too heavy. Even the government of China, which persisted in regarding housing as a state responsibility until 1997, finally announced its retreat from this ambitious agenda. The government instructed state enterprises to "stop distributing free housing to employees beginning July 1, 1998 (later deferred to January 1, 1999) and instead to increase cash wages so that employees can buy housing or pay higher rents" [Choi, 1998, 14].

This second approach to the standards problem—channeling adequate public subsidies to raise all housing to a minimum standard of decency—is still a viable long-term objective, but usually only in combination with the third approach previously mentioned—allowing different housing standards for different income groups. In most societies, the redistribution required to house everyone at middle-class standards is politically unattractive, to say the least. Clearly, the higher the standards, the greater the subsidies required to meet them; and the lower the standards, the more realistic the subsidy requirements. Politically, however, the adoption of different standards for different income groups is usually unacceptable, because it is seen by populist and idealistic politicians as discriminating against the poor: "People who readily accept the reality that poor households drive less costly cars and wear less costly clothes than wealthier households will nevertheless balk at accepting the idea that legally required standards of housing quality should be lower in poor neighborhoods than in wealthier ones" [Downs, 1991, 1112]. Thus, for example, the construction of affordable single-room occupancy hotels, a realistic approach to housing homeless men and women, is illegal in most cities where homelessness is pervasive. Unrealistically high standards raise the cost, and hence the price, of new housing everywhere, lead to the abandonment of rental housing by landlords unable to cover the cost of meeting standards from rents, and replace low-quality units with higher-quality ones. All these outcomes have the effect of reducing the supply of low-quality housing while increasing the demand, and hence the price, for the remaining units. Where building codes and standards are enforced, the long-term result is an increase in housing quality, coupled with a decrease in affordability. This is precisely what has recently happened in the United States:

> [F]rom 1974 to 1987, the number of very low-income families living in severely inadequate housing dropped from more than 10 to less than 2 percent of such families; and the number of such families paying more than half their money income for rent rose from 24 percent to 36 percent. More recent data from HUD show the latter figure to be over 40 percent. In short, America's poorest are spending more to get better housing. [Malpezzi and Green, 1996, 1807]

Insistence on unaffordable standards can have one of two results: it can force households to pay more for housing against their will, or it can force them to live illegally. Experience throughout the world suggests that wherever a large segment of the urban population is unable to afford standard housing, this segment will resort to illegal means for finding housing rather than become homeless, crowd into small spaces, or pay an inordinate share of family income for housing. In parallel, the authorities, unable to force people to pay more for housing and unwilling to assist them financially, inevitably gravitate towards the only remaining approach — tolerating the continued existence of illegal substandard housing.

Even in countries with strong police powers, code enforcement is found to be selective. In new, planned communities housing codes are strictly enforced, and in older middle-class neighborhoods they are less rigorously enforced. "But in low-income areas, were many households live in extremely deteriorated units that clearly violate the law, housing codes are almost totally unenforced" [Downs, 1973, 6]. In general, governments the world over have chosen, sometimes after offering stiff resistance, to protect basic housing rights at the price of shirking their responsibility to uphold the law. Authorities have tolerated illegal housing, recognizing that bad housing is to be preferred to no housing at all and that, since they could offer no viable alternative, they could not continue to destroy illegal housing with impunity.

Surely, from time to time there have been spates of slum clearance, sometimes motivated by development pressures, and at other times ignited by authorities unsure of their power. But, all in all, differential code enforcement has acted to allow millions of people to remain housed and to improve their housing over time, with — or more often without — government assistance. The explanation for the almost universal lax enforcement of codes and standards probably lies in the rather weak motivations underlying it — bad housing is in a different category from crimes against person or property. Although it may create a nuisance for neighbors, the nuisance inflicted by eviction and demolition is no doubt greater.[4] With the advent of modern medicine, the threat of epidemics has subsided and with it the threat that bad housing posed to overall public health. Threats to public safety remain — especially the threat of fire in dense urban neighborhoods that can and should be mitigated by insistence on building with noncombustible, and hence more costly, materials. Even there, authorities have been understandably lax. In developing-country cities, wooden shacks in slums occasionally burn to the ground while fire trucks, for a consideration, stand by to protect adjacent higher-income homeowners and businesses from the spread of fire.

The Regulatory Regime Index

Since the early 1980s, there has been a spate of efforts to measure the stringency of the regulatory environment governing the housing sector, as well as its effect on house prices. Regulatory measures include the percentage of suburban land unavailable for growth [Segal and Srivanasan, 1985, 26]; the percentage of major applications disapproved during the year [Godschalk and Hartzell, 1993]; percentage of disapprovals of public or private proposals to rezone, replan, extend services, or annex land in order to expand the land supply [Godschalk and Hartzell, 1993]; the proportion of applications accepted [Cheshire and Sheppard, 1989, 470]; the number of applications per 1,000 m^2 of the existing stock [Cheshire and Sheppard, 1989, 470]; the regulatory costs of housing — "costs associated with obtaining building permits, paying construction fees and taxes, securing utility service rights, and titling a new home" [Zearley, 1993, 246]; and the length of the development review period [Godschalk and Hartzell, 1993].

The Global Survey of Housing Indicators of 1990 contained a regulatory audit which sought (with only a modicum of success) to include measures of regulatory stringency. There were several questions in the audit about the existence or nonexistence of growth controls, for example. But as it turned out, 85% of the answers were positive. Growth controls, as such, were apparently ubiquitous. Almost all cities had them on the books in one form or another. More empirical measures, such as the *actual* percentage of land unavailable for growth, could not be obtained. A proxy indicator — the land conversion multiplier (see chapter 14) — attempted to measure the premium attached to a change in zoning from rural to urban land. But 20 out of the 53 responding consultants could not obtain a reliable number, so there were too many missing values to use it as a component of the Regulatory Regime Index.

The Regulatory Regime Index thus contains only one measure that is indirectly associated with strict growth controls: *permits delay*, defined as the median length in months to get approvals, permits, and titles for a new, medium size (50–200 unit) residential subdivision in an area at the urban fringe where residential development is permitted. It is assumed that in metropolitan areas where there is strong resistance to residential development, planning permission is likely to be more cumbersome. A second measure tries to capture the effect of zoning and land use controls: *minimum lot size*, defined as the minimum lot size for a single-family housing unit in a new 50–200-unit residential subdivision. It is assumed that in urban fringe communities that practice exclusionary zoning, minimum lot sizes are likely to be larger.

A third measure tries to capture the effect of building codes and standards: *minimum floor area*, defined as the minimum floor space per dwelling unit in private-sector construction. Similarly, it is assumed that building codes and standards that are not sensitive to affordability are likely to require higher minimum floor space per unit.[5]

The Regulatory Regime Index is a composite measure of three indicators — permits delay, minimum lot size, and minimum floor area. In the construction of the index, two of the indicators — minimum lot size and minimum floor area were normalized by dividing them by the median house size. It stands to reason that in cities with much larger houses, minimum lot size and minimum floor area would be larger, increasing gradually as the economy develops and as families are able to afford larger lots and larger houses. Normalizing these measures focuses on the appropriateness of these standards in the actual conditions in the housing market, rather than on their absolute values. Summary values for these three indicators (in their original, rather than normalized, form) and for the Regulatory Regime Index appear in table 11.1.

Permit delays for private-sector subdivisions varied considerably among countries, from a minimum of 2 months in 10 countries (Malawi, Côte d'Ivoire, Turkey, the former Czechoslovakia, Algeria, Russia, Greece, Singapore, Hong Kong, and France) to 20 months or more in nine other countries (Tanzania, Bangladesh, India, the Philippines, Colombia, Poland, Australia, Canada, and the United States). Among regions, Asia stood out with a high median value of 26 months for permits, while the Middle East and North Africa's median value was three months. The global median time required for permits was 6 months, which was identical to that of the industrialized countries, and slightly lower than that of the developing countries as a whole, eight months. There was, therefore, no observable correlation between this indicator and the Development Index.

The median minimum lot size was higher in the industrialized countries, 175 m^2, than in the developing countries as a whole, 100 m^2. The global median was between the two (125 m^2). Again, there was no correlation between this indicator and the Development Index. Among regions, Southern Africa stood out as having a particularly high median value (250 m^2), and Asia as having a particularly low one (64 m^2). Three countries reported no minimum lot size at all (Turkey, France, and Germany). In contrast, seven countries reported minimum lot sizes of 300 square meters or more (Tanzania, Malawi, Nigeria, Ghana, Zimbabwe, Russia, and Australia). Five of these countries were in Southern Africa, all former British colonies that have inherited their zoning and land use laws from their colonial administrations.

Median values for the minimum floor area increased with income among developing countries, and the median value for the developing countries as a whole (30 m^2) was similar to the median value for industrialized countries (25 m^2). As a result, there is a small negative correlation (-0.11) between this indicator and the Development Index. Among regions, the Middle East and North Africa had a particularly high median value (50 m^2), while Eastern Europe had a particularly low one (13 m^2). Ten countries (Nigeria, China, Jordan, Poland, Korea, Israel, Spain, Hong Kong, France, the United States, Sweden, and Japan) reported a zero value for this indicator. Canada reported the maximum value (84 m^2). Only four other countries (Senegal, Tunisia, Algeria, and Australia) reported values greater than 60 m^2.

Once we normalized the values for the minimum lot size and the minimum floor area in the construction of the Regulatory Regime Index, the picture changed. The index increased regularly with income, from a median value of 61 in the low-income countries, to a median value of 88 in the high-income ones. Its correlation with the Development Index was positive and relatively high (+0.51). Regulations, on the whole, appeared to be less severe in the higher-

Table 11.1. The Components of the Regulatory Regime Index, 1990.

Country Groupings	Permits Delay (months)	Minimum Lot Size (m^2)	Minimum Floor Area (m^2)	Regulatory Regime Index
Low-Income Countries	16	150	12	61
Low-Middle Income Countries	6	100	31	65
Upper Middle Income Countries	3	100	35	84
High-Income Countries	8	200	25	88
Southern Africa	6	250	19	62
Asia and the Pacific	26	64	23	68
Middle East and North Africa	3	100	50	72
Latin America and the Caribbean	6	100	34	83
Eastern Europe	5	200	13	74
All Developing Countries	6	100	30	68
Industrialized Countries	8	175	25	88
Global Average	12	171	28	71
Global Minimum	1	0	0	0
Global Median	6	125	28	76
Global Maximum	36	836	84	100
Global Standard Deviation	12	154	22	20
Correlation with Development Index	-0.02	-0.03	-0.11	0.51

Source: Housing Indicators Program [1994].

income countries, once their higher standards of living were taken into account. On the whole, developing countries had a median value of 68, and the industrial-ized countries had a median value of 88. Among developing–country regions, Latin America had a relatively high value (83) and Southern Africa a relatively low one (62). France, which did not have any minimum size restriction and reported a permit delay of two months, obtained the maximum value for this Index. Tanzania, with a minimum lot size of 336 m^2, and a reported permit delay of 36 months obtained the minimum value.

* * *

The regulatory regime has emerged as a key element of the policy environment affecting housing sector performance, and it is likely to gain in importance in the coming years. In an enabling housing policy environment, the regressive eco-nomic effects of growth–control regulations are not be overlooked. While there is ample room for keeping significant parts of the natural environment surround-ing cities for the use and enjoyment of their inhabitants, there is no need to restrict urban growth or to ration the amount of land available for residential develop-ment. The housing impact of environmental legislation aimed at curtailing growth must become a prime concern of the housing sector, restraining those who myopically pursue an environmental agenda while blatantly disregarding basic human needs. Second, in an enabling housing policy environment, pervasive exclusionary zoning practices must be abandoned in favor of those that encourage mixed land uses. There should be no unnecessary restrictions imposed on developers of residential land, allowing them to choose the most efficient combi-nation of land, labor, and capital for constructing housing. The minimal regula-tions necessary to promote health and safety must be transparent and well-understood, and there should be no inordinate delays in obtaining permits. Third, building codes and standards must not act to constrain the production of new affordable housing or the continued occupation of the existing stock of affordable housing. The use of police powers to demolish nonconforming houses en masse without adequate compensation or alternative housing must be abandoned. Housing standards need to be differentiated by income and affordability through consultation with communities affected by such standards, and government agencies owning and managing housing estates must also be subjected to these standards lest they have no incentive to reform them. As long as subsidies are in short supply, as they commonly are, authorities should continue to tolerate sub–standard housing. And to the extent that society is committed to increasing housing standards, such increases have to be accompanied by public subsidies that promote the gradual improvement and rehabilitation of existing units, as well as provide income support to families unable to afford prevailing house prices and rents in the private sector.

12

The Enabling Index

Most governments, both at the central and metropolitan level, do not yet approach housing policy in an integral fashion, nor do they coordinate housing policy with macroeconomic policies, social welfare policies, or urban development policies. They can be said to have some housing policies, but not *a* housing policy. Several European countries have adopted more comprehensive housing policies, moving toward managing the housing sector as a whole. This move has been gradual, and it has been easier in some countries than in others. Norway, Sweden, the Netherlands, and Germany, countries that had "less social divisiveness, and more coherence in managing the economy as a whole" stand out as having made more progress on this front [Pugh, 1980, 191], but on the whole the policy environment of the housing sector is still largely fragmented. Interestingly, in a number of countries, important elements of housing policy are already in place, but they are still not recognized as critical components of a comprehensive housing policy regime.

In this chapter, we focus on two objectives: first, integrating the housing policy regime into a single whole by creating an *Enabling Index*, which is a composite measure of its five components; and second, exploring the relations between the economic, social, and political context of the housing sector and the housing policy regime, with the aim of finding out what factors in this context give rise to a more enabling regime. We do so by employing two multiple regression models, statistical models that seek to explain the variations in the Enabling Index among countries as consequences of variations in their economic, social, and political context.

The Construction of the Enabling Index

The Enabling Index is a single composite measure of the housing policy environment. It provides a summary measure of the complex array of policy instruments discussed at length in chapters 7 to 11. Our key hypothesis — that housing policy matters — cannot be decided upon without resorting to some single measure of the housing policy environment, primitive as that measure may be. We can still examine relationships between individual components of the index and specific aspects of sector performance, but a simple measure of the policy environment as a whole can provide us with the simple insights we require to reduce the complexity of the issues at hand. This is clearly missing from past studies that focus on the effect of one single policy dimension (say the percentage of land unavailable for development) on one single outcome, such as the relative price of substandard housing [Malpezzi and Green, 1996, 1815]. Finally, we cannot avoid such simplification because the amount of data required to measure the effects of each and every instrument in the housing policy environment on each and every measure of sector performance is formidable and unlikely to be available in the foreseeable future.

The structure of the Enabling Index is presented in figure 12.1. A glance at the structure as a whole gives us a sense of the entire spectrum of policy concerns that make up an enabling housing policy environment—from the free exchange of property through negative real interest rates, foreclosure delay, the public housing stock, rent control, infrastructure expenditures, and minimum standards. All of these work together to affect housing sector performance. This complicated construction is surely a first effort. One must hope that a second- and third-generation construction of an index for the housing policy environment will include fewer and better indicators than those presented here and will be much simpler. The present experiment should be viewed only as a first attempt at quantifying the entire housing policy environment. But primitive as it may be, it already yields interesting and powerful results, as we shall see.

The Enabling Index was constructed in identical fashion to the indices presented earlier. It is an equally weighted composite index of five components: three on the demand side (the Property Rights Index, the Housing Finance Regime Index, and the Housing Subsidies Index) and two on the supply side (the Residential Infrastructure Index and the Regulatory Regime Index). Because the components are given equal weights, each contributes one-fifth to the Enabling Index. A subcomponent in turn contributes its share of the component to the overall index. For example, because the Regulatory Regime Index has three subcomponents, the indicator permits delay, for example, contributes a third to the Regulatory Regime Index, and one-fifteenth to the Enabling Index.

The five indices that together make up the Enabling Index are not necessarily independent of each other. Some of them are, in fact, highly correlated with each other.[1] The correlations among the indices are presented in table 12.1.

Summary values for the components of the Enabling Index and the index itself are presented in table 12.2. The first important observation is that the index attained higher values as incomes increased, from a value of 30 in low-income countries to a value of 83 in high-income ones. It also had a relatively high positive correlation with gross national product (GNP) per capita (+0.64). The median value for the developing countries as a whole was 49, while the median value for the industrialized countries was 85. These results strongly suggest that

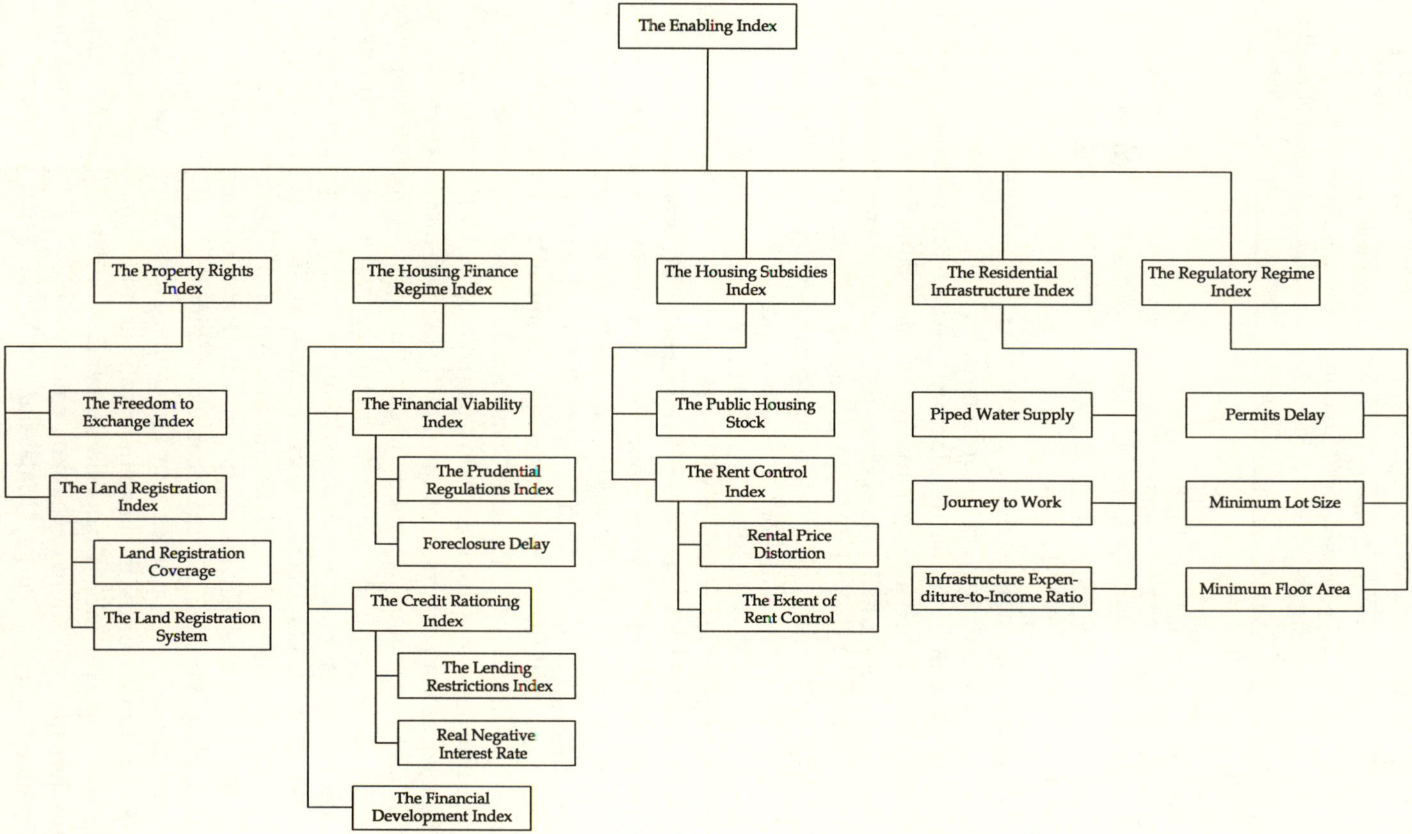

Figure 12.1. The Structure of the Enabling Index.

Table 12.1. The Correlations among the Housing Policy Indices, 1990.

Indices	Property Rights Index	Housing Finance Regime Index	Housing Subsidies Index	Residential Infra-structure Index	Regulatory Regime Index	Enabling Index
Property Rights	1.00					
Housing Finance Regime	0.50	1.00				
Housing Subsidies	0.27	0.55	1.00			
Residential Infrastructure	0.37	0.05	−0.25	1.00		
Regulatory Regime	0.25	0.11	−0.08	0.36	1.00	
Enabling	0.79	0.73	0.49	0.50	0.54	1.00

Source: Housing Indicators Program [1994].

housing policy becomes more enabling as countries become more developed economically, namely that progress toward a more enabling policy environment goes hand in hand with economic development. Among developing country regions, Eastern Europe had a particularly low median value for the index (21). Southern Africa and Asia had values close to the overall median (45 and 50 respectively). The middle East and North Africa had a slightly higher value (56) and Latin America had the highest value among the developing countries (62).

Figure 12.2 presents the values of the Enabling Index for each country (two-letter country labels are given in table 5.1 and table A1), graphed against GNP per capita. GNP per capita is presented in logarithmic form. The regression line between the two variables is also shown (with a correlation coefficient of 0.71). The line divides the sample into two groups of approximately equal size. If we consider the line to be an expected value of the index for each income level, we can see that although a country such as Kenya (KN) had a relatively high value on the index compared to countries of similar income, it had a lower absolute value than, say, Austria (AU). Relative to income, however, Kenya had a more enabling housing policy environment than Austria. Income, therefore, is expected to affect housing sector performance both directly (higher–income countries are expected to have better housing) and indirectly (through its effect on the policy environment). The graph also suggests that index values for the group of high–income countries were more clustered than those of the other three income groups. In fact, the standard deviation of the index for the high–income group was half that of the standard deviation of the rest of the sample.[2] This gives support to our hypothesis that housing policies do tend to converge and become more similar at the higher end of the income distribution.

Among the developing countries, four (Tanzania, China, Poland, and Russia) had values of 10 or less for the Enabling Index, and an additional seven (Malawi, Bangladesh, Madagascar, India, Ghana, the former Czechoslovakia, and Hungary) had values less than 40. Eight developing countries (Senegal, the Philippines, Jordan, Thailand, Jamaica, Turkey, Malaysia, and Mexico) had values of 70 or more for the index, with Mexico attaining the highest value of 87. Among the Industrialized countries, five countries (the United Kingdom, the United States,

Table 12.2. The Components of the Enabling Index, 1990.

Country Groupings	Property Rights Index	Housing Finance Regime index	Housing Subsidies Index	Residential Infra- structure Index	Regula- tory Regime Index	Enabling Index
Low–Income Countries	32	51	96	36	61	30
Low–Middle Income Countries	69	57	93	53	65	58
Upper Middle Income Countries	70	58	87	55	84	59
High–Income Countries	88	73	85	74	88	83
Southern Africa	38	59	94	31	62	45
Asia and the Pacific	74	54	92	48	68	50
Middle East and North Africa	62	54	82	64	72	56
Latin America and the Caribbean	66	59	94	45	83	62
Eastern Europe	36	36	9	62	74	21
All Developing Countries	62	55	91	46	68	49
Industrialized Countries	90	73	85	74	88	85
Global Average	65	61	79	57	71	60
Global Minimum	0	0	0	0	0	0
Global Median	73	62	88	56	76	69
Global Maximum	100	100	100	100	100	100
Global Standard Deviation	29	19	26	22	20	25
Correlation with GNP per capita	0.44	0.44	0.12	0.60	0.34	0.64

Source: Housing Indicators Program [1994].

Norway, Sweden, and Finland) had values higher than 90, with Finland attaining the maximum value of 100. Six industrialized countries (Israel, Spain, Singapore, Hong Kong, the Netherlands, and Austria) had values lower than 80, with the Netherlands attaining the lowest value among them, 57.

The Effects of the Economic, Social, and Political Context on the Housing Policy Environment

The quantitative values for the Enabling Index now make it possible for us to explore, in greater detail, what factors in the economic, social, and political context of the housing sector have a significant effect on the degree of enabling of a given housing policy regime. We already know that the level of economic development matters; looking at the graph, we can already suspect that Communist and former-Communist regimes are likely to have less enabling housing policy regimes. In the following paragraphs we seek to answer these questions with greater confidence, resorting to multiple regression statistical models. Referring back to the diagram illustrating the conceptual model of the housing sector (figure

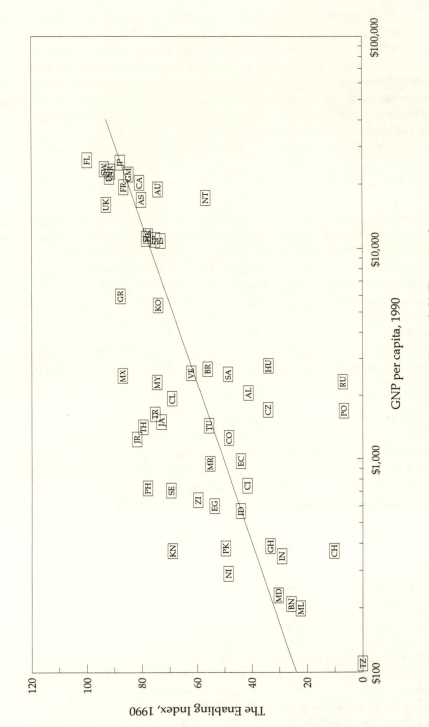

The Enabling Index, 1990

GNP per capita, 1990

Figure 12.2. The Enabling Index and GNP per capita.

6.1), we now focus on the first of six arrows in the diagram – the arrow postulating a causal relationship between the context and the policy environment.

Of 21 contextual indicators, to be discussed in greater detail in chapter 13, only a small number can be expected to have a direct policy impact on the housing policy environment. Among the income indicators, it stands to reason that the level of economic development, measured by GNP per capita, will affect the degree of enabling, as we saw earlier. More developed countries are likely to have more evolved regulatory regimes, more substantial public works programs, and more developed financial sectors. Among the social and political variables, only the Freedom Index (see chapter 13) is likely to affect the degree of enabling. We expect that countries with more democratic rights will have more enabling housing policies. Among the variables measuring the structure of the GNP, both government expenditures as a percentage of GDP and government welfare expenditures as a percentage of all expenditures are policy variables that can have a direct impact on housing policy, either by creating the necessary bureaucratic machinery needed to manage policy or by allocating more funds to residential infrastructure or to housing subsidies. Finally, among the money and interest variables, financial depth (see chapter 13) is likely to be associated with a more developed financial sector and hence with a more enabling housing finance regime.

Two statistical models were constructed to explained the variations in the Enabling Index using these indicators and indices as explanatory variables. The results of the first model are presented in table 12.3. The model had an R-squared of 0.64, indicating that variations in the explanatory variables explained almost two-thirds of the variations in the Index. More important, the model confirms the main hypotheses just discussed. It indicates that higher levels of economic development, measured by GNP per capita, were associated with positive increases in the index. Similarly, decreases in political freedoms and civil liberties (i.e., increases in the Freedom Index) were positively associated with increases in the Enabling Index, as expected. Higher government expenditures were also

Table 12.3. The Effect of the Economic, Social, and Political Context
on the Enabling Index, Model I.

Variable	β–coefficient[a]	t–statistic
Log GNP per capita	0.50	2.03**[b]
The Freedom Index	−0.35	−2.08**
Government expenditure as % of GDP	0.20	1.60*
Welfare expenditures as % of GDP	−0.40	−1.99**
Financial depth	0.20	1.45*
Number of Observations	34	
R-squared and Adjusted R-squared	0.64	0.57
$F_{5,28}$	9.91***	

Source: Housing Indicators Program [1994].

[a] For a definition of the β–coefficient, see chapter 6.

[b] ***,**, and * denote 1%, 5% and 10% levels of confidence, respectively.

associated with higher levels of enabling, as expected. An important result of the model is that welfare expenditure as a percentage of all expenditure was found to have a *negative* relation with the Enabling index — significant at the 5% level — suggesting that the index was not necessarily associated with redistribu-tive welfare policies. In fact, higher levels of the Index were associated with a *more skewed* distribution of income.

If we now add the income distribution variable to the model — *the income share of the lowest 40% of income earners* — we find that it also had a negative relationship with the Enabling Index, significant at the 1% level. This can be observed in Model II, presented in table 12.4. Although this model had fewer observations (27 as against 34) its R-squared was higher, 0.74, suggesting that it explained almost three-quarters of the variations in the Enabling Index. The significantly negative relationship with the income share variable is an important finding, because it suggests that an enabling housing policy environment is *not* associated with a more egalitarian distribution of income, such as, for example, that of the countries of Eastern Europe. In those countries, where political freedoms and civil liberties were still low in 1990, the median value of the income share of the lowest 40% of income earners was 25%, as against a global median of 17%. The Freedom Index did not exert a significant influence on the Enabling Index in this second model, and neither did government expenditures as a percentage of GDP or financial depth.

In interpreting these models we should keep in mind that even though these contextual indicators explained much of the variation in the Enabling Index, they did not explain all the variation. It should not be inferred, therefore, that housing policy as such is simply a logical extension of the economic, social, and political context that gives rise to it. It is not. Although housing policy is but a component of an overall policy environment, and although it is intimately related to policies in other fields, there is still considerable discretion in housing policy making that is not simply derivative of higher levels of policy. There is much to be gained in

Table 12.4. The effect of the economic, social, and political context
on the Enabling Index, Model II.

Variable	β–coefficient[a]	*t*–statistic
Log GNP per capita	0.74	3.13***[b]
The Freedom Index	–0.15	–0.79
Government expenditures as % of GDP	0.10	0.88
Welfare expenditures as % of all Expenditures	–0.45	–2.11**
Financial depth	0.08	0.55
Income share of the lowest 40% of income earners	–0.28	–2.68***
Number of Observations	27	
R-squared and Adjusted R-squared	0.74	0.66
$F_{6,20}$	9.43***	

Source: Housing Indicators Program [1994].
[a] For a definition of the β–coefficient, see chapter 6.
[b] ***,**, and * denote 1%, 5% and 10% levels of confidence, respectively.

housing sector performance from pursuing more-enabling housing policies in a variety of different economic, social, and political contexts.

* * *

The statistical models for the Enabling Index close Part II of this book. In this part, we elaborated on what constitutes an enabling housing policy environment, presenting its five key components in detail, and constructing a measure — the Enabling Index — that allowed us to distinguish between cities and countries on the basis of their housing policy environment. It remains to be demonstrated that a more-enabling policy environment indeed exerts a beneficial impact on housing market conditions and on specific housing market outcomes. This, then, is the central objective of Part III. This part is of a different character. Instead of the broad brush strokes employed Parts I and II, here we needed to use surgical tools in our treatment of large quantities of statistical data, and to follow established procedures lest we let oversight, shoddy workmanship, and imprecise language contaminate the results. This, in turn, rendered the writing more strained, and, given the limitations of the techniques employed, less incisive as well. For the most part, however, it was kept free of jargon and easily accessible to any reader with a minimal understanding of basic economic concepts.

Part III

Housing Policy and Housing Sector Performance

13

The Economic, Social, and Political Context

Part III of this book focuses on two questions of critical importance to the conduct of policies that rely on enabling housing markets to work: (a) how do we monitor housing market performance? and (b) how do we account for variations in housing market conditions and outcomes among cities and countries? This chapter initiates this discussion by examining the economic, social, and political context of the housing sector, with a view to identifying the elements of this context that are expected to have a direct bearing on housing market performance. Recall the conceptual model of the housing sector discussed in chapter 6: these contextual factors may influence housing market performance either indirectly (through their effects on the housing policy environment or on housing market conditions), or directly (as household income, for example, as an element of the context, affects the quantity or quality of housing on the market). Since our key emphasis here is on monitoring and modeling the sector, we shall pay special attention to those elements of the context that are measurable — and indeed have been measured — ignoring or mentioning only in passing factors that at present cannot be properly measured. Such concerns as, for example, the environmental orientation of the political party in power, the balance of power between suburbs and central cities, the distribution of authority among branches of government, the strength of nongovernmental organizations, the prevalence of mutual aid and cooperative traditions, the existence of corrupt bidding practices in the construction sector, religious and supernatural beliefs affecting the form of houses, and government suppression or encouragement of squatter movements have been largely excluded from the analysis in this part of the book. This should not imply, however, that these concerns are less significant than those factors that are measurable. The numbers we use do tell a good story, even a comprehensive one, as we shall see, but not the whole story.

The underlying hypothesis governing the inclusion or exclusion of contextual factors in this study is that the economic, social, and political context of the housing sector significantly affects the housing policy environment, housing market conditions, and housing market outcomes. It should be clear, for example, that bad housing is a reflection of poverty, and that growth in income should improve housing market performance. There is no possible way that a family in Malawi earning $700 a year can have a house of the same quality as a family in Germany earning 50 times that income. Hence household income, and the factors related to household income, are undoubtedly key measures of the context of the housing sector. The question is: What are the other important measures of the context that significantly affect housing? We seek to answer this question by looking for quantitative indicators in five different components of the context: (1) income and the level of economic development; (2) politics and society; (3) demography and geography; (4) the structure of the economy; and (5) financial and fiscal conditions.

Income and the Level of Economic Development

First and foremost, housing sector performance is expected to be strongly influenced by the performance of the economy as a whole. Indicators that measure and compare the level of economic development include the gross national product (GNP) per capita [World Bank,1992, table 1, 218–219] and the average annual growth rate of the gross domestic product (GDP) per capita [World Bank, 1992, table 2, 220–221]. Other indicators include measures of median household income, or the median household income of specific groups, such a renters, women–headed households, or the elderly. Still other indicators include measures of purchasing power parities. They also include measures of the *distribution* of income such as the percentage of the population below the poverty line, the income share of the lowest 40% of income–earning households, or the ratio of income shares of the highest 20% to the lowest 20% of income–earning households [UNDP, 1990, table 16,158–159].

The Global Survey of Housing Indicators of 1990 included data for five income–related indicators: The level of GNP per capita in the country, calculated by dividing the GNP by the country population and measured in U.S. dollars; the rate of change of country GDP between 1980 and 1990 as a measure of economic growth; the city median household income, also measured in dollars; the city median renter household income, also measured in dollars; and the country income share of the lowest 40% of income–earning households measured as a percentage of total national income. Summary values for the five income and economic development indicators are given in table 13.1.

We note immediately in table 13.1 that there was a vast disparity in income between the industrialized countries and the developing countries in the sample — the median GNP per capita for the former is 17 times that of the latter. The maximum GNP per capita in 1990 (that of Finland) was 260 times the minimum (that of Tanzania). Similar, although smaller, disparities were seen in the household income figures because families in the developing countries were considerably larger. The median household income for industrialized countries was eight times that of the developing countries. The maximum household

Table 13.1. Income and Economic Development Indicators, 1990.

Country Groupings	GNP per capita ($)	GDP Growth 1980–1990 (%)	Median Household Income ($)	Median Renter Household Income ($)	Income Share of Lowest 40% (%)
Low–Income Countries	350	4.2	1,241	1,241	19.6
Low–Middle Income Countries	1,110	3.0	3,290	3,111	16.3
Upper Middle Income Countries	2,510	1.6	5,189	4,925	13.6
High–Income Countries	19,275	3.2	29,199	23,446	18.4
Southern Africa	380	2.9	1,415	1,344	10.4
Asia and the Pacific	570	5.5	1,975	1,622	19.7
Middle East and North Africa	1,340	3.8	3,867	3,743	17.0
Latin America and the Caribbean	1,940	2.0	3,696	3,252	11.6
Eastern Europe	2,020	1.4	3,400	3,400	24.8
All Developing Countries	1,110	3.0	3,188	2,906	16.6
Industrialized Countries	19,060	3.1	26,080	23,118	18.4
Global Average	6,607	3.3	11,451	9,579	16.7
Global Minimum	110	0.5	692	692	7.0
Global Median	1,940	3.0	4,158	3,916	17.0
Global Maximum	26,040	9.7	49,667	41,000	25.7
Global Standard Deviation	8,386	2.0	13,365	10,642	4.2
Correlation with Development Index	0.86	–0.04	0.81	0.83	0.36

Sources: Housing Indicators Program [1994]; UNDP [1995, tables 12 and 28]; World Bank [1992, table 2, 220–221].

income — that in the United States — was more than 70 times the minimum (that of Malawi). Annual GDP growth in the period 1980–1990 was almost identical for the industrialized and the developing countries, around 3%, and varied from a global maximum of 9.7% in Korea to a global minimum of 0.5% in the Côte d'Ivoire. During this period, economies in the Asian region grew the fastest, while those in Eastern Europe grew the slowest.

While there were no significant differences in the distribution of income between industrialized and developing countries, there were considerable regional differences. The income share of the lowest 40% of income–earning families in Eastern Europe was almost 25%, with Hungary at a global maximum of 25.7%. In contrast, this share was only 10.4% in Southern Africa and 11.6% in Latin America and the Carribean, with Brazil at a global minimum of 7%.

The five income indicators were clearly not independent from each other. The correlations between median household income and median renter household income and GNP per capita were of the order of 0.95, suggesting that they are almost substitutes for each other — knowing one will enable us to predict the others with good precision. They were also all highly correlated with the Development Index as well, as we shall see at the end of this chapter. The rate of GDP growth was not at all related to the other indicators, and had an almost zero correlation (–0.04) with the Development Index. The latter was, however, positively correlated (+0.36) with the income distribution variable, suggesting that more developed countries tended to have more equitable income distributions.

Politics and Society

There is no doubt that the overall political context affects the housing policy environment. Housing policy is, after all, an extension (or at least a reflection) of the overall political orientation of governments, municipalities, and international agencies. Having said that, there are only a few measurable indicators of the overall political orientation of a given city or country. Countries are often differentiated as having market economies, economies in transition, or centrally planned economies. They can also be classified according to several proposed indices of political development: the Freedom Index [Freedom House, 1990], the Social Insurance Index (the existence of sickness benefit, work injury insurance, parents' cash benefit, child allowance, retirement pension, and unemployment insurance) [Priemus,1994,133], or the Corruption Index.[1]

The *social* context of the housing sector has been measured by a variety of indicators and composite indices. Indicators include the under–5 mortality rate per 1,000 live births (female and male), life expectancy at birth (female and male) [World Bank, 1992, table 32, 280–281], and the crime rate per 1,000 population (by type of crimes) [UNCHS, 1994, 19]. Composite indices include the UNDP Human Development Index (a composite measure of life expectancy, literacy, and real GDP per capita) [UNDP, 1990, 109–111, 128–129], and the Index of Social Progress (a composite index of 36 indicators measuring education, health status, women status, defense effort, economy, demography, disaster vulnerability, political participation, cultural diversity, and welfare effort) [Estes, 1988]. There have also been a number of attempts to classify cities according to a composite measure of their quality of life, using a variety of such indicators [Sufian, 1993].

The Global Survey of Housing Indicators of 1990 included data on four political and social indicators from published sources: The Freedom Index, life expectancy (measured in years), infant mortality (measured per 1,000 live births), and adult illiteracy (measured as a percentage of all adults). The Freedom Index [Freedom House, 1990] is a composite measure of the absence of political freedoms (free elections, de facto opposition, minority rights) and civil liberties (free press, the freedom to organize, equality under the law, independent judiciary).[2] It can be expected to affect the housing policy environment by making housing policy less, rather than more, enabling. Life expectancy and infant mortality may affect housing demand through their effects on population growth. Adult Illiteracy may have an indirect effect on housing demand through its influence on incomes. Summary results for these four indicators appear in table 13.2.

Looking at this table, we note that the Freedom Index decreased substantially with the level of economic development—it had a correlation of –0.75 with the Development Index. Its median value of 1.0 in the industrialized countries was considerably lower than the median value of 4.0 in the developing countries, with Southern Africa being the region with the lowest level of freedom and hence highest median value, 5.5, and with China at the maximum value of 7.0.

Table 13.2. Political and Social Indicators, 1990.

Country Groupings	Freedom Index	Life Expectancy at Birth (years)	Infant Mortality (per thousand)	Adult Illiteracy (%)
Low–Income Countries	5.5	55	98	40
Low–Middle Income Countries	3.5	67	50	20
Upper Middle Income Countries	3.5	70	17	13
High–Income Countries	1.0	77	7	3
Southern Africa	5.5	54	90	40
Asia and the Pacific	3.0	64	41	23
Middle East and North Africa	4.3	66	63	39
Latin America and the Caribbean	2.0	70	37	13
Eastern Europe	4.5	71	15	n.a.
All Developing Countries	4.0	65	57	23
Industrialized Countries	1.0	77	7	3
Global Average	3.3	67	42	21
Global Minimum	1.0	46	5	3
Global Median	3.5	70	32	13
Global Maximum	7.0	79	149	65
Global Standard Deviation	1.8	9	37	20
Correlation with Development Index	–0.75	0.91	–0.89	–0.78

Sources: Freedom House [1990, 18–20]; World Bank [1992, tables 1 and 28].

The three other social indicators were strongly related to the level of economic development, with correlations with the Development Index of the order of 0.8–0.9. As expected, countries with lower incomes had a lower life expectancy. Life expectancy was lowest in Southern Africa with a median value of 54, and highest in the industrialized countries with a median value of 77. Malawi had the lowest value (46) and Japan the highest value (79). Similarly, industrialized countries had much lower rates of infant mortality—7 per 1,000 live births as against 57 for the developing countries as a whole, and 90 for Southern Africa. Again, Japan had the lowest value (5) and Malawi the highest (149). Adult illiteracy was less than 5% in the industrialized countries, 27% in developing countries as a whole, higher in Southern Africa and the Middle East, and up to 65% in Pakistan.

Demography and Geography

The demographic context of the housing sector can be expected to affect it directly through the generation of demand for housing. Demographic indicators include measures of the country population; the urban population and its structure; the urban population as a percentage of total population; the annual growth rate of the urban population [World Bank, 1992, table 31, 278–279]; the annual rate of rural–urban migration, the natural urban growth rate [Kadas,1991, 213–220], and the annual rate of urban or regional outmigration [Gibb and Maclennan, 1991, 304].

Indicators that measure the structure of the population include household size, the rate of household formation, and the number of marriages and divorces [Woodfield, 1989, 70]. Demographic measures of particular segments of the urban population with specific housing attributes include the percentage of married couples with two incomes [Wright, 1993, 267], the proportion of one-person households as a percentage of all households [Kettnaker and Rosberg, 1994, 34], the proportion of the population 65 years in age and above [Colleen and Lindgren, 1994, 75], and the proportion of single-parent households with children [Kettnaker and Rosberg, 1994, 35]. Two other demographic indicators that can be expected to affect the housing sector are the central city growth rate and the growth rate of the rest of the metropolitan area [Malpezzi, 1994, 3].

Geographic indicators that affect the housing sector include measures of the built-up area and its expansion, measures of urban density — such as the gross population density of the city (persons per square kilometer) [Grimes, 1976, 116-126; UNDP, 1990, table 17, 160-161], or the number of dwellings per square kilometer [Boelhouwer and van der Heijden, 1992, 34]. Another important geographic indicator, residential segregation, was found to be difficult to measure and was therefore not included in the Global Survey.[3] Housing sector performance may also be affected by the location of employment opportunities, specifically by the growth of urban employment and its distribution, as measured, for example, by the share of metropolitan job growth outside central city [Coyle, 1978 in Wright, 1993, 270]. Specific environmental indicators that may affect the housing design and production costs include, for example, climatic measures — such as mean annual temperature or the mean precipitation rate — as well as indicators of environmental vulnerability, such as the annual average fatality rate from natural disasters per million population [Estes, 1988, 20, 31-32].

The Global Survey included only four demographic and geographic indicators with a potential affect on housing sector performance: the level of urbanization (measured as a percent of the country population living in urban areas), the annual growth rate of the urban population, the average household size, and the overall urban density (measured in persons per square kilometer of built-up area). Summary values for these four indicators appear in table 13.3.

A cursory look at this table shows that the first three variables were clearly associated with the level of economic development. Their correlations with the Development Index were of the order of 0.80. The level of urbanization increased with economic development from a median of 31% in low-income countries to 78% in high-income ones, and 100% in Singapore. Among the developing countries, Latin America was already highly urbanized in 1990, while Asia and Africa were only one-third urbanized. Malawi was only 12% urbanized. The urban growth rate slowed down considerably as countries became more urbanized and more countries developed economically. The rate slowed down from

Table 13.3. Demographic and Geographic Indicators, 1990.

Country Groupings	Percent Urbanized (%)	Annual City Growth Rate (%)	Household Size	Density (persons per km²)
Low-Income Countries	31	4.4	5.2	10,350
Low-Middle Income Countries	50	3.9	4.6	6,300
Upper Middle Income Countries	73	2.7	4.0	6,600
High-Income Countries	81	1.4	2.6	4,600
Southern Africa	33	4.5	5.0	5,800
Asia and the Pacific	32	3.6	5.0	13,800
Middle East and North Africa	53	3.7	5.2	6,600
Latin America and the Caribbean	73	3.1	4.3	5,700
Eastern Europe	69	0.1	2.6	6,500
All Developing Countries	50	3.7	4.7	6,600
Industrialized Countries	78	1.3	2.6	6,600
Global Average	59	2.8	4.1	9,886
Global Minimum	12	-1.1	1.9	1,600
Global Median	61	3.1	4.1	6,600
Global Maximum	100	6.9	7.7	39,700
Global Standard Deviation	23	1.8	1.5	8,306
Correlation with Development Index	0.76	-0.82	-0.80	-0.01

Sources: Housing Indicators Program [1994]; World Bank [1992, table 31, 278–279].

4.4% per annum in low-income countries to 1.4% in high-income ones. It was the highest in Southern Africa (4.5%), with a maximum of 6.9% in Tanzania, and lowest in Eastern Europe (0.1%). It was actually negative in Moscow in 1990, (–1.1%). Cities in poorer countries, therefore, faced the most severe population pressures and, given their low incomes, the most serious challenges to their housing systems.

Household size also declined with increased levels of economic development. It was the highest in low-income countries (5.2), and half of that value in high-income countries (2.6). Among regions, it was highest in Africa, Asia, and the Middle East, with a maximum of 7.7 in Senegal; it was lowest in Eastern Europe and the industrialized countries, with a minimum of 1.9 in the Netherlands.

The fourth indicator in this table, urban population density, was not at all related to the level of economic development, with identical median values of 6,600 persons per km² in both developing and industrialized countries. It was the highest in Asia and the Pacific, with a maximum of 39,700 persons per km² in Hong Kong, and lowest in the Industrialized countries with 1,600 persons per km² in Washington, D.C. Unlike the first three demographic variables, its correlation with the Development Index was practically zero.

The Structure of the Economy

The resources — both private and public — available for housing are not only a function of the total level of resources in the economy, but also of the allocation of these resources among different uses. The housing sector may therefore be affected by the overall structure of the economy, commonly measured by the share of consumption, savings, and investment in the GDP. Other important measures of the structure of the GDP that may affect housing sector performance include the ratio of private consumption to GDP [World Bank, 1992, table 9, 234–235]; gross domestic savings as a percent of GDP [UNDP, 1990, table 22, 170–171]; personal savings as a percentage of personal disposable income [U.N. data, in McGuire, 1981, 31]; and household debt as a percentage of household disposable income [Renaud, 1994, 29]. All of these measures may have an affect on the ability of households to save for housing. The structure and levels of capital investment may also have a bearing on housing investment, in particular gross fixed capital formation [United Nations, 1992, table 2, 4–6], non–residential investment [Currie, 1990, chart 5], the rates of return on residential and nonresidential investments, and net capital inflows [Renaud, 1994, 10].

The structure of government expenditures in the GDP may also affect housing sector performance. The fiscal deficit as a percentage of GNP [Kaufmann, 1991; UNDP, 1990, table 22, 170–171], for example, may have a direct bearing on levels of housing subsidies. The level of central government expenditure as a percentage of GNP may affect overall public investment in both housing and urban infrastructure. And the percent of central government expenditure devoted to housing, amenities, social security, and welfare [World Bank, 1992, table 11, 238–239] may affect public housing expenditures.

The Global Survey included only four measures of the structure of the GDP: government expenditures as a percentage of GDP; consumption as a percentage of GDP; government welfare expenditures as a percentage of all government expenditures; and gross domestic investment as a percentage of GDP. Summary values for these four indicators appear in table 13.4.

The first indicator, government expenditures as a percentage of the gross domestic product, appeared to increase with the level of economic development, from 10% in low–income countries to 18% in high–income countries, and its correlation with the Development Index was +0.38. It was the lowest in Eastern Europe and Asia, with a minimum of 7% in Poland, and highest in the industrialized countries, with a maximum of 39% in Israel. The second indicator, Consumption as a Percentage of GDP, decreased with the level of economic development, and had a negative correlation (–0.55) with the Development Index. The third indicator, Government welfare expenditures (housing, amenities, social security and welfare) as a percentage of all government expenditures, was much more strongly related to income, with a correlation of almost 0.90 with the Development Index. It increased from a median of 3.6% in low–income countries, to 37.4% in high–income ones. It was the lowest in Africa and Asia, higher in the Middle East,

Table 13.4. Indicators of the Structure of the Gross National Product, 1990.

Country Groupings	Government Expenditure as % of GDP	Consump- tion as % of GDP	Government Welfare Expenditure as % of Total Exp.	Gross Domestic Investment as % of GDP
Low–Income Countries	10.0	70.4	3.6	19.0
Low–Middle Income Countries	14.0	66.3	4.9	22.5
Upper Middle Income Countries	14.5	61.8	22.7	22.0
High–Income Countries	18.0	58.8	37.4	21.5
Southern Africa	12.5	69.9	3.8	18.0
Asia and the Pacific	10.0	62.0	5.8	34.0
Middle East and North Africa	15.0	66.9	13.1	24.5
Latin America and the Caribbean	15.0	64.8	20.1	20.0
Eastern Europe	10.5	63.5	25.3	30.0
All Developing Countries	11.5	64.8	8.0	22.0
Industrialized Countries	18.0	58.8	37.4	21.0
Global Average	14.8	63.7	21.7	23.3
Global Minimum	7.0	44.3	1.5	9.0
Global Median	15.0	63.2	17.8	22.0
Global Maximum	29.0	87.8	55.9	39.0
Global Standard Deviation	5.4	9.3	16.2	7.1
Correlation with Development Index	0.38	–0.55	0.89	0.22

Sources: IMF [1998,166–169]; World Bank [1992, tables 9 and 11].

and still higher in Latin America (20.1%). Its value for Eastern Europe (25.3%) was considerably lower than that of the industrialized countries (37.4%), with a global maximum of 55.9% in Sweden. The fourth indicator, gross domestic investment as a Percentage of the GDP, was weakly related to the level of economic development, and its correlation with the Development Index was +0.22. Its values for the developing countries and for the industrialized countries were quite similar — of the order of 20%, with higher values for Asia, and a global maximum for Singapore at 39%.

Financial and Fiscal Conditions

Overall monetary policy as well as tax and subsidy policies exert a number of powerful effects on the housing sector, many of which have been discussed in detail in previous chapters. Monetary policy and the performance of the financial sector as a whole may affect housing sector performance through their effects on the mortgage market and on the availability of credit for construction. Measures related to their performance include the prime interest rate, the nominal and real time-deposit rate [Renaud, 1989, 6], and the financial depth of the economy (M2/GDP).[4] Overall inflation, measured as the annual change in the consumer price index [Renaud, 1989, 6] may also have an affect on the mortgage market. High inflation is typically not conducive to mortgage lending, and indexation systems designed to correct for inflation tend to collapse when inflation exceeds 50% per annum [Buckley, 1996, 88].

Four general money and interest indicators were included in the Global Survey: the prime interest rate, the deposit interest rate, the average annual rate of inflation between 1980 and 1990, and the country's financial depth measured as the ratio of the quantity of money and quasi-money (M2) and GDP [IMF, 1998, country tables, 180–923]. The difference between the two rates (prime minus deposit) may be seen as an indicator of the efficiency and competitiveness of the financial sector as a whole. The differences between each rate and the rate of inflation are the *real* prime and deposit rates, that may be either positive or negative. The summary values for these indicators appear in table 13.5.

The global median values for the prime and deposit interest rates in 1990 were 14.9% and 12.8%, respectively. Given the global median inflation rate of 9.5% in 1990, the median real rates were 5.4% and 3.3%, respectively. Both the prime and the deposit interest rates appeared to decrease with the level of economic development, but both had almost negligible correlations with the Development Index (−0.3 and −0.09, respectively). Their raw values were, of course, strongly related to the annual rate of inflation. Interest rates were higher in countries with higher levels of inflation. The deposit rate was at a maximum in Brazil, which also had the highest value for the rate of inflation in the sample in 1990. The prime rate was at a minimum in Japan (6.0%), while the deposit rate was at a minimum in Germany (3.5%). The average annual rate of inflation in the 1980s was higher

Table 13.5. Money and Interest Indicators, 1990.

Country Groupings	Prime Interest Rate (%)	Deposit Interest Rate (%)	Annual Inflation 1980–1990 (%)	Financial Depth (M2/GDP)
Low–Income Countries	17	16	10	0.13
Low–Middle Income Countries	17	14	11	0.26
Upper Middle Income Countries	28	18	14	0.29
High–Income Countries	12	9	6	0.45
Southern Africa	17	15	15	0.10
Asia and the Pacific	15	12	7	0.31
Middle East and North Africa	12	9	7	0.37
Latin America and the Caribbean	31	32	25	0.13
Eastern Europe	80	15	9	0.37
All Developing Countries	20	15	11	0.23
Industrialized Countries	12	9	6	0.46
Global Average	25	42	20	0.35
Global Minimum	6	4	2	0.03
Global Median	15	13	8	0.31
Global Maximum	217	1,067	284	1.04
Global Standard Deviation	33	155	41	0.24
Correlation with Development Index	−0.03	−0.06	−0.09	0.51

Sources: Housing Indicators Program [1994]; World Bank [1992, table 1, 218–219].

in the developing countries as a whole (11%) than in the industrialized countries (6%), and had a very small negative correlation (–0.09) with the Development Index.

The fourth indicator, financial depth, measures the ratio of the quantity of money in the economy (M2) and the GDP. A high value for this indicator could be associated with a more developed financial sector, a factor that could be a precondition for a more developed housing finance sector. This indicator did appear to have a positive relationship with the level of economic development, with a correlation of +0.51 with the Development Index. Its global median value was 0.31. Median values increased from 0.13 in the low–income countries to 0.45 in the high–income countries. Among the developing countries, the values were low in Africa and Latin America, with a minimum value of 0.03 in Ghana. The values were higher in the Middle East and in Eastern Europe, with a maximum value of 1.04 in Malaysia.

The Development Index

All in all, data on 21 indicators of the economic, social, and political context of the housing sector have been discussed so far. It is easy to conclude from our short review of these indicators that underlying most of the context indicators was the level of economic development. Indeed, if we take the GNP per capita as the simplest measure of economic development, we note that most of the indicators discussed here were correlated with it in one way or another. The actual correlations are summarized in table 13.6; half of the correlations with GNP per capita were greater than 0.5, and five more were above 0.25.

Grouping these highly correlated indicators into one composite index has considerable merit. It can give us a measure that can go beyond GNP per capita to include social and demographic indicators, indicators that are more distributive in character and more in line with our intuitive perception of "development." An important attempt to create such a composite measure was indeed made by the United Nations Development Programme (UNDP) in 1990. The Human Development Index developed by UNDP is a composite index of three indicators — real GDP per capita, life expectancy, and adult literacy) [UNDP, 1990, 109–111, 128–129]. In line with our discussion of composite indices in Chapter 4, we can use our considerably–larger number of context indicators to create a more comprehensive *Development Index*.

This index was constructed from 12 of the indicators listed in table 13.6.[5] Summary values for the index are given in table 13.7. Individual country values are given in table A1. As expected, the Development Index increased with income, from a median value of 16 in the low–income countries to a value of 86 in the high–income countries. Among the developing countries, it was lowest in southern Africa (15), higher in Asia and the Middle East, still higher in Latin America, and the highest in Eastern Europe (65), almost double the median for the developing countries as a whole. The range of variation in the index was 100

Table 13.6. The Context Indicators and their Correlation with
GNP per Capita and with the Development Index, 1990.

Indicator	Correlation with GNP per Capita	Correlation with the Development Index
Gross national product per capita[a]	1.00	0.86
Change in GNP per capita 1980–1990[b]	-0.04	-0.04
Median household income[a]	0.95	0.81
Median renter household income	0.93	0.83
Income share of lowest 40% of population[a]	0.25	0.36
The freedom index[a]	-0.73	-0.75
Life expectancy at birth[a]	0.69	0.91
Infant mortality per 1,000 live births[a]	-0.65	-0.89
Adult illiteracy[a]	-0.64	-0.78
Percent of country population in urban areas[a]	0.60	0.76
Annual rate of city population growth[a]	-0.57	-0.82
Household size[a]	-0.69	-0.80
Gross urban population density[b]	-0.07	-0.01
Government expenditures as a % of GDP	0.41	0.38
Consumption as a % of GDP	-0.43	-0.55
Government welfare expenditure as a % of Expenditures[a]	0.83	0.88
Gross domestic investment as a % of GDP[b]	0.04	0.22
The prime interest rate	-0.26	-0.03
The deposit interest rate[b]	-0.13	-0.06
The annual rate of inflation[b]	-0.16	-0.09
Country financial depth (M2/GDP)[a]	0.39	0.51

Source: Housing Indicators Program [1994].
[a]   Components of the Development Index.
[b]   Correlation with GNP per capita smaller, in absolute value, than 0.25.

— it reached its maximum of 100 in Japan and its minimum of 0 in Tanzania. Table 13.6 shows that it was highly correlated with income measures, with the Freedom Index, with key social indicators, with the welfare orientation of government, with a number of demographic indicators, and with financial depth. Not surprisingly, the index was highly correlated (the correlation coefficient is +0.90) with the Human Development Index mentioned previously, which is actually a composite index of three of the twelve indicators that make up the Development Index. It was not correlated, however, with the rate of economic growth, with the share of investment in GDP, with interest rates and inflation, or with urban population density.

The Development Index was used in the following chapters in place of GNP per capita as a single composite measure for the context of the housing sector taken as a whole. In the foregoing statistical analysis, however, we did not use the Development Index; we instead identified particular context indicators that were expected to exert a significant influence on the particular aspect of housing that we sought to explain. In short, *development* by itself explains a considerable

Table 13.7. The Development Index, 1990.

Country Groupings	Development Index
Low–Income Countries	16
Low–Middle Income Countries	35
Upper Middle Income Countries	44
High–Income Countries	86
Southern Africa	15
Asia and the Pacific	37
Middle East and North Africa	34
Latin America and the Caribbean	41
Eastern Europe	65
All Developing Countries	34
Industrialized Countries	85
Global Average	49
Global Minimum	0
Global Median	42
Global Maximum	100
Global Standard Deviation	29

Source: Housing Indicators Program [1994].

amount of variation in housing outcomes, but not enough. For a more comprehensive understanding of housing policy, we need a more refined explanation of the various effects of the economic, social, and political context on the housing sector, one that development as a single cause cannot bring out.

* * *

This chapter summarizes the first of four elements in our model of the housing sector presented in chapter 6 — the economic, social, and political context of the housing sector. Part II of the book elaborated on the second element of our model — the housing policy environment. Chapters 14, 15 and 16 will elaborate on housing market conditions, the third element in our model.

14

The Availability of Land

Land and Housing

The first essential condition for a vibrant and well-functioning housing sector is the availability of residential land, in ample supply and at affordable prices. For example, throughout the twentieth, when land in the rapidly urbanizing developing countries was available and affordable, poor migrants to the cities could and did house themselves — gradually building houses and communities through self-help and mutual aid — without government aid, without access to mortgage credit, and without entering the formal housing market. Access to land in these cities was indeed the key to affordable housing, and in many places it still is.

In this chapter we focus on the factors that affect the supply of urban land for housing. Other than geographical features (such as steep or muddy slopes or flood-prone river beds) that limit the availability of buildable urban land, the key influences on the availability of residential land are three components of the housing policy environment: the property rights regime, infrastructure development, and the regulatory regime. A fourth factor affecting the supply of residential land is the competition from other land uses or land hoarding as a form of saving, as a hedge against inflation, or as speculative investment.

The property rights regime affects the availability of land in a number of ways. First, a more primitive regime, with more land being part of the commons or with private persons and public agencies having weak or unenforceable claims on land, allows for the alienation of lands for residential use at no (financial) cost:

> Customary chiefs, religious leaders, patrons, and grass root political bureaucracies have been instrumental in settling new migrants to the city on public, private, and customary land. Initially, these submarkets did not involve any form of transaction or exchange of money as a price for the plot, rather, the act of "settling" implied a formal act of allegiance, symbolic subservience, and integration into a client network under the authority of a local patron. [Durand-Lasserve, 1990, 47]

Second, when formal land markets are not sufficiently developed, they may give rise to informal land markets. Formal land markets require proper surveying and title registration, and development of such lands for housing requires conformance to subdivision regulations, zoning and land use ordinances, and infrastructure standards. When formal land markets are weak and regulatory enforcement is uneven or nonexistent, informal markets on the fringes of cities supply affordable residential sites, often replacing squatting on common lands, disputed lands, or lands with weak claims.

Both squatter settlements and informal land subdivisions slowly give way to formal land markets. But the speeds at which the regularization of squatter settlements, or the provision of public infrastructure services in informal land subdivisions, occur are very much a question of policy. Enabling housing policy regimes in the developing countries have been faster to recognize that such settlements provide the only affordable housing alternative available, have refrained from demolitions and evictions, have pronounced that these settlements are here to stay, and have engaged in connecting these settlements to urban infrastructure networks. Nonenabling regimes have continued to harass and evict squatter families and have used the squatters' illegality as a means of gaining political leverage over the settlements as well as an excuse for failing to provide infrastructure.

Infrastructure policy by itself affects the availability of land as well. First, the extension of roads and services to new areas bring more land into urban use. When roads, water supply, electricity, sewerage systems, and telecommunication lines are extended into new areas, the supply of land increases. Conversely, when they are artificially constrained, the supply of residential land is restricted. Payne [1982], for example, documents the role of the Turkish *dolmus*—the popular jitneys—in initially providing cheap transport access to newly settled areas around Ankara and then restricting and even denying it:

> The development of these popular transport systems at the time of the city's rapid growth enabled new areas to be opened up for settlement and ensured a steady supply of land at low cost . . . [D]uring the 1970s, the operators exerted influence through their unions to restrict any expansion of their transport network to cope with increased demand. This not only enabled them to increase their rates and reduce "turnaround" times, but also raised the transfer value of their vehicles and their licence plates, since both are a secure form of high income. [127, 134]

Infrastructure policy can be directly engaged in residential land development, through planning for urban expansion and through the coordinated provision of integrated service networks. Conversely, it can ignore land development completely, focusing only on the extension of each network in relative isolation from other networks. At one end of the scale, as in Korea [Yoon, 1994, 58–59] and Tunisia [Hardoy and Satterthwaite, 1989, 130], government agencies take over the land development function. They acquire peripheral urban land, develop it, and then sell it to private developers. In land pooling and readjustment schemes in Japan for example, rural land owners pool their lands, and, together with government agencies, provide it with infrastructure, and then reallocate the remaining land among them for sale to urban users.

Sites–and–services projects, promoted by the World Bank during the 1970s and 1980s, can also be seen as governmental attempts to simulate and micromanage the informal land development process, by developing minimal infrastructure and selling serviced sites to households who then build on them. In terms of scale, however, such direct public involvement methods have usually provided considerably less residential land than indirect methods of land development. Indirect methods coordinate the expansion of trunk infrastructure services by central government agencies into new development areas, leaving the extension of secondary networks to lower levels of government, and the provision of services within macroblocks to the developers of land subdivisions. The developers of land subdivisions may be in the formal or informal sector, organized communities, or nongovernmental organizations.

Infrastructure planning, in and of itself, may also affect the availability of land for the urban poor. Lim [1983], for example, noted that haphazard and less–than–optimal land use and road layouts have increased the land available to the poor for housing, allowing them to use the less accessible, and the least desirable plots that exist in between the more formal plots, for housing. On the other hand, "when proper urban land use planning is introduced, block layouts are made regular, all plots become equally accessible, and the land values of the entire area are largely equalized. The result is that no room is left for the poor" [397].

The regulatory regime, as we already noted, also acts to reduce or restrain the availability of land. Urban growth controls, restrictions on land use, restrictions on density, restrictions on building form, and insistence on high standards — however noble their intentions may be — all act to limit and constrain the supply of residential land in general, and hence the supply of affordable residential land in particular. Regulations may also restrict the supply of land to a specific segment of the market, while choking off supply to other market segments. The Delhi Development Authority, for example, froze 30,000 hectares of land around New Delhi between 1959 and 1964, announcing its intention to purchase it and then lease it out "to individuals and cooperative societies on an equitable basis, so that the benefit of planned growth accrues to the common man" [Buch, quoted in Sarin, 1983, 242]. Most of this land was never acquired by the authority; instead it was sold illegally by the original landowners for the construction of unauthorized colonies that largely served the middle–class [Sarin,1983, 242–244], and that were eventually legalized.

In addition, regulations may have the effect of clouding property rights and thus slowing down market transactions. The Indian Urban Land (Ceiling and Regulation) Act of 1976 had such an effect. The Act decreed that any vacant urban land in excess of a ceiling ranging from 500 to 2,000 m^2 could be acquired by the government at nominal cost. "[T]he transfer of all urban property was frozen except after securing permission from the competent authority, in order to prevent evasion of the law." Almost all landowners filed for exemptions, and by 1981, only 2% of vacant land was acquired by the government [Sarin, 1983, 245]. In the meantime, the act had the effect of slowing the land market to a near standstill for a few years.

Finally, the availability of land for residential development is affected by the competition for land from other land users and from land hoarders. For example, where no other investment opportunities are available or under conditions of rampant inflation, people may have no choice but to hoard land. By restricting land supply, hoarding may have the effect of increasing land prices, creating a further incentive to hoard land. In general, the taxation of vacant land to force it into use and other attempts to restrain land speculation have been less than effective. Only the development of investment alternatives or the control of inflation can really remove the incentives to hoard land. In addition, an unrestricted supply of land for residential development reduces the incentive for speculation in land, as land becomes no more and no less profitable to hold than other, possibly more liquid, assets.

With the singular exception of the settlement of customary lands at the periphery of cities, which may involve nonmonetary transactions (and, in a few cases, the nationalization of land following a revolution), the supply of land is informed by land prices. We should expect the following:

- land in growing and richer cities will be more expensive than land in shrinking and poorer ones;
- land in larger and denser cities will be more expensive than land in smaller and more dispersed ones;
- land in more developed markets will be more expensive than land in more primitive ones;
- land with legal title will be more expensive than either land with a clouded title, land in illegal occupation, or land threatened by clearance;
- centrally located land or land near places of employment will be more expensive than peripheral land located away from employment opportunities;
- land with good transport access will be more expensive than land with little or no transport access;
- lands with a full complement of amenities will be more expensive than land lacking in such amenities;
- land protected from environmental hazards will be more expensive than land in disaster-prone or hazardous locations;
- land in cities with strict growth controls will be more expensive than land in cities with lax controls;
- land in stable and safe communities will be more expensive than land in transient and crime-ridden ones; and
- land in cities with many nonresidential uses competing for it will be more expensive than land with few such competitors.

Measures of Land Availability

While it is sensible to expect that land prices reflect all the qualities just listed, collecting land price data and building models that can demonstrate these relationships statistically is an altogether different matter. There are numerous studies that show land prices declining as distance from the city center decreases, or increasing as the result of growth controls. There are also studies that show land prices in squatter settlements increasing with the age of the settlement, with regularization of tenure, or with improved infrastructure. All in all, however, studies that link land prices to the host of possible effects mentioned here are few and far between. While land prices are regularly assessed by tax authorities in many countries, good and accurate land data are difficult to obtain, let alone compile into meaningful aggregate measures, such as the average land cost per plot [Peterson et al., 1991, 42], or the annual land price increase [Renaud, 1989, 6].

The Global Survey of Housing Indicators of 1990 obtained three measures of land availability, and all three relied on expert estimates of land prices based on conversations with real estate brokers, rather than on inclusive surveys. The following discussion should therefore be viewed as a preliminary exercise in paving a roadway to future, more robust analyses, rather than one seeking to arrive at authoritative conclusions.

Consultants were asked to obtain two values — a median raw–land price and a median serviced-land price in a typical area on the urban fringe now undergoing development — and to use the ratio of these two values to obtain a measure of the premium associated with the provision of urban infrastructure, the land development multiplier. The latter was taken to be a measure of scarcity of urban infrastructure. When it is high, it indicates that the provision of infrastructure is in short supply, hence making serviced land highly profitable. When it is low, it indicates that bringing urban services to raw land is not especially difficult, and that the process of transforming raw land to serviced land is free of bottlenecks, rationing, or budgetary limitations. More precisely:

1. *the raw–land price* is defined as the median price of raw, undeveloped land in an area currently being developed;
2. *the serviced–land price* is defined as the median land price of a developed plot at the urban fringe in a typical subdivision; and
3. *the land development multiplier* is defined as the ratio between the serviced-land price and the raw-land price.

Since, when these prices are compared among countries, they are found to be highly correlated with household incomes, for international comparisons we need to define two additional measures that normalize them by income:

4. *the raw–land price–to–income ratio* is defined as the ratio of the raw–land price and median household income; and
5. *the serviced–land price–to–income ratio* is defined as the ratio of the serviced–land price and median household income.

These two measures are indeed measures of the affordability of urban land. One of these measures — the raw–land price-to-income ratio — yields very similar results to that of the serviced–land price-to-income ratio, and will not be discussed further. Data for a third land indicator were obtained in the Global Survey:

6. *the land conversion multiplier* is defined as the ratio between the median land price of an unserviced plot on the urban fringe given planning permission for residential development, and the median price of a nearby plot in rural–agricultural use without such permission.

This latter indicator seeks to measure the premium associated with converting rural to urban land. When its value is low, it suggests that there are no serious urban growth controls that limit residential expansion. When it is high, it suggests that regulations do limit urban expansion, and that they are likely to affect land prices and hence house prices. The summary results for these measures of land availability are presented in table 14.1.

The raw–land price exhibited a much lower correlation with the Development Index (+0.39) than, say, construction cost (+0.75). There were also very wide disparities between different countries in the same region. In the industrialized countries, for example, the reported value was $50 per m^2 or less for nine countries, and over $300 in four other countries: $331 in Singapore, $727 in Germany, $1,280 in Hong Kong and $1,490 in Japan. Among developing countries, the variations were not so extreme. There were only three countries with values over $50: Thailand ($58) which experienced a building boom at the end of the 1980s; Jamaica ($62); and Korea ($809), where land development was still seriously lagging behind demand. The developing countries as a whole had lower median values for this indicator, $7, as against $47 for the industrialized countries. Among developing country regions, Southern Africa and Latin America had exceptionally low median raw–land prices ($3 and $4 per m^2, respectively). Four countries in Southern Africa (Tanzania, Malawi, Nigeria, and Ghana) reported median values of less than $1 for one sq.m. of raw land. Asian countries reported the highest median value among the developing countries, $24 per m^2 of raw land.

The serviced–land price, although higher than raw–land prices, exhibited a very similar pattern, a relatively low correlation with the Development Index (+0.41), wide disparities within regions, and higher median values for the industrialized countries — $140 per m^2, in comparison with the developing countries as a whole, $29 per m^2. Among developing-country regions, the Middle East and North Africa had the highest median value, $90 per m^2, followed by Asia ($70), and Eastern Europe ($60). Southern Africa and Latin America, which reported low raw–land prices, also report low serviced land prices ($13 and $14 per m^2, respectively). Two African countries (Tanzania and Nigeria) reported median values of less than $2 per m^2, while Japan reported a median value of $2,980, more than a thousandfold multiple of that of Tanzania and a much higher multiple than the income multiple between these countries.

Table 14.1. Measures of Land Availability, 1990.

Country Groupings	Raw Land Price ($/m²)	Serviced Land Price ($/m²)	Serviced Land Price–to–Income Ratio (%)	Land Development Multiplier	Land Conversion Multiplier
Low–Income Countries	2	12	0.7	3.8	1.8
Low–Middle Income Countries	8	63	2.1	4.0	3.9
Upper Middle Income Countries	6	41	0.8	5.2	5.2
High–Income Countries	47	125	0.7	2.4	6.3
Southern Africa	3	13	0.4	5.6	2.7
Asia and the Pacific	24	70	2.5	2.6	2.2
Middle East and North Africa	10	90	2.8	5.0	4.8
Latin America and the Caribbean	4	14	0.5	3.4	4.5
Eastern Europe	11	60	1.3	3.7	3.9
All Developing Countries	7	29	1.1	4.0	3.4
Industrialized Countries	47	140	0.8	2.4	6.3
Global Average	124	219	1.9	4.7	11.1
Global Minimum	0	1	0.1	1.1	0.8
Global Median	18	69	0.9	3.5	4.4
Global Maximum	1,488	2,977	10.2	16.6	115.0
Global Standard Deviation	317	501	2.2	3.7	23.0
Correlation with Development Index	0.39	0.41	0.07	–0.39	0.38

Source: Housing Indicators Program [1994].

The serviced–land price–to–income ratio seeks to focus on the price of land relative to income, in other words on the affordability of land. Indeed, in Dar es Salaam, Tanzania, a square meter of land costs only 0.2% of annual household income, while in Tokyo it costs 7.8%. Residential land was much less affordable in Tokyo than in Dar es Salaam. This indicator, once normalized by income, no longer exhibited a correlation with the Development Index (+0.07). Residential land appeared to be slightly more affordable in the developing countries as a whole, where a square meter of serviced land cost 0.8% of annual household income, than in the industrialized countries where it cost 1.1% of income. Among developing–country regions, however, two regions reported higher–than–median values — 2.5% in Asia, and 2.8% in the Middle East and North Africa. All in all, more than 20 countries reported values of less than 1% for this indicator, with eight countries (Tanzania, Nigeria, South Africa, Brazil, Australia, Canada, Norway, and Sweden) reporting values of 0.2% or less. In contrast, seven countries (Thailand, Bangladesh, Zimbabwe, Madagascar, Egypt, Japan, and Hong Kong) reported median values of more than 3%, with Hong Kong reporting the maximum value for this indicator, 10.2%.

The land development multiplier simply measured the ratio of the serviced -land price and the raw-land price, and hence the premium (and indirectly the cost) associated with servicing land. The multiplier was lower in the industrialized countries (2.4) than in the developing countries as a whole (4.0) and therefore exhibited a negative correlation with the Development Index (-0.39). Among developing-country regions, it was higher than the median value in Southern Africa (5.6) and in the Middle East and North Africa (5.0). Among the five countries that reported raw-land prices above $300, four had low values for multiplier: 1.3 for Korea, 1.3 for Singapore, 1.2 for Hong Kong, and 1.1 for Germany. This suggests that in these land markets, the multiplier largely reflected the actual cost of providing infrastructure rather than any premium associated with servicing land. It was 2.0 for Japan, however, suggesting that in this case there was still a substantial premium associated with servicing land, which was much higher than the expected cost of servicing it. The land development multiplier reached very high values, attaining a maximum of 16.6 in Malawi. Altogether, nine other countries (Mexico, South Africa, the Philippines, Kenya, Egypt, Turkey, Spain, Ghana ,and Zimbabwe) reported values of 6.0 or more for this indicator. Surely, these high values reflect, in part, the cost of providing infrastructure, in Africa for example. But they may also reflect artificial land shortages created by lags, rationing, budgetary limits, or regulatory barriers in infrastructure provision.

The land conversion multiplier focuses on the regulatory and property-rights regimes, seeking to measure the premium associated with converting rural to urban land, a premium associated exclusively with the policy regime. On the whole, the median value for the sample as a whole was found to be quite high (4.4), suggesting that there is a very significant global difficulty in converting rural land to urban land. The median value for this multiplier was found to be still higher in the industrialized countries (6.3) in comparison with the developing countries as a whole (3.4). It was also found to be positively correlated with the Development Index (+0.38). Both findings suggest that in more developed countries there were stricter restrictions on converting rural land to urban land, or alternatively that as countries developed more restrictions were being placed on urban expansion. Among developing countries, the Middle East and North Africa and Latin America were found to have higher than median values (4.8 and 4.5, respectively). Lower than median values were reported for Asia (2.2) and Southern Africa (2.7). Six countries (Nigeria, Kenya, Jordan, Tanzania, Thailand, and Russia) reported values of 2.0 or less for this indicator. In these countries, land conversion may be said to be rather smooth and free of regulatory obstacles. In contrast, five countries report values of 10.0 or more: Morocco (10.0), Japan (10.4), Zimbabwe (13.3), Netherlands (80.0), and Norway (115.0). In the latter two especially, it appeared virtually impossible to covert rural land to urban land.

The Determinants of Land Availability

Given these five measures of the availability of residential land, the question is: What is responsible for the wide variations among countries along these measures? To begin with, the previous discussion suggests that a number of these measures are affected by the level of economic development, which can be represented by the GNP per capita. Prices may also be affected by the level of urbanization of the country as a whole, a measure highly correlated with GNP per capita. They may also be affected by the size and the density of the city – larger cities may command higher land prices on the urban fringe to reflect the greater access they provide to a wide range of urban services, and denser cities may command higher land prices to reflect the more intensive use of land. Land prices may also be affected by rates of growth, both of the economy as a whole and of the urban population, as growth exerts greater pressures for developing urban land, thereby leading to higher land prices. Finally, prices may be influenced by the housing policy environment – better infrastructure, a more enabling property rights regime and a more sensible regulatory regime may lead to lower land prices. The results of four statistical models of land availability are summarized in Table 14.2. The model for the raw-land price is not included in the discussion, because it provides very similar results to that of the serviced-land price model.

The four models in table 14.2 all posit six explanatory variables: the GNP per capita (in logarithmic form), the GNP growth rate 1980-1990, the urban growth rate, the city population (in logarithmic form), the city's density (in logarithmic form) and the Enabling Index. The model for the serviced-land price is presented in the top row in the table. It has only 26 observations because of the inclusion of the density variable, for which many values are missing. The model has a R-squared of 0.49, explaining nearly half the observed variation in the serviced-land price. It did not yield very interesting results. As expected, this price was higher for higher-income countries, and higher for higher-density cities. The Enabling Index (in its present construction, which does not incorporate limits on urban growth) had no appreciable effects on land prices, and neither did the rate of economic growth, the rate of urban population growth, or city size.

The second model, presented in the second row in table 14.2, replaced the serviced land price with the serviced-land price-to-income ratio, thus normalizing it by income and transforming it into a measure of the affordability of land. This model had a higher R-squared value of 0.70 explaining a larger portion of the variation than the first indicator. In this model, the GNP per capita still had a significant effect on land prices, and the effect of density was now more significant than before. In addition, the serviced-land price-to-income ratio was significantly affected by the rate of economic growth. Faster growing economies were associated with higher values for this indicator than slower-growing ones. The model tells us that density exerted the strongest influence on the serviced land price-to-income ratio, followed by the level of economic development, and

Table 14.2. The Determinants of Land Price and Availability.

Variable	Log of GNP per Capita	GNP Growth Rate 1980-1990	Urban Growth Rate	Log of City Population	Log of Density (persons per km²)	The Enabling Index	No. of observations	R-squared & Adjusted R-squared	F-Value
Serviced land price ($/m²)	0.84[a]	0.16	0.12	0.08	0.57	-0.16	26	0.49	$F_{6,19}$
	1.71*[b]	0.62	0.32	0.35	2.26**[c]	-0.50		0.33	3.06**[b]
Serviced land price-to-income ratio	0.52	0.35	0.12	0.06	0.64	-0.12	26	0.70	$F_{6,19}$
	1.60*	2.05**	0.46	0.42	3.76***	-0.54		0.61	7.46***
The land development multiplier	-0.97	-0.13	-0.48	-0.22	-0.09	0.26	25	0.44	$F_{6,18}$
	-2.33**	-0.64	-1.46*	-1.22	-0.45	0.91		0.26	2.40*
The land conversion multiplier	0.62	-0.07	-0.01	-0.40	0.04	-0.10	22	0.22	$F_{6,15}$
	2.40**	-0.36	-0.03	-2.26**	0.23	-0.55		0.18	5.77***

Source: Housing Indicators Program [1994].

[a] Figures in the top rows are standardized β–coefficients.
[b] Figures in italics denote t– and F–statistics.
[c] ***, **, and * denote 1%, 5% and 10% levels of confidence, respectively.

by the level of economic growth. Again, the Enabling Index did not exert a significant effect on land prices, and neither did city size or the rate of urban population growth.

The third model, presented in the third row in table 14.2, poses the land development multiplier as the dependent variable, with the same explanatory variables as in the earlier two models. This model had an R-squared value of 0.44, explaining less than half of the variation in the indicator. The only two variables that appeared to exert a significant influence on the Land development multiplier were the level of economic development and the rate of urban population growth. More developed countries had lower multipliers, as we saw before. Similarly, cities with faster-growing populations, not faster-growing economies, had lower premiums associated with land development. Again, there was no significant effect of the enabling index, the city's population, or density.

The fourth model, presented in the fourth row in table 14.2, examined the determinants of the land conversion multiplier. The model had a considerably lower R-squared value of 0.22, explaining less than a quarter of the variation in the land conversion multiplier. This multiplier, as expected, increased significantly with the level of economic development: more-developed countries tended to place more restrictions on urban growth than less-developed ones. It also decreased significantly with city size, suggesting that urban growth controls may be more prevalent in smaller cities than in larger ones. Again, the Enabling Index, in its present construction, did not exert a significant effect on the land conversion multiplier, and neither did the GNP growth rate, the rate of urban population growth, or density.

* * *

To conclude, given that the Enabling Index did not incorporate an effective measure of the existence of growth controls — such as the percentage of land unavailable for development — it was not found to have a significant statistical effect on the availability of land. No doubt, there is already some statistical evidence that does demonstrate the effect of strict regulations and growth controls on land prices. The discussion of the escalation of land prices in California in the 1970s in chapter 11 is one important example, and there are others. This effect appears to be widespread and rather worrisome, but the Global Survey data could not demonstrate it conclusively. Land prices were found to be significantly higher in more developed economies and in cities with higher densities, even when normalized for income. In addition, when normalized for income, land prices were found to be less affordable in cities in faster-growing economies than in cities in slower-growing ones. The premium associated with providing raw land with infrastructure, the land development multiplier, was also found to be lower in more developed countries and in faster-growing cities. Finally, the premium associated with converting land from rural to urban use, the land conversion multiplier, was found to increase significantly with the level of economic development: more-developed countries tended to place more restrictions on urban growth than less–developed ones. It also decreased significantly with city size, suggesting that urban growth controls may be more prevalent in smaller cities than in larger ones. All in all, however, the land price data collected for this study were found wanting. Patterns did begin to emerge, but a deeper understanding of the multiple effects of contextual and policy variables must await more systematic comparative studies in the years to come.

15

Conditions in the Residential Construction Sector

A second set of housing market conditions – the conditions in the residential construction sector – requires a deeper understanding of house-building as seen from the perspective of the builders themselves. Ample and affordable housing relies heavily on the builders' ability to produce it inexpensively and quickly, as well as to respond creatively to changes in the context and the policy environment governing the sector. Whether or not conditions in the house-building industry allow it to do so is of fundamental concern to housing policy. An enabling housing policy should create conditions for that industry that, at the very least, lower construction costs for a given level of quality. In this chapter we introduce the perspective of builders. We then discuss monitoring and measurement in the residential construction sector, and finally, we investigate what accounts for the variations in conditions in the sector.

The Perspective of Builders

Building is the making of places to dwell. In the words of Heidegger: "The nature of building is letting dwell. . . Only if we are capable of dwelling, only then can we build" [Heidegger, 1971, 108]. The making of houses to dwell is rooted very deeply in us: "The passion for building enclosures, or for adopting, for taking possession of an enclosed volume under a chair or table as a cozy place for making a home, is one of the commonest of all children's games" [Isaacs, 1933, quoted in Rykwert, 1981, 191]. It is a primitive creative urge that connects us to our basic nature. In a fundamental sense, we are all home builders:

> The primitive hut – the home of the first man – is therefore no incidental concern of theorists, no casual ingredient of myth or ritual. The return to origins always implies a rethinking of what you do customarily, an attempt to renew the validity of your everyday actions, or simply a recall of the natural (or even divine) sanction for your repeating them for a season. In the present rethinking of why we build and what we build for, the primitive hut will, I suggest, retain its validity as a reminder of the original and therefore essential meaning of all building for people. [Rykwert, 1981, 200]

From ancient times to the present day, people the world over built their own homes, or participated — in one form or another — in bringing it into being. Surely, specialization, the division of labor, mechanization, the development of sophisticated markets, and the intervention of activist governments moved many of us away from the original act of building our own abode with our own hands. But we are still fascinated watching a house spring up from the ground. There is still magic in the making of places and this magic still attracts many home builders — often clouding their better judgment regarding the strictly economic sense of their pursuits. In the house building industry, it should be noted, some people are not in it for the money, even though most may be in it to make a living.

A typical building industry includes a large number of distinctive home builders. These include those who find, assemble, and subdivide land for residential development; the manufacturers and distributers of a great variety of building materials; people in the building trades, contractors and subcontractors; corporations engaged in the development and marketing of housing estates; public agencies engaged in the production of residential infrastructure and amenities; and housing authorities building and managing the public housing stock. A builder can be a single person with a toolbox building a squatter house, a small crew remodeling an apartment, or a large industrial conglomerate building an entire new town. Builders can also be individual households engaged in building, renovating, or extending their own house in a variety of capacities. They can be government agencies, semigovernment agencies, cooperatives, private corporations, or nonprofit organizations. And they can also be combinations of those producers — households participating in a government self-help housing scheme, or a group of private companies building public housing for a local authority.

To a large extent, the industry is typically fragmented with many types of builders operating in the same market. The structure of the building industry indeed varies from the highly fragmented (say in the present-day United States) to the highly monopolistic (say in pre-1990 Russia). Mature as the industry in the United States may be, the majority of building firms have one or more partners or family members and no employees at all. In 1992, for example, the *Census of Construction* reported that of nearly 2 million businesses operating in the construction industry, 65% had only self-employed workers and no paid employees on their payroll. Lest one suspect that the industry is gradually consolidating, an earlier census reported that in 1967 there were only 54% of construction firms without employees on their payrolls [Finkel, 1997, 32].

The structure of the industry in the United States — and in all other open-market economies — very clearly fits the definition of a fragmented industry given by Porter [1990] as "an industry in which no firm has a significant market share and can strongly influence the industry outcome" [191]. It shares a large number of inherent characteristics with other fragmented industries: low barriers to entry, low capital requirements, high transportation costs, high inventory costs or erratic sales fluctuations, no monopolies on inputs (such as land, materials, equipment, or labor), no proprietary technology, no customer loyalty, diseconomies of scale in at least some important aspects, low overhead, a highly diverse product, heavy creative content, close local regulation and control, local image and local contacts, diverse market needs, and high product differentiation [Porter, 1990, 7-13, 196-200].

"The underlying structure of a fragmented industry makes dominance futile unless that structure can be fundamentally changed. Barring this, a company trying to gain a dominant share of a fragmented industry is usually doomed to failure" [Porter, 1990, 210]. And while companies have usually stayed out of the race to dominance (most clearly in residential construction), governments have not. Indeed, practically all governments were seduced, at one time or another during the twentieth century, into playing a dominant role in housing construction, promising mass production of "machines for living" with firm convictions in the existence of vast economies of scale. The dirigiste city-state of Singapore stands out as a fine and singular example of a successful government dominance in housing production, successful in the sense of efficient and productive — not necessarily in the sense of meeting the rich diversity of needs of its population. All other countries, with rapidly urbanizing China the last to give in, have been gradually trimming their failing state construction conglomerates, and moving toward a higher level of fragmentation.

How do builders perceive a well-functioning housing sector? From the perspective of builders, in a well-functioning housing sector licensing requirements, regulations, or monopolistic practices do not impede any builder or group of builders from engaging in residential construction. Regulations do not restrict producers from creating a large variety of housing arrangements and combinations, substituting among different inputs and characteristics to meet changing conditions. There are many entrepreneurs who can participate in housing production at all scales, there is sufficient incentive for them to enter the sector, and there is normal risk of business failure. Producers engage in building for all income groups, do not shy away from any segment of the housing market, and pay sufficient attention to renovation of the existing stock, as well as to rental housing. At the same time, dwellers themselves can also engage in self-help or self-managed building of houses, extensions, renovation, or repairs without necessarily requiring professional assistance.

Housing production typically moves through a number of stages as economies mature, as consumer preferences change, as more sophisticated markets develop, as mortgages become available, as property rights become established, as the enforcement of regulations takes hold, and as builders are able to assemble larger amounts of capital. Similarly, housing production evolves as building technology develops, as more work formerly done on the construction site can be prefabricated, as entrepreneurs and workers become more organized, as information becomes more reliable, and as governments refine and adjust their interventions in the sector. To take one example, in Bangkok between 1974 and 1984, the share of land-and-house projects (with optional mortgage-financing) grew from 3.7%

to 14.4% of the total stock, the share of public housing grew from 3.5% to 4.3%, and the share of slums declined from 25.2% to 17.8% of the stock [Angel and Dowall, 1987, table 3.5, 31].

Varied as they may be, home builders are subject to a common set of problems. They are all subject to high fluctuations in the demand for housing, some inherent in the product itself, and some the result of government monetary policies that are essential to the regulation of overall economic activity. Because of the long life of houses, the existing stock of dwellings is very large in relation to annual production. New annual production is typically of the order of 2% to 3% of the total housing stock, and therefore "small fluctuations in the demand for the stock of buildings and works will have very large repercussions on the demand for the buildings and works created by the industry" [Hillebrandt, 1974, 11].

Demand for new housing fluctuates both seasonally and cyclically. For example, records from seventeenth century city of Hull in England note that, between 1653 and 1678, bricklayers worked 11% of their total annual man–days in winter, 22.3% in spring, 38.2% in summer and 28.5% in autumn [Woodward, 1995, 135]. More recent records for the United States, for example, show 75% more housing starts in June than in January [Rosen, 1979, table 6.1, 118]. Rosen noted that:

> Seasonal fluctuations are one of the all–pervasive characteristics of housing markets in general, and of the new residential construction market in particular. Wide-spread shut-downs and curtailment of activities, a 25 percent decline in production and employment, a swelling of the unemployment and relief roles, idle plants, and capital equipment, and sharp rise in the inventory of unsold products are all consequences of the normal seasonal (defined as fluctuations within an annual period occurring on a regular basis over a number of years) decline in the residential construction industry. [xvii]

Rosen observed that the technology for building in winter indeed exists, but that demand for new houses picks up in the summer largely because people schedule their moves to coincide with the school year and because marriages take place predominantly in the summer.

Short–term housing cycles are no less severe. In the United States, for example, between 1953 and 1975, activity in new residential construction underwent seven full short–term cycles, occurring approximately every three and one–half years [Rosen, 1979, 118]. Topel and Rosen [1988] reported that for the 1963–84 period "an expansion doubles the output of new homes and a contraction cuts it in half" [720]. Many analysts noted that these cycles were largely influenced by monetary policy, where the tightening or expansion of credit by the federal government was used to constrain or accelerate housing starts, and therefore to reduce inflationary pressures or to jump–start the economy. Since new construction is such a small fraction of total housing demand, its curtailment to, say, two-thirds of its average output will reduce overall housing consumption by only 1%. It has been suggested, therefore, that "the industry would be wise to accept that it is subject to fluctuations and that both it and government must find ways to alleviate some of the undesirable effects of fluctuations" [Hillebrandt, 1974, 22].

In a well-functioning housing sector, severe fluctuations in production during economic downturns are cushioned — by allowing interest rates to attain market levels rather than by rationing mortgage credit, or by channeling credit to the mortgage market through public institutions.[1] Furthermore, the housing sector does not take the full brunt of the impact of monetary policy; and the burden is shared with other segments of the construction sector, for example, through the phasing of public works projects.

Beyond being subject to sometimes-severe fluctuations in demand and in the availability of credit, home builders face additional problems that usually have to do with their being part of a broader construction sector, the regulation of their activity by government, and constraints or irregularities in the supply of essential inputs — land, labor and expertise, materials, equipment, working capital, and information. Construction volume in a typical city usually breaks down into one-third to one-half residential building, one-fourth to one-third non- residential building, and one-fourth to one-third public works (utilities, highways, streets, dams, water supply, sewerage and drainage, and military construction) [U.S. Department of Commerce, 1978, in Lange and Mills, 1979, table 5-6, 107; Whitehead, 1974, 22]. Governments, larger construction firms, and international firms are usually much more involved in public works than in residential construction. And this can mean that building codes, technological developments, building-material rationing, or collective bargaining agreements take place without the active participation of home builders. In a well-functioning housing sector, home builders have a powerful voice in such matters, commensurate with their overall share in overall production, not with the size of their individual firms.

In a well-functioning housing sector, all construction inputs are in adequate supply; there are no shortages and no rationing. There is an adequate supply of desirable land where residential neighborhoods can be built. Infrastructure networks are adequate, and they reach out to new residential developments in a timely fashion. An adequate variety of standardized building materials is available, locally produced or imported if necessary, as is construction equipment, and those can be transported efficiently to building sites. The quality of building materials is controlled. Sufficient numbers of skilled and unskilled construction workers in all the building trades are available. Well-trained and experienced building professionals — engineers, land surveyors, architects, planners, quantity surveyors, accountants, lawyers, real-estate economists, and construction managers are in adequate supply.

In addition, costs of all construction inputs are stable and predictable, and allow construction of dwelling units in a wide range of prices to meet all housing demand. Adequate construction financing is available. The residential construction sector is not discriminated against by special tariffs or controls, and it can freely compete for investment funds in capital markets.

Finally, regulations concerning land development, land use, building, land tenure, taxation, or special programs are well defined and predictable, and government application of these is efficient, timely, and uniform. Beyond that, builders are not prevented from adopting innovations in the use of new materials, building designs, construction methods, mass production techniques, and management practices. Contracts among all actors are enforceable, and the settling of disputes is reliable and efficient. Builders can respond to changing demand without the undue delay caused by unpredictable and time-consuming regulatory practices. And there is adequate information to enable them to forecast the demand for their products with reasonable certainty.

In general, there are no fundamental conflicts among home builders, beyond those attributed to unfair competition: large monopoly producers, particularly in quarrying or material production, often seek to bar entry of smaller new producers into the sector. Others have been found to engage in corrupt bidding practices to win large public works contracts at the expense of more efficient competitors. Public housing agencies often excused themselves from regulations binding on the private sector, while arguing against a regulatory reform that will enable private-sector producers to meet low-income housing demand. Still, the over-riding common interests of home builders far outweigh their knack for unfair competition. It is in their interest to create and implement a vision of a well-functioning housing sector that protects all home builders, resolves the conflicts among them, and allows them a wide range of choices while ensuring that competition among them is strong and fair.

Monitoring and Measurement in the Residential Construction Sector

How do we monitor the residential construction sector? The structure of the sector is often measured by the number of construction firms with a given number of employees [United Nations, 1992, table 12, 64-70; Whitehead, 1974, 38]; building and construction business failures as percent of all failures [Whitehead, 1974, 38]; construction industry employment [United Nations, 1992, table 11, 62-63], and unemployment [Colleen, 1994b, 82]. Measures of the levels of construction cost and its components include the house construction cost per square meter [Grimes, 1976, 131-143; Whitehead, 1974, 28]; the house construction cost index [Strassmann, 1982, 92]; input and output price indices, and wholesale price indices of building materials [United Nations, 1992, tables 13-15, 71-82]; and the transaction cost (taxes and other costs) as a percentage of house price [Bramley, 1994, 89].

The Global Survey of Housing Indicators of 1990 assembled data on five indicators reflecting conditions in the residential construction sector:

1. *construction cost,* defined as the present replacement cost (labor, materials, on-site infrastructure, management and contractor profits) per square meter of a median–priced dwelling unit;
2. *building time,* defined as the median time (in months), from the start of construction to completion, of a median–priced dwelling unit;
3. *industrial concentration,* defined as the percentage of new formal-sector housing units placed on the market by the five largest developers (either private or public) in a given year;
4. *the skill ratio,* defined as the ratio between the median wage of a construction worker with at least five years of experience in a skilled trade (e.g. carpentry or masonry) and the median wage of an unskilled construction laborer; and
5. *the import share of construction,* defined as the percentage share (in value terms) of residential construction materials that are imported in a given year.

Of particular interest to housing market outcomes are two of these five indicators, construction cost and building time. The first, construction cost, is expected to have a direct effect on housing supply — higher costs of construction are expected to lead to higher costs of supplying housing, and hence to a reduced supply of housing units for a given level of demand. The second indicator, building time, may have an adverse effect on the responsiveness of supply to changes in demand, or in econometric terms, on the price elasticity of supply. The summary values for the conditions in the construction sector are shown in table 15.1.

Not surprisingly, the cost of construction per square meter of a median–priced house or flat varied with the level of economic development. It was more than 10 times higher in high–income countries than in low–income ones, and it had a very high degree of correlation (+0.75) with the Development Index. Among developing–country regions, it was lowest in Southern Africa and Asia, and highest in Latin America. The median value for industrialized countries, $749, was more than five times that of the median value for the developing countries, $142. The minimum value reported for this indicator was $17 in Malawi. In addition to Malawi, 10 other countries reported value of less than $100: four in Africa (Tanzania, Madagascar, Nigeria, and Ghana), four in Asia (China, Pakistan, India, and Indonesia), and Egypt and Venezuela. Among the industrialized countries, six countries (Austria, Germany, Norway, Sweden, Finland, and Japan) reported values higher than $1,000. Japan had by far the highest value ($2,604), more than 50% higher than the next highest value, $1,734 for Finland.

No orderly pattern could be observed for building time, except that it was higher than expected in the Eastern European countries that relied largely on the construction of prefabricated high–rise apartments with outdated technology.

Table 15.1. Conditions in the Construction Sector, 1990.

Country Groupings	Construc-tion Cost ($/m²)	Building Time (months)	Industrial Concent-ration (%)	Skill Ratio	Import Share of Construc-tion (%)
Low–Income Countries	77	11	32	2.3	11
Low–Middle Income Countries	156	8	32	2.0	20
Upper Middle Income Countries	203	18	55	1.9	9
High–Income Countries	870	10	23	1.4	11
Southern Africa	91	5	32	2.4	23
Asia and the Pacific	100	12	54	2.0	5
Middle East and North Africa	153	11	30	2.0	25
Latin America and the Caribbean	171	10	59	2.0	10
Eastern Europe	149	27	46	1.8	7
All Developing Countries	142	12	44	2.0	11
Industrialized Countries	749	10	22	1.4	11
Global Average	428	13	41	1.9	17
Global Minimum	17	2	1	1.1	0
Global Median	171	12	33	1.9	11
Global Maximum	2,604	37	100	4.5	80
Global Standard Deviation	513	9	28	0.7	17
Correlation with Development Index	0.75	0.02	–0.10	–0.43	–0.13

Source: Housing Indicators Program [1994].

Seven countries reported values equal to or higher than 24 months: Poland, 37 months; Nigeria, 36; Zimbabwe and the former Czechoslovakia, 30 each; Tanzania, 28, and India and Malaysia, 24 each. Values of 3 months or less were reported by eight countries: Malawi, Kenya, Indonesia, Côte d'Ivoire, and South Africa, 2 months; and the Philippines, Australia, and Austria, 3 months.

A high value for industrial concentration suggests that large numbers of housing units are built by a small number of construction conglomerates. The maximum value for this indicator, 100% concentration, was found in Moscow, where in 1990, as we noted earlier, all construction was still under the auspices of the all–powerful Moscow Construction Committee. Hungary and Poland, that were never as centralized as the Soviet Union, reported values of less than 50% for this indicator. Four countries reported very low values for this indicator: Nigeria and Greece (1%), Jordan (4%), and Thailand (9%). All in all, industrial concentration was found to be twice as high in the developing countries as a whole (44%) than in the industrialized countries (22%), suggesting that economic development was not associated with the creation of monopolies in the residential construction sector, but rather with increased fragmentation. The typical house construction industry remains largely fragmented, especially in modern car–oriented cities with expansive suburban fringes. This does not preclude the movement toward concentration and globalization both in the housing finance sector and in the urban infrastructure sector discussed in the earlier chapters.

The skill ratio indicator has been proposed as a measure of the shortage of skilled construction workers, and at the same time of a more developed building industry. It was assumed that if there is no shortage of skilled construction workers, their wages will be closer to those of unskilled workers. Also, it was assumed that the utilization of more advanced building technologies will tend to lower the wage differential between skilled and unskilled workers. The industrialized countries as a whole had a lower median value for this indicator, 1.4, compared with the value for the developing countries as a whole, 2.0. The skill ratio indeed had a negative correlation with the Development Index (–0.43) and decreased as income increased, from 2.3 in low–income countries to 1.4 in high–income ones. Values of 3.0 or more for the skill ratio were reported for six countries: Malawi, Zimbabwe, South Africa, China, India, and Poland. Poland reported a maximum value of 4.5. In contrast, six countries reported values of 1.2 or less for the skill ratio: Madagascar, Colombia, Spain, Australia, Austria, and Norway.

Generally, the most basic imports in the construction sector are cement (or the energy to produce cement), primary metals, and construction machinery. The import share of construction is sometimes seen as a factor in increasing construction costs because of the high costs of imports compared with local building materials, and in delaying the development of the local building materials industry. This perception often results in restrictions on imports of building materials and equipment, which may have the opposite effect of restricting productivity growth and increasing construction costs. No orderly pattern could be observed for this indicator in the Global Survey. Southern Africa and the Middle East reported more than double the median values (26% and 25%, respectively) than all other regions (11%). The Asian region reported a low median value of 5%, and Eastern Europe a low value of 7%. Five countries reported importing more than a third (in value terms) of the materials necessary to build a median–priced house: Kenya (37%), Côte d'Ivoire (35%), Ecuador (40%), Hong Kong (70%), and Singapore (80%). In contrast, seven countries (South Africa, China, India, Indonesia, Brazil, Mexico, and Spain) reported importing no materials at all for building median–priced houses.

Construction cost, which has a key influence on housing supply and hence on housing outcomes, is expected to be affected by all the other conditions in the construction sector: the efficiency of construction, which may be captured by building time and possibly by the skill ratio; the existence of price–setting monopolies which may be captured by industrial concentration; the shortage of skilled construction labor, which may be captured by the skill ratio; and the dependence on high–priced or high–duty imports, which may be captured by the import share of construction. It may also be affected by the economic, social, and political context and by the housing policy environment. In particular, higher–income countries with developed construction technology are expected to be more efficient, and hence to have relatively lower construction costs. Conversely, higher–density cities, where buildings need to be higher, are expected to have higher construction costs. Countries with more enabling housing policies are expected to have lower construction costs.

Construction Cost Indices

Can we determine statistically how each one of these conditions affects construction costs? When we model construction cost as a function of household income, density, the Enabling Index, and conditions in the construction sector, we obtain very robust models, with cost rising significantly with incomes, and going down significantly in more enabling housing policy regimes. Other factors are overshadowed, however, by the overriding influence of household income. But construction costs also reflect quality. They are much higher in high–income countries than in low–income ones, mainly because the quality of construction is much higher in the former than in the latter. For a more informative comparison, we need to compare construction costs for units of similar quality.

For simplicity's sake, we first assume that the quality of construction varies linearly with household income. Countries with similar median household incomes are assumed a priori to have similar quality housing. We can then define a new normalized indicator, the construction–cost–to–income ratio, and examine variations in this indicator with conditions in the construction sector:

1. The *construction–cost–to–income ratio*, defined as the ratio of the construction cost for one square meter of a median–priced house and annual median household income.

To obtain a greater degree of precision, we can also normalize construction costs by the level of quality. This requires the introduction of a Construction Quality Index. Given the data limitations of the Global Survey of housing Indicators, only a primitive quality index could be defined:

2. The *Construction Quality Index*, defined as an equally weighted sum of three indicators: permanent structures, quality attributes, and the annual median household income.

The permanent structures indicator was defined as the percentage of dwelling units that were likely to last 20 years or more given normal maintenance and repair, and taking into account environmental hazards. The quality attributes indicator was a discrete measure of the number of positive answers to questions about the presence of seven basic amenities in the median–priced house – piped water to the unit, water–borne sewage, electricity, central heating, air conditioning, elevators, and paved roads adjacent to the house. As these two indicators were deemed to be insufficient to distinguish the quality of construction associated with higher levels of income, annual median household income was added as a third factor to the index, assuming, as we did before, that construction quality varied in direct proportion to income. The resulting index is a simple, yet a rather crude, measure of housing quality, at least in part because it fails to distinguish between permanent structures of varying quality. Yet with the help of this index we can estimate an expected construction cost for a given level of quality, and derive the *construction cost premium*:

3.   The construction cost premium is the ratio between the observed construction cost in a given country and the expected construction cost for the Construction Quality Index in that country.

A value greater than 1 for this measure will indicate that construction costs are higher than expected, while a value lower than 1 will indicate that they are lower than expected. The expected construction cost for each country in the sample was obtained by fitting a regression line to the equation:

$$\ln C_i = a + bU_i,$$

where $\ln C_i$ was the natural logarithm of the reported construction cost for country i, and U_i the value of the construction quality index for country i. The resulting graph showing the scatter of country values as well as the regression line is given in figure 15.1. The logarithm of the construction cost and the quality of construction were highly correlated, with an R-squared of +0.68, suggesting that differences in quality, crudely measured by the Construction Quality Index, explained more than two-thirds of the variations in construction costs in our sample. Summary values for the construction cost-to-income ratio, permanent structures, quality attributes, the Construction Quality Index, and the construction cost premium are presented in table 15.2.

We note at the outset that the construction cost-to-income ratio declined with increasing incomes, from 7.2% in low-income countries to 3.7% in high-income ones. It also exhibited a negative correlation (-0.31) with the Development Index. These results suggest that, if the quality of construction indeed varied in proportion to incomes, construction costs rose slower than incomes. While there were no large variations among developing countries, the median for the developing countries as a whole (4.9%) was higher than that of the industrialized countries (3.6%). This indicator attained a maximum value of 10.8% in Tunisia, and a minimum value of 1% in the United States. Among the industrialized countries, the values for this indicator were especially high in the Netherlands (6.9%) and Japan (6.8%), both countries with lower than expected scores for the Enabling Index. Among the low-income countries, values were especially high for Tanzania (8.8%), India (8.7%), and China (8.3%), also countries with lower than expected scores for the Enabling Index.

The percentage of permanent structures reported for all countries was very high, with an average of 91% and a standard deviation of 13%. All the industrialized countries reported values of 99% or higher, with the exception of Hong Kong that still had squatter settlements and where only 90% of structures were permanent. All the Eastern European countries, that had virtually no informal housing, reported values in excess of 98%. The percentage of permanent structures increased with income, and was highly correlated with the Development Index (+0.63); but it quickly increased to very high values and thus failed to differentiate meaningfully among industrialized countries. Only seven countries (Malawi,

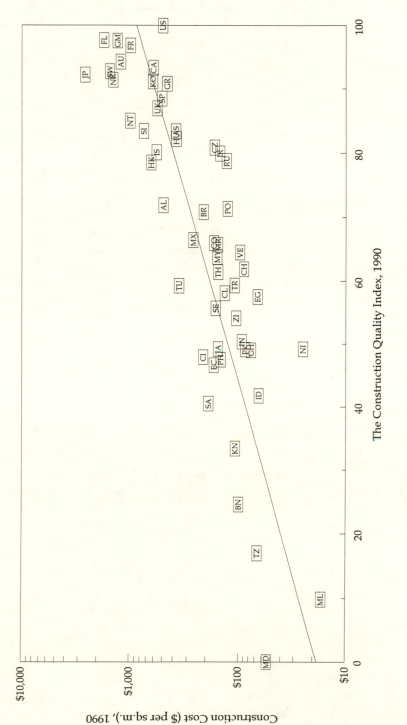

Figure 15.1. Construction Cost and Housing Quality

Table 15.2. Construction Cost Indices, 1990.

Country Groupings	Construction Cost–to–Income Ratio (%)	Permanent Structures (%)	Quality Attri–butes	Construction Quality Index	Construc–tion Cost Premium
Low–Income Countries	7.2	76	2	42	0.7
Low–Middle Income Countries	4.9	94	4	58	0.8
Upper Middle Income Countries	4.0	97	4	71	0.8
High–Income Countries	3.7	100	5	92	1.6
Southern Africa	6.1	79	2	44	1.3
Asia and the Pacific	4.8	86	4	50	0.7
Middle East and North Africa	4.4	95	4	63	0.6
Latin America and the Caribbean	4.2	90	4	65	0.8
Eastern Europe	5.1	99	6	80	0.4
All Developing Countries	4.9	94	4	58	0.7
Industrialized Countries	3.6	100	5	91	1.6
Global Average	4.7	91	4	66	1.2
Global Minimum	1.0	43	0	0	0.2
Global Median	4.2	97	4	66	0.9
Global Maximum	10.8	100	6	100	4.0
Global Standard Deviation	2.1	13	2	23	0.7
Correlation with Development Index	–0.31	0.63	0.78	0.89	0.22

Source: Housing Indicators Program [1994].

Madagascar, Kenya, South Africa, Indonesia, and Ecuador) reported values of 70% or less, and of these only Madagascar reported a value of less than half (43%).

The quality attributes indicator again varied with income, increasing from a median value of 2 in low–income countries to 5 in high–income ones, and having a highly–positive correlation with the Development Index (+0.78). Of all regions, Eastern Europe reported the maximum value of 6 as its median value for this indicator. Southern Africa had the lowest median value of 2, with two African countries (Tanzania and Malawi) reporting a value of 0 for this indicator.

The Construction Quality Index increased with income, as expected. Its median value for the industrialized countries (91) was considerably higher than the median value for the developing countries as a whole (58). Southern Africa had a low median value for this indicator, and three countries in Southern Africa (Tanzania, Malawi, and Madagascar) had scores of less than 20. Among the developing countries, Eastern Europe had an exceptionally high median value for this indicator (80), again attributable to the lack of an informal housing sector. Of the industrialized countries, 10 countries reported values of 90 or higher, and four countries values of 95 or higher: France (97), Germany and Finland (98 each), and the United States (100).

The construction cost premium, already normalized for quality, still exhibited a small positive correlation (+0.22) with the Development Index. It increased gradually with income, from 0.7 in the low-income countries to 1.6 in the high-income ones. The developing countries as a whole had a lower median value for the premium (0.7) than the industrialized countries (1.6). Construction costs for a given level of quality, as measured by the Construction Quality Index, were found to be lower in the developing countries than in the industrialized ones.

The Determinants of Residential Construction Costs

Given these more sensitive, yet rather elementary, indices of construction cost, we can now attempt to answer the question: How do the context, the housing policy environment, and conditions in the construction sector affect construction costs? To answer this question, we construct a number of models that seek to explain the variations in the construction cost-to-income ratio and the construction cost premium by variations in the conditions in the construction sector, per capita incomes, density, and the housing policy environment. These models are shown in table 15.3 .

The table presents two models for the construction cost-to-income ratio. Because of a large number of missing values for the density measure, there are only 23 observations in the first model, appearing in the top line in the table. This model had an R-squared of 0.59, indicating that it explained more than half of the variation in the construction-cost-to-income ratio. Three explanatory variables in the model that were statistically significant: the Enabling Index, the skill ratio, and industrial concentration. Countries with more enabling housing policies had significantly lower construction costs. Countries with higher skill ratios had lower construction costs. And countries with higher levels of industrial concentration had higher construction cost-to-income ratios. The enabling index had the strongest effect on the construction cost-to-income ratio, followed by the skill ratio and then by industrial concentration.

The effect of the skill ratio became statistically insignificant when we excluded density from the model in order to increase the number of observations. The results of this second model are shown on the second line of table 15.3. This model contained a considerably larger number of observations, 42 as against 23. The Enabling Index was now significant at the 1% level, and the only other significant variable was industrial concentration. Their effects on the construction cost-to-income ratio are very similar to those of the first model, and the results of the second model confirm the results of the first one.

For comparison, we also model the construction cost premium as a function of the same variables as those in the second model, again without the density variable. This third model is presented on the third line of table 15.3. It had a

Table 15.3. The Determinants of Construction Cost Indices.

Variable	Log of GNP per capita	Log of Density (persons/km²)	Building Time (months)	Industrial Concentration	Skill Ratio	Import Share of Construction	Enabling Index	No. of observations	R-squared & Adjusted R-squared	F-Value
Construction Cost-to-Income Ratio (Model I)	-0.30 [a]	-0.05	0.24	0.29	-0.56	0.03	-0.61	23	0.59	$F_{7,15}$ [b]
	-0.98 [b]	-0.23	1.13	1.39*	-1.88**	0.15	-2.09** [c]		0.39	3.04**
Construction Cost-to-Income Ratio (Model II)	-0.15	– [d]	0.00	0.27	-0.21	0.16	-0.61	42	0.44	$F_{7,35}$
	-0.77	– [d]	0.01	1.78**	-1.11	1.10	-2.80***		0.34	4.54***
Construction Cost Premium	0.23	– [d]	-0.22	0.19	-0.33	0.16	-0.46	42	0.34	$F_{7,35}$
	1.32	– [d]	-1.68*	1.45*	-2.03**	1.29	-2.43***		0.22	2.97**

Source: Housing Indicators Program [1994].

[a] Figures in the top rows are standardized β-coefficients.

[b] Figures in italics denote *t*- and *F*-statistics.

[c] ***, **, and * denote 1%, 5% and 10% levels of confidence, respectively.

[d] Log of Density not included in this model.

lower R-squared value of 0.34, explaining only one-third of the variation in the construction cost premium. Again, construction was found to be significantly more expensive in non-enabling policy environments. The premium increased with higher levels of industrial concentration, and, as in the first model, cities with higher skill ratios had lower construction cost premiums. Finally, cities with higher building times had lower, rather than higher, construction cost premiums, suggesting that faster construction did not necessarily mean cheaper construction. The Enabling Index exerted the strongest effect on the construction cost premium, followed by building time, the skill ratio, and then industrial concentration. Altogether, six models were built with construction cost and the construction-cost-to-income ratio as dependent variables, and the variables listed in the previous tables as independent ones (once including and once excluding density). In none of the models were density or the import share of construction found to be significant in explaining variations in construction costs. The data did not, therefore, support the contentions that either higher density or higher import shares lead to increased construction costs of median-priced houses.

* * *

To conclude, accounting for differences in quality, all models suggested that a more enabling environment was associated with significantly lower construction costs. In addition, all models suggest that increased levels of industrial concentration were associated with increased construction costs, or conversely, that increased fragmentation in the residential construction industry was associated with lower costs. The effects of other variables varied from one model to another, and given our data we cannot determine with confidence that these variables significantly influenced construction costs in one way or another.

16

The Availability of Mortgage Credit

A third set of housing market conditions, the actual conditions in the housing finance industry, calls for a more thorough investigation of the housing sector as seen through yet another perspective—the perspective of those who lend for housing. Housing policy is intimately tied to the development of the housing finance industry because ample and affordable housing relies heavily on the ability of the financial sector to provide ample and affordable credit for housing. How do mortgage markets develop? What accounts for the variations in the availability of credit among countries? The creation of an effective, vibrant, and responsible housing finance regime is indeed one of the five key components of an enabling housing policy regime. But does a more-enabling housing finance regime indeed result in more credit becoming available for housing? In this chapter we seek to explore these questions.

Conditions in the Housing Finance Sector

There is an undeniable economic logic in borrowing money for building or buying a house:

> Housing yields a stream of services over a period of years and it is therefore logical that it should be paid for over a period of years by means of loan repayments rather than in one lump sum. If people had to pay for their housing in one go then very few would be able to afford housing until very late in life. Loan finance is therefore essential to make an owner–occupied housing market work with full efficiency. [Boleat and Coles, 1987, 11]

Indeed, borrowing for housing is a global phenomenon. At one extreme we find slum dwellers in Madras, India, building their permanent houses with 37% of the funds mobilized from savings, 20% from selling property, and the rest from loans (19% from pawnbrokers, 9% from relatives, 8% from money lenders, and 5% from a government agency) [Marudachalam, 1991, 243]. At the other extreme we find the home mortgage market of the United States, that in 1994 consisted of some $3 trillion of household mortgage debt, nearly all of it held by private-sector financial institutions [Weicher, 1994, 47]. Our own calculations suggest that global urban housing sector could provide potential collateral for tens of trillions of mortgage debt.[1]

We can distinguish three stages in the development of lending for housing, each involving different types of lenders: (a) direct lending, (b) mortgage banking, and (c) securitization. Direct lending is a simple face-to-face transaction between a borrower and a lender. Mortgage banking is once removed: a mortgage bank lends the money for housing from deposits that it collects from savers. Securitization is twice (or more) removed: mortgage loans are originated by one institution, sold to a second institution that collects the mortgage payments and then sells tradable securities (backed by these payments) in the capital market to yet a third institution. The latter can be a pension fund, an insurance fund, or a mutual fund — either domestic or international — that then may sell shares to individual investors.

The great majority of houses in the developing countries are still built with personal savings and direct lending from relatives, employers, neighbors, groups who save together in rotating credit societies (also known as "chit funds"), and unregulated moneylenders and pawnbrokers.[2] Brick houses in the squatter settlements on the outskirts of Lima, Peru, for example, were built in small spurts over many years, as small savings and loans were accumulated [Turner, 1967; Turner, 1968]. Dwellers often used their own labor, or acted as their own contractors, obtaining construction labor and expertise when needed. Lending for such construction was largely based on trust and personal connections, often involving personal guarantees from friends and relatives. Typically, titles were clouded and lenders could not rely on the legal system to enforce contracts. They could only rely on the borrowers' and the guarantors' need to protect their good name. Loans were necessarily small and of short duration, and borrowers were forced to maintain their good credit standing because of their need to obtain loans regularly. Under such circumstances, however, housing credit was always in short supply and there was considerably less housing that what could be afforded by dwellers given their savings and incomes. There is no question that for the majority of families the issue has always been access to credit, not its cost.

A quantum leap in access to credit, and hence to much better housing, occurs when lenders can issue long-term mortgage loans — typically of 10-30 years duration — using the house as collateral to secure the loan. Legally, a mortgage is a claim on one's property granted to a lender, in order to secure the repayment of a loan. The lender receives a pledge that if the owner fails to repay the loan or breaks the loan agreement (e.g., by not maintaining the property or not insuring it), the lender can take legal possession of the property and then sell it to repay the loan. A house is a particularly good form of collateral because it is a form of wealth that, in principle, can be transferred with less loss of value in the transfer than is the case with most other assets. It is, in short, a highly redeployable asset.

The theoretical value of mortgage loans aside, there are several necessary conditions for mortgage lending to develop in practice. Three of them concern the legal environment for lending: titles must be clear and transferable, contracts must be enforceable, and foreclosure — the legal possession of the property by the lender in case of default — must be allowed to proceed without undue delay.

Beyond these three basic legal conditions, there are also a number of institutional, political, and economic requirements for mortgage lending to flourish. When incomes are very low and people spend very little on housing, the administrative costs of issuing housing loans may be too high to make them worthwhile for lenders or borrowers. This is especially true when incomes are irregular and the collection of payments, to be effective, must be at the home or the workplace of the borrower at less than monthly intervals — a typical practice of high–interest money lenders in slums.[3] Beyond this requirement, mortgage lending cannot develop in countries with a high level of political instability, in countries with a high level of corruption in the banking system or where banking systems have collapsed, in countries with a very high level of inflation, or in countries with shortages of development capital that require the rationing of credit.[4]

However, when the political and economic conditions are favorable, the gradual transition from direct lending to mortgage banking normally results in the creation of a host of institutions that collect deposits and issue mortgage loans. These can be building societies, savings–and–loan associations (S&Ls), finance companies, savings banks, commercial banks, or credit unions. In a well–functioning housing finance system, these lenders are not subject to undue lending risk. Lenders are protected against a number of contingencies: that borrowers default on their payments, that houses used as collateral are damaged or destroyed, that the value of houses used a collateral falls below the value of loans, that they are forced to issue long–term loans against short–term deposits, that they lose potential interest payments from the early pre–payment of loans (usually in periods of falling interest rates), or that their loans lose their value through inflation. These risks can be reduced or averted when lenders are able to introduce a number of instruments: reliable valuations and records that ascertain house values and incomes, prudential regulations that limit default by tailoring loans to incomes and house values, adjustable interest rates that combat maturity and early-repayment risks, and indexed mortgages or graduated–payment loans that limit the effects of inflation on both lenders and borrowers.

Mortgage lending under these conditions can grow quite rapidly, as the experience of Malaysia in the 1970s and 1980s demonstrates:

> The most striking feature of the development of the Malaysian housing finance system has been the growth of housing credit provided by commercial banks and finance companies, whose outstanding portfolios of mortgage credit grew at compound rates of 28.5 and 29.3 percent respectively from 1970 to 1985, in each case implying a growth in loans outstanding by a factor of 70 in 15 years. Taking into account all sources of housing credit,

outstanding credit grew at a rate of 26.5 percent over the same time period. [Mayo, 1990, 4–5]

Unfortunately, the growth and development of mortgage banking is not unidirectional. Mortgage banks are subject to a number of additional regulatory risks that can either stunt their growth or bring about their collapse after periods of rapid growth. The government-backed insurance of deposits — coupled with the absence of proper monitoring of adherence to prudential regulations (minimum capital requirements, balance sheet constraints, adequate valuation and borrower selection services, and maximum loan-to-value ratios and loan-to-income ratios) that restrain lending — allowed many S&Ls in the United States to take inordinately high risks with their insured deposits: Residential mortgage borrowers paid a much lower rate at failing or failed S&Ls during the 1980s, for example, than they did at solvent S&Ls [Do and Schilling, 1993]. Overoptimistic commercial and office real estate loans brought down a large number of associations in the United States in the late 1980s, resulting in a massive cost to taxpayers that will have to be met by legislated appropriations. Estimates vary, but the order of magnitude is clear: "The savings and loan debacle is the costliest scandal in the country's history. Bailing out the S&L industry will cost taxpayers at least $500 billion over the next few years and more than $1 trillion over the next several decades, once the cost of borrowing the money is added" [Day, 1993, 9].

A different yet fatal collapse destroyed the mortgage banking systems in a number of Latin American countries in the 1970s and the 1980s, when banks were forced to extend mortgage loans at below-market interest rates, to rely on deposits at below-market interest rates, and to use lending instruments that could not keep up with rampant inflation. In a well-functioning housing finance sector, depositors are not forced to save — and lenders are not forced to lend — at below-market interest rates, and housing subsidies are not funneled through the financial sector. Lending interest rates are higher than deposit rates, and the spread between them is sufficient to cover the risks incurred and the cost of administering the loans. In addition, mortgage lending institutions are not subject to severe fluctuations in the supply of credit that can often lead to their collapse. Imposed interest-rate ceilings that drain their financial resources in periods of credit crunch are removed, and they are allowed to compete for funds on equal terms with borrowers in other economic sectors.

Housing finance systems have undergone a third transformation — the development of securitization. Securitization itself — since it required the pooling of mortgages — could only be made possible through the standardization of mortgage instruments. It required the establishment of uniform underwriting criteria, common documentation, common terms of insurance, and common methods to determine interest rates with limited lender discretion. Given standard practices, securitization then made it possible for housing finance institutions to ameliorate three major risks: to reduce overall default risk through the pooling of large numbers of mortgages, to reduce regional default risk through a broader geographic coverage that avoided the violent swings of local building cycles, and to reduce maturity risk through the packaging of long-term mortgage debt in the form of tradable securities on the capital market.

This development made it possible to massively increase the funds that were available for housing finance, especially as it became clear that mortgage-backed securities were, in fact, highly desirable financial assets. Buckley [1996], for example, has shown that house prices are, on average, 3.8 times *less* volatile than stock market prices in countries along the entire spectrum of economic development: Argentina, Brazil, Italy, Korea, Malaysia, the United Kingdom, and the United States [19]. In the United States in the mid-1990s, the interest rate increase required to cover mortgage default risk was of the order of 0.5%, compared to 3.5% required to cover the risk of corporate debt [18].

The standardization of mortgage-backed securities made them highly uniform products, the trading of which was no longer restricted within national boundaries. In total contrast to the inherent fragmentation of the building industry, the housing finance system is gradually globalizing, becoming consolidated into what some analysts claim is already an oligopoly [Ball, 1990, 204], dominated by a very small number of major institutions. In the United States by 1992, to cite one example, two government-backed private institutions — FNMA (Fannie Mae) and FHLMC (Freddie Mac) — had issued more than 60% of all mortgage-backed securities and accounted for more than two-thirds of the growth in this sector [Weicher, 1994, table 1, 52].

It is not at all clear that such concentration is either efficient or sustainable in the long run, and that mortgage borrowers are indeed being offered competitive market interest rates, commensurate with the low risk associated with lending for housing. Ball, for example, claimed that because of information limitations still prevalent in this sector, larger institutions tend to have an advantage, even though there are no economies of scale in issuing mortgage-backed securities and even though they are not efficient [Ball, 1990, 208-209]. In a well-functioning housing finance system, efficient lenders can enter the market and survive, not subject to the price fixing strategies of dominant lenders that can sustain losses for long periods — because of their size, or because of their ability to offset them through cross-subsidies between their different operations. The recent rise of dominant institutions in housing finance raises doubts whether the voices of the lenders and borrowers along the entire spectrum of lending for housing will continue to be heard, and whether the housing finance system as a whole will move towards higher levels of efficiency and long-term stability. As this short discussion makes clear, lenders can and do vastly increase access to affordable housing credit when the policy environment enables them to do so. For them, the policies and the legal environment governing the sustainability of the financial sector are the two essential ingredients for the development of extensive and efficient systems of housing finance.

Measuring the Availability of Mortgage Credit

What indicators can be used to assess the conditions in the housing finance industry? The extent and structure of mortgage lending are the most-often used measures of the distribution of mortgage loans. Generally, the more widespread mortgage lending is, the broader its coverage of all income and minority groups. The extent of mortgage lending is measured by the aggregate loan-to-value ratio (outstanding mortgage loans as a percentage of the total value of the housing stock) [Mayo, 1990, 6]; the housing credit portfolio (outstanding mortgage loans as a percentage of all loans) [Mayo, 1990, 4, 10-1]; the number of square meters financed, the number of housing loans issued, or the number of clients benefitting from housing loans [Inter-American Housing Union, 1989, 12]; and the annual residential mortgage originations by building type and lender type [U.S. HUD, 1994, 20-21; Papa, 1992, 110; Shilling and Sirmans, 1993, 19]. Specific distributional measures of mortgage lending include the percentage of mortgages above a specified limit [Hills, 1991b, 199-200]; and the lowest-income decile receiving formal housing finance [Tanphiphat and Simapichaichet, 1990].[5]

The conditions in the mortgage market are usually measured by the prevailing interest rates, by the rate of arrears and negative equity, and by the extent of the mortgage insurance and secondary-mortgage markets. These include the mortgage interest rate (nominal and real) [Renaud, 1989, 6]; the mortgage yield spread (difference between average commercial mortgage rate and 10-year treasury bill rate) [Vandell et al., 1992, 11]; the annual net operating costs (before losses) as a percent of total assets of financial institutions [Wennberg, 1994, 204]; the shares of fixed and adjustable mortgage interest rates [U.S. HUD, 1994, 17; Bramley, 1994,90]; the annual number of arrears and repossessions per 1,000 mortgages [Bramley, 1994, 80]; the share of outstanding loans in arrears [Struyk et al., 1990, 330]; the percentage of past due mortgages, 90-days past due, and foreclosure starts [U.S. HUD, 1994, 22]; the percentage of recent buyers with negative equity [Dorling, 1994]; and the ratio of net equity withdrawal to personal disposable income [Muellbauer,1990,52].

The Global Survey of Housing Indicators collected data on three aspects of performance of the housing finance sector: the extent of mortgage lending, the price of loans, and the effective administration of loans. Specifically, data were collected on four housing finance indicators:

1. *the housing credit portfolio,* defined as the ratio of total mortgage loans to all outstanding loans in both commercial and government financial institutions;

2. *the credit-to-value ratio,* defined as the ratio of mortgage loans for housing last year to total investment in housing (in both the formal and informal sectors) last year;

3. *the mortgage-to-prime difference,* defined as the average difference in percentage points between interest rates on mortgages in both commercial

and government financial institutions and the prime interest rate in the commercial banking system; and

4. *the mortgage arrears rate,* defined as the percentage of mortgage loans that are three or more months in arrears in both commercial and government financial institutions.

The first of these two indicators measures the extent, and hence the availability, of mortgage loans to finance housing. The mortgage–to–prime difference reflects two different aspects of the housing finance sector. It can reflect (especially when it is highly negative) the existence of subsidized or below–market mortgage interest rates.   Or, in the absence of implicit mortgage interest subsidies, it can reflect the efficiency in mortgage lending – mortgage interest rates are expected to be lower than interest rates for corporate loans, reflecting the lesser risks associated with mortgage lending as against commercial lending. Whether they are, in fact, lower and how much lower is a measure of the competitiveness and efficiency of the housing finance industry. Finally, the mortgage arrears rate is a measure of the development of mortgage institutions, the stability of mortgage–to–income levels, or the stability of the prices of homes. High rates of arrears may reflect lax credit administration, unaffordably high mortgage– to–income ratios, or the collapse of the housing market. The summary values for these indicators obtained in the Global Survey are presented in table 16.1.

Table 16.1. The Availability of Mortgage Credit, 1990.

Country Groupings	Housing Credit Portfolio (%)	Credit– to–Value– Ratio (%)	Mortgage– to–Prime Difference (%)	Mortgage Arrears Rate (%)
Low–Income Countries	3	10	0.1	12
Low–Middle Income Countries	8	31	0.5	10
Upper Middle Income Countries	18	41	–0.4	5
High–Income Countries	23	87	0.5	1
Southern Africa	5	11	0.7	10
Asia and the Pacific	5	47	0.8	14
Middle East and North Africa	7	20	–2.2	20
Latin America and the Caribbean	20	29	3.2	6
Eastern Europe	18	33	–72.6	10
All Developing Countries	7	26	0.1	10
Industrialized Countries	23	87	0.5	1
Global Average	15	50	–4.9	10
Global Minimum	0	0	–102.4	0
Global Median	14	43	0.2	5
Global Maximum	44	150	10.1	42
Global Standard Deviation	12	39	18.9	12
Correlation with Development Index	0.60	0.70	–0.08	–0.34

Source: Housing Indicators Program [1994].

The proportion of housing loans to all loans in the banking sector increased dramatically with economic development. The median value of the housing credit portfolio increased steadily from 3% in low–income countries to 23% in high–income ones. The median value for the developing countries as a whole (7%) was less than one third that of the industrialized countries (23%). It is not surprising, therefore, that this indicator was highly correlated (+0.60) with the Development Index. Among developing country regions, mortgage lending was most developed in Latin America and least developed in Southern Africa and Asia. All in all, five countries (Tanzania, China, Senegal, Algeria, and Russia) reported housing finance portfolios of less than 2% of overall lending. Among the higher–income countries, Korea reported an exceptionally low value (5.2%), having rationed credit to the housing sector for many years. The next lowest values, those for Greece and Japan, were more than double that of Korea. Five countries (Brazil, the United Kingdom, Germany, Norway, and the United States) reported values for this indicator in excess of 30%. The United States attained the maximum value of 43.6% for this indicator, implying that close to half the loans held by banking institutions in 1990 were in fact housing loans.

The second indicator to measure the extent and proliferation of mortgage lending is the credit–to–value ratio. This indicator had a high degree of correlation with the housing credit portfolio (+0.61), and was even more influenced by the level of economic development than the latter—its correlation with the Development Index was higher (+0.70). The credit–to–value ratio rose from 10% in low–income countries to 87% in high–income ones. The median value for the industrialized countries (87%) was more than triple that of the developing countries as a whole (26%). This number should not be taken to suggest that the average new mortgage loan amounts to, say, 87% of the value of the house, because a considerable amount of new mortgage credit was extended as home–equity loans (for purposes other than housing) secured by existing housing. Indeed, the value of this indicator can be higher than 100%, and it is. Five countries (Spain, the Netherlands, the United States, Finland, and Hong Kong) report values higher than 100%. In contrast, seven countries (Tanzania, Ghana, the Côte d'Ivoire, Bangladesh, Russia, Algeria, and China) reported values of less than 10% for this indicator.

The data for the mortgage–to–prime difference are difficult to interpret because the indicator is affected by two completely different factors: below–market interest rates (which are enforced by decree), and the competitiveness of mortgage lending institutions (which lowers the rate by increasing the efficiency of lending). Because the two effects are mixed, no pattern emerged from the raw data for the sample as whole. There was no difference at all between countries with different incomes, and the correlation with the Development Index was practically zero.

Finally, the data for the mortgage arrears rate again displayed a clear pattern. This indicator had a negative correlation (–0.34) with the Development Index, and it decreased as income increased from a high of 12% in low–income countries to a low of 1% in high-income countries. The median value for the developing countries as a whole was 10%, while that of the industrialized countries was only 1%. Among developing country regions, the median value for the arrears rate appeared to be highest in the Middle East and North Africa (20%) and lowest in Latin America (6%). The arrears rate was surprisingly high in a number of high-income countries, however. Israel reported a very high value of 36% in 1990, possibly associated with the high mortgage-to-income ratios attributable to inflation, while four other countries (the United Kingdom, Austria, the Nether-lands, and Canada) all reported values higher than 5%. In contrast, five industri-alized countries (Australia, the United States, Japan, Finland, and France) reported arrear values of 1% or less. Five developing countries (India, Côte d'Ivoire, Turkey, Algeria, and Brazil) reported arrear values in excess of 25%. Again, in contrast, four developing countries (Kenya, the former Czechoslovakia, Mexico, and South Africa) reported arrear values of 1% or less.

The Determinants of the Availability of Mortgage Credit

All in all, although the level of economic development did explain a considerable part of the variation in these four mortgage credit indicators, there were still considerable variations both between income groups and between regions. A question arises as to whether we can account for these differences. We can assume, for example, that the availability of credit will be influenced by interest rates, or rather by real interest rates adjusted for inflation. We can also assume that it will be hindered by hyperinflation; that it should be higher in countries with greater financial depth; and that it should be affected by the housing policy environment in general, and by the housing finance regime in particular.

Several statistical models were constructed to test these conjectures. Only two countries in the sample, Brazil and Poland, reported the existence of hyperinfla-tion in 1990, not a sufficient number to test the hyperinflation hypothesis. With each of the four credit indicators as a dependent variable, four models were tested with the level of economic development,[6] the real prime interest rate, financial depth, and the Housing Finance Regime Index as explanatory variables. The statistical models testing the effects of these variables on the availability of mortgage credit are presented in table 16.2.

The first model in table 16.2 explores the variations in the housing credit portfolio among different countries. The model had an R-squared of 0.52, suggesting that the variation in the explanatory variables accounted for more than half of the variation in the housing credit portfolio. The model tells us that the level of development, as measured by GNP per capita, had the most powerful effect on the housing credit portfolio, and that the other three variables — the real prime interest rate, financial depth, and the Housing Finance Regime Index — all had more modest effects, roughly of the same level of magnitude. The higher the real interest rate, the lower was the extent of mortgage lending. Second, given that increased financial depth was associated with higher levels of economic development, we find that financial depth did not, in and of itself, increase the availability of mortgage credit. In fact, holding incomes constant, mortgage credit was found to be slightly more abundant in countries with lower levels of financial depth. Finally, the availability of credit, as measured by the housing credit portfolio could not be said to be significantly influenced by a more enabling housing finance regime, although the model did suggest a modest increase.

The Housing Finance Regime Index was found to exert a significant influence on the availability of credit, however, when it was measured by the credit-to-value ratio, as can be seen from the second model, presented in the second line of table 16.2. This model had an R-squared of 0.63, suggesting that the variables in the model explained almost two-thirds of the variation in the sample. In this model, the level of development was again found to be highly significant. It had a considerably more powerful effect on the credit-to-value ratio than that exerted by the Housing Finance Regime Index. The latter did, however, exert a significant positive influence on the availability of credit—the higher the index, the more credit was indeed available. The two other independent variables in the model— the real prime interest rate and financial depth—could not be said to have a significant influence on the availability of credit as measured by the credit-to-value ratio.

The model for the mortgage-to-prime difference was not statistically significant, probably because it lumped together countries with subsidized or below-market mortgage rates with countries with market rates. Although mortgage lending is considerably less risky than lending for commercial or industrial enterprises, as we noted earlier, mortgage interest rates on the whole were still higher than prime interest rates in the great majority of countries. Only four countries (Kenya, Canada, the United States, and Norway) reported mortgage interest rates that were lower than prime interest rates.

The last model in table 16.2 examined variations in the mortgage arrears rate. The model had an R-squared of 0.34, suggesting that the independent variables explained one-third of the variation in the arrears rate in our sample. The results of the model are quite clear. First, arrears rates decreased significantly as per capita income increased, as we have already seen. Second, arrears increased significantly as real interest rates increased. The latter were usually associated with higher mortgage-to-income ratios that became unaffordable. Finally, when the housing finance regime became more developed, arrears decreased. The level of economic development, measured by GNP per capita, exerted the most powerful influence on the level of arrears, while the real interest rate and the Housing Finance Regime Index exerted a weaker influence of a similar magnitude.

* * *

To summarize, the development of mortgage finance is an essential condition for channeling savings into the housing sector. The housing policy

Table 16.2. The Determinants of the Availability of Mortgage Credit.

Variable	Log of GNP per capita	Real Prime Interest Rate	Financial Depth (M2/GDP)	Housing Finance Regime Index	No. of Obser- vations	R-squared & Adjusted R-squared	F-Value
Housing Credit Portfolio	0.74[a] *5.28***[b]*	-0.17 *-1.35**	-0.17 *-1.32**	0.21 *1.27*	40	0.52 0.46	$F_{4,35}$ *9.46***[b]*
Credit-to-Value Ratio	0.68 *5.85***[c]*	-0.07 *-0.73*	0.04 *0.38*	0.19 *1.45**	38	0.63 0.59	$F_{4,33}$ *14.28****
Mortgage Arrears Rate	-0.38 *-2.36***	0.29 *2.21***	0.17 *1.04*	-0.25 *-1.42**	33	0.34 0.25	$F_{4,28}$ *3.62***

Source: Housing Indicators Program [1994].

[a] Figures in the top rows are standardized β–coefficients.

[b] Figures in italics denote *t*– and *F*–statistics.

[c] ***, **, and * denote 1%, 5% and 10% levels of confidence, respectively.

environment can contribute to the increased availability of mortgage finance by (a) improving property rights; (b) securing transactions and enforcing contracts; (c) insisting on a rapid and reliable foreclosure procedure; (d) creating the necessary regulatory framework for the development of mortgage institutions; and (e) insuring, guaranteeing, and supporting the development mortgage lending institutions in their initial stages. In general, as the results of our statistical analysis confirm, the availability of mortgage credit increased largely as the result of overall economic development. For countries in similar levels of development, the financial depth of the economy was not found to be a highly significant factor in increasing mortgage lending. A more enabling housing finance regime, on the other hand, was found to have a modest influence both on the availability of credit and on lowering mortgage arrears. In conclusion, we also note that, all in all, unregulated mortgage interest rates in 1990, that were expected to be lower than prime interest rates because of the lower risks involved, were still, on average, not as low as expected. Mortgage lending markets were still not as competitive and not as efficient as they could be, and there is ample room for expansion of access to credit and for cheaper credit in the years to come.

* * *

This concludes our discussion of the *conditions* in the housing market, the third element of our model of the housing sector. Chapters 17–23 will elaborate on three key questions regarding housing market *outcomes*, the fourth and last element of the model: (a) how do we define the housing outcomes that matter, (b) how do these outcomes vary from one place to another, and (c) what accounts for the variations in outcomes in different places?

17

House Prices, Rents, and Affordability

The housing problem can be characterized as the presence of a large number of urban families living in what society–at–large considers to be unacceptable housing conditions. The problem, posed this way, necessarily focuses on bad housing conditions. When bad housing is plentiful, however, it enables poor families to spend less on housing. When there are many poor families that can only afford bad housing, housing conditions simply reflect poverty — poor people cannot afford to house themselves at standards acceptable to "society–at–large." Surely, when economies develop and people come out of poverty, they either invest in the improvement of their existing houses or move away from slums and into better housing. Economic growth and the distribution of the benefits of growth can therefore be expected to lead to a better housing stock, and to provide a partial solution to the housing problem. Bad housing then gradually gives way to better housing. If, however, bad housing is destroyed faster than warranted and is no longer plentiful, the quality of the housing stock improves but poor families face a shortage of affordable housing and need to spend a larger portion of their meager incomes on shelter. The housing problem then becomes an affordability problem. The lack of affordability is a no less severe problem than bad housing, but a less visible one. Bad housing is a visible sign of poverty. Families that spend more than half their incomes on housing are not.

Housing problems, visible or not, are largely affordability problems. Poor people in some countries live in "substandard" houses because they cannot afford better ones; in other countries poor people live in "standard" houses, pay an inordinate share of their incomes for shelter, and are further impoverished by their housing.

The concept of affordability brings together these three factors: the quality of housing available, the price of housing, and the income of families seeking to buy or rent housing. Low–quality housing is likely to be available at lower prices or rents and hence be more affordable. Conversely, high–quality housing is likely to be more expensive and hence less affordable. The housing problem is therefore intimately tied to house prices and rents. They are the connecting links between housing quality on the one hand, and family incomes on the other. A discussion of the housing problem that does not attend to house prices and rents will therefore be severely flawed. If we take a country's level of economic development and its distribution of income as given, then low house prices and rents are the key to affordable housing. They are also, as we shall see in the chapters that follow, the key to better housing. Why, we should ask, are house prices and rents low in some places and high in others? Is it because of the different economic, social, and political conditions in different countries? Because of differences in their housing policy environment? Or because of differences in the conditions their housing markets face?

This chapter seeks to answer these questions. First, it defines a number of price, rent, and affordability indicators, presents the data collected in the Global Survey on these indicators, and accounts for the variations in these values between cities and countries using the statistical model for the price of housing presented in chapter 6. Second, it proceeds to define a number of hedonic price and rent indices that measure the price per unit of value of housing as well as the rent per unit of value of housing services, and then to account for the differences in these indices among cities and countries. As expected, house prices, rents, and affordability measures were all found to be significantly influenced, in varying degrees, by all three elements — the context, the policy environment, and housing market conditions.

House Price, Rent, and Affordability Measures

National statistical agencies in a number of countries regularly collect data on house prices and rents as important components of the Cost of Living Index. Direct measures of house prices include the average, median, and constant-quality prices of existing and new homes [Smith et al., 1988, 32; U.S. HUD, 1994, 13]; annual house price appreciation [Renaud, 1989, 6; Smith et al., 1988, 32]; and house price fluctuations (range of peak-to-trough percentage change in real house prices during a house price cycle) [Bramley, 1994, 83]. Examples of direct measures of rent are the median rent [U.S. HUD, 1994, 14] and rent increases relative to the consumer price index [United Nations, 1992, table 8, 50–51; Smith et al., 1988, 32].

Income–based measures of housing affordability include the house price–to–income ratio [Renaud, 1991; McGuire, 1981, 58]; the rent–to–income ratio [Strassmann, 1982, 49; McGuire, 1981, 58]; the ratio of median family income to the income needed to purchase the median–priced home based on current interest rates and underwriting standards [U.S. HUD, 1994, 14]; the ratio of house prices and land prices to disposable income per capita [Muellbauer, 1990, 55]; the ratio of land price (per m^2) to the minimum salary [Gilbert and Varley, 1991, 51]; and the percentage of households unable to afford a basic formal–sector house [Grimes, 1976, 148–157]. Expenditure–based measures of housing affordability include housing expenditure as percent of total household expenditures [Strassmann, 1982, 210; Boelhouwer and van der Heijden, 1992, 31]; housing consumption as a percent of private consumption [Hårsman and Quigley, 1991, 15]; the percentage of household expenditures devoted to housing, utilities, and transport [Grimes, 1976, 147]; and real annual housing consumption per capita, corrected for purchasing power parities [OECD data in Colleen, 1994a, 61–62].

The Global Survey of Housing Indicators collected data for three measures of affordability:

1. *the house-price-to-income ratio,* defined as the ratio of the median house price and the median household income;
2. *the rent-to-income ratio,* defined as the ratio of the median annual rent of a dwelling unit and the median annual household income of renters; and
3. *down–market penetration,* defined as a the ratio of the lowest-priced (unsubsidized) formal dwelling unit produced by the private sector in significant quantities (not less than two percent of annual housing production) and the median annual household income.

Data were also obtained for two additional indicators – the *median house value* and the *median annual rental value* – used as intermediate values in the calculation of the first two indicators.[1]

The house price-to-income ratio and the rent-to-income ratio are key measures of both housing affordability and the overall performance of the housing market. When housing prices are high relative to incomes, for example, a smaller fraction of the population will be able to purchase housing. Just as important, deviations of this indicator from the global norm suggest that there are serious distortions in the housing market. When its value is inordinately high, such distortions may be restricting housing supply or inflating housing demand. Conversely, when its value is exceptionally low, the value of houses may be kept artificially low by low–quality construction, insufferable environmental conditions, insecurity of tenure, absence of housing finance, or a lack of consumer confidence in the economy.

The rent–to–income ratio is a proxy measure of housing expenditure as a percent of income. When it is exceptionally high it may be an indication of the existence of supply bottlenecks in the rental housing sector. Conversely, when it is exceptionally low it may be an indication of the prevalence of rent control and the consequent absence of incentives for suppliers to engage in the production of rental housing.

The third indicator of housing affordability – down–market penetration – is a measure of the degree of the affordability of the lowest–priced new house produced by the formal private sector. Low–income people are generally restricted to obtaining new housing in the informal sector – in squatter settlements, slums, or informal land subdivisions; or in "filtered–down" older formal–sector housing. The formal private sector usually produces new housing for higher–income families, but does not market housing to lower–income groups. In many countries, the formal private sector produces individual houses or apartments buildings but does not produce houses in land-and-house developments in significant numbers. In some countries, however, the formal private sector has been willing and able to produce housing affordable to lower-income people without any public supports, incentives, or subsidies. This indicator measures the degree of penetration of new formal residential construction down- market. Summary results from the Global Survey of Housing Indicators for the three indicators of house prices, rents, and affordability are presented in table 17.1.

The global median value for the house price-to-income ratio is 4.2, suggesting that in 1990 median-income urban families paid slightly more than four annual household incomes for purchasing a median-priced house. This indicator did not display a clear and systematic relationship to the level of development, although it had a positive correlation with the Development Index (+0.33). It was particularly low in low-income countries (3.3). The value for the developing countries as a whole (3.7) was somewhat lower than the median value for industrialized countries (4.6).

Among developing-country regions, Southern Africa and Latin America reported lower than median values (2.2 and 2.4, respectively) while the Middle East and North Africa and Eastern Europe reported higher-than-median values (6.4 and 7.0, respectively). In addition, there were great variations among countries within regions. Five out of seven countries that reported median values of 2.0 or less for the house price-to-income ratio were in Southern Africa, but

Table 17.1. Housing Affordability Measures, 1990.

Country Groupings	House Price-to-Income Ratio	Rent-to-Income Ratio (%)	Down-Market Penetration
Low-Income Countries	3.3	10.0	6.9
Low-Middle Income Countries	4.5	16.2	3.6
Upper Middle Income Countries	4.4	14.6	3.4
High-Income Countries	4.6	18.1	2.6
Southern Africa	2.2	10.0	3.7
Asia and the Pacific	5.0	18.6	2.5
Middle East and North Africa	6.4	14.7	5.1
Latin America and the Caribbean	2.4	19.8	3.9
Eastern Europe	7.0	4.2	2.6
All Developing Countries	3.7	14.0	3.5
Industrialized Countries	4.6	18.0	2.6
Global Average	5.0	15.8	4.5
Global Minimum	0.7	0.1	0.8
Global Median	4.2	16.2	3.4
Global Maximum	14.8	37.7	16.7
Global Standard Deviation	2.9	8.4	3.9
Correlation with Development Index	0.33	0.12	−0.30

Source: Housing Indicators Program [1994].

Pakistan and Venezuela also reported values lower than 2.0. Among countries reporting exceptionally high values for this indicator, four (India, Hong Kong, Morocco, and the United Kingdom) reported median values between 7.0 and 9.0. Six countries (China, Algeria, Poland, Korea, Germany, and Japan) reported values higher than 9.0; China reported the maximum value of 14.8 for this indicator.

The rent–to–income ratio had a global median of 16.2% and a global standard deviation of 8.4%, suggesting that the majority of renting urban families paid between 8% and 25% of their income on rent. There was no systematic variation among income groups. The median value for the developing countries as a whole (14%) was somewhat lower than that of the industrialized countries (18%). There were no great variations among developing–country regions, except that the median value for Eastern Europe was exceptionally low (4.2%), reflecting the prevalence of rent control. Among countries with little or no rent control, seven countries reported rent–to–income ratios of 12% or less: four in Southern Africa (Malawi, Kenya, Nigeria, and South Africa); one is Asia (Bangladesh); and two in Europe (Norway and Sweden). The median value for countries with little or no rent control was 18.5%, while the median value for countries with modest to severe measures of rent control was 7.8%. Only three countries in the latter group, however, reported values of less than 6% (Russia, the former Czechoslovakia, and Tanzania). Seven countries, all with little or no rent control (India, Malaysia, Singapore, Korea, Chile, Mexico, and Turkey), reported values of 25% or more for this indicator. Korea reported an exceptionally high value (35.2%), reflecting the serious shortages of rental housing in Seoul. Singapore reported the highest value (37.7%), reflecting the fact that the rental market served largely higher–income families in 1990.

The global median value for down–market penetration was 3.4, slightly less than the median value for the house price–to–income ratio. This means that, in general, the formal sector did reach below–median income households, but not much below the median. To cite a specific example, in 1986 the Thai private sector initiated at least 37 new projects in Bangkok with more than 6,800 low–cost housing units. These were usually row houses with an average of 50 m^2 of floor area, located on small plots (averaging 160 m^2) in outlying suburbs. Seventy-five percent of these units were priced between $7,000 and $8,000, and, with available financing, were affordable[2] by 55% of Bangkok households [Angel and Dowall, 1987, 38–43]. Down–market penetration had a negative correlation of –0.30 with the Development Index. The value reported for the industrialized countries (2.6) was lower than the value reported for the developing countries (3.5). In general, the private sector in more–developed countries went further down–market than in less–developed ones. Among developing–country regions, Southern Africa, the Middle East and North Africa, and Latin America had above–median values for this indicator.

In the following section, we seek to explain the variations in these three measures of housing affordability using the statistical models for house prices and rents developed in chapter 6.

Modeling House Prices and Rents as Measures of Affordability

We now know that there were significant differences in house prices, rents, and affordability among different countries. The question is: what accounts for these differences? More particularly, we must ask whether differences in the housing policy environment accounted for these differences: does a more enabling regime result in more affordable housing? It is one thing to answer these questions in limited comparisons between pairs of countries, for example, and quite another to answer them by comparing all the countries in our sample, the objective of the following analysis..

Each one of the statistical models presented here, as well as in the following section, is a particular variant of the price model developed in chapter 6 using a different definition for the price of housing. To be of use for place-to-place comparisons, the price of housing can be normalized in one of two ways: (a) median house prices and rents can be normalized by household incomes; and (b) median house prices and rents can be normalized by housing quality. Our aim is to explore each of these different measures, because each measure reveals a different aspect of the price of housing, and there is, as yet, not single measure that can subsume all others without becoming too abstract. At the same time, to reduce the complexity of the presentation and to ensure consistency among the different models, we selected specific explanatory variables for the models, and we retained those same explanatory variables, with minor changes, in this chapter and in the following ones.

For the income variable we selected the logarithm of median household income because income by itself is highly nonlinear. For the demographic variable we selected the city population growth rate which is postulated to have a strong effect on housing demand. For the availability of housing finance we used the housing credit portfolio.[3] For the construction cost variable we used the construction cost-to-income ratio, and for the land price variable we used the serviced land price-to-income ratio. Both cost variables were normalized by income to indicate more specifically where input costs were high relative to incomes. Finally, for the policy environment we used the Enabling Index.

The reader should note that two of the six explanatory variables were part of the economic, social, and political context (household income and the city population growth rate); one variable represented the housing policy environment (the Enabling Index); and three variables represented housing market conditions (the housing credit portfolio, the construction cost-to-income ratio, and the land price-to-income ratio). We already know from our earlier models of housing market conditions that the Enabling Index was found to have a significant

Table 17.2. The Determinants of Housing Affordability Measures.

Variable	Log of Household Income	City Population Growth Rate	Housing Credit Portfolio	Construction Cost-to-Income Ratio	Land Cost-to-Income Ratio	Enabling Index	No. of Observations	R-squared & Adjusted R-squared	F-Value
House price-to-income ratio	0.34[a]	-0.37	-0.05	0.11	0.45	-0.28	45	0.63	$F_{6,38}$
	1.95**[b]	-3.43***[c]	-0.44	1.06	5.03***	-2.08**		0.57	10.81***[b]
Rent-to-income ratio	0.15	0.35	-0.11	0.05	-0.05	0.61	45	0.40	$F_{6,38}$
	0.59	2.22**	-0.61	0.31	-0.38	3.00***		0.30	4.20***
Down-market penetration	0.04	0.05	0.07	0.31	0.14	-0.42	37	0.32	$F_{6,30}$
	0.13	0.20	0.33	1.68*	0.83	-1.51*		0.18	2.34*

Source: Housing Indicators Program [1994].

[a] Figures in the top rows are standardized β–coefficients.

[b] Figures in italics denote *t*– and *F*–statistics.

[c] ***, **, and * denote 1%, 5% and 10% levels of confidence, respectively.

negative effect on the construction cost–to–income ratio, a negative (but not significant) effect on the land price–to–income ratio, and a positive (but not significant) effect on the housing credit portfolio. In other words, in the models presented here, the housing policy environment may affect house price not only directly, but also indirectly through its effect on housing market conditions.

The Determinants of House Prices and Rents Normalized by Income

The first set of models investigated the factors affecting the three measures of affordability presented earlier: the house price–to–income ratio, the rent–to–income ratio, and down–market penetration. The results for these models are summarized in table 17.2. The model for the house price–to–income ratio is presented on the top line of this table. The model had a high R–squared (0.63), suggesting that the explanatory variables explain almost two–thirds of the variations in the values of this indicator in our sample of cities. The model as a whole tells us[4] that the land price–to–income ratio had the most powerful effect on the house price–to–income ratio, followed by the city population growth rate, the level of economic development, and the Enabling Index.

Several aspects of this model merit our attention. First, land prices exerted a highly significant effect on affordability, considerably more significant than did construction costs—houses were significantly less affordable in cities with high land cost–to–income ratios. Second, houses were significantly more affordable in rapidly growing cities. The faster the growth of the city, the more affordable was its housing. These two results both suggest that limits to urban growth[5], that act to limit the supply of residential land, are likely to making housing less affordable. Third, this model showed that as income increased, houses became significantly less affordable. In other words, the share of income devoted to houses tended to increase as incomes increased. Housing consumed a higher share of incomes in cities and countries with higher levels of economic development. Finally, we note that the Enabling Index had a significantly negative relationship with the house price–to– income ratio. This is an important result: a more enabling housing policy environment was found to be associated with significantly higher levels of affordability as measured by the house price–to–income ratio.

The results for the second affordability measure, the rent–to–income ratio, are presented on the second line of table 17.2. This model had an R–squared of +0.40, suggesting that the variables used in the model explained more than one–third of the variation in rent–to–income ratios in our sample of cities. Only two of the explanatory variables, the city population growth rate and the Enabling Index, exerted a significant influence on the rent–to–income ratio. The effect of the city population growth rate, however, was opposite to its effect on the house price–to–income ratio. Cities with higher rates of population growth had lower house price–to–income ratios but *higher* rent–to–income ratios. Similarly, a higher degree of enabling was found to increase the rent–to–income ratio, rather than decrease it. This was largely due to the nonenabling effect of rent control, that tended to depress rental values. Clearly, where rent control was rampant, rents are significantly lower. Restricting the model to cities with little or no rent control did not reveal a clear pattern — the model became weak and no longer statistically significant. The explanatory power of the rent-to-income ratio model presented here therefore leaves much to be desired.

The results for the third affordability measure, down-market penetration, appear on the bottom line of table 17.2. This model had a lower R-squared value than the previous two models, 0.31, suggesting that the variables used in the model explained less than one-third of the variation in down-market penetration in our sample of cities. Only two of the explanatory variables, the construction cost-to-income ratio and the Enabling Index exerted a small, yet statistically significant, influence on down-market penetration. First, the private sector in cities with lower construction costs went further down-market than it did in cities with higher construction costs. Second, the private sector went further down-market in cities with more enabling housing policy regimes than it did in cities with less enabling ones.

House Prices and Rents Normalized by Quality

Prices and rents reflect the interaction of demand and supply in the housing market, but, more basically, they also reflect the different qualities and attributes of houses. Since the late 1960s, a number of housing researchers have attempted to explain the variation in house prices in terms of their qualities and attributes. One survey of empirical work carried out in the early 1970s lists a large number of locational, house-related, neighborhood-related, and environmental attributes that have been used to explain the variation in house prices in different cities. These attributes included travel time and distance from the central business district, accessibility to employment and schools, age of dwelling, structure type, number of storeys, floor area of dwelling, number of bathrooms, existence of various amenities, neighborhood quality, and air quality [Ball, 1973]. The method for estimating "hedonic" house prices — house prices as functions of their attributes and qualities — was described in Rosen [1974], and was similar to that employed in the present study. House prices were taken to be dependent variables in a multiple regression equation, with housing characteristics and attribute measures as independent variables. Once the coefficients of the independent variables were estimated, it was then possible to predict or estimate the hedonic price of any bundle of house attributes. Houses could then be differentiated by quality, and their prices could be estimated empirically as a linear sum of a set of products, each product being an attribute measure multiplied by its corresponding coefficient in the regression equation.

Unfortunately, the Global Survey of Housing Indicators collected only meager data on the quality and attributes of the housing stock. A Construction Quality Index was derived earlier (see chapter 15) as an equally weighted sum of three indicators for which values were collected in the Global Survey: permanent structures, the quality attributes of the median–priced house, and median household income. We use the Construction Quality Index here to obtain a number of price and rent indices that are normalized by quality. To obtain a hedonic house price index, we follow the same procedure used earlier to obtain the Construction Cost Premium. First we defined the *Housing Price Index* as the ratio between the reported price per square meter of the median–priced house and the estimated price per square meter of the median–priced house. In other words, the Housing Price Index measured the price paid for one dollar's worth of housing of *constant quality*. The estimated price for each country in the sample was obtained by fitting a regression line to the quadratic equation:

(1) $\ln p_i = a + bU_i + cU_i^2,$

where $\ln p_i$ was the natural logarithm of the reported price for country i, U_i the value of the Construction Quality Index for country i, and U_i^2 the square of this value. The resulting graph showing the scatter of country values as well as the regression line is given in figure 17.1. The logarithm of the price and the quality of construction were highly correlated, with an R–squared of +0.69 suggesting that differences in quality explain more than two–thirds of the differences in price. India (ID), Zimbabwe (ZI), and Turkey (TR) fell directly on the regression line, suggesting that reported and estimated house prices were almost identical there. Their Housing Price Indices were $1.02, $1.02, and $1.00 respectively. Pakistan (PK) reported considerably less expensive houses with a relatively high quality, and thus had a value for the Index of $0.46. Families in Karachi paid less than half a dollar for one dollar's worth of constant-quality housing. A similar hedonic price was estimated for rents: the *Housing Rent Index* was defined as the ratio between the reported rent per square meter of the median–priced house and the estimated rent per square meter of the median–priced house. In other words, the Housing Rent Index measured the rent paid for one dollar's worth of housing services of constant quality. The estimated rental values were obtained by fitting a regression line to the linear equation:

(2) $\ln r_i = a + bU_i,$

where $\ln r_i$ was the natural logarithm of the reported annual rent for country i, and U_i the value of the Construction Quality Index for that country. In this case, however, the sample was restricted to countries with little or no rent control. Ten countries with severe rent control were eliminated in the calculation of estimated rents. The resulting graph showing the scatter of country values as well as the regression line is given in figure 17.2. The logarithm of the rent and the quality of construction were also highly correlated, with an R–squared value of +0.71 suggesting that, in the absence of rent control, differences in quality explained more than two–thirds of the differences in rents in our sample.

The Housing Price Index and the Housing Rent Index were used to construct two additional indices: The *Weighted Housing Price Index* and the *Home Ownership Premium*: The Weighted Housing Price Index was defined as the sum of two

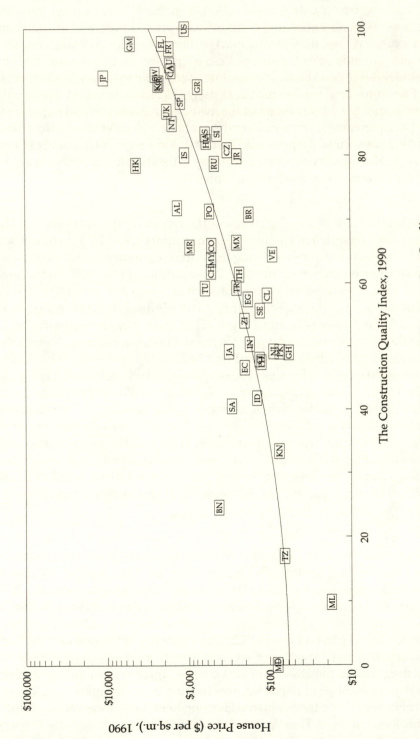

Figure 17.1. House Prices and Construction Quality.

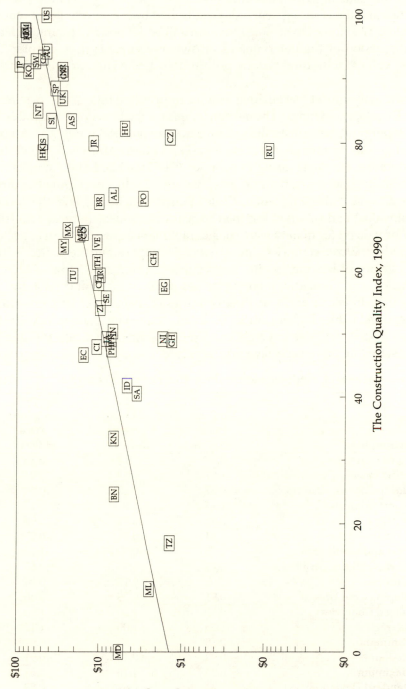

Figure 17.2. Annual Rents and Construction Quality.

products: the Housing Price Index multiplied by the percentage of home-owning households and the Housing Rent Index multiplied by the percentage of renting households. The Home Ownership Premium will be defined and examined later, in our discussion of the determinants of owner-occupancy (see chapter 23). Summary values for the three hedonic price indices defined here are given in table 17.3.

We note at the outset that all three hedonic indices had little or no correlation with the Development Index. The median values for the Housing Price Index for the developing and the industrialized countries were practically identical. Among developing-country regions, the Middle East and North Africa had higher than expected values for the Housing Price Index ($1.75), while Latin America and Eastern Europe had lower than expected values. Eight developing countries (Nigeria, Ghana, Pakistan, Jordan, Chile, Venezuela, Brazil, and the former Czechoslovakia) had values of less than $0.50 for this index. In these countries, houses normalized for quality were considerably less expensive than expected. Among industrialized countries, three (Greece, Singapore, and the United States) reported values of less than $0.50. Five countries (Morocco, Tunisia, Algeria, South Africa, and Germany) reported values between $2.00 and $3.00 for the Housing Price Index. In addition, three countries (Bangladesh, Hong Kong, and Japan) reported values higher than $3.00. Japan attained the maximum value for this index ($6.35). In these last eight countries, houses normalized for quality were considerably more expensive than expected, clearly a cause for concern.

Table 17.3. Hedonic House Price and Rent Indices, 1990.

Country Groupings	The Housing Price Index ($)	The Housing Rent Index ($)	The Weighted Price Index ($)
Low-Income Countries	0.97	0.74	0.87
Low-Middle Income Countries	1.01	0.89	0.94
Upper Middle Income Countries	0.67	0.60	0.54
High-Income Countries	1.15	1.26	1.17
Southern Africa	0.82	0.82	0.94
Asia and the Pacific	1.14	0.81	0.87
Middle East and North Africa	1.75	0.59	1.18
Latin America and the Caribbean	0.71	0.93	0.83
Eastern Europe	0.67	0.10	0.24
All Developing Countries	0.91	0.75	0.86
Industrialized Countries	0.92	1.20	1.14
Global Average	1.35	1.00	1.12
Global Minimum	0.28	0.00	0.01
Global Median	0.92	0.86	0.91
Global Maximum	6.35	4.10	3.81
Global Standard Deviation	1.31	0.69	0.82
Correlation with Development Index	0.12	0.03	0.08

Source: Housing Indicators Program [1994].

The Housing Rent Index was especially low in Eastern Europe, where rent control was still pervasive in 1990. It was also lower than expected in the Middle East and North Africa. All in all, there was altogether less variation in the Rent Index than in the Housing Price Index—the standard deviation in the former ($0.65) was roughly half that of the latter ($1.28). Only six countries (Bangladesh, Madagascar, Ecuador, Malaysia, Hong Kong, and Japan) reported values in excess of $1.75 for the Rent Index.

The Weighted House Price Index displayed similar properties to the two indices from which it was constructed, as was to be expected. Among developing-country regions, median weighted house prices were especially low in Eastern Europe ($0.24) and somewhat higher than expected in Southern Africa ($0.94). All in all, 10 countries (all developing countries) reported values of $0.50 or less for this index: Nigeria, Ghana, China, Egypt, Jordan, Venezuela, Brazil, the former Czechoslovakia, Russia, and Hungary. In contrast, five countries (Bangladesh, Madagascar, Tunisia, Hong Kong, and Japan) reported values in excess of $2.00 . Japan again attained the maximum value for this index ($3.81).

The Determinants of House Prices and Rents Normalized by Quality

What accounts for the variations in house prices and rents once we normalize them by the quality of construction? Using the same explanatory variables as before, we now examine the statistical models for the three hedonic indices previously discussed. The Housing Rent Index and the Weighted Price Index were modeled for the sample as a whole, as well as for countries with little or no rent control. The summary results for these models are presented in table 17.4.

At the outset, we note that the explanatory variables that have a significant influence in all the models were more or less the same: household income, the city population growth rate, the construction cost-to-income ratio, the land price-to-income ratio, and the Enabling Index (except that the Enabling Index did not exert a statistically significant effect on the Housing Rent Index). The housing credit portfolio did not have a significant influence on any of the hedonic price indices.

The model for the Housing Price Index is presented in the top row of table 17.4. The model had an R-squared value of 0.58, implying that the independent variables explained more than half of the variations in the index. The model yielded similar results to that of the house price-to-income ratio presented in table 17.2 above. The effects of the explanatory variables, however, were found to be stronger than before. The model tells us that, again, the land price-to-income ratio had the most powerful effect on the Housing Price Index, followed by the level of income, the Enabling Index, the construction cost-to- income ratio, and the city population growth rate.

First, land prices were found to have a more significant effect on the index than construction costs. Normalizing for quality, houses of similar quality were significantly less affordable in cities with high land price-to-income ratios. Construction costs did, however, exert a similar, but weaker, effect on the index.

Table 17.4. The Determinants of Hedonic House Price and Rent Indices.

Variable	Log of Household Income	City Population Growth Rate	Housing Credit Portfolio	Construction Cost-to-Income Ratio	Land Cost-to-Income Ratio	Enabling Index	No. of Observations	R-squared & Adjusted R-squared	F-Value
Housing Price Index	0.59 [a]	0.21	0.10	0.24	0.72	-0.33	45	0.58	$F_{6,38}$
	2.55*** [b]	*1.47**	*0.62*	*1.78*** [c]	*6.14****	*-1.85***		0.52	*8.81**** [b]
Housing Rent Index, Model I	0.62	0.58	-0.08	0.27	0.30	-0.04	45	0.41	$F_{6,38}$
	2.35**	*3.61****	*-0.43*	*1.75***	*2.22***	*-0.17*		0.32	*4.39****
Housing Rent Index, Model II (countries with little or no rent control)	0.53	0.42	-0.00	0.34	0.35	-0.32	38	0.42	$F_{6,31}$
	1.79**	*1.81***	*-0.01*	*2.07***	*2.45***	*-1.16*		0.30	*3.69****
Weighted Housing Price Index, Model I	0.68	0.45	0.07	0.29	0.63	-0.23	45	0.58	$F_{6,38}$
	3.02***	*3.24****	*0.46*	*2.15***	*5.45****	*-1.31**		0.52	*8.88****
Weighted Housing Price Index, Model II (countries with little or no rent control)	0.48	0.09	0.16	0.32	0.74	-0.61	38	-0.61	$F_{6,31}$
	2.13**	*0.49*	*1.14*	*2.56****	*6.78****	*-2.91****		-2.91	*12.4****

Source: Housing Indicators Program [1994].

[a] Figures in the top rows are standardized β-coefficients.

[b] Figures in italics denote *t*- and *F*-statistics.

[c] ***, **, and * denote 1%, 5% and 10% levels of confidence, respectively.

Second, this model showed again that as income increased, houses — this time of similar quality — become significantly less affordable. In other words, the share of income devoted to houses tended to increase as the level of economic development increased. Third, a key difference between this model and the earlier model for the house price-to-income ratio emerged: the sign for the effect of the city population growth rate was here reversed. Median-priced houses were indeed more affordable in rapidly growing cities, but they were generally of lower quality. Quality housing, however, cost significantly more in rapidly growing cities, where the price per unit of quality appeared to be higher.

Finally, we note that the Enabling Index again had a significantly negative relationship with the Housing Price Index. This is yet another confirmation of our basic conjecture, that a more enabling housing policy environment is associated with significantly higher levels of affordability as measured by the Housing Price Index. Normalizing for quality, house prices were significantly less expensive in enabling housing policy regimes than in nonenabling ones, another key result. To conclude, house prices for a given level of quality increased significantly with higher land prices and higher construction costs, higher levels of economic development as measured by household income, and higher city population growth rates; they decreased, however, when the housing policy environment was more enabling.

A similar model for the Housing Rent Index for the sample as a whole is presented in the second line of table 17.4. The model had an R-squared value of +0.41. In this model, however, more of the explanatory variables exerted a significant influence on the index than on the rent-to-income ratio presented earlier (table 17.2). The model tells us that the level of economic development, measured by household income, had the most powerful effect on the Housing Rent Index, followed by the city population growth rate, the land price-to-income ratio, and the construction cost-to-income ratio. This model showed again that as income increased, rents for houses of similar quality became significantly less affordable. In this model, as in the earlier model, the city population growth rate exerted an upward influence on rents. Similarly, normalizing for quality, rents for houses of similar quality were significantly less affordable is cities with high land cost-to-income ratios. Construction costs exerted a similar, although somewhat weaker, effect on the Index. Here, however, the Enabling Index had no significant effect, either positive or negative, on hedonic rents regardless of the presence or absence of rent control.

To neutralize the effect of rent control on the Housing Rent Index altogether, the same model was tested for countries with little or no rent control, by eliminating 10 countries with substantial rent control from the sample. The results of this modified model appear on the third line of in table 17.4. Again, the model had a similar R-squared value of +0.42. Again, the same variables exerted an upward pressure on the Housing Rent Index. It is important to note, however, that in this model the Enabling Index did exert a downward pressure on the Rent Index, similar in magnitude to those of the land price-to-income ratio and the construction cost–to–income ratio, although not a statistically significant one. In other words, in countries with little or no rent control, enabling housing policies may also result in reduced rents as well, in addition to reduced house prices, when both are normalized for quality.

The combined effects of the explanatory variables on the house price and rent indices became more accentuated in the statistical models for the Weighted Housing Price Index, both for the sample as a whole and for countries with little or no rent control. Summary values for the model for the sample as a whole are presented in the fourth line of table 17.4. The model had a high R–squared value of +0.58, explaining more than half of the variation in the index in our sample. And in this model, the Enabling Index did exert a statistically significant downward pressure on the Weighted Housing Price Index.

This downward pressure became stronger when the sample was restricted to countries with little or no rent control (bottom line of table 17.4). The resulting model had an R–squared of +0.61, explaining more than 60% of the variation in the Weighted Index in the restricted sample of 38 countries where data were available. We note that in this model, the city population growth rate did not exert a significant influence on the index. Four other explanatory variables did exert a significant upward influence on hedonic rents—household income, the land price–to–income ratio, the construction cost–to–income ratio, and the Enabling Index. This model showed again that as income increased, the weighted prices for houses of similar quality became significantly less affordable. Similarly, normalizing for quality, weighted housing prices for houses of similar quality were significantly less affordable in cities with high land cost–to–income ratios. Again, construction costs exerted a similar, although weaker, effect on the index.

Finally, we note that the Enabling Index exerted a significant downward pressure on the Weighted Housing Price Index in countries with little or no rent control. Its effect was second only to that of the land price–to–income ratio. In other words, in countries with little or no rent control, enabling housing policies result in reduced prices and rents, when these are normalized by quality and weighted by the shares of households who own and rent their homes.

* * *

In conclusion, we see that using different measures of house prices and rents we obtain a significant and consistent set of statistical results. All in all, the eight models presented and discussed in this chapter provide us with a broad understanding of how prices and rents vary across countries and cities with different economic and demographic conditions, different housing market conditions, and different housing policy regimes.

We summarize our findings as follows: First, house prices and rents, whether normalized by income or by quality, were generally found to be higher in countries with higher levels of household incomes. In other words, housing did not become more affordable as countries became more developed. People paid a higher share of their incomes for housing in richer countries than in poorer ones.

Second, the effect of the urban growth rate on prices and rents was generally positive; faster growth rates were associated with higher prices and rents. As an important exception, median–priced houses were found to be more affordable (having a significantly lower house price–to–income ratio) in cities with higher population growth rates. Median–price houses in these cities may indeed have been more affordable, but they were generally of lower quality. Rents, regardless of quality, were less affordable in faster growing cities. Normalized for quality, house prices and rents were both significantly less affordable in faster growing cities. Third, land prices generally exerted a strong and significant upward influence on house prices and rents. Of all the explanatory variables, land prices exerted the strongest influence on house prices and a less pronounced influence on rents. Fourth, higher construction costs lead to significant increases in both house prices and rents.

Finally, a more enabling housing policy environment, measured by the Enabling Index, affected prices, rents, and affordability both directly and indirectly. It affected them indirectly through its effect on housing market conditions discussed earlier, particularly through its significant influence on reducing construction costs. It also affected them directly in a number of ways. A more enabling housing policy regime significantly reduced the house price–to–income ratio and thus increased affordability. It significantly increased down–market penetration by the formal private sector. It also led to significantly lower house prices normalized by quality, as measured by the Housing Price Index. Neutralizing the effect of rent control, a more enabling housing policy environment led to lower hedonic rents in countries with little or no rent control. It also significantly reduced the overall price of housing normalized by quality, measured by the Weighted Housing Price Index, in countries with little or no rent control. Given these robust results we can only conclude that, insofar as the housing problem is one of affordability, housing policy indeed matters. Enabling housing policies tend to lower house prices and rents.

18

Housing Conditions and the "Quantity" of Housing

What finally matters in the conduct of housing policy is the reality of housing conditions — the actual houses, apartments, and other forms of shelter in which people live — even though housing policy must remain quite removed from this reality. The basic objective of housing policy is to meet real housing needs. It is therefore the quantity and quality of the material places we inhabit, as well as their suitability to our needs, that are the ultimate measures of the success or failure of housing policy. But housing policy, by its very nature, is and must be sweeping rather than particular. It cannot and should not attend to the form and function of every single house even though it is precisely the conditions of every single house that are its ultimate concerns. It must of necessity care for the state of the housing sector as a whole. This raises serious conceptual and practical difficulties, because it is not at all clear that the collection of houses as a whole can be grasped by housing policy makers as a single entity, and whether it can be measured in a manner that preserves and highlights the essential characteristics that matter to dwellers.

Conceptually, the problem of attending to the collection of houses as a whole is simplified when we perceive it as a market, as we have done so far. In the abstract terms of economics, the entire stock of houses is then reduced to bundles of quantities and qualities that command a price in the market. These bundles, whether perceived as material assets or as flows of services emanating from these assets, are then bought and sold; market equilibrium is attained when the overall quantity demanded at a given price is equal to the overall quantity that suppliers are willing to offer at that price.

From the perspective of housing policy, the conceptual focus on quantities demanded and supplied in the housing market is of primary importance because it enables us to focus on the housing sector as a whole. We can then monitor the overall performance of the sector, enabling it to function efficiently and equitably, and ensuring that it does not fail to generate an adequate quantity of housing. But while the focus on the quantity of housing is (conceptually) quite acceptable and indeed attractive, there remains a serious and rather intractable practical problem: What is the quantity of housing and how do we measure it? In this chapter, we articulate the perspective of dwellers as to what matters to them in housing, and then attempt to translate their concerns into several sets of measures of housing *quantity*.

The Perspective of Dwellers

The housing literature is awash with discussions of housing needs. It is universally agreed that housing is a basic need, in the sense of being a universal need at the most primitive level, a level we share with numerous insects, birds, and animals that need a place to dwell. There is an inherent difficulty, however, in agreeing about the basic requirements of dwellings.

An important perspective on the most basic requirements of dwellings is provided by the homeless. Homeless people talk of their need for a place to lie down and sleep, protected from the elements, and safe from thieves and molesters. They talk of their need for a place they can lock, in which to store their possessions, meager as these may be: the homeless "cavemen" of Sao Paolo, for example, put locks on the doors of the places they inhabit, where they "have a large number of 'identification objects' such as decorations, pictures, and religious symbols" [Taschner and Rabinovich, 1997, 27]. Homeless people also talk of their need for a home address and a place to bathe as being basic requirements for getting a job [Anderson et al., 1993, 125]. They also talk of a home as a basic requirement for having a modicum of human dignity.

For most of us who are well housed, "home" is a comfortable and familiar place of rest and work, a place to be away from strangers, and a place to invite people in. It is a store of possessions, a repository of old traditions, and a display — grand or modest — of our tastes, values, and status. It is a shelter from the elements, and a meeting point for our families, friends, neighbors, and associates. It is a private "fortress" in which we live by our own rules, creating our own unique expressions of beauty and respect, being as free as we can be from the impositions of the outside world. Our homes and their surroundings thus have qualities that give them a practical value as abodes, as the stage sets for the unfolding of our lives. But they also have deeply spiritual values.

For Mark Twain, for example, the home transformed itself into a living object: "Our house was not unsentient matter — it had a heart and a soul, and eyes to see with; and approvals and solicitudes and deep sympathies; it was of us, and we were in its confidence and lived in its grace and in the peace of its benedictions. We never came home from an absence that its face did not light up and speak out in eloquent welcome — and we could not enter it unmoved" [Clemens, 1917, in Rybczynski, 1989, 171]. For Bachelard [1958], the home was a psychic retreat: "[I]f I were asked to name the chief benefit of the house, I should say: the house shelters daydreaming, the house protects the dreamer, the house allows one to dream in peace" [6]. For Ruskin [1880], the home was a sanctuary: "I say that if men lived like men indeed, their houses would be temples — temples which we should hardly dare to injure, and in which it would make us holy to be permitted to live" [179].[1]

Many of these attributes would be very difficult to measure. But reading between the lines, they inform us about what would be of value in a well functioning housing sector. From the perspective of dwellers, the housing sector as a whole is well functioning when everyone is properly housed and no one is homeless. There is a separate dwelling unit for every household, no households need double up, newlyweds can find their own private home, and grown–up unmarried children can move out. Extended families can live together in one dwelling unit, or in adjacent dwelling units. Living space is adequate and can be modified by the inhabitants to meet their changing needs. House designs and layouts respect cultural traditions. There is adequate fresh air and natural light. Structures are safe and provide adequate protection from weather, fire, natural disasters, and unwelcome intruders. Buildings are properly maintained and are in good repair.

There is a sufficient variety of housing arrangements with different combinations of housing attributes such as space, quality, location, and tenure to meet all needs, and households may freely choose among different housing options. Moving from one place to another is simple and efficient, there are sufficient vacancies to choose from, and adequate information is available to ensure efficient choice.

In a well functioning housing sector, neighborhoods are pleasant and safe. Street noise is kept to a reasonable level. Infrastructure services — roads and pedestrian paths, transport, water supply, sewerage, drainage, garbage collection, electricity, and the like — are responsive to need, available, affordable, and reliable. Public amenities — schools, parks and playgrounds, police and fire protection, hospitals and clinics — are also responsive, available, affordable, and reliable. The air is clean. Location provides good access to employment, markets, and amenities. A number of transport alternatives are available, and they are affordable and reliable.

Neighborhoods are also stable and there is no threat of wholesale eviction without an established legal process that includes proper consultation with the residents, adequate compensation for loss of their property or their tenancy rights, and sufficient lead time to find or create new homes. Tenure in all its forms is secure, documented in enforceable contracts, and protected by due process of law. Tenure acquired through adverse possession is recognized by law and tenure rights of squatters accumulate through prolonged stay. Migration into the city is not restricted, and no discrimination in access to housing is tolerated anywhere.

Also, in a well functioning housing sector, there is a responsive, adequately financed and well managed social safety net (consistent with the resources available) that guarantees that households that cannot afford minimum standard housing, whether temporarily or permanently, are provided with such housing or with some form of assistance to enable them to procure or create it themselves.

People are not forced by law to consume more (or less) housing services or housing qualities than they prefer to consume. Housing consumers are protected from exploitation and fraud. They are also insured against serious risks — from the destruction of their homes brought about by wars, earthquakes, or floods, to the damage to their homes resulting from fire or structural collapse.

Residents have a say in the determination of building forms as well as opportunities to participate directly in the management and construction of houses and neighborhoods. For many, like Rybczynski [1989] for example, there is value in building their own nests themselves: "The most beautiful house in the world is the one that you build for yourself" [186]. Households have a right of access to information and expertise that can assist them in promoting and protecting the quality and value of their houses, neighborhoods, and cities through participation in the political process. The issue for them is often not "What is to be built?" but rather "How is it to be built?" [Angel, 1983, 11]. Houses can be built gradually over a long period of time. Households are not held to building standards that they can ill afford; and they are not prevented from using the dwelling unit for income-generating activities as long as they do not infringe on their neighbors' rights. Residents can organize freely to protect their houses and neighborhoods. Laws governing housing are realistic, well understood, and appreciated by dwellers; and such laws are tailored to their economic resources. Interaction with government agencies in the pursuit of building permits, land documents, or public services is cordial, fair, and efficient.

Clearly, each one of the qualities and attributes described here has a price. Each household, with its limited resources, prefers some of these qualities to others and prefers spending on housing not more than necessary for it to have the desired qualities it seeks. Again, from the perspective of dwellers, the housing sector as a whole is well functioning when housing expenditures — be they payments for house purchases, mortgages, or rents; the cost of land, labor, and materials; repair and maintenance expenditures; utility rates; insurance premiums; and taxes — do not take up an undue portion of household income, and households can choose to consume more or less housing if they so desire.

There is a sufficient variety of housing arrangements and combinations — from the very inexpensive to the very expensive — that provides affordable shelter to all income groups. House prices and rents, as well as total housing expenditures, are not subject to undue variability. Housing finance, in the form of a variety of mortgage instruments, is available to smooth housing expenditures over time and to allow households to save and invest. Savings are adequate for down payments, and dwelling units are accepted as sufficient collateral. Houses and dwelling units are economic assets that can accumulate value over time, that can be freely bought and sold by their owners, and that can be used as collateral for securing loans. Housing transactions costs are low and do not deter households from moving when necessary. Taxes on residential and other real properties are fairly distributed, efficiently collected, and sufficient to finance public infrastructure services and amenities to those properties at adequate levels.

Unfortunately, despite many common needs and aspirations, housing consumers are not a homogeneous group that necessarily shares a common vision of what a well functioning housing sector may be. Dwellers include households of every size — from the extended family to the single-person household, from the very rich to the very poor. They include owner-occupiers: those who own their house outright, those who own houses mortgaged to banks, those who own apartments in condominiums, those who share their houses in cooperative ownership, those who own their houses but rent the land on which they are situated, and those who own their houses and have squatters rights to land or occupy land without any rights at all. They also include renters: those who pay market rents for houses and flats, those who are assisted in their rent payments, and those who live in rent-controlled tenements. And these renters may occupy units owned by public, semipublic, nonprofit, or private landlords in a variety of contractual arrangements — from long-term leases contracts to short-term verbal agreements. Dwellers also include people who live in institutional or employee housing — worker or student dormitories, houses of public servants, homeless shelters, residential hotels, group houses for the elderly or the infirm, hospices, orphanages, mental hospitals, monasteries, communes, army barracks, prisons, and servants' quarters.

An Array of Measures of Housing "Quantity"

In the abstract, from the perspective of the economic theory of housing markets, any measurable quantity of housing will do. Indeed, in our models of the housing market presented in chapter 6, we posited an abstract quantity of housing demanded, which is assumed to increase when the price of housing decreases. In contrast, the abstract quantity of houses that producers are willing to supply is assumed to increase when the price of housing increases. Finally, when the market is in equilibrium, the equilibrium price of housing is determined when the quantity demanded is equal to the quantity supplied. The equilibrium quantity of housing in the market is thus determined simultaneously with the equilibrium price of housing.

In truth, there is no single entity or measure that corresponds to this equilibrium quantity of housing in the market. In fact, there is no single housing market in any sizable city. Houses, as we saw earlier, are a highly differentiated "product." In addition, they all occupy unique locations that makes them all different yet again. Good information on what is available is scant and incomplete. Only a small part of the stock, of the order of 2% to 4%, is produced in any given year, and builders cannot respond quickly to changes in demand. Existing houses, not only new ones, are on the market for sale, and they often undergo expansion, maintenance, and repair. These characteristics make the housing sector far removed from a "perfect" market. Still, we can and do seek to monitor changes in this market by measuring the quantity or quantities of housing regularly, quantities that represent what for us are important dimensions. Different measures of quantity necessarily focus on different dimensions of the housing sector, aspects that may be of great concern to some but not to others.

In the following chapters, we introduce and discuss a broad array of measures of housing quantity, each one highlighting an important dimension of the sector. For some readers, this exercise may seem burdensome. Is there not a *single* measure of housing quantity, they may ask, that best characterizes the housing condition of the city as a whole? There may very well be such a measure, and its pursuit is definitely worthwhile. For the time being, however, in the absence a single satisfactory measure, we can benefit from examining several measures of housing quantity, noting what they hide and what they reveal; whose interests they serve; how difficult they are to collect; how sensitive they are to policy changes; and what they explain to us about the mechanisms driving the sector. Some of these measures will survive the test of history, others will be modified, and new ones will be introduced; in due time (sooner, we hope, rather than later) we shall have a robust and dynamic set of measures of housing quantity that can guide and inform housing policy.

In chapters 19–23 we focus on five different kinds of measures of the quantity of housing. These measures, taken together, seek to cover as many of the housing characteristics discussed in the previous section as possible. Clearly, absolute quantities of housing, whatever they may be, cannot be usefully compared among different places, although they can be used to compare between different time periods in a single city (for example, to monitor rates of growth). Because our analysis is inherently comparative, we have no use for, say, the number of dwellings or the total amount of residential floor space in the city. And so again we face the issue of normalization. Each quantity needs to be normalized, so that it can be usefully compared.

In chapter 19, we focus on *dwelling units and living space* measures of housing quantity. Here we normalize the number of units and the amount of living space by numbers of people and households in the city to obtain measures of the adequacy of the housing stock in terms of dwelling units and living space. The measures introduced are dwelling units per 1,000 people, households per dwelling unit, median house size (floor area per household), persons per room, and floor area per person.

In chapter 20, we focus on quantifying aspects of the *quality* of the housing stock. Following our earlier procedure for prices and rents, here we construct a number of hedonic quantity indices, where the quantity of housing in a median–priced house is measured in units of identical quality, hence normalizing it in terms of quality. The quality indicators discussed are the hedonic house value, the hedonic annual rental value, the weighted hedonic house value, and the hedonic house value per person.

In chapter 21, we measure the housing stock in terms of its monetary *value*. Here we discuss the value of houses and the value of the stream of annual rents. The measures discussed are the median house value and the median annual rental value; the ratio of the value of the housing stock and the gross city product (GCP), and the house value–to–income ratio.

In chapter 22, we focus on indicators of annual housing *production and invest-ment*, that are measures of new additions to the existing quantity of housing in the city. They are, therefore, measures of the quantity or value of housing produced in a given year, normalized by the population of the city, the GCP, or the housing stock as a whole. The measures introduced are housing stock growth, annual housing production in units per thousand, and gross urban housing investment (the value of new stock–to–GCP Ratio). In this chapter we also introduce two annual measures related to production and investment: the vacancy rate and residential mobility.

Finally, in chapter 23, we look at the *tenure* aspects of the housing stock. The home ownership premium, the proportion of owner–occupied dwellings, unau-thorized housing, squatter housing, and homelessness are introduced as ten-ure–based measures of the quantity of housing, normalized as fractions of the housing stock or the total population in the city.

In each chapter we follow a similar procedure. First, we explore the literature in search of relevant measures and models of that aspect of the quantity of housing which is the subject of the chapter, define a set of indicators and indices of that aspect of the quantity of housing, and discuss their merits and limitations. Second, we present and summarize the values for these indicators and indices as reported in the Global Survey of Housing Indicators of 1990.

Third, using the equation for the quantity of housing introduced in chapter 6, we present a set of econometric models that seek to find the key variables in the economic, social, and political context, the housing policy environment, and housing market conditions that exert a statistically significant effect on each of these indicators or indices. We use a multiple–regression model to test whether any of the coefficients of these independent variables is significantly different than zero. If it is, the model suggests that differences in that variable are associated with significant differences in the quantity in question.

Measuring the Supply and Demand of Housing "Quantity"

Finally, using the elasticity equations developed in chapter 6, we investigate the structural characteristics of the demand and supply of each measure of quantity; specifically, their sensitivity or responsiveness to changes in incomes, prices, and the policy environment. Of specific interest to us in the foregoing discussion are the income elasticity of demand, the price elasticity of demand, and the policy elasticity of demand on the one hand; and the price elasticity of supply, and the policy elasticity of supply on the other.

The empirical literature on the income and price elasticities of housing demand is quite substantial, but the results are, on the whole, rather unsatisfactory. Empirical estimates vary considerably depending on the definition of the quantity in question; on whether incomes are current incomes or permanent incomes; on how the demand equations are specified; and on whether two-stage least-square methods or reduced-form equations are used in the estimates to eliminate aggregation bias. In general, however, a number of patterns do emerge from these demand studies. First, income elasticity estimates appear to be more reliable than price elasticity estimates. Second, income elasticities appear to be larger in absolute value than price elasticities, and opposite in sign as expected. An early study by deLeeuw [1971] estimated income elasticities to be of the order of 1.0. In a review of 14 housing demand studies in the United States, Mayo [1981b] concluded that "[a]mong the analyses reviewed here that calculate permanent income elasticities, and that appear to be *relatively* free of major biases, the range of income elasticities for renters is from 0.25 to 0.70 with most in the 0.3 to 0.5 range, and for owners from 0.36 to 0.87 with most in the 0.5 to 0.7 range" [103]. Mayo did not find reliable income elasticities higher than unity. A later study by Harmon [1988] found income elasticities in various studies to vary between 0.14 and 1.27; the study also showed that the lower estimates are associated with nonmovers and the higher ones with recent movers [176-177].

In their summary of a large number of developing-country studies, Malpezzi and Mayo [1987] reported income elasticities for renters that vary from 0.16 to 0.80 and income elasticities for owners that vary from 0.62 to 1.19. These studies reported price elasticities of demand that are smaller by comparison, with the median values for renters and owners equal to -0.3 and -0.2, respectively. The two authors also report their own calculations of income elasticities for owners in 14 cities in the developing countries, finding a median value of 0.46 in a range varying from 0.17 to 1.11; and a median value for renters of 0.49 in a range varying from 0.31 to 0.88 [690, 698]. The great variations in estimates of the elasticity of demand are rather unfortunate, if only because of their potential usefulness for policy. We cannot assume, for example, as is common in the design of housing assistance programs, that all households can and will spend 20% to 25% of their incomes on housing, or that this percentage can be used as a reliable measure of affordability of housing in different places and among different income groups.

Less attention has been paid to supply elasticities, and virtually no attention to the effects of policies on either demand and supply or on the income or price elasticities of demand and supply. Follain [1979], for example, showed that the hypothesis that the long-term supply elasticity of new construction in the United States is infinite cannot be rejected. A World Bank study estimated the supply price elasticities in Korea (0.10-0.40) and Malaysia (0.14-0.46), and associated these differences with nonenabling housing policies and consequently rising house prices in in the early 1980s. In contrast, it found supply price elasticities to be much higher in Thailand (6.6-10.2), and associated them with a more enabling regime and falling prices during the same period [Malpezzi and Mayo,

1997]. This study is one of the only ones to suggest that policy differences may have an effect on elasticities. In the chapters that follow, we devote a section in each chapter to modeling demand and supply elasticities in our sample of 53 countries, attempting to measure the policy elasticities of demand and supply as well. Needless to say, throughout the following discussion we focus especially on the effects of the policy environment on the particular conditions in the housing sector that are measured by the quantity indicator or index in question.

19

Dwelling Units and Living Space

The most basic perception of the adequacy of housing is that there be an adequate number of dwellings to house the entire population. This perception is rather simplistic, of course, because it does not contain any information about adequacy in terms of quality, crowding, affordability, location, or tenure choice. Whitehead [1991], for example, remarked that when the Conservative government came to power in the United Kingdom in 1979, "[I]t rejected this wider approach to evaluating housing need. In evidence to the Select Committee on Environment, the Secretary of State started by stressing the 'largest crude surplus of houses over households that we have ever had in this country' (House of Commons, 1981) as justification for cutting the amount of public resources allocated to housing" [879]. Crude measures are often advanced in support of crude policies. Still, precisely because such measures are often used in policy discussions, they merit a more detailed analysis.

Unit and Space Measures of the Quantity of Housing

The simplest way to compare two cities, in terms of the adequacy of their housing, is to compare their respective numbers of dwelling units, normalized by their respective populations. This approach leads us to the first, and most common, indicator for measuring the quantity of housing: *dwelling units per 1,000 people*, defined as the ratio of the total number of dwelling units in the city and the total population in the city (measured in thousands). This indicator is a rather gross measure of the adequacy of the housing stock, because, among its other shortcomings, it fails to account for differences in household size. Clearly, an adequate number of units per 1,000 people for cities with larger households will be smaller than an adequate number of units per 1,000 people for cities with smaller households.

From the perspective of the adequacy of the number of dwellings, an important requirement is that every family or household be housed in its own private unit, and that households need not double up. The appropriate measure in this case is a second quantity indicator: *households per occupied dwelling unit*, defined as the ratio of the total number of households in the city and the total number of occupied dwelling units of all types. There is no question that this is a more useful indicator for measuring the quantity of housing, because it allows each family the privacy of its own home. Unfortunately, it presents serious problems of measurement, if only because the definition of what constitutes a household is bound up with the house it occupies.

Intuitively, we consider a household to be a nuclear family — a couple and their children. Adult children who live with their parents, for example, are still considered part of the household, and when they move out they form new households, alone or with others. In contrast, young married couples who live with their parents, are considered a new and separate household sharing the house. The common, and rather loose, definition of a household is a family group eating together at one table. In some countries, extended families with married children live and eat together as one household. In other countries, complete strangers are forced to share an apartment with a single kitchen, but they all eat separately. Families everywhere rent rooms. In all countries, single people share rooms and apartments and eat together. For these reasons, where data gathering is less sophisticated, the number of households is often determined by simply equating it to the number of occupied dwelling units. And this procedure renders the indicator quite meaningless.

The indicator is especially valuable when it measures the number of households that are doubled up against their will and wish to occupy separate households. Young married couples who cannot move to a private home are the most common case. But there are more severe cases: In the late 1980s, an acquaintance of mine in Moscow divorced her drunken husband, an officer in the former KGB, because he was abusive toward her and her son. Yet they had to stay together in the same apartment for several years because neither could afford to move. She had to bring a woman friend to sleep over because she was afraid to be with her ex-husband alone.[1] Clearly then, a more careful measurement of this indicator is needed, if it is to reveal the number of households who are doubling up against their will, an important measure of the adequacy of the housing stock.

Over and above the question of whether every household occupies a separate unit or not, a more basic measure of the adequacy of housing may be the amount of floor space the household occupies. Dwelling units, in and of themselves, can be large or small. When they are very small, overcrowding results. Overcrowding, or lack of adequate space, is a prime policy concern because it hinders privacy and intimacy; and it makes the separation of different activities, such as cooking, eating, studying, sleeping, and entertaining rather difficult. The size of houses therefore matters.

The concern with the adequate size of dwelling units is incorporated in a third indicator of housing quantity: *median house size*, defined as the usable floor area of habitable rooms in the median–priced dwelling, including bathrooms, internal corridors, and closets. Covered semiprivate spaces, such as corridors, inner courtyards, or verandahs are included in this definition, if used by the household for cooking, eating, sleeping, and other domestic activities. But this indicator, while useful as a gross measure of overcrowding, also fails to account for household size. Small houses may be adequate for single–person households, but not for large families.

To account for the amount of space that individuals need to occupy, we have to introduce a more refined measure. Two indicators are commonly used to measure overcrowding: *persons per room*, defined as the ratio between the median number of persons in a dwelling unit and the median number of rooms in a dwelling unit[2]; and *floor area per person*, defined as the median usable floor area per person in the city in a given year.

The first of these two measures fails to account for different sizes of rooms and is hence less satisfactory that the second one, but the second one is more difficult to measure in household surveys. The amount of floor area per person is indeed the most useful basic measure of the adequacy of space. Its usefulness was clearly evident in former Communist countries, where housing production was often measured by the total amount of floor space, in millions of square meters, built in a given year [e.g., Russian Federation, 1990]. The summary results reported in the Global Survey of Housing Indicators of 1990 for these five unit and space measures of housing quantity appear in table 19.1.

The median value of dwelling units per 1,000 people was more than double in the industrialized countries than in the developing countries, 446 as against 197. The indicator had a high correlation with the Development Index (+0.86). It was

Table 19.1. Unit and Space Measures of Housing Quantity, 1990.

Country Groupings	Dwellings per 1,000 People	Households per Occupied Dwelling Unit	Median House Size (m²)	Persons per Room	Floor Area per Person (m²)
Low–Income Countries	204	1.13	31	2.5	7.1
Low–Middle Income Countries	195	1.19	47	2.0	9.4
Upper Middle Income Countries	225	1.06	67	1.3	15.9
High–Income Countries	446	1.01	75	0.7	31.5
Southern Africa	202	1.05	39	2.3	7.8
Asia and the Pacific	182	1.23	48	2.0	10.2
Middle East and North Africa	195	1.20	56	2.1	9.3
Latin America and the Caribbean	221	1.14	67	1.5	15.6
Eastern Europe	368	1.08	54	1.2	20.6
All Developing Countries	197	1.12	52	2.0	10.1
Industrialized Countries	446	1.00	75	0.7	31.0
Global Average	280	1.15	61	1.7	18.0
Global Minimum	91	0.79	20	0.4	3.7
Global Median	229	1.07	62	1.5	15.3
Global Maximum	575	2.06	180	5.5	68.7
Global Standard Deviation	129	0.28	31	1.0	13.0
Correlation with Development Index	0.86	-0.36	0.51	-0.77	0.78

Source: Housing Indicators Program [1994].

roughly similar among developing countries, hovering around the global median of 229. Among developing–country regions, Eastern Europe was the only exception, with a median value of 368 dwelling units per 1,000 people. Five developing countries reported values of less than 150 for this indicator: Madagascar, Zimbabwe, Bangladesh, Jordan, and Algeria. By contrast, three industrialized countries reported values of more than 500: Austria, Germany, and Japan.

The median value for households per occupied dwelling unit had a small negative correlation with the Development Index (–0.36), as expected. The value for the industrialized countries was essentially 1.00, and the value for the developing countries as a whole was 1.12. The problems of definition of this indicator rendered the reported results somewhat suspect, but, all in all, the reported numbers did not suggest severe problems of doubling up of households. Values were higher than expected in Asia and in the Middle East and North Africa, 1.23 and 1.20 respectively. Four countries (Madagascar, Zimbabwe, Jordan[3], and Korea) reported values of more than 1.50 for this indicator, exposing severe doubling up of households. In contrast, four countries (the former Czechoslovakia, Venezuela, Greece, and Japan) reported values of less than 0.90. In these countries, considerably more occupied dwelling units than households were reported, suggesting either measurement errors or that a significant number of households had second homes within city limits.

Median house size increased regularly with income, as expected, but considerably slower than income. The median value for the high–income countries (75 m^2 of floor space) was only 2.5 times that of the low–income countries (31 m^2), although the multiple of their respective median household incomes was almost 25. Among developing country regions, there were really no great variations in median house size from an overall median of 52 m^2. Houses in Latin America were reported to be somewhat larger, and those in Southern Africa somewhat smaller. Five countries (Tanzania, Malawi, Kenya, Bangladesh, and Hong Kong) reported median house sizes of less than 30 m^2. In addition to Hong Kong, two more industrialized countries reported values of less than 50 m^2: the Netherlands and Japan. In contrast, three countries (Venezuela, Canada, and the United States) reported median values higher than 100 m^2, with the United States attaining a maximum value for the sample as a whole (180 m^2).

The two crowding indicators, persons per room and floor area per person, shared very similar results. They both had similarly high correlations with the Development Index (0.77 and 0.78, respectively). The number of persons per room decreased regularly and floor area per person increased regularly with increasing incomes , as expected. There were 0.7 persons per room, considerably less than one, in the industrialized countries, and a median floor area per person of 31 m^2. By contrast, the median number of persons per room for the developing countries as a whole was 2.0, and the median value for floor area per person was 10.1 m^2. Among developing country regions, overcrowding as measured by these indicators was less acute in Eastern Europe (where the reported median values were 1.2 and 20.6 m^2, respectively), than in all other regions. Data for floor area per person was also available for 1995, as shown in table A27. There were no significant differences in the observed values between the two time periods.

The Determinants of Unit and Space Measures of Housing Quantity

The question of interest in housing policy is what accounts for these differences. Our simple model of the housing sector tells us to expect these quantities to be affected by the economic, social, and political context: by housing market conditions: and by the housing policy environment. The quantities in question were assumed a priori to be affected by the same set of variables: three contextual variables (the median household income,[4] the city population growth rate, and household size), three housing market conditions (the housing credit portfolio, the construction cost–to–income ratio, and the land–cost–to–income ratio), and one housing policy variable (the Enabling Index). These variables are essentially the same variables used in the house price models in chapter 17, with the addition of one contextual variable — household size — that is assumed to have a significant effect on quantities but not necessarily on prices. Summary results for four unit and space measures of the quantity of housing are presented in table 19.2. [5]

The models all had high R-squared values, ranging from 0.61 to 0.85, implying that they explain considerably more than half of the variations in these quantity measures in our sample. We should note at the outset that two of the explanatory variables — the housing credit portfolio and the Enabling Index — did not exert a significant direct influence on any of the four quantity measures. This means that the availability of housing finance and a more or less enabling housing policy environment did not affect the number and size of housing units or the degree of overcrowding one way or another. It implies that these quantities were unaffected by whether housing policies are enabling or nonenabling, and that the more interventionist housing policy regimes succeeded in producing roughly equivalent amounts of housing units and floor space as the more enabling regimes.

All the models show that these quantity measures were significantly affected, to a similar degree, by household incomes. As expected, when incomes increased, the number of units and their size increased significantly, while the degree of overcrowding decreased significantly. The rapid growth of cities appears to have had a modest, though significant, negative effect on two of the four quantity measures presented here, the number of dwelling units per 1,000 people and the number of persons per room.

The second demographic variable in the model, household size, exerted a significant negative effect on the quantity of housing as measured by three of the four variables in this group. First, cities with larger households required a smaller number of dwelling units to house them. Second, larger households were more crowded than smaller households; in other words, the floor area of

Table 19.2. The Determinants of Unit and Space Measures of Housing Quantity.

Variable	Log of Household Income	City Population Growth Rate	Household Size	Housing Credit Portfolio	Construction Cost-to-Income Ratio	Land Cost-to-Income Ratio	Enabling Index	No. of Observations	R-squared & Adjusted R-squared	F-Value
Dwelling Units per 1,000 People	0.28 [a]	-0.22	-0.62	0.02	0.22	-0.09	0.04	44	0.85	$F_{7,36}$ [b]
	*1.83** [b]*	*-2.37***	*-4.85*** [c]*	*0.18*	*2.74****	*-1.30*	*0.34*		0.82	*28.98*** [b]*
Median House Size	0.46	0.02	0.10	0.05	-0.35	-0.26	0.11	45	0.61	$F_{7,37}$
	*1.85***	*0.10*	*0.47*	*0.33*	*-2.68****	*-2.26***	*0.61*		0.54	*8.37****
Persons per Room	-0.35	0.20	0.35	-0.04	0.12	0.14	0.06	43	0.70	$F_{7,35}$
	*-1.56**	*1.46**	*1.81***	*-0.26*	*1.04*	*1.12*	*0.36*		0.64	*11.70****
Floor Area per Person	0.40	0.03	-0.38	0.11	-0.16	-0.26	0.09	45	0.76	$F_{7,37}$
	*2.03***	*0.24*	*-2.29***	*0.94*	*-1.52**	*-2.83****	*0.58*		0.72	*16.84****

Source: Housing Indicators Program [1994].

a   Figures in the top rows are standardized β–coefficients.

b   Figures in italics denote *t*– and *F*-statistics.

c   ***, **, and * denote 1%, 5% and 10% levels of confidence, respectively.

dwellings or the number of rooms increased less than proportionately to accommodate increases in household size.

Two housing market conditions had significant effects on these quantities of housing–the cost of construction and the price of land. Surprisingly, increases in the construction cost-to-income ratio were associated with increases in the number of dwelling units per 1,000 people, suggesting that this measure of housing quantity was less influenced by market forces and more influenced by policy considerations outside the housing market. The other two measures of housing quantity – median house price and floor area per person – appeared to decrease significantly, though modestly, when construction costs increased. Finally, the price of residential land exerted a modest, yet significant, negative effect on two of the four measure of quantity discussed here – the median house size and the amount of floor area per person. The models suggest[6] a number of conclusions. First, household size had the strongest effect on the number of dwelling units per 1,000 people, followed by household income, the urban growth rate, and construction costs. Second, household income had the strongest effect on median house size, followed by construction costs and land costs. Third, median income and household size had the strongest effect on persons per room, followed by the urban growth rate. And fourth, household income had the strongest effect on floor area per person, followed by household size, land prices, and construction costs.

The Demand and Supply of Dwelling Units and Residential Living Space

What accounts for variations in the demand and supply of the quantity of housing, as measured by the five indicators introduced in this chapter? In this section, we focus on the effects of household income, the price of housing, the demographic variables (the urban growth rate and household size), the availability of credit, and the policy environment on housing demand; we also examine the effects of the price of housing, construction cost, land price, and the housing policy environment on housing supply. We estimate two models for each index, one for the quantity demanded (from which we derive the estimated the income elasticity, price elasticity, and policy elasticity of demand) and one for the quantity supplied (from which we derive the price elasticity and the policy elasticity of supply). The elasticity estimates for four of the five quantities just discussed are given in table 19.3 below.[7]

We note at the outset that the four demand models all had high R-squared values, ranging from 0.68 to 0.86. The income elasticity of demand was significantly different from zero in all four models. It was very small (0.09) for dwelling units per 1,000 people, and ranged from 0.34 to 0.38 in the three other models. The price elasticity of demand was not significantly different from zero for dwelling units per 1,000 people. For the median house size and the floor area per person measures the price elasticity of demand was roughly the same (–0.64 and

Table 19.3. The Income, Price and Policy Elasticities of Unit and Space Measures of Housing Quantity.

Variable	Income Elasticity of Demand	Price Elasticity of Demand	Price Elasticity of Supply	Policy Elasticity of Demand	Policy Elasticity of Supply	No. of Obser-vations	Demand Model R-squared & Adjusted R-squared	Demand Model F-value	Supply Model R-squared & Adjusted R-squared	Supply Model F-value
Dwelling Units per 1,000 People	0.09 [a] / 1.68* [b]	-0.12 / -1.11	- [d] / - [d]	-0.03 / -0.48	- [d] / - [d]	42	0.82 / 0.79	$F_{6,35}$ / 26.8*** [c]	0.09 / -0.01	$F_{4,37}$ / 0.94 [b d]
Median House Size (m²)	0.38 / 5.05***	-0.64 / -4.46***	-0.01 / -0.07	0.09 / 0.98	0.24 / 3.16***	43	0.68 / 0.63	$F_{6,36}$ / 12.8***	0.59 / 0.54	$F_{4,38}$ / 13.5***
Persons Per Room	-0.34 / -5.13***	0.35 / 2.65***	-0.52 / -1.82**	0.16 / 1.95**	-0.08 / -0.64	41	0.86 / 0.83	$F_{6,34}$ / 34.1***	0.38 / 0.31	$F_{4,36}$ / 5.5***
Floor Area per Person (m²)	0.36 / 4.87***	-0.67 / -4.74***	0.14 / 0.47	0.09 / 0.98	0.28 / 2.27**	43	0.85 / 0.82	$F_{6,36}$ / 32.9***	0.44 / 0.38	$F_{4,38}$ / 7.4***

Source: Housing Indicators Program [1994].

[a]   Figures in the top rows are elasticities.

[b]   Figures in italics denote t– and F–statistics.

[c]   ***, **, and * denote 1%, 5% and 10% levels of confidence, respectively.

[d]   Supply model not statistically significant.

–0.67, respectively). For the persons per room measure it was smaller and positive as expected (0.35). The policy environment exerted a modest, yet significant, influence on housing demand in only one of the four measures, persons per room; and this influence was surprisingly positive rather than negative. The policy elasticity of the demand for persons per room was 0.16, suggesting that a less–enabling policy environment was associated with a higher demand for living space.

The supply models were also statistically significant, although less powerful than the demand models. One of them, for dwelling units per 1,000 people, was not statistically significant at all; and the other three had R–squared values ranging from 0.38 to 0.59. Only the price elasticity of the supply of persons per room was significantly different from zero, attaining a value of –0.52. As the price of housing increased, crowding (measured by the number of persons per room) increased substantially. In two of the supply models, the policy elasticity of supply was significantly different from zero. As the policy environment became more enabling, the supply of housing measured either by the median house size or by the amount of floor area per person increased modestly, yet significantly. The policy elasticity measures for the two were 0.24 and 0.28 respectively.

* * *

In conclusion, we note that the unit and space indicators of the quantity of housing exhibited a number of systematic regularities. As expected, the economic, social, and political context exerted a significant and measurable effect on the degree of overcrowding. First, as incomes increased, overcrowding (measured by any one of the indicators) decreased significantly. Income was also found to have a significant effect on the demand for housing as measured by house size, persons per room, or floor area per person. The income elasticities of demand for these quantities of housing were found to be of the order of 0.34 to 0.38. House prices were also found to have a significant effect on the demand for housing as measured by these three indicators. The price elasticities of demand for these quantities of housing were found to be in the range of –0.35 to –0.67. House prices were also found to have a significant effect on the supply of housing as measured by the number of persons per room. The price elasticity of the quantity of housing supplied, measured by persons per room, was found to be of the order of –0.52.

Second, household size was found to have a significant effect on overcrowding. Cities with larger households had, on the whole, proportionally fewer dwelling units, as expected. Furthermore, dwelling units in these cities had less space per person than the dwelling units in cities with smaller households. Third, faster–growing cities were associated with modest levels of overcrowding—they had a relatively smaller number of dwelling units and a higher number of persons per room.

Housing market conditions affected overcrowding as well. Both higher construction costs and higher land prices had modest, yet significant, lowering effects on the size of houses and on the amount of floor area per person. On the other hand, the availability of mortgage credit did not have a significant effect on overcrowding as measured by any of these indicators.

Finally we observe that a more enabling housing policy environment was found to increase the supply of housing (as measured by the median house size or by the amount of floor area per person) significantly. It also had a small, yet significant, effect on increasing overcrowding (measured by the number of persons per room). Other than that, the housing policy environment did not exert a significant effect, whether positive or negative, on any of the basic quantity measures of housing presented in this chapter or on the demand and supply of these quantities. Basic shelter was found to be available in equal measures in both enabling and nonenabling policy regimes. Having said that, the housing policy environment was found to exert a considerably stronger upward effect on the quantity of housing, once quantity was measured in units of quality, the subject of the next chapter.

20

Housing Quality

The issue of the quality of housing has been the central issue in a housing policy debate that started in the industrializing European countries during the nineteenth century and continued in developing countries during the twentieth. The debate even narrowed occasionally to the question of "What constitutes a house?" or, in other words, to the question "When does a hovel, a shack, a shanty, or a plastic-and-cardboard contraption become a house?"

We already elaborated on this debate in our discussion of building codes and standards (see chapter 11). On one side of the debate stand those who believe that there is a minimum quality of housing (which they can sensibly define), below which human habitations become inhuman and can no longer be called houses. And it is indeed a short step from this position to decree such inhuman habitations invisible and nonexistent insofar as counting houses is concerned, to point to their state of disrepair and squalor as clear signs of moral degradation, and to demand their immediate removal and replacement with sturdy houses on solid foundations, houses that befit humans and are worthy of their name.

On the other side of the debate stand those who believe that houses reflect poverty; that the poor make rational decisions about how much housing they can afford to consume; that bad housing is not antisocial; and that, when people are given a stake in the houses and neighborhoods they occupy, they invest their labor and their savings in improving their houses over time. In the industrialized countries, this debate has more recently centered on issues of urban redevelopment versus rehabilitation, renewal, and conservation. In the developing countries, this debate has centered on the demolition of slums and the eviction of their dwellers versus slum upgrading and tenure regularization.

This debate is likely to be with us well into the new century, but there is no question that, as of this writing, most societies have now shied away from agreeing on a morally acceptable standard of housing and then ensuring that all their citizens are decently housed, as of right, in such standard housing. Surely, slums and squatter settlements continue to be destroyed for one reason or another, but clearly not with a commitment to replace them with decent houses for their original inhabitants. Singapore stands alone in its commitment, as well as its success, in replacing virtually all its slums and shantytowns with sparkling–white high–rise apartments of an increasing and enviable quality. But Singapore is unique, as we said before, being an island city–state with no rural–urban migration at all. Almost all sensible governments in other countries have had to stop, willingly or grudgingly, their unrealistic attempts to replace their substandard housing with good quality housing, and to focus instead on the gradual rehabilitation, renewal, and preservation of their housing stock. One might say that in the closing years of the twentieth century, we witnessed a silent revolution of lowered expectations.

In an important sense, the insistence on changing the word "housing" to *shelter* in the recent past reflects the position of those who have willingly lowered their expectations, and who believe (as I do) that hovels and shanties are indeed houses, or at least houses in the making, insofar as they provide the bare minimum that people demand from houses — shelter from the elements, a sense of privacy, a store of one's possessions, and a place to call home. This position, needless to say, does not mean that the housing status–quo is either desirable or acceptable. Far from it. It does mean that, in general, miserably bad housing should not be delegitimized and senselessly destroyed, but rather legitimized and gradually improved over time. It also means, as we noted earlier, that arbitrarily high minimum housing standards are counterproductive, because quality simply reflects poverty, and poor people cannot afford to live in houses that are beyond their means.

In the previous chapter we discussed a number of measures that focused on *shelter*, insofar as they looked at living space without inquiring about the quality of that living space. As such, these indicators are important indicators, especially in the poorer countries, because they focus on the most basic dimension of housing — living space — regardless of its quality. But the quality of housing does matter. It matters to all of us, rich and poor alike. People the world over invest more of their work and their savings in improving the quality of their houses than on anything else.

What do we mean by the quality of houses? In chapter 18 we focused on this issue from the perspective of dwellers, the most important perspective on housing quality. To summarize our earlier discussion, we emphasize again that houses embody many different qualities, some of which are not easy to articulate, let alone measure. Other than adequate living space, the solidity and stability of structures is important, and so is their state of repair. Comfort is important and, as we noted earlier, the definition of comfort changes as technology advances. Privacy is crucial and so is personal safety. Variety is essential if all needs are to be met. Services and neighborhoods amenities are critical and so is access to jobs, schools, and markets. Beyond these basic requirements, there are myriad spiritual, aesthetic, symbolic, and status characteristics that are hard to define and may only be in the eye of the beholder, but they no doubt give houses *quality*. The difficulty in defining what constitutes quality in housing makes the effort of measuring it precisely almost insurmountable. Surely, there have been valiant attempts at defining and measuring housing quality, all with different purposes in mind, and all falling short of a simple, transparent, and inclusive measure that we can use to measure overall housing sector performance. Such a simple and acceptable measure still eludes us, but the housing literature does offer us a glimpse of the possibilities inherent in the measurement of housing quality.

Hedonic Measures of the Quality of Housing

Several indicators in the literature seek to measure the quality of physical structures. The age of structures is often used as a proxy for a quality measure [Kadas, 1991, 226]. Other measures involve reference to an arbitrary standard of housing, that may vary considerably from country to country. These may include the percentage of "permanent," "upgradable," and "nonupgradable" dwelling units in the housing stock [Robert A. Nathan Associates and the Urban Institute, 1984, 49]; or the "incipient," "consolidating," and "consolidated" households in squatter settlements (based on a consolidation index that includes building materials and finishes of house, presence of water, drainage, and electricity, material possessions, and degree of specificity of room function) [Ward, 1982]. There are some measures of specific problems with dilapidated housing: additional heating required, heating broken in one or more places, cracks in ceilings and walls, holes in floors, broken plaster and peeling paint, and rodent infestation [Stegman, 1988, 131].

There are several indicators that measure the existence of basic amenities in the home, with different definitions of these amenities and with an emphasis on either their lack or their presence: the number of units with "full comfort" (bath and toilet), "partial comfort" (bath or toilet), and "no comfort" (neither bath nor toilet) [Kadas, 1991, 223–226]; the percentage of dwellings with basic amenities (piped water, fixed bath or shower, central heating) [United Nations, 1992, table 18, 92–99]; dwellings lacking basic amenities (toilet inside dwelling, fixed bath in a bathroom, wash basin, sink, hot and cold water at three points) [Whitehead, 1974, 9]; percentage of households with connections to electricity [UNCHS, 1994, 22]; telephone lines per 1,000 people [UNCHS, 1994, 30]; and access to outdoor space within a specified time [OECD, 1982, 39].

Two types of indicators that relate to the city as a whole have a direct impact on the quality of the residential environment: environmental indicators and residential access indicators. Environmental quality indicators include the accumulated daily concentrations of air pollutants in excess of the World Health Organization's standards; carbon dioxide emissions per capita [World Bank, 1992, 11]; solid waste generated per capita per day; percentage of population enjoying regular solid waste collection [UNCHS, 1994, 28]; and the annual average fatality rate from natural disasters per million population [Estes, 1988, 20, 31–32].

Residential access indicators include the average trip cost and speed for work trips (by public and private transport); automobile ownership per 1,000 people; number of buses per 1,000 people; the average daily commute (in minutes) and the change in the average daily commute [Malpezzi, 1994, 8]. A large number of these measures have been used by housing researchers to estimate the hedonic house prices discussed earlier (see chapter 17).

Finally, there have been a number of attempts to create indicators of housing satisfaction. Some of these measure the percentage of respondents who mention a given complaint. For example, a Japanese study included the difficulty of maintaining privacy, plus high rents, pollution, little sunlight, poor ventilation, shoddy facilities, old and rundown houses, too little space, and no garden space as common complaints.[1]

The Global Survey of Housing Indicators of 1990 assembled very little information on the quality of housing. Only two questions—one on the percentage of permanent structures and another that asked for the enumeration of the basic qualities of the median-priced house—focused on the quality of houses directly. And in addition, there were two questions—one on the percentage of houses with a piped water supply and another on the length of the journey to work—that inquired about the quality of residential amenities and access to jobs. The latter two were incorporated, as we saw earlier, as measures of the quality of residential infrastructure and formed components of the Residential Infrastructure Index (see Chapter 10). The first two were incorporated into the Construction Quality Index. This index was derived as an equally weighted sum of three indicators: permanent structures, quality attributes, and the annual median household income (see chapter 15).

The Construction Quality Index was already used in the calculation of hedonic prices and rents (see chapter 17) as is common in the literature. We calculated a Housing Price Index for every country, an index that measures the price paid in that country for one unit's worth of housing of *constant quality*. A similar Housing Rent Index was calculated, as well as a Weighted Housing Price Index. The Weighted Housing Price Index was obtained by summing two products: the Housing Price Index multiplied by the percentage of home-owning households and the Housing Rent Index multiplied by the percentage of renting households. Given these three price indices, we can now construct four parallel indices that measure the *quantity* of housing in units of constant quality in the cities in the sample.

More precisely, we can construct four indices that measure the dollar value, the rental value, and the weighted dollar value of the median-priced house, plus the weighted dollar value of the median-priced house per person in each city in units of constant quality. The hedonic house value was derived simply by dividing the reported median house price by the estimated Housing Price Index. Similarly, the hedonic annual rental value was derived simply by dividing the reported median annual rent by the estimated Housing Rent Index. To take a simple example, the median house price in Paris in 1990 was $136,452. The Housing Price Index was estimated at $0.70, implying that Parisians paid $0.70 for $1.00 worth of constant quality housing. The hedonic house value in Paris was therefore $136,452/$0.70 = $193,174. Parisian owner–occupiers were living in houses that were worth more, in terms of quality, than what they in fact paid for them. In contrast, Parisians paid a median annual rent of $6,392 in 1990. The Housing Rent Index was estimated at $1.47, implying that Parisians paid $1.47 in rent for $1.00 worth of rent of constant quality housing. The hedonic annual rental value in Paris was therefore $6,392/$1.47 = $4,356. Parisians tenants were living in houses that were worth less, in terms of quality, than what they paid for them.

The Weighted Housing Price Index is more difficult to calculate. To derive it, we first need to estimate the capitalized value of the stream of hedonic annual rental values. We do this by estimating an interim indicator, the *hedonic rent–to–value ratio*. The hedonic rent–to–value ratio is defined as the ratio between the annual hedonic rental value and the hedonic house value in the city. This ratio is a measure of the rate of capitalization of the housing stock normalized for quality, or of the rental stream in units of quality from housing property normalized for quality.

The hedonic rent–to–value ratio for the countries in our sample was found to decline with increasing incomes, from a median value of 5.1% in the low–income countries, to a median value of 2.7% in the high–income countries. This index therefore had a strong negative correlation with the Development Index, –0.71. The strong relationship of this index to income is graphed in figure 20.1. Two estimates were calculated for the estimated hedonic rent–to–value ratio for each country, a linear estimate and a quadratic estimate. Both are shown in figure 20.1. The linear estimate was calculated for all but the three lowest–income countries (Tanzania, Malawi, and Madagascar) which were found to have very low values for this index. Its R–squared is 0.78. The quadratic estimate was calculated for the sample as a whole. It R–squared is 0.70.[2] In general, except for the very low–income countries, the index fell with increasing incomes (as expected) because the stream of rental incomes and the time horizon of owners were both longer in the higher–income countries.[3]

Given an estimated value of this ratio for each country in our sample, we can calculate the Weighted Housing Price Index by summing two algebraic expressions: the hedonic house value multiplied by the percentage of home–owning households; and the hedonic annual rental value, multiplied by the percentage of renting households and divided by the estimated hedonic rent–to–value ratio. This may sound more complicated than it really is. We return to our Paris example. The actual hedonic rent–to–value ratio can be obtained simply by dividing the hedonic annual rental value by the hedonic house value: $4,356/$193,174 = 2.25%. The estimated hedonic rent–to–value ratio for Paris was found in the regression analysis to be 2.5%. Owner–occupancy in Paris in 1990 was

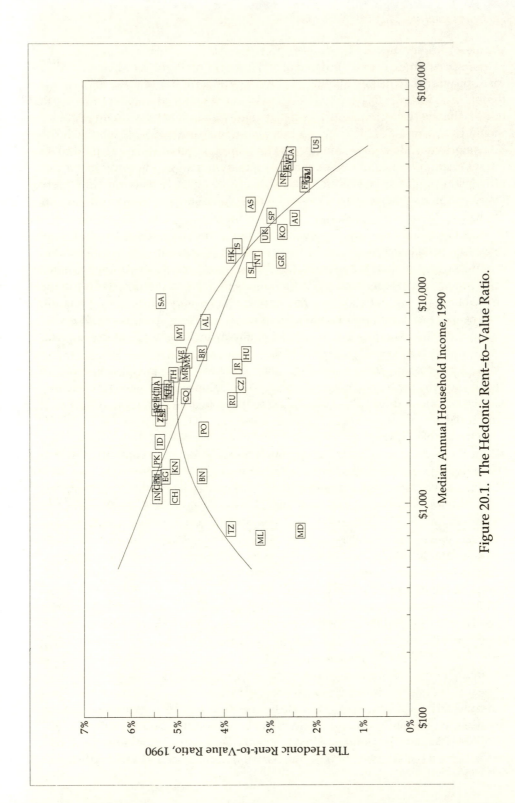

Figure 20.1. The Hedonic Rent-to-Value Ratio.

42.9%. The Weighted Housing Price Index for Paris therefore equals 42.9% × $193,174 + (100% – 42.9%) × $4,356/2.5% = $181,359.

Finally, a fourth hedonic measure of the quantity of housing, the hedonic house value per person, was derived by dividing the Weighted Housing Price Index by household size. This measure is similar to the measure of the amount of floor area per person discussed in chapter 19, except that it measures units of housing quality per person instead of units of floor space. The summary values for these four hedonic measures of the quantity of housing appear in table 20.1.

Examining this table, we can immediately observe that all four hedonic measures display a similar and consistent relationship to income. All can be seen to increase with income, and all display high degrees of correlation with the Development Index, ranging from +0.60 to +0.70.[4] However, the rate of increase with increasing income varies among them. The reported median for the hedonic house value per person for the industrialized countries is more than 20 times that of the reported median for the developing countries as a whole; the multiple for the hedonic house value is 12.5; the multiple for the weighted hedonic house value is 10; and the multiple for the hedonic annual rental value is only 6. This suggests, first of all, that individuals experience higher increases in housing quality with income than do households, largely because increases in income are accompanied by shrinking household sizes. Second, with increased incomes, house values increased at double the pace as rents for a housing unit of identical quality.

Among developing–country regions, Eastern Europe attained higher than

Table 20.1. Quality Measures of Housing Quantity, 1990.

Country Groupings	Hedonic House Value ($)	Hedonic Annual Rental Value ($)	Weighted Hedonic House Value ($)	Hedonic House Value per Person ($)
Low–Income Countries	6,001	323	6,285	1,178
Low–Middle Income Countries	11,010	559	11,461	1,983
Upper Middle Income Countries	32,576	1,345	29,453	6,416
High–Income Countries	129,421	3,270	121,138	42,923
Southern Africa	6,456	349	7,032	1,391
Asia and the Pacific	8,648	443	9,492	1,942
Middle East and North Africa	14,639	764	15,318	3,489
Latin America and the Caribbean	15,982	838	16,214	3,815
Eastern Europe	42,998	1,567	35,571	12,581
All Developing Countries	10,093	519	10,415	2,349
Industrialized Countries	126,529	3,112	102,829	49,606
Global Average	58,316	1,697	58,322	21,640
Global Minimum	1,483	42	1,280	213
Global Median	20,445	962	20,030	4,642
Global Maximum	542,354	10,820	588,138	224,480
Global Standard Deviation	87,717	1,878	93,010	37,483
Correlation with Development Index	0.63	0.70	0.60	0.64

Source: Housing Indicators Program [1994].

expected values for all four hedonic indices. This occurred partly because the quality of housing in this region was relatively high compared to other developing countries — largely due to of the absence of unauthorized housing and squatter housing. But these values are also high because the Construction Quality Index failed to distinguish more subtle differences in housing quality. There is no question that, in comparison to the quality of construction in Western Europe, for example, the ancient methods of prefabrication and the shoddy, almost reckless, construction of public housing flats in the years before the collapse of Eastern European Communism left much to be desired. Still, flawed though they were, they were produced in ample supply and they did score high values on the index. In general, values for Latin America and for the Middle East and North Africa were also consistently higher than the developing-country median values, while values for Southern Africa and Asia were consistently lower than the developing-country median values.

The Determinants of Quality Measures of Housing Quantity

Following the procedure established in the previous chapters, we now investigate the statistical models for these four hedonic quality indices, using the same model structure and the same set of explanatory variables representing the economic, social, and political context; the housing policy environment; and market housing conditions. The summary results of these four models appear in table 20.2.

At first inspection, we can see that the four models are essentially similar. All the models had reasonably high R-squared values, ranging from 0.56 to 0.66, suggesting that these models explain more than half of the variations in the hedonic measures of the quantity of housing. Again, as in the models discussed in chapter 19, the housing credit portfolio and the Enabling Index did not exert a significant direct influence on any of these quantity measures.

In all four models, the explanatory variable that exerted the strongest pressure on the quantity of housing measured in terms of quality units is household income. Comparing these models with the models of the quantity of housing in chapter 19, we can see that income exerted considerably more influence on the quantity of housing measured in terms of quality than on the quality of housing measured simply in terms of units and floor space.

Put another way, the amounts of dwelling units and living space are quantity measures of basic housing needs, needs that must be satisfied even at very low levels of income and that increase much less than proportionately with increased incomes. Housing quality measures, on the other hand, are associated with improved living conditions and creature comforts. In countries with higher household incomes, households actively seek to improve the quality of their houses, with the result that the quantities of housing they consume (measured in units of constant quality) do appear to vary in direct proportion to income.

The second explanatory variable found to have a significant, though more modest, impact on three of the four hedonic measures is the rate of urban growth.

Table 20.2. The Determinants of Quality Measures of Housing Quantity.

Variable	Log of Household Income	City Population Growth Rate	Household Size	Housing Credit Portfolio	Construction Cost-to-Income Ratio	Land Cost-to-Income Ratio	Enabling Index	No. of Observations	R-squared & Adjusted R-squared	F-Value
Hedonic House Value	0.71 [a]	0.22	-0.18	0.08	-0.18	-0.13	-0.09	45	0.57	$F_{7,37}$
	2.69*** [b]	1.32 [c]	-0.80	0.50	-1.29	-1.04	-0.46		0.49	7.1*** [b]
Hedonic Annual Rental Value	0.76	0.14	-0.14	0.03	-0.20	-0.15	-0.06	45	0.66	$F_{7,37}$
	3.23***	0.94	-0.69	0.23	-1.63*	-1.43*	-0.37		0.60	10.5***
Weighted Hedonic House Value	0.71	0.26	-0.17	0.10	-0.19	-0.12	-0.10	45	0.56	$F_{7,37}$
	2.62***	1.53*	-0.75	0.61	-1.35*	-0.99	-0.48		0.47	6.6***
Hedonic House Value per Person	0.63	0.25	-0.29	0.12	-0.12	-0.14	-0.05	45	0.58	$F_{7,37}$
	2.40**	1.51*	-1.31*	0.78	-0.89	-1.21	-0.25		0.50	7.3***

Source: Housing Indicators Program [1994].

[a] Figures in the top rows are standardized β–coefficients.

[b] Figures in italics denote *t*– and *F*–statistics.

[c] ***, **, and * denote 1%, 5% and 10% levels of confidence, respectively.

Generally speaking, cities that grow more rapidly were found to have *higher* quality housing that slower–growing ones. These findings suggest that unrestricted urban growth may be an important condition for improving the housing conditions of the majority, and that restrictions on growth may be counterproductive, as we suggested earlier (chapter 11).

Household size, the third explanatory variable, did not have a significant effect on the hedonic measures of quantity of housing, except in the case of the hedonic house value per person. As noted in the discussion of floor area per person, the quantity of housing – in this case measured in units of quality – increased less than proportionately with household size. Holding other variables constant, bigger households, in general, lived in houses where the quality of housing per person is considerably lower than that of smaller households.

Finally, two housing market conditions exerted a significant, though more modest, negative effect on these hedonic measures of the quality of housing: the cost of construction and the price of residential land. In all four models, higher input costs were associated with lower values for the four indices, although only three of the values were statistically significant. Higher construction and land costs thus tended to reduce the equilibrium values for the quantity of housing measured in units of housing quality.

The Demand and Supply of Housing Quality

The effect of housing policy on these hedonic measures of the quantity of housing became more pronounced when we shifted our focus from the equilibrium quantities modeled in the previous section to the quantities demanded and supplied. Following the same procedure outlined in chapter 6, we now investigate the effects of household income, the estimated price of housing, mortgage credit, and the policy environment on the demand for the four hedonic measures of housing quantity; we also examine the effect of the estimated price of housing, the inputs costs of land and construction, and the policy environment on the supply of these quantities. We estimate two models for each index, one for the quantity demanded (from which we derive the estimated the income elasticity, price elasticity, and policy elasticity of demand) and one for the quantity supplied (from which we derive the price elasticity and the policy elasticity of supply). The results of these calculations appear in table 20.3.

A cursory look at the table reveals that all the demand models have high R–squared values, ranging from 0.84 to 0.92, suggesting that these models explain more than three–quarters of the variations in the quantity demanded as measured by the hedonic indices in our sample. The R–squared values for the supply models are lower, ranging from 0.41 to 0.48, suggesting that these models explain almost half of the variations in the quantity supplied as measured by the hedonic indices in our sample. Several observations merit our attention. First, we note that the income elasticities of demand were found to be close to unity, ranging from 0.99 to 1.13. These elasticities were considerably higher than those observed

Table 20.3. The Income, Price, and Policy Elasticities of the Quality Measures of Housing Quantity.

Variable	Income Elasticity of Demand	Price Elasticity of Demand	Price Elasticity of Supply	Policy Elasticity of Demand	Policy Elasticity of Supply	No. of Observations	Demand Model R-squared & Adjusted R-squared	Demand Model F-value	Supply Model R-squared & Adjusted R-squared	Supply Model F-value
Hedonic House Value	1.08 [a] / 7.77*** [b]	-0.39 / -2.09**	1.06 / 1.85**	0.16 / 0.94	0.89 / 3.48*** [c]	43	0.88 / 0.86	$F_{6,36}$ 43.6***	0.47 / 0.41	$F_{4,38}$ 8.3*** [b]
Hedonic Annual Rental Value	0.99 / 6.38***	-0.74 / -1.92**	-0.15 / -0.38	0.38 / 2.01**	0.86 / 3.38***	43	0.84 / 0.82	$F_{6,36}$ 31.9***	0.45 / 0.39	$F_{4,38}$ 7.9***
Weighted Hedonic House Value	1.13 / 8.19***	-0.62 / -2.32**	1.01 / 1.63*	0.23 / 1.35*	0.76 / 2.89***	43	0.89 / 0.87	$F_{6,36}$ 46.4***	0.48 / 0.42	$F_{4,38}$ 8.6***
Hedonic House Value per Person	1.13 / 8.19***	-0.62 / -2.32**	1.21 / 1.58*	0.23 / 1.35*	0.79 / 2.45***	43	0.92 / 0.90	$F_{6,36}$ 65.5***	0.41 / 0.35	$F_{4,38}$ 6.7***

Source: Housing Indicators Program [1994].

[a] Figures in the top rows are elasticities.
[b] Figures in italics denote t– and F–statistics.
[c] ***, **, and * denote 1%, 5% and 10% levels of confidence, respectively.

for the raw median house size and the floor area per person not adjusted for quality, that were in the range of 0.34 to 0.38 (see table 19.3). This finding may clarify our earlier discussion of the literature on the income elasticities of demand for housing, that highlighted the observed differences in different studies and attributed them to, among other things, different measures of quantity. The comparison between the two models suggests that these differences may be systematic, namely that the demand for basic shelter is less sensitive to income than the demand for quality or comfort in housing. These findings echo earlier findings by Follain and Jimenez [1985a] who concluded that "[T]he empirical literature on the demand for housing characteristics indicates that the income elasticity of the demand for living space is less than unity while the income elasticity for quality variables is greater than unity" [430–431].

In contrast to the systematic difference in the effect of income, the price elasticities of demand in these models do not vary significantly from those for the raw median house size and the floor area per person not adjusted for quality. In the demand models in the above table they vary between –0.39 and –0.74, and in the earlier models they varied between –0.64 and –0.67. The demand for quality in housing is thus found to be just as sensitive to price as the demand for basic shelter not accounting for quality. We note in passing that the observed elasticities in both demand models are very close to the median value of –0.61 reported by Kravis et al. [1982] in their cross–country comparisons of the price elasticity of rents.

In chapter 19, the price elasticity of supply of the median house size and the floor area per person could not be assumed to be different from zero.[5] In contrast, the price elasticities of supply of the hedonic house value, the weighted hedonic house value, and the hedonic house value per person were all significantly different from zero and ranged from 1.01 to 1.21. This suggests that the supply of housing when the quantity of housing accounts for its quality was more sensitive to price than the supply of basic shelter.

Finally, we note that the housing policy environment exerted a strong and significant upward thrust on both the demand and supply of housing when the quantity of housing accounted for its quality. Again, the effects of the housing policy environment were consistently higher than those observed in the earlier models in chapter 19. In these earlier models, the policy elasticity of demand for the median house size and the floor area per person was found not to be significantly different from zero, and the policy elasticity of supply was in the range of 0.24 to 0.28. In contrast, the policy elasticity of demand for housing (when the quantity demanded accounts for quality) was positive and significantly different from zero in three of the four models, ranging from 0.23 to 0.38. The policy elasticity of the supply (when the quantity supplied accounts for quality) was also found to be positive and considerably higher than the policy elasticity of demand in all four models, ranging from 0.76 to 0.89. It was also consistently higher than the policy elasticity of supply of raw floor space.

* * *

To summarize, when the quantity of housing is measured in terms of units of housing quality, a different perspective of the housing sector emerges — the effect of income on the quantity of housing (and on housing demand and supply) becomes more pronounced than its effect on the quantity of basic shelter. While the ratio of GNP per capita between high–income and low–income countries in the sample was 55:1 in 1990, the ratio of the quantity of housing per person (measured in units of housing quality) was 40:1. And while the ratio of household incomes between high–income and low–income countries was 24:1, the quantity of housing per household (measured in units of housing quality) was 20:1. Gains in housing quality were somewhat lower but roughly commensurate with increased incomes. The ratio of annual rents (measured in units of housing quality) between high–income and low–income countries was only 10:1, because of the expectations of considerably longer rental–income streams in the high-incomes countries. The income elasticity of the demand for both owner–occupied and rental housing (measured in units of quality) was found to be close to unity.

Cities that grow more rapidly were found to have higher quantities of housing than slower–growing ones, and cities with higher construction and land costs tended have lower quantities of housing, when quantities were measured in units of quality.

Finally, while the housing policy environment did not exert a significant effect on the equilibrium quantities of housing measured in units of quality, it did have a significant effect on housing demand and supply — a more enabling policy environment was associated with a higher demand for housing as well as a higher supply of housing, and the effect of the policy environment on housing supply was greater than its effect on housing demand. Both results suggest that there are major efficiency gains to be had for the economy as a whole by making housing policies more enabling.

21

The Value of Housing

The estimated median monetary value of a country's urban housing stock in 1990 was of the order of 1.4 times its gross national product (GNP). The estimated total value of the urban housing stock in the world was of the order of $50 trillion, roughly 2.25 times the gross product of the world at that time,[1] and this great wealth was largely in the hands of home–owning families. The irreversible evolution of universal urban home ownership has resulted in the transfer of both wealth and power from the ruling classes to the masses. Contrary to the now-discredited Marxist view that the ownership of the means of production should be vested in the state, houses – the means of production of housing services – are now universally vested in the hands of the people in a form a of highly decentralized capitalism that could not be imagined before. And there is no doubt that this has limited, rather than strengthened, the hand of the state vis–à–vis the individual in the conduct of urban policy (for better or for worse).

The transformation of housing into a form of wealth (and sometimes the only form of wealth) that households can accumulate over time, has indeed been the greatest motivating force in improving the housing stock worldwide. Basic shelter, it can be sensibly argued, must be built regardless of its economic value. Shelter has a use value that precedes any commodity value it may accumulate later. But as soon as houses start to have a commodity value, the motivations for investing in them and for maintaining them in good order multiply. And it is precisely these motivations – because they can be exercised freely by each household – that lead, in and of themselves, to great improvements in the housing stock.

There is, in fact, an inherent discipline that the market imposes on households in their pursuit of an increased monetary value of their homes. Homes have monetary value as long as they are in demand in the market. And they are in demand only if they have the qualities that people in that particular market want of their houses. To conform to market demand, families need to build and maintain their homes at standards that the market as a whole (or a significant market segment) values, rather than according to their personal whims. Their houses, personalized as they may be, must in fact retain a certain depersonalized set of traits that makes them exchangeable in the market. Lacking those traits, they may not be marketable, or they might fetch a much lower price than they would otherwise. This drive to conformity leads to a natural evolution of housing standards; these are not standards that are imposed arbitrarily by an insensitive bureaucracy, but self-imposed standards brought about by a desire to maximize the value of houses.

When houses form the bulk of personal wealth, as they do in almost all countries, houses are transformed as well. They are no longer perceived as shelter, but as particular forms of saving and investment — especially secure in the face of inflation — among other options of capital accumulation. They also become a major form of collateral for borrowing capital. As a result, homeowners in the millions become, willingly or unwillingly, small "players" in the arena of global capitalism, subject to the whims and uncertainties in capital markets. Their financial fortunes rise and fall with local or global real estate cycles. In the United Kingdom, for example, after major house-price inflation in the early1970s and the later 1980s, house prices fell sharply. Foreclosures and repossessions skyrocketed: "Repossessions had not exceeded 3,000 a year before 1979 but reached 43,000 in 1990 and around 80,000 in 1991 and 1992" [Hallett, 1993, 215]. Surely, the perception of housing as capital can, to our detriment, overwhelm our earlier perception of housing as shelter. It should not. Houses must continue to provide shelter, and can therefore be fully exchanged for other forms of capital only by moving into rented accommodations. In fact, houses are a strange form of wealth, in the sense that they cannot simply be parted with or lost due to speculation since people need them as shelter.

When houses become a form of wealth, secure or less secure, they do affect the economic behavior of households. It has been observed, for example, that in the United Kingdom, during the period of housing asset inflation in the 1980s, households saved less and spent more on nonhousing goods and services, increasing the demand for imported goods, and therefore worsening the balance of payments [Muellbauer and Murphy, 1989]. In some countries, housing wealth has become a major form of retirement income. As people retire, their housing needs are reduced and they can move to lower-value housing or rental housing, investing the balance and using the proceeds as a form of pension. In Russia, where pensions have not been indexed to inflation, the privatization of the housing stock has acted to provide retirees with the only form of social security available after the fall of Communism.

The transformation of housing from basic shelter into wealth should not, however, be conceived of as an unmitigated good. In a fundamental sense, what we observe is a transition from need to greed. In parallel with the lack of agreement on a basic minimum standard of decent housing, there is no shared perception of what constitutes enough housing. Audacious mansions have now become a large part of conspicuous consumption. In response, there have been occasional calls for restricting the accumulation of housing capital, but these have usually been cast in terms of restricting the growth of new housing estates rather than restricting the amount of land or housing that an individual may own. Surely, the housing sector as a whole does gobble up enormous amounts of natural resources, and it occupies vast tracts of virgin or previously agricultural lands. Yet, on the whole, these amounts, in comparison with land used for agriculture or left undisturbed, are rather low. There may be reasons for restricting the size of residential lots or houses, but in general increasing the value of the housing stock and thereby increasing social wealth is beneficial and should be pursued. Public sector policies should indeed seek to maximize the value of housing property, and by extension the property tax base and public revenues from housing, by supplying residential neighborhoods with infrastructure services, while holding and maintaining large tracts of open spaces as parks and playgrounds.

But this prescription is not so simple. The higher the value of housing, the higher its price and the lower its affordability. These are intimately bound together. Surely, existing homeowners will benefit from any policies that lead to an increase in the value of their homes. But their adult children with their young families will not be able to afford the house next door. And neither would be the newcomers to the city who are needed to fuel its growth and prosperity. And here lies an inherent conflict among the haves and have-nots in the housing sector. The housing haves often support high-sounding "anti-sprawl" and open-space conservation policies that choke housing supply in the face of increasing demand, because such policies lead to increased land prices and hence to higher house values. The have-nots, on the other hand, must favor policies that open up housing supply and keep it responsive to changing demand, so that prices are not artificially inflated and houses remain affordable.

There is little doubt that artificially inflated house prices are counterproductive. They do not reflect the basic quantities and qualities discussed in the earlier chapters, but rather an imbalance between demand and supply that allows one group to behave like a monopolist and capture a surplus that would not be there if artificial barriers to supply were removed. Policies that favor choking housing supply in the name of protecting property values are less than enabling, but unfortunately already enjoy massive political support in the outlying suburbs of many cities.

The wealth accumulated in the housing stock lends greater urgency to the pursuit of sensible housing policies. Such policies are still absolutely necessary for attaining the goal of decent and affordable shelter for everyone, but, because of these policies' role in the creation of massive housing wealth, they must also be conceived as part and parcel of managing society's wealth, savings, and investment. To do that, we must begin, as we did before, with trying to measure this wealth.

Value Measures of the Quantity of Housing

The measurement of societal wealth in all its forms has, for one reason or another, not advanced in parallel with measures of the flow of resources, incomes, expenditures, and investments. This is rather unfortunate, because it tends to hide or underplay the role of wealth-poverty in overall poverty, as well as the role of the housing sector in the economy.

There were few measures of housing wealth to be found. Simple housing wealth measures are, of course, simple measures of the average or median value of houses and annual rents. More global measures include the total value of the national housing stock [Mayer,1978, in Wright, 1993, 279]; housing assets as a percent of total wealth [Smith et al., 1988, 31]; the net value of residences as a proportion of total private wealth [U.S. Department of Commerce, 1978]; and housing's share of net capital stock [Peterson et al., 1991, 27]. Very few reliable statistics on these more global measures were found in the literature.

The Global Survey of Housing Indicators collected data on median house prices and rents. These data were used to construct the hedonic price and quantity indices discussed in earlier chapters, as well as to construct a number of measures of the value of the housing stock as a whole. In this chapter we introduce and discuss four value measures of the quantity of housing:

1. the *median house value*, defined as the value of that house in the urban area that has 50% of all the houses — both old and new, both in the formal and the informal sectors — valued above it, and 50% valued below it;

2. the *median annual rental value*, defined as the amount of rent paid annually by that household that has 50% of all households — both in market-rent and controlled-rent dwelling units — paying higher rents, and 50% paying lower rents[2]; and

3. the *value of stock-to-GCP ratio*, defined as the ratio of the total value of the urban housing stock and the Gross City Product (GCP). The total value of the stock is calculated by multiplying the average value[3] of a housing unit by the total number of dwelling units. The gross city product is calculated by multiplying the average household income by the number of households in the city, and dividing it by the consumption-to-GDP ratio.[4]

This third measure calculates the dollar value of the housing stock as a whole and normalizes it by the GCP, so that values can be comparable among cities. It is a similar measure to the housing investment measure used in national accounts, but for two critical differences. First, it pertains to the stock as a whole while investment refers only to new construction and rehabilitation. Second, it includes the value of land, while housing investment calculations view land values as transfers and do not include it. A high value for this indicator does not imply a valuable housing stock in terms of quality. Because monetary values are, in fact, the products of quantity and price, they can be high because of high quantities, high prices, or both high quantities and high prices. Value indices cannot tell us, therefore, whether there is a shortage of housing measured in terms of numbers of dwelling units or living space, nor whether the city in question has a high-quality housing stock or a low-quality one accompanied by high prices.

Because the GCP is not a familiar measure, we also estimated a fourth index from the data in the Global Survey:

4. the *urban housing wealth-to-GNP ratio,* defined as the ratio of the estimated total monetary value of the urban housing stock in a given country and the GNP of the country.

To estimate the total monetary value of the urban housing stock, we assume: (a) that *median* house values reported in the Global Survey for the major city in every country are consistently lower than *average* house values in the city, and (b) that average urban house values for the country as a whole are consistently lower than the average house value reported for the major city (in most cases the largest city in the country) in the Global Survey. We combine these two assumptions into one and assume (c) that the average house value for the country as a whole is approximately equal to the median house value reported in the Global Survey. We further assume (d) that the average value of a rental housing unit is the same as the average value of an owner-occupied housing unit.[5]

Given these assumptions and given the city population and number of dwelling units in the city, we then obtain an average house value per person for every city in our sample. We multiply this average house value per person by the total urban population in the country to obtain an estimate of the total value of the urban housing stock in each country.

The results obtained for 1990 in the Global Survey for these four measures of the quantity of housing in terms of its monetary value are summarized in table 21.1. The median house value and the median annual rental value display very similar patterns. They are both highly correlated with incomes, rising steadily as incomes rise. Consequently, the correlation of these two measures with the Development Index is high, +0.74. While the multiple of household incomes of the industrialized countries in terms of the median income of the developing countries as a whole is of the order of 8:1 (see table 13.1), the corresponding multiple for the median house value is 12:1; and for the median annual rental value it is 10:1. House values and rents thus appear to rise faster than incomes in cross-country comparisons. Both are also subject to greater extremes than differences in household incomes or GNP per capita. The global maximum value for the median house value in the sample is that of Japan ($441,719), and the global minimum is that of Malawi ($506). Similarly, the global maximum for the median annual rental value in the sample is that of the United States ($7,992), and the global minimum is that of Russia in 1990 ($4). The corresponding ratios between the maximum and minimum values and rents are 872:1 and 2,000:1, respectively. In comparison, the ratio between the maximum and minimum

Table 21.1. Value Measures of Housing Quantity, 1990.

Country Groupings	Median House Value ($)	Median Annual Rental Value ($)	Value of Stock-to- GCP Ratio	Urban Housing Wealth-to- GNP Ratio
Low–Income Countries	3,147	130	2.3	0.72
Low–Middle Income Countries	16,205	523	2.2	1.10
Upper Middle Income Countries	23,646	687	2.4	1.74
High–Income Countries	134,137	3,735	2.7	2.56
Southern Africa	3,979	154	1.3	0.59
Asia and the Pacific	8,451	328	2.5	0.90
Middle East and North Africa	19,158	614	3.9	1.44
Latin America and the Caribbean	11,818	682	1.6	0.90
Eastern Europe	24,272	118	3.8	3.06
All Developing Countries	11,001	386	2.3	0.94
Industrialized Countries	132,500	3,700	2.8	2.56
Global Average	62,279	1,635	2.9	1.87
Global Minimum	506	4	0.5	0.07
Global Median	20,315	682	2.6	1.44
Global Maximum	441,719	7,992	9.2	7.05
Global Standard Deviation	88,007	1,972	1.6	1.49
Correlation with Development Index	0.74	0.74	0.39	0.64

Source: Housing Indicators Program [1994].

household income is 71:1, and the ratio between the maximum and minimum GNP per capita in the sample is 235:1.

The third indicator in this group attempts to measure the value of the entire housing stock in the city. The values discussed here are not actual measures of these values, but gross estimates that may be subject to considerable error. The GCP is a gross estimate, using the urban population, household income, and national data for the consumption–to–GDP ratio to calculate it—a procedure that leaves much to be desired. Given these limitations, however, they can still be usefully compared because the same procedure was applied to all the cities in the sample. The value of stock–to–GCP ratio increases modestly with income, in line with our earlier observations — first, that the house price–to–income ratio increases modestly with income, and second that house values rise somewhat faster than household incomes. Its correlation with the Development Index is +0.39, not much different that the correlation of the house price–to–income ratio which is +0.33 (see table 17.1).

The median values for this index are consistently lower, although highly correlated with the house price–to–income ratio. They are lower because they are normalized by the consumption–to–GDP ratio (which had a global median of 0.63 in 1990) and by the ratio of the total number of dwelling units to the total number of households (which had a global median of 0.96). The global median value for this index for the sample as a whole is 2.6 and the global average is 2.9, suggesting that the value of the housing stock in a typical city in 1990 was roughly three times the value of its GCP. The reported value of the stock–to–GCP ratio in the Global Survey for the industrialized countries (2.8) is somewhat higher than that reported for the developing countries as a whole (2.3). Low–income countries have a median of 2.3, the same as the median for the developing countries as a whole. Among developing country regions, Southern Africa reports the lowest median value (1.3), and Latin America the second–lowest value (1.6). The Middle East and North Africa report the highest value (3.9); Eastern Europe reports a similarly high value (3.8). Only three countries, all in Southern Africa, report values of less than 1.0 for this indicator: Malawi, Kenya and South Africa. Six countries, all with high house price–to–income ratios, report values of more than 5.0 for this indica- tor: China, Algeria, Hong Kong, Poland, Germany, and Japan; Japan reported the highest value (9.2).

The fourth measure, the ratio of urban housing wealth to GNP, increased regularly with income, from a median of 0.72 of GNP in low–income countries to a median of 2.56 in high–income countries. It also had a high correlation (+0.64) with the Development Index. Higher–income countries are more heavily urban- ized, have more dwelling units per 1,000 people, and are able to invest more savings in their housing stocks. Hence, they are able to accumulate more urban housing wealth. In other words, not only are these countries richer in terms of income, they are also wealthier. The high–income countries in our sample generated 83% of the total GNP of the countries in the sample in 1990, and possessed 91% of all housing wealth. For the sample as a whole, urban housing wealth had a median value of 1.4 times GNP, but it varied considerably among countries.

Given the considerable variation in the ratio of urban housing wealth to GNP among individual countries, we estimated the total value of urban housing wealth using the median values[6] of the ratios for each of the four income groups in our sample (see table 22.1). The countries in the sample generated $17.5 trillion of a total gross product of $22 trillion of the world in 1990 [World Bank, 1992, table 1, 218–219]. Multiplying the shares of the global product in each income group by the median ratio for this group yielded the total urban housing wealth for each group. Adding these four values yielded a total of $41 trillion as the estimated value of the urban housing stock for all the countries in the sample. The remain- ing gross product, $4.5 trillion, was multiplied by the median value of the the ratio of urban housing wealth to GNP (1.4) to estimate the housing wealth in the countries not included in the sample, yielding an additional urban housing wealth of $6 trillion. The cumulative standard deviation for this calculation was of the order of $35 trillion. We can conclude, therefore, that the total urban housing wealth in the world in 1990 was of the order of $50 (±$35) trillion.

The Determinants of Value Measures of Housing Quantity

Except for incomes, what generally accounts for the variations in these four value measures of the quantity of housing? We attempt to answer this question by investigating the statistical models for these measures, using the same procedure established in the preceding chapters, and the same set of explanatory variables representing the economic, social, and political context; the housing policy environment; and market housing conditions. The summary results for the four value models appear in table 21.2.

The first two value models seek to explain the variations in the monetary values of median–priced houses and median annual rents.[7] The model for the median house value is presented in the top row of table 21.2. It has a very high R-squared (+0.94), implying that the variables used in the model explain more than ninety percent of the variation in house values between cities. Median house values are significantly affected by four of these explanatory variables: household income, the city population growth rate, the land cost–to–income ratio, and the Enabling Index.

The equilibrium value of houses (measured by the median house value) is expected to be higher in high–income countries, in absolute terms, than the corresponding value in low–income countries. The model suggests that the equilibrium quantity of housing measured by the monetary value of houses rises just as fast if not faster than incomes in cross–country comparisons. What is less obvious is the finding that the equilibrium value of houses in rapidly growing cities is lower than the corresponding value in slow growing cities. In other words, population pressure by itself does not result in higher house values when there are no restrictions on housing supply. What does lead to increased monetary house values are high land costs relative to incomes, and, less significantly, high construction costs relative to incomes. Finally, a more enabling policy environment leads to a modest, yet significant, reduction in monetary value of houses.

The second model in table 21.2 poses the median annual rent as a measure of the equilibrium monetary value of houses.[8] Again, the model has a high R-squared (+0.87), suggesting that the selected variables explain more than 80% of the variation in rents in our sample. Three of the explanatory variables in this model exert a significant influence on this measure of the value of the housing stock. Rental values, like house values, are significantly higher in higher–income countries. But, in contrast to house values, rental values are found to be modestly *higher* in rapidly growing cities. They are also significantly higher in cities with more enabling housing policy environments. The explanation for the higher rental values coupled with lower house values in rapidly growing cities may be largely accountable for by the absence of rent control in these regimes.

The third model of the value of housing uses the estimate of monetary value of the entire housing stock in the city, normalized by the annual GCP as the dependent variable. Again, the model has a high R-squared (+0.67) suggesting

Table 21.2. The Determinants of Value Measures of Housing Quantity.

Variable	Log of Household Income	City Population Growth Rate	Household Size	Housing Credit Portfolio	Construction Cost-to-Income Ratio	Land Cost-to-Income Ratio	Enabling Index	No. of Observations	R-squared & Adjusted R-squared	F-Value
Log of Median House Value	1.03 [a], [b] 10.6*** [b]	-0.19 -3.07***	0.09 1.16	-0.02 -0.37	0.06 1.20	0.17 3.89*** [c]	-0.11 -1.47*	45	0.94 0.93	$F_{7,37}$ 82.0*** [b]
Log of Median Annual Rental Value	0.76 5.63***	0.24 2.78***	-0.01 -0.10	–[d] –[d]	0.11 1.53*	-0.01 -0.22	0.43 4.07***	46	0.87 0.85	$F_{6,39}$ 42.4***
Value of Stock-to-GCP Ratio	0.30 1.38*	-0.50 -3.73***	0.12 0.65	0.08 0.63	0.31 2.66***	0.51 5.17***	-0.19 -1.13	44	0.67 0.61	$F_{7,36}$ 10.5***
Urban Housing Wealth-to-GNP Ratio	1.07 3.80***	-0.43 -2.51**	–[e] –[e]	0.01 0.03	0.22 1.32*	0.47 3.27***	-0.40 -1.82**	45	0.69 0.64	$F_{6,38}$ 13.07***

Source: Housing Indicators Program [1994].

[a] Figures in the top rows are standardized β–coefficients.
[b] Figures in italics denote t– and F–statistics.
[c] ***, **, and * denote 1%, 5% and 10% levels of confidence respectively.
[d] Housing credit portfolio not included in this model.
[e] Household size not included in this model.

that the model explains two-thirds of the variation in this index in our sample. The value of stock–to–GCP Ratio is significantly affected by four of the explanatory variables: higher incomes and higher costs of land and construction are associated with higher values for this index, while faster urban growth rates are associated with lower values.

The effect of income on this measure of the value of housing is weaker than its effect on the value of houses and rents, because it is normalized by the GCP which is, in itself, highly correlated with income. This index measures the value of the housing stock relative to incomes, but its value is still higher for higher-income countries, as we saw in table 21.1. The upward influence of land and construction costs on this index strongly suggests that this value measure of quantity is very much biased by the high prices of inputs and does not necessarily mean that cities with high values for this index have a better housing stock. Finally, the downward effect of the urban growth rate on this index is a complex finding that combines the disparate effects we examined earlier, including the lower numbers of dwelling units, higher quality, lower values, and higher rents associated with the rate of urban growth. What matters is the finding that the value of the housing stock is indeed lower in faster-growing cities than in slower-growing ones.

The fourth and final model in this group posits the ratio of urban housing wealth to GNP as the dependent variable. As we saw in table 21.1 earlier, this ratio is significantly influenced by household income – in general, the higher the household income in a given country, the higher the ratio of urban housing wealth to GNP. This ratio is also influenced by four other variables in the model. It is significantly lower in faster-growing cities and in cities with a more enabling housing policy environment, and it is significantly higher in cities with high construction and land costs. This suggests again that housing wealth may be generated by high construction costs and land values that lead to high house prices, and not necessarily by higher numbers of dwelling units or by the higher quality of the housing stock. For example, Japan and Germany, that had unusually high house prices in 1990, also had the highest ratios of urban housing wealth to GNP.

The Demand and Supply of Value in Housing

We now investigate the effects of household income, mortgage credit, and the policy environment on the demand for these four value measures of housing quantity; we also examine the effect of the inputs costs of land and construction and the policy environment on the supply of these quantities, following the same procedure used in earlier chapters. We did not include the estimated price of housing in these demand and supply models because the dependent variables include a price element.[9] We calculate two models for each index, one for the quantity demanded (from which we derive the estimated income elasticity and policy elasticity of demand) and one for the quantity supplied (from which we derive the policy elasticity of supply). The results of these calculations appear in table 21.3.

The demand models for both the median house value and the median annual rental value had high R–squared values of +0.90 and +0.89, respectively. The income elasticity of demand in both models was again close to unity (1.15 and 1.05, respectively), similar in value to those found for the hedonic values and rents in the previous chapter. The policy elasticity of demand was not significant in the value model and significant and positive (+0.43) in the rent model. The policy elasticity of supply was high and significant in both models (0.72 and 1.35, respectively), again similar to that found for the hedonic quantities, and again higher than the policy elasticity of demand.

The demand model for the value of stock–to–GCP ratio was less powerful than the first two models, and had an R–squared value of +0.37 only. The income elasticity of demand in this model was very low (0.16) but statistically significant. The demand model for the urban housing wealth to GNP ratio was robust, with an R–squared value of 0.62 and an income elasticity of +0.55. The demand for urban housing wealth was thus found to be income–elastic, although with an elasticity less than unity.

The supply models for these last two measures were not statistically significant, and their corresponding R–squared values were very low (0.07 and 0.06, respectively). Therefore, the policy elasticity of the supply of housing, as measured by these two ratios, cannot be said to be significantly different from zero.

*   *   *

To conclude, when we measure the quantity of housing in terms of its value we get yet a different perspective on the housing stock than the ones obtained from looking and dwelling units and living space or at housing quality. The three perspectives are, in fact, complementary. Household income was found to have a strong upward effect on house values and rental values, similar in strength to that observed for the parallel hedonic measures of house values and rents discussed in chapter 20. The income elasticities of demand for these two measures were close to unity, similar to those observed earlier for the hedonic measures. Income had a weaker, yet significant, effect on the ratio of urban housing wealth to GNP. The value of the housing stock relative to GNP was thus found to be significantly higher in richer countries.

The urban growth rate had a complex effect on housing quantities. It was found to exert a downward effect on the monetary value of houses, and on the monetary value of houses normalized by income or CGP, in contrast to the upward effect on the value of houses measured in units of quality discussed in chapter 20. On the whole, houses were thus found to be less expensive and of higher quality in faster–growing cities. Rental values and the quality of rental units, on the other hand, were found to be higher in faster–growing cities.

Table 21.3. The Income and Policy Elasticities of Value Measures of Housing Quantity.

Variable	Income Elasticity of Demand	Policy Elasticity of Demand	Policy Elasticity of Supply	No. of Observations	Demand Model		Supply Model	
					R-squared & Adjusted R-squared	F-value	R-squared & Adjusted R-squared	F-value
Median House Value	1.15 [a]	0.14	0.72	47/46 [e]	0.90	$F_{5,41}$	0.23	$F_{3,42}$
	9.75*** [b]	0.89	2.59*** [c]		0.89	76.1***	0.29	5.59*** [b]
Median Annual Rental Value	1.05	0.43	1.35	47/46 [e]	0.89	$F_{5,41}$	0.50	$F_{3,42}$
	9.25***	2.88***	5.81***		0.88	67.0***	0.53	16.0***
Value of Stock-to-GCP Ratio	0.16	0.09	– [d]	45	0.37	$F_{5,39}$	0.07	$F_{3,41}$
	1.47*	0.61	– [d]		0.29	4.61***	0.13	2.04
Urban Housing Wealth-to-GNP Ratio	0.55	-0.16	– [d]	47/46 [e]	0.63	$F_{5,41}$	0.06	$F_{3,42}$
	5.55***	-0.97	– [d]		0.60	17.96***	-0.01	0.84

Source: Housing Indicators Program [1994].

[a] Figures in the top rows are elasticities.

[b] Figures in italics denote *t*- and *F*-statistics.

[c] ***, **, and * denote 1%, 5% and 10% levels of confidence, respectively.

[d] Supply model not statistically significant.

[e] 47 observations for demand model and 46 for supply model.

It is important to see the differences in the effects of construction costs and land prices on the different measures of quantity. Higher than expected construction costs (as measured by the construction cost–to –income ratio) exerted a downward effect on housing quality and on the median house size, but an upward effect on the monetary value of houses. Higher than expected land prices exerted a downward effect on the number of dwelling units, median house size, and housing quality, but exerted a significant upward effect on all three measures of house value. We must suspect, therefore, that the high house values in our sample were not the result of more units, more space, or more quality, but rather the result of high prices, resulting at least in part from the high cost of land and construction.

Finally, we observe that the housing policy environment exerted a significant downward effect on house values, and an upward effect on rental values, the latter probably associated with the absence of rent control in more enabling regimes. In more enabling regimes we again found, as we did in chapter 20, that both the demand and the supply of housing in terms of monetary value were higher. The policy elasticity of demand for both house values and rental values was positive, and quite similar to that observed for the hedonic measures of housing quantity. The policy elasticity of supply for both house values and rental values was higher than the policy elasticity of demand, and again quite similar to that observed for the hedonic measures of housing quantity. The housing policy environment on the whole thus exerted a significant upward effect on housing demand, and an even stronger upward effect on housing supply, when those were measured in the monetary values of houses and rents.

22

Production and Investment, Vacancy, and Mobility

Looking at quantitative and qualitative aspects of the housing stock as a whole is of little interest to home builders, developers, investors, and lenders, because their entire activity in any given year is largely focused on marginal additions to the housing stock and not on the stock as a whole. To encompass these important perspectives, this chapter focuses on changes in quantity rather than on the absolute dimensions of quantity, and on the growth of the housing stock or on the creation of new housing assets rather than on their present size or value. We are not, however, dealing here with the distinction between stocks and flows, between housing as an asset and housing as a flow of housing services. In large measure, the two — stocks and flows — are indeed exchangeable, because the value of a house is determined by the discounted value of the services it provides to dwellers over its lifetime. What is of interest to us here are the changes taking place in the housing sector as a whole, whether in its size or value or in the overall flow of services from the stock as a whole.

It is fruitful, however, to view additions, improvements, or demolitions of the housing stock as marginal adjustments to the stock as a whole to meet new demand, and the process of adding to or subtracting from the stock as a stock–adjustment process [Muth,1960]. Housing demand is thus viewed as demand for the stock as a whole, and housing supply as an adjustment to the stock to meet this demand. This suggests that it may not be sensible to speak of the "demand for new housing," but rather of "new demand for housing" that may or may not be satisfied by the existing housing stock, and may result in a new equilibrium in the housing market. In the new equilibrium old *and* new housing supply together meet old and new housing demand.

Generally speaking, from a comprehensive perspective, it is the long–term, efficient functioning of the sector as a whole that is the prime objective of policy. Having said that, we note that all housing–sector policies that seek to affect changes in the sector must of necessity track small changes in the stock as a whole. An important reason to track one particular measure of the rate of housing production, housing starts, has little to do with housing–sector concerns or with a well functioning housing sector, but with the contribution of housing activity to the economy as a whole. The beginning of construction of houses, measured usually by the number of permits issued, is a "leading" economic indicator, often used as a predictor of future economic activity: "Construction results in the hiring of workers, the production of construction materials and equipment, and the sale of large household appliances such as ranges and refrigerators. In addition, when owners or tenants occupy the housing, they often buy new furniture, carpeting, and other furnishings" [Frumkin, 1994, 184].

From a comparative policy perspective, however, focusing on housing production and investment in a single year is problematic. Since both are stock- adjustment responses, we cannot determine "which way is up?" in the absence of other indicators. It is not at all clear that more new housing is better than less, since an oversupply of housing can lead to high vacancy rates, slow rates of sale, and depressed house prices. In addition, as we noted in chapter 21, a high value of new housing investment may be the result of a few units being built at exorbitant prices, again not necessarily a good sign. Alternatively it may be the result of an upswing in the building cycle, and thus not easily comparable to other countries in different phases of their building cycles.

It is important to keep in mind that in housing, in contrast with, say, the food industry, only a very small part of the stock is produced and sold every year. The global median value of the housing stock growth rate is 2.5%, and the global average is 3.0%. Two-thirds of the cities in the Global Survey of 1990 reported rates between 0.7% and 5.3%. Clearly, the great bulk of the housing stock already exists, and additions to it are only marginal. In addition, housing stock growth rates are subject to rather severe cyclical fluctuations, as we have noted previously (see chapter 15), and can vary greatly from one year to the next.

Doan [1997] studied housing stock growth rates for the United States from 1880 to 1990. In general, the straightline trend showed that rates decreased gradually during this period from 3.1% per annum in 1880 to 2.2% in 1990. The standard deviation from the trend line was ±38%, implying that approximately two-thirds of the time, growth rates were between 62% and 138% of the trend-line estimates.[1] The average ratio of the maximum growth rate and the minimum growth rate in any five-year period from 1880 to 1990 was 2.2, again suggesting that, on average, growth rates either doubled or shrank in half during a typical building cycle. A similar finding is reported by Topel and Rosen [1988] for the 1963-84 period: "an expansion doubles the output of new homes and a contraction cuts it in half" [720]. Atypical and severe downward swings from the trend line were reported by Doan for World War I (23% of the expected trend-line rate in 1917), the Great Depression (12% of the expected rate in 1933, for example), and World War II (16% of the expected rate in 1944, for example). Atypical upward swings were reported for the boom years following the world wars — 156% in 1923 and 193% in 1950, for example. The housing stock growth rate thus multiplied by 6 or more between 1917 and 1923, and by no less than 12 between 1944 and 1950. These wide fluctuations suggest that it may be quite difficult to compare, let alone explain, cross sectional differences in growth rates among countries in any given year, when one country may be at the peak of a building cycle, another at a trough, and yet another somewhere in between. This is a serious limitation of the analysis that follows, and of previous analyses such as those of Burns and Grebler [1977] and Malpezzi [1988].

In the sections that follow, we shall review and define various measures of annual changes in the housing stock, as well as two factors related to these changes, the vacancy rate and annual residential mobility. We shall then discuss the underlying factors that may be responsible for the differences in these annual rates, review previous findings, and present the econometric models that seek to account for these differences in terms of the economic, political, and social context; the housing policy environment; and housing market conditions. Finally, we shall investigate differences in the supply and demand parameters governing these annual rates[2] and attempt to estimate their supply, demand, and policy elasticities.

Measures of Production and Investment, Vacancy, and Mobility

We note at the outset that there are several methodological difficulties in measuring annual changes in the housing stock, as well as incorporating these measures correctly in national accounts. Needless to say, additions to informal–sector housing, that normally proceed without permits, are usually underreported. There are also difficulties in accounting adequately for repairs, additions, and demolitions, as well as changes in the value of the existing housing stock. These are by no means insignificant. For example, "[c]urrent estimates suggest that the value of stock created through maintenance and renovation [in the United States] is about 30 percent of the value of [new] stock created" [Smith et al., 1988, 45]. Finally, there is a serious difficulty, alluded to earlier, in isolating short–term fluctuations from underlying trends, especially for purposes of comparison among countries.

Measures of changes in the housing stock are usually, but not always, derived directly from the indicators used to measure the stock as a whole. Indicators of total new housing production measure it at different stages, and in different units: the number of housing permits issued [U.S. HUD, 1994, 4], housing starts [U.S. HUD, 1994, 10], permanent dwellings completed per 1,000 people [U.S. HUD, 1994, 11; Boelhouwer and van der Heijden, 1992, 35], rooms completed per 1,000 people [United Nations, 1992, table 4, 8–38], square meters completed [Russian Federation, 1990], mobile home shipments [U.S. HUD, 1994, 11], sales of new homes and new homes for sale [U.S. HUD, 1994, 12], and annual housing production by the informal sector in developing countries [Hoffman et al., 1992, 25]. The main indicators that measure the value of new housing production include gross fixed capital formation in residential buildings as a percent of gross domestic product (GDP) [United Nations, 1992, table 2, 4–6; Woodfield, 1989, 68–69; U.S. HUD, 1994, 23] and gross fixed capital formation in residential buildings as a percent of gross fixed capital formation [United Nations, 1992, table 2, 4–6].[3]

Related indicators measure housing consumption as a percentage of gross national product (GNP) [OECD data, in Colleen, 1994a, 59] and housing consumption as a percentage of total private consumption [OECD data, in Colleen, 1994a, 61].

Other indicators measure the quality and space characteristics of new housing production: the average number of rooms per dwelling completed [United Nations, 1992, table 4, 8–38]; average useful floor area per dwelling completed (in m²) [United Nations, 1992, table 4, 8–38]; dwellings completed with piped water, fixed bath, or shower, and central heating [United Nations, 1992, table 4, 8–38]; percent of dwellings completed in one, two, and three or more storeys [United Nations, 1992, table 5, 40–43]; percent of public units in new housing construction [United Nations, 1992, table 4, 8–38; Papa, 1992, 104]; and housing production by type of investor (private, nonprofit/semipublic, and government) [U.N. data, in McGuire, 1981, 83].

Measures of demolitions, additions, or improvements of the housing stock include the total number of dwellings demolished or closed [Whitehead, 1974, 13; United Nations, 1992, table 18, 92–99] and the ratio of the value of improvements to the value of total new construction [Smith et al., 1988, 31]. Finally, indicators of annual residential mobility include the vacancy rate for owned homes and rentals [U.S. HUD, 1994, 25], the average length of vacancy chains (average number of moves initiated by the construction of one new dwelling unit) [Hegedus and Tosics, 1993, 89], the average duration of a rental tenancy [Gilbert, 1987], and residence of less than one year in the present home [Minford et al., 1987, 92]. Although neither the vacancy rate nor annual residential mobility are, in fact, rates of change in the housing stock, we have included them in this discussion; first, because the vacancy rate is an indicator of housing sector performance that has a critical influence on rates of change in the stock, and second, because a significant component of annual residential mobility is associated with moving into new housing.[4]

The Global Survey of Housing Indicators of 1990 collected data on five measures of housing production and investment, vacancy, and mobility. To make them comparable among different countries, all were normalized, either by the number of dwellings in the housing stock, by the urban population, by the total number of households, or by the total urban economic output measured by the gross city product (GCP). These five measures were:

1. the *vacancy rate,* defined as the percentage of the total number of dwelling units that are presently unoccupied;
2. *housing stock growth,* defined as the ratio of the net number of units produced (units produced minus units demolished) in both the formal and informal sectors last year and the total number of dwelling units in the housing stock;

3. *housing production,* defined as the net number of units produced (units produced minus units demolished) in both the formal and informal sectors last year per 1,000 people[5];

4. *gross urban housing investment,* defined as the estimated total investment in housing (including land) last year as a percentage of GCP[6]; and

5. *annual residential mobility,* defined as the percentage of households that moved into their current unit (including new dwelling units) last year.

Summary values for these five measures are presented in table 22.1. The vacancy rate exhibited an observable increase with increased levels of income, from as little as 0.2% of the stock in low–income countries to 5.4% in high–income ones. The median value for the developing countries as a whole was 1.8%, considerably lower than that for the industrialized countries, 5.0%. Its correlation with the Development Index was thus positive (+0.25), but not exceptionally high. Among developing–country regions, vacancy rates were exceptionally low in Southern Africa, and lower than median for the economies in transition in Eastern Europe. Five countries reported no vacancies at all in the surveyed cities, three in Africa (Tanzania, Malawi, and Senegal) and two in Asia (China and Korea). In contrast, Egypt reported a very high vacancy rate (14.5%), largely the result of regulatory distortions that made it more advantageous for owners of residential

Table 22.1. Production and Investment, Vacancy, and Mobility, 1990.

Country Groupings	Vacancy Rate (%)	Housing Stock Growth (%)	Housing Production (units per 1,000 people)	Gross Urban Housing Investment (%)	Annual Residential Mobility (%)
Low–Income Countries	0.2	3.1	5.6	5.1	6.3
Low–Middle Income Countries	2.8	4.0	7.7	10.7	5.0
Upper Middle Income Countries	3.8	2.1	6.1	4.4	4.4
High–Income Countries	5.4	1.5	6.5	4.1	10.4
Southern Africa	0.1	3.1	5.2	3.1	6.8
Asia and the Pacific	2.3	4.7	7.6	12.4	6.0
Middle East and North Africa	9.0	4.0	7.2	15.9	5.0
Latin America and the Caribbean	4.2	3.5	6.0	6.1	3.4
Eastern Europe	1.3	1.1	3.8	3.5	3.9
All Developing Countries	1.8	3.5	6.6	6.9	5.0
Industrialized Countries	5.0	1.4	6.4	4.2	10.8
Global Average	4.0	3.1	6.9	8.3	9.0
Global Minimum	0.0	0.5	1.9	0.7	1.0
Global Median	3.5	2.5	6.5	5.4	7.1
Global Maximum	14.5	12.9	14.8	34.9	26.5
Global Standard Deviation	3.8	2.3	3.4	7.1	5.9
Correlation with Development Index	0.25	–0.40	0.02	–0.14	0.34

Source: Housing Indicators Program [1994].

properties in Cairo to keep them vacant rather than put them on the market [Mayo, 1981a].

Median values for the four income groups for all three growth rates — housing stock growth, housing production, and gross urban housing investment — exhibited the pattern described by Burns and Grebler [1977] and later by Malpezzi [1988]. All three rates appeared first to increase and then to decrease as income increased. They were low in low-income countries, rising to a peak in low-middle income countries and then generally falling as incomes continue to increase. Unfortunately, however, as we shall see, this pattern could not be confirmed statistically by fitting a second-degree curve to the Global Survey data.

What is important (and statistically significant, as we shall see later) is that the rates of housing stock growth and gross urban housing investment can be expected to decrease as economic development takes place. While housing production exhibited no significant differences between developing countries and industrialized countries, the median value for housing stock growth was 3.5% for the developing countries as a whole and only 1.4% for the industrialized countries; the median value for gross urban housing investment was 6.2% for the developing countries as a whole and only 4.2% for the industrialized countries. Housing stock growth had a relatively strong negative correlation with the Development Index (-0.40) and gross urban housing investment showed a weaker correlation (-0.14), while housing production had a correlation close to zero. As countries develop and become more urbanized, population pressure for new homes decreases but this pressure is replaced by the increased demand for new (as well as higher quality) homes occasioned by the reduction in household size. Gross urban housing investment tends to decrease slightly and to become more similar as economies develop: a difference-of-means test between the industrialized countries, with an average value of 6.1%, and the developing countries as a whole, with an average value of 9.1%, was statistically significant at the 1% confidence level. This can be visually observed in figure 22.1.[7] It strongly suggests that industrialized countries had a more homogeneous pattern of investment in housing; in other words, the pattern of investment in housing tended to converge to a lower value at higher levels of economic development.

Among developing-country regions, all three growth indicators were especially low in Eastern Europe, that in 1990 was undergoing serious economic restructuring and a severe housing crisis. Growth indicators were slightly lower than median values for Southern Africa, and especially high in Asia and in the Middle East and North Africa. Without time-series data on annual growth rates, data that may allow us to smooth out cyclical fluctuations, it is not possible to tell whether these differences are structural or due to comparisons between regions at different stages in their building cycles. In global terms, however, the urban housing stock grew at an average rate of 3.1%, and an average of 6.9 new housing units were produced for every 1,000 urban inhabitants. Given that the urban population was half the total world population of 5.284 billion in 1990 [World Bank, 1992, tables 26 and 31], we can estimate that annual global housing

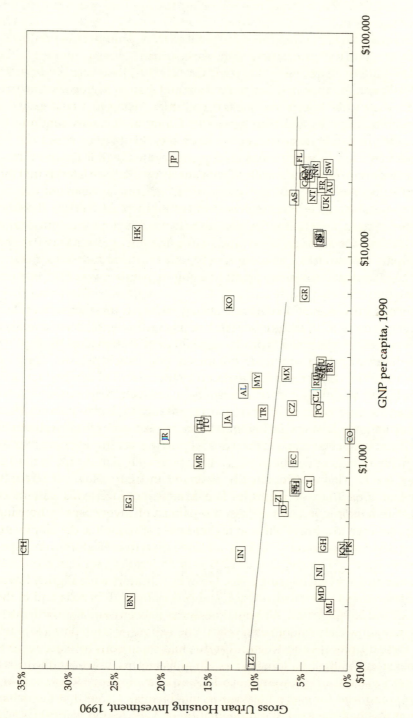

Figure 22.1. Housing Investment and GNP per capita.

production in cities was of the order of 18 million units in that year. Data for 1995 for both housing production and gross urban housing Investment were also collected by the United Nations for 1995 (see table A27). The housing production data exhibited a very similar pattern to the earlier sample, rising and then falling as incomes increase. The rate for Eastern Europe was still lower than expected, rates for Southern Africa and Asia increased slightly, while the global average fell from 6.9 units per 1,000 people in 1990 to 6.1 in 1995. Assuming that the data for the two periods are comparable, this suggests that annual global housing production in cities was of still of the order of 18 million units in 1995.

The 1995 data for the gross urban housing investment was also quite similar to the 1990 data. However, the median values for different income groups appeared to decline steadily as income increased, rather than rising first and then declining. Rates for low–income countries and for Southern Africa were considerably higher than those reported for 1990, as was the rate for Latin America. In contrast, the rate for the Middle East and North Africa was lower than it was in 1990. On the whole, urban housing investment exhibited a decline, from an average of 7.9% in 1990 to 7.3% in 1995, roughly in parallel with the decline in average housing production.

Finally, annual residential mobility displayed a pattern quite distinct from both the vacancy rate and the three growth rates. It was positively correlated with the level of economic development, with a correlation of +0.34 with the Development Index. Its median value for the industrialized countries (10.8%) was more than double that of the developing countries as a whole (5.0%). Among developing–country regions, mobility rates were found to be lower than expected in Latin America and in Eastern Europe. These rates are associated both with a structural propensity to move, that will be discussed later at greater length, as well as with new housing production that results in moves to new dwelling units. There were wide variations in rates of mobility within regions as well. Among the industrialized countries, for example, the annual residential mobility rate reported for the United States (26.5%) was more than three times that of France (8.0%) or Japan (7.2%). Particularly low mobility rates, lower than 3%, were reported for four countries: Jamaica, Mexico, Poland, and Algeria.

Explaining Variations in Production and Investment, Vacancy, and Mobility

What accounts for the differences in rates of production and investment, vacancy, and residential mobility among different cities and countries? We attempt to answer this question first, by reviewing the available literature, and second, by investigating the statistical models for these measures. In exploring the models, we use the same procedure established in the preceding chapters, and a similar set of explanatory variables[8] representing the economic, social, and political context; the housing policy environment; and market housing conditions. The summary results for these models appear in table 22.2.

Table 22.2. The Determinants of Production and Investment, Vacancy, and Mobility.

Variable	Log of GNP per capita	City Population Growth Rate	Construction Cost-to-Income Ratio	Land Cost-to-Income Ratio	Enabling Index	The Vacancy Rate	Owner Occupancy	No. of Observations	R-squared & Adjusted R-squared	F-Value
Vacancy Rate	-0.34 [a]	-0.31	0.22	0.09	0.66	– [d]	– [e]	42	0.28	$F_{5,36}$
	-1.17 [b]	-1.47 [c]	1.27	0.62	2.85***	– [d]	– [e]		0.18	2.76** [b]
Housing Stock Growth	-0.55	0.31	-0.11	0.18	0.23	0.27	– [e]	41	0.47	$F_{6,34}$
	-2.02**	1.59*	-0.71	1.35*	0.99	1.74**	– [e]		0.38	5.10***
Housing Production (units per 1,000 people)	0.06	0.36	-0.06	0.29	-0.04	0.26	– [e]	42	0.27	$F_{6,35}$
	0.21	1.71**	-0.39	2.11**	-0.14	1.63*	– [e]		0.15	2.20*
Gross Urban Housing Investment	-0.34	0.03	0.08	0.51	0.17	0.20	– [e]	42	0.58	$F_{6,35}$
	-1.67**	0.21	0.64	5.05***	0.96	1.75**	– [e]		0.50	7.92***
Residential Mobility	0.79	0.65	-0.31	-0.12	0.12	-0.13	-0.32	39	0.48	$F_{7,31}$
	2.91***	3.07***	-1.91**	-0.86	0.49	-0.81	-1.74**		0.36	4.03***

Source: Housing Indicators Program [1994].

[a] Figures in the top rows are standardized β–coefficients.

[b] Figures in italics denote *t*– and *F*–statistics.

[c] ***, **, and * denote 1%, 5% and 10% levels of confidence, respectively.

[d] Vacancy Rate not included in this model.

[e] Owner Occupancy not included in this model.

We focus first on the vacancy rate. This rate is an important measure of housing market performance. A certain number of vacancies is necessary to enable households to move freely from one place to another. High vacancy rates, however, imply an oversupply of housing, create pressures to reduce prices and rents, and can lead to the collapse of the residential real estate market. Low vacancy rates in turn create pressures for higher prices and rents that make houses less affordable. This suggests that there is a "natural" vacancy rate at which prices remain stable. In the United States, for example, "[a]n often cited rule of thumb has been that the vacancy rate needed to maintain stable prices in a well functioning market is about 5 percent" [Kingsley and Turner, 1993, 10]. More generally, recent research suggests that "the 'natural' vacancy level varies substantially between markets and may sometime exceed the 5 percent threshold," without leading to significant changes in prices and rents [Kingsley and Turner, 1993, 11, quoting Apgar, 1993].

The "natural" vacancy rate may be higher than expected because of persistent structural deficiencies in particular housing submarkets. Turner and Edwards [1993] note, for example, that in American cities, there are "a surprisingly large number of units affordable to very low income renters" in moderate and high income zones. These units tend to remain vacant, however, because of racial barriers and limited information that prevent African-Americans and Hispanic families from moving into white neighborhoods [Quoted in Kingsley and Turner, 1993, 13]. They also observe that, in general, the poorer the neighborhood, the higher the vacancy rate: In Philadelphia, for example, "29 percent of all rental units were vacant. . . in the poorest zones, compared to 12 percent. . . in the moderate-income zones." Many of these units were found to be so physically deficient that they were nearly uninhabitable. Alternatively, they were located "in such undesirable neighborhoods that poor people are willing to pay extremely high rents to avoid them" [Turner and Edwards, 1993, quoted in Kingsley and Turner, 1993, 12-13].

In addition, we should expect that the "natural" vacancy rate will be higher in housing sectors that rely on the market for the allocation of houses among consumers; the rate should be lower in housing sectors that rely on administrative allocation through waiting lists or that place upper limits on prices and rents. In other words, we should expect that the vacancy rate will be higher in the more-enabling housing policy environments. It should also be lower in cities that are experiencing strong demand-side pressures, either through higher family incomes or through higher rates of urban growth, pressures that may keep vacancy rates lower than their "natural" levels.

The model for the vacancy rate is presented on the top line of table 22.2. Its R-squared of 0.28 implies that the variables used in the model explain one-quarter of the variation in vacancy rates in our sample. Of all the explanatory variables, only the city population growth rate and the Enabling Index had a statistically significant influence on the vacancy rate. In general, faster-growing cities were found to have lower than expected vacancy rates. In contrast, cities with a more–enabling housing policy environment had significantly higher vacancy rates. The median vacancy rate for the less–enabling half of our sample was 1.0%, compared with 4.9% for the more–enabling half of the sample. The latter value was more in line with the "natural" vacancy rate expected in well functioning housing markets.

Can the same explanatory variables used in the models in earlier chapter account for differences in housing sector growth and in housing production and investment among cities and countries? There are indeed a number of earlier works that seek to explain variations in these indicators, both among countries and between different time periods, using similar variables.

On the demand side, it has been observed that increasing family incomes, higher rates of rural–urban migration, and urban population growth lead to higher rates of housing production and investment. In Greece, for example, "[t]he increase in the income per capita allowed young couples to acquire and maintain houses separate from their parents. This, in turn, resulted in the decrease in the average size of household" [Donatos, 1995, 1481]. Burns and Grebler, in a landmark comparative study, posited a model for housing investment (the share of housing in total output) as a function of the level of economic development (measured by GNP per capita), national population growth, and the rate of urbanization (measured by the ratio of urban growth to population growth). Using data for 39 countries for two time periods, 1963–19666 and 1967–1970, they were able to demonstrate that housing investment rises with the level of economic development, peaks, and then declines. The models for the two periods had R–squared values of 0.61 and 0.51, respectively [Burns and Grebler, 1977, table 2.5, 30].

Capital transfers from abroad (by overseas workers or expatriates, for example) had been noted to have a significant effect on housing investment as well. This was particularly evident in Dhaka, Bangladesh during the construction boom in the Persian Gulf in the late 1970s and early 1980s, and in Cuenca, Ecuador during the 1990s. Such transfers from abroad can also be speculative investments in residential real estate by international capital, especially during building booms.

Several writers have commented that, since housing is both a consumption good and an investment good, investment in housing is also affected by alternative investment opportunities: "Resources are highly mobile between the single–family housing investment sector and other sectors in the economy" [Topel and Rosen, 1988, 719]. It has also been observed that the availability and cost of mortgage credit affect new investment in housing. There is no question that chronic shortages of credit for housing, such as those observed in Korea during several decades of rapid economic growth, led to severe housing shortages. But even minute changes in the availability of credit can affect housing investment decisions: "In both the U.S. and Japan, rises in the interest rate bring about substantial declines in housing investment" [Chang and Linneman, 1990, 65]. Clearly, so does increased inflation [Donatos, 1995,1481]. Conversely, changes in tax and subsidy policies that make mortgage credit less expensive or channel more funds in to the housing sector tend to increase demand and to have a positive effect on production and investment.

If subsidies and tax relief are directed to the supply side, they *may* also lead to increased overall housing supply although it has been observed [Murray, 1993] that, in the United States at least, subsidized housing has simply displaced nonsubsidized housing without adding to the overall supply. To take another example, in Venezuela during 1960–1999, the formal private sector did not produce housing for any but the top quintile of the housing market, and subsidized housing was the only formal housing available for the rest of the market. Again, subsidized housing may have only displaced the production of housing in the informal sector, that by 1999 housed more than half of the population of the country [CONAVI, 1999, 4]. There is no question, however, that the availability and cost of credit to builders also effects new housing investment, as do the cost of inputs to the construction process: "Factor prices are positively correlated with the level of new construction" [Topel and Rosen, 1988, 718]. It has also been suggested that, because houses in tropical countries need less insulation and heating, they should be consistently less expensive, thus demanding less investment per unit [Renaud, 1980, 399].

The most important effects on production and investment, however, are the critical housing shortages that are the consequence of wars, civil wars, and natural disasters. Postwar construction is usually high due to large scale destruction of the housing stock, large flows of refugees, or the freezing of construction activity to make resources available for the war effort. Finally, rates of production and investment are critically related to the vacancy rate discussed earlier, but their relation to the vacancy rate in any single year is complex: higher rates of production can lead to overinvestment and therefore to high vacancy rates. Conversely, high vacancy rates can be a sign to producers to lower production. In turn, high rates of production and high vacancy rates may both be common features of active housing markets.

Using the data from the Global Survey of Housing Indicators of 1990, we attempt to replicate a number of the earlier statistical results as well as to test some of the conjectures advanced in the literature. The final models for housing stock growth, housing production, and gross urban housing investment are presented in table 22.2. The models for housing stock growth and gross urban housing investment have R–squared values of 0.47 and 0.58, respectively, suggesting that the independent variables used in the models explain half of the variation in these variables in our sample. The model for housing production is weaker, with an R– squared value of 0.27, implying that the variables used in the model explain only one–quarter of the variation in housing production in the sample.

Preliminary model tests have not yielded any significant effects of the availability of credit, the rate of inflation, or the size of the informal sector on any of these indicators. Similarly, attempts to replicate the results reported by Burns and Grebler, and later by Malpezzi, using a number of functional forms have failed as well. In contrast with these earlier writers, and with the pattern that seemed to emerge in table 22.1, the 1990 data suggest that both housing stock growth and gross urban housing investment decline significantly (at the 5% level of confidence) with higher levels of economic development, as measured by GNP per capita. The difference in the results may be explained by the larger sample of countries in the 1990 survey, by the inclusion of informal-sector housing in the calculations, or by the inclusion of the value of land in the calculation of gross urban housing investment. It stands to reason that housing stock growth will decline with increased levels of development, simply because more houses are already built, and rural-urban migration as well as the natural birth rate have subsided. Investment in housing, however, also measures increases in quality of construction that people demand. The 1990 data suggest that in all stages of economic development, the demand for more housing outweighed the demand for better housing, so that, in the final analysis, cities in more developed countries spent a smaller share of their overall output on housing.

The 1990 data also confirm that the demand-side pressure occasioned by faster rates of urban growth significantly affected housing stock growth and housing production. Rapidly growing cities produced more houses to shelter their new populations. Most of this rapid growth was accommodated, however, in low-cost housing in the informal sector and hence the gross urban housing investment was not significantly affected by the urban growth rate.

Three supply-side factors were included in these models: the construction cost-to-income ratio, the land cost-to-income ratio, and the vacancy rate. It was postulated that high factor prices will have a negative effect on housing production and investment. The construction cost-to-income ratio did not affect any of the three rates significantly at all. The effect of the land cost-to-income ratio, however, was significant in all three models and had a positive, rather than a negative effect, on all three rates. It is easy to see that gross urban housing investment rates were significantly higher in cities with high land prices. The strong effect of land prices suggests that a substantial share of expenditure on housing is funneled to paying for residential land, and that high rates of housing expenditure and investment may not necessarily mean high quality or quantity of housing but simply high land prices. Housing stock growth was found to be higher in cities with higher land values. This is possibly due to the higher demand for residential land occasioned by high rates of housing stock growth, suggesting that in this particular case the causal relationship may indeed be reversed.

Finally, all three rates had a positive and significant relationship with the vacancy rate. These results suggest that in international comparisons, strong growth rates in active markets were associated with relatively high vacancy rates — both signs of a well functioning housing sector. We note, in conclusion, that in none of the three models did the Enabling Index exert a significant influence, although it was found to be positively associated with both housing stock growth and gross urban housing investment.

Can the same factors explain cross–country variations in residential mobility? Residential mobility can really be viewed from two quite different perspectives: a broad historical one, plus a narrower shorter–term one that is more in keeping with the annual changes in the rates of production and investment. The broad historical perspective views intraurban residential mobility as an extension of rural–urban migration and the resulting upward social and economic mobility of the new urban households: "Upwards social and economic mobility has historically gone hand–in–hand with residential mobility, as families 'trade up' to increasingly desirable homes and neighborhoods" [Kingsley and Turner, 1993, 1]. Such social mobility was at the root of the great intraurban migrations from city to suburb and from tenancy to home ownership during the second half of the twentieth century. In the rapidly growing cities of the developing countries, similar patterns have been observed. Edwards, for example, paraphrases Turner [1968] who studied Latin American cities in the mid–1960s, explaining that:

> [r]ecent arrivals in the city (the "bridgeheaders") trade–off a high value on accessibility to central–city jobs against a low value on the need for space and security (for home ownership). They live in rental tenements in the city centre. Progress along the family cycle and a rising income alters the parameters of household demand and therefore changes the weights placed on each residential priority. A higher value on the need for space to accommodate a growing family and on the security and independence conferred by home ownership is traded against a lower value on accessibility. The household becomes a "consolidator," owning land in the urban periphery, and gradually extending the dwelling. [Edwards, 1993, 132]

These global mobility trends are only generalizations. In a real housing market, families move out of the central city and back into the central city, into home ownership and back into rental accommodations, in and out of poverty, and in and out of marriage. There is no single pattern that can adequately describe the multiplicity of residential shifts in a single year. Students of mobility, however, have identified several key factors that shape and constrain moves from place to place.

Increased or reduced income, changes in the life cycle of families, the preference to own or rent, the need to reduce overcrowding, the doubling–up of households, the need to release home equity for other uses, seeking a location closer to work, and the desire to move to a better neighborhood or a better school district have all been cited as reasons why families move. There is no question that more affluent people have more opportunities and therefore more propensity to move. The uncoupling of doubled–up households accounts for a significant proportion of moves in tight housing markets: "[T]he share of uncoupling of overall mobility in Moscow (42%) far exceeds the percentage of uncoupling averaged among urban areas (22%) throughout the U.S. in 1993" [Lee and Struyk, 1996, 661]. More generally, this latter observation suggests that cities with higher levels of households per dwelling unit are likely to have higher rates of mobility, a result that could not be statistically confirmed by data from the Global Survey.

Conversely, racial and economic barriers, xenophobia, high transaction costs, home ownership in and of itself, a high incidence of multifamily housing that cannot be modified to meet changing space needs, high mortgage payments that keep families in stable but lower-paying jobs, negative equity, and rent control have all been named as responsible for restricting residential mobility, and hence labor mobility and upward social and economic mobility as well. It is in this latter sense that the housing sector, by failing to allow for *adequate* residential mobility, can frustrate people's aspirations for a better life. This is not to suggest, however, that very high rates of mobility are always desirable, because they can indeed be indications of the breakdown of communities and of a lack of stability and continuity in the home, school, and neighborhood life of urban families.

Very low rates of mobility, however, are no doubt an obstacle to the betterment of life no matter what their cause. When transaction costs are high, for example, they can and will inhibit desirable moves. And very often, these costs are a direct result of government policy: "In Europe, transfer taxes alone range from 2-3 per cent in Britain, 5 per cent for Germany and Denmark, 9-11 per cent for France and Spain, 13 per cent for Italy and 14-16 per cent for Greece and Belgium, to a 9.5-19.5 per cent range for Portugal" [Mouillart and Occhipinti, 1990, in Strassmann, 1991, 763]. Several studies have commented on the adverse effect of rent control on residential mobility: "Freezing rents at nominal levels in times of great destruction, migration, or rising inflation has lead to a near total cessation of rental building, as in Portugal in the late 1970s; to the passive abandonment of tenements to their occupants, as in Sri Lanka at the same time; to systems of illegal 'key payment,' as in Egypt; or to bartered chains of moves, as in Eastern Europe under Communism. All lower mobility" [Strassmann, 1991, 762]. Using the ratio between the house price-to-income ratio and the rent-to-income ratio as a measure of the degree of government intervention (via rent control) in the housing market, Strassmann modeled residential mobility as a function of this ratio using data from the mid-1970s to the mid-1980s for a 16-country sample. The model had an R-squared value of 0.75 [768]. He concluded that "[r]esidential mobility, especially intraurban residential mobility, will be slowed in proportion to the strength of housing market intervention by governments" [759]. He did not, however, find a significant correlation between mobility and owner-occupancy. Strassmann's findings suggest that cities with greater rent control will, on the whole, have lower rates of residential mobility, a reasonable expectation that again could not be confirmed by our data from the Global Survey. Neither the Rent Control Index nor the Enabling Index which embodies it were found to affect residential mobility significantly. Owner-occupancy, in contrast to his findings, did have a significant effect on residential mobility, as we shall see below.

Finally, a downward swing in house prices can leave families stranded in homes that may have lower values than their mortgage liabilities. Such homes cannot be left without incurring a loss, and they cannot provide owners with the equity that is necessary for a down payment for a new home. Henley, using British data, concluded that the "widespread experience of negative equity in the early 1990s had a significant adverse impact on residential mobility and on housing market transactions" [Henley, 1998, 426].

The model for residential mobility is presented on the bottom line of table 22.2. It has an R-squared of 0.48, implying that it explains almost half of the variation in residential mobility in our sample. The model used the same explanatory variables as those of the earlier models, adding owner-occupancy. As expected, residential mobility was found to be significantly higher in higher-income countries and in faster-growing cities. In contrast, it was found to be significantly lower in cities with higher construction costs and higher rates of owner- occupancy. Neither the vacancy rate nor the enabling index (or the Rent Control Index) were found to be significantly associated with higher rates of residential mobility. Among all the explanatory variables, only the level of economic development and the rate of urban growth had a strong effect on mobility.

The Demand and Supply of Housing Production and Investment, Vacancy, and Mobility

As we noted earlier, it may not be sensible to speak of the "demand for new housing," and hence of the demand for housing stock growth, housing production, or housing investment. The demand for new housing cannot be separated from the demand for old housing. The foregoing analysis, which — in parallel with earlier chapters — examines the demand, supply, and policy elasticities of the indicators in question must therefore be interpreted with caution.

Following the same procedure outlined in chapter 6, we now investigate the effects of income, prices, population growth, and the policy environment on the demand for the vacancy rate, housing stock growth, production and investment and residential mobility; we also examine the effect of prices, the inputs costs of land and construction, and the policy environment (and the vacancy rate for the latter four indicators) on the supply of these quantities. We examine two models for each indicator, one for the quantity demanded (from which we derive the estimated income elasticity, price elasticity, and policy elasticity of demand), and one for the quantity supplied (from which we derive the price elasticity and policy elasticity of supply). In all five models, the weighted price index is used as the price variable. The models appear in table 22.3. As the table shows, all of the models, with the exception of the supply model for housing production, were found to be statistically significant.

The demand and supply models for the vacancy rate appear on the top line of table 22.3. The models have R-squared values of 0.29 and 0.28, respectively, suggesting that the variables used explain less than a third of the variation in the quantity demanded and the quantity supplied in our sample. The models indicate that neither income nor price appear to have an effect on the demand or the supply of vacant homes. In contrast, the policy environment was found to have

Table 22.3. The Income, Price, and Policy Elasticities of Housing Production and Investment, Vacancy, and Mobility.

Variable	Income Elasticity of Demand	Price Elasticity of Demand	Price Elasticity of Supply	Policy Elasticity of Demand	Policy Elasticity of Supply	No. of Observations	Demand Model		Supply Model	
							R-squared & Adjusted R-squared	F-value	R-squared & Adjusted R-squared	F-value
The Vacancy Rate	-0.24 -0.84	0.61 0.89	-0.03 -0.04	1.14 3.11***	1.03 3.14***	39	0.29 0.20	$F_{4,34}$ 3.44**	0.28 0.19	$F_{4,34}$ 3.27**
Housing Stock Growth	-0.14 -1.35*	0.29 1.17	0.39 0.95	0.03 0.20	-0.20 -1.03	42	0.50 0.44	$F_{4,37}$ 9.18***	0.08 -0.07	$F_{5,32}$ 0.53
Housing Production (units per 1,000 people)	0.13 1.51*	0.22 1.06	0.61 2.54***	-0.12 -1.06	-0.20 -1.76**	43	0.24 0.16	$F_{4,38}$ 2.96**	0.25 0.14	$F_{5,33}$ 2.22*
Gross Urban Housing Investment	-0.15 -1.08	1.07 3.15***	0.52 1.47*	0.02 0.08	-0.20 -1.19	43	0.25 0.17	$F_{4,38}$ 3.14**	0.34 0.24	$F_{5,33}$ 3.42**
Residential Mobility	0.49 4.44***	-0.40 -1.49*	0.84 2.63***	-0.16 -1.13	0.23 1.53*	38	0.43 0.36	$F_{4,33}$ 6.29***	0.46 0.35	$F_{6,29}$ 4.10***

Source: Housing Indicators Program [1994].

[a] Figures in the top rows are elasticities.

[b] Figures in italics denote t– and F-statistics.

[c] ***, **, and * denote 1%, 5% and 10% levels of confidence, respectively.

[d] Housing Credit Portfolio not included in this model.

a strong effect on both. An enabling housing policy environment was associated with a higher level of demand for vacancies, because a higher level of vacant homes on the market acts to increase choices for consumers. In parallel, an enabling policy environment led to a greater supply of vacant properties, and producers were willing to build houses and put them on the market even if they could not be immediately occupied. Nonenabling housing policies tend to constrain vacancies below a "natural" vacancy rate, the rate that can keep housing prices stable while ensuring ample opportunities for market transactions.

The demand model for housing stock growth, shown in the second row of table 22.3, had an R-squared value of 0.50, implying that it explains half of the variation in housing stock growth in the sample. The demand for stock growth declined significantly as income increased, but was not influenced by neither prices nor by the policy environment. The supply model for this indicator was not statistically significant.

The demand and supply models for housing production, shown on the following line in the table, had R-squared values of 0.24 and 0.25 respectively, implying that they explain only one-quarter of the variation in demand and supply of housing production in the sample. The demand for housing production (in new units per 1,000 people) was found to increase modestly, rather than decrease, with increased income. The income elasticity of demand for new housing production was +0.13. This may have occurred because, in higher income countries with smaller household sizes, relatively more units are produced to accommodate 1,000 people than in lower-income countries with larger household sizes.

The supply of new housing units per 1,000 people was found to be responsive to house prices, with a price elasticity of +0.61. Higher house prices lead to higher supplies of new housing. In contrast, the supply of new housing units (measured in units per 1,000 people) was reduced in more enabling housing policy regimes. The policy elasticity of supply was found to be significantly negative. This finding corresponds to observations that in countries where levels of housing production are determined administratively, the number of units produced is not responsive to prices, independent of demand fluctuations, and possibly higher than levels of production in more market-oriented policy regimes.

The demand and supply models for gross urban housing investment, shown on the fourth line of table 22.3, had R-squared values of 0.27 and 0.39 respectively, implying that they explain roughly one-third of the variations in housing investment in the sample. In parallel with stock growth, the demand for new housing investment declined with increasing income, although not significantly. The demand for new investment had a positive price elasticity as well, found to be +1.12. This is not surprising, because housing investment is measured in value, not in quantities, and therefore contains a price element. Investment is expected to be higher when prices are higher. This leaves open the question of whether investment was higher because of high house prices or because of the greater number of units produced; at least, however, it suggests that high investment values may be associated with high prices. In parallel with the finding on housing production, the supply of new housing investment was found to be responsive to house prices, with a similar supply price elasticity of +0.55. Higher house prices lead to higher investments in new housing. In contrast, the supply of new housing investment (measured in the value of new housing units) was found to be reduced in more–enabling housing policy regimes. The policy elasticity of the supply of housing investment was indeed modestly negative. Countries with more enabling housing policy regimes were found to invest less, rather than more, in housing. This finding, taken together with our earlier findings regarding the conditions of the housing stock in enabling and non-enabling regimes in earlier chapters, suggests that nonenabling regimes may produce more and invest more in housing but get *less,* in terms of the performance, out of their housing sectors.

Finally, the demand and supply models for residential mobility appear on the bottom line of table 22.3. The models had R–squared values of 0.43 and 0.44, respectively, implying that they explain more than 40% of the variation in the demand and supply of residential mobility in the sample. The demand for residential mobility increased significantly with income, and the income elasticity of demand was +0.49. As expected, it decreased significantly when house prices increased. The price elasticity of demand for residential mobility was –0.40. Demand for mobility was not significantly affected by the policy environment, but supply was.[9] This supply is found to be significantly elastic (+0.82) with respect to house prices. Higher house prices give positive signals to suppliers of housing to create more opportunities for residential mobility. Similarly, enabling policy regimes create significantly more opportunities for residential mobility than nonenabling ones.

* * *

To conclude this chapter, we summarize our findings. The level of economic development, measured in terms of household incomes or GNP per capita, was found to have a different relationship with rates of housing stock growth, housing production, and housing investment than that postulated by earlier studies. Instead of increasing, reaching a plateau, and then decreasing, both housing stock growth and gross urban housing investment were found to decrease significantly with higher levels of economic development, and the income elasticities of demand for both were found to be negative. The level of economic development was not found to have a significant effect on the vacancy rate, but a rather robust effect on the equilibrium values of residential mobility and on the demand for residential mobility. Higher incomes were clearly associated with higher levels of mobility.

The urban population growth rate had a statistically significant effect on four of the five measures discussed in this chapter. Vacancy rates were significantly lower and residential mobility higher in the more rapidly growing cities. Housing stock growth and housing production per 1,000 inhabitants were both significantly higher in these cities as well. Housing investment, on the other hand, did not vary appreciably with changes in the urban growth rate.

Factor costs and house prices were found to affect these measures as well. Vacancy rates were modestly (but not significantly) higher and residential mobility rates were lower in cities with higher construction cost-to-income ratios. The demand for residential mobility was found to be significantly lower when house prices were high, while the "supply" of residential mobility was found to be significantly higher when house prices were high.

Construction costs did not have an appreciable effect on rates of investment and growth in the housing sector, but land prices did. Higher land prices were found to be associated with all three growth rate — housing stock growth, housing production, and growth urban housing investment. This could well be the result of growth pressures on land prices, although throughout this study we have assumed that land prices were exogenous to the housing market. Land prices had a particularly strong effect on gross urban housing investment, suggesting that high levels of investment were associated with high land prices, rather than with higher levels of housing production measured in units. The price elasticity of demand for housing investment was found to be significantly positive, again suggesting that higher levels of housing investment may be associated with high house prices, rather than with larger quantities or higher quality. The price elasticity of supply for both housing production and housing investment was also found to be significantly positive, suggesting that suppliers responded positively to new demand for housing. All three growth rate were found to be significantly associated with the vacancy rate. Higher vacancy rates implied higher levels of housing production, investment, and growth.

Finally, a more enabling housing policy environment was found to have a significant positive effect on the vacancy rate, on the demand and supply of vacant residential properties, and on the "supply" of residential mobility. It was not found to have an appreciably positive effect on any of the rates of housing sector growth. In fact, the policy elasticity of the supply of housing production (measured in new units per 1,000 people) was found to be modestly negative, implying that new housing production may indeed be higher in nonenabling regimes. In light of our many findings in the earlier chapters that housing sector performance was considerably better in the more-enabling housing policy regimes, we may conclude that housing conditions in enabling policy environments were better despite lower levels of production and investment in housing. Given our mixed results, however, it is safer to conclude that our data do not support either the contention that enabling policies improve housing production and investment rates or that nonenabling policies engender higher levels of production and investment.

23

Tenure

What are the rights of dwellers to the houses they occupy and how protected are those rights? Do dwellers have the right to occupy their homes without the arbitrary threat of eviction? Do they have the right to own houses as private property that can be exchanged at will? Is the right to a minimum dwelling guaranteed by the state? How do these specific bundles of rights affect housing conditions? To what extent are they protected by existing legislation and enforcement? There is little doubt that the issues surrounding these tenure rights to housing have been central to the housing policy debate. Indeed, from a comprehensive perspective on housing policy, each dwelling unit must be perceived of as a bundle of rights, and housing policy must concern itself with the tenure composition the housing stock – in other words, with ensuring that the bundle of rights associated individual housing units meets societal objectives and expectations.

The distribution of bundles of rights to housing is of key importance to society as a whole, because it affects the behavior of people towards their homes, particularly their care and maintenance of their homes and the investment of their savings in home improvements. It also affects the distribution of national wealth and the contribution of wealth-poverty to income–poverty. Finally, the distribution of rights to housing also affects affects the balance of power between the public and the private sector.

And not only are those bundles of rights important to society as a whole, they are of great importance to dwellers as well. Studies in both developing and developed countries indeed suggest that tenure choice is the single most important determinant of housing demand for all households, overshadowing the importance of both the quality of structures and the amount of living space [Borsch–Supan, 1987; Stahl and Struyk, 1985; Mehta and Mehta, 1989]. It stands to reason, therefore, that many of the housing policy debates are informed by monitoring the tenure composition of housing markets – the proportion of houses in different categories of tenure.

Payne [1997], in a comprehensive review of urban land tenure and residential property rights in developing countries, distinguished a large number of gradations in tenure rights and noted the different circumstances in which each bundle of rights provided the appropriate context for specific kinds of housing. In this chapter we shall limit ourselves to five key tenure distinctions:

1. privately owned versus publicly owned housing;
2. owner–occupied versus rental housing;
3. formal–sector housing versus informal–sector housing;[1]
4. legal versus illegal occupation of residential land; and
5. the housed versus the homeless.[2]

We note at the outset that households may have good reasons, given their circumstances, to opt for any combination of these forms of tenure; and that societies may have good reasons, given their circumstances, to encourage, allow, tolerate, or prohibit any one of these forms. We can also observe that particular households often change their tenure when their circumstances change, and that particular societies often opt to change housing tenure en masse, transforming public housing to private housing and vice versa, transforming tenants to home-owners, transforming squatters to legal occupiers of land, and sheltering or chasing away the homeless. What is important to keep in mind, however, is that all forms of tenure provide a place to stay in the city, that each and every one of them is problematic in some way, and that often the promotion of one form of tenure displaces or disadvantages another. In other words, all forms of tenure contribute to the total housing supply and all are, in some sense, interchangeable. Homelessness, we need to remember, is also a legitimate housing option, one that provides housing of zero quality, usually at zero price, and with some location advantages in terms of access to income–earning opportunities and in terms of drawing attention to one's plight. Many pavement dwellers in India and Brazil, for example, are reported to have adequate housing outside the city but need to stay somewhere in the city — anywhere in fact — to stay alive [Taschner and Rabinovich, 1997, 26].

Surely, in an ideal world with no resource constraints, both individual house-holds and society as a whole may opt overwhelmingly to be housed rather than homeless, to occupy land legally, to have decent houses that fall well within codes and ordinances, to own rather than to rent, and to live in privately owned houses rather than in public housing estates. The reality of resource limitations, alterna-tive investment opportunities, ideological commitments, and simple prefer-ences — say for remaining mobile and unencumbered — creates a much more complex picture, one in which the housing market as a whole contains a rich mixture of different tenures. This mixture is a dynamic one as well, with some forms of tenure gradually disappearing and others taking their place. During the second half of the twentieth century, for example, we witnessed in many countries the rise and fall of public housing construction, the privatization of the public housing stock, the weakening of private investment in rental housing, the gradual rise of home ownership, the massive growth of informal or extra–legal housing, the rise and fall of squatter movements, and the reemergence of new forms of homelessness in cities where it has all but disappeared.

From the point of view of housing policy, it is of critical importance to monitor the composition of housing tenures and to understand what it is that affects this composition. Indeed, in recent history, affecting this composition was often a stated objective of the highest priority in national housing policy. But priorities change. For example, public housing, which was at peak in the years following World War II, is now rarely advocated as a sensible route to increasing housing supply. Public housing stocks are diminishing everywhere. Chapter 9 discussed public housing in greater detail and provided cross-sectional data on the relative size of the public housing stock (see table 9.1). Hence, it will not be discussed further here. The rationale for granting individual property rights in housing was also discussed in greater detail earlier (see chapter 7). But given that greater access to home ownership is still a central housing policy objective, we shall present measures of owner–occupancy and discuss them at greater length in this chapter. In addition, we shall also focus on measuring the contribution of the informal sector to the housing stock; on the reemergence of homelessness as a serious housing policy issue; and on explaining the variation in the levels of home ownership, informal housing, squatter housing, and homelessness (as well as their demand and supply) in different cities and countries.

Home Ownership

There are only a few cross–national studies of home ownership, and they focus on the cultural differences in the perceptions of owning a home in different countries, on the different legal and institutional frameworks governing tenure rights, on the difficulties in articulating universal definitions of tenure and ownership, on the explanations of the differences in home ownership rates between different countries and periods, and, finally, on the effects of government policies on rates of home ownership.

At the household level, there is no question that in many countries owning a home is a preferred option for many families, and that many still fail to realize it because, for one reason or another, it remains outside their reach. Recognizing this pent–up demand, many governments promote home ownership, although often without a clear vision as to its social merits or as to how it is to be promoted. On the positive side, there is no doubt that home ownership has greatly increased housing investment, care, maintenance, improvement, and upgrading of houses by their owners; that it has channeled large amounts of savings and credit to the housing sector; that it has led to a vast redistribution of societal wealth to individual households; that it has diminished the role of the state in the direct provision of housing; and that it has accelerated the development of real estate markets in housing.

In parallel, serious objections against home ownership were raised in early Communist writings, for example, and Communist regimes tended to discourage it in favor of collective or state ownership. Marxist critics in market economies complained that home ownership "was deliberately and intentionally fostered by governments and capitalist interests in an attempt to bolster the bourgeois social order" [Saunders, 1990, 29]. Saunders reviews Marxist claims that home ownership was fostered to (a) broaden vested interests in the survival of private property regimes; (b) create and reinforce divisions within the working classes by helping the higher strata of workers to own housing; (c) dissipate the revolutionary fervor of the masses by making them dependent on the regular jobs necessary to make regular mortgages payments; (d) encourage workers to withdraw into the privacy of their homes and away from social life; and (e) create a market for mass consumer goods [29–33]. Gilbert [1991], writing about government intervention in the housing sector in the developing countries, observes that "[s]elf–help home ownership has been viewed as a means of pacifying the poor" [13]. Examining the history of state intervention to promote home ownership, Saunders concludes that there is little evidence for such intentional behavioral on the part of states to actively (or, for that matter, effectively) promote home ownership: "Like so many other social changes, the expansion of home ownership was planned by nobody, and its consequences have been largely unintended and often unforeseen" [36]. This is not so say that state action to remove barriers to home ownership — facilitating the formation of credit markets, removing discrimination in the granting of credit, tolerating squatters, and regularizing tenure in squatter settlements — has not been instrumental in creating a level playing field for households to choose freely between tenure options.

In the postwar years, home ownership expanded in a large number of industrialized countries. As table 23.1 shows, among 20 industrialized countries, owner–occupancy rates grew by one–third, on average, from 43% shortly after the war to 59% in 1990, and ownership has now become the dominant form of tenure. The most rapid growth can be observed in the United Kingdom and in Ireland. Japan was the only country where owner–occupancy rates declined in the postwar years, while rates in Sweden and Germany remained relatively stable, and relatively low, throughout the period in question. Growth spurts in home ownership have taken place at different time periods in different countries and, on the whole, there is no observed tendency for growth rates in individual countries to be slowing down or reaching stable plateaus. There is little empirical evidence of the growth of home ownership in the developing countries, but, as we shall see later, owner–occupancy rates there are not substantially different from those of the industrialized countries.

It is of growing concern to housing policy makers that governments tend to focus their energies on home ownership and neglect the maintenance of rental markets. Gilbert and Varley [1991], for example, observed that in Mexico, "rental housing has received little by way of funding" [12], in comparison with government programs aimed at home ownership. They noted that "[i]n most parts of the third world, tenants and landlords have become 'invisible'". [Grennel, 1972, in Gilbert and Varley, 1991, 12]. Rental tenements in central cities have been

Table 23.1. The Growth of Home Ownership, 1945–90.

Country	1945–1950	1960	1970	1980	1990
Australia	53%	63%	67%	71%	70%
Austria	36%	38%	41%	48%	55%
Belgium	39%	50%	55%	59%	63%
Canada	66%	66%	60%	62%	64%
Denmark	n.a.	43%	49%	52%	51%
France	n.a.	41%	45%	51%	54%
Finland	n.a.	57%	59%	61%	67%
Greece	n.a.	n.a.	n.a.	70%	77%
Ireland	n.a.	n.a.	71%	76%	81%
Italy	40%	45%	50%	59%	67%
Japan	n.a.	71%	59%	62%	61%
Netherlands	28%	29%	35%	42%	44%
Norway	n.a.	n.a.	53%	59%	59%
Portugal	n.a.	n.a.	n.a.	57%	58%
Spain	n.a.	n.a.	64%	73%	76%
Sweden	38%	36%	35%	41%	42%
Switzerland	n.a.	n.a.	28%	30%	30%
United Kingdom	29%	42%	49%	56%	68%
United States	57%	64%	65%	68%	64%
Germany	n.a.	n.a.	36%	40%	38%
Average	43%	50%	51%	57%	59%
Standard Deviation	12%	13%	12%	12%	13%

Source: Doling [1997, table 9.1, 159].

largely viewed as "slums of despair," and negative attitudes toward exploitative landlords and the "rentier" class have prevented governments from objective assessments of the rental sector, an essential component in any well functioning housing market. In the making of housing policy, it is undoubtedly the balance between ownership and tenure that should be of prime concern. And the key to the attainment of this balance is the creation of a level playing field, where those competing for resources for investing in or constructing housing for rental or ownership can compete fairly, and where consumers can choose freely between one form of tenure and the other.

A number of reasons have been advanced to explain the growth in home ownership and the variations in home ownership rates among countries. These shall be discussed in greater detail later in the context of attempting to model global variations statistically. Such models cannot, however, be expected to explain the deeper meanings of home ownership to dwellers, and the consequent intensity of the desire for home ownership, a desire that can sometimes over-shadow the simple user–cost calculus of households. As Saunders concludes: "[H]ome ownership may also be desired for its own sake, as an emotional expression of autonomy, security, and personal identity... [T]he desire to own a house is an expression of a specific set of cultural values" [Saunders, 1990, 39].

Informal–sector Housing

In comparison to the industrialized economies, the great majority of the developing market economies in Latin America, Asia, and Africa have not been able to attain levels of economic development that could enable them to provide decent–standard housing either through mass public housing construction or through the formal private sector. Grimes [1976], for example, estimated that, in 1970 for example, 47% of the households in Bogota, 35% in Hong Kong, 63% in Madras, 55% in Mexico City, and 68% in Nairobi could not afford the least expensive urban house produced by the formal private sector, regardless of its location [table 5.5, 70]. More recent data is provided by the indicator of down-market penetration (see table 17.1): the global median value of the lowest–priced house produced by the formal sector was 2.3 median household incomes in 1990, still less than affordable for the majority of the poor. Hence, while the formal housing sector produced the bulk of housing for higher–income groups, and while public housing was of limited scope everywhere—except in Hong Kong and Singapore—most low–income housing in the developing market economies was and is produced by the informal housing sector. A significant share of urban housing for the poor in these countries is *informal* or illegal—occupying land illegally (squatting), or built in land subdivisions that do not conform to zoning ordinances and planning regulations. Most of it is built with varying amounts of self–help, self–management, and mutual aid, without conforming to building codes, without adequate infrastructure, without any state subsidies, and without any formal housing finance.

While it is important to understand why such a substantial informal housing sector emerged with such force in Latin America, Asia, and Africa in the twentieth century, we should remember that informal and illegal construction was by no means restricted to these continents. There are records of "a whole clandestine proliferation of hovels and shanties on lands of doubtful ownership in 17th century London" [Braudel, 1976, 83]. According to Braudel, who wrote on the pre–industrial city in Europe, every town, throughout history, had an informal fringe: "All the towns in the world, beginning with those in the West, had their suburbs. Just as a strong tree is never without shoots at its foot, so towns are never without suburbs. They are the manifestations of its strength, even if they are wretched fringes, shanty towns" [66].

Such informal housing has been a feature of cities throughout their history. Hardoy [1982] noted that in Latin America during the colonial period, for example, the formal city was planned and constructed by professional builders, while "the lower–income groups, unskilled Indians, and mestizos without regular employment, built their small houses further away. Like the pre–Colombian city, the colonial city was largely self–built" [26]. De Ramon [1978] described two communities that developed outside the official boundary of Santiago de Chile in the seventeenth century:

In both slums there were mestizos, freed Indians, and Negroes, and poor Spaniards; both had irregular streets and very humble buildings, of indigenous style, called 'ranchos', built of mud and straw...; neither had any of the few public services available at that time to the rest of the city, and both were located far from the city centre, in unhealthy areas...these new areas did not form part of the administrative area of the city and as such were not represented in the deliberations of the Council nor indeed did that organization have much interest in them." [122]

The *Ordenanza Sobre Ranchos* of 1857 actually prohibited the construction of ranchos within Santiago proper, but decreed that outside those limits huts of straw and mud could be built [Gilbert, 1990, 19]. These ranchos were, no doubt, variations on rural housing forms. Similar "suburbs" developed on the outskirts of the planned colonial cities in Asia and Africa.

With the onset of rapid urbanization in these continents — largely a twentieth-century phenomenon — these practices gained momentum for a number of reasons. First, urbanization was more rapid than its earlier counterpart in Europe and North America, and beyond the capacities of a less-organized formal private sector to supply. Second, while the poor in Europe and North America were restricted to the city proper because of lack of transport, the development of mass transportation in the twentieth century made vast tracts of land available for low-rise residential development with traditional building technologies. Third, the transition from colonialism to independence was accompanied by the emergence of populist nationalist governments that had an interest in enlisting the support and the loyalty of the urban masses, while preventing social upheaval and revolution; this made these governments less likely to engage in frustrating the constructive energies of their peoples. Fourth, the supply of land for squatting, either through organized invasions or through gradual encroachment, was substantial:

Its sources were the "crown properties" which the newly independent governments inherited from the colonial administrations, nonagricultural waste land in the fringe of rapidly growing cities, and abandoned private lands not suitable for commercialized urban development. Discontinuities in state power and the use of the land issue in political infighting provided the institutional framework within which vacant land could be occupied without substantial opposition. [Baross and Van der Linden, 1990, 1-2]

And fifth, the poor could not afford to pay for fully serviced land in planned subdivisions zoned for residential development, but they could afford to pay for unserviced land in squatter settlements or illegal commercial subdivisions that did not conform to planning and zoning regulations. In his study of Peruvian cities, De Soto [1989] explains that such illegal settlements have been cheap, affordable, and indeed suitable to the needs of the poor: "First, the informals occupy the land, then they build on it, next they install infrastructures, and only at the end do they acquire ownership. This is exactly the reverse of what happens in the formal world" [17].

Although the focus of attention in many policy discussions has been on squatters, it appears that the bulk of home builders in the informal sector in developing countries actually bought land in informal land subdivisions [Baross, 1990, 69]. These land subdivisions increased land supply by using land not zoned residential, and by ignoring (and indeed overcoming) the shortages of infrastructure grids. They could provide less expensive plots by avoiding the expenses for high-standard infrastructure services, and by disregarding fees and delays in receiving permits. Furthermore, they facilitated home building without access to housing finance, by allowing for houses to be constructed over time [Baross, 1990, 63–69]. The distinction between informal sector housing as a whole and squatter housing as a subset of informal housing will become clearer when we define the indicators measured in the Global Survey.

We should keep in mind that informal-sector housing also exists in the industrialized countries, although the process by which it is created is usually quite different. Houses that do not meet codes and regulations or squatter houses are, in general, not created anew in large numbers.[3] Instead, they are formed in the process of neglect, dilapidation, and abandonment of houses that originally did meet codes and regulations and were inhabited and cared for at acceptable levels of maintenance and repair. Formal-sector housing thus becomes informal-sector housing through a process of "filtering down." Dilapidation and neglect occurred, in the United States for example, when middle-income people abandoned central cities for the suburbs, lowering the demand for houses in older neighborhoods. They also occurred where controlled rents or the low-incomes of dwellers were insufficient to keep housing in good order.

Squatting in the cities of industrialized countries, especially since the late 1960s, has been a form of militant direct action in defiance of the law and the government, a form of protest aimed at focusing attention on social injustice as a whole or on the housing plight of specific groups of poor people. Squatting has taken place in abandoned government buildings, in army barracks, in privately owned housing, and most particularly in public housing. Angotti [1977], writing about housing in Italy during the late 1970s, describes the process of squatting:

> Housing units under construction are watched carefully by local groups of tenants. They are taken over only when completed to the point of being livable, but not complete enough to be rentable. Many squatting actions take place in vacant housing that is finished but held off the market for speculation or other reasons. . . Most squatting, however, takes place in public housing. Public housing authorities. . . are reluctant to send in the police to evict working class families. [49–50]

Homelessness

Homelessness, to be distinguished from squatting or living in inadequate or low-quality housing, is best understood as "the end of the spectrum of poor housing outcomes" [Honig and Filer, 1993, 248]. The definition of what constitutes homelessness — say, for purposes of measurement — is quite controversial, as we shall see. What is important to note, regardless of the definition, is that homelessness is fundamentally both a poverty problem and a housing problem — that poverty breeds homelessness, and that homelessness exacerbates poverty.

There have always been philosophies that advocate the voluntary abandonment of material possessions, including one's home, in search of spiritual enlightenment. The monastic tradition in Buddhism, for example, is referred to in the Buddhist canon as a "venturing forth into homelessness." Except during the rainy season, monks are to follow "the wandering life of the ascetic or the beggar, depending on their livelihood on the gifts of the laity, their only shelter the trees of the forest or booths constructed of leaves and branches" [Hastings, 1916, 797]. In contrast, modern urban homelessness is, as most surveys confirm, largely involuntary. A survey of homeless people in England concluded that "they all wished for a decent and clean place to live with congenial company and to be able to choose and control their way of life" [Deacon and Walker, 1995, 357]. In San Francisco, 94% of homeless people surveyed cited "no place to live indoors" as by far the most important issue they faced [Ball and Havassy, 1984, in Wright and Rubin, 1991, 938]. The homeless at the start of the twenty-first century are clearly not "romantic vagabonds who have traded the rat race of modern urban civilization for a life uncomplicated by mortgage or rent payments, ringing telephones, surly bosses, nagging spouses, and truculent children" [Wright and Rubin, 1991, 938].

The phenomenon of homelessness, or the absence of a home, leads us to seek a definition of what constitutes a *home* in the mind of someone who does not have one — a much lower minimum, to be sure, than one held by those who are comfortably housed. Such a minimal definition is advanced by Jencks [1994], for example: "a fixed address where they could leave their possessions, return whenever they wished, and sleep in peace" [3]. Listening to the homeless, a place to wash oneself may need to be added to this basic definition: "Your clothes are dirty, you're dirty, and everything. No one's gonna want you working for them if you're like that" [Anderson et al., 1993, 14]. Most employers will not employ a person with an unkempt appearance and with no street address. The absence of a home is clearly an instrument of social exclusion, and, as such, one that exacerbates poverty. In the words of a homeless person: "I think it's everybody's worst fear, getting thrown out of your house. You grow up with the idea that your house is your home... That is your base. And as soon as that's taken away, it's like everything you ever hoped or wished for has been taken away. If you don't have a house, your chances of a decent life in the future are completely gone.

How can you plan your future and your work or your family life and your social life if you don't have a place to live?" [Anderson et al., 1993, 78].

The simplest, and to my mind the most satisfactory, explanation for homelessness is an economic one. The urban supply of housing has a minimum price associated with it, and below that price no housing can be supplied.[4] In some cities, where there is ample informal housing and squatter housing, that minimum price may be quite low, and even very low–income people can find a place to live. But in other cities, most often in the industrialized countries or in economies in transition, the low end of the housing supply spectrum has been largely curtailed hand in hand with increased levels of poverty. In the United States, for example, "[i]n twelve large cities surveyed between 1978 and 1983, the amount of inexpensive rental housing available to poor families dropped precipitously, averaging 30%. At the same time, the number of households living at or below the poverty level in the same cities increased by 36%" [Rossi, 1989, 182]. Very inexpensive housing has simply disappeared, at the same time as the housing budgets of the very poor have shrunk. During the Great Depression in the United States and after World War II in Europe, shantytowns sprouted to accommodate those without adequate means to house themselves in conventional housing. No comparable phenomenon was permitted to occur in Eastern Europe during the Communist era, and in Western Europe and North America in the 1970s and 1980s. On the contrary, in the United States, for example, very low–cost housing, such as single room occupancy (SRO) hotels, disappeared in great numbers: "In New York City there was an overall 60 percent loss of SRO hotel rooms between 1975 and 1981" [Wright and Rubin, 1991, 943]. And "between 1970 and 1985 more than half the SRO units in downtown Los Angeles had been demolished" [Hamilton, Rabinowitz and Altshuler, Inc.,1987, in Rossi, 1989, 182].

The main reasons for the disappearance of the lower end of the low–cost housing stock are, on the one hand, the deterioration, abandonment, and destruction without replacement of the old and dilapidated housing stock and other forms of inexpensive housing; and on the other hand, the redevelopment and gentrification of urban neighborhoods. These changes have come about as a result of the combined actions of governments and the private sector. Governments, particularly local governments, have often accelerated the abandonment of neighborhoods, first, by their insistence both on rent control and on minimum standards that could not be sustained by landlords forced to accept low rents; second, by prohibiting rooming houses; and third, by their removal of crucial stabilizing public services, such as fire and police protection, from neighborhoods in decline [Wallace, 1989, 1586].

The disappearance of low–cost housing was accompanied by higher levels of impoverishment and unemployment that surfaced in cities of industrialized countries in the 1970s and 1980s, as income inequality increased and public benefits to the poor declined. Casual day–labor opportunities of Skid Row residents, for instance, shrunk considerably as did their incomes. In Chicago, for example, "the constant–dollar income of the Skid Row residents in 1958 was at least three times the income of the current homeless" [Rossi, 1989, 185]. The ranks of the homeless poor everywhere were added to by a number of groups of disadvantaged groups – those released from mental hospitals who had nowhere to go, drug and alcohol abusers, persons abandoned by their families or escaping from unbearable domestic violence, released prisoners, and the long–term unemployed. What characterizes all these groups is their exclusion from the labor market and their consequent limited ability to earn an adequate income, their exclusion from the support networks of family and friends, and their limited access to public assistance services. It is not their pathology that rendered them homeless. It is rather that their pathology rendered them poor, and their poverty then excluded them from minimum–cost housing.

Surely, many of these groups require special assistance. But in the last analysis, at the basis of their problems there is a housing problem: "Even if there was a way to stabilize the mentally–ill homeless, or treat the alcoholic and drug–addicted homeless, or reintegrate the estranged homeless with their families and friends, almost all would still be poor. And as poor people, they would then face the same housing problem that all poor people face – an insufficient and dwindling supply of low–income housing" [Wright and Rubin, 1991, 947]. Without the solution of the housing problem of the poor, efforts to address many other special needs will be largely fruitless.

The rise of homelessness in the 1980s and the 1990s has prompted governments, as well as academic researchers and advocates of the homeless, to attempt to measure the levels of homelessness, to examine its causes, and to propose preventive measures as well as cures. The accurate measurement of the homeless population has proved to be much more difficult that at first imagined, for reasons that will be discussed in the following section.

Tenure Measures of Housing Quantity

Measures of housing tenure should, in principle, be simple proportions of the total housing stock. Measuring these proportions is quite straightforward in the formal housing sector, whether public or private, owner–occupied or rented, although several commentators have noted that tenure boundaries are often fuzzy and that the perceptions of different tenures tend to vary among cultures [e.g., Marcuse, 1994]. Typical measures are the proportions of dwellings completed by type of investor/owner (state and local governments, other public bodies, private persons, cooperatives, and other private bodies) [United Nations, 1992, table 6, 44–47]; the home ownership rate [U.S. HUD, 1994, 25], the home ownership rate for recently married couples [Madge, 1976, table 13, in Department of the Environment, 1977b, 82] and the average age of owners and renters. As expected, however, there are serious problems in underreporting dwelling units and households in the informal sector, and very serious deficiencies in counting the homeless. The first of these difficulties is gradually being corrected. The 1995 population and housing census of Nicaragua, for example, was based on a careful and systematic inclusion of urban informal housing in its surveys. Census tables included measures of security of tenure, as well as the quality of building materials in all residential communities [Nicaragua National Institute of Statistics and Census, 1995]. Typical measures of the informal housing sector as a whole include slums and squatter settlements as a percent of city population [Grimes, 1976, 116–126; Gilbert, 1990, 20]; land development in illegal subdivisions (hectares) by year [Molina, 1990, 302]; forced eviction of people from private or public land, in absolute numbers [Audefroy, 1994, 11]; and the rate of eviction (number of people evicted per year as percent of total slum population) [Khan, 1994, 29].

There are still a number of inherent difficulties in counting the homeless, and although several estimates have been published [Flood, 1993, 122; Neil et al., 1992], there is sometimes a tenfold difference between one estimate and another. The first difficulty is in agreeing on a simple, consistent, practical definition of the homeless that would allow surveyors in different cities to measure it with a degree of precision and comparability. Such an agreement has not been forthcoming. For some, daytime street dwellers—vagrants, beggars, and drunkards—are perceived as homeless even though they may not be. For the maximalists, anyone living in substandard housing; anyone living in abandoned housing; any squatter in a commercial, industrial or residential building or on public or private land; anyone living in a shelter; anyone living in a refugee resettlement center; anyone living in a residential hotel or a hostel; any live-in partner without a lease agreement; anyone doubling-up involuntarily; and anyone sleeping at night in streets and other public places is homeless. This broad definition, needless to say, inflates the number of the homeless, suggests that the problem is surprisingly widespread, and demands the immediate devotion of considerable societal resources to combat it. Jencks [1994], for example, suggests that for the advocates of the homeless it is important to portray it as a "big" problem involving millions of people: "If you want to hold the attention of the mass media, breaking the 'million barrier' is important" [2].

For the minimalists, only people sleeping at night in streets and other public places (parks and transportation terminals for example)—places that are designated and used for purposes other than housing and therefore cannot be converted to permanent housing use—are homeless. Squatters, to be distinguished from the homeless, are a category onto themselves, as are those living in unauthorized or substandard housing. Given this definition, those in homeless shelters should not be considered homeless as long as they are sheltered. A shelter, like an army barrack, is a solution (albeit a temporary one) to the housing problem, and counting its residents as homeless makes it a part of the problem rather than a part of the solution.[5] Homeless shelters and barracks, in one form or another, are integral parts of any well functioning housing system. This minimalist definition, while deflating the number of the homeless, puts the problem is a more manageable perspective without in any way diminishing its severity or seriousness. It also corresponds to the often-voiced public demand for remedial action regarding the *visibly* homeless, those seen sleeping in the rough on sidewalks, in doorways in parks, and under bridges.

A further difficulty in definition is that for some researchers homelessness is a one–year count (the number of people designated as homeless at least once during a given year) while for others it is a one–night count (the number of people who are homeless on any one night) [O'Flaherty, 1996, 18]. The two definitions are not at all consistent. Again, the latter one is intuitively correct, but it requires a serious and persistent nighttime measurement effort, a dangerous and possibly less–rewarding effort than winning an argument about definitions than can inflate the counts of the homeless without venturing out of doors. Unfortunately, there is little doubt that the debate on the definition, and hence the number, of the homeless has now been politicized, data have been collected using different definitions, and, as a result, the comparative statistical analysis of homelessness, its causes, and its remedies has suffered.

The Global Survey of Housing Indicators collected data on five tenure measures, all defined as proportions of the total housing stock, the total population, or the total number of households:

1.   the *public housing stock*, defined as the percentage of the total number of dwelling units in the urban area that is owned, managed, and controlled by the public sector[6];
2.   *owner–occupancy*, defined as the percentage of all households who own the dwelling units that they occupy;
3.   *unauthorized housing*, defined as the percentage of the total housing stock in the urban area that is not in compliance with current regulations concerning land ownership, land use and zoning, and building construction;
4.   *squatter housing*, defined as the percentage of the total housing stock in the urban area that is currently occupying land illegally[7]; and
5.   *homelessness*, defined as the number of people per thousand of the urban area population who sleep outside dwelling units (e.g., on streets, in parks, railroad stations, and under bridges) or in temporary shelter in charitable institutions.[8]

To explore the attractiveness of home ownership vis–à–vis rental, an additional index was constructed:

6.   the *Home Ownership Premium*, defined as the ratio of the hedonic house price index and the hedonic rent index.

The hedonic indices were defined and presented earlier (chapter 17 and table 17.3). The Home Ownership Premium measures the *relative* price of owning — rather than renting — one unit of identical housing quality. When it is higher than 1.0 it suggests that there is a premium to pay for owning rather than renting a home. Conversely, when it is lower than unity, it suggests that owning a home is more economical than renting one. Summary values for the Home Ownership Premium and for four ownership and tenure indicators are presented in table 23.2.

The Home Ownership Premium did not exhibit a strong variation either among countries in different levels of economic development or among regions. Its correlation with the Development Index was insignificant (+0.07). There were wide variations in the values of this index within income groups and within regions, as we can see by examining table A26. Among the 10 Sub–Saharan African countries in the sample, for example, five countries had values below 1.0 and three had values above 2.0. Countries with strong rent control regimes had considerably higher Home Ownership Premiums. The median value for Eastern Europe, 8.3 in 1990, was much higher than the values for all other regions.[9] The value for the industrialized countries as a whole (0.9) was less than unity, suggesting that home ownership in 1990 did not carry a premium there and was, in fact, less expensive than rental. The global median for this index (1.1) was also close to unity, again suggesting that, on the whole, there were no significant affordability barriers to home ownership in the world at large in this period. In other words, on the whole the costs of renting or owning a home were not significantly different.

In parallel with the Home Ownership Premium, owner–occupancy was also found to be unrelated to the Development Index, with a correlation very close to zero (–0.03). Economic development, by itself, did not necessarily lead to higher levels of home ownership. The global median value for owner–occupancy was found to be 55%, with a slightly higher value for the industrialized countries (57%) than for the developing countries as a whole (48%). Only low–income countries

Table 23.2. Measures of Home Ownership and Tenure, 1990.

Country Groupings	Home Ownership Premium	Owner–Occupancy (%)	Unauthorized housing (%)	Squatter Housing (%)	Homelessness (persons per thousand)
Low–Income Countries	1.7	33	64	17	3.3
Low–Middle Income Countries	1.2	59	27	16	0.2
Upper Middle Income Countries	0.9	57	9	4	1.1
High–Income Countries	0.9	59	0	0	1.3
Southern Africa	1.0	35	56	26	1.9
Asia and the Pacific	1.1	48	48	6	1.9
Middle East and North Africa	2.1	53	23	10	0.1
Latin America and the Caribbean	0.7	65	27	25	2.1
Eastern Europe	8.3	24	0	0	1.0
All Developing Countries	1.4	48	32	12	0.9
Industrialized Countries	0.9	57	0	0	1.0
Global Average	5.8	50	25	12	2.2
Global Minimum	0.2	0	0	0	0.0
Global Median	1.1	55	15	4	0.9
Global Maximum	201.4	90	78	71	11.5
Global Standard Deviation	27.2	22	27	18	2.7
Correlation with Development Index	0.07	–0.03	–0.78	–0.64	0.01

Source: Housing Indicators Program [1994].

stood out as having a low median value for this measure (33%). Among develop-ing-country regions, Eastern Europe stood out as having a very low median value of owner-occupancy in 1990 (24%) followed by Southern Africa (35%). The former value was low because of the large and subsidized public housing sector, the latter because of the prevalence of informal-sector house and room rentals in poor communities. There was a great variation in owner-occupancy within regions, however. Among the cities in the industrialized countries, the cities in the Netherlands, Germany, and Austria in the Global Survey stood out as having very low values for this measure (all less than 20%), while Singapore, Spain, Israel, and Australia had values above 70%. Among developing countries, five countries had values in excess of 70%: Pakistan, Jordan, Ecuador, Chile, and Mexico. At the lower end of the spectrum (except China and the Eastern European countries) no country had a value lower than 20%.

In contrast to owner-occupancy, unauthorized housing, the key measure of the size of the informal housing sector, was clearly associated with lower levels of economic development. Its median value decreased steadily as incomes increased, from 64% in the low-income countries to 0% in the high-income countries. Its median value for the developing countries as a whole was 32%, compared with 0% for the industrialized countries; and its correlation with the Development Index was highly negative (-0.78). At higher levels of economic development, most housing was supplied by the formal sector; at low levels most housing was supplied by the informal sector. This is an expected finding, pointing out the reliance of lower-income countries on the informal sector for the production of substantial portions of the housing stock, and underscoring its importance. The reliance on the informal sector varied among developing-country regions. It was high in Southern Africa (56%) and Asia (48%), much lower in the Middle East and North Africa (23%) and in Latin America (27%), and nonexistent in Eastern Europe. Among developing countries, six countries in the sample had 70% of more of their city's housing stock in Unauthorized Housing: three in Southern Africa (Malawi, Nigeria, and Kenya) and three in Asia (Bangladesh, Indonesia, and the Philippines). The global median value for this indicator was 15%, and the global average was 25%, suggesting that as much as one-sixth and possibly up to one-quarter of the global urban housing stock may be in the informal sector.

Global data for unauthorized housing is also available for 1995 (see table A27). A comparison between 1990 and 1995 suggests that, on the whole, unauthorized housing increased between the two periods, from a global average of 25% to 31%. Increases in informal housing were especially steep in Eastern Europe (and, surprisingly, in the industrialized countries), and to a lesser extent in the Middle East and North Africa. Both Southern Africa and Asia reported decreases in the proportion of their housing stocks in the informal sector.

Squatter housing formed an important subset of unauthorized housing, and was therefore highly correlated with it (+0.64). The median global value for squatter housing was 4%, roughly a quarter of the respective global median value for unauthorized housing. Among developing-country regions, however, while the correlation was still strong, this proportion varied widely, from one-eighth in Asia, to roughly one-half in Southern Africa, to more than nine-tenths in Latin America. In general, squatter housing behaved in a very similar manner to unauthorized housing. It declined significantly with rising incomes, from 17% in the low-income countries to 0% in the high-income ones, and its correlation with the Development Index was high and negative (-0.64). Among developing-country regions it was higher than the median in both Southern Africa (26%) and Latin America (25%). In contrast, both Asia (6%) and the Middle East and North Africa (10%) had lower-than-median values. Again, both Eastern Europe and the industrialized countries had no squatter housing to speak of. Only four countries reported values for this measure in excess of 50%: Tanzania, Malawi, Turkey, and Venezuela.

Finally, the reported values on homelessness — keeping in mind the controversies in the definition of homelessness discussed earlier as well as the difficulties in obtaining accurate data — did not show a regular pattern at all. The global median value for this indicator was 1.0 person per thousand, with little variation between the median values for the developing countries as a whole (0.9) and the industrialized countries (1.0). Homelessness appeared to have a small, yet negative, correlation with the Development Index (-0.15), suggesting at the very least that it is not significantly related to lower levels of economic development. Industrialized countries (many of which have truncated supplies of lower-income housing) had slightly higher levels of homelessness than did developing countries (that have more ample supplies of inexpensive unauthorized housing). Among developing-country regions, Latin America, Southern Africa, and Asia had median values roughly double the global median value, while the Middle East and North Africa had a very low median value (0.1 persons per thousand). Seven countries, some of them high-income countries, reported that more than 5 persons per thousand were homeless in 1990: Bangladesh, Madagascar, Tunisia, Hungary, the Netherlands, France, and Finland. In contrast, eight countries, some of them low-income countries, reported no homelessness at all: Tanzania, Malawi, Morocco, Jordan, Poland, the former Czechoslovakia, Greece, and Hong Kong.

The Determinants of Tenure Measures of Housing Quantity

What accounts for these differences in tenure measures of housing quantity? We now attempt to answer this question by investigating a number of statistical models for these measures, including the Home Ownership Premium, using the same procedure established in the preceding chapters, and the same set of explanatory variables representing the economic, social, and political context; the housing policy environment; and market housing conditions.

There have been a number of studies that have attempted to examine the available statistical evidence in an effort to explain variations in home ownership rates, for example, both among countries and between different time periods.

Oxley, for example, in a comparative statistical study of five European countries was able to demonstrate that "[d]ifferences in cost and availability of mortgages were vital in explaining variations in home ownership rates between countries" [Oxley, 1988, 3, in Saunders, 1990, 36]. Pahl suggested that the growth of household incomes "has enabled such a rapid spread of owner–occupation beyond the middle class since the Second World War" [Pahl, 1984, 231, in Saunders, 1990, 38]. This and similar claims have been disputed by researchers who insist that "the size of a country's home ownership sector is not related to the level of national prosperity" [Doling, 1997, 160]. Gilbert and Varley [1991] suggest that, among other factors, the growth in home ownership can be explained by the explosive growth of single–family homes occasioned by the advent of trains, trams, buses, and the private automobile [18].

Doling [1997], Kemeny [1992], and a number of other writers suggest that rates of owner–occupancy are correlated with collective versus private modes of consumption. Schmidt [1989] has shown, for example, that rates of home ownership are highly correlated with a preference for welfare in government policy, measured by the welfare expenditures of government as a percentage of the Gross Domestic Product [quoted in Doling, 1997, 163]. Doling also quotes *The Economist* as suggesting that "[h]istorically, there has been a fairly close link between rates of home ownership and inflation; high–inflation countries tend to have the highest rates of owner–occupation. . . as property has been a popular hedge against rising prices" ["I Owe, I Owe," 1992–1993, 97, in Doling, 1997, 165].

Finally, government policies promoting home ownership, such as the mortgage tax relief, the neglect of the rental sector mentioned earlier, and antirental legislation such as rent control, have also been mentioned as factors in the growth of owner–occupation. The data from the Global Survey allows us to investigate a number of these claims on a global scale, as we shall now proceed to do.

The model for the Home Ownership Premium is presented in the top row of table 23.3. It used the same explanatory variables as those used in other models of housing quantity in the earlier chapters. Its R–squared of 0.44 implies that the explanatory variables used in the model explained more than 40% of the variation in the Home Ownership Premium. A high premium, as we saw before, is associated with a higher cost of owning as against renting a home. The model suggests that higher household incomes were not associated with higher or lower premiums, but that four other variables had a statistically significant downward effect on the premium — the city population growth rate, the housing credit portfolio, the construction cost–to–income ratio, and the Enabling Index. Owning a home was less expensive relative to renting one in faster–growing cities, in cities where there was ample mortgage credit, in cities with relatively low construction costs, and in cities that had a more enabling housing policy environment. The strongest effects on the premium were those exerted by the Enabling Index, followed by the city population growth rate, and the housing credit portfolio.

Table 23.3. The Determinants of Home Ownership and Tenure.

Variable	Log of Household Income	City Population Growth Rate	Household Size	Housing Credit Portfolio	Construction Cost-to-Income Ratio	Land Cost-to-Income Ratio	Enabling Index	Estimated Home Ownership Premium	No. of Observations	R-squared & Adjusted R-squared	F-Value
Home Ownership Premium	0.17 [a]	-0.57	0.08	-0.42	-0.22	-0.10	-0.59	–[d]	45	0.44	$F_{7,37}$
	0.55 [b]	*-2.91**** [c]	*0.30*	*-2.20****	*-1.32**	*-0.70*	*-2.51****	–[d]		0.33	*4.1**** [b]
Owner–Occupancy (Model I)	-0.06	0.23	0.31	0.32	-0.10	-0.09	0.46	–[d]	45	0.43	$F_{7,37}$
	-0.21	*1.30*	*1.31**	*1.86***	*-0.66*	*-0.67*	*2.15***	–[d]		0.32	*4.0****
Owner–Occupancy (Model II)	0.12	–[e]	–[e]	–[e]	-0.49	-0.30	–[e]	-0.78	45	0.37	$F_{4,40}$
	0.85	–[e]	–[e]	–[e]	*-3.1****	*-2.25***	–[e]	*-4.12****		0.30	*5.8****
Unauthorized Housing	-0.85	0.29	-0.12	-0.03	-0.04	-0.04	0.30	–[d]	45	0.68	$F_{7,37}$
	-4.0***	*2.14***	*-0.64*	*-0.24*	*-0.35*	*-0.45*	*1.84***	–[d]		0.62	*11.1****
Squatter Housing	-0.66	0.40	-0.32	0.00	-0.06	-0.20	0.19	–[d]	43	0.50	$F_{7,35}$
	-2.5***	*2.43****	*-1.44**	*0.01*	*-0.43*	*-1.63**	*0.94*	–[d]		0.40	*4.9****
Homelessness [f] (persons per 1,000)	0.15	0.07	0.01	0.26	0.44	-0.07	-0.21	–[d]	42	0.21	$F_{7,3}$
	0.41	*0.33*	*0.02*	*1.15*	*2.40*	*-0.47*	*-0.74*	–[d]		0.05	*1.32*

Source: Housing Indicators Program [1994].

[a] Figures in the top row are standardized β-coefficients.

[b] Figures in italics denote *t*- and *F*-statistics.

[c] ***, **, and * denote 1%, 5% and 10% levels of confidence, respectively.

[d] Estimated Home Ownership Premium not included in this model.

[e] City population growth rate, household size, housing credit portfolio, and Enabling Index not included in this model.

[f] Model not statistically significant, shown for inspection only.

Three statistical models for owner–occupancy were constructed, the first one using the same variables as those used in the premium model. The second one used the premium as an independent variable, together with household income, construction cost, and land cost. We will discuss those two models together before introducing the third one. The first model is presented in the second row of table 23.3. The model had an R–squared of 0.43, implying that the independent variables used in the model explained more than 40% of the variation in owner–occupancy rates. In this model, household income, the city population growth rate, household size, construction costs, and land costs do not appear to exert a significant effect on home ownership. Home ownership was significantly higher, however, in cities with higher household sizes, in cities with ample mortgage credit, and in cities with a more enabling housing policy environment. The strongest effects on owner–occupancy were those exerted by the enabling index, followed by the housing credit portfolio.

The second model for owner–occupancy is presented in the third row of table 23.3. The model had an R–squared of 0.37, implying that the independent variables used in the model explain more than one-third of the variation in owner occupancy. In this model, the Home Ownership Premium acts as an explanatory variable replacing several independent variables used in the first model, including those that exert a strong influence on it – the city population growth rate, the housing credit portfolio, and the Enabling Index.

In addition to the Premium, household income, the construction cost-to-income ratio, and the land cost-to-income ratio also appear as independent variables. Except for household income, all the independent variables in the model had statistically significant downward effects on owner–occupancy. High Home Ownership Premiums, high construction costs, and high land costs relative to incomes all result in lower levels of home ownership. The effect of the Home Ownership Premium was the strongest, followed by the construction cost-to-income ratio. When we look at both models for owner–occupancy together, we can conclude that the policy environment as well as the availability of credit affected levels of home ownership both directly and indirectly (through their effect on the relative price of owning versus renting), but that household income did not exert a significant effect on these levels.

Following Schmidt and Doling, we now construct a third model of owner–occupancy, which brings in the welfare orientation of government and the long-term rate of inflation as independent variables instead of land and construction costs. This model is presented in table 23.4. We note at the outset that the welfare orientation of government has already been shown to have a significantly negative effect on the Enabling Index (see tables 12.3 and 12.4). The model had an R–squared of 0.40, implying that the variation in the independent variables used in the model explained 40% of the variation in owner–occupancy rates. Higher welfare expenditures as a percent of government expenditures are found to be associated with significantly lower rates of owner–occupancy.

Table 23.4. The Determinants of Owner–Occupancy (Model III).

Variable	β–coefficient	t–statistic
Log of Household Income	0.75	2.07** [a]
Household Size	0.50	1.93**
Housing Credit Portfolio	0.35	1.65*
Welfare Expenditures as % of GDP	-0.83	-3.07***
Enabling Index	0.15	0.51
Inflation 1980–1990	0.20	1.72**
Number of Observations	32	
R-squared and Adjusted R-squared	0.52	0.40
$F_{6,25}$		4.47***

Source: Housing Indicators Program [1994].

[a]   ***, **, and * denote 1%, 5% and 10% levels of confidence, respectively.

Home ownership rates were found to be significantly higher in countries with higher long-term rates of inflation. In agreement with our earlier models, larger household sizes were also associated with higher levels of home ownership. In this model, however, the effect of the Enabling Index on home ownership was obscured by the effect of welfare expenditures, and, surprisingly, household income did exert a significant influence on home ownership rates. We cannot conclude, therefore, given the conflicting results in the three models, whether or not household incomes have a significant effect on home ownership rates. A word of caution in interpreting these three models: As table 23.5 shows, there were strong cross-correlations among five of the six variables in this model that made it difficult to isolate their independent effects.

The model for unauthorized housing is presented in the fourth row of table 23.3. This model had an R-squared of 0.68, implying that the independent variables used in the model explained more than two-thirds of the variation in unauthorized housing. This was largely due to the high association between higher household incomes and lower levels of unauthorized housing, as we noted before. The only other independent variables in the model that significantly affected unauthorized housing were the city population growth rate and the

Table 23.5. Correlations Among the Determinants of
Owner Occupancy (Model III).

Variable	Median Household Income	Household Size	Government Welfare Expenditure as % of all Exp.	Housing Credit Portfolio	Enabling Index
Median Household Income	1.00				
Household Size	-0.63	1.00			
Governement Welfare Expenditure as % of all Exp.	0.75	-0.76	1.00		
Housing Credit Portfolio	0.60	-0.53	0.70	1.00	
Enabling Index	0.65	-0.28	0.48	0.51	1.00

Source: Housing Indicators Program [1994].

Enabling Index. Both were associated with higher levels of unauthorized housing. Faster-growing cities tended to have more unauthorized housing, because the formal sector was unable to serve the high demand for new housing. Similarly, countries with a more enabling housing policy environment allowed for more unauthorized housing to be created to meet housing demand. The effect of household income on unauthorized housing was the strongest, followed by the effect of the Enabling Index and the city population growth rate.

The model for squatter housing is presented in the fifth row of table 23.2. The model has a R-squared value of 0.50, implying that the independent variables used in the model explained one-half of the variation in squatter housing in our sample. The results of the model were quite different from those for unauthorized housing, although the strong negative effect of household incomes and the strong positive effect of the city population growth rate were similar in both. In this model, however, both household size and the land cost-to-income ratio were found to have significantly negative effects on the proportion of squatter housing in the housing stock. In countries with similar levels of income and urban growth, squatter housing was found to be associated with smaller households, although on its own it did have a positive correlation with household size (+0.41), and with access to cheaper land. The effect of household income on squatter housing was the strongest, followed by the effect of the city population growth rate, household size, and the land cost-to-income ratio. The Enabling Index, the housing credit portfolio, and construction cost were not found to have a significant impact on squatter housing. Finally, the model for homelessness using the Global Survey data and the same explanatory variables did not yield any significant or meaningful statistical results. It is presented on the sixth row of table 23.3 for inspection only.

Viewed in a global perspective, homelessness did not display a regular pattern beyond the general observations advanced in the previous section. The published single-country quantitative research on the causes of homelessness does suggest several explanations. Honig and Filer [1993], for example, investigated the causes of intercity variation in homelessness in 50 U.S. metropolitan areas in 1984, analyzing data from the U.S. Department of Housing and Urban Development (HUD). They found homelessness to be significantly higher when the level of rents in the lowest-rent ten percent of all apartments was high, and the vacancy rate in the lowest rent ten percent of all apartments was low. Homelessness was also higher in larger cities, and in cities with a higher percentage of African-Americans. It was found to be lower in cities with a faster growth in employment and a higher share of service jobs. O'Flaherty [1996], in a book centered on the economics of homelessness, based his explanations of homelessness on various sources of data for the United States, focusing on the disappearance of the lowest-cost housing, on the increased price of housing at the low end of the spectrum, and on increased income inequality, but dismissing the effect of rent control or individual pathology on levels of homelessness. Quigley [1996], in a review of O'Flaherty's book noted that "the incidence of homelessness is also greater in cities with temperate climates" [1937]. Wallace and Bassuk [1991], in their attempts to predict future levels of homelessness, found that "homeless families are more likely to have a history of housing instability. . . homeless families are more likely to have lived in overcrowded housing" [487]. Future comparative studies of homelessness must await the collection of *comparable* cross-national data, and such studies will definitely benefit from these earlier models in the setting up of their explanatory frameworks.

The Demand and Supply of Housing Tenure

Following the same procedure outlined in chapter 6, we now investigate the effects of household income, mortgage credit, and the policy environment on the demand for three tenure measures of housing quantity: owner occupancy, unauthorized housing, and squatter housing; we also examine the effect of the inputs costs of land and construction and the policy environment on the supply of these quantities.[10] We investigate two models for each indicator, one for the quantity demanded (from which we derive the estimated income elasticity, price elasticity, and policy elasticities of demand) and one for the quantity supplied (from which we derive the price elasticity and policy elasticity of supply). In all models, the explanatory variable for the price is the Weighted Price Index. The models appear in table 23.6.

The table shows that none of the models for the quantity supplied was robust enough to yield statistically significant results. In the case of homelessness, the demand model was not statistically significant either, while the supply model was discarded altogether — the supply of homelessness is not exactly a well-defined concept. The demand model for owner-occupancy had an R-squared of 0.37, indicating that the model explained more than one-third of the variation in the demand for owner-occupancy. The income elasticity of demand in the model was modest, +0.23, much smaller than the values close to unity found for quality and value measures, but still statistically significant. Income was thus found to have a modest positive effect on the demand for home ownership, although, as we saw earlier, it was not clear whether or not it had a significant effect on the equilibrium quantities of owner-occupancy. The price elasticity of demand for owner-occupancy was also modest, –0.25, but not statistically significant. The policy elasticity of the demand for home ownership was close to zero and not significant at all, although it was earlier found to have a significant effect on the equilibrium values of owner-occupancy.

The demand models for unauthorized housing and squatter housing, also shown in table 23.6, were quite similar. They both had R-squared values of 0.76 and 0.77 respectively, implying that they explained three-quarters of the variation in unauthorized housing and squatter housing in our sample. Of the income, price, and policy elasticities of demand, only the income elasticities were statistically significant, both at the 1% level. Both elasticities were negative and higher than unity (–1.27 and –1.46, respectively), implying that the demand for unautho-

Table 23.6. The Income, Price, and Policy Elasticities of Housing Tenure.

Variable	Income Elasticity of Demand	Price Elasticity of Demand	Price Elasticity of Supply	Policy Elasticity of Demand	Policy Elasticity of Supply	No. of Observations	Demand Model		Supply Model	
							R-squared & Adjusted R-squared	F-value	R-squared & Adjusted R-squared	F-value
Owner Occupancy	0.23 [a]	-0.25	– [d]	-0.03	– [d]	43	0.37	$F_{6,36}$	0.07	$F_{4,38}$
	*2.13** [b]*	*-1.21*	*– [d]*	*-0.26*	*– [d]*		*0.27*	*3.52****	*0.16*	*1.78 [b]*
Unauthorized Housing	-1.27	0.06	– [d]	-0.03	– [d]	43	0.76	$F_{6,36}$	-0.01	$F_{4,38}$
	*-3.08*** [c]*	*0.07*	*– [d]*	*-0.06*	*– [d]*		*0.72*	*19.12****	*0.09*	*0.92*
Squatter housing	-1.46	0.39	– [d]	0.23	– [d]	41	0.77	$F_{6,34}$	0.06	$F_{4,36}$
	*-3.55****	*0.48*	*– [d]*	*0.46*	*– [d]*		*0.73*	*18.77****	*0.15*	*1.59*

Source: Housing Indicators Program [1994].

[a] Figures in the top row are elasticities.

[b] Figures in italics denote *t*– and *F*–statistics.

[c] ***, **, and * denote 1%, 5% and 10% levels of confidence, respectively.

[d] Supply model not statistically significant.

rized housing and squatter housing is indeed income–elastic but negative – an incremental increase, say, of 10%, in income results in a more–than– proportional incremental decrease in both unauthorized housing and squatter housing.

*   *   *

To conclude, when we look at the quantity of housing in terms of the composition of tenures, a different, yet important, perspective on the housing stock emerges that cannot be discerned or deduced from our earlier perspectives on quantity measured in terms of dwelling units, living space, quality, or value. Moreover, the effects of the context, the policy environment, and housing market conditions on tenure composition are markedly different from those observed earlier.

It is not clear, for example, whether household income exerted an appreciable effect on either home ownership rates nor on homelessness. It exerted a small, yet statistically significant, positive effect on the demand for home ownership. It did exert a strong negative effect on levels of unauthorized housing and squatter housing, as expected. When incomes rose, the demand for unauthorized housing and squatter housing decreased appreciably. The elasticities of demand for both were negative and greater than unity.

The statistical analysis supports the finding by Schmidt reported earlier: higher welfare expenditures as a percent of government expenditures were indeed associated with significantly lower rates of owner–occupancy. It also supports the claims of *The Economist* mentioned earlier: home ownership rates were significantly higher in countries with higher long–term rates of inflation.

The urban growth rate had a positive effect on home ownership rates, as well as on unauthorized housing and squatter housing, but no appreciable effect on homelessness. It had a significant downward effect on the home ownership premium, thereby making the relative price of owning, as against renting, lower in faster–growing cities. Faster–growing cities also gave rise to higher levels of unauthorized housing and squatter housing, that were the only practical ways to meet growing housing demand in the absence of adequate public housing or affordable formal–sector housing. Larger households were found to be significantly associated with higher levels of home ownership, as well as with lower levels of squatter housing.

The availability of credit, as measured by the housing credit portfolio, was associated with significantly lower Home Ownership Premiums and significantly higher levels of home ownership. Credit, as expected, rendered home ownership more attractive than rental by lowering the initial payments for housing and streamlining them over a long period of time.

The cost of construction affected tenure choice in a number of ways. Higher construction cost–to–income ratios were associated with lower levels of owner–occupancy, as were higher land cost–to–income ratios. The latter also discouraged squatting on valuable land, and was associated with significantly lower levels of squatter housing.

Finally, the degree of enabling of the housing policy environment, as measured by the Enabling Index, had a strong downward effect on the home ownership premium, making home ownership more affordable, and a strong upward effect on the equilibrium level of owner occupancy itself. It also had a positive upward effect on unauthorized housing, making it easier to meet housing needs, but no appreciable effect on either squatter housing or levels of homelessness. Finally, the policy environment was not found to have statistically significant effects on either the demand or the supply of any of the tenure measures of housing quantity. Still, there is no doubt that the policy environment exerted a strong effect on the compositions of housing tenure, and thus on another key area of housing outcomes, outcomes that are of primary concerns to housing policy.

Conclusion

A vision for the future of housing policy cannot, and should not, be a static utopian one. Ridding society of its slums in the name of a vision of "city beautiful" is no remedy for housing ills, if the remaining houses and apartments are overcrowded or unaffordable. Replacing all unacceptable housing with standard housing en masse, through public action, is not an option either—it is unnecessary, undesirable, inefficient, and fiscally impossible. The static vision of the urban master plan towards which we all must strive is long dead. Cities, and the residential sectors within them, can no longer be perceived as moving towards some stable equilibrium state. Both are engaged in a continuous process of reinventing themselves, and are they likely to do so for a long time to come. As Bauman [1999] aptly observes: "A truly autonomous society cannot exist in any other form but that of its own project: that is, as a society which admits an ever expanding freedom of self-examination, critique and reform, rather than a pre-given pattern of happiness, as its only purpose and *raison d'être*" [81]. A vision for the future of the housing sector must therefore, of necessity, be a dynamic one, where housing policy seeks to ensure that certain parameters or qualities of the sector remain within acceptable norms, while all else remains free to change. Furthermore, these norms and the policies employed to attain them can also be expected to change over time. In short, there cannot be an emphatic final answer to the housing question. In this sense, the answers given in this book are grounded, as they must be, in the historical context of cities at the dawn of the new millennium.

Housing policy at the beginning of this millennium is in the midst of a major transformation. Policy intervention in the housing sector has now come of age. We now know, in broad terms, how the sector works and how it is affected by the broad economic, social, and political context on the one hand, and by the housing policy environment on the other. We understand the futility of intervention in housing at the project level while the sector as a whole remains dysfunctional. We recognize that the sector is made up of interconnected markets, and that intervention in these markets is essentially corrective—enabling markets to work and protecting them from failure. We realize that enabling markets to work requires setting limits and providing support, while relinquishing control. We acknowledge that no one – however influential and powerful – can be in control. And, as it turns out, monopolistic market dominance of the house- building industry is inherently inefficient as well. The modern housing sector has emerged as a fragmented market, with millions of decision-makers participating in giving it form and substance. There are players large and small. At one end of the spectrum, secondary mortgage markets and urban infrastructure consortiums are undergoing a process of global integration. At the other end, builders continue to work alone, or with family members and friends, to build the majority of houses everywhere. And in the middle of the spectrum, there are residential neighborhoods that need to be improved as a whole, and where focused place-based interventions – rather than people-based interventions – are the necessary means to attain housing goals.

Modern housing policy is grounded in the realization that the coming together of people to build the great cities of today has been, in the main, a process that has generated great wealth. Much of this wealth is in houses, largely in the hands of home owning families, families who now own the means of production of housing services they can enjoy for years on end. Can government be relied upon to protect and secure this great wealth? To enable it to grow and flourish? To further extend it to all segments of society? This is surely not a trivial matter. What has been painstakingly gained can be lost and squandered, and what will be amassed by future generations housing themselves can and will be vast. The global march of people from their villages into the cities is still far from over, and is unlikely to reach a plateau before the urban housing stock doubles in size in the next 30 years and reaches many times its present value.

This book presented a coherent and comprehensive view of the housing sector – focusing on its context, its policy environment, its market conditions, its outcomes, and the relationships among them. It established the groundwork for a vision of housing policy in the new millennium. Such a vision must now be informed by a perception of the housing sector as a self-organizing system, a system both largely capable of taking care of itself and permanently in need of corrective action. And it is government housing policy that must, of necessity, provide such corrective action.

In broad terms, housing policy now faces four major challenges – the challenge of regulating the housing sector effectively, the challenge of monitoring it intelligently, the challenge of reforming public housing institutions wisely, and the challenge of creating and administering a new generation of housing programs and projects efficiently and equitably. Needless to say, these four challenges are intractably bound to each other.

The first housing policy challenge is the challenge of *regulation*. The housing sector cannot function effectively without a set of enforceable rules – rules that limit harmful behavior without crushing the vitality of the sector or its ability to meet needs. There is nothing simple or natural about such sets of rules. They do not come into being by themselves. They have to be invented, discovered, and rediscovered by groups of people who look for them intentionally. These rules must command sufficient attention and political support to be passed into law, and once legislated, they must be effectively enforced. Once enforced, they have to be monitored to gauge their effects and then modified from time to time to remain effective. Good rules with prompt enforcement mechanisms are hard to come by, and the search for them must continue. So must the search for understanding what makes them good rules.

The relationships between the rule systems and the systems they govern is only gradually discovered and understood. We can only now begin to point to the effects of the housing policy environment on housing sector performance and to see that housing policy matters — that more enabling housing policies lead to more beneficial housing outcomes — but the evidence, although substantial, is still scarce. There is still no established procedure (definitely not in the housing sector) for monitoring the effects of policies and modifying them regularly to better meet their objectives. As governments take on more regulatory — rather than activist — roles in the sector, the process of regulation and policy–making must, of necessity, be refined. It must also be better informed. Presently, regulators in many sectors are largely informed by interested parties — those who have already understood that they are likely to benefit most (or hurt most) by changes in the regulatory environment. For other interested parties, taking an interest in the regulatory environment must be preceded by a clear understanding of its effects. There is a need, therefore, for a better understanding of the effects of the regulatory environment on housing sector performance. And while the effects of regulations on individual corporations can easily be gauged by corporate lawyers and accountants, the regulations' broader effects on the housing sector as a whole (and on vulnerable groups within it) can rarely be perceived reliably without broader measurement.

The second housing policy challenge to municipal and central governments, international organizations, and academic researchers is, therefore, the challenge of intelligent *measurement*. Again, initial progress has been made in this field and we now have the beginning of a solid system of housing indicators. But it is only a beginning. There is a need to invent and refine housing indicators and the means of measuring them cheaply and precisely. There is a need to embark upon new global and regional initiatives to collect housing indicators systematically: such initiatives have the great advantage of starting a process of collecting internationally comparable indicators — indicators that, once published, attract many more cities and countries that see the value of comparing themselves to others. And comparable indicators are necessary, first and foremost, for refining and extending our use of global norms. Global norms are very effective means for the conduct of housing policy. They provide realistic measures of what is attainable, because they measure what has been already attained in similar places elsewhere.

National and municipal housing policy is now becoming globalized, informed, as it is, by what is happening elsewhere. The adoption of new policies already in place in other countries should be accompanied by reliable measures of their success or failure, in other words, by internationally comparable indicators. We must undertake such global initiatives as collaborations among international organizations, government agencies, and academic institutions. We must encourage census bureaus and government statistical organizations to participate, and we must compel them to undertake fundamental reforms so as to enable them to take more relevant and up-to-date measurements of the housing sector. Governments must support (both politically and financially) appropriate and effective measurement in the housing sector — measurement that can inform policy and that can benefit broad segments of society. Housing markets, with their complex interconnections and public-goods aspects, fail to generate such information themselves.

But even if governments recognized the underlying economic logic calling for their intervention to protect housing markets from failure — even if they were armed with a profound understanding of how to correct market failures and with measurement systems that could reliably gauge the effects of such corrective actions — we would still have no assurances that governments can or will intervene effectively. It is not at all clear that governments will necessarily have the right incentives to intervene effectively. Governments in general, and government housing institutions in particular, often pursue their own institutional agendas and are not always obliged to act at the behest or interest of any other groups, let alone for the benefit of society as a whole.

The third housing policy challenge, therefore, is the radical reform of government *institutions* in the housing sector. There is surely a dire need to revitalize central-government and local-government housing agencies, eliminating their earlier mandates — to build and manage public housing or to lend at below-market interest rates — in the process. New knowledge-rich housing agencies must be wisely compelled into existence, simplifying and unifying their mission in the process. Such agencies must, of necessity, have precise mandates and the correct set of incentives to work towards attaining them. This again is not a simple requirement. Corruption, greed, ignorance, and a host of hidden agendas often prevent housing agencies from operating either efficiently or effectively. In some places, how they can be transformed into the essential institutions for enabling the housing sector to work remains an enigma. In some places, the ground is fertile for far-reaching transformations. In other places, fundamental reforms have already been implemented.

The basic mandate of the new generation of housing institutions is to undertake the responsibility of managing the housing sector as a whole, as a key economic sector. They must act as watchdogs — protecting the interests of the sector in policy-making circles — and engage in the initiation and follow-up of regulatory and policy reforms. Such institutions need broad mandates, mandates that will enable them to act in all five component areas of enabling housing policy — the property rights regime, the housing finance regime, the housing subsidies and tax regime, the provision of residential infrastructure, and the regulation of housing and land development. They must consolidate and improve the monitoring of the housing sector, collaborating in the process with similar agencies worldwide. And they must attract, or generate themselves, substantial public resources in the process and administer these funds efficiently and equitably. To do this effectively, they must be grounded in a political agenda that can draw broad public support — one that is based on a well-founded case for specific interventions in the housing sector, and that can demonstrate that it can intervene in an accountable, affordable, and transparent manner.

The fourth challenge of housing policy must be, therefore, the design and implementation of a new generation of housing-related *projects and programs* that are supported by public funds. The allocation of public resources in the housing sector — and particularly in the form of housing subsidies — must be rethought. There is no question that, in general, we must use public resources to support the housing sector where it fails to be self-supporting. We must provide adequate public funds to maintain a broad-based social safety net for the homeless or the ill-housed and to ensure a minimum standard of decency in housing. We must engender and sustain a political commitment to ameliorate poverty through coordinated place-based action in residential neighborhoods, and a municipal obligation to manage and prepare for urban growth that can accommodate all housing needs. Yet the design of effective and popular public support programs for housing is not self-evident. Public resources are, of necessity, limited, and must be used judiciously to harness the resources of all the actors in the housing sector.

First, adequate resources must be available for programs that build the necessary human capacity to implement regulatory changes, to manage projects and programs, and to deepen our understanding of the workings of these projects and programs as well as that of the sector as a whole. Second, adequate resources must be available for people-based programs — be they public, private, or voluntary — that target direct housing assistance to individuals and families in dire need. Third, adequate resources must be available for place-based programs and projects aimed at upgrading the existing low-quality housing stock — whether through land titling, infrastructure improvements, rehabilitation, small construction loans, densification, or land sharing — as a means of ameliorating the ill effects of housing as a cause, rather than as a consequence, of poverty. Fourth, adequate resources must be available for extending and coordinating urban residential infrastructure grids on the fringes of growing cities, to ensure an adequate supply of land for housing. These grids must, however, stop at the macroblock level, where the public supply of public goods is mandated, and not attempt to provide serviced sites to individual plots. The informal market in many countries has been profitably providing informal land subdivisions for many many years — sites-and-services by another name — while governments, together with the World Bank, have struggled to reinvent them.

Surely, in times of grave crises — in the aftermath of wars and natural disasters, for example — governments must temporarily intervene directly in the financing, construction, and management of housing, only to withdraw later as the housing sector stabilizes again. In parallel, governments may have a role in initiating programs and projects that can later be emulated or taken over by the private or voluntary sector — mortgage finance and mortgage insurance, trunk infrastructure provision, building-material production, or temporary support for the down-market penetration of the residential construction sector, to name a few examples. Initiating with the purpose of retreating is, after all, yet another from of enabling action.

To conclude, we must reflect on the fact that none of the challenges proposed here is easy. It is easier to build a few thousand housing units than to reform housing policy. It is easier to give away a few subsidized home loans than to administer foreclosure laws and banking regulations that enable mortgage finance institutions to massively increase lending at market rates. It is easier to perpetuate rent control for the few than to bring about a healthy rental market for the many. It is easier to bestow a new and ill-targeted housing subsidy than to withdraw a regressive one. It is easier to let the stock of low-cost housing — or single-room-occupancy housing — be destroyed than to maintain and expand it. It is easier to administer top-down housing programs than to engage communities in upgrading their settlements. It is easier to insist on upholding law-and-order than to grant land titles to squatters that have occupied common or idle lands and built sustainable communities. It is easier to raze poor neighborhoods to the ground — to make way for more lucrative develop-ments — than to uplift them from poverty through rehabilitation. It is easier to perpetuate bankrupt housing institutions that have lost their sense of mission than to abolish them. It is easier to prevent people from building what they want, and what they can afford, than to enable them to build what they need through appropriate regulations. And it is easier to champion limits to urban growth than to allow cities to accommodate everyone — and to become powerful engines of economic growth, knowledge, and culture — by preparing for urban growth.

Yet, whether change in the right direction seems easy or not, there is no question that the housing policy environment, seen from a global perspective, is becoming more and more enabling. Housing policies the world over, sometimes forcefully and sometimes hesitantly, are gradually converging to an enabling mode. And as they do, housing sector performance improves. Enabling housing policies, as this book has shown, are both sensible and plausible, and result in significantly better housing. They should be pursued.

Appendix:
Country (City) Tables

The precise definitions for all the indicators and composite indices presented in the following tables were given throughout the text. Unless otherwise noted, the source of all indicator data for these tables was the Global Survey of Housing Indicators of 1990, conducted by the Housing Indicators Program, a joint program of the U.N. Centre for Human Settlements (Habitat) and the World Bank. Some preliminary indicator data were circulated in 1992, but the results of the Global Survey were only finalized in 1994 [Housing Indicators Program, 1994] and were not published before.

The country (city) tables are arranged in order of increasing 1990 values for GNP per capita. The tables are divided into four income groups: (a) low–income countries ($110 – $590), (b) low–middle income countries ($600 – $1,700), (c) upper middle income countries ($1,710 – $6,000), and (d) high–income countries ($10,000 and above).

Values for the composite indices were computed directly from 1990 indicator data from the Global Survey, and the methods of computation of these indices were also explained in the text. Composite indices were computed for all the cities in the sample. In the absence of the raw data required for the construction of a particular composite index for a given country (city), the median value for its region (and in the case of Scandinavia and the Indian Subcontinent, the median value for its subregion) was used instead. The city of Bratislava, which was in Czechoslovakia in 1990, is now in Slovakia, and Hong Kong is now a part of China.

The summary tables given in the text correspond exactly to the country (city) tables. There is one summary table for every one of the tables. The summary tables provide median values for four income groups, five developing–country regions, the developing countries as a whole, and the industrialized countries as a whole. They also provide global averages, minimums, maximums, medians, and standard deviations for each indicator and composite index. Finally, they also provide the degree of correlation between each indicator or composite index and the Development Index.

Table A1. The Countries and Cities in th e Global Survey, 1990. [a]

Country (City)	Label	Country Population (millions)	GNP per capita ($)	City Population	Development Index
Tanzania (Dar es Salaam)	TZ	24.5	110	1,566,290	0
Malawi (Lilongwe)	ML	8.5	200	378,867	1
Bangladesh (Dhaka)	BN	106.7	210	5,225,000	16
Madagascar (Antananarivo)	MD	11.7	230	852,500	4
Nigeria (Ibadan)	NI	115.5	290	5,668,978	4
India (New Delhi)	IN	849.5	350	8,427,083	29
Kenya (Nairobi)	KN	24.2	370	1,413,300	16
China (Beijing)	CH	1,133.7	370	6,984,0C.)	37
Pakistan (Karachi)	PK	112.4	380	8,160,000	16
Ghana (Kumasi)	GH	14.9	390	1,387,873	19
Indonesia (Jakarta)	ID	178.2	570	8,222,515	30
Egypt (Cairo)	EG	52.1	600	6,068,695	37
Zimbabwe (Harare)	ZI	9.8	640	1,474,500	20
Senegal (Dakar)	SE	7.4	710	1,630,000	13
Philippines (Manila)	PH	61.5	730	7,928,867	37
Côte d'Ivoire (Abidjan)	CI	11.9	750	1,934,398	17
Morocco (Rabat)	MR	25.1	950	1,050,700	25
Ecuador (Quito)	EC	10.3	980	1,100,847	30
Jordan (Amman)	JR	3.2	1,240	1,300,000	40
Colombia (Bogota)	CO	32.3	1,260	4,907,600	37
Thailand (Bangkok)	TH	55.8	1,420	6,019,055	48
Tunisia (Tunis)	TU	8.1	1,440	1,631,000	34
Jamaica (Kingston)	JA	2.4	1,500	587,798	57
Turkey (Istanbul)	TR	56.1	1,630	7,309,190	34
Poland (Warsaw)	PO	38.2	1,690	1,655,700	67
Slovakia (Bratislava)	CZ	15.7	1,710	441,000	65
Chile (Santiago)	CL	13.2	1,940	4,767,638	41
Algeria (Algiers)	AL	25.1	2,060	1,826,617	31
Malaysia (Kuala Lumpur)	MY	17.9	2,320	1,232,900	45
Russia (Moscow)	RU	148.1	2,330	8,789,200	64
Mexico (Monterrey)	MX	86.2	2,490	2,532,349	37
South Africa (Johannesburg)	SA	35.9	2,530	8,740,700	28
Venezuela (Caracas)	VE	19.7	2,560	3,775,897	42
Brazil (Rio de Janeiro)	BR	150.4	2,680	6,009,397	42
Hungary (Budapest)	HU	10.6	2,780	2,016,774	64
Korea, Republic of (Seoul)	KO	42.8	5,400	10,618,500	59
Greece (Athens)	GR	10.1	5,990	3,075,000	76
Israel (Tel Aviv)	IS	4.7	10,920	1,318,000	76
Spain (Madrid)	SP	39.0	11,020	4,845,851	76
Singapore (Singapore)	SI	3.0	11,160	2,690,100	61
Hong Kong (Hong Kong)	HK	5.8	11,490	5,800,600	70
United Kingdom (London)	UK	57.4	16,100	6,760,000	85
Australia (Melbourne)	AS	17.1	17,000	3,035,758	78
Netherlands (Amsterdam)	NT	14.9	17,320	695,221	87
Austria (Vienna)	AU	7.7	19,060	1,503,194	92
France (Paris)	FR	56.4	19,490	10,650,600	89
Canada (Toronto)	CA	26.5	20,470	3,838,744	84
United States (Washington, D.C.)	US	250.0	21,790	3,923,574	84
Germany (Munich)	GM	79.5	22,320	1,277,576	94
Norway (Oslo)	NR	4.2	23,120	462,000	88
Sweden (Stockholm)	SW	8.6	23,660	1,500,000	99
Japan (Tokyo)	JP	123.5	25,430	8,163,573	100
Finland (Helsinki)	FL	5.0	26,040	830,600	90

Sources: Housing Indicators Program [1994]; World Bank [1992, Table 1, 218–219].

[a]   For definitions and summary values, see chapter 13.

Table A2. Income and Economic Development Indicators, 1990. [a]

Country (City)	GNP per capita ($)	GNP Growth 1980–1990 (%)	Median Household Income ($)	Median Renter Household Income($)	Income Share of Lowest 40.0%(%)
Tanzania (Dar es Salaam)	110	2.8	763	928	8.1
Malawi (Lilongwe)	200	2.9	692	692	n.a.
Bangladesh (Dhaka)	210	4.3	1,352	1,082	22.9
Madagascar (Antananarivo)	230	1.1	747	833	n.a.
Nigeria (Ibadan)	290	1.4	1,331	1,331	n.a.
India (New Delhi)	350	5.3	1,084	1,312	21.3
Kenya (Nairobi)	370	4.2	1,500	1,357	10.1
China (Beijing)	370	9.5	1,079	1,079	17.4
Pakistan (Karachi)	380	6.3	1,622	1,622	21.3
Ghana (Kumasi)	390	3.0	1,241	1,241	18.3
Indonesia (Jakarta)	570	5.5	1,975	1,501	20.8
Egypt (Cairo)	600	5.0	1,345	1,345	n.a.
Zimbabwe (Harare)	640	2.9	2,538	2,538	10.3
Senegal (Dakar)	710	3.0	2,714	2,714	10.5
Philippines (Manila)	730	0.9	3,058	3,294	16.6
Côte d'Ivoire (Abidjan)	750	0.5	3,418	3,418	19.2
Morocco (Rabat)	950	4.0	4,158	4,158	17.1
Ecuador (Quito)	980	2.0	2,843	2,843	n.a.
Jordan (Amman)	1,240	1.7	4,511	4,511	16.8
Colombia (Bogota)	1,260	3.7	3,252	3,252	11.2
Thailand (Bangkok)	1,420	7.6	4,132	3,916	15.5
Tunisia (Tunis)	1,440	3.6	3,327	3,327	16.3
Jamaica (Kingston)	1,500	1.6	3,696	2,969	15.9
Turkey (Istanbul)	1,630	5.1	3,576	2,800	n.a.
Poland (Warsaw)	1,690	1.8	2,265	2,265	23.9
Slovakia (Bratislava)	1,710	1.4	3,677	3,677	n.a.
Chile (Santiago)	1,940	3.2	3,433	2,489	10.5
Algeria (Algiers)	2,060	3.1	7,335	7,335	17.9
Malaysia (Kuala Lumpur)	2,320	5.2	6,539	6,539	12.9
Russia (Moscow)	2,330	1.0	3,123	3,123	n.a.
Mexico (Monterrey)	2,490	1.0	4,810	4,810	11.9
South Africa (Johannesburg)	2,530	1.3	9,201	3,475	n.a.
Venezuela (Caracas)	2,560	1.0	5,123	5,040	14.3
Brazil (Rio de Janeiro)	2,680	2.7	5,204	4,741	7.0
Hungary (Budapest)	2,780	1.3	5,173	5,173	25.7
Korea (Seoul)	5,400	9.7	19,400	16,250	19.7
Greece (Athens)	5,990	1.8	14,229	13,573	n.a.
Israel (Tel Aviv)	10,920	3.2	16,680	16,680	18.4
Spain (Madrid)	11,020	3.1	23,118	23,118	15.0
Singapore (Singapore)	11,160	6.4	12,860	8,527	15.0
Hong Kong (Hong Kong)	11,490	7.1	15,077	15,077	16.2
United Kingdom (London)	16,100	3.1	18,764	8,631	16.3
Australia (Melbourne)	17,000	3.4	26,080	22,560	15.5
Netherlands (Amsterdam)	17,320	1.9	14,494	13,961	20.1
Austria (Vienna)	19,060	2.1	22,537	22,537	n.a.
France (Paris)	19,490	2.2	32,319	31,048	18.4
Canada (Toronto)	20,470	3.4	44,702	31,124	17.5
United States (Washington, D.C.)	21,790	3.4	49,667	32,542	14.7
Germany (Munich)	22,320	2.1	35,764	29,664	19.5
Norway (Oslo)	23,120	2.9	34,375	27,477	19.0
Sweden (Stockholm)	23,660	2.2	41,000	41,000	21.2
Japan (Tokyo)	25,430	4.1	38,229	23,773	21.9
Finland (Helsinki)	26,040	3.4	35,770	27,390	18.4

Sources: World Bank [1992, table 2, 220-221];UNDP [1995, tables 12 and 28]; Housing Indicators Program [1994].

[a] For definitions and summary values, see chapter 13.

Table A3. Political and Social Indicators, 1990. [a]

Country (City)	Freedom Index	Life Expectancy at Birth (years)	Infant Mortality (per thousand)	Adult Illiteracy (%)
Tanzania (Dar es Salaam)	6.0	48	115	n.a.
Malawi (Lilongwe)	6.5	46	149	n.a.
Bangladesh (Dhaka)	4.0	52	105	65
Madagascar (Antananarivo)	4.5	51	116	20
Nigeria (Ibadan)	5.5	52	98	49
India (New Delhi)	2.5	59	92	52
Kenya (Nairobi)	6.0	59	67	31
China (Beijing)	7.0	70	29	27
Pakistan (Karachi)	3.0	56	103	65
Ghana (Kumasi)	5.5	55	85	40
Indonesia (Jakarta)	5.0	62	61	23
Egypt (Cairo)	4.5	60	66	52
Zimbabwe (Harare)	5.0	61	49	33
Senegal (Dakar)	3.5	47	81	62
Philippines (Manila)	2.5	64	41	10
Côte d'Ivoire (Abidjan)	5.5	55	95	46
Morocco (Rabat)	4.0	62	67	51
Ecuador (Quito)	2.0	66	55	14
Jordan (Amman)	5.0	67	51	20
Colombia (Bogota)	3.5	69	37	13
Thailand (Bangkok)	2.5	76	27	7
Tunisia (Tunis)	4.0	67	44	35
Jamaica (Kingston)	2.0	73	16	3
Turkey (Istanbul)	3.0	67	60	19
Poland (Warsaw)	3.5	71	16	n.a.
Slovakia (Bratislava)	6.0	72	12	n.a.
Chile (Santiago)	3.5	72	17	7
Algeria (Algiers)	5.5	65	67	43
Malaysia (Kuala Lumpur)	4.5	70	16	22
Russia (Moscow)	5.5	n.a.	n.a.	n.a.
Mexico (Monterrey)	3.5	70	39	13
South Africa (Johannesburg)	5.5	62	66	n.a.
Venezuela (Caracas)	2.0	70	34	12
Brazil (Rio de Janeiro)	2.0	66	57	19
Hungary (Budapest)	3.5	71	15	n.a.
Korea (Seoul)	2.5	71	17	3
Greece (Athens)	1.5	77	11	7
Israel (Tel Aviv)	2.0	76	10	n.a.
Spain (Madrid)	1.0	76	8	5
Singapore (Singapore)	4.0	74	7	n.a.
Hong Kong (Hong Kong)	3.5	78	7	n.a.
United Kingdom (London)	1.0	76	8	<3
Australia (Melbourne)	1.0	77	8	<3
Netherlands (Amsterdam)	1.0	77	7	<3
Austria (Vienna)	1.0	76	8	<3
France (Paris)	1.5	77	7	<3
Canada (Toronto)	1.0	77	7	<3
United States (Washington, D.C.)	1.0	76	9	<3
Germany (Munich)	1.0	76	7	<3
Norway (Oslo)	1.0	77	8	<3
Sweden (Stockholm)	1.0	78	6	<3
Japan (Tokyo)	1.0	79	5	<3
Finland (Helsinki)	1.0	76	6	<3

Sources: Freedom House [1990,18–20]; World Bank [1992, tables 1 and 28].

[a]   For definitions and summary values, see chapter 13.

Table A4. Demographic and Geographic indicators, 1990. [a]

Country (City)	Percent Urbanized (%)	Annual City Growth Rate (%)	Household Size	Density (persons per km2)
Tanzania (Dar es Salaam)	33	6.9	4.3	3,500
Malawi (Lilongwe)	12	4.2	4.3	8,300
Bangladesh (Dhaka)	16	5.3	5.3	29,000
Madagascar (Antananarivo)	25	6.8	6.0	n.a.
Nigeria (Ibadan)	35	4.8	6.0	n.a.
India (New Delhi)	27	2.6	5.6	19,300
Kenya (Nairobi)	24	5.0	4.0	n.a.
China (Beijing)	56	3.6	3.3	n.a.
Pakistan (Karachi)	32	4.4	5.9	n.a.
Ghana (Kumasi)	33	3.4	5.2	5,800
Indonesia (Jakarta)	31	4.1	4.7	12,400
Egypt (Cairo)	47	2.1	4.1	n.a.
Zimbabwe (Harare)	28	5.0	4.5	n.a.
Senegal (Dakar)	38	4.0	7.7	6,300
Philippines (Manila)	43	3.6	5.2	13,800
Côte d'Ivoire (Abidjan)	40	3.8	5.3	n.a.
Morocco (Rabat)	48	4.2	5.3	n.a.
Ecuador (Quito)	56	5.8	3.9	n.a.
Jordan (Amman)	61	3.5	6.2	n.a.
Colombia (Bogota)	70	3.5	4.7	n.a.
Thailand (Bangkok)	23	4.2	4.5	4,900
Tunisia (Tunis)	54	3.9	5.0	n.a.
Jamaica (Kingston)	52	1.3	3.8	n.a.
Turkey (Istanbul)	61	5.0	4.2	n.a.
Poland (Warsaw)	62	0.0	2.6	n.a.
Slovakia (Bratislava)	78	2.1	3.2	n.a.
Chile (Santiago)	86	3.1	4.3	10,200
Algeria (Algiers)	52	2.9	7.4	6,600
Malaysia (Kuala Lumpur)	43	3.5	5.0	6,900
Russia (Moscow)	75	–1.1	2.6	9,200
Mexico (Monterrey)	73	3.8	4.8	6,300
South Africa (Johannesburg)	60	4.0	4.8	3,900
Venezuela (Caracas)	84	1.6	7.0	4,400
Brazil (Rio de Janeiro)	75	2.4	3.2	5,100
Hungary (Budapest)	61	0.1	2.5	3,800
Korea (Seoul)	72	3.1	3.8	17,500
Greece (Athens)	63	0.5	3.0	10,400
Israel (Tel Aviv)	92	1.8	3.1	17,000
Spain (Madrid)	78	1.3	2.9	n.a.
Singapore (Singapore)	100	3.3	4.1	8,600
Hong Kong (Hong Kong)	94	2.1	3.6	39,700
United Kingdom (London)	89	0.0	2.4	n.a.
Australia (Melbourne)	86	1.5	3.3	n.a.
Netherlands (Amsterdam)	89	1.9	1.9	3,500
Austria (Vienna)	58	0.7	2.1	n.a.
France (Paris)	74	0.1	2.5	4,600
Canada (Toronto)	77	2.9	2.9	n.a.
United States (Washington, D.C.)	75	2.6	2.6	1,600
Germany (Munich)	84	0.6	1.9	4,100
Norway (Oslo)	75	0.7	2.0	3,000
Sweden (Stockholm)	84	1.0	1.9	n.a.
Japan (Tokyo)	77	0.7	2.6	17,000
Finland (Helsinki)	60	1.5	2.1	n.a.

Sources: Housing Indicators Program [1994]; World Bank [1992, table 31,278–279].

[a] For definitions and summary values, see chapter 13.

Table A5. Indicators of the Structure of the Gross National Product, 1990. [a]

Country (City)	Government Expenditure as % of GDP	Consump-tion as % of GDP	Government Welfare Expenditure as of Total Exp.	Gross Domestic Investment as % of GDP
Tanzania (Dar es Salaam)	10	86.7	n.a.	25
Malawi (Lilongwe)	15	70.4	3.2	19
Bangladesh (Dhaka)	9	87.8	8.0	12
Madagascar (Antananarivo)	9	77.8	n.a.	17
Nigeria (Ibadan)	11	69.3	n.a.	15
India (New Delhi)	12	67.6	6.9	23
Kenya (Nairobi)	18	61.8	3.6	24
China (Beijing)	8	54.4	n.a.	39
Pakistan (Karachi)	15	72.6	3.1	19
Ghana (Kumasi)	8	81.5	11.9	15
Indonesia (Jakarta)	9	61.4	1.5	36
Egypt (Cairo)	10	77.2	17.8	23
Zimbabwe (Harare)	26	58.5	3.9	21
Senegal (Dakar)	14	74.6	n.a.	13
Philippines (Manila)	9	75.3	2.3	22
Côte d'Ivoire (Abidjan)	18	64.6	n.a.	10
Morocco (Rabat)	16	66.2	n.a.	26
Ecuador (Quito)	8	71.1	2.5	19
Jordan (Amman)	24	76.0	11.7	19
Colombia (Bogota)	10	66.4	n.a.	19
Thailand (Bangkok)	10	62.0	5.8	37
Tunisia (Tunis)	16	64.3	14.4	27
Jamaica (Kingston)	15	62.5	n.a.	30
Turkey (Istanbul)	14	67.5	3.6	23
Poland (Warsaw)	7	64.2	n.a.	31
Slovakia (Bratislava)	10	44.3	33.9	30
Chile (Santiago)	18	67.6	n.a.	20
Algeria (Algiers)	13	49.6	n.a.	33
Malaysia (Kuala Lumpur)	10	47.4	n.a.	34
Russia (Moscow)	11	n.a.	13.0	n.a.
Mexico (Monterrey)	19	64.1	n.a.	20
South Africa (Johannesburg)	9	53.7	n.a.	19
Venezuela (Caracas)	16	64.8	20.1	9
Brazil (Rio de Janeiro)	11	61.8	35.3	22
Hungary (Budapest)	21	63.5	25.3	23
Korea (Seoul)	21	52.8	12.2	37
Greece (Athens)	21	70.0	n.a.	19
Israel (Tel Aviv)	29	58.8	24.3	18
Spain (Madrid)	15	63.6	37.7	26
Singapore (Singapore)	11	48.5	11.7	39
Hong Kong (Hong Kong)	8	60.5	n.a.	28
United Kingdom (London)	20	62.8	34.8	19
Australia (Melbourne)	18	59.1	29.7	21
Netherlands (Amsterdam)	15	61.0	42.3	21
Austria (Vienna)	18	56.5	48.2	25
France (Paris)	18	60.8	46.4	22
Canada (Toronto)	20	58.8	37.0	21
United States (Washington, D.C.)	18	67.0	28.2	16
Germany (Munich)	18	55.5	48.2	22
Norway (Oslo)	21	52.8	39.2	21
Sweden (Stockholm)	27	53.0	55.9	21
Japan (Tokyo)	9	58.2	n.a.	33
Finland (Helsinki)	21	55.4	35.1	27

Sources: IMF [1998, 166–169]; World Bank [1992, tables 9 and 11].

[a]   For definitions and summary values, see chapter 13.

Table A6. Money and Interest Indicators, 1990. [a]

Country (City)	Prime Interest Rate (%)	Deposit Interest Rate (%)	Annual Inflation 1980–1990 (%)	Financial Depth (M2/GDP)
Tanzania (Dar es Salaam)	27.0	26.0	25.8	n.a.
Malawi (Lilongwe)	15.0	14.4	14.7	0.10
Bangladesh (Dhaka)	10.8	12.5	9.6	0.23
Madagascar (Antananarivo)	15.8	13.0	17.1	0.04
Nigeria (Ibadan)	17.0	17.3	17.7	0.09
India (New Delhi)	16.5	9.0	7.9	0.31
Kenya (Nairobi)	19.0	15.8	9.2	0.16
China (Beijing)	n.a.	n.a.	5.8	0.31
Pakistan (Karachi)	n.a.	n.a.	6.7	0.09
Ghana (Kumasi)	27.0	27.0	42.5	0.03
Indonesia (Jakarta)	21.9	18.4	8.4	0.23
Egypt (Cairo)	n.a.	n.a.	11.8	0.64
Zimbabwe (Harare)	9.3	9.8	10.8	0.18
Senegal (Dakar)	14.0	8.0	6.7	0.76
Philippines (Manila)	19.9	16.9	14.9	0.24
Côte d'Ivoire (Abidjan)	n.a.	n.a.	2.3	0.10
Morocco (Rabat)	12.5	8.5	7.2	0.15
Ecuador (Quito)	53.3	42.8	36.6	0.08
Jordan (Amman)	11.0	7.5	7.3	0.77
Colombia (Bogota)	31.2	30.8	24.8	0.08
Thailand (Bangkok)	14.8	11.9	3.4	0.58
Tunisia (Tunis)	11.8	8.5	7.4	0.27
Jamaica (Kingston)	30.0	20.0	18.3	0.33
Turkey (Istanbul)	90.0	57.0	43.2	0.16
Poland (Warsaw)	217.4	230.6	54.3	0.46
Slovakia (Bratislava)	n.a.	n.a.	1.9	0.40
Chile (Santiago)	30.3	36.6	20.5	0.13
Algeria (Algiers)	n.a.	n.a.	6.6	0.47
Malaysia (Kuala Lumpur)	7.5	7.3	1.6	1.04
Russia (Moscow)	79.8	13.3	n.a.	0.13
Mexico (Monterrey)	29.1	31.8	70.3	0.27
South Africa (Johannesburg)	19.6	14.8	14.4	0.21
Venezuela (Caracas)	35.0	22.0	14.4	0.07
Brazil (Rio de Janeiro)	n.a.	1066.6	284.3	0.21
Hungary (Budapest)	28.0	15.0	9.0	0.33
Korea (Seoul)	10.0	10.0	5.1	0.31
Greece (Athens)	22.2	21.8	18.0	0.53
Israel (Tel Aviv)	22.5	16.7	101.4	0.71
Spain (Madrid)	16.0	10.8	9.2	0.41
Singapore (Singapore)	7.7	5.5	1.7	0.68
Hong Kong (Hong Kong)	9.0	6.5	7.2	n.a.
United Kingdom (London)	14.9	13.9	5.8	0.59
Australia (Melbourne)	11.7	11.0	7.4	0.42
Netherlands (Amsterdam)	11.5	4.6	1.9	0.61
Austria (Vienna)	11.5	6.3	3.6	0.75
France (Paris)	12.0	4.5	6.1	0.42
Canada (Toronto)	14.1	12.8	4.4	0.32
United States (Washington, D.C.)	10.0	8.2	3.7	0.44
Germany (Munich)	6.3	3.5	2.7	0.44
Norway (Oslo)	14.2	8.9	5.5	0.16
Sweden (Stockholm)	12.4	10.3	7.4	n.a.
Japan (Tokyo)	6.0	5.8	1.5	0.82
Finland (Helsinki)	12.4	10.0	6.8	0.46

Sources: Housing Indicators Program [1994]; World Bank [1992, table 1, 218–9].

[a] For definitions and summary values, see chapter 13.

Table A7. The Property Rights Index, 1990. [a]

Country (City)	Freedom of Exchange Index	Land Registration Index	Property Rights Index
Tanzania (Dar es Salaam)	70	7	14
Malawi (Lilongwe)	55	57	38
Bangladesh (Dhaka)	82	85	77
Madagascar (Antananarivo)	9	50	0
Nigeria (Ibadan)	55	56	37
India (New Delhi)	18	56	11
Kenya (Nairobi)	81	93	81
China (Beijing)	0	85	18
Pakistan (Karachi)	n.a.	n.a.	75
Ghana (Kumasi)	36	24	2
Indonesia (Jakarta)	100	0	32
Egypt (Cairo)	100	n.a.	85
Zimbabwe (Harare)	91	100	93
Senegal (Dakar)	91	85	83
Philippines (Manila)	91	100	93
Côte d'Ivoire (Abidjan)	91	6	29
Morocco (Rabat)	81	n.a.	62
Ecuador (Quito)	36	60	26
Jordan (Amman)	100	100	100
Colombia (Bogota)	100	50	66
Thailand (Bangkok)	100	100	100
Tunisia (Tunis)	82	50	52
Jamaica (Kingston)	91	68	71
Turkey (Istanbul)	91	55	62
Poland (Warsaw)	73	36	36
Slovakia (Bratislava)	73	n.a.	36
Chile (Santiago)	55	85	57
Algeria (Algiers)	55	82	55
Malaysia (Kuala Lumpur)	55	100	67
Russia (Moscow)	14	n.a.	18
Mexico (Monterrey)	100	n.a.	85
South Africa (Johannesburg)	73	100	80
Venezuela (Caracas)	91	33	47
Brazil (Rio de Janeiro)	91	100	93
Hungary (Budapest)	91	71	73
Korea (Seoul)	64	100	74
Greece (Athens)	100	100	100
Israel (Tel Aviv)	36	100	54
Spain (Madrid)	82	n.a.	87
Singapore (Singapore)	82	100	87
Hong Kong (Hong Kong)	73	100	80
United Kingdom (London)	100	n.a.	100
Australia (Melbourne)	100	85	90
Netherlands (Amsterdam)	18	100	41
Austria (Vienna)	52	n.a.	65
France (Paris)	91	100	93
Canada (Toronto)	90	100	93
United States (Washington, D.C.)	91	100	93
Germany (Munich)	82	100	87
Norway (Oslo)	100	100	100
Sweden (Stockholm)	91	100	93
Japan (Tokyo)	52	100	65
Finland (Helsinki)	n.a.	100	90

Source: Housing Indicators Program [1994].

[a]   For definitions and summary values, see chapter 7.

Table A8. The Components of the Financial Viability Index, 1990. [a]

Country (City)	Prudential Regulations Index	Foreclosure Delay (months)	Financial Viability Index
Tanzania (Dar es Salaam)	27	n.a.	54
Malawi (Lilongwe)	100	6	97
Bangladesh (Dhaka)	76	n.a.	44
Madagascar (Antananarivo)	51	5	69
Nigeria (Ibadan)	51	63	30
India (New Delhi)	51	84	30
Kenya (Nairobi)	76	8	81
China (Beijing)	0	n.a.	0
Pakistan (Karachi)	63	n.a.	37
Ghana (Kumasi)	76	n.a.	75
Indonesia (Jakarta)	51	72	30
Egypt (Cairo)	76	24	67
Zimbabwe (Harare)	100	4	98
Senegal (Dakar)	100	6	97
Philippines (Manila)	100	18	86
Côte d'Ivoire (Abidjan)	27	6	54
Morocco (Rabat)	51	n.a.	74
Ecuador (Quito)	76	12	77
Jordan (Amman)	76	3	85
Colombia (Bogota)	76	48	46
Thailand (Bangkok)	100	12	91
Tunisia (Tunis)	76	24	67
Jamaica (Kingston)	100	6	97
Turkey (Istanbul)	2	6	40
Poland (Warsaw)	76	n.a.	44
Slovakia (Bratislava)	100	n.a.	58
Chile (Santiago)	27	7	53
Algeria (Algiers)	63	n.a.	66
Malaysia (Kuala Lumpur)	100	2	100
Russia (Moscow)	51	n.a.	30
Mexico (Monterrey)	100	6	97
South Africa (Johannesburg)	27	5	55
Venezuela (Caracas)	100	12	91
Brazil (Rio de Janeiro)	100	12	91
Hungary (Budapest)	27	n.a.	15
Korea (Seoul)	76	2	86
Greece (Athens)	76	2	86
Israel (Tel Aviv)	76	n.a.	85
Spain (Madrid)	76	24	67
Singapore (Singapore)	76	3	85
Hong Kong (Hong Kong)	76	4	84
United Kingdom (London)	51	3	71
Australia (Melbourne)	51	2	72
Netherlands (Amsterdam)	27	6	54
Austria (Vienna)	27	7	53
France (Paris)	27	12	49
Canada (Toronto)	76	3	85
United States (Washington, D.C.)	100	5	98
Germany (Munich)	2	3	43
Norway (Oslo)	76	n.a.	85
Sweden (Stockholm)	100	3	99
Japan (Tokyo)	27	n.a.	57
Finland (Helsinki)	100	6	97

Source: Housing Indicators Program [1994].

[a]   For definitions and summary values, see chapter 8.

Table A9. The Components of the Credit Rationing Index, 1990. [a]

Country (City)	Lending Restrictions Index	Negative Real Interest Rate (%)	Credit Rationing Index
Tanzania (Dar es Salaam)	73	−4.8	77
Malawi (Lilongwe)	36	− [b]	61
Bangladesh (Dhaka)	64	− [b]	78
Madagascar (Antananarivo)	100	− [b]	100
Nigeria (Ibadan)	73	− [b]	83
India (New Delhi)	64	− [b]	78
Kenya (Nairobi)	100	− [b]	100
China (Beijing)	0	−3.1	34
Pakistan (Karachi)	64	−9.1	65
Ghana (Kumasi)	64	−22.3	47
Indonesia (Jakarta)	91	− [b]	94
Egypt (Cairo)	73	−16.8	60
Zimbabwe (Harare)	73	−3.9	78
Senegal (Dakar)	82	− [b]	89
Philippines (Manila)	100	− [b]	100
Côte d'Ivoire (Abidjan)	55	− [b]	72
Morocco (Rabat)	55	− [b]	72
Ecuador (Quito)	55	−15.0	51
Jordan (Amman)	55	−7.7	61
Colombia (Bogota)	64	− [b]	78
Thailand (Bangkok)	73	− [b]	83
Tunisia (Tunis)	91	− [b]	94
Jamaica (Kingston)	91	− [b]	94
Turkey (Istanbul)	100	− [b]	100
Poland (Warsaw)	73	−40.0	28
Slovakia (Bratislava)	73	−10.0	69
Chile (Santiago)	100	− [b]	100
Algeria (Algiers)	55	−16.6	49
Malaysia (Kuala Lumpur)	64	− [b]	78
Russia (Moscow)	82	n.a.	89
Mexico (Monterrey)	64	− [b]	78
South Africa (Johannesburg)	82	− [b]	89
Venezuela (Caracas)	82	−19.4	62
Brazil (Rio de Janeiro)	27	−40.0	0
Hungary (Budapest)	100	−21.3	71
Korea (Seoul)	55	− [b]	72
Greece (Athens)	82	−0.4	88
Israel (Tel Aviv)	91	− [b]	94
Spain (Madrid)	91	− [b]	94
Singapore (Singapore)	82	− [b]	89
Hong Kong (Hong Kong)	100	n.a.	100
United Kingdom (London)	100	− [b]	100
Australia (Melbourne)	100	− [b]	100
Netherlands (Amsterdam)	64	− [b]	78
Austria (Vienna)	100	− [b]	100
France (Paris)	64	− [b]	78
Canada (Toronto)	100	− [b]	100
United States (Washington, D.C.)	100	− [b]	100
Germany (Munich)	73	− [b]	83
Norway (Oslo)	91	− [b]	94
Sweden (Stockholm)	91	− [b]	94
Japan (Tokyo)	91	− [b]	94
Finland (Helsinki)	91	− [b]	94

Source: Housing Indicators Program [1994].

[a]   For definitions and summary values, see chapter 8.

[b]   Interest rates were positive in 1990.

Table A10. The Housing Finance Regime Index, 1990. [a]

Country (City)	Financial Viability Index	Credit Rationing Index	Financial Development Index	Housing Finance Regime Index
Tanzania (Dar es Salaam)	54	77	47	56
Malawi (Lilongwe)	97	61	29	55
Bangladesh (Dhaka)	44	78	18	45
Madagascar (Antananarivo)	69	100	18	66
Nigeria (Ibadan)	30	83	41	51
India (New Delhi)	30	78	53	51
Kenya (Nairobi)	81	100	53	80
China (Beijing)	0	34	0	0
Pakistan (Karachi)	37	65	35	40
Ghana (Kumasi)	75	47	53	47
Indonesia (Jakarta)	30	94	29	54
Egypt (Cairo)	67	60	35	47
Zimbabwe (Harare)	98	78	53	73
Senegal (Dakar)	97	89	76	86
Philippines (Manila)	86	100	65	85
Côte d'Ivoire (Abidjan)	54	72	41	52
Morocco (Rabat)	74	72	35	56
Ecuador (Quito)	77	51	41	47
Jordan (Amman)	85	61	29	51
Colombia (Bogota)	46	78	59	58
Thailand (Bangkok)	91	83	29	66
Tunisia (Tunis)	67	94	18	62
Jamaica (Kingston)	97	94	88	93
Turkey (Istanbul)	40	100	18	57
Poland (Warsaw)	44	28	29	19
Slovakia (Bratislava)	58	69	29	48
Chile (Santiago)	53	100	71	77
Algeria (Algiers)	66	49	18	35
Malaysia (Kuala Lumpur)	100	78	76	80
Russia (Moscow)	30	89	6	43
Mexico (Monterrey)	97	78	88	83
South Africa (Johannesburg)	55	89	41	62
Venezuela (Caracas)	91	62	47	59
Brazil (Rio de Janeiro)	91	0	59	26
Hungary (Budapest)	15	71	6	28
Korea (Seoul)	86	72	24	56
Greece (Athens)	86	88	18	64
Israel (Tel Aviv)	85	94	35	73
Spain (Madrid)	67	94	53	73
Singapore (Singapore)	85	89	12	62
Hong Kong (Hong Kong)	84	100	35	76
United Kingdom (London)	71	100	71	83
Australia (Melbourne)	72	100	53	77
Netherlands (Amsterdam)	54	78	35	53
Austria (Vienna)	53	100	12	59
France (Paris)	49	78	88	68
Canada (Toronto)	85	100	82	91
United States (Washington, D.C.)	98	100	100	100
Germany (Munich)	43	83	88	69
Norway (Oslo)	85	94	24	69
Sweden (Stockholm)	99	94	71	88
Japan (Tokyo)	57	94	41	66
Finland (Helsinki)	97	94	47	80

Source: Housing Indicators Program [1994].

[a] For definitions and summary values, see chapter 8.

Table A11. The Components of the Housing Subsidies Index, 1990. [a]

Country (City)	Public Housing Stock (%)	Rental Price Distortion (%)	Extent of Rent Control (%)	Rent Control Index	Housing Subsidies Index
Tanzania (Dar es Salaam)	16	41	100	40	63
Malawi (Lilongwe)	14	n.a.	n.a.	95	91
Bangladesh (Dhaka)	15	n.a.	n.a.	98	92
Madagascar (Antananarivo)	2	44	8	95	98
Nigeria (Ibadan)	10	100	0	100	96
India (New Delhi)	6	n.a.	n.a.	98	97
Kenya (Nairobi)	2	100	0	100	100
China (Beijing)	97	2	100	0	0
Pakistan (Karachi)	5	n.a.	n.a.	98	98
Ghana (Kumasi)	13	10	15	86	88
Indonesia (Jakarta)	2	100	0	100	100
Egypt (Cairo)	29	20	80	35	53
Zimbabwe (Harare)	2	55	26	88	94
Senegal (Dakar)	6	67	2	99	98
Philippines (Manila)	30	82	31	94	82
Côte d'Ivoire (Abidjan)	9	30	12	91	92
Morocco (Rabat)	15	100	0	100	93
Ecuador (Quito)	7	22	n.a.	97	96
Jordan (Amman)	12	73	100	73	81
Colombia (Bogota)	12	n.a.	n.a.	100	94
Thailand (Bangkok)	10	100	0	100	95
Tunisia (Tunis)	15	10	23	79	83
Jamaica (Kingston)	30	100	0	100	85
Turkey (Istanbul)	5	100	0	100	98
Poland (Warsaw)	n.a.	6	100	4	7
Slovakia (Bratislava)	86	10	100	9	10
Chile (Santiago)	26	100	0	100	87
Algeria (Algiers)	25	13	35	69	72
Malaysia (Kuala Lumpur)	19	8	6	94	88
Russia (Moscow)	90	2	100	0	4
Mexico (Monterrey)	n.a.	64	3	99	95
South Africa (Johannesburg)	8	77	24	94	94
Venezuela (Caracas)	9	100	0	100	96
Brazil (Rio de Janeiro)	7	75	83	79	87
Hungary (Budapest)	n.a.	7	95	11	10
Korea (Seoul)	53	48	3	98	72
Greece (Athens)	0	79	95	80	91
Israel (Tel Aviv)	22	11	15	86	83
Spain (Madrid)	9	37	77	51	72
Singapore (Singapore)	79	10	5	95	57
Hong Kong (Hong Kong)	64	62	58	78	56
United Kingdom (London)	21	68	26	92	86
Australia (Melbourne)	10	100	0	100	95
Netherlands (Amsterdam)	69	100	0	100	64
Austria (Vienna)	15	37	35	78	82
France (Paris)	30	73	21	94	82
Canada (Toronto)	8	85	100	85	89
United States (Washington, D.C.)	1	77	15	96	99
Germany (Munich)	1	64	18	93	97
Norway (Oslo)	7	66	34	88	91
Sweden (Stockholm)	30	100	0	100	85
Japan (Tokyo)	8	100	0	100	97
Finland (Helsinki)	31	100	0	100	85

Source: Housing Indicators Program [1994].

[a]   For definitions and summary values, see chapter 9.

Table A12. Housing Subsidies, 1990. [a]

Country (City)	Housing Subsidies (%)	Targeted Subsidies (%)
Tanzania (Dar es Salaam)	n.a.	n.a.
Malawi (Lilongwe)	n.a.	0.0
Bangladesh (Dhaka)	0.0	10.0
Madagascar (Antananarivo)	1.2	0.0
Nigeria (Ibadan)	8.4	7.2
India (New Delhi)	n.a.	n.a.
Kenya (Nairobi)	n.a.	27.0
China (Beijing)	n.a.	n.a.
Pakistan (Karachi)	n.a.	n.a.
Ghana (Kumasi)	n.a.	n.a.
Indonesia (Jakarta)	1.1	24.6
Egypt (Cairo)	n.a.	n.a.
Zimbabwe (Harare)	n.a.	50.0
Senegal (Dakar)	0.2	100.0
Philippines (Manila)	1.4	5.9
Côte d'Ivoire (Abidjan)	n.a.	n.a.
Morocco (Rabat)	n.a.	n.a.
Ecuador (Quito)	6.1	6.3
Jordan (Amman)	11.0	60.0
Colombia (Bogota)	0.0	n.a.
Thailand (Bangkok)	0.3	52.6
Tunisia (Tunis)	1.1	25.0
Jamaica (Kingston)	n.a.	n.a.
Turkey (Istanbul)	n.a.	n.a.
Poland (Warsaw)	6.9	6.0
Slovakia (Bratislava)	8.5	n.a.
Chile (Santiago)	2.9	50.0
Algeria (Algiers)	n.a.	n.a.
Malaysia (Kuala Lumpur)	n.a.	n.a.
Russia (Moscow)	n.a.	n.a.
Mexico (Monterrey)	n.a.	n.a.
South Africa (Johannesburg)	0.7	56.5
Venezuela (Caracas)	5.6	15.5
Brazil (Rio de Janeiro)	9.1	47.5
Hungary (Budapest)	14.2	37.5
Korea (Seoul)	11.9	35.7
Greece (Athens)	2.3	30.0
Israel (Tel Aviv)	1.3	80.0
Spain (Madrid)	5.3	70.0
Singapore (Singapore)	5.5	80.0
Hong Kong (Hong Kong)	9.1	51.0
United Kingdom (London)	n.a.	39.4
Australia (Melbourne)	8.1	42.5
Netherlands (Amsterdam)	6.9	80.0
Austria (Vienna)	8.1	42.5
France (Paris)	13.5	75.0
Canada (Toronto)	1.3	60.0
United States (Washington, D.C.)	3.8	15.3
Germany (Munich)	2.2	n.a.
Norway (Oslo)	5.8	23.0
Sweden (Stockholm)	10.3	50.0
Japan (Tokyo)	4.1	n.a.
Finland (Helsinki)	15.0	38.0

Source: Housing Indicators Program [1994].

[a]   For definitions and summary values, see chapter 9.

Table A13. The Components of the Residential Infrastructure Index, 1990. [a]

Country (City)	Piped Water Supply (%)	Journey to Work (minutes)	Infrastructure Expenditures–to–Income Ratio (%)	The Residential Infrastructure index
Tanzania (Dar es Salaam)	79	50	1.1	32
Malawi (Lilongwe)	31	60	n.a.	5
Bangladesh (Dhaka)	60	45	4.7	36
Madagascar (Antananarivo)	36	60	0.8	0
Nigeria (Ibadan)	63	26	n.a.	45
India (New Delhi)	38	59	7.7	24
Kenya (Nairobi)	40	24	4.0	37
China (Beijing)	86	25	13.5	92
Pakistan (Karachi)	66	52	n.a.	44
Ghana (Kumasi)	49	35	10.0	54
Indonesia (Jakarta)	66	40	2.0	34
Egypt (Cairo)	71	40	8.1	56
Zimbabwe (Harare)	97	56	3.2	44
Senegal (Dakar)	49	35	2.9	31
Philippines (Manila)	66	30	7.7	59
Côte d'Ivoire (Abidjan)	33	38	3.1	21
Morocco (Rabat)	86	25	1.5	53
Ecuador (Quito)	76	56	9.1	52
Jordan (Amman)	97	30	8.1	77
Colombia (Bogota)	99	90	8.2	39
Thailand (Bangkok)	100	91	10.9	48
Tunisia (Tunis)	86	37	13.0	83
Jamaica (Kingston)	87	60	2.8	35
Turkey (Istanbul)	94	40	8.8	71
Poland (Warsaw)	98	45	5.7	60
Slovakia (Bratislava)	99	40	5.7	64
Chile (Santiago)	99	51	2.4	46
Algeria (Algiers)	95	30	1.3	54
Malaysia (Kuala Lumpur)	94	34	6.2	67
Russia (Moscow)	100	56	0.9	38
Mexico (Monterrey)	91	25	1.4	56
South Africa (Johannesburg)	52	59	3.2	18
Venezuela (Caracas)	70	39	4.1	43
Brazil (Rio de Janeiro)	97	107	13.8	45
Hungary (Budapest)	99	34	5.9	69
Korea (Seoul)	100	37	8.8	77
Greece (Athens)	100	40	7.4	70
Israel (Tel Aviv)	100	32	n.a.	75
Spain (Madrid)	95	33	2.3	56
Singapore (Singapore)	100	30	10.9	88
Hong Kong (Hong Kong)	95	45	7.3	64
United Kingdom (London)	100	30	7.2	76
Australia (Melbourne)	100	25	5.5	74
Netherlands (Amsterdam)	100	18	9.2	90
Austria (Vienna)	95	25	12.6	94
France (Paris)	97	40	7.2	68
Canada (Toronto)	100	26	3.4	67
United States (Washington, D.C.)	100	29	7.2	77
Germany (Munich)	99	25	1.4	61
Norway (Oslo)	100	20	4.1	73
Sweden (Stockholm)	98	33	5.8	69
Japan (Tokyo)	100	40	12.0	85
Finland (Helsinki)	99	21	12.9	100

Source: Housing Indicators Program [1994].

[a]   For definitions and summary values, see chapter 10.

Table A14. The Components of the Regulatory Regime Index, 1990. [a]

Country (City)	Permits Delay (months)	Minimum Lot Size (m2)	Minimum Floor Area (m2)	Regulatory Regime Index
Tanzania (Dar es Salaam)	36	336	n.a.	0
Malawi (Lilongwe)	2	375	n.a.	42
Bangladesh (Dhaka)	36	135	40	4
Madagascar (Antananarivo)	4	150	9	77
Nigeria (Ibadan)	3	474	0	72
India (New Delhi)	36	26	23	60
Kenya (Nairobi)	6	100	17	63
China (Beijing)	24	n.a.	0	76
Pakistan (Karachi)	n.a.	n.a.	n.a.	57
Ghana (Kumasi)	8	445	n.a.	61
Indonesia (Jakarta)	28	90	12	68
Egypt (Cairo)	3	100	40	77
Zimbabwe (Harare)	6	300	50	38
Senegal (Dakar)	7	150	71	65
Philippines (Manila)	36	32	20	64
Côte d'Ivoire (Abidjan)	2	100	19	84
Morocco (Rabat)	3	60	n.a.	59
Ecuador (Quito)	6	90	36	66
Jordan (Amman)	1	250	0	90
Colombia (Bogota)	36	22	40	49
Thailand (Bangkok)	11	64	25	84
Tunisia (Tunis)	12	100	60	42
Jamaica (Kingston)	6	268	7	81
Turkey (Istanbul)	2	0	n.a.	87
Poland (Warsaw)	36	200	0	58
Slovakia (Bratislava)	2	n.a.	n.a.	89
Chile (Santiago)	3	100	34	85
Algeria (Algiers)	2	200	67	68
Malaysia (Kuala Lumpur)	18	91	43	68
Russia (Moscow)	2	400	n.a.	69
Mexico (Monterrey)	3	60	33	89
South Africa (Johannesburg)	24	200	35	56
Venezuela (Caracas)	3	100	45	90
Brazil (Rio de Janeiro)	6	125	30	83
Hungary (Budapest)	7	150	26	79
Korea (Seoul)	3	60	n.a.	92
Greece (Athens)	2	50	35	90
Israel (Tel Aviv)	18	200	0	80
Spain (Madrid)	8	200	0	88
Singapore (Singapore)	2	150	30	88
Hong Kong (Hong Kong)	2	20	0	100
United Kingdom (London)	5	n.a.	36	81
Australia (Melbourne)	36	300	75	57
Netherlands (Amsterdam)	16	120	24	69
Austria (Vienna)	9	250	35	71
France (Paris)	2	0	n.a.	97
Canada (Toronto)	30	279	84	54
United States (Washington, D.C.)	36	836	n.a.	54
Germany (Munich)	7	0	25	90
Norway (Oslo)	n.a.	n.a.	n.a.	91
Sweden (Stockholm)	4	250	0	89
Japan (Tokyo)	8	30	0	95
Finland (Helsinki)	n.a.	n.a.	n.a.	87

Source: Housing Indicators Program [1994].

[a]   For definitions and summary values, see chapter 11.

Table A15. The Components of the Enabling Index, 1990. [a]

Country (City)	Property Rights Index	Housing Finance Regime index	Housing Subsidies Index	Residential Infra- structure Index	Regula- tory Regime Index	Enabling Index
Tanzania (Dar es Salaam)	14	56	63	32	0	0
Malawi (Lilongwe)	38	55	91	5	42	22
Bangladesh (Dhaka)	77	45	92	36	4	26
Madagascar (Antananarivo)	0	66	98	0	77	30
Nigeria (Ibadan)	37	51	96	45	72	49
India (New Delhi)	11	51	97	24	60	29
Kenya (Nairobi)	81	80	100	37	63	69
China (Beijing)	18	0	0	92	76	10
Pakistan (Karachi)	75	40	98	44	57	50
Ghana (Kumasi)	2	47	88	54	61	33
Indonesia (Jakarta)	32	54	100	34	68	44
Egypt (Cairo)	85	47	53	56	77	54
Zimbabwe (Harare)	93	73	94	44	38	60
Senegal (Dakar)	83	86	98	31	65	70
Philippines (Manila)	93	85	82	59	64	78
Côte d'Ivoire (Abidjan)	29	52	92	21	84	42
Morocco (Rabat)	62	56	93	53	59	55
Ecuador (Quito)	26	47	96	52	66	44
Jordan (Amman)	100	51	81	77	90	82
Colombia (Bogota)	66	58	94	39	49	49
Thailand (Bangkok)	100	66	95	48	84	80
Tunisia (Tunis)	52	62	83	83	42	56
Jamaica (Kingston)	71	93	85	35	81	73
Turkey (Istanbul)	62	57	98	71	87	75
Poland (Warsaw)	36	19	7	60	58	7
Slovakia (Bratislava)	36	48	10	64	89	34
Chile (Santiago)	57	77	87	46	85	69
Algeria (Algiers)	55	35	72	54	68	41
Malaysia (Kuala Lumpur)	67	80	88	67	68	75
Russia (Moscow)	18	43	4	38	69	7
Mexico (Monterrey)	85	83	95	56	89	87
South Africa (Johannesburg)	80	62	94	18	56	49
Venezuela (Caracas)	47	59	96	43	90	62
Brazil (Rio de Janeiro)	93	26	87	45	83	56
Hungary (Budapest)	73	28	10	69	79	34
Korea (Seoul)	74	56	72	77	92	74
Greece (Athens)	100	64	91	70	90	88
Israel (Tel Aviv)	54	73	83	75	80	73
Spain (Madrid)	87	73	72	56	88	75
Singapore (Singapore)	87	62	57	88	88	79
Hong Kong (Hong Kong)	80	76	56	64	100	78
United Kingdom (London)	100	83	86	76	81	93
Australia (Melbourne)	90	77	95	74	57	80
Netherlands (Amsterdam)	41	53	64	90	69	57
Austria (Vienna)	65	59	82	94	71	74
France (Paris)	93	68	82	68	97	87
Canada (Toronto)	93	91	89	67	54	81
United States (Washington, D.C.)	93	100	99	77	54	92
Germany (Munich)	87	69	97	61	90	85
Norway (Oslo)	100	69	91	73	91	92
Sweden (Stockholm)	93	88	85	69	89	94
Japan (Tokyo)	65	66	97	85	95	88
Finland (Helsinki)	90	80	85	100	87	100

Source: Housing Indicators Program [1994].

[a]   For definitions and summary values, see chapter 12.

Table A16. Measures of Land Availability, 1990. [a]

Country (City)	Raw Land Price ($/m2)	Serviced Land Price ($/m2)	Serviced Land Price- to-Income Ratio (%)	Land Develop- ment Multiplier	Land Conversion Multiplier
Tanzania (Dar es Salaam)	0.5	1.3	0.2	2.5	1.7
Malawi (Lilongwe)	0.2	2.6	0.4	16.6	n.a.
Bangladesh (Dhaka)	30.0	60.0	4.4	2.0	2.0
Madagascar (Antananarivo)	7.2	36.0	4.8	5.0	2.4
Nigeria (Ibadan)	0.7	1.4	0.1	2.0	1.1
India (New Delhi)	n.a.	n.a.	n.a.	n.a.	n.a.
Kenya (Nairobi)	2.5	20.3	1.4	8.3	1.2
China (Beijing)	n.a.	n.a.	n.a.	n.a.	n.a.
Pakistan (Karachi)	n.a.	n.a.	n.a.	3.8	n.a.
Ghana (Kumasi)	0.3	3.6	0.3	12.5	2.7
Indonesia (Jakarta)	9.2	20.0	1.0	2.2	n.a.
Egypt (Cairo)	9.0	89.7	6.7	10.0	n.a.
Zimbabwe (Harare)	7.6	114.0	4.5	15.0	13.3
Senegal (Dakar)	2.6	10.3	0.4	4.0	3.8
Philippines (Manila)	5.9	39.2	1.3	6.7	2.2
Côte d'Ivoire (Abidjan)	7.8	19.5	0.6	2.5	7.5
Morocco (Rabat)	23.5	118.0	2.8	5.0	10.0
Ecuador (Quito)	4.0	16.0	0.6	4.0	4.0
Jordan (Amman)	5.3	22.5	0.5	4.2	1.6
Colombia (Bogota)	3.0	8.6	0.3	2.9	n.a.
Thailand (Bangkok)	57.6	149.5	3.6	2.6	1.8
Tunisia (Tunis)	17.9	65.7	2.0	3.7	3.0
Jamaica (Kingston)	62.3	81.0	2.2	1.3	9.2
Turkey (Istanbul)	10.2	102.4	2.9	10.0	n.a.
Poland (Warsaw)	25.0	60.0	2.6	2.4	n.a.
Slovakia (Bratislava)	n.a.	n.a.	n.a.	n.a.	n.a.
Chile (Santiago)	4.4	12.4	0.4	2.8	0.8
Algeria (Algiers)	n.a.	n.a.	n.a.	n.a.	6.7
Malaysia (Kuala Lumpur)	18.3	79.6	1.2	4.3	5.5
Russia (Moscow)	3.0	11.1	0.4	3.7	1.8
Mexico (Monterrey)	6.8	40.7	0.8	6.0	5.0
South Africa (Johannesburg)	2.7	16.5	0.2	6.2	8.4
Venezuela (Caracas)	n.a.	n.a.	n.a.	n.a.	2.0
Brazil (Rio de Janeiro)	1.2	12.6	0.2	10.4	40.0
Hungary (Budapest)	11.4	68.5	1.3	6.0	6.0
Korea (Seoul)	809.0	1,052.0	5.4	1.3	3.8
Greece (Athens)	n.a.	350.0	2.5	n.a.	n.a.
Israel (Tel Aviv)	50.0	125.0	0.7	2.5	6.7
Spain (Madrid)	25.8	309.3	1.3	12.0	n.a.
Singapore (Singapore)	331.0	413.8	3.2	1.3	6.0
Hong Kong (Hong Kong)	1,282.1	1,538.5	10.2	1.2	n.a.
United Kingdom (London)	195.5	469.3	2.5	2.4	n.a.
Australia (Melbourne)	28.0	60.6	0.2	2.2	n.a.
Netherlands (Amsterdam)	47.1	121.9	0.8	2.6	80.0
Austria (Vienna)	126.2	154.2	0.7	1.2	n.a.
France (Paris)	25.9	108.2	0.3	4.2	n.a.
Canada (Toronto)	34.0	110.7	0.2	3.3	2.7
United States (Washington,D.C.)	36.0	72.0	0.1	2.0	n.a.
Germany (Munich)	726.7	766.7	2.1	1.1	4.8
Norway (Oslo)	31.0	78.0	0.2	2.5	115.0
Sweden (Stockholm)	17.5	70.2	0.2	4.0	5.0
Japan (Tokyo)	1,488.1	2,976.8	7.8	2.0	10.4
Finland (Helsinki)	n.a.	n.a.	n.a.	n.a.	n.a.

Source: Housing Indicators Program [1994].

[a]   For definitions and summary values, see chapter 14.

Table A17. Conditions in the Construction Sector, 1990. [a]

Country (City)	Construction Cost ($/m2)	Building Time (months)	Industrial Concent- ration (%)	Skill Ratio	Import Share of Construction (%)
Tanzania (Dar es Salaam)	67	28	54	2.7	10
Malawi (Lilongwe)	17	2	26	3.0	6
Bangladesh (Dhaka)	100	6	15	2.0	30
Madagascar (Antananarivo)	54	6	31	1.2	29
Nigeria (Ibadan)	25	36	1	2.3	23
India (New Delhi)	94	24	85	3.3	0
Kenya (Nairobi)	108	2	32	2.5	37
China (Beijing)	90	17	46	3.0	0
Pakistan (Karachi)	87	12	n.a.	2.1	11
Ghana (Kumasi)	77	11	n.a.	2.0	n.a.
Indonesia (Jakarta)	65	2	n.a.	1.5	0
Egypt (Cairo)	67	8	29	1.8	19
Zimbabwe (Harare)	106	30	32	3.0	10
Senegal (Dakar)	165	4	91	1.7	45
Philippines (Manila)	148	3	54	1.4	7
Côte d'Ivoire (Abidjan)	215	2	12	2.0	35
Morocco (Rabat)	157	14	23	n.a.	25
Ecuador (Quito)	171	8	55	2.5	40
Jordan (Amman)	150	4	4	2.0	28
Colombia (Bogota)	171	6	n.a.	1.1	0
Thailand (Bangkok)	156	5	9	2.1	3
Tunisia (Tunis)	359	22	65	2.1	25
Jamaica (Kingston)	157	12	94	1.4	20
Turkey (Istanbul)	110	16	30	2.0	10
Poland (Warsaw)	128	37	44	4.5	7
Slovakia (Bratislava)	168	30	n.a.	1.5	2
Chile (Santiago)	136	6	33	1.5	26
Algeria (Algiers)	495	6	33	1.2	25
Malaysia (Kuala Lumpur)	159	24	75	1.8	5
Russia (Moscow)	130	13	100	1.5	n.a.
Mexico (Monterrey)	267	12	74	2.5	0
South Africa (Johannesburg)	192	2	85	3.0	0
Venezuela (Caracas)	98	n.a.	15	2.0	n.a.
Brazil (Rio de Janeiro)	214	18	64	2.5	0
Hungary (Budapest)	379	23	46	2.2	13
Korea (Seoul)	617	18	55	2.0	15
Greece (Athens)	456	18	1	1.4	20
Israel (Tel Aviv)	570	18	40	1.5	22
Spain (Madrid)	510	18	13	1.1	0
Singapore (Singapore)	749	9	90	1.6	70
Hong Kong (Hong Kong)	641	30	88	2.0	80
United Kingdom (London)	560	20	n.a.	1.4	n.a.
Australia (Melbourne)	383	3	14	1.1	11
Netherlands (Amsterdam)	997	13	69	1.5	10
Austria (Vienna)	1,215	3	14	1.1	11
France (Paris)	990	8	13	1.5	5
Canada (Toronto)	608	6	40	1.2	10
United States (Washington, D.C.)	500	4	24	2.0	2
Germany (Munich)	1,305	8	41	1.5	12
Norway (Oslo)	1,426	12	n.a.	1.1	18
Sweden (Stockholm)	1,527	10	20	1.3	9
Japan (Tokyo)	2,604	12	10	2.0	n.a.
Finland (Helsinki)	1,734	9	22	1.3	10

Source: Housing Indicators Program [1994].

[a]   For definitions and summary values, see chapter 15.

Table A18. Construction Cost Indices, 1990. [a]

Country (City)	Construction Cost to–Income Ratio (%)	Permanent Structures (%)	Quality Attributes	Construction Quality Index	Construction Cost Premium
Tanzania (Dar es Salaam)	8.8	76	0	17	1.9
Malawi (Lilongwe)	2.4	67	0	10	0.6
Bangladesh (Dhaka)	7.4	55	3	25	2.1
Madagascar (Antananarivo)	7.2	43	1	0	2.9
Nigeria (Ibadan)	1.9	100	2	49	0.2
India (New Delhi)	8.7	86	4	50	0.7
Kenya (Nairobi)	7.2	67	3	33	1.6
China (Beijing)	8.3	94	5	62	0.4
Pakistan (Karachi)	5.4	97	2	49	0.7
Ghana (Kumasi)	6.2	100	2	49	0.6
Indonesia (Jakarta)	3.3	67	4	42	0.7
Egypt (Cairo)	5.0	94	4	58	0.4
Zimbabwe (Harare)	4.2	83	4	54	0.7
Senegal (Dakar)	6.1	84	4	56	1.0
Philippines (Manila)	4.8	80	3	48	1.3
Côte d'Ivoire (Abidjan)	6.3	88	2	48	1.8
Morocco (Rabat)	3.8	94	4	66	0.7
Ecuador (Quito)	6.0	70	4	47	1.5
Jordan (Amman)	3.3	97	6	80	0.4
Colombia (Bogota)	5.3	97	4	66	0.7
Thailand (Bangkok)	3.8	97	3	61	0.8
Tunisia (Tunis)	10.8	96	3	59	2.0
Jamaica (Kingston)	4.2	80	3	49	1.3
Turkey (Istanbul)	3.1	95	3	59	0.6
Poland (Warsaw)	5.7	100	5	71	0.4
Slovakia (Bratislava)	4.6	100	6	81	0.4
Chile (Santiago)	4.0	85	4	58	0.8
Algeria (Algiers)	6.7	97	4	72	1.7
Malaysia (Kuala Lumpur)	2.4	86	4	64	0.7
Russia (Moscow)	4.2	99	6	79	0.3
Mexico (Monterrey)	5.5	93	4	66	1.1
South Africa (Johannesburg)	2.1	66	2	41	2.2
Venezuela (Caracas)	1.9	90	4	65	0.4
Brazil (Rio de Janeiro)	4.1	99	4	71	0.8
Hungary (Budapest)	7.3	98	6	82	0.9
Korea (Seoul)	3.2	97	6	91	1.0
Greece (Athens)	3.2	100	6	91	0.7
Israel (Tel Aviv)	3.4	100	4	80	1.4
Spain (Madrid)	2.2	100	5	88	0.9
Singapore (Singapore)	5.8	99	5	83	1.6
Hong Kong (Hong Kong)	4.3	90	5	79	1.7
United Kingdom (London)	3.0	100	5	87	1.1
Australia (Melbourne)	1.5	100	4	83	0.8
Netherlands (Amsterdam)	6.9	100	5	85	2.0
Austria (Vienna)	5.4	100	6	94	1.7
France (Paris)	3.1	100	6	97	1.3
Canada (Toronto)	1.4	100	5	93	0.9
United States (Washington, D.C.)	1.0	100	6	100	0.6
Germany (Munich)	3.6	100	6	98	1.6
Norway (Oslo)	4.1	100	5	91	2.3
Sweden (Stockholm)	3.7	100	5	93	2.3
Japan (Tokyo)	6.8	100	5	92	4.0
Finland (Helsinki)	4.8	100	6	98	2.2

Source: Housing Indicators Program [1994].

[a]   For definitions and summary values, see chapter 15.

Table A19. The Availability of Mortgage Credit, 1990. [a]

Country (City)	Housing Credit Portfolio (%)	Credit–to–Value–Ratio (%)	Mortgage–to–Prime Difference (%)	Mortgage Arrears Rate (%)
Tanzania (Dar es Salaam)	0	3	4	n.a.
Malawi (Lilongwe)	5	n.a.	0	n.a.
Bangladesh (Dhaka)	3	2	5	18
Madagascar (Antananarivo)	2	13	1	14
Nigeria (Ibadan)	n.a.	n.a.	2	10
India (New Delhi)	2	14	-3	33
Kenya (Nairobi)	6	12	-1	0
China (Beijing)	0	0	n.a.	5
Pakistan (Karachi)	9	n.a.	n.a.	n.a.
Ghana (Kumasi)	3	8	-12	n.a.
Indonesia (Jakarta)	3	35	-10	n.a.
Egypt (Cairo)	7	74	n.a.	n.a.
Zimbabwe (Harare)	10	33	4	10
Senegal (Dakar)	2	11	2	6
Philippines (Manila)	7	58	3	n.a.
Côte d'Ivoire (Abidjan)	9	8	n.a.	26
Morocco (Rabat)	7	21	-2	n.a.
Ecuador (Quito)	22	29	-20	3
Jordan (Amman)	19	34	-3	10
Colombia (Bogota)	11	60	10	9
Thailand (Bangkok)	7	66	1	14
Tunisia (Tunis)	8	20	0	11
Jamaica (Kingston)	22	28	3	20
Turkey (Istanbul)	3	7	-15	30
Poland (Warsaw)	18	33	-102	n.a.
Slovakia (Bratislava)	n.a.	n.a.	n.a.	0
Chile (Santiago)	20	44	3	n.a.
Algeria (Algiers)	0	0	n.a.	42
Malaysia (Kuala Lumpur)	22	73	2	n.a.
Russia (Moscow)	0	1	-73	10
Mexico (Monterrey)	18	77	8	0
South Africa (Johannesburg)	39	75	0	1
Venezuela (Caracas)	17	24	-14	2
Brazil (Rio de Janeiro)	33	21	n.a.	40
Hungary (Budapest)	29	41	-20	20
Korea (Seoul)	5	62	-0	5
Greece (Athens)	11	45	-2	0
Israel (Tel Aviv)	14	65	1	36
Spain (Madrid)	25	118	1	1
Singapore (Singapore)	15	41	-2	3
Hong Kong (Hong Kong)	19	150	2	5
United Kingdom (London)	37	98	0	0
Australia (Melbourne)	24	83	2	1
Netherlands (Amsterdam)	16	126	-3	7
Austria (Vienna)	25	73	2	5
France (Paris)	17	47	-3	0
Canada (Toronto)	28	55	-1	8
United States (Washington, D.C.)	44	131	0	1
Germany (Munich)	36	n.a.	3	1
Norway (Oslo)	36	80	-1	n.a.
Sweden (Stockholm)	20	90	2	n.a.
Japan (Tokyo)	11	93	0	1
Finland (Helsinki)	23	129	1	0

Source: Housing Indicators Program [1994].

[a]   For definitions and summary values, see chapter 16.

Table A20. Housing Affordability Measures, 1990. [a]

Country (City)	House Price-to-Income Ratio	Rent-to-Income Ratio (%)	Down-Market Penetration
Tanzania (Dar es Salaam)	1.9	3.3	13.5
Malawi (Lilongwe)	0.7	10.0	7.7
Bangladesh (Dhaka)	6.3	12.0	16.7
Madagascar (Antananarivo)	3.3	20.8	1.0
Nigeria (Ibadan)	3.6	6.9	0.8
India (New Delhi)	7.7	25.0	n.a.
Kenya (Nairobi)	1.0	10.0	6.9
China (Beijing)	14.8	6.3	n.a.
Pakistan (Karachi)	1.9	18.6	n.a.
Ghana (Kumasi)	2.5	5.8	n.a.
Indonesia (Jakarta)	3.5	14.7	1.1
Egypt (Cairo)	6.7	6.0	n.a.
Zimbabwe (Harare)	2.8	13.5	3.7
Senegal (Dakar)	3.0	19.2	7.0
Philippines (Manila)	2.6	13.6	1.2
Côte d'Ivoire (Abidjan)	1.4	13.2	3.5
Morocco (Rabat)	7.2	13.0	5.1
Ecuador (Quito)	2.4	18.5	2.1
Jordan (Amman)	3.4	16.3	2.7
Colombia (Bogota)	6.5	19.8	5.7
Thailand (Bangkok)	4.1	20.0	1.7
Tunisia (Tunis)	6.1	20.7	8.6
Jamaica (Kingston)	4.9	16.2	2.7
Turkey (Istanbul)	5.0	25.0	5.0
Poland (Warsaw)	10.8	5.8	n.a.
Slovakia (Bratislava)	6.5	2.9	1.3
Chile (Santiago)	2.1	27.8	5.1
Algeria (Algiers)	11.7	5.8	n.a.
Malaysia (Kuala Lumpur)	5.0	26.2	3.4
Russia (Moscow)	7.4	0.1	n.a.
Mexico (Monterrey)	3.7	36.4	2.5
South Africa (Johannesburg)	1.7	5.3	1.2
Venezuela (Caracas)	2.0	23.8	n.a.
Brazil (Rio de Janeiro)	2.3	14.4	14.2
Hungary (Budapest)	6.6	5.6	3.9
Korea (Seoul)	9.3	35.2	3.5
Greece (Athens)	3.8	14.8	1.6
Israel (Tel Aviv)	5.0	22.6	1.1
Spain (Madrid)	3.7	10.4	n.a.
Singapore (Singapore)	2.8	37.7	10.7
Hong Kong (Hong Kong)	7.4	8.4	8.6
United Kingdom (London)	7.2	24.9	n.a.
Australia (Melbourne)	3.9	16.4	2.8
Netherlands (Amsterdam)	4.8	18.2	6.9
Austria (Vienna)	4.7	12.5	n.a.
France (Paris)	4.2	20.6	1.1
Canada (Toronto)	4.2	18.4	2.5
United States (Washington, D.C.)	3.9	24.6	1.8
Germany (Munich)	9.6	18.0	2.6
Norway (Oslo)	5.5	8.6	n.a.
Sweden (Stockholm)	4.6	11.0	2.0
Japan (Tokyo)	11.6	16.2	3.5
Finland (Helsinki)	3.7	18.7	n.a.

Source: Housing Indicators Program [1994].

[a]   For definitions and summary values, see chapter 17.

Table A21. Hedonic House Price and Rent Indices, 1990. [a]

Country (City)	Housing Price Index ($)	Housing Rent Index ($)	Weighted Price Index ($)
Tanzania (Dar es Salaam)	0.97	0.53	0.65
Malawi (Lilongwe)	0.28	1.20	0.90
Bangladesh (Dhaka)	5.44	1.87	2.94
Madagascar (Antananarivo)	1.37	4.10	3.11
Nigeria (Ibadan)	0.55	0.19	0.41
India (New Delhi)	1.02	0.74	0.87
Kenya (Nairobi)	0.80	1.36	1.20
China (Beijing)	1.84	0.15	0.28
Pakistan (Karachi)	0.46	0.81	0.52
Ghana (Kumasi)	0.36	0.15	0.21
Indonesia (Jakarta)	1.14	0.68	0.94
Egypt (Cairo)	0.79	0.13	0.35
Zimbabwe (Harare)	1.02	0.92	0.98
Senegal (Dakar)	0.61	0.73	0.66
Philippines (Manila)	0.82	0.86	0.84
Côte d'Ivoire (Abidjan)	0.85	1.27	1.18
Morocco (Rabat)	2.79	1.05	1.85
Ecuador (Quito)	1.36	1.94	1.48
Jordan (Amman)	0.32	0.42	0.35
Colombia (Bogota)	1.48	0.94	1.28
Thailand (Bangkok)	0.84	0.75	0.81
Tunisia (Tunis)	2.49	1.62	2.20
Jamaica (Kingston)	1.92	0.93	1.34
Turkey (Istanbul)	1.00	0.75	0.90
Poland (Warsaw)	1.18	0.14	0.51
Slovakia (Bratislava)	0.40	0.05	0.10
Chile (Santiago)	0.45	0.82	0.52
Algeria (Algiers)	2.87	0.33	1.46
Malaysia (Kuala Lumpur)	1.67	1.78	1.71
Russia (Moscow)	0.66	0.00	0.01
Mexico (Monterrey)	0.71	1.44	0.83
South Africa (Johannesburg)	2.44	0.54	1.76
Venezuela (Caracas)	0.28	0.68	0.42
Brazil (Rio de Janeiro)	0.39	0.51	0.44
Hungary (Budapest)	0.67	0.16	0.39
Korea (Seoul)	1.46	1.71	1.61
Greece (Athens)	0.48	0.65	0.56
Israel (Tel Aviv)	1.42	1.72	1.48
Spain (Madrid)	0.92	0.88	0.91
Singapore (Singapore)	0.46	1.20	0.53
Hong Kong (Hong Kong)	6.28	1.85	3.75
United Kingdom (London)	1.51	0.77	1.19
Australia (Melbourne)	0.64	0.69	0.65
Netherlands (Amsterdam)	1.48	1.64	1.63
Austria (Vienna)	0.84	0.91	0.89
France (Paris)	0.70	1.47	1.14
Canada (Toronto)	0.86	1.04	0.93
United States (Washington, D.C.)	0.36	0.74	0.51
Germany (Munich)	2.02	1.44	1.53
Norway (Oslo)	1.39	0.65	1.19
Sweden (Stockholm)	1.42	1.32	1.36
Japan (Tokyo)	6.35	2.11	3.81
Finland (Helsinki)	0.82	1.46	1.06

Source: Housing Indicators Program [1994].

[a] For definitions and summary values, see chapter 17.

Table A22. Unit and Space Measures of Housing Quantity, 1990. [a]

Country (City)	Dwellings per 1,000 People	Households per Occupied Dwelling unit	Median House Size (m2)	Persons per Room	Floor Area per Person (m2)
Tanzania (Dar es Salaam)	229	1.006	21.6	2.2	5.0
Malawi (Lilongwe)	222	1.046	28.6	1.8	6.6
Bangladesh (Dhaka)	140	1.358	19.8	3.5	3.7
Madagascar (Antananarivo)	91	1.827	30.4	5.5	5.1
Nigeria (Ibadan)	179	0.931	54.0	2.0	9.0
India (New Delhi)	162	1.120	47.7	2.5	8.6
Kenya (Nairobi)	214	n.a.	20.3	3.7	5.1
China (Beijing)	217	1.408	30.5	1.5	9.3
Pakistan (Karachi)	n.a.	n.a.	41.7	3.0	7.1
Ghana (Kumasi)	261	n.a.	54.1	2.9	10.4
Indonesia (Jakarta)	194	1.137	48.1	1.3	10.2
Egypt (Cairo)	195	1.465	49.2	1.5	12.0
Zimbabwe (Harare)	109	2.056	35.0	2.3	7.8
Senegal (Dakar)	129	1.000	62.7	2.3	8.1
Philippines (Manila)	181	1.099	62.4	3.0	12.0
Côte d'Ivoire (Abidjan)	208	n.a.	42.1	2.2	7.9
Morocco (Rabat)	n.a.	n.a.	31.2	2.3	6.0
Ecuador (Quito)	221	1.178	33.6	1.7	8.6
Jordan (Amman)	97	1.868	62.0	3.3	10.0
Colombia (Bogota)	168	1.307	40.9	1.7	8.8
Thailand (Bangkok)	183	1.325	73.8	2.0	16.5
Tunisia (Tunis)	198	1.100	32.7	1.9	6.5
Jamaica (Kingston)	247	1.111	58.1	1.5	15.3
Turkey (Istanbul)	198	1.200	71.4	2.0	17.0
Poland (Warsaw)	356	1.085	45.0	0.9	17.4
Slovakia (Bratislava)	379	0.856	74.2	1.1	23.2
Chile (Santiago)	248	0.989	67.5	1.2	15.9
Algeria (Algiers)	142	1.046	63.2	2.6	8.5
Malaysia (Kuala Lumpur)	202	1.030	62.5	1.7	12.5
Russia (Moscow)	303	1.273	49.7	1.5	18.0
Mexico (Monterrey)	170	1.347	71.7	1.1	15.6
South Africa (Johannesburg)	196	1.073	53.3	n.a.	11.1
Venezuela (Caracas)	177	0.808	112.0	2.0	16.0
Brazil (Rio de Janeiro)	293	1.135	67.1	1.0	19.4
Hungary (Budapest)	389	1.066	58.1	1.3	23.5
Korea (Seoul)	140	1.896	77.6	1.5	13.0
Greece (Athens)	450	0.787	72.5	0.8	24.5
Israel (Tel Aviv)	285	1.193	76.9	1.0	24.8
Spain (Madrid)	441	0.884	69.8	0.6	24.4
Singapore (Singapore)	254	1.020	82.9	1.4	20.0
Hong Kong (Hong Kong)	322	0.906	25.5	n.a.	7.1
United Kingdom (London)	446	1.002	75.9	0.8	31.9
Australia (Melbourne)	329	0.999	167.3	0.7	50.7
Netherlands (Amsterdam)	474	1.129	45.1	0.6	23.8
Austria (Vienna)	575	0.960	64.3	0.9	31.0
France (Paris)	446	0.953	81.6	0.8	32.4
Canada (Toronto)	352	1.000	117.4	0.5	41.1
United States (Washington, D.C.)	397	1.027	179.9	0.4	68.7
Germany (Munich)	513	1.030	67.7	0.6	35.0
Norway (Oslo)	481	1.048	84.0	0.5	42.0
Sweden (Stockholm)	485	1.101	75.0	0.6	40.0
Japan (Tokyo)	527	0.803	40.9	0.8	15.8
Finland (Helsinki)	471	1.036	63.8	0.7	30.4

Source: Housing Indicators Program [1994].

[a] For definitions and summary values, see chapter 19.

Table A23. Quality Measures of Housing Quantity, 1990. [a]

Country (City)	Hedonic House Value ($)	Hedonic Annual Rental Value ($)	Weighted Hedonic House Value ($)	Hedonic House Value per Person ($)
Tanzania (Dar es Salaam)	1,483	57	1,373	317
Malawi (Lilongwe)	1,790	58	1,511	351
Bangladesh (Dhaka)	1,553	70	1,497	281
Madagascar (Antananarivo)	1,791	42	1,280	213
Nigeria (Ibadan)	8,806	480	9,330	1,555
India (New Delhi)	8,142	443	8,941	1,611
Kenya (Nairobi)	1,965	99	2,050	512
China (Beijing)	8,648	438	9,492	2,903
Pakistan (Karachi)	6,791	370	6,948	1,178
Ghana (Kumasi)	8,760	478	9,815	1,888
Indonesia (Jakarta)	6,001	323	6,285	1,330
Egypt (Cairo)	11,366	598	12,258	2,990
Zimbabwe (Harare)	6,974	375	7,204	1,601
Senegal (Dakar)	13,339	711	13,837	1,788
Philippines (Manila)	9,532	520	10,096	1,942
Côte d'Ivoire (Abidjan)	6,539	357	7,145	1,341
Morocco (Rabat)	10,654	516	10,665	2,024
Ecuador (Quito)	4,974	271	5,093	1,306
Jordan (Amman)	47,141	1,754	44,487	7,175
Colombia (Bogota)	14,185	684	14,113	3,033
Thailand (Bangkok)	20,445	1,040	20,795	4,642
Tunisia (Tunis)	8,162	424	8,333	1,651
Jamaica (Kingston)	9,492	517	10,165	2,675
Turkey (Istanbul)	17,912	930	18,378	4,376
Poland (Warsaw)	20,699	920	19,464	7,529
Slovakia (Bratislava)	59,696	2,173	46,698	14,593
Chile (Santiago)	15,982	838	16,214	3,815
Algeria (Algiers)	29,938	1,318	29,507	3,987
Malaysia (Kuala Lumpur)	19,407	962	20,030	4,006
Russia (Moscow)	35,134	1,344	27,480	10,569
Mexico (Monterrey)	25,436	1,220	25,454	5,303
South Africa (Johannesburg)	6,372	341	6,918	1,441
Venezuela (Caracas)	36,006	1,771	36,462	5,209
Brazil (Rio de Janeiro)	30,017	1,345	29,399	9,102
Hungary (Budapest)	50,862	1,791	43,662	17,645
Korea (Seoul)	122,567	3,341	107,850	28,683
Greece (Athens)	111,831	3,083	97,627	32,982
Israel (Tel Aviv)	59,041	2,189	59,298	19,117
Spain (Madrid)	91,981	2,723	90,660	31,670
Singapore (Singapore)	78,468	2,675	77,387	18,673
Hong Kong (Hong Kong)	17,837	686	18,047	5,015
United Kingdom (London)	90,110	2,791	86,112	36,241
Australia (Melbourne)	157,620	5,384	164,641	49,891
Netherlands (Amsterdam)	47,252	1,544	41,041	21,659
Austria (Vienna)	126,529	3,112	102,829	49,606
France (Paris)	193,974	4,356	181,359	72,030
Canada (Toronto)	216,695	5,496	247,284	86,575
United States (Washington, D.C.)	542,354	10,820	588,138	224,480
Germany (Munich)	170,103	3,717	160,890	83,193
Norway (Oslo)	135,254	3,656	139,446	69,723
Sweden (Stockholm)	132,314	3,428	151,136	80,606
Japan (Tokyo)	69,568	1,833	77,746	30,018
Finland (Helsinki)	161,273	3,515	157,212	74,863

Source: Housing Indicators Program [1994].

[a]   For definitions and summary values, see chapter 20.

Table A24. Value Measures of Housing Quantity, 1990. ^a

Country (City)	Median House Price	Median Annual Rent	Value of Housing Stock-to-GCP Ratio	Urban Housing Wealth-to-GNP Ratio
Tanzania (Dar es Salaam)	$1,433	$30	1.6	0.99
Malawi (Lilongwe)	$506	$69	0.5	0.07
Bangladesh (Dhaka)	$8,451	$130	4.1	0.90
Madagascar (Antananarivo)	$2,453	$173	1.4	0.24
Nigeria (Ibadan)	$4,810	$92	2.7	1.04
India (New Delhi)	$8,300	$328	4.7	1.04
Kenya (Nairobi)	$1,563	$136	0.6	0.22
China (Beijing)	$15,945	$68	5.7	5.24
Pakistan (Karachi)	$3,130	$302	n.a.	0.45
Ghana (Kumasi)	$3,147	$72	2.8	0.69
Indonesia (Jakarta)	$6,839	$221	1.9	0.72
Egypt (Cairo)	$8,969	$81	4.1	1.37
Zimbabwe (Harare)	$7,096	$343	1.1	0.34
Senegal (Dakar)	$8,180	$521	2.2	0.57
Philippines (Manila)	$7,843	$447	1.8	0.84
Cote d'Ivoire (Abidjan)	$5,556	$453	1.2	0.62
Morocco (Rabat)	$29,737	$541	n.a.	2.84
Ecuador (Quito)	$6,767	$525	1.5	0.85
Jordan (Amman)	$15,271	$736	1.5	0.73
Colombia (Bogota)	$21,033	$644	3.4	1.96
Thailand (Bangkok)	$17,138	$783	2.1	0.51
Tunisia (Tunis)	$20,315	$688	3.9	1.51
Jamaica (Kingston)	$18,258	$480	2.9	1.56
Turkey (Istanbul)	$18,000	$700	2.8	1.34
Poland (Warsaw)	$24,487	$131	6.4	3.20
Slovakia (Bratislava)	$24,056	$106	3.5	4.16
Chile (Santiago)	$7,184	$691	1.5	0.79
Algeria (Algiers)	$85,789	$429	6.1	3.07
Malaysia (Kuala Lumpur)	$32,407	$1,711	2.4	1.21
Russia (Moscow)	$23,236	$4	2.5	2.26
Mexico (Monterrey)	$18,000	$1,751	2.0	0.90
South Africa (Johannesburg)	$15,560	$185	0.9	0.72
Venezuela (Caracas)	$10,184	$1,200	1.6	0.59
Brazil (Rio de Janeiro)	$11,818	$682	1.3	0.97
Hungary (Budapest)	$34,272	$288	4.0	2.92
Korea (Seoul)	$179,500	$5,720	2.6	3.36
Greece (Athens)	$54,070	$2,009	3.5	2.56
Israel (Tel Aviv)	$83,880	$3,770	2.6	2.01
Spain (Madrid)	$84,844	$2,404	2.9	2.65
Singapore (Singapore)	$35,862	$3,211	1.4	0.82
Hong Kong (Hong Kong)	$112,022	$1,266	5.2	2.95
United Kingdom (London)	$135,774	$2,145	4.8	3.34
Australia (Melbourne)	$100,960	$3,700	2.5	1.68
Netherlands (Amsterdam)	$69,935	$2,534	2.6	1.70
Austria (Vienna)	$105,926	$2,817	3.2	1.85
France (Paris)	$136,452	$6,392	2.9	2.31
Canada (Toronto)	$186,855	$5,734	2.5	2.47
United States (Washington, D.C.)	$194,150	$7,992	2.7	2.65
Germany (Munich)	$343,333	$5,339	5.3	6.63
Norway (Oslo)	$187,500	$2,363	2.8	2.92
Sweden (Stockholm)	$187,780	$4,510	2.2	3.23
Japan (Tokyo)	$441,719	$3,863	9.2	7.05
Finland (Helsinki)	$132,500	$5,130	2.0	1.44

Source: Housing Indicators Program [1994].

^a For definitions and summary values, see chapter 21.

Table A25. Production and Investment, Vacancy, and Mobility, 1990. [a]

Country (City)	Vacancy Rate (%)	Housing Stock Growth (%)	Housing Production (units per 1,000 people)	Gross Urban Housing Investment (%)	Annual Residential Mobility
Tanzania (Dar es Salaam)	0.0	6.5	14.8	10.4	5.0
Malawi (Lilongwe)	0.0	4.2	9.3	2.1	7.0
Bangladesh (Dhaka)	1.0	5.7	8.0	23.4	6.0
Madagascar (Antananarivo)	0.3	2.1	1.9	3.0	6.6
Nigeria (Ibadan)	0.1	1.2	2.1	3.2	8.0
India (New Delhi)	0.8	2.5	4.1	11.7	4.6
Kenya (Nairobi)	n.a.	1.3	2.7	0.7	n.a.
China (Beijing)	0.0	6.1	13.3	34.9	13.0
Pakistan (Karachi)	n.a.	n.a.	n.a.	n.a.	5.3
Ghana (Kumasi)	n.a.	1.0	2.6	2.8	4.6
Indonesia (Jakarta)	4.1	3.6	7.1	7.1	11.9
Egypt (Cairo)	14.5	5.8	11.2	23.7	3.1
Zimbabwe (Harare)	0.8	7.1	7.7	7.7	6.5
Senegal (Dakar)	0.0	2.6	3.4	6.0	18.0
Philippines (Manila)	3.5	3.2	5.7	5.8	4.1
Côte d'Ivoire (Abidjan)	n.a.	3.7	7.8	4.3	n.a.
Morocco (Rabat)	1.0	n.a.	6.5	16.2	n.a.
Ecuador (Quito)	1.6	4.2	9.3	6.1	3.4
Jordan (Amman)	10.8	12.9	12.5	19.9	8.8
Colombia (Bogota)	2.0	3.6	6.0	11.9	n.a.
Thailand (Bangkok)	8.0	7.7	14.1	16.2	16.1
Tunisia (Tunis)	9.0	4.0	7.8	15.5	8.5
Jamaica (Kingston)	4.2	4.6	11.3	13.3	1.0
Turkey (Istanbul)	n.a.	3.3	6.6	9.4	5.0
Poland (Warsaw)	0.0	0.5	1.9	3.4	2.6
Slovakia (Bratislava)	3.6	1.8	6.8	6.3	3.4
Chile (Santiago)	4.2	2.5	6.2	3.7	n.a.
Algeria (Algiers)	8.9	1.9	2.7	11.6	1.5
Malaysia (Kuala Lumpur)	3.8	4.3	8.6	10.1	4.1
Russia (Moscow)	0.1	1.5	4.5	3.7	4.9
Mexico (Monterrey)	9.2	3.5	6.0	6.9	2.8
South Africa (Johannesburg)	1.0	3.6	7.0	3.1	17.5
Venezuela (Caracas)	n.a.	2.2	3.9	3.5	6.4
Brazil (Rio de Janeiro)	7.0	1.7	4.9	2.2	4.0
Hungary (Budapest)	2.4	0.8	3.0	3.2	4.4
Korea (Seoul)	0.0	5.1	7.2	13.2	24.3
Greece (Athens)	4.6	1.4	6.4	5.0	12.0
Israel (Tel Aviv)	5.0	1.3	3.8	3.5	10.0
Spain (Madrid)	10.4	1.1	4.9	3.2	9.0
Singapore (Singapore)	6.9	2.5	6.4	3.6	6.1
Hong Kong (Hong Kong)	4.7	4.4	14.2	23.0	6.9
United Kingdom (London)	5.7	0.6	2.6	2.8	13.3
Australia (Melbourne)	7.9	2.5	8.2	6.2	15.2
Netherlands (Amsterdam)	1.3	1.6	7.6	4.2	20.2
Austria (Vienna)	12.6	0.8	4.4	2.4	10.8
France (Paris)	6.5	1.1	5.0	3.2	8.0
Canada (Toronto)	0.5	2.1	7.3	5.1	20.9
United States (Washington, D.C.)	6.3	1.7	6.6	4.5	26.5
Germany (Munich)	2.1	1.0	5.0	5.2	9.1
Norway (Oslo)	0.8	1.4	6.9	4.0	9.3
Sweden (Stockholm)	0.1	1.2	5.6	2.6	13.7
Japan (Tokyo)	8.8	2.1	11.0	19.2	7.2
Finland (Helsinki)	2.3	2.8	13.3	5.7	11.0

Source: Housing Indicators Program [1994].

[a] For definitions and summary values, see chapter 22.

Table A26. Measures of Home Ownership and Tenure, 1990. [a]

Country (City)	Home Ownership Premium	Owner Occu- pancy (%)	Unautho- rized Housing (%)	Squatter Housing (%)	Homeless- ness (persons per thousand)
Tanzania (Dar es Salaam)	1.8	27	64	51	0.0
Malawi (Lilongwe)	0.2	33	71	71	0.0
Bangladesh (Dhaka)	2.9	30	78	10	11.5
Madagascar (Antananarivo)	0.3	36	49	4	6.5
Nigeria (Ibadan)	2.9	62	75	n.a.	1.9
India (New Delhi)	1.4	48	48	17	4.2
Kenya (Nairobi)	0.6	29	75	37	3.5
China (Beijing)	12.0	8	12	3	0.0
Pakistan (Karachi)	0.6	83	51	44	n.a.
Ghana (Kumasi)	2.4	28	40	n.a.	n.a.
Indonesia (Jakarta)	1.7	56	70	3	3.3
Egypt (Cairo)	5.8	32	65	4	0.1
Zimbabwe (Harare)	1.1	66	18	18	0.8
Senegal (Dakar)	0.8	57	67	30	n.a.
Philippines (Manila)	1.0	48	76	6	0.1
Côte d'Ivoire (Abidjan)	0.7	21	25	17	n.a.
Morocco (Rabat)	2.7	46	16	6	0.0
Ecuador (Quito)	0.7	79	54	40	0.6
Jordan (Amman)	0.8	75	15	15	0.0
Colombia (Bogota)	1.6	62	8	8	3.0
Thailand (Bangkok)	1.1	68	17	3	0.3
Tunisia (Tunis)	1.5	67	29	29	6.4
Jamaica (Kingston)	2.1	41	50	33	3.6
Turkey (Istanbul)	1.3	60	51	51	0.1
Poland (Warsaw)	8.3	35	0	0	0.0
Slovakia (Bratislava)	8.3	14	0	0	0.0
Chile (Santiago)	0.5	80	20	n.a.	1.3
Algeria (Algiers)	8.8	45	4	4	0.9
Malaysia (Kuala Lumpur)	0.9	59	12	12	4.1
Russia (Moscow)	201.4	0	0	0	1.9
Mexico (Monterrey)	0.5	83	16	4	0.5
South Africa (Johannesburg)	4.5	64	34	22	n.a.
Venezuela (Caracas)	0.4	65	54	54	n.a.
Brazil (Rio de Janeiro)	0.8	62	27	16	3.3
Hungary (Budapest)	4.2	45	1	1	5.0
Korea (Seoul)	0.9	40	6	5	0.4
Greece (Athens)	0.7	55	4	1	0.0
Israel (Tel Aviv)	0.8	80	2	0	0.1
Spain (Madrid)	1.0	74	0	0	1.7
Singapore (Singapore)	0.4	90	1	1	0.1
Hong Kong (Hong Kong)	3.4	43	5	3	0.0
United Kingdom (London)	2.0	57	0	0	3.0
Australia (Melbourne)	0.9	73	0	0	0.4
Netherlands (Amsterdam)	0.9	9	0	0	8.9
Austria (Vienna)	0.9	17	0	0	2.7
France (Paris)	0.5	43	0	0	5.6
Canada (Toronto)	0.8	60	5	0	1.0
United States (Washington,D.C.)	0.5	61	5	0	3.6
Germany (Munich)	1.4	17	1	0	0.9
Norway (Oslo)	2.1	74	0	0	4.0
Sweden (Stockholm)	1.1	45	0	0	0.3
Japan (Tokyo)	3.0	40	0	0	0.2
Finland (Helsinki)	0.6	63	0	0	7.7

Source: Housing Indicators Program [1994].

[a] For definitions and summary values, see chapter 23.

Table A27. A Comparison of Summary Values for Ten Housing Indicators for 1990 and 1995.

Country Groupings	House Price-to-Income Ratio 1990	1995	Rent-to-Income Ratio (%) 1990	1995	Floor Area per Person (m²) 1990	1995	Permanent Structures (%) 1990	1995	Unauthorized Housing (%) 1990	1995
Low-Income Countries	3.3	7.4	10.0	28.7	7.1	7.7	76	62	64.0	52.5
Low-Middle Income Countries	4.5	8.8	16.2	15.4	9.4	13.2	94	78	27.1	27.1
Upper Middle Income Countries	4.4	8.3	14.6	11.7	15.9	17.3	97	92	9.4	14.5
High-Income Countries	4.6	4.7	18.1	18.0	31.5	31.4	100	96	0.1	3.8
Southern Africa	2.2	6.9	10.0	27.3	7.8	8.0	79	61	56.4	51.4
Asia and the Pacific	5.0	9.4	18.6	23.7	10.2	9.5	86	73	48.3	41.2
Middle East and North Africa	6.4	9.7	14.7	17.8	9.3	12.6	95	84	22.7	25.9
Latin America and the Caribbean	2.4	3.8	19.8	20.2	15.6	14.7	90	80	26.8	26.4
Eastern Europe	7.0	12.2	4.2	4.4	20.6	17.8	99	98	0.0	5.7
All Developing Countries	3.7	7.9	14.0	21.5	10.1	11.2	94	73	31.5	36.0
Industrialized Countries	4.6	4.4	18.0	18.9	31.0	34.5	100	98	0.1	2.2
Global Average	5.0	7.5	15.8	21.2	18.0	13.6	91	76	24.9	31.3

Country Groupings	Land Development Multiplier 1990	1995	Infrastructure Expenditures per capita 1990	1995	The Housing Credit Portfolio (%) 1990	1995	Housing Production (units per 1,000 people) 1990	1995	Value of New Stock-to-GCP Ratio (%) 1990	1995
Low-Income Countries	3.8	5.0	$15	$16	3	7	5.6	5.4	3.2	10.0
Low-Middle Income Countries	4.0	3.9	$48	$48	9	12	7.7	8.5	8.6	6.2
Upper Middle Income Countries	5.2	4.6	$62	$136	18	20	6.1	5.6	4.4	5.1
High-Income Countries	2.4	5.3	$706	$421	24	27	6.5	4.8	4.1	3.2
Southern Africa	5.6	5.2	$17	$22	5	8	5.2	5.7	3.1	8.9
Asia and the Pacific	2.6	3.8	$45	$25	5	5	7.6	9.3	11.7	9.0
Middle East and North Africa	5.0	6.0	$51	$71	7	10	7.2	5.5	15.9	8.8
Latin America and the Caribbean	3.4	4.6	$30	$138	20	24	6.0	7.3	3.7	7.0
Eastern Europe	3.7	5.5	$50	$80	18	8	3.8	2.6	3.5	3.9
All Developing Countries	4.0	4.9	$27	$59	7	11	6.6	6.2	6.2	7.6
Industrialized Countries	2.4	3.9	$621	$623	23	35	6.4	5.2	4.2	3.5
Global Average	4.7	4.8	$291	$96	15	13	6.9	6.1	7.9	7.3

Sources: Housing Indicators Program [1994]; United Nations data for the Habitat II Conference, in Flood [1997].

Notes

Chapter 2 (pages 23–28):

1.   In the United Kingdom "in 1987 the value of residential buildings accounted for approximately 40 percent of total personal sector wealth" [Meen, 1990, 30].

2.   Data for housing investment as a percentage of gross fixed capital formation and as a percentage of the gross domestic product (GDP) in 22 Western European countries and the United States for the years 1980, 1988, 1989, 1990 and 1991 was obtained from United Nations, 1992, table 2, pp. 4–6. The median value for housing investment as a percentage of gross fixed capital formation was 25%, with two-thirds of the values falling between 20% and 31%. The median value for housing investment as a percentage of the gross domestic product was 5.1%, with two-thirds of the values falling between 3.7% and 7.2%.

Chapter 4 (pages 37–55):

1.   Nicaragua. National Institute of Statistics and Census, 1995, summarized in Internationale Projekt Consult, 1998, table 3, 3.

2.   Flood, 1997, table 13, 1656 reports an average value of 3.8 for Latin America and the Caribbean. See also table A27.

3.   Data obtained from the Banco Central for October 1996, adjusted for inflation, quoted in Internationale Projekt Consult, 1998, table 7, 10.

4.   A fourth use of indicators – the administrative, nonmarket allocation of resources to localities for programs or projects based on observed indicator values – has been in practice in Great Britain and Australia, as well as in all centrally planned economies, and will be discussed in later chapters only in passing.

5.   The United Nations Economic Commission for Europe's *Annual Bulletin of Housing and Building Statistics for Europe* is an exception. See, for example, United Nations, 1992.

6.   With the sad exception of cities engaged in war or civil war.

Chapter 5 (pages 56–66):

1.   The work by Burns and Grebler [1977] is an exception. Using U.N. statistics, it examines *one* observed empirical regularity – the change in the national level of housing investment as per capita income increased. There are several journal articles (see for example Annez and Wheaton, 1984) that examine global empirical regularities in the housing sector, many of which will be reviewed here, but not books.

2.   Examples of the latter are Donnison [1967]; McGuire [1981]; Donnison and Ungerson [1982]; Baross and van der Linden [1990]; Van Vliet [1990]; and Hårsman and Quigley [1991].

3.   For a discussion of the 1985–1994 global real estate cycle, see Renaud [1994].

4.   Resolution 1993/77 of the United Nations Commission on Human Rights, for example, proclaims forced evictions to be a gross violation of human rights.

5.   Schmidt [1989], who set out to test the "convergence" theory empirically in 18 countries could not find statistical confirmation for it, concluding that "institutional and ideological factors loom large" [89].

6.   Nicaragua, for example, adopted the California building code, practically in its entirety, after the earthquake in Managua in 1973.

7.   UNCHS (Habitat) now manages the Urban Observatory , a web page devoted to urban indicators — www.urbanobservatory.org.

8.   The final selection of cities for the survey, beyond the criteria discussed here, also depended on identifying a distinguished housing expert who was a recognized authority on housing in his or her country, and had access to official and academic sources of data. Most of these consultants (more than 75%) were contracted to do the work. The rest, mostly members of the European Housing Research Network, volunteered.

9.   Data for South Africa and the Russian Federation were collected and included in the Survey in 1992.

10.   See UNCHS [1993]; and Angel et al. [1993, 23–42].

11.   The largest city in the country.

Chapter 6 (pages 67–80):

1.   A seventh relationship — the effects of housing market outcomes on the economic, social, and political context — is only explored in passing because of data limitations. The present study does not shed much more light on these effects than that provided by earlier studies [e.g., Ermisch, 1990].

2.   In the longer term, land and construction prices, for example, cannot be assumed to be independent of housing demand. In this study, it is assumed that they are, but occasionally reversed causality is discussed as well.

3.   For a state-of-the-art review of housing market research, see, for example, Smith et al. [1988].

4.   In this context, housing tenure measures, as well as measures of residential mobility, are taken to be specific aspects of housing quantity and quality.

5.   The other two housing market conditions — the availability of construction finance and subsidies — will be discussed only in passing. As we noted earlier, failure to obtain good data on subsidies, beyond those presented in chapter 9, made it difficult to include them in modeling housing market conditions.

6.   We standardize each data item by subtracting from it the average value for the sample as a whole, and dividing the result by the standard deviation for the sample as a whole. The β-coefficients are also referred to as z-scores in the statistical literature [see, for example, Freund and Simon, 1997, 89].

7.   Initially, I also attempted to test whether the income and price elasticities, in and of themselves, were significantly different for enabling and nonenabling housing policy environments. I divided the sample into two discrete groups (an enabling group and a nonenabling group). I then introduced a dummy variable K, which takes on the value 1 for enabling regimes and a value of 0 for non-enabling regimes. K now replaced the Enabling Index P in equations (10) and (11). I also introduced the products of both $\ln Y$

and $\ln p^*_h$ and K as new variables in the demand equation, and the product of $\ln p^*_h$ and K as a new variable in the supply equation. I then rewrote the two equations as:

$$(12) \quad \ln Q_d = g_0 + g_1 \ln Y + g_2 \ln D + g_3 \ln p^*_h + g_4 \ln F + g_5 K$$
$$+ g_6 K \ln Y + g_7 K \ln p^*_h; \text{ and}$$

$$(13) \quad \ln Q_s = h_0 + h_1 \ln C + h_2 \ln L + h_3 \ln p^*_h + h_4 K + h_5 K \ln p^*_h .$$

Clearly, for nonenabling regimes, K and all the products involving K are 0. The estimated coefficients g_1, g_3, and h_3 therefore represent the elasticities for nonenabling regimes. In turn, the estimated coefficients $(g_1 + g_6)$, $(g_3 + g_7)$ and $(h_3 + h_5)$ represent the elasticities for enabling regimes, and if we can determine that one or more of these coefficients are significantly different from 0, then we can conclude that the respective elasticities for enabling regimes are significantly different that those of nonenabling regimes. Unfortunately, the estimation of the effect of the policy environment on demand and supply elasticities did not yield any statistically significant results, and such effects must await more detailed comparative studies. One such study did find that stricter regulatory regimes in Malaysia and Korea resulted in lower price elasticities of supply, in comparison with Thailand, which was found to have a less restrictive regulatory regime [Malpezzi and Mayo, 1997].

Chapter 8 (pages 96–108):

1.   The first recorded terminating building club was in Birmingham in 1775 [Boddy 1980, 5–6, in Saunders 1990, 19].

2.   Condominium and cooperative legislation, enabling the ownership and exchange of apartments, is an essential prerequisite for providing long-term finance for this market segment.

3.   An additional regulatory concern, not included in the survey, is the existence (or nonexistence) of regulations to combat discrimination in mortgage lending.

4.   A maximum upper limit for this indicator was calculated by adding two standard deviations to the mean of the reported values. Missing values were estimated from regional and subregional medians.

5.   In any given country, if real interest rates were positive, a 0% interest rate was assigned in the calculation of the Credit Rationing Index.

6.   It would have been worthwhile to include in the survey quantitative indicators that measure some aspects of housing finance development — for example, secondary market development (defined as residential mortgage sales on the secondary market as a percentage of mortgage originations [McGuire, 1981, 151]), or mortgage insurance development (defined as the number of mortgage insurance applications received and endorsed [U.S. HUD, 1994, 18] as a percentage of all mortgages).

Chapter 9 (pages 109–131):

1.   In the ensuing discussions the term "subsidies" incorporates both subsidies and taxes.

2.   The Housing Allowances experiment, undertaken in the United States during the 1970s is an exception; see Hamilton [1979].

3.   Commonly of the order of 0.3–1.5. A value of +1.0 seems to be the best estimate [Rosen, 1979]. See discussion of income elasticities in chapters 19–23.

4.   Where they were not stigmatized and in short supply, they were often appropriated by higher-income groups.

5.   Subsidies that support operating expenses tend to delay or prevent efficient operation.

6.   The taxation of the imputed rental income of owner–occupiers will lead to a better utilization of the housing stock and to the elimination of an unnecessary advantage to owner–occupiers over renters.

7.   Property taxes have been found to be extremely regressive in run–down neighborhoods, often accelerating property abandonment. In Baltimore in 1970, for example, where reassessment was not forthcoming in the face of lower property values, property taxes in blighted neighborhoods were found to be 14.9% of the market value of the property as against 1.5% in the rest of the city [Peterson, 1973, 111].

8.   This is an inferior measure to one that measured the same percentage in new construction rather than in the stock as a whole, because many countries with substantial public housing no longer engage in new production.

Chapter 10 (pages 132–148):

1.   Construction volume in a typical city in a given year usually breaks down into 1/3 to 1/2 residential building, 1/4 to 1/3 nonresidential building, and 1/4 to 1/3 public works (utilities, highways, streets, dams, sewerage and water supply, and military construction). For data on the United States for the period 1958–1977, see U.S. Department of Commerce [1978], in Lange and Mills [1979, table 5–6, 107].

2.   Land use surveys in major U.S. cities between 1945 and 1960, for example, found 39.0% of all developed land in residential use, 10.9% in commercial use, 4.8% in industrial use, 19.7% in public use, and 25.7% in use for roads and highways [Niedercorn and Hearle, 1964, table 1, 106].

3.   For such a survey, see World Bank [1994].

4.   In the case of solid–waste disposal it may be limited to enforcement of households' obligations to disposal and the regulation of private–sector collection and disposal.

5.   In the majority of cases, "tolls charged directly to users do not cover the full cost of roads" [World Bank, 1994, 97].

6.   Pennsylvania has been experimenting with separating the property tax into two: "Fifteen cities in Pennsylvania... are lowering the taxes on buildings, thereby encouraging improvement and renovations, while raising the tax on land values, thus discouraging land speculation" [Hartzok, 1997, 205]. The split tax is widely used in Australia and New Zealand, and has been in use in Pittsburgh since 1913. In Pittsburgh in 1985, the tax on land was more than six times the tax on improvements [Carlson, 1985, 1].

7.   The purchase of public right–of–way is most transparent where only the minimum necessary amount of land is bought. Occasionally, a case is made for purchasing additional land that can then be sold at market prices to recover costs, or used as collateral for loans. In 1871, "the Canadian House of Commons adopted a policy of land grants as a way to subsidize railway construction without having to raise the rate of taxation" [World Bank, 1994, 94].

8.   It should be noted that builders and developers have a stake in putting pressures on politicians and planners to direct public roads toward their lands; builders and developers also have an interest in contributing right–of–way or paying for such roads themselves, as another way of capturing the unearned increment. In Bangkok, for example, in areas ripe for urban development where no public roads exist, rural landowners contribute land along the edges of their sites for road right–of–way [Angel et al., 1987, 71–72].

9.   Unless, of course, several such services are provided by a single company.

10.   There are exceptions to this pattern. In urban Nicaragua, for example, where there are many illegal connections to the water and electricity networks that are tolerated by the authorities, formalizing and upgrading connections is likely to lead to considerably higher costs.

11.   Such subsidies were provided in Bogota and Medellin, Colombia, in the early 1980s [World Bank, 1994, 81].

12.   In upgrading infrastructure in slums and squatter settlements, care must be taken to avoid mass dislocation of the original residents through gentrification.   Where infrastructure improvements are modest and the increase in tenure security is gradual, the original settlers are usually able to stay in the community. A study of an upgraded settlement in Madras, India, reported little dislocation of the original residents [Robben, 1984]. In Mexico City and Tunis, on the other hand, one-third of the original residents ere displaced by higher income households [Ferchiou, 1982].

Chapter 11 (pages 149–166):

1.   Fear of rural–urban migration is still cited by officials as their rationale for not improving urban housing conditions, although it is widely acknowledged that the housing occupied by new migrants is notoriously worse that their previous rural dwellings.

2.   In Japan, for example, which has a high degree of industrial concentration in the construction sector, the practice of bid–rigging in large contracts was pervasive and practically taken for granted well into the 1990s [Woodall, 1996].

3.   Similar exclusionary practices are reported in Great Britain [Young and Kramer, 1978], even though Britain has a much more centralized local government structure.

4.   What is more surprising is that authorities, mostly in the developing countries, have had to tolerate (for a time) invasions of land for housing by squatters, which *is* a crime against property. Upon closer examination, however, most (but not all) squatting has occurred on public land or land in disputed ownership, and it was not seen as a threat to private property owners. Squatters have usually been respectful of occupied land, whether in agricultural or in urban use, and have refrained from encroaching upon it.

5.   An indicator that may better capture the impact of the regulatory regime on the housing sector is the *regulatory premium*, defined as the percentage increase in the cost of the lowest-priced unit produced by the formal sector (and conforming to land subdivision and building regulations), and the cost of a similar–quality unit produced by the informal sector (and not conforming to regulations).

Chapter 12 (pages 167–175):

1.   The correlations among various policy dimensions should make it possible to design simpler overall measures of housing policy in the future.

2.   The difference between their variances was significant at the 1% level of confidence.

Chapter 13 (pages 179–191):

1.   The Corruption Index is based on several published surveys that are analyzed and published regularly by Transparency International [Crosette,1995, 2]; see also www.transparency.de.

2.   The Freedom Index is therefore high in countries that have fewer freedoms, and lower in countries with more freedom.

3.   It is possible, but not simple, to measure the overall level of segregation in a city by urban residential segregation, defined as the maximum ratio of the highest and the lowest concentrations of any minority group (defined in terms of income, race, tribe, or place of origin) in any two census tracts in the city.

4.   An additional measure, not included in the Global Survey, is banking sector credit, defined as the ratio of total credit in the banking sector and the GDP. This measure indicates the overall strength of the financial sector, which has a direct bearing on the strength of the housing finance sector.

5.   The 12 indicators chosen for constructing the Development Index were those that were associated with the intuitive notion of "development" — higher GNP per capita, higher household incomes, a better income distribution, more freedom, higher life expectancy, lower infant mortality, lower adult illiteracy, more government expenditures on welfare, higher levels of urbanization, slower rates of urban growth, smaller households, and greater financial depth. The individual indicator values were each normalized by subtracting the average value for the sample as a whole and dividing by the standard deviation for the sample as a whole. The index was constructed as an equally weighted sum of the 12 indicators and then normalized again on a range of 0–100. Out of a total of 636 (i.e., 12 × 53) values used to construct the index, there were 47 missing values. These were replaced by regional median values (and in the case of Scandinavia and the Indian subcontinent with subregional medians) to calculate the index for all the countries in the sample.

Chapter 15 (pages 204–219):

1.   This is one of the key responsibilities in the charters of the Federal National Mortgage Association (Fannie Mae) and the Federal Home Loan Mortgage Corporation (Freddie Mac) in the United States, but it is not clear that they can or do, in fact, fulfill it in periods of strong economic downturns [Weicher, 1994, 56–60].

Chapter 16 (pages 220–231):

1.   Given the value of urban housing in 1990 (see calculation in chapter 21, 288).

2.   Direct lending is often found in the developed countries as well, either in the form of a loan for a down payment or where developers of new housing, as well as families selling their own homes, are forced to grant loans to buyers when there are restrictions on the supply of bank financing for housing.

3.   Relying in such cases on group loans to credit unions or cooperatives is less than satisfactory, because they rarely have adequate means of disciplining offenders.

4.   And even when these conditions are met, governments may need to step in and facilitate mortgage lending before the private sector joins the fray. The Federal Housing Administration (FHA), for example, has led the way in demonstrating the feasibility of long–term self–amortizing loans in the United States in the 1930s by creating an insurance fund that guarantees mortgage loans.

5.   An alternative distributional measure may be the mortgage loan structure, defined as the respective shares of the total mortgage portfolio in several loan–amount categories (e.g., below one annual median household income, between 1 and 2 median incomes, and above 2 median incomes) [Woodward and Weicher, 1989, 311].

6.   Measured by the logarithm of GNP per capita.

Chapter 17 (pages 232–249):

1.   These will be presented and discussed at greater length in chapter 18 as additional measures of the quantity of housing. Value measures are often used to measure the quantity of housing in the literature (see, for example, Follain,1979, and Mayo, 1981b].

2.   Assuming a household pays no more than 25% of its monthly income on housing.

3.   The level of urbanization was not included; it was highly correlated with the logarithm of median household income (+0.74) and with the city population growth rate (−0.62). Household size has been eliminated in the price models (but not in the quantity models); it was also highly correlated with the city population growth rate (+0.63). The credit-to-value ratio was not included; it yielded very similar results to the housing credit portfolio.

4.   Through a comparison of its β–coefficients.

5.   Unfortunately, we have not been able to incorporate a forceful measure of this policy dimension into the Enabling Index.

Chapter 18 (pages 250–258):

1.   For a more elaborate exposition of the house as temple see Lawlor [1994].

Chapter 19 (pages 259–268):

1.   For a more general discussion of this phenomenon in Russia, see Lee and Struyk [1996, 661].

2.   An alternative measure to persons per room is the number of crowded dwellings (dwellings in which the number of persons exceeds the number of rooms); see, for example, McGuire [1981, 111].

3.   The high value for Jordan reflected a temporary upsurge occasioned by the massive inflow of returnees from the Persian Gulf in 1990.

4.   In logarithmic form.

5.   The model for the fifth measure — households per dwelling unit — was not statistically significant and was therefore excluded from the foregoing discussion.

6.   Through comparisons of their β–coefficients.

7.   The demand and supply models for the fifth measure — households per dwelling unit — were also not statistically significant.

Chapter 20 (pages 269–281):

1.   Survey results reported in *Japan Economic Journal* (May 22, 1979) quoted in McGuire [1981, 229].

2.   The latter quadratic estimate was used to calculate the Weighted Housing Price Index in chapter 17.

3.   Country data and summary data for the hedonic rent-to-value ratio are not shown here. They can be easily calculated from table A23. The statistical models for this index were weak and not robust, and therefore they are also not shown.

4.   The association with household income should be interpreted with caution, because household income is one of the three components of the Construction Quality Index. Still, we should remember that the other two components of the index are also highly correlated with household income.

5.   Because their *t*-statistics were not significant at the 10% level of confidence.

Chapter 21 (pages 282–294):

1.   With a standard error term of ±35 trillion (see calculation on page 288).

2.   It should be noted here that median rent is not necessarily the rent on the median-valued house, although we have assumed this to be the case in our analysis.

3.   The median value is estimated to be in the range of 0.7 times the average value. The average value of a dwelling unit in the city is then derived from the median house value in that city by dividing it by 0.7.

4.   Data for the consumption-to-GDP Ratio for 1990 are given in IMF [1998, 166-169].
he median value for this ratio in our sample was 0.63. The median ratio of the number of
dwelling units and the number of households was 0.96. These ratios explain why the
median values for this index are consistently lower than the house value-to-income ratios.
5.   The Global Survey asked for the value of a median-priced house without
distinguishing between owner-occupied units and rental units, and therefore the value for
the median-priced house was used for both. In reality, there are good reasons to suspect
that rental units will be smaller and of lower quality than owner-occupied units.
6.   Median values were assumed to be more reliable than average values, because they
are less subject to the undue influence of extreme values.
7.   Because house values and rents vary with incomes, and because the income variable
in our model is the logarithm of median household income, we use their logarithms rather
than their actual values as dependent variables.
8.   Again, we used the logarithm of rent as the dependent variable in the model. The
housing credit portfolio was not used an an independent variable in this model, as it was
not postulated to have a strong influence on rents.
9.   For example, Malpezzi and Mayo [1987], in their comparative study of the income
elasticity of housing demand in eight developing countries, use the rental value as a
dependent variable, and income and household size as the independent variables
[691-697].

Chapter 22 (pages 295-314):

1.   The trend rates and standard deviations were calculated directly from the data tables
provided by Doan [1998, table A, 182-183]. My calculations vary slightly from those
reported by Doan in the text.
2.   With the proviso that the demand for and supply of new housing are not clear
concepts and must be approached with caution.
3.   Information on the profitability of housing investment—for example, the return on
housing investment (defined as the ratio of the rate of return on housing investment and
the rate of return on common stocks in a given year)—could provide a useful measure of
the vitality of the housing sector.
4.   Alternatively, the vacancy rate may be considered another quantity measure—similar
to dwelling units per 1,000 people—that describes the relationship between households
and dwelling units in the sector at large. Residential mobility is not inherently associated
with any group of housing indicators, and may need to be treated on its own.
5.   The only difference between the last two measures is in their denominators; one is
normalized by the number of dwelling units and one by the urban population. Housing
production is a commonly used measure in international comparisons, but because
household size varies considerably from country to country, the same value of housing
production may house three times the number of households in Nigeria (where household
size is 6.0) than in Norway (where household size is 2.0). This indicator was, therefore,
found to be less than satisfactory, and was included mainly for purposes of completeness.
6.   Because this estimate includes the value of land (which is not normally included in
calculations of housing investment as a share of the GDP in national accounts) the values
reported in the following tables and in the Appendix table are considerably larger. This
indicator was estimated by the following formula: gross urban housing investment = (new
dwelling units) x (median house price)/ [(number of households) x (median household
income) x (consumption-to-GDP Ratio)].

7.   We estimated the regression lines separately for developing countries and industrialized countries. The correlation coefficients for both lines were not significant at all.

8.   In all the models, we used GNP per capita as a measure of the level of economic development, instead of household income, to make comparisons with the existing literature more transparent.

9.   It is difficult to grasp intuitively what the "supply of residential mobility" might be.

Chapter 23 (pages 315–339):

1.   In this discussion, we view the distinction between formal–sector and informal–sector housing as a tenure distinction because the two sectors involve different bundles of rights. In particular, informal–sector housing, because of its usual failure to conform to rules and regulations governing construction, land subdivision, and land use, offers dwellers considerably less protection from unscrupulous promoters of informal housing, from neighbors, and from the authorities.

2.   We also examine homelessness as a form of tenure, perceiving it as a bundle of rights, including the right to be visibly homeless and the right of the homeless to minimum basic housing guaranteed by the state.

3.   There are exceptions to this rule. In Italy, for example, informal–sector housing that is developed along very similar lines to that practiced in developing countries is referred to as *Abusivismo*. It is widespread and includes both low–income housing, higher income housing, and speculative development. It was estimated that by 1975 "one out of every four inhabitants of Rome lived in an unauthorized structure" [Guttenberg, 1988, 266].

4.   The minimum price must at least cover the operating cost of maintaining it at the legally accepted or culturally expected standard, as well as the opportunity cost of the land that it occupies.

5.   If shelters do not eliminate homelessness, then the resources presently invested in shelters should be redirected toward housing solutions, such as cubicle hotels, that do eliminate homelessness. "Especially falling short are the mass dormitory shelters in our largest cities that offer no privacy, little security, for persons or possessions, and little more than beds and sanitary facilities" [Rossi, 1989, 204].

6.   We have already discussed the proportion of the housing stock in public ownership (see chapter 9). Summary data for this indicator appears in table 9.1 and the data for each city appears in table A11.

7.   This definition failed to include built structures that are occupied illegally by squatters. Squatter settlements that are recognized by the authorities as permanent settlements and that are provided with documentation to this effect have been excluded from the definition.

8.   This definition includes the population of homeless shelters, following the practice in the United States and elsewhere, so as to enable consultants to use available data. A similar approach was adopted by O'Flaherty [1996] as a compromise (in spite of his objection to the definition) to facilitate his economic analysis.

9.   At the time of writing, the median value was already significantly lower than it was in 1990.

10.   The Home Ownership Premium cannot be considered a quantity outcome; it is, in fact, a price outcome.

References

Alm, J., and R. Buckley. 1994. "Decentralization, Privatization, and the Solvency of Local Governments in Reforming Economies: The Case of Budapest," *Environment and Planning C* 12: 333–346.

Al-Wansharisi, Ahmad, 1909. *La Pierre de Touche des Fetouas*, vol. 2. n.d. Reprinted in *Archives Marocaines* 13: 310–311.

Anderson, I., P. Kemp and D. Quilgars. 1993. *Single Homeless People*. London: Her Majesty's Printing Office.

Andrusz, Gregory D. 1984. *Housing and Urban Development in the USSR*. New York: State University of New York Press.

Angel, Shlomo. 1983. "Upgrading Slum Infrastructure: Divergent Objectives in Search of a Consensus," *Third World Planning Review* 5 (No. 1, February): 5–22.

———, 1986. "Where Have All the People Gone? — Urbanization and Counter Urbanization in Thailand." In United Nations Centre for Human Settlements, *Spontaneous Settlement Formation in Rural Regions*, vol. 2: Case Studies. Nairobi: United Nations Centre for Human Settlements, 35–47.

Angel, Shlomo, Raymon W. Archer, Sidhijai Tanphiphat and Emiel A. Wegelin. eds., 1983. *Land for Housing the Poor*. Singapore: Select Books.

Angel, Shlomo, and Somsook Boonyabancha. 1988. "Land Sharing as an Alternative to Eviction." *Third World Planning Review* 10 (No. 2, May): 107–127.

Angel, Shlomo, David Dowall et al. 1987. *The Land and Housing Markets of Bangkok: Strategies for Public Sector Participation*. Bangkok: The Bangkok Land Management Study, Planning and Development Collaborative International.

Angel, Shlomo, Stephen K. Mayo, and William L. Stevens. 1993. "The Housing Indicators Program: A Report on Progress and Plans for the Future." *Netherlands Journal of Housing and the Built Environment* 8 (No.1): 13–48.

Angel, Shlomo, and Sopon Pornchokchai. 1990. "The Informal Land Subdivision Market in Bangkok." In *The Transformation of Land Supply Systems in Third World Cities*, edited by Paul Baross and Jan van der Linden. Aldershot: Avebury, 169–191.

Angotti, Thomas. 1977. *Housing in Italy: Urban Development and Political Change*. New York: Praeger Special Studies.

Annez, Philippe, and William Wheaton. 1984. "Economic Development and the Housing Sector: A Cross–National Model." *Economic Development and Cultural Change* 32 (No. 4): 749–766.

Apgar, William C. 1993. "An Abundance of Housing for All but the Poor." *Housing Markets and Residential Mobility*, edited by G. Thomas Kingsley and Margaret Austin Turner. Washington, D.C.: The Urban Institute Press, 99–123.

Arecchi, A. 1985. "Dakar." *Cities* 2 (No. 3): 198–211.

Audefroy, Joel. 1994. "Eviction Trends Worldwide and the Role of Local Authorities in Implementing the Right to Housing." *Environment and Urbanization* 6 (No. 1, April): 8–24.

Aufhauser, E., M. M. Fischer, and H. Schonhofer,, 1991. "The Vienna Housing Market: Structure, Problems and Policies." In *Housing Markets and Housing Institutions: An International Comparison*, edited by Björn Hårsman and John M. Quigley. Boston: Kluwer, 235–281.

Bachelard, Gaston. 1958. *La Poétique de l'Espace* (The Poetics of Space). English ed., 1994. Boston: Beacon Press.

Bahl, Roy W. 1979. "The Practice of Urban Property Taxation in Less Developed Countries." In *The Taxation of Urban Property in less Developed Countries*, edited by Roy W. Bahl, Madison: University of Wisconsin press, 9–47.

Ball, J. F., and B. E. Havassy. 1984. "A Survey of the Problems and Needs of Homeless Consumers of Acute Psychiatric Services." *Hospital and Community Psychiatry* 35: 917–921.

Ball, Michael. 1973. "Recent Empirical Work on the Determinants of Relative House Prices." *Urban Studies* 10 (No. 2): 213–233.

Ball, Michael J. 1990. *Under One Roof: Retail Banking and the International Mortgage Finance Revolution*. New York: St. Martin's press.

Barlow, J., and A. King. 1992. "The State, the Market and Competitive Strategy: The House-building Industry in the United Kingdom, France and Sweden." *Environment and Planning A* 24 (No.3, March): 381–400.

Baross, Paul, 1990. "Sequencing Land Development: The Price Implications of Legal and Illegal Settlement Growth." In *The Transformation of Land Supply Systems in Third World Cities*, edited by Paul Baross and Jan van der Linden. Aldershot: Avebury, 57–82.

Baross, Paul, and Jan van der Linden. 1990. *The Transformation of Land Supply Systems in Third World Cities*. Aldershot: Avebury.

Bartlett, Will, and Glen Bramley, eds. 1994. *European Housing Finance: Single Market or Mosaic?* Bristol: SAUS Publications.

Bauer, R. A., ed. 1966. *Social Indicators*. Cambridge, Mass.: MIT Press.

Bauman, Zygmunt. 1999. *In Search of Politics*. Stanford, Calif.: Stanford University Press.

Becker, Charles M., Andrew M. Hamer, and Andrew R. Morrison. 1994. *Beyond Urban Bias in Africa: Urbanization in the Era of Structural Adjustment*. Portsmouth: Heinemann.

Benevolo, Leonardo, 1993. *The European City*, Blackwell, Oxford.

Beng–Huat, Chua. 1997. *Political Legitimacy and Housing: Stakeholding in Singapore*. London: Routledge.

Bertaud, Alain, and Bertrand Renaud. 1997. "Socialist Cities without Land Markets." *Journal of Urban Economics* 41: 137–151.

Best, Richard. 1996. "Successes, Failures, and Prospects for Public Housing Policy in the United Kingdom." *Housing Policy Debate* 7 (Issue 3): 535–562.

Bi, A. T. G. 1996. "Private Company and State Partnership in the Management of Water Supply and Sewage Services: The Case of SODECI in Côte d'Ivoire." In *Managing Water Resources for Large Cities and Towns* edited by K. Ray and A. Dzikus. Nairobi: U.N. Centre for Human Settlements, 90–102.

Boddy, M. 1980. *The Building Societies*. London: Macmillan.

Boelhouwer, Peter, and Harry van der Heijden. 1992. *Housing Systems in Europe, Part I: A Comparative Study of Housing Policy*. Delft: Delft University Press.

Boleat, Mark, and Adrian Coles. 1987. *The Mortgage Market*. London: Allen and Unwin.

Borsch-Supan, A. 1987. *Econometric Analysis of Discrete Choice with Applications on the Demand for Housing in the U.S. and West Germany*. Lecture Notes in Economics and Mathematical Systems vol. 296. New York: Springer.

Bradshaw, John, 1988. *Healing the Shame that Binds You.*. Deerfield Beach, Fla.: Health Communications.

Bramley, Glen. 1994. "The Economic Fundamentals: Housing Finance and National Economies." In *Report of the 11th International School*. Münster: The International Union of Housing Finance Institutions, July, 53–90.

Bratt, Rachel G., Langley C. Keyes, Alex Schwartz, and Avis C. Vidal. 1994. "Confronting the Management Challenge in the Non–Profit Sector." New York: Community Development Research Center.

Braudel, Fernand. 1976. "Pre–Modern Towns." In *The Early Modern Town: A Reader*, edited by Peter Clark. London: Longman, 53–90.

Buckley, Robert M. 1993. "Mortgage Design under Inflation and Real Wage Uncertainty." *World Development* 231 (No. 3): 455–464.

———. 1996. *Housing Finance in Developing Countries*. London: Macmillan.

Buckley, Robert M., and Eugene N. Gurenko. 1995. "Housing Demand in Russia: Rationing Revisited." Unpublished manuscript. Washington, D.C.: Urban Development Division, World Bank.

Buckley, Robert, and Renaud. Bertrand. 1987. "Housing Finance in Developing Countries: Guidelines for Bank Operations." Draft. Washington, D.C.: Water and Urban Development Department, World Bank.

Burnett, John. 1986. *A Social History of Housing 1815–1985*. 2nd ed. London: Methuen.

Burns, Leland S., and Leo Grebler. 1977. *The Housing of Nations: Analysis and Policy in a Comparative Framework*. London: MacMillan.

Carlson, Eugene. 1985. "Regions: It's the Land Tax, by George, that Sets Pennsylvania Apart." *The Wall Street journal* (Eastern Ed.) March 12, 1.

Carrizosa, M., C. Fajardo, and R. Suescun. 1982. *Análisis Económico del Sistema de Valor Constante en Colombia*. Bogota: Centro de Estudios sobre Desarollo Economico. Universidad de Los Andes.

Case, Karl E. 1991. "Investors, Developers and Supply–side Subsidies: How Much Is Enough?." *Housing Policy Debate* 2 (Issue 2): 341–356.

Chang, Chin–Oh, and Peter Linneman. 1990. "Forecasting Housing Investment in Developing Countries." *Growth and Change* 21 (No. 1, Winter): 59–72.

Cheshire, Paul, and Stephen Sheppard. 1989. "British Planning Policy and Access to Housing: Some Empirical Estimates." *Urban Studies* 26 (No. 5): 469–485.

Choi, Songsu. 1998. "A Housing Market in the Making." *The China Business Review* 25 (No. 6, November–December): 14–19.

Clemens, Samuel [Mark Twain]. 1917. *Mark Twain's Letters*. New York: Harper.

Coles, Adrian. 1994. "The Building Society System." In *Report of the 11th International School*. Münster: The International Union of Housing Finance Institutions, July, 137–162.

Colleen, Leif. 1994. "Housing and the National Economy." In *Housing in Sweden in an International Perspective*, edited by Eva Hedman. Karlsrona: Boverket, 55–64.

———, 1994a. "Building Costs." In *Housing in Sweden in an International Perspective*, edited by Eva Hedman. Karlsrona: Boverket, 77–85.

Colleen, Leif, and Pia Lindgren. 1994. "Housing Construction." In *Housing in Sweden in an International Perspective*, edited by Eva Hedman. Karlsrona: Boverket, 65–75.

Consejo Nacional de Vivienda (CONAVI). 1999. *Política de Vivienda 1999–2004: Qué Hacer y Cómo Hacerlo*. Caracas: Government of Venezuela.

Cox, Kevin R., ed. 1978. *Urbanization and Conflict in Market Societies*. Chicago: Maaroufa.

Coyle, J. S. 1978. "Job Meccas for the '80s." *Money* 7 (May): 40–47.

Crossette, Barbara. 1995. "A Global Gauge of Greased Palms." *The New York Times*. August 20 (Week in Review): 2.

Currie, Lauchlin. 1990. "Residential Building as a Leading Sector." Unpublished paper. Bogota: Universidad de Los Andes.

Das, S. K. 1981. "Case Study: Bombay, India." In *Urban Slums: Slums and Squatter Settlements in the ESCAP Region*, edited by Madhu Sarin. Bangkok: United Nations Economic and Social Commission for Asia and the Pacific.

Day, Cathleen. 1993. *S&L Hell: The People and Politics behind the $1 Trillion Savings and Loan Scandal*. New York: Norton.

Dayal, John, and Ajoy Bose. 1977. *Delhi under Emergency*. New Delhi: Ess Ess Publications.

De Soto, Hernando. 1989. *The Other Path: The Invisible Revolution in the Third World*. New York: Harper and Row.

De Ramon, A. 1978. "Suburbios y Arrabales en un Area Metropolitana: el Caso de Santiago de Chile." In *Ensayos Histórico–Sociales Sobre la Urbanización en América Latina*, edited by Jorge E. Hardoy, et al. CLASCO. Buenos Aires: Ediciones SIAP, 113–130.

Deacon, A., J. Vincent, and R. Walker. 1995. "Whose Choice? Hostels or Homes? Policies for Single Homeless People." *Housing Studies* 10 (No. 3): 345–363.

deLeeuw, F. 1971. "The Demand for Housing—A Review of Cross-Section Evidence." *Review of Economics and Statistics* 53 (No. 1, February): 1–10.

Department of the Environment. 1977a. *Housing Policy: A Consultation Document*. Cmnd 6581. London: Her Majesty's Stationery office.

———. 1977b. *Housing Policy: Technical Volume—Part III*. London: Her Majesty's Stationery Office.

Do, A. Quang, and James D. Shilling. 1993. "The Cost of Mortgage Credit during the 1980s." Madison: Center of Urban Land Economics Research, University of Wisconsin.

Doan, Mason C. 1997. *American Housing Production 1880–2000*. Lanham, Md.: University Press of America.

Doebele, William A., ed. 1982. *Land Readjustment: A Different Approach for Financing Urbanization*. Lexington, Mass.: D. C. Heath.

Doebele, William A., Orville F. Grimes, and Johannes F. Linn. 1979. "Participation of Beneficiaries in Financing Urban Services: Valorization Charges in Bogota, Colombia." *Land Economics* 55 (No.1, February): 73–92.

Doling, John. 1997. *Comparative Housing Policy: Government and Housing in Advanced Industrial Countries*. London: Macmillan.

Donatos, George. 1995. "Quantitative Analysis of Investment in New Housing in Greece." *Urban Studies* 32 (No. 9): 1475–1487.

Donnison, David. 1967. *The Government of Housing*. Harmondsworth, U.K.: Penguin.

———. 1980. "A Policy for Housing." *New Society* 54 (No.938, November): 283–284.

Donnison, David, and C. Ungerson. 1982. *Housing Policy*. Harmondsworth, U.K.: Penguin.

Donovan, R. 1994. "Phoenix, Arizona: Privatization of Solid Waste Water Services." *The Urban Age* (October): 14.

Dorling, Daniel. 1994. "Negative Equity: The Nature and Incidence of Britain's Latest Housing Crisis." In *European Housing Finance: Single Market or Mosaic?* Edited by Will Bartlett and Glen Bramley. Bristol, U.K.: SAUS Publications, Bristol University.

Downs, Anthony. 1973. *Opening Up the Suburbs: An Urban Strategy for America.* New Haven, Conn.: Yale University Press.

———. 1988. "The Real Problem with Suburban Anti-Growth Policies." in *The Brookings Review* (Spring): 23–29.

———. 1991. "The Advisory Commission on Regulatory Barriers to Affordable Housing: Its Behavior and Accomplishments." *Housing Policy Debate* 2 (Issue 4): 1095 –1137.

Durand-Lasserve, Alain. 1990. "Articulation Between Formal and Informal Land Markets in Cities in Developing Countries: Issues and Trends." In *The Transformation of Land Supply Systems in Third World Cities,* edited by Paul Baross and Jan van der Linden. Aldershot: Avebury, 37–56.

Durand-Lasserve, Alain, and Raul Pajoni. 1995. "Synthesis of Case Studies: A Seminar Introduction." In *Integration of Irregular Settlements: Current Questions in Asia and Latin America,* edited by Valerie Clerk, Alain Durand-Lasserve, Francisco Luciano, Raul Pajoni, and Laurent Vidal. Paris: Groupment de Reserche Interurba, AITEC.

Eberstadt, Nicholas. 1995. *The Tyranny of Numbers: Mismeasurement and Misrule.* Washington, D.C.: AEI Press.

Edelman, Marian Wright. 1980. *Portrait of Inequality: Black and White Children in America.* Washington, D.C.: Children's Defense Fund.

Edwards, Michael. 1993. "Residential Mobility in a Changing Housing Market: The Case of Bucaramanga, Colombia." *Urban Studies* 20 (No. 2): 131–145.

Emmanuel, D. 1994. "An Analysis of the Market for Housing: Two Examples." In *Urban and Regional Development: Theory, Analysis and Policy,* edited by P. Gemitis, et al. Athens: Themelio, 265–306.

Engels, Friedrich. 1872. *The Housing Question.* English ed. translated by C. P. Dutt. New York: International Publishers, 1935.

———. 1892. *The Condition of the Working Class in England.* first published 1892. Reprinted Oxford: Blackwell, 1958.

Ermisch, John, ed. 1990. *Housing and the National Economy.* Aldershot: Avebury.

Estes, Richard J. 1988. *Trends in World Social Development: The Social Progress of Nations 1970-1987.* New York: Praeger.

Fainstein, Susan. 1997. "Justice, Politics, and the Creation of Urban Space." In *The Urbanization of Injustice,* edited by Andy Merrifield and Erik Swyngedouw, New York: New York University Press, 18–44.

Ferchiou, Ridha. 1982. "The Indirect Effects of New Housing Construction in Developing Countries." *Urban Studies* 19 (No. 2): 167–176.

Finkel, Gerald. 1997. *The Economics of the Construction Industry.* Armonk, N.Y.: M.E. Sharpe.

Fischel, William A. 1995. *Regulatory Takings: Law, Economics, and Politics.* Cambridge, Mass.: Harvard University press.

Flagler Management Group. 1989. "Measuring the Size of the Implicit Subsidies in the Low Cost Home Ownership (KPR) Program in Indonesia: a Preliminary Attempt." Unpublished report submitted to the Office of the State Minister of Housing and the World Bank.

Flood, Joe. 1993. "Housing Indicators in Australia: a Consultative Method." *Netherlands Journal of Housing and the Built Environment* 8 (No.1): 95–124.

———. 1997. "Urban and Housing Indicators." *Urban Studies* 34 (No. 10): 1635–1665.

Follain, James R. 1979. "The Price Elasticity of the Long-Run Supply of New Housing Construction." *Land Economics* 55 (No.2): 190–199.

Follain, James R., and Emmanuel Jimenez. 1985a. "The Demand for Housing Characteristics in Developing Countries." *Urban Studies* 22 (No. 5): 421–432.

———. 1985b. "Estimating the Demand for Housing Characteristics: A Survey and Critique." *Regional Science and Urban Economics* 15: 77–107.

Forrest, Ray, and Alan Murie. 1985. "Restructuring the Welfare State: Privatization of Public Housing in Britain." In *Housing Needs and Policy Approaches: Trends in Thirteen Countries,* edited by Willem van Vliet, Elisabeth Huttman, and Sylvia Fava. Durham, N.C.: Duke University Press, 97–109.

Francis, John G. 1993. *The Politics of Regulation: A Comparative Perspective.* Oxford: Blackwell.

Freedom House. 1990. *Freedom at Issue: Freedom around the World 1990.* New York: Freedom House.

Freund, John E., and Gary A. Simon. 1997. *Modern Elementary Statistics.* 9th ed. Upper Saddle River, N.J.: Prentice Hall.

Frumkin, Norman. 1994. *Guide to Economic Indicators.* 2nd ed. Armonk, N.Y.: M.E. Sharpe.

Gans, Herbert. 1962. *The Urban Villagers: Group and Class in the Life of Italian Americans.* New York: Free Press.

Gibb, Andrew, and Duncan Maclennan. 1991. "Glasgow: From Mean City to Miles Better." In *Housing Markets and Housing Institutions: An International Comparison,* edited by Björn Hårsman and John M. Quigley. Boston: Kluwer, 283–327.

Gilbert, Alan. 1983. "The Tenants of Self-help Housing: Choice and Constraint in the Housing Markets of Developing Countries." *Development and Change* 14: 449–477.

———. 1987. "Latin America's Urban Poor: Shanty Dwellers or Renters of Rooms?." *Cities* (February): 43–51.

———. 1990. "The Costs and Benefits of Illegality and Irregularity in the Supply of land." In *The Transformation of Land Supply Systems in Third World Cities,* edited by Paul Baross and Jan van der Linden. Aldershot: Avebury, 17–36.

Gilbert, Alan, and Ann Varley. 1991. *Landlord and Tenant: Housing the Poor in Urban Mexico.* London: Routledge.

Gillette, Clayton P. 1994. "The Private Provision of Public Goods; Principles and Implications." In *A Fourth Way?: Privatization, Property and the Emergence of New Market Economies,* edited by Gregory S. Alexander and Grazyna Skapska. New York: Routledge, 95–116.

Glasser, Irene. 1994. *Homelessness in Global Perspective.* New York: G.K. Hall.

Godschalk, David R., and David J. Hartzell. 1993. "Development Supply Constraints from Government Growth Management in Major MSAs." Paper presented at the Prudential Real Estate Investment Strategy Conference. Pinehurst, N.C., May.

Goetz, Edward G. 1993. *Shelter Burden: Local Politics and Progressive Housing Policy.* Philadelphia: Temple University Press.

Goldsmith, Mike. 1995. "Autonomy and City Limits." In *Theories of Urban Politics,* edited by David Judge, Garry Stoker, and Harold Wolman. London: Sage, 228–252.

Goode, Richard. 1987. "Obstacles to Tax Reform in Developing Countries" In *The Relevance of Public Finance to Policy Making,* edited by Hans M. van der Kar, and Barbara L. Wolfe. Detroit, Mich.: Wayne State University Press, 213–223.

Goodman, John L. 1992. "National Information Systems for Decision Making in Housing and Mortgage Finance." Unpublished paper. Washington, D.C.: U.S. Federal Reserve.

Grennel, P. 1972. "Planning for Invisible People: Some Consequences of Bureaucratic Values and Practices." In *Freedom to Build: Dweller Control of the Housing Process*, edited by J. F. C. Turner, and R. Fichter. Houndsmill: Macmillan, 95–121.

Grimes, Orville Jr. 1976. *Housing for Low Income Urban Families*. A World Bank Research Publication. Baltimore, Md.: Johns Hopkins University Press.

Grunfeld, Frans. 1985. "Segregation trends in the Netherlands." In *Housing Needs and Policy Approaches: Trends in Thirteen Countries*, edited by Willem Van Vliet. Durham, N.C.: Duke University Press, 276–290.

Guttenberg, Albert. 1988. "*Abusivismo* and the *Borgate* of Rome." In *Spontaneous Shelter: International Perspectives and Prospects*, edited by Carl V. Patton. Philadelphia: Temple University Press, 258–276.

Hagred, Ulrika. 1994. "The Housing Stock — Age, Quality and Forms of Tenures." In *Housing in Sweden in an International Perspective*, edited by Eva Hedman. Karlsrona: Boverket, 15–31.

Hair, Joseph F., Rolph E. Anderson, Ronald L. Tatham, and Bernie J. Grablowsky. 1979. *Multivariate Data Analysis with Readings*. Tulsa, Okla.: Petroleum Publishing Company.

Hallett, Graham. 1993. "The New Housing Shortage: An International Review." In *The New Housing Shortage: Housing Affordability in Europe and the USA*, edited by Graham Hallett. New York: Routledge, 207–265.

Hamer, Andrew. 1985. "Bogota's Unregulated Subdivisions: The Myth and Reality of Incremental Housing Construction." Staff Working Paper no. 734. Washington, D.C.: World Bank.

Hamilton, Rabinowitz, and Altshuler, Inc. 1987. "The Challenging Face of Misery: Los Angeles' Skid Row in Transition, Housing and Social Services Needs of Central City East." Los Angeles: Community Development Agency.

Hamilton, William R. 1979. *A Social Experiment in Program Administration: The Housing Allowances Administrative Agency Experiment*. Cambridge, Mass.: Abt Books.

Harding, Alan.1995. "Elite Theory and Growth Machines." In *Theories of Urban Politics*, edited by David Judge, Garry Stoker, and Harold Wolman. London: Sage, 35–53.

Hardoy, Jorge E. 1982. "The Building of Latin American Cities." In *Urbanization in Contemporary Latin America*, edited by Alan G. Gilbert. Chichester, U.K.: John Wiley, 19–34.

Hardoy, Jorge E., and David Satterthwaite. 1989. *Squatter Citizen: Life in the Urban Third World*. London: Earthscan Publications.

Harlow, Michael. 1995. *The People's Home: Social Rented Housing in Europe and America*. Oxford: Blackwell.

Harmon, Oscar R. 1988. "The Income Elasticity of Demand for Single-Family Owner-Occupied Housing: An Empirical Reconciliation." *Journal of Urban Economics* 24: 173–185.

Harpham, Trudy, Tim Lusty and Patrick Vaughan. 1988. *In the Shadow of the City: Community Health and the Urban Poor*. New York: Oxford University Press.

Harpham, Trudy, Patrick Vaughan, and Susan Rifkin. 1985. *Health and the Urban Poor in Developing Countries*. EPC Publication 5. London: London School of Hygiene and Tropical Medicine.

Hårsman, Björn, and John M. Quigley, eds. 1991. *Housing Markets and Housing Institutions: An International Comparison*. Boston: Kluwer.

Hartzok, Alanna. 1997. "Pennsylvania's Success with Local Property Tax Reform: The Split Rate Tax." *American Journal of Economics and Sociology* 56 (Issue 2, April): 205–213.

Harvey, David. 1997. "The Environment of Justice." In *The Urbanization of Injustice*, edited by Andy Merrifield, and Erik Swyngedouw. New York: New York University Press, 65–99.

————. 1977. "Government Policies, Financial Institutions and Neighborhood Change in United States Cities." In *Captive Cities*, edited by Michael Harloe. London: Wiley.

Hassan, Arif. 1988. "A Low Cost Sewer System by Low Income Pakistanis." In *Building Community: A Third World Case Book*, edited by Bertha Turner. London: Building Community Books, 81–88.

Hastings, James, ed. 1916. *Encyclopaedia of Religion and Ethics*, vol. 8. New York: Charles Scribner's Sons.

Hayek, Friedrich A. von. 1988. *The Fatal Conceit: The Errors of Socialism*. Vol. 1 of *The Collected Works of F.A. Hayek*, edited by W.W. Bartley III. Chicago: University of Chicago Press.

Hederstierna, Anders. 1994. "Housing Expenditure." In *Housing in Sweden in an International Perspective*, edited by Eva Hedman. Karlsrona: Boverket, 45–54.

Hedman, Eva, ed. 1994. *Housing in Sweden in an International Perspective*. Karlsrona: Boverket

Heerma, Enneus. 1993. "Housing Indicators: A Tool for Housing Policy." *Netherlands Journal of Housing and the Built Environment* 8 (No.1): 125–130.

Hegedus, Jozsef, and Ivan Tosics. 1993. "Housing Indicators in Transitional Economies: A New Tool for Policy Making." *Netherlands Journal of Housing and the Built Environment* 8 (No.1): 85–94.

Hegedus, Joszef, Stephen K. Mayo, and Ivan Tosics. 1996. *Transition of the Housing Sector in the East–Central European Countries*. Budapest: Metropolitan Research Institute.

Heidegger, Martin. 1971. "Building, Dwelling, Thinking." In *Poetry, Language, Thought* by Martin Heidegger, translated by Albert Hofstader. New York: Harper and Row, 143–161.

Henley, Andrew. 1998. "Residential Mobility, Housing Equity, and the Labour Market." *The Economic Journal* 108 (March): 414–427.

Hesse, J. J. 1991. "Local Government in a Federal State — The Case of West Germany." In *Local Government and Urban Affairs in International Perspective*, edited by J. J. Hesse. Baden Baden: Nomos Verlagsgesellschaft.

Hillebrandt, Patricia M. 1974. *Economic Theory and the Construction Industry*. London: Macmillan.

Hillman, Mayer.1996. "In Favour of the Compact City." In *The Compact City: A Sustainable Urban Form*, edited by Mike Jenks, Elisabeth Burton, and Katie Williams. London: E&FN Spon, 36–44.

Hills, John. 1991a. "Distributional Effects of Housing Subsidies in the United Kingdom." *Journal of Public Economics* 44: 321–352.

————. 1991b. *Unravelling Housing Finance: Subsidies, Benefits, and Taxation*. Oxford: Oxford University Press.

Hiorns, Frederick R. 1956. *Town Building in History*. London: George G. Harrap.

Hoffman, Michael, Barbara Haupt, and Raymond J. Struyk. 1992. *International Housing Markets: What We Know; What We Need to Know*. Washington, D.C.: Fannie Mae Office of Housing Policy Research.

Holcombe, Randall G., 1995. *Public Policy and the Quality of Life: Market Incentives vs. Government Planning*. Westport, Conn.: Greenwood press.

Honig, Margorie, and Randall K. Filer. 1993. "Causes of Intercity Variations in Homelessness." *The American Economic Review* 83 (No. 1, March): 248–255.

House of Commons Environment Committee. 1981. *Enquiry into Implications of Government's Expenditure Plans 1980–81 to 1983–84 for the Housing Policies of the Department of the Environment*. HC 383. i–ii. London: Her Majesty's Stationery Office.

Housing Indicators Program. 1991. *The Extensive Survey Instrument.* Joint Program of the World Bank and the U.N. Centre for Human Settlements (Habitat). Washington, D.C.: World Bank.

Housing Indicators Program. 1994. *The Global Survey of Housing Indicators–1990.* Final survey results. Unpublished. Joint Program of the World Bank and the U.N. Centre for Human Settlements (Habitat). Washington, D.C.: World Bank.

Howenstine, E. Jay. 1986. "The Consumer Housing Subsidy Approach Versus Producer Housing Subsidies." *Cities* (February): 24–40.

Hughes, G. A. 1980. "Housing and the Tax System." In *Public Policy and the Tax System,* edited by G.A. Hughes and G.M. Heal. Boston: George Allen and Unwin.

Hughes, Harold K. 1969. "Utopias and Cybernetic Cultures." In *Cybernetics and the Management of Large systems,* edited by Edmond M. Dewan. New York: Spartan Press. 1–24.

Husung, Sabine, and Peter G. Lieser. 1996. "GreenBelt Frankfurt." In *Local Places in the Age of the Global City,* edited by Roger Keil, Gerda G. Wekerle, and David V. J. Bell. Montreal: Black Rose Books, 211–222.

"I Owe, I Owe, So Off to Work I Go." 1993. *The Economist* (1992–1993), December 26 – January 8, 95–97.

Indrakumar, S. 1977. "Analysis and Evaluation of Sri Lanka's Ceiling on Housing Property Law." M.Sc. thesis. Bangkok: Asian Institute of Technology.

Inter–American Housing Union. 1989. *The Private System of Housing Financing in Chile 1930–1988.* Cuaderno no. 141. Lima, Peru: Secretariat of the Inter–American Housing Union.

International Monetary Fund (IMF). 1998. *International Financial Statistics Yearbook 1998.* Washington D.C.: IMF.

Internationale Projekt Consult, GmbH. 1998. "Análisis de la Demanda Habitational y Reflectiones Sobre el Diseño de un Programa de Vivienda en Nicaragua." Frankfurt: Internationale Projekt Consult.

International Union of Housing Finance Institutions. 1994. *Report of the 11th International School.* Münster, July.

Isaacs, Susan S. 1972. *Social Development in Young Children.* New York: Shocken Books.

Jacobs, Jane. 1961. *The Death and Life of Great American Cities.* New York: Random House.

Jagmohan. 1978. *Island of Truth.* New Delhi: Vikas Publishing House.

Jencks, Christopher. 1994. *The Homeless.* Cambridge, Mass.: Harvard University Press.

Jensen, R. 1995. "Managed Competition: A Tool for Achieving Excellence in Government." Paper presented at the regional seminar on Megacities Management in Asia and the Pacific. Manila: Asian Development Bank.

Jones, Bryan D. 1995. "Bureaucrats and Urban Politics: Who Controls? Who Benefits?" In *Theories of Urban Politics,* edited by David Judge, Garry Stoker, and Harold Wolman. London: Sage, 72–95.

Judge, David, Garry Stoker, and Harold Wolman, eds. 1995. *Theories of Urban Politics.* London: Sage Publications.

Kadas, Sandor. 1991. "Analysis of the Housing Sector, the Housing Market, and Housing Policy in the Budapest Metropolitan Area." In *Housing Markets and Housing Institutions: An International Comparison,* edited by Björn Hårsman and John M. Quigley. Boston: Kluwer, 207–234.

Karn, Valerie, and Harold Wolman. 1992. *Comparing Housing Systems: Housing Performance and Housing Policy in the United States and Britain.* Oxford: Clarendon Press.

Kaufmann, Dani. 1991. "The Forgotten Rationale for Policy Reform: The Productivity of Investment Projects." Paper presented at the Infrastructure and Urban Development Division, World Bank. Wasihngton D.C.: World Bank. April.

Keane, Thomas H. et al. 1991. *"Not in My Back Yard": Removing Barriers to Affordable Housing.* Report to President Bush and Secretary Jack Kemp by the Advisory Commission on Regulatory Barriers to Affordable Housing. Washington D.C.

Kemeny, Jim. 1977. "A Political Sociology of Home Ownership in Australia." *Australian and New Zealand Journal of Sociology* 13: 47–59.

———. 1992. *Housing and Social Theory.* London: Routledge.

Kettnaker, Volkmar, and Gustav Rosberg. 1994. "Households and Space Standards." In *Housing in Sweden in an International Perspective,* edited by Eva Hedman. Karlsrona: Boverket, 33–43.

Keyes, Langley C., Alex Schwartz, Avis C. Vidal, and Rachel G. Bratt. 1996. "Networks and Non-profits: Opportunities and Challenges in the Era of Federal Devolution." *Housing Policy Debate* 7 (Issue 2): 201–211.

Khan, Shahed Anwer. 1994. "Attributes of Informal Settlements Affecting Their Vulnerability to Eviction: A Case Study of Bangkok." *Environment and Urbanization* 6 (No. 1, April): 25–39.

Kim, Kyung–Hwan. 1997. "Housing Finance and Urban Infrastructure Finance." *Urban Studies* 34 (No.10): 1597–1620.

King, Robert G., and Ross Levine. 1993. "Finance and Growth: Schumpeter Might Be Right." *Quarterly Journal of Economics* 108 (No. 3): 717–737.

Kingsley, G. Thomas, and Margaret Austin Turner. 1993. "Housing Markets and Residential Mobility: An Overview." In *Housing Markets and Residential Mobility,* edited by G. Thomas Kingsley and Margaret Austin Turner.. Washington D.C.: The Urban Institute Press, 1–37.

Kravis, Irving B., Alan Heston, and Robert Summers. 1982. *World Product and Income: International Comparisons of Real Gross Product.* Baltimore, Md.: Johns Hopkins University Press.

Kresl, Peter Karl, and Balwant Singh. 1994. *The Competitiveness of Cities.* Paper presented to the Cities and the Global Economy Conference. Melbourne. November.

Kumar, Y. 1980. "An Exploratory Study of the Progress of Habitat–Hyderabad." M.Sc. thesis. Bangkok: Asian Institute of Technology.

Lai, Richard Tseng–Yu. 1988. *Law in Urban Design and Planning.* New York: Van Nostrand.

Lange, Julian E., and Daniel Quinn Mills. 1979. *The Construction Industry: Balance Wheel of the Economy.* Lexington, Mass.: D. C. Heath.

Lanjouw, Jean O. and Philip I. Levy, 1998. "Untitled: A Study of Formal and Informal Property Rights in Urban Ecuador." Economic Growth Center, Yale University, Center Discussion Paper 788, New Haven, April.

Lawlor, Anthony. 1994. *The Temple in the House: Finding the Sacred in Everyday Architecture.* New York: Putnam.

Le Corbusier. 1927. *Towards a New Architecture.* Reprinted, New York: Praeger Publishers, 1960.

———. 1943. *The Athens Charter.* Paris: La Librarie Pion. Reprinted, New York: Grossman, 1973.

Lee, Lisa, and Raymond J. Struyk. 1996. "Residential Mobility in Moscow during the Transition." *Journal of Urban and Regional Research* 20 (No.4, December): 656–670.

Leo, Christopher. 1997. "City Politics in an Era of Globalization." In *Reconstructing Urban Regime Theory: Regulating Urban Politics in a Global Economy*, edited by Mickey Lauria, Thousand Oaks, Calif.: Sage Publications.

Leveau, Remy.1985. "Public Property and Control of Property Rights: Their Effects on Social Structure in Morocco." In *Property, Social Structure, and Law in the Modern Middle East*, edited by Ann Elisabeth Mayer. Albany: State University of New York Press, 61–84.

Levine, Ross. 1997. "Financial Development and Economic Growth: Views and Agenda." *Journal of Economic Literature* 35 (June): 688–726.

Lim, William S. W. 1983. "Land Acquisition for Housing with Singapore as a Case Study." In *Land for Housing the Poor*, edited by Shlomo Angel et al. Singapore: Select Books, 393–410.

Lindgren, Pia. 1994. Table appendix in *Housing in Sweden in an International Perspective*, edited by Eva Hedman. Karlsrona: Boverket, 145–151.

Linn, Johannes F. 1983. *Cities in the Developing World: Policies for Their Equitable and Efficient Growth*. New York: Oxford University Press.

Lorraine, Dominique. 1997. "Introduction: The Expansion of the Market." In *The Privatization of Urban Services in Europe*, edited by Dominique Lorrain and Gerry Stoker, London: Pinter, 1–26.

Lujanen, Martti. 1993. "How Useful Are Housing Indicators as a Tool for Housing Policy in Europe?" *Netherlands Journal of Housing and the Built Environment* 8 (No.1): 77–84.

Mackay, Donald A. 1987. *The Building of Manhattan*. New York: Harper and Row.

Maclennan, Duncan, and Kenneth Gibb. 1993. "Housing Indicators and Research for Policy from the Perspective of Applied Economics." *Netherlands Journal of Housing and the Built Environment* 8 (No.1): 49–60.

Madge, J. 1976. *The Housing Experience of Newly Married Couples. Progress Report*. London: Centre for Studies in Social Policy.

Magnussen, Warren. 1996. *The Search for Political Space: Globalization, Social Movements, and the Urban Political Experience*. Toronto: University of Toronto Press.

Majone, Giandomenico. 1997. "From the Positive to the Regulatory State; Causes and Consequences of Changes in the Mode of Governance." *Journal of Public Policy* 17 (No. 2): 139–167.

Malpass, Peter, and Alan Murie. 1982. *Housing Policy and Practice*. London: Macmillan.

Malpezzi, Stephen. 1988. "Urban Housing and Financial Markets: Some International Comparisons." Working paper. Washington, D.C.: World Bank.

———. 1994. *Wisconsin Metropolitan Housing Markets: Some Simple Comparisons to Other Metro Areas*. Center for Urban Land Economics Research, Working Paper Series. Madison: School of Business, University of Wisconsin.

———. 1999. "The Regulation of Urban Development: Lessons from International Experience." Unpublished draft. Madison: Department of Real Estate and Urban Economics, University of Wisconsin.

Malpezzi, Stephen, and Gwendolyn Ball. 1991. *Rent Control in Developing Countries*. Technical paper. Washington, D.C.: World Bank.

Malpezzi, Stephen, and Richard K. Green. 1996. "What Has Happened to the Bottom of the U. S. Housing Market?." *Urban Studies* 33 (No.10): 1807–1820.

Malpezzi, Stephen, and Stephen K. Mayo. 1987. "The Demand for Housing in Developing Countries: Empirical Estimates from Household Data." *Economic Development and Cultural Change* 35 (No. 4, July): 687–721.

————. 1997. "Getting Housing Incentives Right: A Case Study of the Effects of Regulation, Taxes, and Subsidies on Housing Supply in Malaysia." *Land Economics* 73 (No. 3, August): 372–391.

Mangin, William. 1967. "Latin American Squatter Settlements: A Problem and a Solution." *Latin American Research Review* 2 (No. 3): 65–98.

Marcuse, Peter. 1994. "Property Rights, Tenure, and Ownership: Towards Clarity in Concept." In *Social Rented Housing in Europe: Policy, Tenure and Design*, edited by B. Danermark and I. Elander. Housing and Urban Policy Studies 9. Delft: Delft University Press.

Martin, Richard. 1979. "Land Tenure and Title Registration." Paper presented to the Seminar on Improving Low Income Residential Areas in South East Asian Cities. Bandung.

Marudachalam, V. M. 1991. "Slum Finances in Madras." *Habitat International* 15 (Nos. 1–2): 239–246.

Mathey, Kosta, ed. 1990. *Housing Policies in the Socialist Third World*. London: Mansell.

Mayer, Martin. 1978. *The Builders: Houses, People, Neighborhoods, Government, Money*. New York: W. W. Norton.

Mayo, Stephen K. 1981a. *Informal Housing in Egypt*. Cambridge, Mass.: Abt Associates.

————. 1981b. "Theory and Estimation of the Economics of Housing Demand." *Journal of Urban Economics* 10: 99–116.

————. 1990. *Housing Finance Development: Experiences in Malaysia and Thailand and Implications for Indonesia*. Paper prepared for the Office of the State Minister for Housing, Indonesia. Infrastructure and Urban Development Department. Washington, D.C.: World Bank.

Mayo, Stephen K., and David G. Gross. 1987. "Sites-and-services and Subsidies: The Economics of Low-Cost Housing in Developing Countries." *World Bank Economic Review* 1 (No. 2): 301–335.

McGuire, Chester C. 1981. *International Housing Policies: A Comparative Analysis*. Lexington, Mass.: Lexington Books.

Mearns, Andrew, et al. 1883. *The Bitter Cry of Outcast London: An Inquiry into the Conditions of the Abject Poor*. Extracts reprinted in *The Idea of the City in Nineteenth Century Britain*, edited by B. I. Coleman. London: Routledge and Kegan Paul, 1973, 172–174.

Meen, Geoffrey. 1990. "The Macroeconomic Effects of Housing Market Policies Under Alternative Mortgage Conditions." In *Housing and The National Economy*, edited by John Ermisch. London: Avebury, 28–42.

Mehta, M., and D. Mehta. 1989. *Metropolitan Housing Market: A Study of Ahmedabad*. New Delhi: Sage Publications.

Mengisteab, Kidane. 1995. "A Partnership of the State and the Market in African Development: What Is an Appropriate Strategy Mix?." In *Beyond Economic Liberalization in Africa: Structural Adjustment and the Alternatives*, edited by Kidane Mengisteab and B. Ikubolajeh Logan. London: Zed Books, 163–181.

Merrifield, Andy, and Erik Swyngedouw, eds. 1997. *The Urbanization of Injustice*. New York: New York University Press.

Merrill, Robert. 1971. "Toward a Structural Housing Policy: An Analysis of Chile's Low Income Housing Program." Ph.D. dissertation, Cornell University.

Miller, Alice. 1981. *The Drama of the Gifted Child: The Search for the True Self*. New York: Basic Books.

Milne, Alistair. 1992. "The Private Sector Finance of Affordable Housing in South Africa." London: Center for Economic Forecasting, London Business School.

Minford, Patrick, Michael Peel and Paul Ashton. 1987. *The Housing Morass: Regulation, Immobility and Unemployment*. Hobart Paperback no. 25. London: Institute of Economic Affairs.

Moehring, Eugene P. 1981. *Public Works and the Patterns of Urban Real Estate Growth in Manhattan*, 1835–1894. New York: Arno Press.

Mohai, Paul, and Bunyan Bryant. 1992. "Environmental Racism: Reviewing the Evidence." In *Race and the Incidence of Environmental Hazards*, edited by Bunyan Bryant and Paul Mohai. Boulder, Colo.: Westview press, 163–176.

Molina, Umberto. 1990. "Bogota: Competition and Substitutions between Urban Land Markets." In *The Transformation of Land Supply Systems in Third World Cities*, edited by Paul Baross and Jan van der Linden. Aldershot: Avebury, 295–307.

Moses, Robert. 1970. *Public Works: A Dangerous Trade*. New York: McGraw–Hill.

Mouillart and Occhipinti. 1990. "Le Logement et-il un Frein a la Mobilité en Europe?" *Les Cahiers du Credit Mutuel* (April): 22–29.

Muellbauer, John. 1990. "The Housing Market and the U.K. Economy: Problems and Opportunities." In *Housing and The National Economy*, edited by John Ermisch. London: Avebury, 48–71.

Muellbauer, John, and J. Murphy. 1989. *Why Has U.K. Personal Savings Collapsed?* Report Prepared for Credit Suisse, London Office.

Murie, Alan. 1983. *Housing Inequality and Deprivation*. London: Heinemann.

Murray, Michael P. 1993. *Subsidized and Unsubsidized Housing Stocks 1937–1987: Crowding Out and Cointegration*. Unpublished manuscript, Bates College.

Muth, Richard F. 1960. "The Demand for Non–Farm Housing." In *The Demand for Durable Goods*, edited by Arnold C. Harberger. Chicago: University of Chicago Press.

Neil, C. C., et al. 1992. *Homelessness in Australia*, volume 1: *Conceptual Issues*. Melbourne: Ministerial Advisory Committee on Homelessness and Housing.

New Jersey Supreme Court. 1975. *Southern Burlington County N.A.A.C.P. v. Township of Mount Laurel*. March 24.

Newton, Peter, and Maryann Wulff. 1985. "State Intervention in Urban Housing Markets: Melbourne, 1945–1980." In *Housing Needs and Policy Approaches: Trends in Thirteen Countries*, edited by Willem Van Vliet. Durham, N.C.: Duke University Press, 110–127.

Newton, Kenneth. 1978. "Conflict Avoidance and Conflict Suppression: The Case of Urban Politics in the United States." In *Urbanization and Conflict in Market Societies* , edited by Kevin R. Cox. Chicago: Maaroufa, 76–93.

Nicaragua. National Institute of Statistics and Census. 1995. *National Census of Nicaragua–1995*. Managua: Government of Nicaragua.

Niedercorn, John H., and Edward F. R. Hearle. 1964. "Land Use Trends in Forty–Eight Large American Cities." *Land Economics* 40 (No. 1): 105–109.

Noguchi, Yukio. 1990. *Baburu no Keizaigaku, (The Economics of the Bubble)*, Tokyo: Nihon Keizai Sinbunsha.

Norwood, Hugh C. 1979. "Port Moresby: Pattern of Settlement among Migrant and Urban Villagers." In *Going through Changes: Villagers, Settlers and Development in Papua New Guinea*, edited by C. A. Valentine and B. L. Valentine. Port Moresby: Institute of Papua New Guinea Studies, 73–90.

O'Flaherty, Brendan. 1996. *Making Room: The Economics of Homelessness*. Cambridge, Mass.: Harvard University Press.

Organization for Economic Co–operation and Development (OECD). 1982. *The OECD List of Social Indicators*. Paris: OECD.

Osborne, David E., and Ted Gaebler. 1992. *Reinventing Government: How the Entrepreneurial Spirit is Transforming the Public Sector.* Reading, Mass.: Addison–Wesley.

Oxley, Michael. 1988. "Tenure Change in Eastern Europe." Paper presented at the International Research Conference on Housing Policy and Innovation. Amsterdam.

———. 1991. "The Aims and Methods of Comparative Housing Research," *Scandinavian Journal of Housing and Planning Research* 8: 67–77.

———. 1993. "Social Housing in the European Community." European Housing Research Working Papers Series no. 2. Leicester, U.K.: De Monfort University.

Paccione, Michael. 1990. *Urban Problems: An Applied Urban Analysis.* New York: Routledge.

Pahl, R. 1984. *Divisions of Labour.* Oxford: Blackwell.

Papa, Oscar. 1992. *Housing Systems in Europe, Part II: A Comparative Study of Housing Finance.* Delft: Delft University Press.

Patton, Carl V., ed. 1988. *Spontaneous Shelter: International Perspectives and Prospects.* Philadelphia: Temple University Press.

Payne, Geoffrey K. 1982. "Self–Help Housing: a Critique of the Gecekondus of Ankara." In *Self–Help Housing: A Critique*, edited by Peter M. Ward. London: Mansell, 117–139.

———. 1997. *Urban Land Tenure and Property Rights in Developing Countries: A Review.* London: IT Publications, Overseas Development Administration.

Pejovich, Svetozar. 1990. *The Economics of Property Rights: Towards a Theory of Comparative Systems.* Dordrecht: Kluwer.

———. 1995. *Economic Analysis of Institutions and Systems.* Kluwer. Dordrecht.

Peterson, George E. 1973. "The Property Tax and Low–income Housing Markets." in *Property Tax Reform.* edited by George E. Peterson. The Urban Institute. Washington, D.C.

Peterson, George E., G. Thomas Kingsley, and Jeffrey P. Telgarsky. 1991. *Urban Economies and National Development.* Washington, D.C.: Office of Housing and Urban Development Programs, U.S. Agency for International Development.

Platt, Rutherford H. 1991. *Land Use Control: Geography, Law and Public Policy.* Englewood Cliffs, N.J.: Prentice Hall.

Polinsky, A. 1977. "The Demand for Housing: A Study in Specification and Grouping." *Econometrica* 45 (No. 2): 447–461.

Porter, Michael. 1990. *The Competitive Advantage of Nations.* New York: The Free Press.

Priemus, Hugo. 1994. "Housing Markets, Housing Policies, and Housing Finance in an Integrating Europe." In *Report of the 11th International School.* Münster: The International Union of Housing Finance Institutions, July, 109–136.

Pugh, Cedric. 1980. *Housing in Capitalist Societies.* Westmead: Gower Publishing

———. n.d. *Housing Policy Development in Developing Countries: The World Bank and Internationalization 1972–1993.* London: The Royal Institution of Chartered Surveyors.

Quigley, John M. 1996. "The Homeless." *Journal of Economic Literature* 34 (December): 1935–1941.

Ramanathan, Ramu. 1992. *Introductory Econometrics with Applications.* 2nd ed. Orlando, Fla.: Harcourt, Brace, Janovich.

Ramirez, Ronaldo. 1978. "The Housing Queue." Paper presented to the Special Seminar on People's Participation and Government Inputs in Low Cost Housing, Bouwcentrum International, Rotterdam.

Renaud, Bertrand. 1980. "Resource Allocation to Housing Investment: Comments and Further Results." *Economic Development and Cultural Change* 28 (No. 2, January): 389–399.

———. 1989. "Understanding the Collateral Qualities of Housing for Financial Development: The Korean 'Chonse' as Effective Response to Financial Sector Shortcomings."

398 References

Discussion paper. Washington, D.C.: Infrastructure and Urban Development Department, The World Bank.

———. 1991. *Affordability, Price-Income Ratio and Housing Performance: An International Perspective.* Working paper. Washington, D.C.: Urban Development Division, The World Bank.

———. 1993. "Confronting a Distorted Housing Market: Can Korean Policies Break with the Past?" In *Social Issues in Korea: Korean and American Perspectives,* edited by Lawrence B. Krause and Fun-Koo Park. Seoul: Korea Development Institute.

———. 1994. "The 1985-1994 Global Real Estate Cycle: Are There Lasting Behavioral and Regulatory Lessons?" Paper presented at the Annual Conference of the American Real Estate and Urban Economics Association. Washington, D.C.

Renaud, Bertrand, Ming Zhang, and Stefan Koeberle. 1998. "How the Thai Real Estate Boom Undid Financial Institutions. What Can Be Done?" Paper delivered at the NESDB-World Bank Conference on Thai Dynamic Economic Recovery and Competitiveness. Bangkok.

Reserve Bank of India. 1978. *The Shah Report on Finance for Housing Schemes.* Bombay: Reserve Bank of India.

Robben, Pieter. 1984. "Improvement and the Better-Off: Displacement as a Consequence of Squatter Settlement Upgrading." Geografische en Planologische Notities 24. Amsterdam: Vrise University.

Robert A. Nathan Associates and the Urban Institute. 1984. *Preparing a National Housing Needs Assessment.* Occasional Paper Series. Washington, D.C.: Office of Housing and Urban Programs, U.S. Agency for International Development.

Rodwin, Lloyd, ed. 1987. *Shelter, Settlement, and Development.* Boston: Allen and Unwin.

Roman, Rolf-Eric, Peter Bengtsson, and Jessica Johansson. 1994. "The Volume of Housing Subsidies." In *Housing in Sweden in an International Perspective,* edited by Eva Hedman. Karlsrona: Boverket, 125-134.

Rose, Carol M. 1994. *Property and Persuasion: Essays on the History, Theory, and Rhetoric of Private Ownership.* Boulder, Colo.: Westview Press.

Rosen, H. S. 1979. "Owner Occupied Housing and the Federal Income Tax: Estimates and Simulation." *Journal of Urban Economics* 6 (April): 247-266.

Rosen, Kenneth T. 1979. *Seasonal Cycles in the Housing Market: Patterns, Costs, and Policies,* Cambridge, Mass.: MIT Press.

Rosen, Sherwin. 1974. "Hedonic Prices and Implicit Markets: Product Differentiation in Pure Competition." *Journal of Political Economy* 82 (No. 1): 34-55.

Rossi, Peter H. 1989. *Down and Out in America: The Origins of Homelessness.* Chicago: University of Chicago Press.

Ruskin, John. 1880. *The Seven Lamps of Architecture.* Reprinted, New York: Dover, 1989.

Russian Federation. 1990. *National Statistical Yearbook.* Moscow: Russian Federation.

Ryan, Joseph E. "Survey Methodology." *Freedom Review* 22 (No. 1): 13-15.

Rybczynski, Witold. 1986. *Home: A Short History of an Idea.* Harmondsworth, U.K.: Penguin Books.

———. 1989. *The Most Beautiful House in the World.* Harmondsworth, U.K.: Penguin Books.

Rykwert, Joseph. 1981. *On Adam's House in Paradise: The Idea of the Primitive Hut in Architectural History.* 2nd ed. Cambridge, Mass.: MIT Press.

Sandbrook, Richard. 1993. *The Politics of Africa's Economic Recovery.* Cambridge, U.K.: Cambridge University Press.

Sarin, Madhu. 1983. "The Rich, the Poor, and the Land Question." In *Land for Housing the Poor,* edited by Shlomo Angel et al. Singapore: Select Books, 237-253.

————, ed. 1981. *Urban Slums: Slums and Squatter Settlements in the ESCAP Region*. Bangkok: United Nations Economic and Social Commission for Asia and the Pacific.

Saunders, Peter. 1990. *A Nation of Home Owners*. London: Unwin Hyman.

Schmidt, S. 1989. "Convergence Theory, Labor Movements, and Corporatism: The Case of Housing." *Scandinavian Housing and Planning Research* 6 (No. 2): 83–101.

Schon, Donald A. 1987. "Institutional Learning in Shelter and Settlement Policies." In *Shelter, Settlement and Development*, edited by Lloyd Rodwin. Boston: Allen and Unwin.

Schuringa,M., A. K. Salahudin, E. Meyer, and K. S. Yap. 1979. *Baldia Evaluation Survey Report: A Study of Improvement of Living Conditions in a Katchi Abadi*. Unpublished. Karachi: Karachi Slum Improvement Project.

Scott, M. 1989. *A New View of Economic Growth*. Oxford: Clarendon Press.

Segal, David, and Philip Srinivasan. 1985. "The Impact of Suburban Growth Restrictions on U.S. Housing Price Inflation, 1975–1978." *Urban Geography* 6 (No. 1): 14–26.

Shilling, James D., And C. F. Sirmans. 1993. *The Evaluation of Pass Through Mortgage Backed Securities*. Working Paper Series, Center for Urban Land Economics Research. Madison: School of Business, University of Wisconsin.

Shrader-Frechette, Kristin. 1993. "Practical Steps and Ethical Justifications." In *Policy for Land: Law and Ethics*, edited by Lynton Keith Caldwell and Kristin Shrader-Frechette. Lanham: Rowman and Littlefield, 227–312.

Sillince, J. A. A., ed. 1990. *Housing Policies in Eastern Europe and the Soviet Union*. New York: Routledge.

Simon, David. 1992. *Cities, Capital and Development: African Cities in the World Economy*. London: Belhaven Press.

Smith, Lawrence B., Kenneth T. Rosen, and George Fallis. 1988. "Recent Developments in Economic Models of Housing Markets." *Journal of Economic Literature* 26 (March): 29–64.

Stahl, Konrad, and Raymond J. Struyk, eds. 1985. *U.S. and West German Housing Markets*. Washington, D.C.: Urban Institute Press.

Stegman, Michael A. 1988. *Housing and Vacancy Report: New York City, 1987*. New York: Department of Housing Preservation and Development, City of New York.

Stone, Douglas, and William T. Ziemba. 1993. "Land and Stock Prices in Japan." *Journal of Economic Perspectives* 7 (No. 3, Summer): 149–165.

Strassmann, W. Paul. 1982. *The Transformation of Urban Housing: The Experience of Upgrading in Cartagena*. Baltimore, Md.: Johns Hopkins University Press.

————. 1984. "The Timing of Urban Infrastructure and Housing Improvements by Owner Occupants." *Urban Studies* 12 (No. 7): 743–753.

————. 1991. "Housing Market Interventions and Residential Mobility: An International Comparison." *Urban Studies* 28 (No. 5): 759–771.

Stren, Richard E. 1989. "Urban Housing in Africa: The Changing Role of Government Policy." In *Housing the Urban Poor in Africa*, edited by Philip Amis and Peter Lloyd, Manchester: Manchester University Press, 35–53.

Struyk, Raymond J., Michael Hoffman, and Harold Katsura. 1990. *The Market for Housing in Urban Indonesia*. Washington, D.C.: Urban Institute Press.

Struyk, Raymond J., and Nadezhda B. Kosareva. 1994. *Transition in the Russian Housing Sector: 1991–1994*. Working paper. Washington, D.C.: The Urban Institute.

Sufian, Abu Zafar Muhammad. 1993. "A Multivariate Analysis of the Determinants of Urban Quality of Life in the World's Largest Metropolitan Areas." *Urban Studies* 30 (No.8): 1319–1329.

Sutcliffe, Anthony. 1981. *Towards the Planned City: Germany, Britain, the United States, and France 1780–1914*. New York: St. Martin's.

Tafuri, Manfredo. 1976. *Architecture and Utopia: Design and Capitalist Development*. Translated by Barbara Luigia La Penta. Cambridge, Mass.: MIT Press.

Tanphiphat, Sidhijai, and Pratak Simapichaichet. 1990. "Thailand Case Study: Private Sector Housing at Scale: Land, Finance, and Development." In *Third International Shelter Conference, Volume II: Case Studies*. Washington, D.C.: National association of Realtors.

Taschner, Suzana Pasternak, and Elaine Pedreira Rabinovich. 1997. "The Homeless in São Paolo: Spatial Arrangements." In *International Critical Perspectives on Homelessness*, edited by Mary Jo Huth and Talmadge Wright. Westport: Praeger, 13–30.

Taylor, John. 1987. "Evaluation of the Jakarta Kampung Improvement Project." In *Shelter Upgrading for the Urban Poor*, edited by Reinhard Skinner, John Taylor, and Emiel A. Wegelin. Manila: Island Publishing.

Topel, Robert and Sherwin Rosen. 1988. "Housing Investment in the United States." *Journal of Political Economy* 96 (No. 4): 718–740.

Tuccillo, John A., and Sean A. Burns. 1990. *The Contribution of Housing to National Economic Development*. Paper prepared for the Third International Shelter Conference. Washington, D.C.: National Association of Realtors.

Turner, Bengt. "Housing Indicators: A Tool for Research?", *Netherlands Journal of Housing and the Built Environment* 8 (No.1): 61–66..

Turner, John F. C. 1967. "Barriers and Channels for Housing Development in Modernizing Countries." *Journal of the American Institute of Planners* 33 (No. 3): 167–181.

———. 1968. "Housing Priorities, Settlement Patterns, and Urban Development in Modernizing Countries." *Journal of the American Institute of Planners* 34 (No. 6): 354–363.

———. 1972. "Housing as a Verb." In *Freedom to Build: Dweller Control of the Housing Process*, edited by J. F. C. Turner, and R. Fichter. Houndsmill: Macmillan, 148–175.

Turner, Margaret Austin, and John G. Edwards. 1993. "Affordable Rental Housing in Metropolitan Neighborhoods." In *Housing Markets and Residential Mobility*, edited by G. Thomas Kingsley and Margaret Austin Turner.. Washington D.C.: The Urban Institute Press, 125–160.

U.S. Bureau of the Census. 1993. *1990 Census of Population and Housing*. Washington, D.C.: U.S. Department of Commerce.

U.S. Department of Commerce. 1978. *Value of New Construction Put in Place*. Bureau of Census, C–30 Series (Construction). Washington, D.C.: Government Printing Office.

U.S. Department of Housing and Urban Development (HUD). 1994. *U.S. Housing Market Conditions, 3rd Quarter 1994*. Washington, D.C.: Office and Policy Development and Research. U.S. Department of Housing and Urban Development.

United Nations. 1992. *Annual Bulletin of Housing and Building Statistics for Europe*. New York: United Nations Economic Commission for Europe, United Nations.

———. 1993. *World Urbanization Prospects: The 1992 Revision*. New York: Department of Economic and Social Information and Policy Analysis.

———. 1998. *World Urbanization Prospects: The 1996 Revision*. New York: Department of Economic and Social Information and Policy Analysis.

United Nations Centre for Human Settlements (UNCHS). 1993. *Shelter Sector Performance Indicators*. Report of the Executive Director to the Human Settlements Commission, Fourteenth Session. Nairobi: UNCHS.

———. 1994. *Report of the International Expert Group Meeting on Urban Indicators*. Nairobi: UNCHS.

United Nations Commission on Human Settlements. 1988. *Global Shelter Strategy to the Year 2000*. New York: United Nations.

United Nations Development Programme (UNDP). 1990. *Human Development Report 1990*. New York: Oxford University Press.

United Nations Development Programme (UNDP). 1995. *Human Development Report 1995*. New York: Oxford University Press.

Urban Institute. 1996. *Summary of Habitat II Urban Finance Colloquium*. Washington, D.C.: Urban Institute.

Van der Linden, Jan. 1977. *The Bastis of Karachi–Types and Dynamics*. Amsterdam: Free University.

———. 1981. "Actors in Squatment Upgrading." *Open House International* 6 (No. 1): 36–43.

Van Vliet, Willem, ed. 1990. *International Handbook of Housing Policies and Practices*. New York: Greenwood Press.

Van Vliet, Willem, Elisabeth Huttman, and Sylvia Fava, eds. 1985. *Housing Needs and Policy Approaches: Trends in Thirteen Countries*. Durham, N.C.: Duke University Press.

Vandell, Kerry D., Walter C. Barnes, James D. Shilling, and Richard K. Green. 1992. *Toward a Secondary Commercial Mortgage Market: Standardization and Credit Risk Evaluation Issues*. Center for Urban Land Economics Research, Working Paper Series. Madison: School of Business, University of Wisconsin.

Villani, Kevin E. 1979. "The Tax Subsidy to Housing in an Inflationary Environment: Implications for after Tax Housing Costs." Working paper. Washington, D.C.: U.S. Department of Housing and Urban Development.

Wallace, R. 1989. "'Homelessness,' Contagious Destruction of Housing, and Municipal Service Cuts in New York City: 1. The Demographics of a Housing Deficit." *Environment and Planning A* 21: 1585–1603.

Wallace, R., and E. Bassuk. 1991. "Housing Famine and Homelessness: How the Low-Income Housing Crisis Affects Families with Inadequate Supports." *Environment and Planning A* 2: 485–498.

Ward, Peter M. 1978. "Self Help Housing in Mexico City: Social and Economic Determinants of Success." *Town Planning Review* 49 (No. 1): 38–50.

———. 1982. "The Practice and Potential of Self-help in Mexico City." In *Self Help Housing; A Critique*, edited by Peter M. Ward. London: Mansell, 175–208.

———. 1990. "The Politics and Costs of Illegal Land Development for Self-Help Housing in Mexico City." In *The Transformation of Land Supply Systems in Third World Cities*, edited by Paul Baross and Jan van der Linden. Aldershot: Avebury, 133–168.

———, ed. 1982. *Self Help Housing; A Critique*. London: Mansell.

Weicher, John C. 1990. "The Voucher/Production Debate." In *Building Foundations: Housing and Federal Policy*, edited by Denise Dipasquale and Langley C. Keyes. Philadelphia: University of Pennsylvania Press, 263–291.

———. 1994. "The New Structure of the Housing Finance System." St. Louis: Federal Reserve Bank of St. Louis.

Weisman, Leslie Kanes. 1994. *Discrimination by Design: A Feminist Critique of the Man–Made Environment*. Champagne–Urbana: University of Illinois Press.

Wennberg, Trond E. 1994. "Mortgage Banking System — Northern Europe." In *Report of the 11th International School*. Münster: The International Union of Housing Finance Institutions, July, 191–212.

Whitehead, Christine M. E. 1974. *The U.K. Housing Market: An Econometric Model*. London/Lexington, Mass.: Saxon House/Lexington Books.

————. 1991. "From Need to Affordability: An Analysis of U.K. Housing Objectives." *Urban Studies* 28 (No. 6): 871–887.

Whitehead, Christine M. E., and Mark Kleinman. 1990. "The Viability of the Privately Rented Housing Market." In *Housing and The National Economy*, edited by John Ermisch. London: Avebury, 113–134.

Williamson, Oliver E. 1985. *The Economic Institutions of Capitalism*. New York: The Free Press.

Woodall, Brian. 1996. *Japan under Construction: Corruption, Politics, and Public Works*. Berkeley: University of California Press.

Woodfield, Anthony. 1989. *Housing and Economic Adjustment*. New York: Taylor and Francis.

Woodward, Donald. 1995. *Men at Work: Labourers and Building Craftsmen in the Towns of Northern England, 1450–1750*. New York: Cambridge University Press.

Woodward, Susan E., and John C. Weicher. 1989. "Goring the Wrong Ox: a Defense of the Mortgage Interest Deduction." *National Tax Journal* 42 (No. 3): 301–313.

World Bank. 1992. *World Development Report – 1992: Development and the Environment*. New York: Oxford University Press.

————. 1993. *Housing: Enabling Markets to Work*. A World Bank Policy Paper. Washington, D.C.: World Bank.

————. 1993. *Russia Housing Reform and Privatization. Vol. I: Main Report*. Washington, D.C.: World Bank.

————. 1994. *World Development Report – 1994: Infrastructure for Development*. New York: Oxford University Press.

————. 1997. *World Development Report – 1997: The State in a Changing World*. New York: Oxford University Press.

Wren, Christopher S. 1995. "The G.I.'s Don't Carry a Marshall Plan." *The New York Times*, December 17, 14.

Wright, James D., and Beth A. Rubin. 1991. "Is Homelessness a Housing Problem?" *Housing Policy Debate* 2 (Issue 3): 937–956.

Wright, Gwendolyn. 1993. *Building the Dream: A Social History of Housing in America*. Cambridge, Mass.: MIT Press.

WuDunn, Sheryl. 1999. "Japan Bets on a Wired World to Win Back Its Global Niche." *The New York Times*, August 30, A8.

Yates, Judith. 1994. "Private Finance for Social Housing in Australia." *Housing Policy Debate* 5 (Issue 2): 177–202.

Yoon, Il–Seong. 1994. *Housing in a Newly Industrialized Economy: The Case of South Korea*. Aldershot: Avebury.

Young, Ben, and John Kramer. 1978. "Local Exclusionary Policies in Britain: The Case of Suburban Defense in a Metropolitan System." In *Urbanization and Conflict in Market Societies* , edited by Kevin R. Cox. Chicago: Maaroufa, 229–251.

Zearley, Thomas Lee. 1993. "Creating an Enabling Environment for Housing: Recent Reforms in Mexico." *Housing Policy Debate* 4 (Issue 2): 239–249.

Index